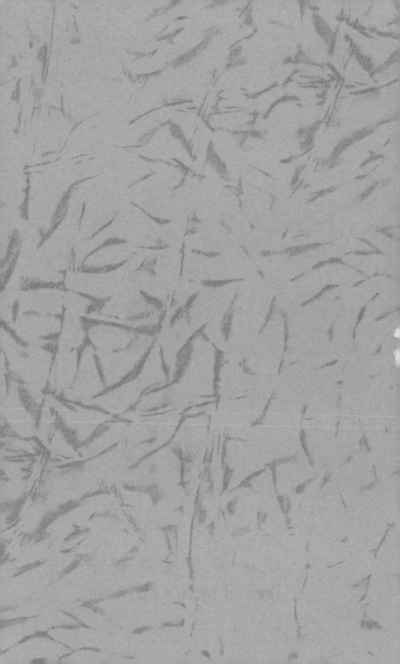

英汉双向法律词典

主编：何高大　编写：毛莉萍　池晓　　王建国　章通天

ENGLISH-CHINESE AND CHINESE-ENGLISH DICTIONARY OF

LAW

上海交通大学出版社

图书在版编目（CIP）数据

英汉双向法律词典/何高大主编．—上海：上海交通
大学出版社，2002
ISBN 7-313-02891-1

Ⅰ．英…　Ⅱ．何…　Ⅲ．法律－词典－英、汉
Ⅳ．D9－61

中国版本图书馆 CIP 数据核字（2001）第 084551 号

英汉双向法律词典
何高大　主编
上海交通大学出版社出版发行
（上海市番禺路 877 号　邮政编码 200030）
电话：64071208　出版人：张天蔚
常熟市印刷二厂印刷　全国新华书店经销
开本：787mm×960mm　1/32　印张：30.25　字数：1356 千字
2002 年 1 月第 1 版　2002 年 1 月第 1 次印刷
印数：1～6050
ISBN 7－313－02891－1/D·071　定价：42.00 元

前　言

在崭新的 21 世纪，一个人的书柜里如果没有一部英语词典，就好像他不属于这个时代的。对部分技术人员来说，他最需要的词典就是他所从事的专业方面的英语词典，《英汉双向法律词典》正是为广大从事法律工作的专业人才编著的。

这是一部时代性很强的专业英语工具书。从开始收集资料到今天出版用了三年时间。三年间，语言创新突飞猛进，新的思想和专业术语层出不穷，每一次审读、每一次整理，我们都及时地将新的内容插入，所以说这是一部和时代同步的词典。

法律词汇涉及广泛，为避免词典庞大而不实用，我们大力删除已过时了多年的词条。但收词多少为宜，确实费了我们一番周折。为此，我们参阅了诸多国内外新出版的专业词典和杂志，又经专业人员认定，最后编入了近 50000 词条，仍难免挂一漏万。

本词典还有一个显著的特点是具有从汉语查到相应英语词条的功能。词典前一部分和一般英汉词典没有什么区别，但后一部分为汉英检词索引。该索引按《汉语拼音方案》字母表排序，根据每个汉语词条后标注的页数和行数，从英汉部分即可查到相关词条。一本词典，两种功能，极大地方便了读者使用。

本词典虽经反复修改和补充，但时代的变化日新月异，绝不敢言最新、最好。我们可以得到一点欣慰的是，这确是一部我们用力、用心编著的词典。希望为您所用，希望为您喜欢，希望得到您的赐教。

编者

2001 年 10 月

目录

体例说明

1.词典分为前后两部分,前半部为英汉部分,后半部分为汉英部分。

2.英汉部分的每个词条中缝都标有行数,以备查阅。

3.汉英部分按汉语拼音排序,每个汉语词条后都注有页数和行数,由此即可查到相对的英语词条。

A

a basket of currencies "一揽子"货币

a bipantite contract 一式两份的合同

a bon droit（拉）合理

a branch of an enterprise 企业分支机关

a broker's fee 佣金

a case pertaining to death sentence 判处死刑的案件

a case pertaining to death sentence with a two-year reprieve 判处死刑缓期二年执行的案件

a certain number 若干

a change of cabinet 内阁更迭

a change of government 政府更迭

a citizen's disappearance 失踪案件

a clear and unambiguous explanation 确切的解释

a complete set of codes 全套法典

a constitutional government in which there are three independent branches 三权分立政体

a contract by dccd 书面合同（注：英美法中分点）

a contract of mortgage 质押契据

a court of first instance 初审法院

a crime in preparation 犯罪预备

a criminal case filed for reexamination of the death penalty 报送死刑复核的案件

a day not juridical 不开庭日

a departure from terms 违背条款

A false cause does not vitiate a contract 虚伪原因不影响合同效力

a foreign trade operator acting as an agent 接受委托的对外贸易经营者

a formal notification of reeducation-through-labour 劳教通知书

a general cessation of the constitution 全面废除宪法

A general clause does not refer to things expressed（英） 一般条款是不涉及业务特别明示的内容的

a general contractor 总承包人

a great beginning 一个伟大的创举

a great deal of economic analysis 大量的经济分析

a guarantee of real right 物的担保

a host of fact 大量事实

a hostile element 敌对分子

A judge cannot be a witness in his own cause 法官在自己的案件中不得当证人

a judge in Hades 判官

A judge ought always to regard equity 法官应当始终考虑公平原则

A later statute takes away the effect of a prior one 后法取代前法

a lengthy peaceful reign 长治久安

a letter of confirmation 确认书

a letter of hypothecation 质押书

a lien agreement 典契

a lien tenancy 典租制

a long standing issue 长期存在的问题

a lump sum 一次性报酬

a manner contrary to honest commercial practices 违反诚实的商业惯例

a matter of the whole 全局性问题

a mensa et thoro （拉） 分居（注：指夫妻分居）

a middleman's fee 佣金

a mortgage deed 质押契据

a party not in office 在野党

a permanent tenancy 永佃权

a person of full age and capacity 完全民事行为能力人

a portion of the power 部分权力

a precise definition 确切的定义

a presumption of law and right 不容反证的法律推定

a priori theories of law and justice 法律与正义先验论

a proportion with yearly progressive decrease 逐年递减比例

a proportion with yearly progressive increase 逐年递增比例

a protective organization of regeneration 更生保护组织

a public prosecuting speech 公诉词

A right does not rise out of a wrong 侵权不得产生权利

a series of 一系列

a simple contract 简式合同（注：指英美法中分类）

a sin unpunishable by law 法律不能处罚的罪

a small majority 微弱多数

a standing contract 继续契约

a statutory age limit 法定年龄限制

a system of campaigning for post 竞选制

a system of matriarchy 母权制度

a tenancy in perpetuity 永佃权

a term of five years 任期五年

a time of turmoil 动乱时期

a transaction infringing public policy and morals 与公共政策和道德相抵触的行为

a unitary multinational state 统一的多民族的国家

a unitary system of ownership of the means of production by the whole people 单一的生产资料全民所有制

a warehousing contract 仓储合同

a whole set 全套

ab agendo（拉） 无行为能力的，丧失行为能力的

ab confectionis（拉） 从缔约之日起

ab intestato（拉） 无遗嘱继承，无遗嘱继承的，未立遗嘱的

ab invito （拉） 非出于自愿，不情愿地

ab origine（拉） 从起源

abagendo（拉） 无行为能力

abandon 背弃,弃权,委付

abandon a patent 放弃专利权

abandon drug habits 戒毒

abandon evil and do good 改恶从善

abandon the right 放弃的权利

abandoned 无主的,被遗弃的

abandoned goods 无主财物

abandoned infant 弃婴

abandoned riverbed 废河床

abandoned woman 被遗弃的妇女

abandonee 弃物受领人,受委付人（注：多指海上保险）,被遗弃者

abandonment 委付,放弃

abandonment loss 势弃损失

abandonment of action 撤诉

abandonment of appeal 撤回上诉

abandonment of contract 否认合同

abandonment of domicile 废止住所(或户籍)

abandonment of right 权利的放弃,弃权

abandonment of solicitation 教唆中止

abandum 遗弃物

abate 减轻,撤销,废除

abate a debt 减免债务

abate a price 降价

abate an action 撤销诉讼

abatement 废除,撤销

abatement of action 中止诉讼

abatement of criminal punishment 免除刑罚

abatement of debts 减免债务,废除债务

abatement of legacies 放弃遗赠

abatement of nuisance 减少妨害干扰,排除妨害

abatement of purchase-money 减低买卖

abatement order 废除令

abbreviation convention 缩写约定

abdicate 退位

abdicated monarch 退位君主

abduct and traffic people 拐卖人口

abductor 拐骗犯

aberrant personality 变态心理

aberration 无行为能力,错误行为

abesse(注:二大陆法) 不出庭

abet incite 唆使

abetted offense 被教唆的犯罪

abettor 违意犯

abeyance 无主,搁置

abeyance of seizin 中止地产占有

abeyant 无主

abidance by law 守法

abidance by the rules 遵守规则

abide by 遵守

abide by contracts 信守合同

abide by promise 遵守诺言

abide by the contract 遵守合同

abide by the law 遵守法律

abiding by contracts and keeping promises 重合同,守信用

abiding place 住所

abili(拉) 不在犯罪现场

ability 能力

ability to bargain 交易能力

① ability to borrow 借债能力

② ability to pay 支付能力,偿付能力

④ pay ability of bearing taxation 负税能力

⑥ ability to repay in foreign exchange 外汇偿付能力

⑧ ability to repay loan 偿还借款能力,借款偿还能力

⑩ abject of manufacture 加工对象

⑪ abjudicate 判为不法

⑫ abjuration of the realm 弃国宣誓(英)

⑭ able to make payment 有支付能力

⑯ able-bodied citizen 有能力的公民

⑱ abligatio pura et simplex(拉) 无条件债务

⑳ abnormal fixation 变态固着

㉑ abnormal personality 变态人格

㉒ abnormal psychology 变态心理

㉓ abnormal risk 异常危险

㉔ abode 住所地

㉕ abolish 取消,撤销,废除,废止,革除

㉗ abolish a system 废除某一制度

㉘ abolish improper rules and regulations 取消不合理的规章制度

㉚ abolish outmoded regulations and irrational practices 革除陈规陋习

㉝ abolished 废除的

㉞ abolisher 废除者

㉟ abolishment 取消

㊱ abolishment of law 法律的废除,法律的废止,法律废止

㊳ abolitio restitutio famiae(拉) 恢复名誉

㊵ abolition 取消

㊶ abolition act 废奴法(英 1807-1838)

㊸ abolition of administrative act 行政行为的废止

㊺ abominable crime 兽奸罪

㊻ aboriginal title(美) 原始所有权

㊼ above par 票面价值以上,超出

面值

above the line 往事账

above-ground structures 地上建筑物

abrasion 皮外损伤

abridge 剥夺

abridge sb of his rights 剥夺某人权利

abridgements of statutes 法规节略

abrogate 废除,撤销,废止

abrogate a judgment, repeal a judgment, repeal a court decision 撤销判决

abrogate a treaty 废除条约

abrogate a unequal treaty 废除不平等条约

abrogation 废除

abrogation of judgment 撤销判决

abrogation of right 取消权利

abscond 逃匿,潜逃

abscond to avoid punishment 逃避惩罚

absence 失踪

absence of consideration 缺乏约因,缺乏对价

absence of discernment 无意识

absence of proof 缺乏证据

absence without reason 旷工

absentee 居住国外者

absentee ownership 不在地主所有权

absolute 绝对的

absolute acceptance 无条件承兑,无条件接受

absolute advantage 独占优势

absolute and relative impossibility 绝对不能犯与相对不能犯

absolute and universal prohibition 绝对普通禁止

absolute assignment 全部转让,绝对转让

absolute bill 绝对诉状

absolute contraband 绝对禁制品

absolute conveyance 无条件权利或财产让与,无条件转让

absolute cover 绝对保险额

absolute deed 无抵押契据

absolute defence 绝对抗辩

absolute delivery 无条件交付

absolute disability 完全无行为能力

absolute discharge 完全清偿

absolute duty 绝对义务

absolute endorsement 绝对背书

absolute equity 绝对平衡法

absolute estate 不附条件之地产权

absolute fact 确凿事实

absolute full cover 全部保证

absolute guaranty 绝对担保,无条件担保

absolute immunity 绝对豁免

absolute indeterminate sentence 绝对不定期刑

absolute invalidity 绝对无效

absolute legacy 无条件遗赠

absolute liability 绝对责任,绝对赔偿责任

absolute majority 绝对多数

absolute monarchy 君主专制,君主专制政体

absolute monopoly 绝对垄断

absolute net loss 绝对净损

absolute obligation 绝对义务

absolute order 立即完全生效决定

absolute ownership 绝对所有权,绝对所有

absolute par 绝对平价

absolute price 绝对价格

absolute price competition 绝对价格竞争

absolute promise 无条件承诺

absolute proof 确凿的证据

absolute quota 绝对配额

absolute quotas 绝对配额

absolute responsibility 绝对责任

absolute right 绝对权利

absolute sale 无条件销售

absolute sovereignty 绝对主权

absolute title 绝对所有权

absolute veto power 绝对多数否决权

absolute warrantor 绝对保证人

absolutely determinate statutory punishment 绝对确定法定刑

absolutely indeterminate statutory punishment 绝对不确定法定刑

absolution 赦免

absolutism 绝对性,专制主义

absolutism test 绝对主义法定刑

absolve 免除

absolve sb from an obligation 免除某人的一项债务

absorb foreign capital 吸收外资,吸引外资

absorb foreign investment 引进外国资本

absorb idle capital 吸收闲散资金

absorption consolidation 合并

absorption principle 吸收原则

abstain from an act 不作为

abstain from pleading 放弃申辩权

abstain from replying 不答辩

abstain from voting 弃权

abstainer 弃权者

abstention 弃权

abstract administrative act 抽象行政行为

abstract contract 无因契约

abstract danger theory 抽象危险说

abstract juristic act 无因法律行为

abstract labour 抽象劳动

abstract misdemeanor 抽象轻过失

abstract negligence 抽象过失

abstract of record 案卷摘录

abstract of title 产权说明,所有权证明摘要

abstract right of action 抽象诉权

abstraction of electricity 窃用电力

abstraction of water 窃取用水

abstraction principle 抽象原则

abundant financial resources 资金雄厚

abuse 弊端,滥用

abuse of (one's) authority 滥用职权

abuse of a dominant position 滥用支配地位

abuse of authority 滥用权力

abuse of civil rights 权力滥用

abuse of discretion 滥用自由裁量权

abuse of environment 环境污染

abuse of flag 旗帜的滥用

abuse of judicial discretion 滥用司法裁决权

abuse of justice 滥用司法

abuse of law 滥用法律

abuse of police authorities 滥用警察权力

abuse of power 滥用权力,权力滥用

abuse of privileges 滥用特权

abuse of process 滥用诉讼程序

abuse of public prosecution 公诉滥用论

abuse of right 滥用权利,权利滥用,权利的滥用

abuse of the power of agency 滥用代理权

abuse of the right of representation 代理权滥用

abuse one's authority 滥用职权

abuse one's official capacity 滥用职权

abuse one's official power 滥用职权

abuse one's official powers 滥用职权

abuse one's power 滥用职权

abuse power for personal gain 以权谋私

abuttals 地界

abutter 相邻业主

academic degree 学位

academic degrees system 学位制

度

academic interpretation　学理解释

academic rank　学衔

academy　学校,学院,学会

acceding party　加入一方

acceding state　参加国

accelerate　促进

accelerated growth　加速增长

acceleration　加速促进

acceleration clause　提前偿付条款,提前条款

accept　承兑,认可,收容,承认,受理

accept a bill of exchange　承兑汇票

accept a commission　接受委托

accept a complaint　受理控诉

accept a draft　承兑汇票

accept a judgment　服从判决

accept and hear a case　受理案件

accept insurance　承保

accept sb's bid　接受某人投标

acceptable quality level　可接受质量标准

acceptance　受盘,承兑,承诺,受理

acceptance at complaint only　告诉才处理

acceptance bank　承兑银行

acceptance bill　承兑汇票,承兑票据,银行承兑的票据

acceptance business　票据承兑业

acceptance by a part of the drawees　一部分付款人承兑

acceptance by intervention　参加承兑

acceptance certificate　验收合格证,验收单

acceptance commission　承兑手续费,承兑费用

acceptance condition　合格条件

acceptance credit　承兑信用,承兑信贷

acceptance credit (/letter of cred-it)　承兑信用证

acceptance criterion　验收标准

acceptance fee　承兑费用

acceptance fee (for an arbitration case)　案件处理费

acceptance for carriage　承运

acceptance for honor　参加承兑

acceptance in blank　空白承兑,不记名承兑

acceptance in default　受领迟延

acceptance line　承兑限额

acceptance of action　起诉成立

acceptance of delivery　接受转让

acceptance of goods　接受货物

acceptance of object　标的之受领,标的物之领受

acceptance of offer　受盘,承诺

acceptance of partial performance　部分履行之受领

acceptance of proposal　确认要求

acceptance of protest　接受抗诉

acceptance of punishment　服罪

acceptance of sentence　接受判决

acceptance of service　接受送达

acceptance of single lot　单批接受

acceptance of succession　接受继承

acceptance of treaty　条约的接受

acceptance rate　票据贴现率,承兑利率

acceptance supra protest　代承兑拒付汇票

accepted　已接受,被承兑人,接受者,承诺人,承揽人

accepted draft bill　已承兑汇票

accepted meaning　公认的含义

accepted standard of civilization　公认的文明标准

accepting bank　承兑银行

accepting citizenship　接受国籍

acceptio (拉)　承诺

acceptor　接受者,承揽人,承兑人,承诺人

acceptor for honor　参加承兑人

access to court　申诉权利

access to (the) market　市场准入

accessio　添附

accessio（拉）附随

accessio cedit principali　（拉）从物属于主物所有人

accessio naturalis（拉）自然添附

accessio possessionis（拉）前占有人占有期间的并算,财产的添附

accession clause　加入条款

accession compensatory amount　加入补偿费

accession of sovereign　王位的继承

accession to treaty　条约的加入

accessorial criminal　从犯

accessory　帮凶,帮助犯

accessory administrative measure　辅助的行政措施

accessory after the event　事后从犯

accessory and coerced offender　主犯,从犯,胁从犯

accessory before the event　事前从犯

accessory charges　附加指控

accessory claim　附加权利要求,附属要求

accessory contract　附属合同,所附的合同,从契约,从合同

accessory criminal law　附属刑法

accessory debtor　从属债务人

accessory during the fact　在场从犯

accessory law　辅助性的法律

accessory obligation　附带义务,从义务

accessory on the scene　在场从犯

accessory punishment　从刑,附加刑

accessory right　从权利

accessory risk　附加险

accessory things　从物

accessory to another accessory　从犯的从犯

accessory to smuggling　走私帮助犯

accident　意外,偶然事故,意外事件

accident and indemnity　意外事故及损害赔偿

accident at sea　海上事故

accident collision　意外碰撞

accident damage　意外事故损害,意外事故损失

accident in handling　装卸意外事故

accident in loading　装货中的意外事故

accident in transit　途中意外事故

accident insurance　意外保险

accident involving civil liability　民事责任事故

accident involving criminal responsibility　刑事责任事故

accident report　海事报告

accident victim　事故受害人

accidental　意外,附属物

accidental cause　偶因

accidental damage　意外损失

accidental death　非真实性犯罪人,意外死亡

accidental destruction　意外毁损

accidental force　不可抗力

accidental injury　偶然伤害,意外伤害

accidental injury to third person　意外伤害第三人

accidental killing　偶然杀人

accidental loss of deed　契据之意外遗失

accidental losses　意外损失

accidental obstacle　意外障碍

accidental omission　意外遗漏

accidental phenomena　偶然现象

accidental price charges　偶然的价格变动

accidental way damage　途中意外损坏

accidentia（拉）偶然因素

accommodate sth to circumstances 变通

accommodated party 借款当事人

accommodation 通融资金,借贷,通融关系人,贷款

accommodation bill 空头票据,通融汇票,通融汇划票据

accommodation note 通融票据

accommodation party 通融当事人,汇票担保人

accomplice 帮凶,同案犯,共犯,伙同犯

accomplice before the perpetration of a crime 事前共犯

accomplice during the perpetration of a crime, confederates in the course of a crime 事中共犯

accomplice in insurance fraud 保险诈骗的共犯

accomplice liability 从犯刑事责任

accomplice under duress 胁从犯

accomplice witness 共犯证人

accomplices after the perpetration of a crime 事后共犯

accomplished crime 既遂犯

accomplished fact 既成事实

accomplished offense 既遂

accomplishment of a crime 犯罪既遂

accord 给予

accord and satisfaction 和解与清偿

accord priority to 给予优先权

accord with 符合

according to 依照,依据,根据

according to faculties and functions 依职权

according to law 依照法律,按照法律规定,按照法律,依照法律规定,依法

according to provision of law 依照法律规定

according to the customs 按照惯例

according to the provisions of eco-nomic law 按经济法律规定

account books 会计账簿

account charges 账户费用

account day (股票市场)结账日

account in figures (票证等)小写金额

account of bill 票据的票面金额

account of payments 支出账户(付款账户)

account of receipts 收入账户

account opening form 开户登记日

account price 记账价格

account purchase 赊购

account receivable 应收账款

account sales 销售清单

account system 会计制度

accountability 可说明性

accountability in management 管理责任

accountability unit 责任单位

accountable 负有解释的义务

accountant 会计师

accountant arrangement method 会计处理方法

accountant certificate 会计师查账证书

accountant general 总会计师,会计主任

accountant in bankruptcy 破产主核算员

accountant in charge 会计主管人员

accountant subject 会计主体

accountant's practice qualification certificate(s) 会计从业资格证书

accountant(s) 会计,财务会计

accountants' comments 会计师意见书

accountants' opinions 会计师意见书

accounting 会计

accounting achieve(s) 会计档案

accounting act 会计法

accounting and auditing services 查账验证业务

accounting archives　会计档案

accounting book　会计账簿

accounting codes　会计准则

accounting cycle　会计循环

accounting disciplines　会计核算纪律

accounting document　会计凭证

accounting documentation　会计资料

accounting dollar　记账美元

accounting dossiers　会计档案

accounting exposure　会计风险

accounting firm　会计事务所

accounting inspection　会计检查

accounting items　会计事项,会计科目

accounting law　会计法

accounting law and regulations　会计法规

accounting law in a broad sense　广义会计法

accounting law in a limited sense　狭义会计法

accounting law in a narrow sense　狭义会计法

accounting legislation　会计立法

accounting management　财务会计管理

accounting manual　会计规程

accounting office(s)　会计机构,会计人员

accounting on the accrual basis　权责发生制

accounting period　会计核算期间

accounting personal　会计人员

accounting practice　会计核算,会计实务

accounting price　核算价格

accounting prices　记账价格

accounting principle　会计准则

accounting principles　会计原则

accounting privilege　会计特权

accounting record　会计账册

accounting regulation　会计规程

accounting regulations　会计法规

accounting relation　会计关系

accounting relationship　会计关系

accounting report form　会计报表

accounting rule　会计规程

accounting standard　会计准则

accounting supervision　会计监督

accounting supervision and examination　会计监督检查

accounting surplus　账面金额

accounting system　会计制度

accounting unit　核算单位,记账单位

accounting voucher　会计凭证

accounting year　会计年度

accounting(s)　会计人员

accounts of assured　保险人账户

accounts receivable insurance　应收账款保险

accredit (to)　强制承兑

accredited agency　派驻机构

accredited organization of public security　公安派驻机构

accredits　承认资格

accretion　添附

accrual basis　权益发生制

accrual concept　权益发生概念

accrued taxes　纳税储备

accumulated profit　累计利润

accumulated savings　累进储金

accumulated surplus　历年结余

accumulation fund　公积金

accumulation trust　储蓄信托

accumulative penalty　加重处罚

accumulative sentence　累计判决

accusation　罪名

accusation evidence　检察证据

accusation function　控诉职能

accusational system　控诉制

accusatory instrument　控告起诉书

accusatory pleading　控告起诉书

accusatory procedure　弹劾式诉讼,控告式诉讼程序

accuse　控告

accuser 控告人

achieve the goal 达到目的

acknowledg(e)ment of debt 承认债务

acknowledge 认领,承认

acknowledg(e)ment 承认,认领

acknowledge and approve 认诺

acknowledgement by the debtor of debt 债务人承认债务

acknowledgment of a debt 债务证明

acknowledgment or receipt 收据

acquiesce 默许

acquiescence 默认权利侵害,默许,默认

acquiescent 默许的,默认的

acquire 收购,让受,取得

acquire(to) 兼并

acquire by fraud 诈欺取得

acquired nationality 取得国籍

acquired right 既得权利,既约权益

acquirement(/acquisition) of nationality 取得国籍

acquirer 让受人(方)

acquirers primus (拉) 第一取得人

acquiring enterprise 购方企业

acquiring party 让受人(方)

acquisitio(拉) 取得

acquisition 兼并,收购,取得

acquisition by occupancy 占有取得

acquisition of nationality by descent 因血缘取得国籍

acquisition of ownership 所有权取得

acquisition of property right 取得财产权

acquisition price 购买价格

acquisition theory of crime 犯罪学习论

acquisition without consideration 无偿取得

acquisitive prescription 取得时效

acquisitor 取得人

acquisitum 占有物

acquit 判决无罪,免除

acquittance of responsibility 免除责任

acreage estate company 地产公司

acreage property 大块土地

acreage reserve program 保留耕地面积计划

across-the-board adjustment 全面调整

across-the-board tariff reduction 全面降低关税

act 条例

act against 违反

act against duty 违反义务的行为

act as a commission agent 代销

act as a counterweight to 抗衡

act as regent 摄政

act as sales agent 代销

act compelled by threats 威胁强迫行为

act decree 法令

act done by mistake of fact 事实错误行为

act for sinking evidence 隐匿证据行为

act going against the law 与法律相抵触的行为

act in excess of authority 越权行为

act in good faith 善意行事

act in law 法律上行为,法律行为

act in prospect of death 死后行为

act in violation of regulations 违章行为

act in violation of the administrative order 违反行政管理秩序的行为

act in violation of the stipulations 违反规定行为

act in-the-law 民事法律行为

act of a party 当事人行为

act of a third person 第三人行

为

act of abducting a child　诱拐儿童行为

act of accepting bribes　收受贿赂行为

act of accession　加入他人已订立的合同行为

act of adhesion　加入行为

act of administration　行政行为

act of agency　代理行为

act of altering certificates of bank settlement　变造银行结算凭证行为

act of altering currency　变造货币行为

act of altering financial instruments and cards　变造金融证券行为

act of altering official documents, certificates or seals　变造公文、证件或印章行为

act of altering state currency　变造国家货币行为

act of altering the business license of financial operations　变造经营金融业务许可证行为

act of authentication　认证行为

act of authority　授权行为

act of authorization　授权行为

act of authorizing the power to impose penalties　授权处罚的行为

act of bankruptcy　破产行为

act of cheating others out of letter of credit　骗取信用证的行为

act of civil litigation　民事诉讼行为

act of commission　作为

act of concealing criminal evidence　隐匿罪证行为

act of concealing postal materials　隐匿邮件电报行为

act of concealment　隐匿行为

act of congress　国会法案

act of consideration　有偿行为

act of corruption　腐化行为

act of court　法院备忘录

act of delegating other organizations to impose penalties　委托处罚的行为

act of denunciation　毁约行为

act of disposition　处分行为

act of disrupting the order of social administration　妨害社会管理秩序行为

act of disturbing traffic order　扰乱交通秩序行为

act of embezzlement　侵吞行为

act of execution　执行行为

act of fabricating false grounds of introducing capital, projects and others to swindle out of loans　编造引进资金、项目等虚假理由的诈骗贷款行为

act of falsifying of official documents　伪造公文行为

act of fraud by pledging falsified certificate of property rights to obtain a bank loan　使用虚假的产权证明作担保的诈骗贷款行为

act of fraud by pledging falsified certifying documents to obtain a bank loan　使用虚假的证明文件的诈骗贷款行为

act of fraud by pledging falsified economic contracts to obtain a bank loan　使用虚假的经济合同的诈骗贷款行为

act of God　天灾(不可抗力),自然灾害,不可抗力行为,不可抗力

act of government　政府行为

act of grace　特赦

act of hegemonism　霸权主义行为

act of indemnity　赦免法

act of infringement　侵权行为

act of investigation　侦查行为

act of jeopardizing business secret　妨害商业秘密行为

act of knowingly holding, using, or transporting forged currencies　明知是伪造的货币而持

有使用、运输的行为

act of knowingly using forged, mutilated of disused instruments 明知是伪造、变造、作废的票据而使用的行为

act of larceny 盗窃行为

act of manufacturing or selling bogus medicines 制造、贩卖假药行为

act of manufacturing or selling fake or inferior products 制造、销售伪劣产品行为

act of manufacturing or selling inferior medical equipment 制造、销售劣质医疗器械行为

act of manufacturing or selling inferior or harmful foodstuff 制造、销售劣质有害食品行为

act of manufacturing, or selling fake and inferior pesticides 制造、销售假劣农药行为

act of manufacturing, selling or transporting narcotics 制造、贩卖、运输毒品行为

act of notary public 公证行为

act of official duty 法定职务行为

act of omission 不作为，相行为

act of parliament 条例

act of people's representatives 人民代表性

act of perpetrating 实行行为

act of pooling public deposits in disguised form 变相吸收公众存款行为

act of producing pornographic books or pictures 制作淫书淫画行为

act of producing, selling or misusing dangerous drugs and narcotics 制造、销售、滥用危险药品和毒品行为

act of purpose 目的行为说

act of ratification 批准行为、追认行为

act of representation 表意行为

act of reprisals 报复行为

① act of rescue 紧急避险
② act of sale 销售活动
③ act of self-defense 防卫行为
④ act of settlement 王位继承法
⑤ act of state 国家行为,治理行为
⑥ act of state doctrine 国家行为主义
⑧ act of supremacy 最高权力条例
⑨ act of swindling 欺骗行为
⑩ act of taking bribes 收受贿赂行为
⑫ act of taking the credit card of another as one's own 冒用他人信用卡的行为
⑮ act of the seller 卖方行为
⑯ act of tort 侵权行为
⑰ act of transgressing customs control rules 违反海关监管规定的行为
⑲ act of unfair competition 不正当竞争行为
㉒ act of union（英）合并法
㉓ act of violence 使用暴力行为,暴行,暴力行为
㉕ act of war 战争行为
㉖ act of willfully selling commodities that utter false registered trademarks 故意销售假冒注册商标和商品的行为
㉚ act on the enjoyment of civil rights by foreigners and on the application of foreign Laws 外国人享有民事权利及外国法律适用法
㉟ act one's age 从事适龄行为
㊱ act or omission 作为或不作为
㊲ act or other expressions of repentance 悔改表现
㊳ act prohibiting combinations is restraint of trade（加）禁止限制性贸易的合并法
㊷ act that subjects one's person to indignity 人身侮辱的行为
㊹ act to execute a crime 着手实行犯罪
㊻ act without compensation 无补偿行为,无偿行为

act without legal effect 无效法律行为

act without responsibility 不负责任的行为

acte authentique（港） 在公证人前所签订之契约或字据

actio（拉） 诉讼

actio ad interesse（拉） 损害赔偿的诉讼

actio civilis（拉） 民事诉权

actio commodati（拉） 使用借贷诉讼

actio damni injunia 要求赔偿损失的诉讼

actio de peculio（拉） 损害赔偿的诉讼

actio duplex（拉） 双重住所地主义

actio ex contratu（拉） 由合同引起的诉讼

actio hypothecaria（拉） 质物诉讼

actio in personam（拉） 对人诉讼

actio in rem（拉） 对物诉讼

actio matnimonialis（拉） 根据委托契约的诉讼

actio mixta（拉） 混合诉讼

actio negatoria（拉） 排除妨碍所有权之诉，所有权侵害诉讼

actio punliana（拉） 撤销诈欺行为之诉

actio quod metus causa（拉） 取消强迫订立的契约的诉讼，基于胁迫订立之诉

action 诉,诉讼,战斗

action at law 法律诉讼

action by the community relating to nature conservation 共同体保护自然界行动

action for administrative compensation 行政赔偿诉讼

action for alteration 变更法律关系之诉

action for collision 船舶碰撞索赔诉讼

action for compensation for loss 损害赔偿的诉讼

action for confirming jural relations 法律关系确认之诉

action for damages 损害赔偿的诉讼

action for deceit 因欺诈提起的诉讼

action for indemnity 赔偿诉讼，损害赔偿的诉讼，要求赔偿的诉讼

action for inheritance 继承诉讼

action for mesne profits 要求收回中间收益诉

action for possession 占有诉法

action for property 财产诉讼

action for registration 登记诉讼

actlon for restitution 退还原物诉讼

action for the alteration of legal relations 变更法律关系之诉

action founded in contract 根据合同提起的诉讼

action in chief 本诉,本诉讼

action in person 对人诉讼

action in personam（拉） 对人诉讼

action in rem（拉） 对物诉讼,对物诉讼制度

action of appeal for annulment of administrative directives 取消裁决之诉

action of appeal for annulment of disciplinary sanctions 取消处分之诉

action of assumpsit 违约损害赔偿之诉

action of certificate 证书诉讼

action of contract 契约诉讼

action of creation 创设之诉

action of detinue 收回非法占有动产之诉

action of election 选举诉讼

action of enforcement 执行之诉（给付之诉）

action of first instance 一审案件

action of keeping 保管行为

action of nullity 要求宣告无效

的诉讼

action of parties（日） 当事人诉讼

action of performance 要求履行的诉讼

action of procedure 程序意义上的诉讼

action of public authorities（日）机关诉讼

action of real action 产权诉讼

action of real property 不动产诉讼

action of realty 不动产诉讼

action of replevin （动产）返还之诉

action of subrogation 主张代位权之诉

action of veal right 物权诉讼

action of wastes 毁损诉讼

action on a contract 合同诉讼

action on fraudulent copying of trademark 仿冒商标的诉讼

action on procedural alteration 程序变更之诉

action on properties 财产案件

action on the case 令状诉讼

action popular 民众诉讼

action to recover the price 要求支付价金的诉讼

actions mixed 人权物权混合诉讼

active 现行,积极性

active ability 行为能力

active capital 活动资本,有收差的资本

active citizens 积极公民

active constitution of a crime 积极犯罪构成

active counterrevolutionary 现行反革命分子

active crime 现行犯罪

active criminal 现行犯

active debt 活动债务

active defense 积极抗辩

active duty 现役

active duty commission 服现役

active intent 积极故意

① active intervention 积极干预
② active labour force 劳动适龄人
③ 口
④ active negligence 积极过失,故
⑤ 意过失
⑥ active partner 经营合伙人
⑦ active restraint 积极限制
⑧ active right of claim 积极请求
⑨ 权
⑩ active stage of psychosis 精神疾
⑪ 病发病期
⑫ active trust 自动的信托,有经
⑬ 营权的信托
⑭ acts forbidden under civil law 民
⑮ 法所禁止的行为
⑯ acts in action 诉讼行为
⑰ acts of selling and purchasing
⑱ counterfeit currencies 出售、
⑲ 购买伪造的货币行为
⑳ actual acknowledgment 实际知
㉑ 悉
㉒ actual amount rate of interest paid
㉓ 实际支付利息数额
㉔ actual authority 实际权限,实际
㉕ 权力
㉖ actual budget 决算
㉗ actual cancellation 实际撤销
㉘ actual capacity to repay 实际偿
㉙ 还能力
㉚ actual carrier 实际承运人
㉛ actual cash value 实际现金价值
㉜ actual conditions 具体条件
㉝ actual contractor 实际订约人
㉞ actual damage 实际损害,实际
㉟ 损失
㊱ actual damage offense 实害犯
㊲ actual debts 实际债务
㊳ actual delivered price 目的地交
㊴ 货实际价格
㊵ actual delivery 实际交付,实际
㊶ 交货
㊷ actual discharge 实际清偿
㊸ actual dishonor 拒绝承兑
㊹ actual fault 实际过失
㊺ actual fault of the carrier 承运
㊻ 人本人的过失
㊼ actual fault or privity 实际过失

或私谋

actual handing over　实际支付

actual harm　实际伤害

actual harmful intent　实害故意

actual holder　实际占有人

actual intent　直接故意

actual loss　实际损失

actual notice　实际通知

actual performance　实际履行

actual plural offense　实际数罪

actual possession　实际占有

actual price　实际价格,实价

actual rate　实际汇率

actual requirement　现实的要求

actual residence　实际住所

actual service　实际送达

actual shipment　实际装运

actual strength　实力

actual total loss　实际全损,实际损失,绝对全损

actual value　实际价格

actuary　(保险公司)统计员、保险统计专家

actus injura（拉）侵权行为

actus reus（拉）不正当行为,犯罪行为

actus solemnis（拉）要式行为

actus traditionis（拉）交付行为

ad arbitrium（拉）任意

ad colligenda bona（defuncti）（拉）特别遗产管理状

ad hoc diplomacy　特别外交

ad hoc inspection and repair　临时检修

ad hoc plenipotentiary　特别全权代表

ad hoc settlement　特殊财产授予

ad instantian partis（拉）统一方要求

ad interide bene esse（拉）暂时

ad judicium（拉）合情合理的

ad libitum（拉）无限期

ad ralorem duty/tax　从价税

ad ralorem taxation　从价征税

ad referendum　待请示

ad referendum contract　暂定合

① 同,草签合同

② ad unum onnes（拉）全体

③ ad usum（拉）依照习惯

④ ad valorem（拉）接价,从价

⑤ ad valorem duties　从价税

⑥ ad valorem import duties（拉）

⑦ 从价进口税

⑧ ad valorem import duty（拉）从

⑨ 价进口税

⑩ ad valorem method（拉）从价方

⑪ 法,从价法

⑫ ad valorem property tax（拉）从

⑬ 价财产税

⑭ ad valorem rate of duty（拉）从

⑮ 价税率

⑯ ad valorem taxation of customs

⑰ duties（拉）从价计征关税

⑱ adaptability of punishment　刑罚

⑲ 适应能力

⑳ adaptation to prison　监狱适应

㉑ adaptation, accommodation　变通

㉒ 办法

㉓ add　附加,补充

㉔ add up several punishments　数

㉕ 刑相加

㉖ added damages　附加损失赔偿,

㉗ 追加损害赔偿

㉘ addictive narcotic　麻醉品

㉙ adding mortgage　加添抵押,增

㉚ 加抵押

㉛ addltion of parties　当事人的追

㉜ 加

㉝ additional　附加

㉞ additional articles　附加条款,增

㉟ 订条款

㊱ additional assessment　补充评

㊲ 税,追加课税

㊳ additional benefit　附加利益

㊴ additional budget　追加预算

㊵ additional clause　(单据,证件中

㊶ 的)附加条款

㊷ additional commitment authority

㊸ 追加的承诺权

㊹ additional conditions　附加条件

㊺ additional duty　追加关税

㊻ additional funds　额外资金

㊼ additional imposition of fines　附

科罚金

additional interest　附加利息

additional investment　额外投资,追加投资

additional legacy　附加遗赠

additional losses　扩大的损失

additional mark　附加标志

additional order　增订货,追加订单,追加订货

additional paid-up insurance　已缴的附加险

additional payment　追加付款

additional premium　追加保费,附加保费,额外保费

additional protocol　附加议定书

additional provision　补充规定

additional provisions　附加条款

additional purchase　附条件购买

additional quantity　追加数量

additional regulation　补充规定

additional remark　补充说明

additional right　额外权利

additional risk　附加险

additional risks of cargo insurance　货物保险附加险别

additional service　追加服务

address　地址

address for contract service　合同送达地址

address inquiries to　质询

adduce　提出理由

adduce evidence　举证,提出证据

adequacy criterion　恰当性标准

adequacy of sentencing　量刑适当

adequate　适当

adequate cause　充分理由

adequate compensation　适当补偿

adequate consideration　适当的对价,适当约因

adequate insurance　充分保险

adequate measures　适当措施

adequate opportunity for consultation　适当的协商机会

adequate remedy　定额补偿

① adequate reparation　适当赔偿
② adherence contract　附和契约
③ adherence to a contract　信守合同
④ 同
⑤ (to) adhere to Leadership by the
⑥ Communist Party of China　坚
⑦ 持中国共产党的领导
⑧ (to) adhere to the people's demo-
⑨ cratic dictatorship　坚持人民
⑩ 民主专政
⑪ adhering motion　附议
⑫ adhesion contract　定式合同,附
⑬ 延缓条件(民事)法律行为,附
⑭ 意合同,订不订由你的合同
⑮ aditing agency　审计组织
⑯ adjacent property　周围房地产
⑰ adjacent region　邻区
⑱ adjacent relation　相邻关系,相
⑲ 邻权
⑳ adjacent waters　毗邻水域
㉑ adjective　有关程序的
㉒ adjective law　程序法
㉓ adjoining area　相邻地位
㉔ adjoining building　毗邻建筑物
㉕ adjoining property　周围房地产
㉖ adjourn　休会
㉗ adjourn a meeting　闭会
㉘ adjourn the court　休庭
㉙ adjourned sale　延期销售
㉚ adjournment　闭会,休会
㉛ adjournment of trial　审判延期
㉜ adjournment sine die　无限期休
㉝ 庭,无限期休会
㉞ adjournment term　休庭后继续
㉟ 开庭的期间
㊱ adjudicate　判决
㊲ adjudicate according to law　依
㊳ 法裁决
㊴ adjudicate on a matter　判定某
㊵ 事件
㊶ adjudication　裁决,法庭裁决,
㊷ 裁判
㊸ adjudication clause　裁判条款
㊹ adjudication disappearance　宣告
㊺ 失踪
㊻ adjudication in force　发生法律
㊼ 效力的裁判

adjudication of bankruptcy 宣告破产

adjudication of civil action with criminal case 刑事司法处分

adjudication of death 宣告死亡

adjudication of punishment 刑罚裁量

adjudicative power 审判权

adjudicator 审判员

adjudicatory organization of the state 国家审判机关,国家审判权

adjudicatory personnel 审判人员

adjudicatory power 判决权

adjudicatory power of the state 国家审判权

adjunct account 附加账户

adjusted basis 调整基数

adjusted tax on salaries/wages 工资调节税

adjustment fee 理算费用

adjustment of agricultural structure 调整农业结构

adjustment of exchange rate 调整汇率

adjustment of the par values 调整平价

adjustment range 调整幅度

adjustment tax 调节税

adminicular evidence 辅助证据,补充证据

administer 实施,监管

administer by law 依法行政

administered price 管理价格,管制价格

administering authority 管理当局

administering methods of macro-control law 宏观调控法的调整方法

administering of property 财产管理

administrative document 行政公文

administrative regulation made and promulgated in line with faculty and power 依职权制定、发布的行政法规

administrative department in charge of culture 文化行政主管部门

administration 管理,行政管理,行政,经营管理机构,监管

administration bill 政府法案

administration by law 依法行政

administration concerning the grassland 草原管理工作

administration litigation law 行政诉讼法

administration of audiovisual products 音像制品行政管理

administration of business operation and utilization wildlife 野生动物经营利用管理

administration of classified state-owned property 国有资产的分类管理

administration of communications 交通行政管理

administration of crop seed production and management 农作物种子生产经营管理

administration of domestication and breeding of wildlife 野生动物驯养繁殖管理

administration of education 教育管理

administration of environment of the economic open area 对外经济开放地区环境管理

administration of estate 物业管理

administration of financial institution abroad 境外金融机构管理

administration of freight transportation entering and leaving the country 进出国境货运的监管

administration of health 卫生管理

administration of health law 卫生行政法

administration of Hong Kong 港人治港

administration of justice 司法裁判,司法行政,司法

administration of law 执法,司法,法律的实施

administration of pharmaceutical trading enterprise 药品经营企业管理

administration of prison affairs 狱政

administration of product quality certification 产品质量认证管理

administration of public order at hotels 旅馆业治安管理

administration of public security 公安行政管理

administration of special types of trades 特种行业管理

administration of statistic forms 统计报表管理

administration of statistical data 统计资料的管理

administration of tax revenue 税收管理

administration of territory 领土管理

administration of the foreign exchange involved in investment abroad 境外投资外汇管理

administration of the prevention and control 消防管理

administration of water transport 水路运输管理

administration of wildlife 野生动物管理

administration of wildlife resource 野生动物资源管理

administration on the registration of periodicals 期刊登记管理

administrative decision 管理决策

administrative 行政执行法,行政法规,行政诉讼制度

administrative act 行政行为

administrative act by application 应申请的行政行为

administrative act by resorting to administrative measures 采取行政措施的行政行为

administrative act by the function 主动的行政行为

administrative act for postal management 邮政管理行政行为

administrative act in respect of road traffic 道路交通行政行为

administrative act in respect of traffic safety in waters of fishing harbors 渔港水域交通安全管理行为

administrative act in violation of law 违法行政行为

administrative act of formulating statutory documents 制定法律文件的行政行为

administrative act of law 行政法律行为

administrative act of the customs 海关行政行为

administrative act of watertraffic 水路交通管理行政行为

administrative act on water conservancy 水利行政行为

administrative act to one's discretion 行政自由裁量行为

administrative action 经营管理决定,行政行动,行政诉讼

administrative action concerning foreign interests 涉外行政诉讼

administrative action for financial control 金融管理行政诉讼

administrative action in the army 军内行政诉讼

administrative action of communications 交通行政诉讼

administrative action of taxation 税务行政诉讼

administrative action on price control 价格管理行政诉讼

administrative action on punishment concerning contagious diseases 传染病处罚行政诉讼

administrative action on urban planning management 城市规划管理行政诉讼

administrative activity 行政活动

administrative adjudication 行政裁决,行政裁判,行政审查

administrative advice 行政咨询

administrative affair 行政事务

administrative agent 行政人员

administrative agreement 行政协定

administrative apparatus 管理机构

administrative appeal 行政复议,行政控诉

administrative complaint 行政申诉

administrative appeal of audit 审计复议

administrative appeal on price control 价格管理行政复议

administrative appraisal 行政鉴定

administrative approval 行政批准

administrative arbitrariness 行政强制

administrative arbitration 行政仲裁

administrative area 行政区划,行政区域

administrative arrangement 行政安排

administrative assistant 行政协理

administrative attachment 行政拘留

administrative audit (review) 经营管理审计

administrative authorities 行政主管

administrative authority 行政当局,行政权

administrative authority in charge of labour 劳动行政主管部门

administrative authorization 行政授权

administrative autonomy 行政自主

administrative award 行政奖励

administrative award and punishment 行政奖惩

administrative behavior 管理行为

administrative board 行政委员会

administrative bodies of the State Council 国务院办事机构

administrative body 行政机关

administrative boundary 行政疆界

administrative budget 行政预算,经营管理预算

administrative bureau for industry and commerce 工商行政管理局

administrative bureau of post and telecommunications 邮电管理局

administrative business 行政事务

administrative capacity 行政资格

administrative capacity for performance 行政行为能力

administrative capacity of disposal 行政行为能力

administrative case 行政案件

administrative case for audit 审计行政案件

administrative case for civil affairs 民政行政案件

administrative case for urban construction 城市建设行政案件

administrative case of finance 财政行政案件

administrative case of first instance 第一审行政案件

administrative case of second instance 二审行政案件

administrative case of transportation 交通运输行政案件

administrative case on family

planning 计划生育行政案件

administrative case on grassland 草原行政案件

administrative case on technical supervision 技术监督行政案件

administrative cases of fishery 渔业行政案件

administrative certificate 行政证书

administrative certification 行政证明

administrative charges 行政性收费

administrative circular 行政通报

administrative code 行政法典，管理规章

administrative coercion 行政强制

administrative coercive measure 行政强制措施

administrative coercive power 行政强制权

administrative coercive procedure 行政强制程序

administrative committee 行政委员会

administrative committee of reeducation-through-labour 劳动教养管理委员会

administrative compensation 行政赔偿

administrative compensation case 行政赔偿案件

administrative compensation law 行政赔偿法

administrative competence 行政资格，行政权限

administrative complaint 行政诉状

administrative conciliation 行政调解

administrative conference 行政会议

administrative confirmation 行政确认

administrative consultation 行政协商

administrative consulting 行政咨询

administrative contract 行政合同，行政契约

administrative control 行政控制

administrative control of a state 国家行政管理

administrative control of measuring instrument 计量器具管理

administrative controversy 行政纠纷案

administrative council 行政理事会

administrative counterpart 行政相对人

administrative court 行政法庭，行政法院

administrative decision 行政决定

administrative decrees 行政法规

administrative department 行政部门，行政管理部门

administrative department for animal husbandry 畜牧行政管理部门

administrative department for aquatic products industry 水产业行政管理

administrative department for archives 档案行政管理部门

administrative department for audiovisual products 音像制品行政管理部门

administrative department for catering and service trade 饮食服务业行政管理部门

administrative department for coal mining 煤矿行政管理部门

administrative department for cultural relics 文物行政管理部门

administrative department for education 教育行政部门

administrative department for fisheries 渔业行政管理部门

administrative department for justice 司法行政部门

administrative department for justice of the People's Republic of China 中华人民共和国司法行政机关

administrative department for labour 劳动管理部门

administrative department for pharmaceuticals 药品行政管理部门

administrative department for pharmacy 医药行政管理部门

administrative department for religious affairs 宗教事务行政主管部门

administrative department for tobacco 烟草专卖行政主管部门

administrative department in charge of agriculture 农业行政主管部门

administrative department in charge of animal husbandry 牧业行政主管部门,畜牧行政主管部门

administrative department in charge of auto industry 汽车工业主管部门

administrative department in charge of civil aviation 民用航空主管部门

administrative department in charge of communication 交通行政主管部门

administrative department in charge of education 教育行政主管部门

administrative department in charge of electric power industry 电子工业主管部门

administrative department in charge of family planning 计划生育行政主管部门

administrative department in charge of food hygiene 食品

administrative department in charge of forestry 林业行政主管部门

administrative department in charge of forests 森林行政主管部门

administrative department in charge of health 卫生行政主管部门

administrative department in charge of mineral resources 矿产资源行政主管部门

administrative department in charge of personnel matters 人事行政主管部门

administrative department in charge of post and telecommunications 邮电行政主管部门

administrative department in charge of post service 邮政主管部门

administrative department in charge of railroads 铁道行政主管部门

administrative department in charge of realty management 物业管理行政主管部门

administrative department in charge of supervision 监察行政主管部门

administrative department in charge of telecommunications 电信主管部门

administrative department in charge of the coal industry 煤炭工业主管部门

administrative department in charge of the transport service 运输业行政主管部门

administrative department in charge of tourist industry 旅游业行政主管部门

administrative department in charge of urban planning 城市规划行政主管部门

administrative department in

charge of water conservancy 水利行政主管部门

administrative department of public security 公安行政机关

administrative department of the state in charge of oceanology 国家海洋行政主管部门

administrative department under reconsideration 被复议机关

administrative departments in charge of audit 审计行政主管部门

administrative deposition 行政听审

administrative detention 行政拘留

administrative determination 行政裁决

administrative directive 行政指示

administrative disciplinary measure 行政处分

administrative disciplinary measures for medical malpractices caused by irresponsibility 医疗责任事故行政处分

administrative discretion 行政裁量

administrative disposal 行政处分

administrative disposing power 行政处理权

administrative dispute 行政纠纷,行政争议

administrative distribution (of recourse) 行政配置

administrative division 行政区划,行政区域,行政审判庭,行政诉讼审判庭

administrative document 行政文献

administrative duties 行政职责

administrative economic law 行政经济法

administrative employee 行政雇员

administrative enforcement of law 行政执法

administrative examination 行政审查

administrative execution 行政执行

administrative expense 行政费

administrative fact 行政事实

administrative faculties 行政权限

administrative file 行政案卷

administrative fine 行政罚款

administrative function 行政职能

administrative functionary 行政人员

administrative functions and powers 行政职权

administrative guidance 行政指导

administrative guide 行政指导

administrative handling 行政处理

administrative hearing 行政听审

administrative immunity 行政免除

administrative implementation 行政执行

administrative implementations law of administrative execution 行政执行法

administrative indictment 行政诉状

administrative information 行政情报,行政信息

administrative inquiry 行政调查

administrative inspection 行政检查

administrative instruction 行政指令

administrative instrument 行政文件

administrative integrity 行政完整

administrative interference 行政干涉

administrative interpretation 行

政解释

administrative intervention 行政干预

administrative investigation 行政调查

administrative judge 行政法官

administrative judgment 行政判决

administrative judicature 行政司法

administrative judicial relation 行政法律关系

administrative jural relation 行政法律关系

administrative jural relations of audit 审计行政法律关系

administrative jural relations of civil affairs 民政行政法律关系

administrative jurisdiction 行政管辖

administrative jurisprudence 行政法学

administrative jurisprudence system 行政法学体系

administrative justice 行政司法

administrative law 行政法,行政法律,行政行为法

administrative law for industry and commerce 工商行政法

administrative law of audit 审计行政法

administrative law of civil affairs 民政行政法

administrative law of communications 交通行政法

administrative law of culture 文化行政法

administrative law of culture and education 文教行政法

administrative law of education 教育行政法

administrative law of finance 财政行政法

administrative law of foreign affairs 外事行政法

administrative law of justice 司法行政法

administrative law of physical culture and sports 体育行政法

administrative law of public security 公安行政法

administrative law of science and technology 科技行政法

administrative law of self-government 自治行政法

administrative law of the customs 海关行政法

administrative law of urban construction 城建行政法

administrative law system 行政法制度,行政法体系

administrative laws and regulations 行政法规

administrative laws of finance 财政行政法

administrative legal construction 行政法制建设

administrative legal norm 行政法律规范

administrative legal relations of supervision 监察行政法律关系

administrative legal relationship 行政法律关系

administrative legal relationship of civil affairs 民政行政法律关系

administrative legal relationship of justice 司法行政法律关系

administrative legal relationship of physical culture and sports 体育行政法津关系

administrative legal supervision 行政法制监督

administrative legal supervision in administrative proceedings 行政诉讼中的行政法制监督

administrative legal system 行政法律制度,行政法制

administrative legality 行政法制

administrative legislation 行政立法

administrative legislation act 行

政立法行为

administrative legislation power 行政立法权

administrative legislation system 行政立法体制

administrative licensing act 行政许可行为

administrative licensing procedure 行政许可程序

administrative line 行政界限

administrative litigation 行政诉讼

administrative malfeasance 行政违法行为

administrative means 行政方法,行政手段,行政管理手段

administrative measure by one's discretion 自由裁量的行政措施

administrative measure taken according to power 依职权的行政措施

administrative measure taken upon application 依申请的行政措施

administrative measures 行政措施,行政处分

administrative mediation 行政调解

administrative norm 行政规范

administrative notice 行政告知,行政通知

administrative notification 行政通知

administrative obligation 行政职责

administrative of foreign affairs 外交行政

administrative of public security 治安行政

administrative offender 行政犯

administrative office 行署,管理机构

administrative office decision 经营管理机构

administrative office for industry and commerce 工商所

administrative office in charge of salt industry 盐业主管机构

administrative office of the U.S. courts 美国联邦法院管理署

administrative official 行政官员

administrative omission 行政不作为

administrative order 行政管理秩序,行政序列,行政命令

administrative organ 经营管理机构,管理机构

administrative organ of postal service 邮政管理机关

administrative organic law 行政组织法

administrative organization 行政机关,行政组织

administrative organization for commodity inspection 商检行政机关

administrative organization for culture 文化行政管理机关

administrative organization for fisheries 渔业管理机构

administrative organization for industry and commerce 工商行政机关

administrative organization for law enforcement 行政执法机关

administrative organization for reform-through-labour 劳动改造工作管理机关

administrative organization for urban construction 城建行政管理机关

administrative organization for water traffic 水路交通行政管理机关

administrative organization of copyright 版权管理机关

administrative organization of health 卫生行政机关

administrative organization of justice 司法行政机关

administrative organization of physical culture and sports 体

育行政管理机关

administrative organization of reconsideration 复议机关

administrative organization of science and technology 科技行政管理机关

administrative organization/authority for tax revenue collection 税收征收管理机关

administrative pact 行政协议

administrative penalties imposed by taxation authorities 税务管理行政处罚

administrative penalties in entry and exit control 出入境管理行政处罚

administrative penalties in forestry 森林管理行政处罚

administrative penalties law 行政处罚法

administrative penalties of finance 财政行政处罚

administrative penalties which restrict the right to freedom of the person 限制人身自由的行政处罚

administrative penalty 行政罚款,行政处罚

administrative penalty in respect of health 卫生行政处罚

administrative penalty in respect of road traffic control 道路交通管理行政处罚

administrative penalty in respect of road traffic control 道路交通管理行政处罚

administrative penalty which restricts the right to disposing capacity 限制行为能力的行政处罚

administrative petition 行政请愿

administrative petition of public security management 治安管理行政申诉

administrative pleadings 行政答辩状

administrative post 行政职务

administrative power 管理权,行政权力,治权

administrative power of the customs 海关管理权

administrative power to one's discretion 行政自由裁量权

administrative prerogative 行政特权

administrative privilege 行政特权

administrative procedural jurisprudence 行政诉讼法学

administrative procedure 行政诉讼,行政程序,行政争讼

administrative procedure in the narrow sense 狭义的行政诉讼法

administrative procedure law 行政争讼法,行政程序法,行政诉讼法

administrative procedure law in the broad sense 广义的行政诉讼法

administrative procedure legislation 行政程序立法

administrative proceedings 行政诉讼

administrative provisions 行政规定

administrative punishment 行政解决,行政处罚

administrative punishment concerning food hygiene 食品卫生行政处罚

administrative punishment concerning traffic control 交通管理行政处罚

administrative punishment for violations against control of entering and leaving China 入出境管理行政处罚

administrative punishment in entry and exit control 出境入境管理行政处罚

administrative punishment in grassland supervision 草原管

理行政处罚

administrative punishment in management of contagious diseases 传染病管理行政处罚

administrative punishment in management of contagious diseases 传染病行管理行政处罚

administrative punishment in respect to supervision of fishery 渔业行政管理行政处罚

administrative punishment in supervision of water resource 水资源管理行政处罚

administrative punishment of financial control 金融管理行政处罚

administrative punishment of industry and commerce 工商行政管理处罚

administrative punishment of inflicting obligations 科以义务的行政处罚

administrative punishment of traffic control of inland rivers 内河交通管理行政处罚

administrative punishment on price control 价格管理行政处罚

administrative reconsideration 行政复查,行政复议

administrative reconsideration concerning traffic control 交通管理行政复议

administrative reconsideration for industry and commerce 工商管理行政复议

administrative reconsideration in respect of health 卫生行政复议

administrative reconsideration of the customs 海关行政复议

administrative reconsideration on taxation 税务行政复议

administrative reconsideration on urban planning management 城市规划管理行政复议

administrative record 行政案卷

administrative recuperation 行政补偿

administrative region 行政区

administrative regional division of the People's Republic of China 中华人民共和国行政区划

administrative registration 行政登记

administrative regulation for enforcement of law and others 执行的行政法规

administrative regulation made and promulgated upon entrustment 委托制定、发布的行政法规

administrative regulations 行政管理法规,行政法规

administrative regulations of mineral resources 矿产资源行政法规

administrative relation 行政关系

administrative remedy 行政救济

administrative reply 行政批复

administrative request for instruction 行政请示

administrative requisition 行政征调

administrative resolution 行政决议

administrative responsibility 行政责任

administrative responsibility system 行政责任制

administrative review 行政复议

administrative review in management of contagious diseases 传染病管理行政复议

administrative review of finance 财政行政复议

administrative review term 行政复议期间

administrative rules 管理规章,行政规章

administrative ruling 行政裁定

administrative ruling in writing 行政裁定书

administrative sanction 行政处分,行政制裁

administrative sanction of the customs 海关行政处罚

administrative sanctions 行政拘留

administrative self-government 行政自治

administrative staff 行政管理人员,管理人员

administrative standard 行政规范

administrative statistics 行政统计

administrative structure of building industry and capital construction（or investment）建筑业和基建管理体制

administrative supervision 行政监督,行政监察

administrative supply 行政给付

administrative system 行政制度

administrative system of finance 财政管理机构

administrative system of importation of technology 技术进口管理制度

administrative time limit 行政时限

administrative tort 行政侵权

administrative treaty 行政条约

administrative trial 行政审查

administrative tribunal 行政法庭,行政裁判所,行政诉讼法庭

administrative union 行政组合,行政同盟

administrative unit 行政单位

administrative verification 行政确认

administrative village 行政村

administrative zone 行政区

administrator 行政长官,管理人员

administrator of an estate 物业管理人

administrator of property 物业管理人

admiralty 海事法

admiralty court of the People's Republic of China 中华人民共和国海事法庭

admiralty courts of the U.S.A. 美国海事法庭

admissibility of evidence 证据的可采性

admissible assets 可税资产

admissible plea 可以受理的抗辩

admission by investment 投资入伙

admission of a debt 承认债务

admission of a new member 新会员国的接纳

admission of alien 外国人入境许可

admission of facts 承认事实

admission of liability 承认责任,承认负有责任

admission of partner 入伙

admission of securities to listing 证券上市指南

admission(s) 承认

admissions 被告口供,被告人口供

admit 承认

admit by examination 招考

admit one's guilt 认罪,领罪

admit one's guilty 伏罪

adobe 砖坯砌成的建筑物

adopt 采取,收养

adopt a dictatorial policy 采用专制政策

adopt a series of measures 采取一系列措施

adopt safety measures 采取安全措施

adopted 被收养,被收养人

adopted minor 被收养未成年人

adopted on first reading 一读通过

adoption 收养关系

adoption by acquiescence 默认通过

adoption by consensus 以协商一致方式通过

adoption of children act 儿童收养法

adpromissiones（拉） 保证契约

adult 成年人

adult child 成年子女

adulterate 掺假

adulteration 掺假,掺杂

adulteratio（拉） 伪造货币

adulterator 伪造者

adultery 通奸罪

advance 垫款,预付款项,提出,预付,促进

advance against bills 凭汇票发放贷款

advance buying for the season's needs 因季节需要提前购买

advance by overdraft 透支

advance charge 预付费用

advance deposits 预存款项,预缴押金

advance freight 预付运费

advance guarantee 预付款退还担保

advance in cash 预付现金

advance money on security 预付保证金

advance on sale 预收贷款

advance payment 预购定金,预付,提前付款

advance payment 提前付款,预付

advance received on contract 按合同预收款项

advance shipment 提前装船

advance the delivery 提前交货

advance upon collateral（security） 证券担保贷款

advanced bill of loading 预借提单

advanced deposit 进口押金制度

advanced equipment 先进设备

advanced experience 先进经验

advanced payment 预付款项,预付

advanced technique 先进技术

advanced technology 先进技术

advancement of the time limit for delivery of goods 提前交货

advances from customers 顾客预付款

advances on construction 预付建筑工程款

advances received 暂收款,预收款

advance-in-price clause 涨价条款

advantage in competition 竞争优势

advantages and disadvantages 利弊

adventure 投机活动

adversary 对方当事人

adversary doctrine 辩论原则

adversary proceedings 辩论式的诉讼程序,辩论式诉讼,辩论主义诉讼程序,当事人主义诉讼程序

adversary system 辩论制度,当事人主义,对抗制

adverse party 他方当事人

adverse possession 无合法所有权之拥有,无权拥有

adverse verdict 不利的裁决

advertise for workers 招工

advertisement regulation act（英） 广告管理法

advertisement tax 广告税

advertisement to offer a prize or reward 悬赏广告

advertiser 广告人

advertising agency 广告公司,广告代理

advertising agency organization 广告事业委员会

advertising association 广告协会

advertising contract 广告合同

advertising cost 广告费

advertising department 广告部门

advertising design 广告设计

advertising goal　广告目的

advertising institute　广告协会

advertising marks　广告商标

advertising media　广告媒介

advertising of public utility　社会公益广告

advertising planning　广告策划

advertising production corporation　广告制作公司

advertising rates　广告费率

advertising restriction　广告限制

advertising standard authority（美）广告标准局

advice　通知

advice and pay　通知付款

advice for collection　托收委托书

advice for collection of documentary bill　跟单汇票把收委托书

advice note　通知单

advice of arrival　货物运到通知书，到货通知

advice of bill accepted　承付票据通知

advice of bill collected　票款收到通知

advice of bill paid　票据付款通知，票款付讫通知

advice of charge　付款通知

advice of claims　索赔通知

advice of collection　收款通知书

advice of delivery　货到通知书

advice of drawing　汇款通知书，提款通知

advice of loss　损失通知

advice of payment　付款通知

advice of shipment goods　发货通知

advice of shipping　装运通知

advice on evidence　证据指导

advise　通知

adviser　参事

advising（notifying）bank　通知行

advisory body　咨询机关

advisory jurisdiction　咨询管辖权

advisory letter of commutation　减刑建议书

advisory office　参事室

advisory paper for revocation of a parole　撤销假释建议书

advisory referendum or plebiscite　咨询性的全民公决

advocacy system of criminal action　刑事诉讼的辩论原则

advocacy system of criminal proceedings　刑事诉讼的辩论原则

advocate　辩护律师，辩护人，律师，辩护

aerial navigation　航空

aerial piracy　空中强盗行为

aerial space　大气空间

aerial traffic　空中交通

aeronautical meteorological service　航空气象服务

aeroplane crash　空难

aerospace　大气空间

aerospace law　大气空间法

affairs concerning nationals residing abroad　侨务

affairs of state　朝政

affected person　受损失的人

affective impulse crisis　激情危象

affective psychosis　情感性精神病

affidavit evidence　誓证

affidavit of defense　辩护宣誓书

affiliate　分支机构（附属公司），关系人，分支机构

affiliate enterprises　关系企业

affiliated agency　分支机构

affiliated association　下属社团

affiliated enterprise　分支企业

affiliated notes to accounting statement(s)　会计报表附注

affiliated to a ministry　部属的

affiliation　联营

affirm　维持，确认

affirmation　确认

affirmative　确定的

affirmative action 确认行为

affirmative active 积极行动

affirmative covenant 保单

affirmative defence 肯定抗辩

affirmative evidence 积极证据

affirmative plea 积极抗辩

affirmative view on causation of omission 不作为因果关系肯定说

affirmative vote 赞成票

affirmative warranty 确认保证

affix 签署

affix a name 签名

affix a seal 加盖

affix one's signature 具名(签押)

affix one's signature to an agreement 在协议上签名

afford proof 提供证据

afford us useful lessons 提供有益的经验教训

afforestation 森林覆盖率

afforested zones holding off sandstorms 防护林带

affreightment in a general ship 件杂货运输合同

affront 冒犯

aforesaid right 上项权利

African convention on the conservation of nature and natural resources (1968) 保护自然和自然资源的非洲公约

after care 更生保护

after care measure 更生保护处分

after date 出票后

after sight 见票后

after sight bill 见票后定期付款汇票

after the event 事后

after-arrival-of-goods draft 货物到达后见票即付汇票

after-quired property clause 后约财产条款

after-sales service 售后服务

after-tax deduction 纳税后扣除

after-tax net income 纳税后净收入

after-tax profits 纳税后利润

after-tax yield 付税后收益

afterwards 事后

against 凭…支付(交换)

against all risks 保金险,保一切险

against bribery 反贿赂

against one's conscience 违背良心

against one's true intention 违背真实意思

against one's will 违反意志

against public interest 与公共利益相抵触

against the form of the statute 违反法律规定

against the forms of the statute 与法律规定不符

age characteristics of a criminal 犯罪年龄特征

age for criminal responsibility 刑事责任年龄

age for enlistment 征兵年龄,服役年龄

age of consent 合法年龄

age of discretion 责任年龄

age of first offense 始犯年龄

age of majority 法定成年人的年龄

age of responsibility 责任年龄

age old malpractice 积弊

agency 代理店,代理,代理机构,代理人,办事处,代理点子,派出机构,代理权

agency agreement 代办合同,代理契约,代理协议

agency arrangement 代理协议

agency business 代理业务

agency by appointment 指定实际承运人

agency by conduct 意定代理

agency by estoppel 不容否认的代理,表见代理

agency by mandate 委托代理

agency by ratification 追认的代理

agency commission　代理手续费

agency company　代理公司

agency contract　代理合同,代办合同,代理契约

agency department　代理部

agency endorsement　代理背书

agency fee　代理费

agency for execution of reform-through-labour　劳动改造执行机关

agency for food hygiene supervision　食品卫生监督机构

agency for international development　国际开发署

agency marketing　代理处经销

agency of admInistration　派出行政机构

agency of institution of administrative review　行政复议机构

agency of interpretation　解释机构

agency of necessity　必需代理

agency of people's procuratorate　人民检察院派出机构

agency of state　国家机构

agency office　代理处

agency operation of bookkeeping　代理记账业务

agency relation　代理关系

agency rules　机关规章

agency service　代理服务,代理业务

agenda　议事日程

agent　代理人

agent ad litem　法定代理人

agent and patient　权利义务兼有者

agent bank　代理银行

agent bank corresponding bank　代理制

agent by conduct　意定代理人

agent commission　代理费

agent fee　代理费

agent general　总代理

agent middlemen　代理中间商

agent of criminal action　刑事诉讼代理人

① agent of criminal proceedings　刑事诉讼代理人

③ agent of necessity　必需代理人

④ agent of penal proceedings　刑事诉讼代理人

⑥ agent office　代理处

⑦ agent service　代理业务

⑧ agent without authority　未授权代理人

⑩ agent's acts of agency　代理人代理行为

⑫ agent's name　代理人姓名

⑬ agents contract　代理合同

⑭ ager privatus　(拉)私有土地

⑮ aggravated assault　严重侵犯人身,加重企图伤害罪

⑰ aggravated damages　加重赔偿

⑱ aggravated misconduct　严重的不法行为

⑳ aggravated misconduct　严重不法行为

㉒ aggravated negligence　严重过失

㉓ aggravated offence　加重犯

㉔ aggravated offense by circum-stances　情节加重犯

㉖ aggravated penalty　加重刑罚

㉗ aggravating circumstances　加重处罚情节

㉙ aggravating constitution of a crime　加重犯罪构成

㉛ aggravation　加重处罚情节

㉜ aggravation of penalty　加刑

㉝ aggregate　法人团体,集体

㉞ aggregate amount　总金额

㉟ aggregate corporation　合股公司

㊱ aggregate corporation　社团法人

㊲ aggregate demand price　总需求价格

㊳ aggregate investment　投资总量

�40 aggregate liability　债务总额

㊶ aggregate offense　集合犯

㊷ aggregate price　总价,总价格

㊸ aggregate supply　总供给

㊹ aggregate traffic　集中运输

㊺ aggregated consequential offense　结果加重犯

㊻ aggregatio mentium　(拉)意思

一致

aggression 侵略

aggressive policy 侵略政策

aggressive war 侵略战争

aggrieved alien 受害外籍

aggrieved party 受害人

agrarian law 土地法

agrarian reform 土地改革

agree 同意

agree to (or on or with) 商订

agreed currency 约定货币

agreed decision 协议决定

agreed destination 约定目的地

agreed formula 一致同意的方式

agreed limitation of liability 约定赔偿限额

agreed measures for the conservation of antarctic fauna and flora 《保护南极动植物协议措施》1964

agreed par value with the fund 同意的平价

agreed period 约定期限

agreed price 协定价格,议定价格,约定价格

agreed returns 约定退费

agreed stable price 协议稳定价格

agreed terms 约定条件

agreement 协定书,协定(协议),君子协定,合同,一致,契,协约,口头协议,协议,合伙契约

agreement between Japan and the Republic of Korea on the joint development of the continental shelf 《日韩共同共发大陆架协定》

agreement between the government of the People's Republic of China and the government of pakistan on the boundary between china's sinkiang and the contiguous A 《中巴边界条约》

agreement between two sides 双方协议

agreement between undertaking 企业间协议

agreement by piece 计划合同

agreement concerning scientific and technical cooperation 科技合作协定

agreement concerning the industrial property of central America 中美洲工业产权协定

agreement for a lease 租赁协议

agreement in the form of an exchange of letters 换文形式的协议

agreement in writing 书面协定

agreement jurisdiction 协议管辖

agreement jurisdiction principle 协议管辖原则

agreement of honour 信用协议

agreement of labour cooperation 劳务合作协议

agreement of mandate 委任合同

agreement of the people 《人民公约》

agreement of transfer 转让协议

agreement of understanding 非正式协议

agreement on economic co-operation 经济合作协定(注:指少数西欧国家如瑞士,荷兰等签订的有关投资保护协定)

agreement on establishing the world trade organization 建立世界贸易组织协定

agreement on exchange guarantees 外汇保值协定

agreement on helping and educating delinquent children (in the PRC) 帮教协议

agreement on implementation of article VI of the general agreement on tariffs and trade 实行关税与贸易总协定第六条的协定

agreement on import licensing procedures 进口许可证手续

协议

agreement on investment insurance or guarantee 投资保险协定

agreement on investment protection 投资保护协定

agreement on protection of investment 投资保护协定

agreement on scientific and technological cooperation 科技协作合同

agreement on trade-related aspects of intellectual property rights 与贸易有关的知识产权协议

agreement on trade-related investment measures(简写:Trims) 与贸易有关的投资措施协定

agreement on writing a book 图书约稿合同

agreement price 协议价格,合同价格

agreement quotas 协议配额

agreement tariff 协定规则,协定关税

agreementon interpretation and application of articles Ⅵ, X Ⅵ and X Ⅺ Ⅱ of the general agreement on tariffs and trade 关于解释和应用关税与贸易总协定第六条、第十六条和第二十三条的协议

agreements and stipulations of the parties to a contract must be observed agricultural producers' co-operatives 农业生产合作社

agricultural activity 农业活动

agricultural adjustment act of 1963 农业调整法(1963 年)

agricultural adjustment Acts(美) 农业调整法

agricultural automation 农业自动化

agricultural country 农业国

agricultural credit 农业信贷

agricultural gain tax 农业收益税

agricultural holding 农业占用地,农业租借地

agricultural integration 农业一体化

agricultural land 农用土地

agricultural loan 农业贷款

agricultural means of production 农业生产资料

agricultural mechanization 农业机械化,农业现代化

agricultural pricing policy 农业价格政策

agricultural producer's mutual aid organization 农业生产与互助组织

agricultural producers cooperation 农业生产合作社

agricultural producers' cooperative(中) 农业生产合作社

agricultural production mutual aid team(中) 农业生产互助组

agricultural production responsibility system(中) 农业生产责任制

agricultural raw material 农业原料

agricultural resources 农业资源

agricultural stabilizer 农业稳定机制

agricultural tax 农业税

agriculture committee(美) 农业委员会

agriculture industrial-commercial combine 农工商联合企业

agriculture policy 农业政策

agriculture protectionism 农业保护主义

agriculture-processing-marking allied enterprise 农工商联合企业

agro-economic zone 农业经济区

agro-industrial complex 农工联合企业

agro-industrial enterprise 农工企业

agro-pastoral economy 农牧经济

ahead of schedule 提前

ahead of time 提前

aid and abet 教唆

aider and abettor 帮助教唆犯，教唆帮助犯

aide-memoire 外交备忘录

aim of punishment 刑罚目的

air communications 航空通讯

air conservation 防止大气污染

air contaminant 大气污染物

air contamination 大气污染

air control (/supremacy) 制空权

air control area 空中管制区

air defense 防空

air defense forces 防空部队

air defense identification zone 防空识别区

air disaster 空难

air express service 航空急件传送

air harbour 航空港

air information service 航空情报服务

air law 航空法

air letter 航空信

air line 航线

air material 航空器材

air navigation 航空

air pollutant 空气污染物质，大气污染物，大气污染，空气污染

air pollution administration 大气污染管理

air pollution control 空气污染控制

air pollution control administra-tion (日) 大气污染控制管理局

air pollution control commission (美) 大气污染管制委员会

air pollution control department (美) 大气污染控制署

air pollution control district (美) 大气污染管制区

air pollution control law 空气污染防治法

air pollution control office/APCO (美) 空气污染控制处

air pollution control regulation 空气污染防治条例

air pollution damage 大气污染危害

air pollution index 空气污染指数

air pollution prevention 大气污染防治

air pollution range 大气污染范围

air pollution ratio 大气污染率

air pollution source 空气污染源

air pollution surveillance system 空气污染监测系统

air quality act (美) 大气质量法 (1967)，空气质量法

air quality and emission standard 空气质量和排放标准，大气质量和排放标准

air quality standard 空气质量标准

air raid warning 防空警报

air right 空间所有权

air space 空气空间

air space above sea 海上空间

air space law 航空法即空气空间法

air supremacy 空中交通

air traffic (/transportation) 航空运输

air traffic control 航空管制

air traffic control service 空中交通管制部门

air transport agreement 航空协定

air transportation 空中运输

airborne pollutant 空气传播的污染质

aircraft 航空器

aircraft logbook 航空日志

aircraft seizures 空中劫持

aircrew 机组成员

airfreight 航空货运，空运货物

airlift 空运

airmail 航空信，航空邮件

airport 飞机场,航空邮件

airpost parcel 航空运输包裹

alr-resupply 空中补给

air-supply 空中补给

aitio redhibitouid（拉）解除买卖契约的纠纷

Al shari'a 伊斯兰教教法

alcoholic 酒精性

alcoholic delusion 酒精中毒性妄想症

alcoholic offender 嗜酒犯

alcoholistic psychosis 酒精中毒性精神病

aleration of law 法律的修改

Alexander. Hamilton 亚历山大·汉密尔顿

alien 让步,让与,侨民,外国人

alien act 侨民法

alien and sedition law 外侨和谋叛法（美 1798）

alien company 外国公司

alien corporation 外国公司

alien enemies act 敌侨法

alien enemy 敌侨

alien friend 友侨

alien law 外籍人法

alien property 外侨财产

alien registration act of 1940（Smith act）外侨登记法（史密斯法）

alienability 可让与性

alienable 可让与的

alienage 外侨的法律地位

alienate 让与,转让

alienation 转让

alienation clause 让步条款

alienation of property 财产转让

alienation of the pledge 转让出质物,抵押品的转让

alienator 让步人,转让人

alienee 让受人(方),受让方

alieni juris（拉）他权人

alienism 外侨身份

alieno nomine possidere（拉）代理人代本人管理占有物

aliens checkpost 外办检查站

aliens' act 侨民法

① alignment of the boundary line
② 边界走向
③ aliment 抚养
④ alimentation 抚养
⑤ alio intiuitu（拉）从不同的角度
⑥ 看
⑦ all 全体
⑧ all dimensions 全方位
⑨ all England law report 全英法
⑩ 律报告(英)
⑪ all eventual risks/AER 一切意
⑫ 外风险
⑬ all in all 全部
⑭ All individuals have equal rights to
⑮ get information 每人都有得
⑯ 到信息的平等权利
⑰ All men are equal before the law
⑱ 在法律面前人人平等
⑲ all orders of society 社会各阶层
⑳ all other perils 一切其他风险
㉑ All power belongs to the people
㉒ 一切权力属于人民
㉓ all risk insurance 综合险
㉔ all risks 一切险
㉕ all risks insurance 一切险、全险
㉖ all risks policy 一切险保单,全
㉗ 险保单
㉘ all round price 综合价格
㉙ all told 全部
㉚ all walks of life 各行各业
㉛ all working time saved 节省的
㉜ 全部工作时间
㉝ Allah 真主
㉞ alleged 引证
㉟ alleged cause 引证的理由
㊱ allergy 变态反应
㊲ alliance 联盟,同盟
㊳ alliance of political party 政党
㊴ 联盟
㊵ alliance of workers and peasants
㊶ 工农联盟
㊷ allocate 划拨
㊸ allocate（to）拨款,(资金的)分
㊹ 配
㊺ allocation according to plan 计
㊻ 划调拨
㊼ allocation of foreign exchange 外

汇分配

allocation of funds　拨款

allocation of land use right　土地使用权划拨

allocation of resources　资源配置

allocation price　调拨价格

allocation to the lowest tenderer　减价投标

allocutus（拉）　不服判罪理由的陈述

allodium（拉）　绝对所有权,私有土地

allot　划拨,分配

allotment　分配

allotment issued　已拨款项

allotment of share　股份分配

allow　许可,承认

allow a discount on　打折扣

allow full play to　充分发挥

allow retention　容许保留

allowance　津贴,补助

allowance for damage　货损折扣

allowed by constitution　宪法允许的

all-in contract　总体承包合同

all-in price　包干价格

all-round development　全面发展

almanac　年鉴

alms　捐款

aloof cabinet　超然内阁,官僚内阁

alphabetical Index to BTN and explanatory notes　税目及注释说明字母顺序索引

already existing provisions　原有规定,原有规定

alta proditio（拉）　叛逆罪

alter　变更,变造,改变,更改

alter seals　涂改印章

alter stamps　涂改印章

alter the economic relations　变革经济关系

alter will　变更遗嘱

alteration　变造,修改

alteration of a contract　合同变更

① alteration of administrative act　行政行为的变更

③ alteration of contract　合同的变更

⑤ alteration of guardianship　变更监护关系

⑦ alteration of judicial person　法人变更

⑨ alteration of litigant　当事人的更换

⑪ alterative relief　选择救济

⑫ alternate　签署轮换制,候补

⑬ alternate deputy　候补代表

⑭ alternate member　候补委员

⑮ alternate member of the political bureau　政治局候补委员

⑰ alternative competence　替代职权

⑲ alternative condition　选择条件

⑳ alternative duty　选择税

㉑ alternative form　代替形式

㉒ alternative legacy　未确定具体项目的遗赠

㉔ alternative order　替代订货

㉕ alternative remedy　可代补偿

㉖ alternative voting　选择投票

㉗ amalgamation　联合化,企业合并,合并

㉙ amalgamation of enterprise　企业合并

㉛ ambassador　大使

㉜ ambassador extraordinary and plenipotentiary　特命全权大使

㉟ ambassadorial privilege　大使特权

㊲ ambassador-at-large　无任所大使

㊴ ambidexter　两面受贿

㊵ ambient air　环境空气

㊶ ambient contamination　环境污染

㊸ ambient humidity　环境湿度

㊹ ambient light　环境光照度

㊺ ambient noise　环境噪音

㊻ ambient standard　环境标准

㊼ ambiguously worded　措辞含糊

ambulatory　可变更的

ambulatory appraisement　门诊鉴定

amenable to law　服从法律

amend　改正,修正,修改

amend a judgment　改判

amend the constitution　修改宪法

amend the description　修改说明书

amendatory constitution of crime　修正犯罪构成

amended agreement　修正协定

amended draft　修正草案

amending clause　修正条款

amending statute　修改成文法规

amendment　修改,修正,修正案

amendment act of criminal law　刑法修正法

amendment advice　修改通知

amendment of constitution　宪法修改

amendment of contract　修正合同

amendment to treaty　条约的修正

amendments of constitution of the U.S.A　美国宪法修正案

amends　赔偿

amentia　智力缺陷

America selling price system　美国售价制

American academy of forensic sciences　美国法庭科学学会

American academy of juridical education (AAJE)　美国司法教育学院

American arbitration association　美国仲裁协会

American association for international conciliation (AAIC)　美国国际和解协会

American association for legal and political philosophy　美国法律和政治哲学协会

American association for the comparative study of law　美国法律比较研究协会

American association of criminalogy　美国犯罪学协会

American association of labour legislation (A.A.L.L)　美国劳动立法协会

American association of law libraries　美国法律图书馆协会

American Bankruptcy Reports (Am.B.T.)　《美国破产案例汇编》

American bar association disciplinary rule (ABADR)　《美国律师协会纪律准则》

American Civil Law Journal (Am.Civ.L.J.)　《美国民法杂志》

American civil liberties union　美国民权同盟

American college of trial lawyers (ACTL)　美国出庭律师协会

American institute of international law (AIIL)　美国国际法协会

american journal of international law (AJIL)　美国国际法杂志

American jurisprudence (Am.Jur.)　美国法学

American jurist　美国法学家

American law　美国法

American law institute　美国法律协会,美国法学院

american law institute model code　美国法学会示范法典

american law journal　美国法律杂志

American law of property　美国财产法

american law reports (A.L.R)　美国法律文献资料汇编

american law review　美国法律评论

american lawyer　美国律师

american legal realism　美国法律实在论

american patent law association (APLA)　美国专利法协会

american railway cases (Am.

Rail. Cas.) 美国铁路案件判例

American society of international law (ASLL) 美国国际法学会

amissum quod nescitur hon amittitur (拉) 根本不算损失,不知道的损失

amnesty 赦免,大赦

Amoco Cadiz accident 阿马科·卡蒂兹号事件

amok 癫痫杀人犯

amok syndrome 残暴疯狂综合征

among other things 除其他事项外

amortizable 可分批偿还的

amortization 折旧,分期偿还,转让,清偿

amortize 转让,分期偿还

amount allowable for loss of freight 运费损失金额

amount allowable for loss or damage to cargo 货物损失金额

amount allowable for loss or damage to ship 船舶损失金额

amount drawn 已提取金额

amount in arrear 欠款金额

amount in force 有效金额

amount involved in malfeasance 违法金额

amount of administrative compensation 行政赔偿数额

amount of bond 担保额

amount of capital invested 投资额

amount of compensation 赔偿数额

amount of currency in circulation 货币发行量

amount of damages 损失赔偿金额

amount of debt 债务额

amount of debt secured 受担保债权数额

amount of illegal gains 违法所得金额

amount of indemnity 赔偿数额

amount of limitation of liability 赔偿限额,责任限额

amount of loss 损失额

amount of money equivalent involved in an action 讼争金额

amount of money issued 货币发行量

amount of obligation 债权金额

amount of paper money in circulation 纸币发行量

amount of paper money issue 货币发行量

amount of share 股本额

amount of tax exemption 免税额

amount of tax payment 纳税额

amount of the offset 抵消金额

amount on order 订货数量

ample evidence 充分证据

amplified interpretation 扩充解释,扩张解释

amplify 阐述

amplify economic legislation 健全经济法制

an academic authority in law 法学权威

an account of 报告

An act does not make one guilty, unless the intention be bad. Actio non facit re am, nins mens sit rea (拉) 行为除非具有犯意,否则并不构成犯罪

An act done by oneself, against one's will, is not one's own act 违反自己意愿所作的行为不是本人的行为

An equal has no dominion over an equal 平等者之间无统治权

an error in logic 逻辑上的错误

an execution procedure 执行程序

an expedient measure 权宜之计

an impression made by seal 署押

an incontestable conclusion 确定不移的结论

an invitation to treat (or offer) 要约邀请

an official's salary 俸禄

an unwarranted charge 莫须有的罪名

an urgent need 迫切需要

analogical interpretation 类推解释

analogical patterns 类比方式

analogize 推理

analogous contraband 类似禁制品

analogous list price 准订价

analogy 类推,比照类推

analogy explanation 类推解释

analogy in criminal law 刑事类推

analogy of law 法律的推理

analogy procedure 类推程序,类推方法

analysis certificate 化验证书

analysis of legal problems 法律问题的分析

analytical jurisprudence 分析法理学

analyze the detailed circumstances of a crime 分析犯罪情节

anchor lease 长期租约

ancient codes and records 典籍

ancient constitution 古代宪法

ancillary bill of indictment 附加起诉状

ancillary document 附属文件

ancillary investment 辅助投资

ancillary relief 附属救济

ancillary right 附属权益

Andean group 安第斯条约组织

anesthetic crime 麻醉剂犯罪

animal and plant quarantine agency 动植物检疫机关

animal and plant quarantine department 动植物检疫机关

animal and plant quarantine organization of the People's Republic of China 中华人民共和国动植物检疫机关

animal husbandry 牧业

animal or plant pathogenic microorganism 动植物病源微生物

animals and plants 野生动植物,动植物

animus cancellandi（拉） 有废除的意向

animus possidendi（拉） 意图占有

animus revocandi（拉） 撤销的意思

Annecy 法国阿讷西

annexation 领土兼并

annexation de facto 事实上兼并

annexation of property 侵吞财产

annihilate 摧毁

annihilation of punishment 刑罚消灭

annotated 注释

annotated code 注释法典

annotated proof 附注证明

annotation of statute 法规的注释

announce 公布

announce in court 当庭宣读

announcement of court session 开庭公告

announcement of disappearance 失踪声明

announcement of enterprise registration 企业登记公告

annual budget 年支出

annual financial report 决算年度财务报告

annual income 年收入

annual income tax return 年度所得税申报表

annual interest rate 年利率

annual reporting law 决算法

annual return 年度统计表

annual revenue 年收入

annual shareholder's meeting 股东年会

annuitant 年金受惠人

annuities insurance 年金保险

annuity 年金

annuity assurance 年金人寿保险,年金保险

annuity bond 年金债券

annuity certain 定期年金

annuity depreciation method 年金折旧法

annuity due 到期年金

annuity fund 年金基金

annuity in advance 预付年金

annuity method 年金法

annuity payable 应付年金

annuity reserve 年金准备

annuity reversion 年金归属

annuity table 年金表

annuity trust 年金信托

annul 取消,废除,撤销,宣告无效

annul a contract 使契据无效

annul a law firm 撤销律师事务所

annulment 宣告无效

annulment of law 废除法律,废止法律

annus civilis(拉) 民法上的年

annus cuctus(拉) 一年丧期

answer 答辩书

answer(of the defendant) 被告的答辩

answer for a crime 负有罪责

antagonist blocs 敌对集团

antagonistic 敌对

antagonistic contradictions 对抗性矛盾

antecedent intent 事前故意

antecedent supervision 事前监督

antedate 提早日期

antiburglary 反盗窃

antichemical warfare corps 防化兵

anticipate 预见

anticipated freight 预期运费

anticipated interest 预期利息,预计利息

anticipated payment 预付款

anticipated price 预计价格

anticipatory breach 事前违反

anticipatory breach of contract 预期违约,先期违约

anticipatory interest 预计利息

anticipatory self-defense 预先自卫

antidumping code 反倾销法典

antidumping duty 反倾销税

artificial person created by law 法人

antilogy 自相矛盾

antimodification clause 不得修改条例

antinomy 法律上的自相矛盾

antipollution 反污染

antipollution standard 防污标准

antirecession program 经济衰退对策

antisocial behaviour 反社会行为

antisocial personality 反社会人格

antisocial personality disorder 反社会性人格障碍

antisocial psychology 反社会心理

antisociality 反社会性

antisubsidy duty 反补贴税

antitrust 反托拉斯

antitrust guide for international operation(1977)(美) 关于国际经营活动中的反托拉斯指南

antitrust law 反垄断法,反托拉斯法

antitrust laws 反托拉斯法

antitrust legislation 反托拉斯立法

antitrust policy 反托拉斯政策

antiwar pact 反战条约

anti-bounty duty 反补贴税

anti-bribery 反贿赂

anti-corruption 反腐败

anti-dated bill of lading 倒签提单

anti-dumping 反倾销

anti-dumping and countervailing 禁止倾销和限制出口补贴原则

anti-dumping duty 反倾销税

anti-dumping law 反倾销法

anti-feudal 反封建

anti-government 反政府

anti-inflation 反通货膨胀

anti-plunder（of the fish stock）无滥捕(渔业资源)

anti-pollution equipment 防污器材

anti-pollution measure 反污染措施

anti-pollution zone 反污染区

anti-racism 反种族歧视

anti-Semitism 反犹太运动

anti-trust law 反托拉斯法

anti-trust laws 反托拉斯法

anti-trust legislation 反托拉斯立法

any other perils 其他一切风险

Aomen 澳门

Aomori Bank（Aomori） 青森银行(青森)

apartheid 种族隔离

apatistio（拉） 契约

apology 道歉

apostasy 叛教

apostate 背教罪

apostles 使徒

appanage 封地

apparent 显而易见

apparent alteration 显明的更改

apparent condition 表面状况

apparent condition of goods 货物的表面状态

apparent damage 明显损坏

apparent validity 明显的效力

appeal 上诉

appeal against conviction 不服定罪的上诉

appeal against finding 不服裁定的上诉

appeal against punishment 不服判刑的上诉

appeal against sentence 不服判处刑罚的上诉

appeal made against part of a judgment 不服部分判决的上诉

appeal to the higher authorities for help 上访

appealed case 上诉案件

appear before the court 到案

appear in court 出庭

appear in court as a witness 出庭作证

appearance 投案,出庭

appearance bond 出庭保证

appeasement 绥靖

appellant 上诉人（注：指二审中）

appellate committee of the House of Lords 上议院上诉委员会（英）

appellate instance 上诉申请

appellate mode 上诉方式

appellate paper 上诉书

appellate period 上诉期间

appellate petition 上诉状

appellate procedure 上诉程序

appellate review 上诉复审

appellation of origin 原产地名称

appellor 上诉人

appended litigant 被追加的当事人

applicability of treaty 条约的可适用性

applicable criminal punishment 适用刑罚

applicable law 适用的法律,准据法

applicable law for capacity for rights of natural persons 自然人权利能力的准据法

applicable law for disposing capacity of natural persons 自然人行为能力的准据法

applicable law for general average 共同海损的准据法

applicable law for ship collision 船舶碰撞准据法

applicable law of the international commercial arbitration tribunal 国际商事仲裁适用的法律

applicable law to principal question 主要问题的准据法

applicable law to the preliminary question 先决问题的准据法

applicable scope of labour regulations 劳动法规适用范围

applicant 开证申请人

applicant contracting party 申请缔约方

applicant for reconsideration 复议申请人

application 申请,适用,投保单,用途

application by analogy 类推适用

application for adjournment 申请延期

application for administrative reconsideration of the customs 海关行政复议申请书

application for allowance 申请免税额

application for annulment of contract 申请宣告合同无效

application for approval of compulsory summon to court 呈请拘传批示表

application for arbitration 仲裁申请书

application for arbitration of a technology contract 技术合同仲裁申请书

application for bail 请求担保

application for cargo shipment 货物托运单

application for drawback 申请退还税款

application for letter of credit 信用证申请书

application for naturalization 入籍申请

application for payment 请求付款

application for reconsideration 申请复议,复议申请

application for reexamination of rejected assignment 驳回转让复审申请书

application for resignation 辞呈

application form for approval of detention 呈请拘留批示表

application form for approval of search 呈请搜查批示表

application form for approval of summon to court 呈请传唤批示表

application of administrative penalties 行政处罚的适用

application of analogy 类推适用

application of law 法律适用,法律的适用

application of law in civil relations with foreigners 涉外民事关系的法律适用

application of law in foreign civil relation 涉外民事关系的法律适用

application of punishment 刑罚的运用,刑罚适用

application of treaties 条约的适用

application submitted for approval of an arrest 提请批准逮捕书

apply 实行

apply for 申请

apply for according to law 依法申请

apply for an extension of the time limit 申请顺延期限

apply for notarization 申请公证

apply for reconsideration 申请复议

apply for survey 申请检验

apply in a supplementary manner 附加适用

apply stern sanctions against 严厉的制裁

apply the constitution 实施宪法

apply the formalities of the contract 用合同形式

apply the law 实施法律,运用法律

applying for naturalization 申请加入国籍

applying for remittance 托汇

applying the proviso 适用组书

appoint 约定,任命

appoint and dismiss 任免

appoint and remove 任免

appoint people by favouritism 任人惟亲

appoint people on their merits 任人惟贤

appoint persons by favoritism 任人惟亲

appoint persons on their merit 任人惟贤

appointed agency 指定代理

appointed agent 指定代理人

appointed day 约定日期,法定日,指定日期(为实施日)

appointed guardian 选派监护人

appointed surveyor 指定的检验人

appointing unit 代理权指定单位

appointment 约定,任命

appointment and removal of master 船长的任免

appointment of civil servants 公务员的任用

appointment of trustee 受托人的指定

appointment system 委任制

appointment system for factory directors 厂长聘任制

apportion 摊派

apportioned tax 分摊税

apportionment 摊派

appotioned tax 分配税赋

appotionment of liability 责任分担

appraisal of food hygiene 食品卫生评价

appraisal of xerograpic paper 静电复印纸鉴定

appraisal through democratic discussions 民主评议

appraise 权衡,议价

appraise and decide litigious costs 核定诉讼费

appraise the quality of a product 鉴定产品质量

① appraisement of forensic psychiatry 司法精神病学鉴定,司法精神医学鉴定

④ appraiser 鉴定人

⑤ appreciate (to) added value 增值

⑦ appreciation of currency 货币升值

⑨ appreciation of exchange rate 汇率升值

⑪ apprehend 逮捕

⑫ appropriate 适当,划拨,拨出款项,依据,正当

⑭ appropriate amount 适当金额

⑮ appropriate amount of civil liability 适当民事责任

⑰ appropriate arrangement 妥善安排

⑲ appropriate authorities 主管当局

㉑ appropriate body 主管机构,有关机关

㉓ appropriate portion 适当份额

㉔ appropriate preferential treatment 适当照顾

㉖ appropriate proportion 适当比例

㉘ appropriate provisions 恰当的规定

㉚ appropriate readjustment 适当调整

㉜ appropriate sentencing 量刑适当

㉞ appropriate share 适当份额

㉟ appropriation 拨出款项,拨款

㊱ appropriation account 拨款账户

㊲ appropriation budget 拨款预算

㊳ appropriation by force 强行征用

㊵ appropriation committee 拨款委员会

㊷ appropriation of land 土地的占有

㊹ appropriation of profits 利润分配

㊻ appropriation price 调拨价格

㊼ appropriator 占用人

approval 赞同

approval of treaty 条约的赞同

approval sale 试验买卖

approval system for the issuing of securities 证券发行批准制度

approve 赞同,批准

approved school (英) 教养院

approved to cover 承保

approximate equality and parity 大致均等和均势

approximation of laws 法律的接近

appurtenance 附属权利

appurtenant right 从属权利

apt to 易于

aquatic ecosystem 水域生态系统

aquatic products industry 水产业

aquatic resources 水产资源

aquatic wildlife 水生野生动物

arable land 可耕地

araeosystyle 对柱式建筑物

arbiter 仲裁人,仲裁员

arbitrage 套购,套汇,套利

arbitrage exchange rate 套汇率

arbitrage in stocks 股票套购

arbitrage of exchange 套购外汇

arbitrage of stocks and shares 股票套购

arbitral agency 仲裁机构

arbitral agreement 仲裁协定

arbitral award 裁决

arbitral clause 仲裁条款

arbitral decision 仲裁裁决,仲裁决定

arbitral organization 仲裁组织

arbitral procedure 仲裁程序

arbitral review 仲裁复核

arbitral tribunal 仲裁庭

arbitralment 仲裁裁决

arbitrary 专断行为,任意

arbitrary administrative execution 行政强制执行

arbitrary administrative execution act 行政强制执行行为

arbitrary administrative imple-

mentation 行政强制执行

arbitrary assertion 任意断定

arbitrary collection of fees 乱收费

arbitrary decisions by the individual 个人专断

arbitrary fines 乱罚款

arbitrary interpretation 任意解释

arbitrary power 专制的权利

arbitrary price hike 乱涨价

arbitrary taxation 擅自征税

arbitrate 仲裁

arbitration 仲裁,书面仲裁裁决

arbitration act 仲裁法

arbitration agreement 仲裁协议

arbitration agreement over a technology contract 技术合同仲裁协议

arbitration awards 仲裁裁决

arbitration board of technology contract 技术合同仲裁委员会

arbitration by summary procedure 简易仲裁

arbitration by the state 国家仲裁

arbitration clause 仲裁条款

arbitration concerning foreign interests 涉外仲裁

arbitration institute of Stockholm chamber of commerce 斯德哥尔摩商会仲裁院

arbitration institution 仲裁机构

arbitration of contractual dispute 合同纠纷仲裁

arbitration of exchange 两国货币兑换汇率的确定

arbitration of technology contract 技术合同仲裁

arbitration organization for economic contract 经济合同仲裁机关

arbitration rules of China maritime arbitration commission, 1988 中国海事仲裁委员会仲裁规则(1988)

arbitration system　仲裁制度
arbitration treaty　仲裁条约
arbitration tribunal　仲裁庭
arbitration tribunal of technology contract　技术合同仲裁庭
arbitrator　仲裁人,裁决人
arbitrator for technology contracts　技术合同仲裁员
archdeacon　副主教(英)
archidiacenal courts　副主教法庭(英)
archipelagic baseline　群岛基线
archipelagic state　群岛国
archipelagic waters　群岛水域
architectural complex　建筑群
architectural decoration and finishing　建筑装修
architectural ornament　建筑装饰
archive keeping　档案保管
archives　案卷,档案
archives bureau　档案局
archives management　档案管理
archivist　档案管理员
archon　执政官
area　地区
area for settlement　新居民区
area hit by epidemic diseases of animals and plants　动植物疫区
area of application　适用范围
area sampling　抽样面积
Area where a quarantinable infectious disease is epidemic　检疫传染病疫区
argue　辩论
argument　论据
argumentation　论证
arlstocracy　贵族,贵族政治
aristocratic republic　贵族共和国
aristocratic stratum　贵族阶层
Aristotelianism　亚里士多德哲学
Aristotle　亚里士多德
arm's length principle　正常交易原则

① arm's-length pricing　合理定价
② arm's-length transaction　正当
③　交易
④ armament industry　军火工业
⑤ armed conflict　武装冲突
⑥ armed forces　武装部队,部队
⑦ armed injury　持械伤人
⑧ armed mass rebellion　持械聚众
⑨　叛乱
⑩ armed merchantman　武装商人
⑪ armed neutrality　武装中立
⑫ armed police　武装警察
⑬ armed rebellion　叛乱
⑭ armed robbery　持械抢劫
⑮ armistice　停战
⑯ armistice agreement　停战协定
⑰ armistice pact　停战公约
⑱ army　部队
⑲ army's election committee　军队
⑳　选举委员会
㉑ arnont retained by the collective　集体提留
㉒
㉓ arouse the enthusiasm of　调动积
㉔　极性
㉕ arra (拉)　定金,定钱
㉖ arraignment　弹劾
㉗ arranged tax rate　约定税率
㉘ arrangement　安排
㉙ arrangement for employment after serving a sentence　刑满安置
㉚　就业
㉛
㉜ arrangement of shipment　装运
㉝　安排
㉞ arrear of stock　积压商品
㉟ arrearages　欠款
㊱ arrears　欠款
㊲ arrest　逮捕,拘留,扣留,捕拿
㊳ arrest document　逮捕人犯决定
㊴　书
㊵ arrest of judgment　判决的中止
㊶ arrest record　逮捕记录
㊷ arrest vessel　扣船
㊸ arrest warrant　捕票,逮捕证
㊹ arrestable crime　可逮捕罪
㊺ arrested development　受抑制的
㊻　发展
㊼ arrival card　入境证

arrival notice 到达通知
arrival of cargo 货物到达
arrival of goods 到货
arrival of goods/AOG 货
arrival quantity term 到达数量
条件
arrival terms 到货条件
arrival time 到达时间
arrival weight 到达重量
arrive at one's post 到任
arrogate all authority to oneself
大权独揽
arson 放火罪
arson in the first degree 一级放
火罪
arsonist 放火犯
art business registration 企业开
业登记
art of civil adjudication 民事审
判艺术
article 货物,条款,物品
article of association 公司章程,
内部细则
article of property 财物
article receipt 货物收据
articles 节,法则,章程
articles in a statute 法规条文
articles of agreement 协议条款
articles of an enterprise legal person 企业法人章程
articles of confederation 联邦条
例
articles of contraband 违禁品
articles of copartnership 合伙条
款
articles of impeachment 弹劾条
款
articles of partnership 合伙条款
articles of trade 商品
artificial 人为
artificial accretion 人为添附
artificial boundary 人为疆界
artificial island 人工岛屿
artificial person 非自然人,法人
artificially imposed obstacle 人
为的障碍
artificially imposed obstacle clause

① 人为障碍条款
② Aryans 雅利安人
③ as a consequence of an irresistible
④ cause 由于不可抗拒的原因
⑤ as agreed 依照协定
⑥ as certained goods 确定物
⑦ as per sample 与样品相符
⑧ as prescribed by law 依照法律
⑨ 的规定
⑩ as prescribed by laws 由法律规
⑪ 定
⑫ as prescribed for law 依照法律
⑬ 规定
⑭ as provided by law 由法律规定
⑮ as soon as practicable clause 尽
⑯ 速通知条款
⑰ as supplementary 作为补充
⑱ ascend the throne 登基
⑲ ascertain 判明
⑳ ascertain criminal facts 查清犯
㉑ 罪事实
㉒ ascertain facts 查清
㉓ ascertain the facts 查清事实,判
㉔ 明真相,查明事实
㉕ ascertain where the responsibility
㉖ lies 追究责任
㉗ ascertained by law 经法律确认,
㉘ 经法律确认的
㉙ ascertained offense 已然之罪
㉚ ascertainment of foreign law 外
㉛ 国法内容的查明
㉜ ascertainment of the fees for the
㉝ use of technology 技术使用费
㉞ 的确定
㉟ Asia and Pacific Economic Coop-
㊱ eration (简写:APEC) 亚太经
㊲ 济合作组织
㊳ Asia dollar 亚洲美元
㊴ asian dollar market 亚洲美元市
㊵ 场
㊶ asian lease association 亚洲租赁
㊷ 协会
㊸ ask about 询问
㊹ ask for 申请
㊺ ask for a sample 索取样品
㊻ ask for an explanation 质询
㊼ ask for compensation 请求补偿

ask for resignation from one's post 要求退位
asked price 要价
asked quotation 报价单
asking price 索价
aspect 朝向
assassin 暗杀,行刺
assault with intent commit rape 奸淫
assaulting each other 互殴罪
assay certificate 鉴定证明
assemblies of magnates 贵族会议
assembling offense 聚合犯
assembly 代表大会,集会,大会,会议,议会
assembly industry 装配工业
assembly procedure 安装程序
assemblyman 议员
assent 同意
assent and consent 一致通过
assert a claim 主张债权,提出要求
assertion 断定
assertion of rights 维护权利
assertive evidence 本证
assess 考核
assessable 应纳税所得额
assessable income 可免税的收入
assessment 估价,鉴定,评估
assessment at ordinary times 平时考核
assessment of environment management for industrial enterprises 工业企业环境保护考核制度
assessment of environmental quality 环境质量评价
assessment of property 征收财产税
assessment of risks 危险评估
assessment of scientific and technical staff 科技人员考核
assessment of state civil servants 国家公务员的考核
assessment of tax 征税

assessment percentage 估税率
assessor 陪审员,技术顾问
assessor system 陪审制
assets and liabilities management 资产负债管理
assets and liabilities of bank 银行的资产与负债
assets and property trust company 资产与财产信托公司
assets brought into a business 资产投资
assets cover 资产担保
assets settlement 资产决算
assets trust 资产信托
assign 让步,让与,分配,转让
assign ordinary 权利转让
assign property to 财产转让
assign the rights and obligations stipulated in the contract 转让合同的权利义务
assignable 可让与的
assignable contract 可转让的合同
assignatus utitur jure auctoris (拉) 受让人享有此款的权利
assignee 受让人,受让方
assignee of the buyers 买方受让权
assignment 权利让转,转让
assignment by operation of law 依法转让
assignment charge 转让费
assignment of claim application fy right 债权转让
assignment of contract 契约转让,合约转让
assignment of contracts 合同的转让
assignment of debts 转让债权
assignment of indemnity 赔偿金的转让
assignment of interest 权利让与
assignment of policy 保险单转让
assignment of property 产权转让
assignment of right 权利转让

assignor 让步人,转让人

assimilation of world economy 世界经济同质化

assist 辅助

assistance and salvage at sea 海上救助

assistance of others 他人的协助

assistant accountant(s) 会计助理员

assistant judge 助理审判员

assistant notary public 助理公证员

assistant prosecutor 助理检察员

assize 巡回审判

assizes 诏令

assizes of novel disseisin 新不动产回复之诉

associate chief judge 副庭长

associate judge 副审判员

associate justice 最高法院法官

associate presiding 副庭长

associated agency 委托机构,有关的委托机构

associated bank 联营银行

associated bilateral aid 联合双边援助

associated builders and contractors/ABC 联合营造与承包商组织

associated company 关联公司

associated enterprise 组合企业

associated enterprise 联合企业

associated press/A.P(美) 联合社

association 社团

association embracing agriculture 农工商联合企业

association for the disabled 残疾人协会

association of American law school (A.A.L.S) 美国法律学院联合会

association of American law Schools(ALIS) 美国法学院协会

association of natural rubber producing countries 天然橡胶生产国协会

association of securities dealers 证券买卖人协会

association of south east Asian nations(简写:ASEAN) 东南亚国家联盟

association of undertakings 企业联合会

assume 采取,承担

assume civil obligations 承担民事义务

assume obligation 承担义务

assume office 到任,就职

assume the obligations 承担义务

assumed bond 担保债券

assumed liability 承担负债

assuming contract 加工承揽合同

assumpsit 口头合同

assumption of reviewability 假设可审理论

assumption of the risks 自担风险

assurance 财产转让

assure 保证

assure the obligation 负有义务

assured 被保险人

assured tenancy 被保证的租赁

assurer 保险人

astate in expectancy 期待财产

astronautical jurisprudence 太空法学,宇航法学

asylum 庇护

at a low price 低价

at a low value 低价

at a proper place 在适当的地方

at any time 在任何时候

at arm's-length price 正当交易价

at closing time 停止业务活动时间

at court 当庭

at current price 按当时价格,按现行价格

at destination 目的地交货实际价格

at fair price 价格公道

at fault 有过失
at fixed term 定期
at full capacity 全部开工
at godown 在货栈交货,货栈交货
at market price 按市场价格
at one's disposal 自由处分
at our command 由我方处理
at our option 由我方选择
at owner's risk 风险由货主负担
at par 平价发行,与票面价值相等
at railway risk 铁路负责
at shipper's risk 由发货人承担风险
at sight 见票即付
at the appointed time 在指定时间
at the buyer's disposal 买方处置
at the corresponding level 本级
at the expense of 由…负担
at the expiration of one's term of office 届满时
at the expiration of tenure 届满时
at the latest 至迟
at the next higher level 上一级
at the right moment 适时
at the same level 本级
at variance with the facts 不合乎事实
at will 随意的
Athens convention relating to the carriage of passengers and their luggage by sea 海上旅客及其行李运输雅典公约
Atlantic charter 大西洋宪章
atmosphere 大气层
atmospheric contamination 空气污染
atmospheric environment 大气环境
atmospheric impunity 大气污染物
atmospheric monitoring system 大气监测系统
atmospheric pollutant 大气污染物
atmospheric pollution 大气污染
atmospheric protection 大气防护
atmospheric space 大气空间
atomistic competition 单纯竞争
atrium 正厅
atrocious criminal 凶恶犯
attach 附加
attached account 法院查封账户
attached clause 附加条款
attached condition 附带条件
attached party 被追加的当事人
attachment 查封
attachment 诉讼保全
attachment before the institution of an action 诉前保全
attachment of property before the institution of an action 诉前财产保全
attachment of property in litigation 诉讼财产保全
attacking offense 攻击性犯罪
attempt 未遂犯
attempt of crime 犯罪未遂
attempt of solicitation 教唆中遂
attempt to monopolize 企图垄断
attempt where a crime has been carried out 实施终了未遂
attempted assassination 暗杀未遂
attempted murder 谋杀未遂
attempted rape 强奸未遂
attendant in means of transportation 乘务员
attendant trade 有关的贸易
attest function 公证职能
attestation function 证明职能
attestation of weight 重量证明
attesting witness 契约见证人
attic 顶层阁楼
attorney 受权人,受委托人
attorney 代理人,律师
attorney agent 代理律师
attorney fees 律师费

attorney general 总检察长,律政司

attorney general 检察总长

attorney general's bill 呈交给大陪审团的诉状

attorney in fact 代理人

attorney preparing documents for others 代书律师

attorney's certificate 律师资格证书

attorney's license 律师执照

attorney's procuration 律师代理

attornment 转让,土地转让契约

attract merchants by raising prices 用抬价办法引诱客商

attribution 归属(注:指物的所有权归属)

at-once-payment 立即付额

auction 拍卖

auction by tender 不公开拍卖

auction market 拍卖市场

auction price 拍卖价格

auction sample 拍卖样品

auctionalie(拉) 拍卖目录

auctioramentum(拉) 雇佣契约

auctoritas(拉) 权力,同意

audacious behavior 不受约束的行为

audiovisual products 音像制品

audiovisual publishing unit 音像出版单位

audit 审计,查账,稽核,决算

audit accounts 稽核账目

audit administration 审计署

audit basis 审计依据

audit consistency 审计的一致性

audit criteria 审计标准

audit department 稽查部门

audit evidence 审计证据

audit findings 审计结果

audit ground 审计依据

audit independence 审计的独立性

audit objectivity 审计的客观性

audit of expenditure 监督开支

audit of returns 决算审计

audit office's audit universe 审计部门的审计范围

audit office's mandate 审计机关的任务

audit opinion 审计意见

audit procedure 审计程序

audit report 审计报告

audit result 审计结果

audit rights 审计权

audit steps 审计步骤

audit supervision 审计监督,审计监督权

audit system by the end of factory director's tenure 厂长任期终结审计制

audit year 审计年度

audit's firm 审计事务所

auditing 审计

auditing act 审计法

auditing administration 审计署

auditing administrator 审计署署长

auditing advisory committee 审计咨询委员会

auditing authority 审计职权

auditing body 审计机关,审计机构

auditing bureau 审计局

auditing committee 审计委员会,财务审核委员会

auditing department 审计部门

auditing evidence 审计证据

auditing extent of jurisdiction 审计管辖范围

auditing in charge 审计主管

auditing law in a broad sense 广义审计法

auditing law in a limited sense 狭义审计法

auditing law in a narrow sense 狭义审计法

auditing legal system 审计法律制度

auditing of accounts 审计,查账

auditing organization 审计组织

auditing precision 审计的精确

性

auditing principle 审计原则

auditing regulation 审计条例

auditing report(s) 审计报告

auditing setup 审计机构

auditing standard 审计标准

auditing supervision system 审计监督制度

auditing system 稽核制度

auditor 审计师

auditor's certificate 审计证明书

auditor's civil liability 审计师的民事责任

auditor's comments 审计意见书

auditor's criminal liability 审计师的刑事责任

auditor's liability to clients 审计人员的客户的责任

auditor's opinion 审计意见书

auditor's report 审计报告

auditor's responsibility for the detection of fraud 审计人员发现欺诈行为的责任

auditor-general 审计长

auditor-submitted financial reports 审计师的财务报告

austerity program 紧缩计划

aute diem(拉) 到期以前

authentic 权威的

authentic act 公证证书

authentic interpretation 权威解释,权威的解释

authentic text 作准文本

authenticate 鉴定

authenticate contract 鉴定合同,认证合同

authentication 鉴定,签字认证

authentication of treaty 条约的认证

authenticator 确认者

authenticity 真实性,确实性

authoritarianism 独裁主义

authoritative interpretation 权威解释,有权威的解释,有权解释

authoritative person 权威人士

authoritative precedent 权威的判例,权威判例

authoritativeness 权威

authorities concerned 主管当局

authority 委托的权限,权限,授权

authority conferred by constitution 宪法赋予的权力

authority conferred by law 法律赋予权力

authority for postal administration 邮政管理权

authority of administrative penalties 行政处罚权

authority of administrative penalty 行政处罚权

authority of agency 代理权

authority of agent ad litem 诉讼代理权

authority of constitution 宪法权威

authority of law 法律的权威,法律权威

authority of res judicata(拉) 定案权

authority of state 国家权力

authority of the husband 夫权

authority to pay 付款委托书

authority to pay (A/P) 支付授权书

authority to purchase/AP 委托购买证

authority to supervise 监督权

authority vested in the people 属于人民的权力

authorizable 可批准的,可授权的

authorization of agent 代理人委托书

authorization of the investment 投资许可

authorization to pay 付款委托书

authorization to sign 签字授权

authorize 认可

authorize to pay 授权支付

authorized 核准的

authorized agency 有权代理

authorized agent 授权代理人，指定代理人

authorized audit 授权审计

authorized bank 授权银行，外汇指定银行

authorized bank for dealing in foreign exchange 外汇指定银行

authorized by law 经法律许可

authorized by state 国家认可

authorized capital 认购资本，法定资本，注册资本

authorized investment 授权投资

authorized legislation 授权立法

authorized officer 授权人员

authorized organization 受委托组织，被授权组织

authorized representative representative 被授权的代表

authorized representative 授权代表

authorized shares 认购股权

authorized signatory 授权签字人

authorized signature 授权签字，授权签署

authorized size of a government body 政府机关编制

authorized size of an organization 编制

authorized surveyor 授权检验人

authorized unit 被授权单位

authorized use 授权使用

authorizer 授权人

authorizing administrative organization 委托行政机关

authorship 著作权

auto theft 盗用汽车罪

autocracy 专制政体，独裁政治，专制，大会

autocrat 独裁者

autocratic 帝制

autocratic government 专制政府

autocratic leadership 集权型领导

autocratic monarchy 君主专制，君主专制政体，无限君主制，专制君主制，帝制

autocratic rule 独裁

autocratic system 专制制度

autograph 亲笔签名

automated clearing house 自动票据交换所

automated teller machine 自动出纳机，自动取款机

automatic acceptance 自动接受

automatic acquisition 自动取得

automatic approval system 自动核准制

automatic avoidance 自动失效

automatic exception 自动抗辩

automatic expiration 自动到期

automatic naturalization 自动入籍

automatic renewal 自动延长

automatic security 自动担保

automatic system of fingerprint recognition 指纹自动识别系统

automatic termination clause 自动终止条款

automatic transfer service account 自动转账服务账户

automatism 无意识行为

autonomous banner 自治旗

autonomous county 自治县

autonomous county of ethnic minorities 民族县

autonomous county people's congress 自治县人民代表大会

autonomous county people's court 自治县人民法院

autonomous county people's government 自治县人民政府

autonomous county people's prosecutors' office 自治县人民检察院

autonomous investment 自动投资，自主投资

autonomous jurisdiction 自治权

限

autonomous organization 自治机关

autonomous prefecture 自治州

autonomous quotas 自主配额

autonomous region 自治区,自治区域

autonomous regional people's congress 自治区人民代表大会

autonomous tariff 自主关税,自主税则

autonomous tariff system 自主关税制度

autonomous township 自治镇

autonomy 自治,自主权,自治权

autonomy in management 经营自主

autonomy in running schools 办学自主权

autonomy of enterprise 企业自主权

autonomy of party 当事人自治

autonomy of prisoners 犯人自治制度

autonomy of private law 私法自治

autonomy of will 意思自治

autonomy of will of the parties 当事人意思自治

autonomy theory 自治理论

autopsy 尸检,尸体解剖

autrefois acquit (拉) 前经宣告无罪,不应再受审判

autrefois convict (拉) 一罪不二罚

auxiliary 辅助

auxiliary activities 附带经营

auxiliary bodies of the general assembly of the United Nations 联合国大会辅助机构

auxiliary body 辅助机构

auxiliary claim 附带求偿

auxiliary law 辅助性的法律

auxiliary organ 辅助机构

auxiliary penal measure 辅助惩罚措施

auxiliary product 附属产品

auxiliary sources of international law 国际法的辅助渊源

auxiliary work 辅助性工作

availability 有效

availability clause 货币供应条款,欧洲货币供应条款

availability study 可行性研究

available funds 可动用的资金

available stocks of gold 能动用的黄金

avenum (拉) 财物

aver 确证

average 海损

average adjuster 海损理算人

average adjustment 海损理算

average bond 海损分担保证

average clause 填补条款

average clauses 分担条款

average living floor area per capital 人均居住面积

average living space per person 人均居住面积

average policy 海损保单

average premium 平均保险费

average rate of interest 平均利率

average wage 平均工资

aviation 航空

aviation (or aircraft) insurance 航空保险

aviation accident 航空事故,空难

aviation administration 航空行政管理

aviation administrative organization 航空行政管理机关

aviation fire insurance 航空火险

aviation safety 航空安全

Avignon 阿维农

avoid 规避

avoid a contract 撤销合同,宣布合同无效

avoid liability 逃避责任

avoid or minimize the loss 防止或减少损失

avoid the inspection　逃避检验

avoidable　可归无效的,可避免的

avoidable risk　可避免的风险

avoidal　宣告无效

avoidance clause　宣告无效条款

avoidance of contract　宣布合同无效

avoidance of contractual liability　逃避合同责任

avoidance of disposition order　废止财产处分金

avoidance of misrecognition　避免误认

Avoidance of pending peril　避免危险

avoidance of responsibility　逃避责任

await cross-examination　候审

await trial　候审

award　奖励,裁决,裁决书

award an order to return or compensate the property　判令退赔

award and punishment　奖惩

award and punishment of staff and worker in enterprise　企业职工的奖惩

award of arbitration　仲裁决定书

award of compensation　赔偿裁决

award of contract　签订合同

award of maritime arbitration　海事仲裁裁决

award refered by default　缺度裁决

awarding sentence　处断刑

awards and rewards to judges　对法官的奖励

awareness of probability　可能预见

B

bachelor girl quarters 单身(女)宿舍

bachelor of law 法学士

bachelor quarters 单身(男)宿舍

back a check 背书支票

back country 边远地区

back freight 退货运费

back goods 退货

back goods freight 退货运费

back letter 保函

back money 拖欠款

back order 延交定货

back rent 欠租

back to back c/c 背对背信用证

backbencher 后座议员

background materials 背景资料

backlog (keep long is stock) 积压

backpay 补发工资

backwardation 现货升水,延期交割

back-to-back (or ancillary) of credit 背对背信用证

back-to-back loan 背对背贷款

bad character 不良品德

bad cheque 空头支票

bad debt 坏账,呆账

bad debts reserve acount reserve for bad and doubtful 呆账准备金

bad faith 恶意

Bad grammar does not vitiate a contract 语法不通不影响合同效力

bad law 徒具空名的法律

dead letter laws 徒具空名的法律

bad packing 包装不全,包装不善

bad policies 弊政

bad stowage 积载不良

bad title 缺陷产权,无效所有权,有缺点之所有权,不良的所有权

baffleboard 证券交易所行情报

baggage insurance 行李保险

bail 委托,保释,保释金,保人,保证人

bail act 保释法案,保释法庭

bail bond 保释保证书,保释担保,保释协议

bail court (港) 保释法庭

bail dock (英) 犯人受审的房间

bail for somebody 为某人作保

bail in criminal action 刑事诉讼中的保释

bail in criminal proceedings 刑事诉讼中的保释

bail on security 保释

bail out 保释

bail piece 保释誓约,保释证明书

bail process 保释程序

bail system 保释制度

bailable offense 可保释罪行

baile 委托方

bailee 受委托人,受托人

bailee clause 收托人条款

bailee receipt 受托人收据

bailer 狱警

bailiff 法警

bailment 保释,临时委托,寄托买卖,受托,寄托

bailor 寄托人

bailsman 保证人

bait selling 诱售

bait-and-switch 诱购

balance 平衡,结余,差额,权衡

balance between crime and punishment 罪刑均衡

balance between imports and exports 进出口平衡

balance budgets 平衡预算

balance due 欠款

balance of capital movements 资

本收支平衡

balance of external payments　对外支付平衡

balance of financial revenue and expenditure　财政收支平衡

balance of international payments　国际收支平衡

balance of payments　国际收支的资本项目

balance of payments deficit　国际收支逆差

balance of payments on current account　流动项目收支平衡

balance of payments surplus　国际收支顺差

balance of power　势力均衡,权力平衡,实力均衡

balance of profit　利率结余

balance of responsibility　责任平衡

balance of trade　贸易逆差

balance receipts and payments　结算收支

balance sheet　资产负债表

balance sheet date　资产负债表日期,结账日

balance sheet total　资产负债总表

balance the budget　对预算加以平衡

balanced addition　已抵除的增加额

balanced budget　预算平衡

balanced development　平衡发展

balanced economy　平衡经济

balanced growth　平衡增长

balance-sheet showing a loss　资产负债表上表现亏损

balance-sheet showing a profit　资产负债表上表现的盈利

balancing account　平衡项目

balancing doctrine　平衡论

balancing of interests　权益平衡,权益平衡论

ballistics　弹道学

ballooning　股票上账

ballot　选票,候选人名单,投票

权,无记名投票,投票选举

ballot box　投票箱

ballot paper　选票

ballot paper null and void　无效票

ballot ticket　选票

balloter　投票日

balloting committee　投票选举委员会

balloting system　投票制度

ban　查禁,禁止

ban according to law　依法取缔

ban drugs　禁毒

ban on ambient noise　环境噪音禁令

bandit　抢劫犯,拦路强盗,拦路抢劫犯

bandit rebels　叛匪

banditry　盗窃罪

bane　犯罪分子

banish　驱逐出境

banishment　驱逐出境,流放刑,流放国外

bank　银行

bank acceptance　银行承兑汇票,银行承兑

bank acceptance rate　承兑率

bank account　银行来往账,银行往来账,银行账户

bank accounting　银行会计业务

bank balance　银行余额

bank bill　银行汇票

bank cable transfer　银行电汇

bank card　银行卡

bank charge　银行费用,银行手续费

bank check（美）银行支票

bank cheque（英）银行支票

bank clearing　票据交换

bank clerk　银行职员

bank commission　银行佣金,银行手续费

bank consortium　银行团

bank credit　银行信贷,银行信用证,银行信用

bank credit　银行贷款

bank credit card　银行信用卡

bank credit transfer 银行汇票

bank debenture 银行债券,金融债券

bank debt 银行债务

bank deposit 银行存款

bank deposit certificate 银行存款凭证

bank deposit receipt 银行存单

bank discount 银行票据贴现,银行贴现,银行贴现折价

bank draft 银行汇票

bank endorsement 银行背书

bank examination 银行检查

bank exchanges 银行兑换票据

bank failure 银行倾(倒)闭

bank giro credit 银行转账信贷

bank group 集体银行

bank guarantee 银行保证书,银行担保

bank holding company 银行控股公司

bank in dorsement 银行背书

bank interest 银行利息

bank interest rate 银行利率,银行贴现率

bank investment 银行投资

bank invoice 银行发票

bank legislation 银行立法

bank loan 银行贷款

bank management 银行管理

bank merger 银行合并

bank monetary position control 银行头寸管制

bank monopoly capital 银行垄断资本

bank overdraft 银行透支

bank paper 银行票据

bank pass-book 银行存折

bank policy 银行政策

bank post bill 银行汇票

bank prime rate 银行借款最低利率,银行最优惠利率

bank rate 银行利率,银行贴现率

bank rate of rediscount 银行再贴现率

bank rate policy 利率政策、贴现政策

bank refundment guarantee 银行偿付保证书

bank regulating agencies 银行管理机构

bank remittance 银行汇票

bank reserve 银行储备,银行准备金

bank returns 银行收益,银行营业报告

bank robber 抢劫银行犯

bank stamp 银行戳记

bank statement 银行对账单,银行结单

bank syndicate loan 银团贷款

bank term loan 银行定期贷款

bank transfer 银行汇票,银行转账

bank's acceptance bill 银行承兑的票据

bank's bill 银行票据

bank's demand draft 银行限期汇票

bank's exchange settlement 银行结汇

bank's exposure limits 银行风险限额

bank's fund position 银行资金状况

bank's lien 银行留置权

bankbook 银行存折

banking 银行业

banking capital 银行资本

banking center 金融中心

banking consortium 银行财团

banking consortium loan 银团放款

banking facilities 金融机构

banking institution 金融机构

banking law 金融法,银行法

banking operation 银行业务

banking power 贷款能力

banking practice 银行惯例

banking secrecy 银行保密

banking secret 银行保密责任

banking syndicate 财团

banking system 银行制度,金融

体制,金融制度
bankrupt 倒闭
bankruptcy 破产,无偿付能力
bankruptcy act 破产法案
bankruptcy law 破产法
bankruptcy notice 破产通知书
bankruptcy proceeding 破产讼诉
bankrupted factory 倒闭工厂
banni(拉) 流放犯
banter 易货贸易,物物交换
banter away 出卖
banter with trade off 物物交换
bar 法庭,律师
bar and entail 废除产业限定继承权
bar association 律师协会
bar association（香港） 律师公会
bar by lapse of time 过时抗拒
bar committee 律师委员会
bar council 律师委员会
bar examination 律师资格考试
bare 无担保的
bare contract 无担保契约,无条件契约,不附担保的契约
bare majority 勉强多数
bare trust 无担保信托
bareboat charter party 光船租赁合同
bareboat charter with hire purchase 光船租购合同
bargain 交易,协议,谈判,廉价品,订约
bargain money 定金
bargain on spot 即付交易
bargain price 物价
bargainee 买主,买方
bargainer 卖主
bargaining agent 谈判代理人
bargaining right(s) 劳资谈判权
barrator 诉讼教唆犯
barratry 诉讼教唆
barriers between localities 地区封锁
barrister 律师,辩护律师(大律师),出庭律师,辩护律师

① **barrister**（英） 大律师
② **barrister-at-law** 辩护律师
③ **barter** 易货,易货贸易
④ **barter business** 易货交易
⑤ **barter contract** 易货合同
⑥ **barter deal** 易货交易
⑦ **barter scheme** 易货方案
⑧ **barter system** 易货方式
⑨ **barter trade** 易货交易,易货贸易
⑩ 易
⑪ **barter transaction** 易货交易
⑫ **basal value** 基价
⑬ **base component** 基础部分
⑭ **base court**（英） 初级法院
⑮ **base currency for bookkeeping** 记账本位币
⑯
⑰ **base foundation basic** 根本
⑱ **base freight rate** 基本运价
⑲ **base number of deputies** 代表名额基数
⑳ **base of taxation** 征税标准,课税标准
㉑
㉒
㉓ **base on fact** 以事实为根据
㉔ **base period price** 基础价格
㉕ **base price** 基础价格,基价,底价
㉖
㉗ **base rule** 基础规则
㉘ **base structure** 基础结构
㉙ **base time** 基本时间
㉚ **based on** 以…为依据
㉛ **based on alliance of workers and peasants** 以工农联盟为基础
㉜
㉝ **based on custom** 以习惯为依据
㉞ **based on fact** 以事实为依据
㉟ **Basel agreement** 巴塞尔协定
㊱ **Basel commission** 巴塞尔委员会
㊲
㊳ **baseline of territorial sea** 领海基线
㊴
㊵ **basement** 地下室
㊶ **Basibeus** 首席执政官
㊷ **basic** 基本,基价,根本
㊸ **basic accounting unit** 基本核算单位
㊹
㊺ **basic commodities** 基本商品
㊻ **basic constitution of crime** 基本犯罪构成
㊼

basic constitutional document 基本宪法文件

basic credit line 贷款限额

basic currency 基本货币

basic definition 基本定义

basic document 基础文件

basic instrument 基本文件

basic exemption for the classified income tax 分类所约税的基本免税额

basic fingerprint patterns 指纹的基本类型

basic form 基本形式

basic freight 基本运费

basic freight rate 基本运价

basic function 基本职能

basic human rights 基本人权

basic industrial enterprise 基本工业企业

basic industry 基础工业

basic intervention price 基本干预价格

basic labour law 劳动基本法

basic law 根本法,根本大法

basic law courses 基本的法律课程,基本法律课程

Basic Law of the Macao Special Administrative Region 澳门特别行政区基本法

basic law on guardianship (南)监护基本法

basic legal conception and assumption 基本司法概念和假设

basic level 基层单位

basic level economic organization 基层经济组织

basic maxim 基本准则

basic national policy 基本国策

basic norm 基本准则

basic norm of conduct 根本的行为准则

basic norm of law 基本法律规范

basic perils 基本危险

basic people's court 初级人民法院

basic policies 基本方针

basic policy of the state 国策

basic power source 基本能源

basic price 基本价格

basic principle 基本原则

basic principles of administrative law 行政法基本原则

basic principles of administrative procedure 行政程序的基本原则

basic principles of administrative reconsideration 行政复议基本原则

basic principles of constitution 宪法基本原则

basic punishment 基本刑

basic rate 基本汇率,基本运价

basic reason 根本原因

basic regulations 基本规定

basic rights and duties 基本权利和义务

basic rule 基本规则

basic sate policies 基本国策

basic science 基础研究

basic standard 基础标准,基本准则

basic state policy risk 基本风险

basic statue 基本法律

basic system 根本制度

basic system of administrative procedure 行政程序的基本制度

basic systems of administrative reconsideration 行政复议基本制度

basic target price 基本指数价格

basic tasks 根本任务

basic tax rate 基本税率

basic theories of economic law 经济法学的基本理论

basic theory of environmental science 环境科学基础理论

basic time 基本时间

basic unit of state power 基层政权单位

basing-point pricing 基础定价法

basis 基价,依据

basis in custom 根据习惯

basis of assessment 征税标准，课税标准

basis of liability 赔偿责任基础

basis of price 价格基础

basis of punishment 刑罚根据

basket of currencies 一揽子货币

basket purchase 一揽子购买，一揽子购置

bastard 劣质货

Bastille 巴士底

batch 一批

batch by batch and stage by stage 分批分期

batch number 批号

battered child syndrome 受虐儿童综合征

battery 欧击罪

battery to death 欧杀

battle 战斗

battle act 巴特尔法案

battlefield 战场

be a candidate 候补

be accused (of) 被起诉

be an alternate 候补

be an incentive to 对…起鼓励作用

be antagonistic to 对立

be applied concurrently 合并适用

be applied exclusively 单独适用

be applied mutatis mutandis 参照使用

be approved 业经批准

be arrested 被捕

be at fault 有过错

be authorized 被授权

be automatically prolonged 自动延长

be bailed out 取保释放，取保出狱

be behind in payment 拖欠

be benefited 受益

be born 出生

be borne by 由…负担

be borne by the buyer 由买方负担

① be borne by the consumer 由消费者负担
② be bound by law 受法律约束
③ be calculated on the basis of 依…计算
④ be called to account 追究责任
⑤ be called to testify 被传唤作证
⑥ be called to the stand 被传到庭
⑦ be cast for damages 被判决赔偿损失
⑧ be cast in a lawsuit 败诉
⑨ be cast in damages 被判决赔偿损失
⑩ be charged (with) 被起诉
⑪ be charged with 负…责任，承担
⑫ be checked and found to be true 查证属实
⑬ be collectively owned 集体所有
⑭ be commissioned 受托
⑮ be completely in conformity with 完全符合
⑯ be confiscated for the sale 归公
⑰ be conscious of guilt 抱罪
⑱ be constitutional 符合宪法的
⑲ be contagious 传染
⑳ be contrary to 违反
㉑ be contrary to the fact 违背事实
㉒ be contrary to the historical facts 违背历史事实
㉓ be convicted 被判有罪
㉔ be covered by us 由我方负担
㉕ be dealt with according to law 绳之以法
㉖ be dealt with severely according to law 依法从重惩处
㉗ be declared illegal 被宣布为非法
㉘ be deemed 被视为
㉙ be deficient in quantity 数量不足
㉚ be denied entry to 被拒绝入境
㉛ be deprived of 丧失
㉜ be devoted to one's duties 忠于职守
㉝ be disabled 残废
㉞ be discharged from prison 出狱

be divided into 划分为

be divorced from reality 脱离实际

be duly authorized 正式授权

be elected 当选

be elected by a thin majority 得到微弱多数票而当选

be elected by a unanimous vote 全票当选

be elected by an absolute majority 得到绝对多数票而当选

be elected by an over-whelming majority 得到压倒多数票而当选

be enthroned 登基

be entitled to 有权

be entitled to the right 享有权利

be entrusted (with a task) 受托

be excluded 被拒绝入境

be exempted from prosecution 免予起诉

be fit for industrial application 适于工业应用

be fit for the agreed service 适于约定用途

be forced 被迫

be found guilty 被判有罪

be found out and brought to justice 犯案

be guilty of the most heinous crimes 罪大恶极

be hanged 被处绞刑

be held jointly liable 负连带责任

be held-intact 妥善保管

be hostile to 敌视

be imperative 势在必行

be imprisoned 入狱

be in arrears 延滞

be in charge of 负责

be in conformity with law 符合法律

be in conformity with the principle 符合原则

be in error 有过错

be in keeping with 符合

be in line with 符合

be in office 当政，任职

be ln order 符合程序

be in power 当权，当政

be in receipt 收到

be in the box 出庭

be in transit 过境

be indicted (for, on) 被起诉

be informed against to the police 被告发

be kept for inspection 留验

be liable for damage 负赔偿损失责任

be liable for loss 对损失负责

be liable to pay compensation 负赔偿责任

be naturalized 入籍

be naturalized as a Chinese citizen 入中国籍

be not in accordance with the terms and conditions of a credit 与事实不符之陈述

be not in session 闭会

be obviously unfair 显失公平

be operated by a family 家庭经营

be operated by an individual 个人经营

be operation of law 依法

be or go away on official business 出差

be outlawed 被宣布为非法

be outside the law 不合法

be owned by collectives 集体所有

be owned by the state 国家所有

be past due 误期

be placed on probation within the party 留党察看

be present court 到案

be present in court 到庭

be pressed for 缺少

be prompted 受驱使

be protected by law 受法律保护

be punished for a crime 抵罪

be put to death 处以死刑

be put to torture 受刑

be qualified 有资格

be qualified as a legal person 取得法人资格

be rational 合乎情理

be reasonable 合乎情理

be released in court 当庭释放

be released on bail 讨保出狱

be reported 被告发

be responsible for 对…负责

be responsible for their own profits or losses 自负盈亏

be responsible to the people and subject to their supervision 对人民负责,受人民监督

be restricted 受限制

be sacred and inviolable 神圣不可侵犯

be sentenced to death 被处死刑

be sentenced to fixed-term imprisonment 被处有期徒刑

be sentenced to life imprisonment 被处无期徒刑

be short of 缺乏

be stamped 加盖

be strict and fair in meting out rewards and punishment 赏罚严明

be subject to people's supervision 受人民监督

be submitted to a public trial 付诸公判

be subordinated to overall interest 服从全局利益

be suitable to actual circumstances 切合实际

be sure 确信

be sworn in 宣誓就职

be sworn into office 宣誓就职

be taken in custody 被拘留

be tied down to sth(sb) 受限制

be tortured 受刑

be twice-born 改过自新

be under arrest 被捕

be underaged 未达法定年龄

be up to the standard 符合标准

be void 失效

beaches 滩涂

① beak 治安法官

② bear 承担,负担

③ bear a loss 负担损失

④ bear all responsibilities 负全部责任

⑤ 责任

⑥ bear civil liability 承担民事责任

⑦ 任

⑧ bear financial responsibility 承担经济责任

⑨ 担经济责任

⑩ bear joint liability 承担连带责任

⑪ 任,承担法律责任

⑫ bear legal liability 承担法律责任

⑬ 任

⑭ bear market 卖空市场

⑮ bear no responsibility for any other party 不负连带责任

⑯ er party 不负连带责任

⑰ bear on（upon） 施加压力

⑱ bear operation 卖空行为

⑲ bear or assume a legal liability 负法律责任

⑳ 负法律责任

㉑ bear or be changed with the criminal responsibility 负刑事责任

㉒ nal responsibility 负刑事责任

㉓ bear responsibility for all the serious consequences arising therefrom 承担由此产生的一切严重后果

㉔ ous consequences arising there-

㉕ from 承担由此产生的一切

㉖ 严重后果

㉗ bear testimony 提供证据

㉘ bear the civil responsibility 承担民事责任

㉙ 民事责任

㉚ bear the costs 承担一切费用,承担费用

㉛ 承担费用

㉜ bear the criminal responsibility 承担刑事责任

㉝ 承担刑事责任

㉞ bear the liability 承担赔偿责任

㉟ bear the responsibility 承担责任

㊱ bearer bill 不记名汇票

㊲ bearer bond 不记名债券

㊳ bearer check 无记名支票,来人支票

㊴ 支票

㊵ bearer of tax 负税人

㊶ bearer shares 无记名股票

㊷ bearing wall 承重墙

㊸ beat of death 殴打致死

㊹ beat the rap 逃避法律制裁

㊺ beat up 虐待

㊻ beating the gun 先期成交

㊼ become a formidable obstacle to

sth 严重妨碍

become corrupt and degenerate 腐化堕落

become effective 生效,发生法律效力

become feeble and die 衰亡

become invalid 失效

become of age 成年

bedroom suburb 城郊住宅区

beef 告发

before and after clause 前后条款

before the event 事前

before the tribunal of conscience 受良心的裁判

before the tribunal of public opinion 受舆论裁判

beforehand 事前

begin one's life anew 重新做人

behavioral method in public administration 行政行为研究法

behaviour of government 政府行为

behind schedule 误期

Being calculated to deceive 有意欺骗

belated 误期的

belated self-defense 过时防卫

belief 真实相信,信仰

believe 确信

belligerency 交战状态

belligerent 交战者

belligerent community 交战团体

belligerent state 交战国

belongings 财物,财产

below-the-line promotional activity 自营销售

bench 法庭,议席,法官席位,法官,法官席,下议院议员

bench and bar 法官和律师

bench memo 法官备忘录

bench trial 对席判决,法官审理

bench warrant 法院逮捕状,法院拘票,拘传票

benchers 法律学院院监(英)

benefactor 遗赠人

beneficial interest 权益,受益权

beneficial owner 受益所有人

beneficial ownership 受益所有权

beneficial result 效益

beneficial right 受益权

beneficiary 受益人,受益方

beneficiary of remittance 汇款收款人

beneficium competentiae (拉) 少偿还债务的数额以使债务人能维护

beneficium divisionis (拉) 分担利益

benefit 效益,利益,受益,权益

benefit already acquired 既约利益,既得利益

benefit foregone 放弃的权益

benefit of a fall (in price) clause 保值条款

benefit of argument 辩论权

benefit of cession 让与的利益,让与权

benefit of credit 信贷利益

benefit of insurance clause 保险利益条款

benefits 福利

benevolence 仁慈

benevolent government 仁政

benevolent government 王道

benevolent rule 德政

benighted criminal 愚昧性犯罪人

benign transformation of criminal motives 犯罪动机的良性转化

Bentham 边沁

Bentham's utilitarianism 边沁的功利主义

bequeath 遗留给,遗赠动产,遗赠

bequeathal personal property 遗赠动产

Berne convention for the protection of literary and artistic work 保护文学艺术作品伯尔尼公约

berth charter 泊位装货租船合

同

berth terms 班轮条款

best bid 最佳出价

best evidence rule 最佳举证规则，最佳证据规则

best price 最优惠价

best rate 最佳汇率

bestaving 杖诉

bestiality 鲁奸

bet or beth（以色列）法庭

betray 叛变,泄露

betray a secret 泄露秘密

betray one's country treachery 叛国

betrayal of secret 泄露秘密

betrothal gifts 聘礼

betrothal marriage 聘娶婚

betterment 改良

betterment levy 地产增值税

betting and loans (infants) act 未成年人赌博及借款法

between sessions 休会期间

beware of imitations 谨防假冒

beyond a reasonable doubt 无可置疑原则

"Beyond a reasonable doubt" in criminal case 刑事案件中"毫无合理怀疑"的证据原则

beyond controversy 无可争议

beyond jurisdiction 超过权限

beyond one's control 难以约束

beyond reason 不合理

beyond reasonable doubt 无合理怀疑

beyond the borders 境外

beyond the boundaries 境外

beyond the powers 越权

beyond the scope of the power of agency 超越代理权

bicameral system 二院制,两院制

bicameralism 两院制

bid 叫价,出价,投标

bid abstract 标价总表

bid against each other 竞相投标

bid and ask price 出价与讨价

bid bond 履行合同保证书,投

标保证金

bid opening limited 有限开标

bid package 一揽子投标

bid price 买方出价,递价,出价

bid proposal 承包建议书

bid sheet 投标人名单

bid to boost investment 投资鼓励

bid up the price 提价

bidder 投标人

bidding 出价,投票

bidding contract 投标契约

bidding sheet 标(价)单

big business loans 大额商业贷款

big business 大企业

big capitalists 大资本家

big construction item 大型建设项目

big-character poster 大字报

big economic crime 大经济犯罪

big enterpnise 大企业

big-nation chauvinism 大民族主义

big-nationality chauvinism 大民族主义

big pencil 决定权

big pot of rice 大锅饭

big power 大国

bigamy 重婚

bilateral 双务

bilateral (/two way) trade 双边贸易

bilateral account 双边账户

bilateral act 双方民事法律行为,相互民事法律行为,双边行为

bilateral action 双边行为

bilateral agency 双方代理

bilateral agreement 双边协议,双方协议

bilateral business 双边交易

bilateral conflict rules 双边冲突规范

bilateral consultation 双边协商

bilateral contract 双边合同,双边契约,双务合同,双务契约

bilateral discharge 双边解除，双方履行

bilateral investment treaty 双边投资协定

bilateral legal transaction 双方法律行为

bilateral partner 双边合伙

bilateral quotas 双边配额

bilateral taxation agreement 双边税收协定

bilateral transaction 双边交易

bilateral treaty 双边条约

bill 票据

bill accepted 承兑票据

bill account 汇票结算

bill after date 开票后

bill at sight 见票即付的汇票，即期票据

bill book 票据账簿，出纳簿，存折

bill broker 票据经纪人，证券经纪人

bill clerk 票据管理人

bill discounted 贴现票据

bill dishonored 拒付汇票

bill drawn on a letter of credit 信用证汇票

bill for collections 托收票据

bill for remittance 汇票

bill holder 持票人

bill ignored 拒绝受理的诉状

bill market 票据市场

bill of action 诉状

bill of addressing inquiries 质询案

bill of administrative regulation 行政法规案

bill of amendment 修正案

bill of approximate quantities contract 估计工程量单价合同

bill of chattel mortgage 动产抵押契据

bill of complaint 起诉书，起诉状，告诉文书

bill of credit 取款凭单，付款通知书，付款通知

bill of defense 答辩状

bill of entry 报关单

bill of exceptions 抗辩状，抗议诉状

bill of exchange 汇票

bill of goods 货物清单

bill of goods adventure 借贷抵押证书

bill of indictment 告诉文书

bill of lading (B/L) 提单，集装箱提单

bill of lading clause 提单条款

bill of lading issued under charter party 根据租船合签发的提单

bill of Middlessex 米德尔塞克斯式诉状(英)

bill of oblivion 大赦

bill of parcels 货单

bill of rights (美) 权利法，权利法案，民权法案，人权法案，权利宣言

bill of sale 动产抵押据，卖契，抵押借据

bill of sale acts 动产抵押据法例

bill of sale by way of mortgage 通过按揭之动产抵押契据

bill of sight 进口货临时报告单

bill of sufferance 免税单

bill on deposit 以汇票为抵押证券

bill payable after sight 见票后付款的汇票

bill payable at long sight 见票后远期支付汇票

bill payable at sight 见票即付的汇票

bill payable by instalments 分期付款的汇票

bill payable on demand 即付票据

bill signed in acknowledgement of debt 欠条

bill stamp 票据税

bill to bearer 不记名票据

bill to fall due 票据到期，汇票到期

bill to mature 票据到期,汇票到期

bill to order 跟单票据

bill to purchase 出口结汇

bill under deliberation 审议中的法律

bill undue 票期未到

billboard 广告牌

billing 开票,发票

bills 短期国库券,立法议案

bills certifying seizure of properties 没收财物单据

bills committee 法案委员会

bills in chancery 衡平申请状

bills of exchange act 汇票法

bills of freight 运单

bills of payment 付款单

bills rediscounted 再贴现票据

bimetallic standard 复本位制

bin tag 物料标签

binder 临时契约

binding 约束力,有约束力的

binding and enforceable contract 有约束力并可强制执行的契约

binding character 约束性

binding contract 有约束力的契约,附有义务的契约

binding decision 拘束性判决

binding effect 约束效能,约束力

binding effect of usage 约束性的惯例

binding force 约束力

binding instrument 有约束力的文件

binding judgment 拘束性判决

binding law 绝对法

binding nature 约束性

binding norm 强行性规范

binding offer 实盘,有约束力的报价

binding precedent 有约束力的判例,有拘束力的判例,具有约束力的判例

biological factors of crime 犯罪生物因素

① bipartisan system 两党制

② bipartite 一式两份

③ bipartite administrative act 双方行政行为

⑤ bipartite agreement 双方协定

⑥ bipartite punishment system 双罚制

⑧ bipartite wagening contract 双方赌博契约

⑩ birth certificate 出生证

⑪ birth control 计划生育

⑫ birth control necessities 计划生育用品

⑭ birth of a citizen 公民出生

⑮ birth right 生来就有的权利

⑯ birthday 出生日期

⑰ birthplace 出生地

⑱ bishop 主教

⑲ Bishop of Rome 罗马主教

⑳ Bismarck 俾斯麦

㉑ bite mark examination 牙齿痕迹检验

㉓ black codes 黑人法典

㉔ black economy 黑色经济

㉕ black interest 应收利息

㉖ black market 非法交易市场

㉗ black market financing 黑市融资

㉙ black market operation 黑市交易

㉛ black market price 黑市价(格)

㉜ black market sale 黑市销售

㉝ black marketer 黑市商人

㉞ black rate 黑市价(格)

㉟ blackmail 勒索

㊱ blank bill 空白汇票

㊲ blank check 空白支票

㊳ blank constitution of a crime 空白犯罪构成

㊴ blank criminal law 空白刑法

㊶ blank endorsement 空白背书

㊸ blank facts about a crime 空白罪状

㊹ blank form contract 空白合同

㊺ blanked order 长期有效订单

㊻ blanket insurance 总括保险

㊼ blanket mortgage 总括抵押,一

揽子抵押
blanket order 总括订单
blight notice 遭受毁损通知书
blind 盲目
blind drain 地下排水沟
blind imitation 盲目抄袭
blind tract bullet wound 盲管枪弹痕
blindness 盲目广告
bloc group 集团
bloc price 集团价格
bloc trade 集团贸易
bloc transaction 集团交易
block 大厦,大楼
block construction 大型砌块建筑
block limits 地区限额
block number 批号
block offer 成批出售
block sale 成批出售
blockade 封锁
blockade in time of war 战时封锁
blockade of river 河流封锁
blockade on techniques 技术封锁
blockade outward 外向封销
blockaded state 被封锁国家
blocked account 冻结账户
blocking freezing 冻结
blocking statutes "抵制性"立法
blood feud 血亲复仇
blood grouping by bloodstain 血痕血型检验
blood guilt 杀人罪
blood thirstiness 杀人狂
bloodstain examination 血痕检验
blood-type theory of crime 犯罪血型说
blow-off pipe 安全排气管
blue chip rate 优惠利率
bluechip stock 蓝筹码股票
blue-ribbon jury 蓝授带陪审团
blue-sky laws 蓝天法
blunder 错误
blunt instrument injury 钝器伤

board of administration 董事会
board of auditors 审计委员会
board of conciliators 调解委员会
board of criminal injure compensation 刑事伤害赔偿委员会
board of management 管理委员会
board of supervisors (美) 监察委员会,监事会
board of trade 贸易委员会
board officer 董事会成员
body 机关
body corporate 法人实体,法人团体
body of deed 契据文本
body of sea water 海水水域
bog down 停滞
bolster the price 提价
bolt 插销,瑕疵
bona acquisita (拉) 取得的财产
bona adventicia (拉) 特有财产
bona adventicia irregularia (拉) 自由特有财产
bona adventicia regularia (拉) 非自由物财产
bona bonorum (拉) 共有财产
bona caduca (拉) 归序财产
bona fide claim 善意要求
bona fide counterpart 善意相对人
bona fide negotiation 善意磋商
bona fide owner 善意所有人
bona fide possession 善意占有
bona fide purchaser/BFP 善意购买人
bona fide transaction 正当交易
bona immobilia (拉) 不动产
bona indivisibilia (拉) 不可分物
bond 保证人,契约所规定的义务,约据,第三者担保债务,债券,镣铐,保证书,公债券,政府债券,抵押,契约
bond and preferred stock fund 债券和优先股基金
bond certificate 债券
bond collateral loan(s) 债券抵

押贷款,债券抵押借款
bond coupon 债券息票
bond creditor 契约债权人,约据债权人
bond dividends 债券利息
bond expense 债券发行费,债券费用
bond floatation market 债券发行市场,债券浮动市场
bond funds 债券基金
bond holder 债券持有人
bond indenture 债券信托契约
bond interest 债券利息
bond investment 债券投资
bond investment trust 债务投资信托公司,债券投资信托
bond issue 债券发行
bond issue cost 债券发行成本,债券发行费用
bond-issuing expense 债券发行费用
bond loan 债券方式借款
bond market 债务市场,债券市场
bond premium 债券溢价
bond rate 债券利率
bond register 债券簿,债券登记表
bond re-discount 债券再贴现
bond subscription 债券认购
bond table 债券表
bond trustee 证券受托人
bond yield 债券收益
bonded 保税
bonded area 保税区
bonded debt 债券债务
bonded exhibition 保税陈列场
bonded factory 保税工厂
bonded goods 保税货物
bonded shed 保税货棚
bonded system 保税制度
bonded transportation 保税运输
bonded warehouse 保税仓库
bondholder 债券持有人
bonding company 担保公司
bonds held on their books 登记的债券

bonds with warrants 附认购债券
bondsman 保证人,受合同约束的人
bonorum cessio（拉） 财产转让
bonorum collation（拉） 归还受赠物的义务
bonorum possessio（拉） 遗产占有,财产占有
bonorum venditio（拉） 善意的财产互凭
bonus 奖金,一次性租售费
bonus tax 奖金税
boodle 贿赂品
book worship 本本主义
booking note 托送单
bookkeeper 会计
boom and bust 盛衰
boost the price 提价,抬高物价
boot 附约财产,附约利益
boot money 额外补偿金
bootlegging 违法售酒
booty of war 战利品
border 边境,国境
border control 边境管制,边境检查
border control for entries and exits by Chinese citizens 中国公民出境入境管理
border crossing identification card 过境身份证
border defense 边防
border demarcation commission 划分边界委员会
border dispute 边界争端
border duty adjustment 出入境关税调整
border entry or exit pass of the People's Republic of China 中华人民共和国入出境通行证
border incident 边界事件
border inspection agency of the People's Republic of China 中华人民共和国边防检查机关
border police 边境警察

border price 边界价格
border region 边境地区
border tax 边境税
border tax adjustment 边境税的调整
borderline jurisprudence 边缘法学
borderline personality disorder 边缘型人格障碍
borough 自治市
borrow 担保物
borrowed fund 借入资金
borrower 借款人
borrowing needs 贷款要求
borrowing plan 贷款计划
borrowing short 短期借款
borstal institution 少年犯感化院
both contracting parties 缔约双方
both contracting party 缔约方
both litigants 双方当事人
both parties 双方当事人
both signatory states 缔约双方
both to blame collision 双方过失的碰撞
both to blame collision clause 互有过失碰撞条款，船舶互撞均有过失条款
both versions being equally authentic 两种文字具有同等效力
bottom price 最低价
bottomry 押船借款
bottomry bond 押船借款契约
bought deal 包销
bought for cash 现金交易
Boule 四百人议事会
bound 受约束的，约束，负有责任的
bound by law 受法律约束
bound by precedent 受先例约束
bound labour 合同工
boundary line 边界，边界线
boundary pillar 界桩
boundary river 边界河流
boundary rivers 国界河，界河

boundary sign 边界标志
boundary strip 地界
boundary tablet 界碑
boundary treaty 边界条约
boundary treaty between the People's Republic of China and People's Democratic Republic of Laos 中老边界条约
boundary treaty between the People's Republic of China and the Kingdom of Afghanistan 中阿边界条约
boundary treaty between the People's Republic of China and the Kingdom of Nepal 中尼边界条约
boundary treaty between the People's Republic of China and the People's Republic of Mongolia 中蒙边界条约
boundary treaty between the People's Republic of China and the Union of Burma 中缅边界条约
bounty land act（美）土地授予法
bouquet of arrangement 一揽子合同
bouquet reinsurance treaty 一揽子分保合同
bourgeois democracy 资产阶级民主
bourgeoisie 资产阶级
box 保险箱
Boxer Indemnity 庚子赔款（中国 1900 年）
boxing injury 拳击伤
boycott 联合抵制，抵制
bracket light 壁灯
bracket progression 分等递进征税
Brahmanism 婆罗门教
brain damage syndrome 脑损害综合征
brain death 脑死亡
brain organic psychosis 脑器质性精神障碍

branch of people's procuratorate 人民检察院分院

branch office 分支机构,分局

branch secretary 支部书记

branch theory of international criminal law 国际刑法分支说

branches at home and abroad 国内外分支机构

branches of the economy 经济部门

branding the face 黥刑 (墨刑)

brazing bullet wound 擦过枪弹创

breach a contract and tear it to pieces 撕毁合同

breach as to an instalment delivery on payment 违反分批交货或分期付款的义务

Breach before performance is due 合同履行期到期并违约

breach of a duty imposed by law on a person towards another person 违背私人对私人的法律义务

breach of a duty imposed by law on a person towards the public 违背私人对公众的法律义务

breach of agreement 违反协议

breach of an expressed warranty 违反明示的担保

breach of arrestment 擅自处理已查封的财产

breach of blockade 破坏封锁

breach of close 侵入他人土地

breach of condition 违反合同要件

breach of constitution 违宪

breach of contract 违背契约,违反合同,违约

Breach of contract before the performance is due 履行期未到前的违约

breach of contract damages 违约金

breach of duty 违反义务,不负责任

breach of implied warranty of authority (英、美) 违反有代理权的默示担保

breach of justice 违背公正

breach of law 违反法律,违法,不法行为

breach of morality 破坏道德

breach of privilege 侵犯特权,权利侵害

breach of procedural law 程序违法

breach of promise 违背诺言,违约

breach of regulations 违例

breach of statutory duty 违反法定义务,违反法定职责

breach of terms and conditions contracted 违反合同规定

breach of the peace 破坏安宁,妨害安宁

breach of trust 背信罪,违反信托义务

breach of warranty 违背保证,违反保证,违反担保

breach of warranty clause 违反保证条款

breach of warranty of authority 违反代理权保证,违反有代理权的保证

breaches of contract 违约行为

break 违反

break a contract 违约,撕毁合同

break a promise 违反诺言

break bulk agent 卸货代理人

break down the established conventions 打破成规

break even 保本

break even price 保本价

break off an engagement terminate an agreement 解约

break prohibition 犯禁,违禁

break rules and regulations 违章,违规

break rules or regulations 违章

break the criminal law 触犯刑律

break the law 违反法律,触犯法律

break the law and violate discipline 违反法纪

break the law on a serious scale 严重违法

break the peace 扰乱治安

break the routine 打破常规

break with convention 打破常规

breakage clause 破碎险条款

breakage-proof 防破损

breaking of rules and regulations 违章

breakout type of psychopathy 暴发性病态人格

breath specimen 呼吸检样

breath test 呼吸检验

Bremer Landesbank (Bremen) 不来梅地方银行(不来梅)

Bretton woods agreement 布雷顿森林协定

Bretton woods agreement act 布雷顿森林协定法

Bretton woods system 布雷顿森林体系

brevia testate (拉) 契据的初期形式

brib(e)able 可贿赂的

bribe 贿赂,受贿,暗中行贿,贿赂物

bribe money 贿赂金

bribee 受贿者

bribery 贿赂,暗中行贿,行贿罪

bribery and corruption crimes 贪污贿赂罪

bribery at election 贿赂选举罪

bribery of civil servants 贿赂公务人员罪

brief (of a case) 案情摘要

brief and to the point 简明扼要

brigade 生产大队

bring an action 提出诉讼

bring an action against 起诉

bring down a cabinet 倒阁

bring forward 承前

bring in a verdict (陪审团)作出裁决

bring in a verdict of "guilty" 判决有罪

bring in a verdict of "not guilty" 判决无罪

bring into 纳入

bring into effect 实施

bring into force 使生效

bring into play 发挥

bring law into effect 实施法律

bring the initiative of the masses into full play 充分发挥群众的积极性

bring to a satisfactory settlement 妥善处理

bring to justice 绳之以法,归案,依法处理

bring to justice as severely and fast as possible 依法从重从快惩处

bring to the hammer 予以拍卖

bring up 抚养

bringing order out of chaos 拨乱反正

brinkmanship 外交冒险政策

brink-of-war policy 战争边缘政策

British civil police 英国民事警察

British commonwealth of nations 英联邦国家,英联邦

British constitution 英国宪法

British empire 大英帝国

broad interpretation 广义解释

broadcast in court 当庭播放

broaden one's scope of mind 打开思路

broadth of the territorial sea 领海宽度

broken and damaged cargo list 货物残损单

broken deposit indemnities 补偿银行损失条款

broken deposit indemnity 补偿银行损失条款

broker 证券经纪商,经纪人

broker's cover note 保险经纪

人出具的暂保单

broker's lien 经济人留置权

brokerage 经济人佣金,经济义务,回扣

brokerage clause 佣金条款

brokerage contract 行纪合同

brokerage expenses 佣金、经纪费用

brokerage firm 经济商行

brokerage house 经济商行

brokerage lease 经济租赁

brokerage office 经济商行

brokers 经纪人

broker-dealer 经纪自营商

broking 经纪业

bruise 挫伤,擦伤

Brussels tariff nomen clature 布鲁塞尔关税税则目录

brutal torture 非功利性犯罪

Bryan peace treaties 布赖恩和平条约

bucket shop 非法股票经纪业

bucketing 投机倒把,投机活动

Buddha Dharma 佛法

Buddhism 佛教

budget 预算书,计算,财政预算,基本建设预算

budget administrative system 预算管理体制

budget allocations appropriations 预算拨款

budget committee 预算委员会

budget control 预算控制

budget control statement 预算控制报告

budget deficit 预算赤字

budget for local government 地方预算

budget lay-out 预算编制

budget management 预算管理

budget outturn 预算执行结果

budget performance 预算执行情况

budget period 预算期间

budget practice 预算办法

budget presentation 编制预算

budget procedure 预算程序

① budget process 预算程序

② budget proposal 预算提案

③ budget surplus 预算结余

④ budget to be carried over to the next year 跨年度预算

⑤ budget year 预算年度

⑥ budgetary accounting item 预算科目

⑦ budgetary allocations 财政拨款

⑧ budgetary control 预算检查

⑨ budgetary deficit 财政赤字

⑩ budgetary procedure 预算编制程序

⑪ budgetary receipts 预算收入

⑫ budgetary resources 预算经费

⑬ budgetary revenues and expenditures 预算收支

⑭ budgetary technique 预算编制方法

⑮ budgeted cost 计划成本

⑯ buffer country 缓冲国

⑰ buffer stock 缓冲存货

⑱ buffer stock financing facility 缓冲库存贷款

⑲ buffer store 缓冲储备

⑳ bufferstock financing facility 缓冲库存资助

㉑ build by oneself 自营

㉒ buildable area 建筑用地

㉓ builder's risk 船舶建造险

㉔ builders 施工人员

㉕ building 建筑物

㉖ building and installation engineering construction and installation engineering 建筑安装工程

㉗ building area 建筑占地面积

㉘ building authority 建筑管理机关

㉙ building code 建筑法规,建筑条例

㉚ building complex 建筑群

㉛ building concession 建筑许可证

㉜ building cost 建筑物造价

㉝ building cost of projects 工程造价

㉞ building enterprises 建筑业

㉟ building industry 建筑业

building installation enterprise 建筑安装企业

building insurance 建筑物保险

building laws 建筑法规

building lease 租地造房权,建筑租赁合同

building orientation 朝向

building plot 建筑用地

building preservation notice 保护建筑物通知

building projects 土建工程

building property mortgage 房产抵押

building site 建筑工地

building tax 房产税

building taxes 房产税

building tenancy 建筑权

building under construction 在建房屋

building work 建筑工程

build-operate-transfer 建造-经营-转让

build-own-operate 建造-拥有-经营

build-own-operate-sell 建造-拥有-经营-出售

build-own-operate-transfer 建造-拥有-经营-转让

built-in cabinet 壁橱

bulk cargo 散装货

bulk commodity 散装货

bulk freight 散装货

bulk loading 散装装运

bulk purchase 成批采购

bulk sale 成批销售

bulk sales contract 大批大宗销售合同

bulk shipment 散装装运

bulk transfer 成批交易

bulky cargo 超大货物

bulky cargo charges 超大货物运费

bull 买空

bull transaction 多头交易

bull(s) 多头,买方,买空

bullion market 金银市场

bullish 牛市

bulls and bears 买空卖空

bully 威吓

bungalow 带回廊的平房

bunker clause 燃料条款

burden 负担,义务,责任

burden of contract 履行合同责任

burden of pleading 答辩的责任

burden of proof 举证责任,证明责任,提供证据的责任

burden of rebuttal 提出相反证据的责任

burden of taxation burden tax 赋税分担

bureau members 主席团成员

bureau of commerce and industry 工商局

bureau of industry 工业局

bureaucracy 官僚制,官僚主义

bureaucratic comprador's capital 官僚买办资本

bureaucratism 官僚主义

bureaucrat-capitalism 官僚资本主义

burglary 侵入住宅

buried object 埋藏物

burn corpse 焚尸

burn the corpse to cover up a crime 焚尸灭迹

business 商业,企业,经营

business (/commonlaw) trust 商业信托

business accounting 经营核算

business activity 企业活动

business administration 工商管理,企业管理

business agency 派出机构

business agent 营业代理人,业务代理人

business background 企业背景

business building 办公楼

business circle 商检

business combination 企业联合,企业联合

business condition 营业状况

business conglomerate 企业集团

business contract 商业合同

business cooperation network 企业合作网

business corporation 企业公司

business cycles 商业周期

business decision 营业决策

business depression 经济萧条

business development loan 商业小额贷款

business efficiency 经营效率

business enterprise 工商企业

business entity 企业法人

business entity principle 企业个体法人原则

business failure 企业倒闭,企业破产,歇业

business finance 企业资金融通

business fund 经营资金

business group 集团企业

business hours 营业时间

business law 企业法规,商业法

business liability 业务责任

business licence 营业执照

business licence for handling transport business 运输业执照

business license for audiovisual publication 音像制品出版经营许可证

business license for audiovisual wholesaling 音像制品批发经营许可证

business license for lease of audio-visual products 音像制品出租经营许可证

business license for retail sales and broadcasting of audiovisual products 音像制品零售、放映经营许可证

business loans 商业借款,工商贷款,商业贷款

business location 企业场所

business management 企业管理

business management power in administrative law 行政法上的经营权

business management right 经营管理权

business objective 经营目标

business of broker 经济义务

business on consignment 寄售交易

business operation 经营活动,经营

business operator 经营者

business permit 营业执照

business profit 营业利润

business profit tax return 营业税申报书

business purpose 营业范围

business quarter 商业区

business registration 营业登记,商业登记证明

business registration certificate 工商业登记证,营业执照

business regulation 业务章程

business revival 经济复苏

business risk 经营风险

business scope 营业范围

business secret 商业秘密

business speculation 商业投机

business sphere 经营范围

business standing 企业信用、营业信誉

business surplus 营业盈亏

business taxes 工商税,工商业税,营业税

business trade 交易

business traffic 商业运输

business transaction 企业交易,经济业务,交易往来

business trust company 商业信托公司

business volume 交易额

business year 营业年度

businessman's investment 企业家投资

Bustamante code 巴斯塔曼特法典

butterfly spread 价差

but-for causation 无因果关系

but-for income 特定因素收益

buy American act 购买美国货法案

buy and sell 买卖

buy and sell without authorization 私自买卖

buy back 返销,回销

buy for a rise 买入

buy for the account 买入期货

buy forward 买入期货

buy goods wholesale 趸货

buy in 买进

buy long 买空

buy off (out) 赎回,买回

buy on credit 赊欠

buy on credit 赊购

buy up 收购

buy up sth 全部买入

buy wholesale 趸买

buyer 买主,买方

buyer of land 土地买受人

buyer's credit 买方退货,买方信贷

buyer's failure to perform a contract 买方不履行合同

buyer's interest 买方权益

buyer's market 买方市场

buyer's monopoly 买方垄断

buyer's option 买方选择权,买方选择,由买方选择交割日期的远期合同

buyer's strike 买方拒购

buying and selling of foreign currencies 外汇买卖业务

buying and selling of land 土地买卖

buying and selling on commission 代实买卖

buying for current needs 现用采购

buying for ready money 买入

buying in 买入

buying offer 买方发价

① buying party 买方

② buying price 买价,买入价格

③ buying quota 买入限额,购买限额

⑤ buyor credit 买方信贷

⑥ "By a preponderance of evidence" in civil cases 民事案件中"占有优势证据"的原则

⑨ by a simple majority 以简单多数

⑪ by an absolute majority 以绝对多数

⑬ by both party 由双方

⑭ by both sides 由双方

⑮ by consent of the owner 经所有人同意

⑰ by contract 依合同

⑱ by force 凭借暴力

⑲ by inference 根据推理

⑳ by law 次要法规,按照法律

㉑ by letter 用书面方式,用书面

㉒ by mail 以邮寄方式,邮寄

㉓ by means of extortion 以恐吓方法

㉕ by means of fraud 以诈骗方法

㉖ by mutual consent 经双方同意

㉗ by operation of law 依现行法律,依法

㉙ by provision of law 由法律规定

㉚ by public tender 通过公开招标

㉛ by regulations 根据法规

㉜ by right of blood 根据血统

㉝ by strong arm 用强制手段

㉞ by way of exception 作为例外

㉟ by-bidder 抬高售价者

㊱ by-election 补选

㊲ by-law of budget 预算施行规则

㊳ by-laws 内部细则

㊴ bye-election 补选

C

cabinet 内阁
cabinet council 内阁会议
cabinet member 阁员,阁员大臣
cabinet minister 内阁大臣
cabinet secretary 阁员大臣
cabinet system 内阁制
cabinet system of government 内阁制政府
cable confirmation 电报确认书,电传确认书
cable remittance 电汇
cabotage 沿海贸易
cabotage right 沿海航运权
cabstand 出租车停车处
cadaver tanned in peat bog 软尸
cadaveric spasm 尸体痉挛
cadere (拉) 停止
cadre 干部
Cairo conference 开罗会议
calamity 灾害
calculated crime 故意犯罪,预谋犯罪
calculating remuneration in relation to output 联产计酬
calculation 计算
calculation of investigation 侦查推理
Calcutta conference 加尔各答班轮公会
calendar of sentence 判决记录
call a conference 召集会议
call a court to order 开庭
call accounts 核账
call demand for payment 付款要求
call deposit 活期通知存款,通知存款
call for funds 招股,集资
call in a loan 收回贷款
call into play 发挥
call loan 通知贷款
call loans secured 活期抵押放

⑤ 款
⑥ call market 活期存款市场
⑦ call option 买卖期货权,买方期权
⑧
⑨ call out the names of those voted
⑩ 唱票
⑪ call premium on bonds 债券兑回溢价
⑫
⑬ call price 提前赎债价格,通知赎债价格
⑭
⑮ call rate 通知贷款利率
⑯ call to account 质问
⑰ call together 召开,召集
⑱ call up 征集,征兵
⑲ call witness to 请…作证
⑳ calling in question 提出异议
㉑ calumniae 诽谤
㉒ calumniate libel 诽谤
㉓ Calvo clause 卡尔沃条款
㉔ Calvo doctrine 卡尔沃主义
㉕ cambiale jus (拉) 交易法
㉖ cambium (拉) 互易
㉗ Camp David 戴维营
㉘ campaign document 竞选文件
㉙ campaign for 竞选
㉚ campaigner 竞选人
㉛ canal dues 运河通行税
㉜ cancel 撤销,取消
㉝ cancel a contract 撤销合同
㉞ cancel a contract, cancellation of contract 解约
㉟ cancel a purchase 退房
㊱ cancel an administrative decision 撤销行政决定
㊲
㊳ cancel an order 撤销指令,取消订货
㊴
㊵ cancel one's right 权利的撤除
㊶ cancel order 撤销指令
㊷ cancel the contract 取消合同
㊸ canceling one's business licence 吊销营业执照
㊹
㊺ cancellation 退保,取消
㊻ cancellation clause 撤销条款

cancellation of contract 合同的解除,撤销合同,取消合同

cancellation of franchise 取消选举

cancellation of registration 注销登记,取销登记

cancellation of will 撤销遗赠

cancelled 取消的,废除的

cancelling clause 撤销条款,解约条款

cancelling date 解约日,销约日期

candidacy 候选资格,候选人的资格

candidacy list of deputies 代表候选人名单

candidate 候选人,竞选人

candidature 候选资格

candidly confess 供认不讳

cannonist 寺院法学家

cannot stand 不能成立的

canon law 教会法,寺院法

canon of economy 经济法规

canon of professional ethics 职业道德准则

canon of taxation 课税准则

canon shot rule 大炮射程论

capability 能力

capability of imbursement 偿付能力

capability survey 能力审查

capable person 有行为能力的人

capacity 责任能力,生产能力,权能,行为能力,能力,资格

capacity as a subject 主体资格

capacity as a subject of law 法律主体资格

capacity for administrative litigation 行政诉讼行为能力

capacity for civil conduct 民事行为能力

capacity for civil rights 民事权利能力

capacity for criminal responsibility 刑事责任能力

capacity for duties 责任能力,承担义务的能力

capacity for enjoying the right to run schools 办学权利能力

capacity for labour work 劳动力

capacity for prosecution 起诉能力

capacity for responsibility 责任能力,承担义务的能力

capacity for responsibility of juristic person 法人的责任能力

capacity for right of natural person 自然人的权利能力

capacity for rights 权利能力

capacity for rights in administrative litigation 行政诉讼权利能力

capacity of a party 当事人资格,当事人能力

capacity of acceptance 承诺能力

capacity of bearing criminal punishment 接受刑罚能力

capacity of civil right 权利能力

capacity of contract 订约能力

capacity of crime 犯罪能力

capacity of discernment 识别能力

capacity of discernment or control of a female during sex 女性性行为辩认或控制能力

capacity of disposition 行为能力

capacity of enter into legal transactions 法律行为能力

capacity of having private obligation 承担民事义务的能力

capacity of having private right 享受私权的能力,享有民事权利的能力

capacity of intention 意思能力,识别能力

capacity of performance of obligation 债的履行能力

capacity of self-government 自治能力

capacity of testator to devise 遗赠资格

capacity of will 意识能力,自主能力

capacity of witness 证人能力

capacity penalty 能力罚

capacity ratio 生产能力比率

capacity to action 诉讼能力

capacity to be a party 当事人资格

capacity to be party 当事人能力

capacity to bear responsibility 责任能力

capacity to compromise 和解能力

capacity to contract 订约资格,订立契约资格,订立契约能力

capacity to enjoy rights and assume obligations 享受权利及承担义务的能力

capacity to serve a sentence 服刑能力

capacity to stand for election 被选举资格

capax negotii（拉）有行为能力,经营能力

capcity to submit requests 抗辩能力

capias（拉）拘票

capital 首都,国都,资金,资本

capital account 资本项目,资本账户,国际收支的资本项目

capital account balance sheet 资本账户平衡表

capital adequacy ratio 资本充足率

capital adjustment account 资本调整账户

capital and liabilities ratio 资本负债比率

capital appreciation 资本增值

capital bonus 股票红利

capital borrowed 贷入资本

capital case 死刑案件

capital composition 资本结构,资本构成

capital construction 基建

capital construction act 基本建设法

capital construction budget 基本建设预算

capital construction funds 基本建设资金

capital construction investment 基本建设投资

capital construction plan 基本建设计划

capital construction products 基本建设产品

capital construction fundamental 基本建设

capital consumption allowance 折旧费

capital cost recovery 资本回收

capital crime 死罪

capital debentures 资本债券

capital deficit 资本亏损

capital duty 股本税

capital endowment 资本捐赠

capital expenditure 资本支出,资本开支

capital export 资本输出

capital export country 资本输出国

capital flow 资本流动

capital gains 资金收入

capital goods 生产资料

capital goods in the agricultural sector 农业生产资料

capital in cash 现金资本

capital income 资本所得、资本收益

capital inflow 资金流入

capital input 投入资本

capital intensive enterprise 密集资本企业

capital invested 投入资本

capital investment 基本建设投资,投资支出

capital issue 股票发行

capital liabilities 资本负债

capital loan 资本放款,资本借贷

capital market 资本市场

capital net-importer 资本净输入国

capital note and debenture 资本

票据和债券

capital outlay 基本投资

capital paid-in 实缴资本,缴入资本

capital pay-off 投资回收

capital projects found 基本建设项目基金

capital punishment 生命刑,死刑,极刑

capital rating 资产评估

capital ratio 资本比率

capital reserve 资本公积,资本准备

capital stock certificate 股本凭证,股票

capital stock common 普通股票

capital stock issued 已发行股本

capital stock preferred 优先股本

capital stock premium 股本溢价

capital stock tax 股本税

capital structure 资本结构,资本构成

capital structure ratio 资本结构比例

capital sum 资本总额

capital surplus 资本盈余

capital tax 资本税

capital transaction 资本交易

capital transaction account 资本交易账户

capital transfer 资本转移

capital turnover rate 资金周转率,资产周转率

capital works 基建工程,基本建设工程

capital-Intensive project 资本密集项目

capital-labor ratio 资本、劳力比率

capitalist class 资产阶级

capitalist criminal law 资本主义刑法

capitalist system 资本主义制度

capitalization 资本总额

capitalization issue 资本化发行

capitalization rate 资本化率

① capitalize 投资

② capitalize cost 投资成本

③ capitalized cost 投资成本

④ capital-intensive industry 资本密集工业

⑤

⑥ capital-saving technical progress 节约资本的技术进步

⑦

⑧ capitation 人头税

⑨ capitation tax 人头税

⑩ capitis deminutio (拉) 人格减等

⑪ capitulations 领事裁判权条约

⑫ captain of industry 工厂主

⑬ captain on reserve service 预备役上尉

⑭

⑮ caption 法律文件标题

⑯ captive market 垄断市场

⑰ captive shop 附属工厂

⑱ capture 收缴,捕拿

⑲ Caracalla 卡拉卡拉

⑳ cardinal 红衣主教,根本

㉑ cardinal principle 根本原则

㉒ Cardozo 卡多佐

㉓ care and control 照管和监督

㉔ career consul 职业领事

㉕ career plan 企业管理制度

㉖ careless and inadvertent negligence 疏忽大意的过失

㉗

㉘ careless negligence 疏忽大意的过失

㉙

㉚ caretaker cabinet 看守内阁

㉛ caretaker government 看守政府

㉜ cargo 货物

㉝ cargo arrival notice 货物到达通知

㉞

㉟ cargo book 货物清单

㊱ cargo capacity 载货容积

㊲ cargo certificate 货单

㊳ cargo damage survey 载损鉴定,货损检验

㊴

㊵ cargo delivery notice 提货通知

㊶ cargo handling 货物装卸

㊷ cargo in bulk 散装货

㊸ cargo inspection ageney 货物检验机构

㊹

㊺ cargo insurance (航运)货物保险

㊻

㊼ cargo insurance policy 货物保险

单

cargo insurance rate 货物保险费率

cargo insurent 货物保险人

cargo insurer 货物承保人

cargo mark 货物标志

cargo owner 货物所有人,货主

cargo policy 货物保险单

cargo port 运货港

cargo premium 货物保险费

cargo receiver 收货人

cargo reservation 货运保留

cargo service 货运服务

cargo space 载货空间

cargo supervision and control 货运监管

cargo underunite 货物保险人

cargoworthiness 适货

cargoworthiness inspection 适载检验

cargoworthy 适货

Carolingian Dynasty 卡罗林王朝

carriage 载运,运输

carriage documents 运输单证

carriage expense 运费

carriage forward 运费到付

carriage free 运费免付

carriage of container 集装箱运输

carriage of contraband 运载违禁品

carriage of goods by liner 班轮货物运输

carriage of goods by sea 海运货物

carriage paid 运费已付

carriage paid to 运费付至

carried interest 附带权益

carrier 承运人,承运人

carrier at fault 有过失的承运人

carrier liability for delay 承运人因迟延所负的责任

carrier's exceptions 承运人免责

carrier's liabilities in through ① **shipment** 联运承运人责任

② **carrier's liability** 承运人责任

③ **carrier's liability clause** 承运人责任条款

⑤ **carrier's lien** 承运人的留置权

⑥ **carrier's option** 承运人的选择权

⑧ **carring out of law** 执行法律

⑨ **carry into effect** 开始生效,实行,施行

⑪ **carry on an improper business** 不正当经营

⑬ **carry out** 实行,执行,贯彻

⑭ **carry out a contract** 履行合同

⑮ **carry out a death sentence according to law** 明正典刑

⑰ **carry out a selective examination** 抽查

⑲ **carry out earnestly** 切实履行

⑳ **carry out the law** 执法

㉑ **carrying capacity** 载货量

㉒ **carrying capacity of environment** 环境的负担能力

㉔ **carrying costs** 财产维护费

㉕ **carrying out a contract** 契约履行

㉗ **carrying trade** 转口贸易,运输业

㉙ **carrying vessel** 载货船只

㉚ **carry-forward** 预借

㉛ **carry-over** 留用额

㉜ **cartage** 货车运费

㉝ **cartel** 企业联合

㉞ **cartel price** 垄断价格

㉟ **cas fortuit** (拉) 意外事件

㊱ **case** 案例,案件,案子

㊲ **case arising from an indemnity decision** 补偿决定案件

㊳ **case at law** 法律案件

㊴ **case based on informer's accusation** 检察案件

㊷ **case book** 案例汇编

㊸ **case concerning the adjudgement of restricted legal capacity of citizens** 认定公民限制民事行为能力案件

㊼ **case concerning the declaration of**

a person as missing 宣告公民失踪案件

case concerning the determination of a property as ownerless 认定财产无主案件

case concerning the proclamation of death of a missing person 宣告死亡之案件

case facts 案件事实

case for administrative appeal 行政申诉案件

case for administrative reconsideration 行政复议案件

case for new trial 重审案件

case for reconsideration 复议案件

case for retrial 重审案件

case for succession of sperm 精子继承案

case handling efficiency 办案效率

case in point 例证

case involving swindling of state properties 骗取国家财产罪

case involving the violation of regulations 违章案件

case involving the violations of rules 违章案件

case law 判例法,案例法

case law book 判例法书

case law system 判例法系,判例法制度

case method 判例教学法

case of a labour contract case 劳动合同案件

case of a missing person 失踪案件

case of abducting a minor 拐骗未成年人罪

case of abducting and trafficking in people 拐卖人口案件

case of compensation trade 补偿贸易纠纷案件

case of corporate crime 法人犯罪案件

case of criminal complaint filed by procuratorate against a court decision 刑事抗诉案件

case of criminally caused explosion 爆炸案

case of dereliction of duty 渎职犯罪案件

case of disrupting solidarity of the nationalities 破坏各民族团结案

case of drain on state-owned assets 国有资产流失案

case of embezzling funds and articles for disaster relief 挪用救灾、抢险等款物案

case of first impression 没有判决先例的案件,初见案件

case of first instance 初审案件,第一审案件

case of labour payment 劳动报酬案件

case of misappropriation of public funds 挪用公款案

case of releasing a criminal of judicial personnel's own accord 私放罪犯案

case of remuneration for personal service 劳动报酬案件

case of remuneration for labour 劳动报酬案件

case of retaliation and frame-ups 报复陷害案

case of second instance 第二审案件

case of state compensation 国家赔偿案件

case of treason 叛国案

case of violence 暴力罪案

case on alteration of guardianship 变更监护关系案件

case study method 案例研究法

case system 案例制度,案例教学法

case unable to be privately prosecuted 不能自诉的案件

case under renewed ruling 重新裁决案件

casebook 判例集

casement 窗扇

cases in which people were unjustly 冤假错案

cases involving privacy 隐私案件

case-book 判例汇编

cash 现金

cash account 现金账户

cash administration 现金管理

cash against delivery 交货停担，货到付款

cash against documents 交单付现

cash and carry 现金交易

cash articles 代金证券

cash assets 现金资产

cash at bank 活期存款

cash balance 现金余额

cash before delivery 付现后提货

cash benefit 现金收益

cash circulation 现金流通

cash commodity 现货

cash credit 银行透支限额

cash day 付款日

cash deposit 押金

cash deposit in advance 预付现款

cash discount 现金折扣

cash equivalent 现金等值

cash flow-back 现金回笼

cash holding 库存现金

cash holdings 款项

cash in bank 银行存款

cash in bank-special funds 专项基金存款

cash items 现金项目

cash liabilities 流动负债

cash market 现货市场

cash on arrival 货到付款

cash on delivery 货到付款

cash on delivery certificate 货到付款证

cash on delivery commission 货到付款手续费

cash on delivery price 货到付款价格

cash on delivery sale 货到付款销售

cash on hand 库存现金

cash on receipt of merchandise 收货付现

cash on the barrelhead 付现

cash payment 现金支付，现金付款

cash pledge 押金

cash position 头寸

cash price 现金售价，现金价格，现售价格，现货价格

cash receipts and disbursements 现金收支

cash resource 现金资源

cash sale 现金销售

cash settlement 现金结算

cash terms 现付条件，付现条件

cash trade 现金交易

cash transaction 现金交易

cash with order 订货付现，现金订货

cashability 变现能力

cashier 出纳，出纳员，革除，革职

cashier's check 本票，银行本票

cashier's orders 本票，银行本票

cast 辞退

cast a vote 投票

cast a vote of censure 提出不信任案

cast secret ballot 秘密投票

cast the contract on the scrap heap 撕毁合同

caste system 种姓制度（印度）

castration 宫刑

casual condition(s) 偶然条件

casual inspection 不定期检查

casual offender 偶发性犯罪人

casual offender casual offense 偶犯

casual offense 偶发犯

casualties 死伤

casualty 严重伤之事故，受害者

casualty insurance 意外伤害保险，偶然事件保险，意外事故保险

casus（拉） 意外事故

casus clvilis（拉） 民事案件

casus fortuitus（拉） 意外事件，不能避免的偶然事故，不能预见的偶然事故

casus major（拉） 不能避免的偶然事故

casus omissus（拉） 无明文规定者

catalog of prices 价格目录

catalog price 定价

catalogue price 商品目录价格

catch 捕拿

catch pole 法庭执达员

catch quota 捕鱼限额

catch-all exception 杂项除外条款

catch-all exceptions 一揽子免责

catechism Romanus 罗马教义问答

categories of constitution 宪法范畴

categories of subjects of state economic management 国家经济管理主体的种类

category accusation 类罪名

category charge 类罪名

category of Jurisprudence 法学的范畴

category of pollutant discharge 排放污染物种类

category of the product 产品类别

Catholicism 天主教

caucus 党团会议

causa（拉） 原因

causa sine qua non（拉） 根本原因，不可欠缺原因

causa turpis（拉） 不道德的约因，非法的原因

causal juristic act 要因法律行为

causal relationship 因果关系

causality in criminal law 刑法因果关系

causality in negative crimes 不作为犯罪因果关系

causality in negligent offense 过失犯罪因果关系

causality of death 死亡诱因

causality within the meaning of criminal law 刑法意义上的因果关系

causation of crime 犯罪原因论

causative action 要因行为

causative contract 要因合同

causative juristic act 有因行为，要因的法律行为，要因法律行为

cause 案件，原因

cause a person's injury or disability 致人伤残

cause and effect 原因和结果

cause book 被告出庭备忘录

cause damage 造成损害

cause death of another by malicious injury 故意伤害致人死亡

cause death to a person 致人死亡

cause harm 造成损害

cause list 最高法院诉讼案排列表

cause losses 造成损失

cause of a crime 犯罪原因

cause of action 诉讼事由，诉因，案由

cause of action for administration cases 行政案由

cause of bankruptcy 破产原因

cause of challenge 回避事由

cause of civil jurisdiction 民事审判案由

cause of civil lawsuit 民事案由

cause of criminal action 刑事案由

cause of death 死亡原因，死因

cause serious injury to a person 致人重伤

causes beyond volition 意志以外原因

cautio（法） 保释金

cautio pro expensis（拉） 费用担保

caution 警告
caution money 保证金
caution security 保证金
caveat emptor（拉）货物出门概不退还
caveat venditor（拉）卖主当心
cease to bind 失去约束力
cease to exist except in name 名存实亡的
cease to exist of judicial person 法人的终止
cease to have effect 停止生效
cease-fire order 停战令
ceasing the infringing act 停止侵害
cede territory 割地
cede territory and pay indemnities 割地赔款
ceding insurance company 分保公司
ceiling 最高限额
ceiling price 最高限价,最高价格
ceiling quota 最高限额
ceiling top 最高限额
cell 单人牢房
cellar 地下室
censor 保密检查员,监察官
censorship 检查制,审查制度
censorship of books 书报检查制度
censorship of press 出版物的审查
censure motion 不信任动议
censure vote 不信任票
census 户口普查,人口普查,租赁
census areaham（拉）地租
census register 户籍簿,户籍
center lot 中心地段
center of measurement 计量中心
central administrative law 中央行政法
central administrative legislation 中央行政立法
central administrative organization 中央行政机关
central authorities 中央
central commission for discipline inspection of the Communist Party of China 中共中央纪律检察委员会
central committee member 中央委员
central committee of the Communist Party of China 中共中央委员会,中国共产党中央委员会
central criminal court 中央刑事法院
central government 中央政府
central merchandising 集中购买
central military committee of the People's Republic of China 中华人民共和国中央军事委员会
central people's government 中央人民政府
central people's government of the People's Republic of China 中华人民共和国中央人民政府
central planned economy 集中计划经济
central planning system 集中计划体制
central purchasing 集中采购
central rate 中心汇率
central state organs 中央国家机构
central tax 中央税
centralism 集中制
centrality of offenders 犯罪者中心主义
centralization 中央集权
centralization of authority 中央集权,集权制
centralization of power 中央集权,集权
centralization of purchasing 集中采购
centralization system 集权制
centralized decision-making 集

中决策

centralized feudal monarchy 中央集权的封建君主制

centralized government 集权政府

centralized inspection 集中检验

centralized leadership 统一领导

centralized management 集中管理,统一经营,集权管理

centralized operation 集中经营

centralized purchase and contracted marketing 统购色销

centralized purchasing and marketing 统购统销

centralized purchasing 集中采购

centralized type of organization 集权制

centrally administered municipality 直辖市

centrally planned economies 中央计划经济

centrally planned economy country 中央计划经济国家

centre for economic cooperation and integration 经济合作和一体化中心

ceramic tile veneer 瓷砖镶面

cerebral concussion 脑震荡

cerebral contusion 脑挫伤

cerebral injury psychosis 颅脑损伤伴发精神障碍

certa pecuria 金钱债权

certain (**/terminable**) **annuity** 定期年金

certainty of law 法律确定性

certificate 转运证书,商业登记证明,凭证书

certificate by a notary 公证证

certificate for charge of domicile 户口迁移证

certificate for export 出口检验证

certificate for holding and use of firearms for official purposes 公务用枪持枪证件

certificate for inventor 发明人

① 证书

② **certificate for release upon completion of a sentence** 刑满释放证

⑤ **certificate for the certificate of a law firm for practicing** 律师事务所执业证书

⑧ **certificate of acceptance** 验收证明书

⑩ **certificate of addition** 补充证书

⑪ **certificate of agent's authority** 代理权证书

⑬ **certificate of analysis** 化验证书

⑭ **certificate of approval** 批准证书

⑮ **certificate of approval of works** 工程核准证书

⑰ **certificate of authority** 授权证书

⑲ **certificate of authorization** 授权证书,授权书

㉑ **certificate of bank balance** 银行(存、兑)余额证明

㉓ **certificate of capital** 股本说明书

㉕ **certificate of change of name of registrant** 注册人名义变更证明

㉘ **certificate of competency** 合格证书,合格证

㉚ **certificate of completion/COC** 完工证书

㉜ **certificate of death** 死亡证明书

㉝ **certificate of deposit** 存款证书,存款单

㉟ **certificate of disability** 残废证,残废证明书

㊲ **certificate of discovery** 发现证书

㊳ **certificate of dishonour** 拒绝付款

㊶ **certificate of elected deputies** 代表当选证书

㊸ **certificate of enterprise name registration** 企业名称登记证书

㊺ **certificate of honour** 荣誉证书

㊻ **certificate of import license** 进口许可证

certificate of incorporation 营业执照

certificate of indebtedness 债务单据,债务证明

certificate of inspection 检验证明书,合格证

certificate of insurance 保险凭单

certificate of loss or damage 损失或损坏证明书

certificate of manufacture 制造证明书

certificate of manufacturer 厂方证明书,工厂证明书

certificate of merchandise 出厂证明书

certificate of nationality 国籍证明书

certificate of naturalization 入籍证书

certificate of obligation 债权证书

certificate of origin 原产地证书

certificate of origin form A 产地证明书A格式

certificate of origin form DA59 产地证明书DA59格式

certificate of ownership 所有权证书,产权证书

certificate of ownership of land 土地所有权证

certificate of possession (of) land 土地所有权证书

certificate of quality 质量证书,合格证,品质证书

certificate of quantity 数量证明书

certificate of receipt 收货证明书

certificate of receipts 收据,收款凭证

certificate of registration 登记证,注册执照

certificate of registration for books and periodicals 书刊登记证

certificate of registration of a mass organization as legal person 社会团体登记证

certificate of registration of mortgage 抵押登记凭证

certificate of registration of periodicals 期刊登记证

certificate of seal impression 印鉴证期

certificate of security 保证单,担保证书

certificate of shipment 出口证明书

certificate of soundness 合格证书

certificate of superintendent 检验员证明书

certificate of supervision over administration 行政监察证

certificate of surety 担保证书

certificate of tax 税单

certificate of tax payment 纳税证明书,缴款凭证

certificate of timber transportation in forest region 林区木材运输证

certificate of title 产权审查意见书,所有权证书,产权证书

certificate of validity 有效证明书

certificate of value 货价证明书

certificate of weight surveyors' report on weight 重量证明书

certificate on cargo weight and measurements 货物重量与尺码证书

certificate to patent 专利证书

certificates for the right to the use of land 土地使用权证书

certificates of beneficial interest 投资受益证

certification 合格证

certification by a notary 公证证

certification mark 认证标志

certification of fitness 质量合格证

certificator (拉) 偿还债务保证人

certified 有保证的

certified cheque 保付支票

certified public accountant（CPA）注册会计师

certify（美）担保付额

certifying bank 付款保证银行

cert-money 古代人头税

cessamentum（拉）迟延

cessat executio（拉）缓刑

cessation 取消

cessation of infringement 停止侵害

cesser and lien clause 责任终止与留置权条款

cesser clause 责任终止条款，债务中止条款，中止条款，租船免责条款，租船人责任终止条款

cessio in jure（拉）以诉讼方式交出物权

cession 转让，转让财产权益，割让

cession capital 债权转让

cession of administration 行政割让

cession of territory 领土割让

cession of the obligatory right 债权让与

cessionary （财产，权利等）受让人

cessionary 让受人（方），受让方

cestui que trust（拉）信托受益人

cestui que use（拉）有用益权者，用益权的受益人

cestui que vie（拉）生前租赁

CFR（Cost and Freight）成本加运费

CFS to CFS 站到站

CFS to CY 站到场

chain banking 连锁银行

chain contracts 连锁合同

chain discount 连锁折扣

chain firms 连锁商行

chain of causation 因果关系

chain of representation 连锁代理

chain of responsibility 连锁责任

chain stores 连锁商店

chains 镣铐

chairman 主任委员，主席，委员长

chairman of the board of governors 董事长

chairman of the Central People's Government 中央人民政府主席

chairperson 主席，主任委员

chairwoman 主任委员，主席，委员长

challenge a ruling 对裁决提出异议

challenge of a party 当事人请回避

challenge the law personally 以身试法

challenged personnel 被申请回避的人员

chamber 法官室，法官秘密评论室

chamber of commerce 商会

chamber of deputies 众议院

chamber of nationalities 民族院

chamberlain's court 管理大臣法院（英）

chambers of import and export commerce 进出口商会

champerty 帮讼

champtertor 帮讼者

chance event 偶发事件

chance happening 偶然事件

chance verdict 偶然裁决，机令裁决

chancellery 办事处，大法官法庭

chancellor 衡平法院大法官，大法官

chancellor of the legation 使馆主事

chancery division（英）大法官法庭，大法官分庭，大法官庭

chancery master 大法官法庭庭长

chancery（英）大法官法庭

change 加以改变，更迭，更改，

变更,改变

change account 赊销

change hand 转手

change in th functions of government 政府职能转变

change in the amount of properties 财产数额变更

change litigious claims 变更诉讼请求

change of circumstances 环境变迁,环境变化

change of date 期日变更

change of dynasty 改朝换代

change of nationality 改变国籍,变更国籍

change of price 价格变动

change of residence 住所变更

change of territorial 领土的变更

change of the degree of secrets 变更密级

change of title 产权变更,权利的变更

change of venue 变更审判地点

change of working condition 施工条件变更

change one's dwelling place 迁户口,迁居

change one's residence 迁徙

change technology 技术改造

change the line of production 转产

change the original sentence 改判,更改原判

changes of administrative legal relationship 行政法律关系的变动

changing of work 工程变更

changing one's nationality 改变国籍

changment of law 法的变化

channel discount 特殊折扣

channel of distribution 销货渠道

chapter 章

character 人格

character loan 信用贷款

character of obligation 债的性质

character of state 国家性质

characteristic 特性

characteristics of administrative act 行政行为的特征

characteristics of constitution 宪法的特征

characteristics of crime 犯罪特征

characteristics of law 法的基本特征

characterization 定性

charge 责令,控告,税收,责令,邮费

charge by way of legal mortgage 通过合法抵押的土地负担

charge in nature of risk 危险性质变更

charge of land 土地使用费

charge off 冲账

charge on real estate 征收房地产税

charge prepaid 预付费用

charge sb or sth 索价

chargeable period 应税期间

charged 代办

charger 固定费用

charging document 诉讼文书

charging order 基金扣押令

charitable deduction 慈善事业减税

charitable gift 慈善事业减税

Charles Louis Montesquieu 孟德斯鸠,查尔斯·路易斯·孟德斯鸠

Charles The Great 查理大帝

charm price 诱人价格

charter 宪章,契约书,船舶租约,营业执照,宪法,租约

charter by demise 光船租船合同

charter for Hague conference in private international law 海牙国际私法会议章程

charter for international trade organisation 国际贸易组织章

程

charter hire 船舶租金

charter of economic rights and duties of states 各国经济权利和义务宪章

charter of far-east international military court 远东国际军事法庭宪章

charter of incorporation 公司组建章程

charter of international military court of Europe 欧洲国际军事法庭宪章

charter of liberties 自由宪章

charter of the corporate body 法人章程

charter of the United Nations 联合国宪章

charter party 船舶租约,租船合同

charter party agreement 租约

charter party by demise 光船租赁合同

chartered back 回租

chartered carrier 包机运输

chartered period 租期

charterer 船舶承租人,租船人

chartering 船舶租赁

chartering agreement 租船协议

charterparty laytime definitions 1980 (1980年)租船合同术语解释

chartism 宪章运动(英)

chartist 宪章运动者

chartist movement 宪章运动(英)

chattel incoproreal 无形动产

chattel loan 以动产为担保的借贷

chattel mortgage 动产抵押

chattel personal 私人动产

chattel(s) lien 动产留置权

chattel(s) loan 动产担保借贷

chattels real 准不动产

cheap goods 廉价品

cheap in price and excellent in quality 物美价廉

① cheapjack 摊贩

② cheap-john 摊贩

③ cheat 欺骗,欺骗行为

④ cheating 欺骗

⑤ cheating on workmanship and materials 偷工减料

⑦ check 支票,制约,稽核,托运,寄存,考核,制约

⑨ check and balance 制衡,制约与平衡

⑪ check and control doctrine 制约原则

⑬ check and pass judgment on prisoners 对罪犯的考核评审

⑮ check and pass on prisoners 对罪犯的考核评审

⑰ check at ordinary times 平时考核

⑲ check clearing system 支票交换制

㉑ check credit 银行透支

㉒ check drawer 支票出票人

㉓ check holder 支票持票人

㉔ check on household occupants 查户口

㉖ check price 控制价格

㉗ check rate 支票利率

㉘ check replacement 支票挂失

㉙ check residence cards 查户口

㉚ check up 查清

㉛ check up laws and regulations 清理法规

㉝ checkbook money 支票货币

㉞ checking account 支票账户

㉟ checking deposits 支票存款

㊱ checking up on the projects under construction 清理在建项目

㊳ checks and balances 制衡,制约原则

㊴ checks and balances doctrine 制约与平衡原则

㊷ check-off 扣除

㊸ check-up system 考核制度

㊹ cheek and accept the completed capital construction project 基本建设项目竣工验收

㊼ chemical pollution 化学污染

cheque　支票

cheque（check）crossed generally （specially）　普通（特别）划线支票

cheque crossed generally　普通划线支票

cheque crossed specially　特别划线支票

cheque only for account　转账支票

cheque stubs　支票存根

cheque to bearer　来人支票

chief accountant　总会计师

chief administrative officer　行政首长

chief controller　稽核长

chief criminal　首犯

chief executive　行政长官

chief grand justice　首席大法官

chief grand prosecutor　首席大检察官

chief judge　审判长

chief justice　首席法官

chief justice of the United States　美国（高等法院）首席法官

chief lawyer　主任律师

chief of delegation　代表团长

chief of government　政府首脑

chief of staff　参谋长

chief procurator　检察长

chief prosecutor　首席检察院,检察长

chief war criminal　首要战犯

chief whip　议会多数党领袖

child in ward　被监护儿童

children act　少年法令

children court　少年法庭

children of returned overseas Chinese　归侨子女

China commodity inspection bureau　中国商品检验局

China council for the promotion of international trade　中国国际贸易促进委员会

China international economic and trade arbitration commission　中国国际经济贸易仲裁委员会

China lease corporation　中国租赁公司

China licensing executives society　中国国际许可证贸易工作者协会

China maritime arbitration commission　中国海事仲裁委员会

China national chartering corporation time　中国租船公司定期租船合同

China post　中国邮政

China's boundaries　中国的国界

China's national economy　中国国民经济

Chinese group of the international association for the protection of international property　国际保护工业产权协会中国分会

Chinese joint venturer　中国合营者

Chinese law　中国法律

Chinese legal history　中国法制史

Chinese legal system　中华法系,中国法制

Chinese nationality　中国国籍

Chinese nationals residing abroad　华侨

Chinese peasants and workers democratic party　农工民主党

Chinese people's political consultative conference　政协全国委员会

Chinese society of international law　中国国际法学会

Chinese-foreign contractual joint venture　中外合作经营企业

Chinese-foreign cooperative development　中外合作开发

Chinese-foreign cooperative enterprises　中外合作企业

Chinese-foreign equity joint venture　中外合资经营企业

Chinese-foreign joint venture　中外合资经营企业

chit　保单、保证书

choice of criminal mind 犯罪心理选择

choice of law 法律选择,法律的选择,选择法律

choice rules for regulating the conflict of laws 选择适用的冲突规范

cholera 霍乱

choose 推选

choose the form of the contract 选择合同形式

choose through public appraisal 评选

chose 所有物

Christ 基督

Christianity 基督教

chronic alcoholism 慢性酒精中毒

chronic criminal 慢性犯罪人

chronic morphinism 慢性吗啡中毒

church 教会

CIF (cost, insurance and freight) 成本,运费加保险费

CIP (carriage, insurance paid to) 运费保险费付至

circiter(拉) 大约

circuit trial system 巡回审判制度

circuits judicial 美国巡回审判

circular letter 通知

circulars 通知

circulate 流通的

circulate a notice of commendation 通报表扬

circulate a notice of criticism 通报批评

circulating capital 流动资本、周转资金

circulating fund 周转基金,资金

circulating medium 流通货币

circulating notes 流通现钞

circulation market 流动市场,流通市场

circulation of commodity 商品流通

circulation tax 流转税

① circulation volume 流通量

② circumstance 意外,情形

③ circumstanced evidence 环境证据

⑤ circumstances after a crime 罪后情节

⑦ circumstances before a crime 罪前情节

⑨ circumstances for adjudication 定罪情节

⑪ circumstances for discretion 酌定情节

⑬ circumstances for judgment 裁判情节,裁定情节

⑮ circumstances for liberal punishment 从宽情节

⑰ circumstances for severe punishment 从严情节

⑲ circumstances of a case 案件事实情节,案情事实

㉑ circumstances of crime 犯罪情节

㉓ circumstantial evidence 参考证据,环境证据,间接证据

㉕ citation 引证,传票

㉖ cite 引证,传唤,援引

㉗ cite a precedent 援引先例

㉘ cite to appear in court 传唤出庭

㉙ cities and towns 城镇

㉚ citizen (注:在我国也可译为 natural person) 公民

㉜ citizen found incapacity with capacity by the court 被认定为无行为能力的公民

㉟ citizen lawsuit 公民诉讼

㊱ citizen of a state 州公民

㊲ citizen of the People's Republic of China 中华人民共和国公民

㊴ citizen status 公民地位

㊵ citizen subject to petition for a holding of incapacity 被要求认定为无行为能力 的公民

㊸ citizen's duties 公民义务

㊹ citizen's home 公民的住宅

㊺ citizen's lawful privately-owned property 公民私人所有的合法财产

citizen's legitimate private property 公民私有的合法财产

citizen's right of succession to private properties 公民私有财产继承权

citizen's rights 公民权

citizenhood 公民身份

citizenize 赋予公民权

citizenry 公民

citizens' cultural and education rights and liberty 公民的文化教育权利与自由

citizens' freedom of communication and confidentiality of communication 公民的通信自由与通信秘密

citizens' personal liberty 公民的人身自由

citizens' personal property 公民的个人财产

citizens' political rights and liberty 公民的政治权利和自由

citizens' private lawful properties 公民个人的合法财产

citizens' right of accusation 公民的控告权

citizens' right of complaint 公民的申诉权

citizens' right of information 公民的检举权

citizens' right to environment 公民环境权

citizens' right to equality 公民的平等权

citizens' right to make criticisms and suggestions 公民的批评建议权

citizens' right to material assistance 公民的物质帮助权

citizens' right to obtain compensation 公民的取得赔偿权

citizens' right to personal liberty 公民的人身自由权

citizens' right to receive education 公民的受教育权

citizens' right to religious freedom 公民的宗教信仰自由权

citizens' right to rest 公民的休息权

citizens' right to revote 公民复选

citizens' right to vote and right to stand for election 公民的选举权与被选举权

citizens' rights 公民权

citizenship 公民身份，公民权，公民资格，市民权

citizenship by descent 血统国籍

city building 城建

city development 城市发展

city grant 城市建设基金

city heat and gas supply engineering 城市供热供燃气工程

city improvement 城市改建

city law 城市法

city layout 城市布局

city listed independently in the state plan 计划单列市

city noise 城市噪声

city not divided into districts 不设区的市

city pattern 城市格局

city people's congress 市人民代表大会

city people's court 市人民法院

city people's government 市人民政府

city people's procuratorate 市人民检察院

city planning 城市规划

city planning administration 城市规划管理

city proper 城区

city protection 城市保护

city sanitation measures 城市环境卫生措施

city scape 城市风貌

city-state 城邦国家，城邦

city-state democracy 城邦民主制

civil act 民事行为

civil action 民事权利诉讼，民事诉讼

civil action (/process; lawsuit)

民事诉讼

civil activities　民事活动

civil activity　民事活动

civil adjudication　民事审判,民事审判活动

civil adjudication organization　民事审判组织

civil adjudication system　民事审判制度

civil adjudicatory activities　民事审判活动

civil adjudicatory agency　民事审判机构

civil administration　民政,内务

civil administration organization　民政机关

civil affairs department　民政部门

civil agent ad litem　民事诉讼代理人

civil aircraft　民用航空器

civil and commercial law　民商法

civil appeal　民事申诉

civil appraisement of forensic psychiatry　民事司法精神病学鉴定

civil aviation　民用航空

civil capacity of conduct　民事行为能力

civil capacity of right　民事权利能力

civil case　民事案件

civil case against minor　侵害未成年人的民事案件

civil circulation　民事流转

civil claim　民事请求,民事求偿,民事诉讼要求

civil code　民法典

civil commotion marine clause　民事海上保险条款

civil compensation　民事赔偿

civil complaint　民事诉状

civil contempt　藐视法庭(民事上的)

civil controversy　民事争议

civil court (/division of a people's court)　民事法庭,民事审判庭

civil court directive　民事决定

civil damage(s)　民事损害赔偿,民事损害

civil debt　民事占有,民事债务

civil decision　民事裁判,民事判决

civil defendant　民事诉讼被告

civil detention　民事拘留

civil dice　诱骗

civil disability　无民事行为能力

civil dispute　民事争议,民事纠纷

civil dispute arising from traffic accident　因交通事故引起的民事纠纷

civil division　民事法庭

civil duties　公民义务

civil duty　民事义务

civil evidence act　民事证据法

civil evidence law　民事证据法

civil execution　民事执行

civil fines　民事罚款

civil fruits　合法财产孳息(收益)

civil injury　民事侵害,民事损害

civil judicature　民事审判组织

civil jural relation　民事法律关系

civil jurisdiction in relation to foreign ships　对外国船舶的民事管辖权

civil jurisprudence　民法学

civil jurist　民法学家

civil juristic right　民事法律行为

civil juristic act having conditions attached　附条件民事法律行为

civil juristic act(s)　民事法律行为

civil law　民法,大陆法

civil law countries　大陆法系国家

civil law in broad sense　广义民法

civil law in narrow sense　狭义民

法

civil law of the continental law system 大陆民法

civil law system 民法法系,民法法统

civil lawsuit 民事诉讼,民事案件

civil legal relation 民事法律关系

civil legal relation containing foreign element 涉外民事法律关系

civil legislation 民事立法

civil legislative activities 民事立法活动

civil liability 民事责任分摊,民事责任

civil liability for infringement of rights 侵权的民事责任

civil liability for oil pollution damage 油污损害民事责任

civil liability for wrongful acts 侵权的民事责任

civil liability insurance 民事责任保险

civil liberties 公民自由权,民权

civil litigant 民事当事人

civil litigant participants 诉讼参加人

civil litigants 民事诉讼当事人

civil litigation 民事诉讼

civil litigation right 民事诉讼权利

civil litigations activities 民事诉讼活动

civil litigations duty 民事诉讼义务

civil litigations obligation 民事诉讼义务

civil mediation 民事调解

civil object 民事客体

civil obligations 公民义务

civil offence 民事违法行为

civil offender 民事犯

civil offense 民事违法行为

civil official 文官

civil order 民事裁定

① civil panty 民事当事人

② civil penalty 民事罚款

③ civil personnel 文职人员,民政人员

⑤ civil plaint 民事诉状

⑥ civil plaint for retrials 民事申请再审诉状

⑧ civil plaintiff 民事原告

⑨ civil plea against appeal 被上诉答辩状

⑪ civil pleading 民事答辩状

⑫ civil possession 民法上的占有

⑬ civil prisoner 民事犯

⑭ civil procedural law 民事程序法,民事诉讼法

⑯ civil procedure 民事诉讼程序,民事程序

⑱ civil procedure law 民事诉讼程序法,民事诉讼法学

⑳ civil proceedings 民事诉讼,民事审判程序,民事程序

㉒ civil process 民事诉讼程序

㉓ civil property relation 民事财产关系

㉕ civil punishment 民事制裁

㉖ civil relation 民事关系

㉗ civil relation containing foreign element 涉外民事关系

㉘ civil remedies 民事救济

㉚ civil responsibility 民事责任

㉛ civil restriction 民事制裁

㉜ civil rights 公民的权利,民事权利,民权,公民权

㉞ civil rights act 民权法

㉟ civil rights and interests 民事权益

㊱ civil rights and obligations 民事权利和义务

㊳ civil rights bill 民权法案

㊴ civil rights law 民权法

㊵ civil rights movement 民权运动

㊷ civil ruling 民事裁定

㊸ civil ruling paper 民事裁定书

㊹ civil salvage 民间救助

㊺ civil sanction 民事制裁,民事处分

㊼ civil servant 公务员,文官,国家

机关工作人员

civil servant law 公务员法

civil servants act 公务员法

civil servants of state 国家公务员

civil servants' demotion system 公务员降职制度

civil servants' examination system 公务员考核制度

civil servants' welfare system 公务员福利制度

civil servants' wage system 公务员工资制度

civil service 文官,公务员

civil service commission 文官委员会

civil service of state 国家公务员

civil service system 公务员制度

civil service training system 公务员培训制度

civil status of aliens 规定外国人民法律地位的规范

civil subject matter jurisdiction at different levels 民事级别管辖

civil subject(s) 民事主体

civil suit 民事诉讼

civil terrestrial jurisdiction 民事地域管辖

civil trespass 民事侵权行为

civil trial 民事审判

civil tribunal 民事法庭

civil war 南北战争,内战

civil wrong 民事违法,民事过错,民事不法行为,民事过失

civilian 民法学家

civilian agent 民政人员

civilian industry 民用工业

civilian person 平民个人

civilians 平民

civilization 文化

civilized pledge 文明公约

claim 请求权,诉讼请求,索赔条款,索回,索赔,索偿,债权,权利要求,认领

claim a refund 索赔

claim against breach of the contract 违约引起的索赔

claim against property 物权诉讼

claim arising from a defect of the goods 货物瑕疵引起的赔偿

claim arising from breach of the contract 由于违约产生的债权

claim arising from defects of goods 由货物瑕疵而产生的债权

claim barred by reason of time limitation 因时效而受阻的债权

claim based on fraud 因欺诈而产生的诉权

claim based on lack of conformity of the goods 货物不符合同要求引起的索赔

claim based on physical loss or damage 因货物丢失或损失而产生的债权

claim clause 索赔条款

claim compensation 索赔,请求补偿

claim compensation for 要求赔偿

claim compensation for the damage 要求损害赔偿,要求赔偿损失

claim compensation for the loss 要求赔偿损失

claim damages 损坏索赔

claim for charge at random 乱收费

claim for compensation 赔偿要求,请求赔偿,求偿,损害赔偿的诉权,赔偿请求

claim for damages 损害赔偿要求,要求损失赔偿,要求赔偿损失,损坏索赔

claim for indemnification 要求赔偿损失

claim for indemnity, seek redress 要求赔偿

claim for interior quality 质量索赔

claim for payment 要求付款

claim for refund 要求退款,要

求偿还
claim for reimbursement 要求偿还
claim for repair of the vessel 因修理船舶而产生的债权
claim for restitution 恢复原状请求
claim for restitution of advance payment 要求退回预付款
claim for rights 权利主张
claim for salvage 救助报酬请求权
claim in tort 因侵权行为产生的请求权
claim indemnity claim for payment 索赔
claim letter 索赔信件
claim of reconsideration 复议请求
claim of recourse 追偿请求
claim on account of quality 质量索赔
claim on quality 品质索赔
claim ratio 赔付率
claim reimbursement 索赔
claim secured by mortgage 有抵押权担保的债权
claim settlement 理赔
claim stores 联营商业
claim the protection of the law 要求法律保护
claim timelimit 请求权时效
claim to be a king 称帝
claimant 请求权人,索赔人,债权人,贷方,请求人
claimant for administrative compensation 行政赔偿请求人
claimant for compensation 赔偿请求人
claimant for indemnity 赔偿请求人
claimant for judicial redress 司法赔偿请求人
claimer 索赔人
claims 赔偿金
claims document 索赔单据
claims documents 索赔单证

claims for administrative compensation 行政赔偿请求
claims protected by lien 有留置权担保的债权
claims secured by a lien 有留置权担保的债权
clamp down on 钳制
clan 宗族
clan ethnic group 民族
clan system 宗族制度
clarify some facts 澄清事实
clash 冲突
class action 集团诉讼
class contradictions 阶级矛盾
class inspection 等级检验
class of consul 领事的等级
class of pollution 污染等级
class price 等级价格,分类价格
class school of crime 犯罪古典学派
class society 阶级社会
class stamp tax 分等印花税法
class struggle and crime 阶级斗争与犯罪
classes of head of mission 使馆馆长的等级
classification 定类,分类
classification of administrative act 行政行为的分类
classification of administrative legislation 行政立法的分类
classification of constitution 宪法分类
classification of crimes 罪的分类,犯罪分类
classification of evidence 证据的分类
classification of evidence for criminal procedure 刑事诉讼证据的分类
classification of law 法律分类
classification of prisons 监狱分类
classification of punishment 刑罚分类
classification of tariff 税则分级
classification of torts 侵权行为

的类别

classification system of prisoners
犯人分类制度

classified document 保密文件

classified secret 机密

clause 条款,加入条款

clause allowing the choice of port
of discharge 选择卸货港条款

clause of contract 合同条款,契
约条款

clause of regulations 规章条款

clause of restrictions on the use of
technology after the expiration
of the contract 合同期满禁用
条款

clause of restrictly exclusive use
排他性使用条款

clause of statute 法规条款

clause of style 格式条款

clause paramount 首要条款

clause relieving the carrier from
liability 免除承运人责任的
条款

clauses acts 共同条款法

clausula(拉) 约款

Clausula generalis non refertur ad
expressa(拉) 一般条款是不
涉及业务特别明示的内容的

clausum fregit(拉) 不动产占有
侵犯,侵入他人土地

Clayton act(美) 克莱顿法

Clayton antitrust act(美) 克莱
顿反托拉斯法

Clayton. Henry de Lamar 享利·
克莱顿

clean 未载货的

clean acceptance 不带保留条件
的承兑

clean B/L 清洁提单

clean bill 光票

clean bill for collection 光票托
收

clean bill of exchange 不附条件
的汇票

clean bill of lading 清洁提单

clean collection 光票托收

clean credit 无条件信用证

① clean draft 股票汇票

② clean draft(bill) 光票

③ clean hands 清白

④ clean L/C 光票信用证

⑤ clean letter of credit 光票信用
证

⑥ clean loan 无抵押贷款,无抵押
借款

⑦ clean sign 明显标志

⑧ clean state principle 白板原则

⑨ clean up misunderstanding 清除
误解

⑩ clear 明确

⑪ clear and present danger 明确和
现实的危险

⑫ clear away 清除

⑬ clear meaning 明显意义

⑭ clear off 清偿,清偿债务

⑮ clear off one's debts 偿清债务

⑯ clear proof 确证

⑰ clear signs 明显标志

⑱ clear sum 扣除税额外纯得所得
权

⑲ clear the debt 清偿债务

⑳ clear up a criminal case 侦破案
件,破案

㉑ clearance 票据交换、票据交换
总额

㉒ clearance account 清算账户

㉓ clearance clauses 清理条款

㉔ clearance of goods 报关,货物结
关

㉕ clearance of security transaction
证券经纪清算

㉖ cleared goods 已结关货物

㉗ clearing a bill 付清

㉘ clearing account 清算账户

㉙ clearing agent 清算代理

㉚ clearing agreement 清算协定

㉛ clearing bank 清算银行

㉜ clearing corporation 清算公司

㉝ clearing firm 清算商行

㉞ clearing fund 清算基金

㉟ clearing house 票据交换所

㊱ clearing house balance 票据交
换差额

㊲ clearing member 清算成员

clearing off debts 债务清偿

clearing operation 清算业务

clearing price 清算价格

clearing sheet （银行）汇划结算清算

clearing transactions 清算交易

clearing union 清算同盟

clearly stated rights and interests 权益分明

clerestory 长廊

clerical error 书写错误

clerk 书记员

clerk of the House 下议院书记官

client 当事人,委托方

clientage 委托关系

clinch a bargain 达成交易

clinch a deal 成交

clinical death 临床死亡

clinical forensic medicine 临床法医学

clinical period of death 临床死亡期

clinical tests 临床试验

clinical verifications 临床验证

close a bargain 达成协议

close a business 停业营业

close a deal 达成交易

close a meeting 闭会

close a transaction 达成交易

close an account 结账

close confinement 严格限制

close corporation 封闭式公司

close down 停业,查封

close inspection 严格检查

close of debate 辩论终结

close of the war 战争结束

closed account 停止借贷

closed conference 小型公司

closed hearing 不开庭审理

closed indent 限定订单

closed mortgage 限额抵押,定额抵押法

closed sea and semi-closed sea 闭海与半闭海

closed shop 排外企业

closed treaty 封闭性条约,非开放性条约

closed trial 不开庭审理

closedly connected relative 关系密切亲戚

closed-door policy 闭关政策

closed-end fund 封闭型基金

closet 壁橱

closing account 决算

closing day 停业日

closing price（rate）（股票交易所）收盘价格

closure by suture of the skull 颅骨缝愈合

closure of liquidation 清算完结

clothing carring special postal marks 邮政专用标志服

cloud on the title 产权不清

Clovis 克洛维斯

cluster development 成群成片开发

coal law 煤炭法

coal mine safety law 煤矿安全法

coalition government 联合政府

coarse 粗糙的

coast fisheries 沿海渔业

coast line 海岸线

coast town 沿海城镇

coast traffic 沿海运输

coast zone 海岸带

coastal area 沿海地区

coastal city 沿海城市

coastal fisheries 沿海渔业

coastal industry 沿海工业

coastal jurisdiction 沿海管辖权

coastal resources 沿海资源

coastal sea-bed economic area 海岸海床经济区域

coastal state 沿海国

coastal state resource jurisdiction 沿海国家资源管辖权

coastal transport 沿海运输

coastal water 沿海水域

coastal works 沿海作业

coasting trade 沿海贸易

coasting transport 沿海运输

coastland 沿海地区

coastwise carriage　沿海运输

Cocoa producer's alliance-CO-PAL　可可生产者联盟

COD certificate　货到付款证

COD commission　货到付款手续费

COD price　货到付款价格

COD sales　货到付款销售

code　法典

code designation of a military unit　部队番号

code for the settlement of disputes　调解争端的法典

code Justinian　查士丁尼法典

code of cannon law　寺院法法典

code of civil procedure　民事诉讼法典

code of commerce　商法典

code of competition　竞争法规

code of conduct　行为规范,行为准则

code of criminal procedure　刑事诉讼法典

code of ethics　道德准则

code of Gundobad　耿多巴德法典

code of Hammurabi　汉漠拉比法典

code of practice　惯例法,工作守则

code of written law　成文法典

codebtion　共同债务人

codefendant　共同被告人

codge a claim　提出索赔

codification　法律编纂

codification of code　法典编纂

codification of international law　国际法的编纂

codification of laws and regulations　法规编纂

codified law　成文法律

codifier　法律编纂者

codify, compilation　编纂

coequal　相互平等的

coerce　胁迫,强制

coercion policy　强制政策,高压政策

coercive　强制执行

coercive act　胁迫行为

coercive action　胁迫行动

coercive execution　强制执行

coercive force of the state　国家强制力

coercive measure　强制手段

coercive measure against the person　人身强制措施

coercive measures against obstruction of administrative proceedings　对妨害行政诉讼的强制措施

coercive measures against obstruction of civil proceedings　对妨害民事诉讼的强制措施

coercive measures against obstruction of criminal proceedings　对妨害刑事诉讼的强制措施

coercive measures in civil proceedings　民事强制措施

coercive method　强制办法

coercive policy　强制政策

coercive procedure　强制程序

coercive summons　拘传票

cofinance　共同融资

cofinancing　联合贷款

cognate　同宗

cognition　认知

cognition process of investigation　侦查认识过程

cognition theory of crime　认知论犯罪观

cognitive ability　认识能力

cognovit note　被告承认书

coguarantor　共同担保人

cohesion　协调

coin specie　金属货币

coinage act　金属造币法规

coincidence of accomplices　共犯竞合

coincidence of faults　过错竞合

coinsurance　共同保险

coinsurance clause　联保条款,再保险条款

coinsurer　共同约护人

Coke. Edward　爱德华·柯克

cold-shoulder 怠慢

cold-water ordeal 浸冷水神判法

collaborate 合作

collaboration 合作

collapse 倒塌

collateral 附属担保品,抵押品,(不动产)抵押,担保

collateral acceptance 担保承兑

collateral assignment 担保物的转让,间接转让

collateral civil action in administrative proceedings 行政诉讼附带民事诉讼

collateral condition 附带条件

collateral conditions 附加条件

collateral contract 附属合同

collateral loan 有抵押贷款,抵押供款

collateral rights 从属权利

collateral security 从保证,副担保,附加担保物,证券抵押品

collateral security 附属担保品

collateral surety 副担保人,从担保人

collateral warranty 从担保,副担保书

collateralize 提供抵押

collatio(拉) 合并

collect 征集,征收,收缴

collect fees arbitrarily 乱收费

collect on delivery 钱货两清,货到收款

collect rent 收租

collect taxes 征税

collectible 可收回的

collecting bill 代收票据

collecting note 代收本票

collecting post 收容所

collection (银行)代收,托收

collection clause 收款条款

collection commission 托收手续费

collection cost 托收成本

collection discharge licence 排污收费制度

collection of cash 托收现款

collection of customs duty 征收关税

collection of debts 收取债款

collection of documentary bills 托收跟单汇票

collection of drainage dues 排污费征收

collection of evidence 证据的收集

collection of rent 收租

collection on delivery/COD 货到收款

collection order 托收委托书

collection receipt 托收收据

collective 集体

collective act 集体行为

collective advertising 联合广告

collective agreement 集体合同,集体协议

collective agricultural economic organization 农业集体经济组织

collective appraisement 集体鉴定

collective bargain 集体谈判

collective consumption 集体消费

collective economic organization 集体经济组织

collective economy 集体经济

collective enforcement 集体执行

collective enterprise 集体企业

collective farm family 集体农户

collective goods 集体财产

collective guarantee 集体保证

collective head of state 集体元首

collective human rights 集体人权

collective hysteria 癔病集体发作

collective interest 集体利益

collective intervention 集体干涉

collective investment fund 集体投资基金

collective investment institution 集体投资机构

collective land　集体土地

collective leadership　集体领导

collective measure(s)　集体措施

collective measures committee　集体措施委员会

collective naturalization　集体入籍

collective negotiation　集体协商

collective offense　集合犯

collective operation　集体经营

collective organization of the working masses　劳动集体组织

collective ownership　集体所有制,公共所有权,共同所有权

collective ownership by labourers　劳动群众集体所有权

collective ownership of the means of production　生产资料集体所有制

collective ownership system　集体所有制

collective production　集体生产

collective property　集体财产

collective recognition　集体承认

collective relief　集体救济

collective reserve unit　共同储备单位

collective responsibility　集体负责制,集体责任制,集体责任

collective rights　集体权利

collective rule　集体制

collective sanction　集团制裁

collective security　集体安危,集体安全保障

collective security system　集体安全体系

collective selfdefence　集体自卫

collective self-reliance　集体自力更生

collective sovereignty　集体主权

collective welfare　集体福利

collective welfare institutions　集体福利设施

collective will　集体意志

collectively-owned enterprise　集体企业

① collectively-owned unit　集体所有制单位

② collectivism　集体主义

③ collectivization of agriculture　农业集体化

④ collectivization of farming　农业集体化

⑤ college　学校

⑥ college and universities　高校

⑦ college for professional training　大专

⑧ collegial bench　合议庭

⑨ collegial panel　合议庭

⑩ collegial system　合议制,委员会制

⑪ collegiate beach　合议庭

⑫ collegiate bench of judges　审判合议庭

⑬ collegiate bench of judges and people's assessors　审判员及人民陪审员会议庭

⑭ collegiate bench of second instance　第二审合议庭

⑮ collision（insuring）clause　碰撞保险条款

⑯ collision at sea　海上碰撞

⑰ collision liabilities　碰撞责任

⑱ collision liability in hull insurance　(船壳)碰撞责任险

⑲ collision of marine insurance　海洋碰撞险

⑳ collision regulation, regulations for preventing collisions at sea　避碰规则

㉑ collusive action　串通诉讼

㉒ collusive coprincipals　共谋共同正犯

㉓ colonel on reserve service　预备役上校

㉔ colonial power　殖民主义国家

㉕ colonial rule　殖民统治

㉖ colonialism　殖民主义

㉗ colony　侨民

㉘ colourable imitation　假造

㉙ combat readiness　战备

㉚ combatant　战斗员

㉛ combination　联合,联营

combination budget 联合预算

combination of centralization and decentralization 统分结合

combination of democracy with dictatorship 民主和专政相结合

combination of enterprise 联合企业

combination of judicial and executive branches 审执合一

combination of juridical and prosecutorial branches 审检合署

combination of legislative and executive powers 议行合一

combination of punishment and education 惩罚与教育相结合

combination of punishment with leniency 惩办与宽大相结合

combination of punishment with reformation 惩罚和改造相结合

combination of sentence after reduction 先减后并

combination of shares 联合股份

combination system 合并制

combination-deal 联合经营

combinative crime 结合犯

combine 联合企业

combine punishment and control with ideological remolding 惩罚管制与思想改造相结合

combine punishment with leniency 惩办和宽大相结合

combine uniformity and flexibility 统一性与灵活性相结合

combined 并行

combined account 联合账户

combined bill of lading 集装箱提单

combined carrier 联运承运人

combined forwarder 联运代理人

combined industrial and commercial tax 工商统一税

combined jurisdiction 并案管辖

combined management of industry and commerce 工商联营

① combined offer 联合发价

② combined sentence of principal and supplementary punishments 主刑从刑并科

④ combined sentence of principal punishment 主刑并科

⑦ combined transport 联合运输,联运

⑨ combined transport document 多式联运单据或联合运输单据

⑪ combined transport operator 联运经营人

⑬ combined transport operator (CTO) 联运经营人

⑮ combustible 易燃

⑯ come into agreement 达成协议

⑰ come into effect 开始生效

⑱ come into force 生效,发生法律效力,施行

⑳ come into power 执政

㉑ come into terms 达成协议

㉒ come of age 达到法定年龄,成年

㉔ come off the press 出版

㉕ come to an agreement, conclude an agreement 达成协议

㉗ come to terms 商妥,妥协

㉘ come up to the standard 达到标准

㉚ comfort letter 意向书

㉛ comfortably well-off standard 小康水平

㉝ Comintern 共产国际

㉞ comity(of nations) 国际礼让

㉟ comm of pasture 牧场共同权

㊱ commandeer 征用

㊲ commencement and termination of cover (保险)责任起讫

㊳ commencement of risk 风险的开始

㊶ commencement of the limitation period 时效开始

㊸ commencement of war 开战

㊹ commentional mortgage loan 常规抵押贷款

㊻ commerce 商业

㊼ commerce illicit 不法贸易

commercial acceptance 商业承兑

commercial activity 营业行为

commercial adventure 商业投机

commercial advertisement 商业广告

commercial agent 商业代理

commercial and industrial enterprises 工商企业

commercial and industrial laws and regulations 工商法规

commercial area 商业区

commercial articles 商品

commercial aviation 民用航空

commercial bank 商业银行

commercial bank law 商业银行法

commercial bank loans 商业银行贷款

commercial belligerent 交战者间的协定

commercial bill 商业汇票

commercial business 商业企业

commercial circle 商检

commercial code 商法典

commercial competition 商业竞争

commercial contract 商业合同

commercial court 商业法院

commercial credibility 商业信誉

commercial credit company 商业信贷公司

commercial credit insurance 商业信贷保险

commercial deposit 商业存款

commercial discounts 商业折扣

commercial district 商业区

commercial domicile 商业住所

commercial enterprise 商业企业

commercial goodwill 商业信誉

commercial intercourse 商业交往

commercial investment trust company 商业投资信托公司

commercial invoice 发货清单

commercial law 商法,商业法

commercial letter of credit 商业信用证

commercial liability 商业责任

commercial loan 工商贷款,商业贷款

commercial loan rate 商业贷款利率

commercial management 商业经营

commercial object 商业目的

commercial operation 商业经营

commercial paper 商业票据

commercial pledge 商业抵押

commercial production 商业性生产,大规模生产

commercial reputation 商业信誉

commercial residence 商业住所

commercial use 商业用途

commercial world 商检

commercium (拉) 商业

commission 手续费,代理,委员会,佣金,作为,代理权,管理委员会

commission (fee) 佣金,代理费,收取佣金的证券经纪人

commission agency 佣金代理

commission agent 佣金代理人,代理人,代销店,代办商

commission business 委托业务

commission charge 手续费

commission clause 佣金条款

commission contract 委托合同

commission for acceptance 承兑佣金

commission for compilation of the laws and regulations 法规汇编委员会

commission for discipline inspection 纪律检查委员会

commission for ecological environment 生态环境委员会

commission for international industrial development law 国际工业发展法委员会

commission for legal affairs 法制委员

commission for physical culture

and sports 体育运动委员会
commission house 经济商行
commission in charge of government establishments 编制委员会
commission insurance 佣金保险
commission lease 委托租赁
commission merchant 代理人
commission of a crime 犯罪实施
commission of court 法院委托
commission of joint offense 共同犯罪行为
commission on sales 销货佣金
commission rule 委任性规范
commission sale 委托销售
commissioned development contract 委托开发合同
commissioned party 受托方
commissioner 首席行政长官
commissioner of state 国务委员
commissioners of inland revenue 国内税收专员署
commissioning party 委托人,委托方
commit a crime 作案,犯罪
commit an offense 犯罪
commit crimes 为非作歹
commit crimes with firearms 持枪作案
commit oneself 承担义务,使自己受诺言的约束
commit physical assault or murder 行凶抢劫
commitment 保证债务,承诺,拘禁令,义务
commitment available period 贷款有效期
commitment charge 信贷佣金
commitment fees 承诺费
commitment letter 委任书
commitment period 贷款有效期
commitment set forth 规定的义务
commitment to prison 收监执行
committee 委员会
committee for economic development/CED 经济发展委员会

committee for internal and judicial affairs 内务司法委员会
committee for industrial development 工业发展委员会
committee for people's mediation 人民调解委员会
committee for revision of the constitution 宪法修改委员会
committee for the examination and appraisal of judges 法官考评委员会
committee member 委员
committee of active labour reformers 劳动改造积极分子委员会
committee of inspection 监察委员会
committee of superintendence 监督委员会
committee on anti-dumping practices 反倾销委员会
committee on human rights 人权事务委员会
committee on ministers' power 大臣权力监察委员会(英)
committee on natural resources/CNR(美) 自然资源委员会
committee on sanitary and phytosanitary measures 卫生和植物检疫措施委员会
committee on the peaceful uses of outer space 和平利用外层空间委员会
committeeman 工人代表
committing crimes by imitating 模仿法则说
commnunity of goods 财物共有
commodatum(拉) 无偿借贷,使用借贷
commodities 商品
commodities for the home market 内销商品
commodities futures 商品期货
commodities in short supply 紧缺商品
commodities purchased by choice 选购商品

commodity 商品,货物

commodity composition 商品结构

commodity contract 商品交易合同

commodity control list 判定管制货单

commodity dumping 商品倾销

commodity economy 商品经济

commodity exchange tax 商品流通税

commodity housing 商品住宅

commodity information 商品信息

commodity inspecting and testing bureau 商品检验局,商检局

commodity inspection 商品检验

commodity inspection authority 商检机构

commodity inspection certificate 商检证明书,商检证书

commodity inspection label 商检标志

commodity inspection mark 商检标志

commodity inspection marks or sealings 商检标或者封识

commodity market 商品市场

commodity marketing 商品经营,商品销售

commodity name 商品品名

commodity of the same classification 同类商品

commodity price 物价

commodity price control 物价管理

commodity producer 商品生产者

commodity production 商品生产

commodity residential building 商品住宅

commodity sales 商品销售

commodity tax 商品税,货物税

commodum(拉) 收益

common 普遍

common action 普通诉讼

common agreement 共同协议

common agricultural fund 共同农业基金

common agricultural policy/CAP 共同农业政策

common aspiration of the peoples 民心

common attempt 普通未遂

common benefit 共同利益

common carrier(s) 公共承运人,承运商

common criminal 普通刑事犯

common criterion 共同准则

common custom 世俗

common defect 一般瑕疵

common energy policy 共同能源政策

common equity 普通股股本

common fisheries policy 共同渔业政策

common fishery 公海捕鱼权

common fund 共同基金

common goal 共同目标

common goods (苏格兰) 法人的全部财产

common guideline 共同准则

common heritage of mankind 人类的共同财产,人类共同继承的财富,人类共同继承财产

common in soil 矿藏共同权

common intent 共同故意

common intention of parties to prevail 共同意图优先

common interest 共同利害关系

common interest(s) 共同利益,双方利益

common land 共用地

common law 普通法,共同法

common law and equity 普通法和衡平法

common law court 普通法院

common law jurisdiction 习惯法管辖区

common law lien 习惯法,普通法上的留置权

common law system 英美法律体系,普通法系

common law system countries 英美法系国家

common market 共同市场

common meaning 普通意义

common mistake 共有错误

common money bond 普通金钱担保书

common name 通用名称

common needs of society 社会共同需要

common obligation 共同债务

common opinion 普遍意见

common owner 共同共有人,共有人

common ownership 共同共有,共有权

common policy 共同政策

common practice 常规

common principles of interpretation 解释的共同原则

common property 共同资产,公用财产

common proprietor 共同所有人,共同财产所有人

common prosperity 共同繁荣

common purpose 共同目的

common quality 中等品质

common representative 共同代理人

common requisites (elements) 共同要件

common reserve fund 公积金

common resources 共用资源

common right 共有权利

common seal 公用印章

common share (stock) 普通股

common stock 普通股

common will 共同意志

common will of ruling class 统治阶级的共同意志

commonalty 社团法人

commonwealth 联邦,国家,普通法犯罪

commonwealth of independent state 独联体

commonwealth preference 英联邦特惠制

common-disaster clause 共同灾难条款

common-law accident insurance 公认意外保险

common-law action 普通法诉讼

common-law assignment 普通法上的转让,习惯法上的让与

common-law cheat 普通法上的欺骗

common-law crime 普通法上的罪行

common-law exchange 普通法上的兑换

common-law jurisdiction 普通法上的裁判权,普通法上的管辖权

common-law lien 普通法上的留置权

common-law mortgage 普通法上的抵押

common-law negligence 普通法上的过失

common-law negligence actions 普通法上的过失诉讼

common-law power of arrest 普通法上的拘捕权

common-law procedure act 普通诉讼条例

common-law remedy 普通法上的补偿

common-law right 依普通法获得的权利

common-law right of property 普通法上的财产权

commotion in price 价格紊乱

commission merchant 代办商

communal property 公用财产

Commune de Paris 巴黎公社

communication by implication 默示表达

communications 交通

communio bonorum (拉) 财产共有制

communism 共产主义,社会,共同体

community debt 共同债务

community environmental actions

共同体改善环境行动

community income 共同收益

community industry 共同体工业

community land 公共土地

community of interest 利益集团,共同利益

community ownership 集体所有

community preference system 集体优惠制度

community property 公共财产,共有财产

community property system 共同财产制

community responsibility 社会责任

community work 社会工作

commutation 减轻刑罚,减刑

commutation act 课税代纳法

commutation of penalty 减轻惩罚

commutation order 减刑裁定书

commute 折抵

commuter tax 非居民税

compact 契约

compact communities of nationalities 民族聚居区

company 公司

company act 公司法

company contract 公司合同

company deposit 公司在银行的存款

company law 公司法

company of limited liability 有限公司

company of unlimited liability 无限公司

company with reduced capital 减资企业

company with share capital 股份公司

company's articles of association 公司组织章程

comparable price 可比价格

comparative advantage 比较利益

comparative advertising 比较广告

comparative analysis 对比分析

comparative civil law 比较民法

comparative cost 比较成本理论

comparative criminal law 比较刑法学

comparative criminology 比较犯罪,比较犯罪学

comparative design 比较设计方案

comparative economic law 比较经济法

comparative impairment 比较损害

comparative interpretation 比较解释

comparative jurisprudence 比较法学

comparative law 比较法

comparative legal history 比较法制史

comparative negligence 相对疏忽

comparative penal jurisprudence 比较刑法学

comparative penal law 比较刑法

comparative penology 比较监狱学

comparative right 相对权

comparative right of claim 相对请求权

compel 强制,强迫

compendium of classification opinions 分类意见提要

compensating expense 赔偿费

compensability 可补偿性

compensable 可赔偿

compensable according to law 依法补偿

compensate 补偿,赔偿损失,酬金,赔偿

compensate according to law 依法补偿

compensate according to the cost 照价赔偿

compensate debts 偿清债务

compensate for 抵偿

compensate for the damage 赔偿损失

compensate for the losses 赔偿损失

compensating duty 补偿税

compensating measure 赔偿办法

compensating suretyship 赔偿保证

compensating tariff 补偿关税，抵偿关税率

compensatio（拉） 抵消

compensation 补偿，赔偿金，报酬，有偿，赔偿费，赔偿，偿金，赔偿物

compensation claim 赔偿请求

compensation claimant 赔偿请求人

compensation committee 赔偿委员会

compensation committee in the people's court 人民法院赔偿委员会

compensation costs 赔偿费用

compensation elimination 抵销

compensation expenditure 赔偿费用

compensation for a loss 赔偿损失

compensation for appropriation of a water area and seabeach 水面滩涂征用补偿

compensation for building removal 建筑物迁移补偿

compensation for cancellation of contracts 解除合同补偿费

compensation for crops 青苗赔偿费

compensation for damage 侵权损害赔偿，损失赔偿，损害赔偿

compensation for delay 迟交货赔偿

compensation for government tort 行政侵权赔偿

compensation for land 土地补偿费

compensation for liability for government tort 行政侵权责任赔偿

compensation for loss or damage consequent upon collision 船舶碰撞损害赔偿

compensation for loss(es) 赔偿损失

compensation for nondelivery 不交货赔偿

compensation for removal 迁移费

compensation insurance 赔偿险

compensation law 赔偿法

compensation money 赔偿金

compensation of damage 损失赔偿

compensation of equal value 等价有偿

compensation of guardian 监护人报酬

compensation of obligation 债的抵消

compensation of victim 被害人补偿

compensation payment 补偿金

compensation system 补偿制度

compensation trade 补偿贸易

compensation undercontract 约定赔偿

compensative 补偿的

compensator 赔偿人

compensatory 补偿的

compensatory adjustment 补偿性调整

compensatory approach 补偿办法，赔偿方式

compensatory damages 补偿损害赔偿

compensatory finance 赤字财政

compensatory financing 补偿性资金供应

compensatory financing facility 出口波动补偿资助

compensatory payment 补偿金，赔偿金

compensatory replacement of demolished housing 原拆原建

compensatory tax 补偿税

compensatory transfer of technology 技术有偿转让

competence 权限,能力

competence for a post 任职资格

competence in rectification 更正的权力

competence of court 法院管辖权

competence of lawyers 律师资格

competence of witness 证人的作证资格,证人能力

competence penalty 能力罚

competence to conclude treaties 约权

competency 证据法上的作证资格

competency for being taken on the staff 录用资格

competency of evidence 证据资格

competency or employment 录用资格

competent 适格,有法定资格的

competent administrative authorities 行政主管部门

competent administrative department at a higher level 上级行政主管部门

competent authorities 行政主管

competent authorities of the state 国家主管机关

competent authority 主管机关,主管部门

competent authority for labour administration 劳动行政主管部门

competent customs service 海关主管职能部门

competent defendant 符合条件的被告

competent department 主管部门,主管机关

ccompetent department in charge of price 物价主管部门

competent department in charge of price under the State Council (中) 国务院物价主管部门

competent department of taxation under the State Council (中) 国务院税务主管部门

competent departments concerned 有关主管部门

competent jurisdiction 合法管辖权

competent law 适用性的法律

competent national authorities 国家主管机关

competent organ 主管机关

competent organization 主管单位

competent organization for registration 登记主管机关

competent plaintiff 符合条件的原告

competing goods 竞争产品

competing product 竞争产品

competition 竞争,角逐

competition forces 竞争机制

competition law 竞争法

competition mechanism 竞争机制

competition on equal footing 公平竞争

competition policy 竞争政策

competition process 竞争过程

competition system 竞争机制

competition test 竞争标准

competition using unfair practices 不正当竞争

competitive behavior 竞争行为

competitive bidding 公开招标,竞争性投标,竞标

competitive commodities 竞争产品

competitive currency depreciation 竞争性货币贬值

competitive depreciation 竞争性贬值

competitive devaluation 竞争性贬值

competitive edge 竞争界限,竞

competitive inhibition 竞争抑制

competitive investment 竞争性投资,竞争投资

competitive need criteria 竞争需要标准

competitive offer 有竞争性的报价

competitive price 有竞争性的价格,竞争价格,竞争性价格

competitive relation 竞争关系

competitive sale 竞争性销售

complainant informer 控告人

complement 补充

complementary goods 机辅商品

complete action 法律上完全无效的行为,完全生效的行为

complete agreement 完全物权,完全协议

complete annexation 完全兼并

complete application 完整证明书

complete bankruptcy 完全破产

complete capacity for criminal responsibility 完全责任能力

complete economic integration 完全经济一体化,完全的经济体化

complete evidence 证据充分

complete incorporation 全部合并

complete monopoly 完全垄断

complete one's term of imprisonment 服刑期满

complete payment 最后付款

complete restitution 全部归还

complete set of equipment 整套设备

complete sovereignty 完全的主权

complete subordination 完全从属之债

complete transaction 已完成交易

complete willingness of the two parties 双方完全自愿

completely 全然

completely constituted trust 完全成立的信托

completely ignore provisions of law 全然不顾法律规定

completion 竣工,完成交易

completion acceptance 竣工验收

completion date of the project 项目完工日期

completion guarantee 完成担保

completion guarantees of project financing 项目贷款的完工担保协议

completion of a crime 犯罪既遂

completion of a criminal act 犯罪实行终了

completion of contract 完成合同

completion of the liquidation 清算完结

completion time of project 建设工期

complex 复合,错综交杂,联合企业

complex offense 复合罪

complex political offense 复合政治罪

complex tariff 复式关税,复式税则

complex tariff compound duty 复式税则

complexes 联合企业

complicity 共同犯罪行为,共同犯罪

comply with 遵守

component registration authority of enterprise name 企业名称登记主管机关

composite 复合

composite country 复合国

composite economic results 综合经济效益

composite price 综合价格

composite state 复合国,复合制国家

composite system 金银本位复合制

composite treaty 复合条约

composition 契约方案,部分偿还的了结债务的协议,和解,债务和解协议

composition deed 债务和解协议

composition of investment 投资结构

composition of liability for government tort 行政侵权责任构成

composition of malfeasance 违法构成

compound 复合

compound interest 复利

compound larceny 混合盗窃罪

compound motive of crime 复合性犯罪动机

compound rate 复利率

compound tariff 复合税率

compound with creditors 与债权人和解

compounded 以复利计算的

comprador 买办

comprador bourgeoisie 买办资产阶级

comprador's capital 买办资本

comprador-feudal system 买办封建制度

comprehensive insurance 综合保险

comprehensive amount-limited tax credit 税收综合限额抵免

comprehensive analysis 全面分析

comprehensive balancing 综合平衡

comprehensive codification 全面法典化

comprehensive guarantee 综合担保

comprehensive institutional framework 综合体制

comprehensive operation license 综合经营许可证

comprehensive plan 全面计划

comprehensive planning 综合规划

comprehensive program 全面规划

comprehensive regulation 综合调整

comprehensive short-term guarantee 短期信贷综合担保

comprehensive summing-up 全面总结

comprehensive tax credit of limited amount 税收专项限额抵免

comprehensive utilization 综合利用

comprehensive utilization of natural resources 自然资源的综合利用

compress 压缩,压迫

compromise 和解,相互妥协,和解,妥协

comptroller 稽核

compulsive 强制的

compulsive method 强制性方法

compulsory abandonment of drug habits 强制戒毒

compulsory appropriation 强制划拨

compulsory arbitration 强制仲裁

compulsory collection 强制征收

compulsory contribution 强制摊派

compulsory education 义务教育

compulsory education law 义务教育法

compulsory enforcement 强制执行

compulsory enforcement of the order 强制履行

compulsory impost 征税的强制性

compulsory injunction 强制禁令

compulsory insurance 强制保险

compulsory joint venture 强迫性联营

compulsory judicial settlement 强制司法解决

compulsory law 强行法

compulsory licence 强制许可

compulsory liquidation 强制清

算

compulsory loan 强制贷款

compulsory marriage on account of an arrangement 强迫包办婚姻

compulsory means 强制手段

compulsory means of dispute settlement 解决争端的强制方法

compulsory measure 强制措施

compulsory military service 义务兵役制

compulsory militia 义务民兵

compulsory move 强制搬迁

compulsory nonsuit 强制驳回起诉

compulsory performance 强制履行

compulsory power 强制权

compulsory provisions 强制性规定

compulsory purchase 征购

compulsory retirement 强迫退休

compulsory sanction 强制性制裁

compulsory sea perils insurance 强制海事故保险

compulsory serviceman 义务兵

compulsory standard 强制性标准

compulsory voting 强迫投票

compurgation 誓证法,宣誓免责

computatio (拉) 时间的计算

computed price 推算价

computed value 计算价格

computer software 计算机软件

conceal 隐瞒,隐蔽,隐匿谎报销毁会计资料

conceal one's identity 隐名

conceal statistical data 隐瞒统计资料

conceal the price 匿价

concealed damage 隐蔽的损坏

concealed dumping 隐蔽倾销

concealed fraud 隐瞒事实的诈

欺

concealed malice 隐含的恶意

concealed object 隐藏物

concealment 隐瞒

concealment of fact 隐瞒事实真相

concentrated area of nationalities 民族聚居区

concentrated investment 集中投资

concentrating funds 集中资金

concentration of capital 资本积累

concentration of pollution discharge 排放污染物浓度

concept 观念

concept of administrative act 行政行为的概念

concept of constitution 宪法的概念

concept of crime 犯罪概念

concept of economic law 经济法的概念

concept of law 法的概念

concept of public servant 公仆观念

conceptual knowledge 理性认识

concern 财团,涉及

concerned 有关的

concerned party 有关人员

concerned unit 有关单位

concerning 关于

concert identification 秘密辨认

concert party 一致行动的当事人

concerted refusals to deal 共同拒绝交易

concessio (拉) 让步

concession 租界

concession agreement 租让协议,特许协议,租让条约

concession contract 租让合同

concessionaire 租让合承担人,受租让者,特许权享有者,特许权所有人

concessional disposal 廉价处理,特许出售

concessional loan 优惠贷款

concessional rate 让价,优惠价格

concessional terms 优惠利率

concessionary contract 租让合同

concessionary right 租让权利

concessioner 特许权所有人

conciliate 调解

conciliated procedure 调解程序

conciliation 和解,调解

conciliator 调解人

concinnitas(拉) 诈欺

concise expression 简明语言

conclude 推断,签订

conclude a contract 订立合同

conclude a licensing contract 签订实施许可合同

conclude a transaction 达成交易

conclude an agreement 签订合同

conclusion 推论

conclusion of a review 复审结论

conclusion of audit 审计结论

conclusion of contracts 合同的订立

conclusion of investigation 侦查终结

conclusion of law 法律的断定

conclusion of peace 媾和

conclusion of reexamination 复审结论

conclusion of the examination 审查的终结

conclusion of treaties 条约的订立

conclusion of treaty 条约的缔结

conclusion on reinspection 复验结论

conclusions of expert evaluations; expert conclusion 鉴定结论

conclusive 决定性的

conclusive evidence 确切证据,确凿的证据,结论性证据,证据确凿

conclusive judgment 最终判决

conclusive presumption 确定性

① 的推断

② conclusive proof 确证

③ conclusive sentence 最终判决

④ concoct 捏造

⑤ concord 一致性

⑥ concordance 一致性

⑦ concordance of discordant canons 历代教律辑要

⑧ concordat 教廷条约,契约

⑨ concordat pact 契约

⑩ concrete accusation 具体罪名

⑪ concrete conditions in the establishment of a specific crime 构成具体犯罪的具体条件

⑫ concrete duty 具体义务

⑬ concrete justice 具体正义

⑭ concrete measure 具体措施

⑮ concrete right 具体权利

⑯ concrete right of action 具体诉权

⑰ concretespecific 具体

⑱ concubinage 纳妾制

⑲ concubine 情妇

⑳ concurrence deloyable 不公平竞争

㉑ concurrence of faults 过错竞合

㉒ concurrent 并行

㉓ concurrent authority 同等权力

㉔ concurrent competencies 平行权力

㉕ concurrent condition 对流条件

㉖ concurrent crime 竞合犯

㉗ concurrent interests 并存权益

㉘ concurrent negligence 并存过失,共同过失

㉙ concurrent post representation 兼职代表制

㉚ concurrent power 平行权力,共同权力

㉛ concurrent sentencing 合并判决

㉜ concurrent writ 并存法庭命令

㉝ condemn 判定有罪,判罪,坐罪

㉞ condemn sb to 判处

㉟ condemn sb to death 判处死刑

㊱ condemn sb to life imprisonment 判处无期徒刑

㊲ condemn sb to imprisonment 判

处徒刑

condemn without leniency　坐罪不贷

condemnation　捕获船舶裁定，判决没收，国家征用，刑事定罪

condemned building　被宣布为危险的建筑

condenatio tacita（拉）　默许

condense　压缩

condition　条件，解除条件，制约，现象，假定条件

condition clause　基本条款

condition final at shipment　以装船时状态为准

condition for the application of security measures　保安处分适用条件

condition of contract　契约条件

condition of grant　让步条件

condition of punishment　处罚条件

condition of reciprocity　相互条件

condition of sale　拍卖条件，销货条件，买卖条件

condition of the country　国情

condition of uncertainty　不确定条件

condition of validity　有效条件

condition precedent　停止条件，先决条件

conditional　附条件的，附带条件，有条件的

conditional agreement　附条件的协议，有条件协定

conditional civil juristic act subject to a condition　附条件民事法律行为

conditional clause　有条件条款，有条件禁制品

conditional contract　有条件契约，附条件合同

conditional delivery　有条件交付，有条件交货

conditional discharge　附条件负责

conditional duty　有条件的责任

conditional endorsement　有条件的背书

conditional interpretation　有条件解释

conditional legacy　附条件遗赠

conditional loan　有条件贷款

conditional offer　附条件发价，附条件要约

conditional order　有条件订货

conditional prohibition　有条件禁止

conditional promise　有条件允诺

conditional ratification　有条件的批准

conditional recognition　有条件承认

conditional right　附条件权利

conditional rights　相对权

conditional sale　附条件买卖，有条件销售

conditional sale agreement　附条件的买卖协议，有条件之买卖协议

conditional sales contract　有条件买卖合同，有条件销售

conditional subscription　附条件认购

conditional suspension of fine　罚金缓刑制，罚金刑执行犹豫制

conditional termination　附条件终止

conditional time period　附期限

conditional title　有条件之产权

conditional will　附条件遗赠

conditionality　附加条件

conditions for（/terms of）credit　贷款条件

conditions for initiating an administrative action　行政诉讼起诉条件

conditions for loans　贷款条件

conditions of carriage　货运条件

conditions of contract for civil engineering construction, international　土木工程国际合同条件

conditions of contract for electrical and mechanical works including erection site　机电安装工程合同条件

conditions of contract for works of civil engineering construction　土木建筑工程合同条件

conditions of contract for works of civil engineering contract　土木工程施工合同条件

conditions of crime　犯罪条件

conditions of delivery and redelivery　交还船条件

conditions of labour　劳动条件

conditions of taking in for reeducation through labor　收容、劳动教养条件

conditions of the contract　合同条件

conditions of validity　有效条件

conditions unchangeable clause　情势不变条款

condominium（拉）共有

condonatio（拉）赠与

condonatio erpressa（拉）明示的容许

condonatio praesumta（拉）推定的容许

condonation and settlement of the victim　被害人宽恕与和解

conduct　主持

conduct agent　意定代理人

conduct business operation　从事经营

conduct illegal operations　非法经营

conduct its session　主持会议

conduct joint operation　共同经营

conduct operation　从事经营

conduct resulting in treasury obligation　国库债务负担义务

conduct tax　行为税

condusion of a lawsuit　诉讼终结（诉讼终止）

confederacy　邦联

confederal system　邦联制

confederalism　邦联主义

confederate government　邦联政府

confederated states　邦联

confederation　邦联,同盟

confer　商议,商同,谈判

conference　会议

conference agenda　会议议程

conference in private international law of American countries　美洲国家组织国际私法会议

conference on placing orders　订货会

confess and acknowledge　坦白承认

confess one's crimes　坦白交待罪行

confession　承据,供词,坦白

confession and defense of the accused　被告人供述和辩解

confession in collusion　串供

confession of defense　被告人供述和辩解,被告口供

confession of the defendant　被告人自白

conficatory decree　没收令

confide jussio（拉）共同证

confidence vote　信任投票

confidential document　保密文件

confidentiality　保密条款

confidentiality clauses in technology transfer contract　技术转让合同中的保密条款

confine　限制

confirm　认可

confirm an offer　确盘

confirm the agreement　确认协议

confirm the contract in writing　书面确认合同成立

confirmation　确认书,确认

confirmation of cable　电报确认书,电传确认书

confirmation of order　订货确认书

confirmation of sales　销售确认书,售货确认书

confirmation of telegram (cable, telex) 电报(电传)确认书

confirmation of telex 电传确认书,电报确认书

confirmation of the property right 确认所有权

confirmation request 要示确认

confirmation sheet 确认通知书

confirmation tutelar 监护人的追认

confirmatory sample 确认样品

confirmatory test of bloodstain 血痕确证检验

confirmed irrevocable letter of credit 保兑不可撤销的信用证

confirmed L/C 保兑信用证

confirmed thief 惯窃犯

confirming bank 保兑行

confirming(er) bank 保兑行

confiscate 没收,收缴国库

confiscate according to law 依法没收

confiscate illegal gains 没收违法所得

confiscate property 收缴财产

confiscate the property 收缴财产

confiscate unlawful 没收违法所得

confiscated goods 没收的货物

confiscation 没收

confiscation measure 没收处分

confiscation of contraband 没收违禁品

confiscation of illegal gains 没收违法所得

confiscation of land 土地征用

confiscation of property 没收财产

confiscation of unlawful properties 没收非法财物

confiscation order 没收令

confiscation voucher 没收凭证

confiscator 没收人

confiscatory decree 没收法令

confiscatory taxation 没收性赋税,充公赋税

conflict 冲突

conflict between conflict of laws 冲突规范的冲突

conflict between labour and management 劳务冲突

conflict in negotiable 票据法冲突

conflict law 冲突法

conflict of connecting points 连结点的冲突

conflict of interests 利益冲突

conflict of judgment 判决冲突

conflict of jurisdiction over administrative proceedings 行政诉讼的管辖冲突

conflict of law 法律冲突

conflict of law and equity 普通法与衡平法的冲突

conflict of laws 法律上的冲突

conflict of laws 冲突法

conflict of nationalities 国籍的冲突

conflict of qualification 识别冲突

conflict of territorial jurisdiction over 行政诉讼地域管辖冲突

conflict principles 冲突原则

conflict rule 冲突规则

conflict rules 冲突规范

conflict rules of uniform 统一冲突规范

conflict theory 冲突论

conflict to of subject matter jurisdiction over administrative proceedings 行政诉讼级别管辖冲突

conflicting evidence 冲突证据

conflicting rules 抵触的规定

conform to 符合

conform with 合乎

conform with the contract 与合同相符

conforming product 合格产品

conformity certification 合格认证

confront the accused with the accuser 被告与原告对质

confrontation by both sides 证人对质

confrontation of counterclaim purpose 反诉目的的对抗性

confusion of goods 货物的混杂

confusion of obligee and debtor 债权人与债务人混同

conglomerate 多行业联合企业，多种工业联合企业，跨行业公司合并

conglomerate（company） 联合大企业

conglomerate business conglomerate 集团企业

conglomerate combination 多行业企业联合

conglomerate company 多行业联合企业

conglomerate merge 多行业企业合并

conglomeration 居民区

conglomeration integration 多行业企业联合

congnition of defense 防卫意识

congnovit actionem（拉） 被告供认不讳

congregation 集会

congress 大会，议会，国会，代表大会

congress of teaching and administrative staff 教代会

congress of Westphalia 威斯特伐里亚公会

congress' veto power 国会立法否决权

congressional budget office（美） 国会预算局

congressional legislation 国会立法

congressman 国会议员，议员

congressperson 国会议员

congresswoman 国会议员，议员

conjectio（拉） 推定

conjunctio（拉） 合并

conjunctly and severally 有连带责任的

① connecting factors 连结因素
② connecting points 连结点
③ connotation 内涵
④ conpensatory financing of export fluctuation 出口波动补偿条款
⑤
⑥
⑦ conquest 征服
⑧ consanguinity 同宗，血亲
⑨ conscience of guiltiness 罪责感
⑩ conscious activity 主观能动性
⑪ conscious negligence 有意识过失
⑫
⑬ consciousness disorder 意识障碍
⑭ consciousness of administrative law 行政法意识
⑮
⑯ consciousness of citizenship 公民意识
⑰
⑱ conscript 征兵
⑲ conscript father 参议员
⑳ conscription criterion 征兵标准
㉑ conscription law 兵役法，征兵法
㉒
㉓ conscription system 兵役制度
㉔ consecutive 连续的
㉕ Conseil d'etat（法） 法国行政法院
㉖
㉗ consensio（拉） 同意
㉘ consensual act 非要物行为
㉙ consensual jurisdiction 合议管辖
㉚
㉛ consensus 协商一致，协议，君子协定
㉜
㉝ consensus facit legem（拉） 合同即法律，合意产生法律
㉞
㉟ consensus nuptialis（拉） 一致同意
㊱
㊲ consent 同意
㊳ consent in writing 书面同意
㊴ consequence of damage resulted from a crime 犯罪造成的损害后果
㊵
㊶
㊷ consequential crime 间接犯罪
㊸ consequential damage 间接损害
㊹ consequential damage remote loss 间接损失
㊺
㊻ consequential injury 间接伤害
㊼ consequential loss 间接损失

consequential offense 结果犯

conservation area 保护区

conservation cost for land 土地的维护费用

conservation law on natural resources 自然资源保护法

conservation of environment 环境保护

conservation of evidence 证据保金,保金证据

conservation of resources 资源保护

conservation of the living resources of the high seas 公海生物资源的养护

conservation of wild plant 野生植物保护

conservatism principle 稳健原则

conservative ideas 保守思想

conservator （银行）监督员

conservator of the peace 行政司法官

conservatory measure 防护措施

conservatory measure in relation to recourse 关于追索权的保全措施

conservatory measures in arbitration 仲裁保全

conservatory measures in litigation 假扣押

conserve evidence 保全证据

conserve wild plant 野生植物保护

conserved building 被保留的建筑

considerable contract 有偿合同

considerable order 大量采购

consideratio（拉） 商量

consideration 对价（注：指英美法中），约因,有偿,审议,代价

Consideration may be executory and executed, but not past 对价可以是未付的或已付的,但不能够是过时的

Consideration may be executory and executed, but not past （港）对价可以是来付的和已付的,但不能是过时的

Consideration must be legal 对价必须合法

Consideration must be real 对价必须有价值

Consideration must be sufficient, but de need not be adequate 对价必须有价值,但不必相等

Consideration must be valuable 对价必须有价值

considered repealed 实际失效

consign 托运,委托

consign for shipment 托运

consigned goods 寄售品

consignee 收货人,代售人,代售商,收件人（或:收货人）,受托人

consignee's address 收货人地址

consignee's warehouse 收货人仓库

consigner 发货人,交付人

consignment 发货单

consignment agent 寄售代理人

consignment bill 托送单

consignment bill of lading 托送单

consignment expense 寄售费用

consignment goods 寄售品

consignment note 铁路运单

consignment-in 承销

consignment-out 寄售品

consignor 交付人,发货人,委托方,托运人

consist of 由…组成

consistency 一致性

consistency check 一致性检查

consistency of auditing 审计的一致性

consistency principle 一贯原则

consistent policy 一贯政策,一贯方针

consisting of 由…组成

consistory court 宗教法庭,主教法庭

consolidate 强化

consolidate appeals 合并上诉

consolidate the goods 集装货物

consolidated 固定

consolidated bank 合并而成的银行

consolidated debt 合并债务,确定债务

consolidated group 合并集团

consolidated income 合并收益

consolidated mortgage 合并抵押

consolidated returns 合并收益

consolidated tax 货物税

consolidation 集中托运方式,清理债务,合并集团

consolidation by lease 租赁合并

consolidation by merge 吸收合并

consolidation by purchase 购买合并

consolidation of actions 合并诉讼

consolidation of debt 联合债务

consolidation of provisions 合并条款

consolidation statute 统一法规

consolidation within a specified time 限期整顿

consolidator 集运人

consortium 金融财团,财团,企业集团,银行团

conspiracy 结伙阴谋罪,谋反

conspiracy at common law 普通法上的同谋罪

conspiration to overthrow the government 阴谋推翻政府

conspire against the state 谋反

constable 警察,初级警官

constant price 不变价格,固定价格

constituency 选区,选区的选民,全体选民

constituent assembly 国民代表大会,立宪会议,制宪会议

constituent instrument organic law 组织法

constituent power 制宪权

constitute 构成

constitutio criminalias Carolina (拉) 加洛林纳刑法典

constitution 宪法,宪章

constitution amendment 宪法修正案

constitution and legislation on state 宪法,国家法

constitution granted by the sovereign 钦定宪法

constitution made by the people 民定宪法

constitution made by the sovereign and people 协定宪法

constitution of a crime 犯罪构成

constitution of a party 党章

constitution of constitutional government 宪政建设

constitution of facts 事实构成

constitution of five powers 五权宪法

constitution of the apostles 使徒约章

constitution of the realm of Sicily 西西里王国宪法

constitution of the U.S.A. 美利坚合众国宪法

constitution of three powers 三权宪法

constitutional 符合宪法的

constitutional act 宪法行为

constitutional amendment 宪法修正案

constitutional case 宪法判例

constitutional change 宪法变迁

constitutional complaint 宪法控诉

constitutional convention 宪法惯例,修改宪法会议,修宪会议,宪法习惯,制宪会议,立宪君主制

constitutional court 宪法法院

constitutional crisis 宪法危机

constitutional culture 宪法文化

constitutional day 宪法日

constitutional dispute 宪法纠纷

constitutional document 宪法文件

constitutional education 宪法教育

constitutional effect 宪法效力

constitutional freedom 宪法规定的自由,宪法上规定的自由

constitutional government 宪政,立宪政体,立宪政府

constitutional guarantee 宪法保证

constitutional history 制宪史

constitutional initiative 宪法创制,宪法创制权

constitutional jural relation 宪法法律关系

constitutional jurisprudence 宪法学(国家法学)

constitutional law 宪法律例,符合宪法的法律,根本大法,根本法,宪法

constitutional legal relationship 宪法法律关系

constitutional liability 宪法责任

constitutional limitation 宪法限制

constitutional monarchy 君主立宪制度

constitutional movement 立宪运动,宪政运动

constitutional norm 宪法规范

constitutional position 宪法地位

constitutional powers 宪法上规定的权力

constitutional prescription 宪法规定

constitutional principle 宪法原则

constitutional procedure 宪法程序

constitutional process 宪法程序

constitutional regime 立宪政体

constitutional relation 宪法关系

constitutional republic 立宪共和制

constitutional requirement 宪法规定的必要条件

constitutional responsibility 宪法责任

constitutional restriction 宪法限制

constitutional right 宪法权利

constitutional rights 宪法上规定的权利

constitutional sense 宪法意识

constitutional source 宪法渊源

constitutional spirit 宪法精神,宪政精神

constitutionalism 立宪,立宪政府,立宪主义,宪法论,宪政

constitutionalist 立宪派,合宪性,符合宪法

constitutionality presumption 合宪性推定

constitutions of Clarendon 克莱灵顿法(12C英国)

constitution-drafting agency 宪法起草机关

constitution-drafting committee 宪法起草委员会

constitutive elements of a crime 犯罪构成

constitutive elements of crime 犯罪构成要件

constitutive fact 宪法性事实

constitutive law 宪法性法律,组织法

constitutive requirements 构成要件

constitutive requirements of administrative act 行政行为的构成要件

constitutive theory 构成说

constitutum (拉) 无方式契约

constitutum possessorium (拉) 占有的改定

constraint 拘禁

construction and installation work 建筑安装工程

construct by oneself 自营

constructed price 推定价格

constructed value 结构价格

construction (work) in process (CWIP) 在建工程

construction and erection enterprise 建筑安装企业

construction class　建筑等级

construction company　建筑公司

construction cost　工程造价

construction drawings　建设施工图纸

construction engineering　建筑工程

construction enterprise　施工企业

construction field　建筑工地

construction height　安装高度

construction industry　建筑业

construction inspection rules　施工验收规范

construction item　建设项目

construction of criminal law　刑法解释

construction of law　法律阐释，法律解释

construction of references　权限的解释

construction order　基建任务书

construction project　建设项目

construction project contract　工程合同

construction projects　基本建设工程

construction quality　工程质量

construction site　建筑工地

construction tax　建设税

construction unit　建设单位，施工单位

construction work　建设工程

construction work period　建设工期

constructive　推定的

constructive compulsory rape　准强奸罪

constructive crime　推定罪

constructive delivery　推定交货

constructive dishonor　推定拒付

constructive fault or negligence　推定过失

constructive fraud　推定欺诈

constructive intent　推定故意，推定犯意

constructive knowledge　推定知情

constructive larceny　推定盗窃罪

constructive malice　推定恶意，推定通知

constructive note　推定通知

constructive possession　推定占有

constructive seizin　推定依法占有的不动产

constructive sentencing despite unsettled points　存疑判决

constructive service　替代送达

constructive total loss　推定全损

constructive trust　推定信托

constructive trustee　推定受托人

constructor　施工人

constructors　施工人员

construe　推断，解释

consuetude　惯例

consul　领事，执政官

consul electi (拉)　选任领事

consul general　总领事

consulage　签证费

consular agents　领事代理人

consular authentication　领事认证

consular authority　领事权

consular commission　委任文凭（即领事委任状）

consular corps　领事团

consular court　领事法庭

consular decision　领事裁决

consular district　领田

consular functions　领事职务

consular immunity　领事豁免权

consular jurisdiction　领事裁判权

consular officer　领事官员

consular post　领馆

consular privileges　领事特权

consular privileges and immunities　领事特权与豁免

consular regime　领事制度

consular treaty　领事条约

consult　商议，参照，商量，协商

consult service for economy　经

济咨询服务

consult the original　参照原文

consultant　参事

consultatio（拉）答问录

consultation　协商,磋商

consultation machinery　协商机构

consultation on the basis of equality　平等协商

consultative procedure　协商程序

consulted organization　受质询机关

consulting meetings of Antarctica treaty　南极条约协商会议

consulting principle　协商原则

consulting rules　参照规章

consulting service　咨询服务

consumer credit　（消费者）短期信贷

consumer risk　买方风险

consumer sale　消费交易

consumer's product safety act　消费品安全法

consumer-hire agreement　消费租用协议

consumer-hire business　消费租用业务

consumption abroad　境外消费

contact　联系,接触

contacts with overseas parties　对外联系

contain　遏制

container clause　集装箱条款

container consortium　集装箱联合工业

container hire　集装箱租金

container leasing　集装箱租赁

container loading list　装箱清单

container rules of freight conference　航运公会集装箱规则

container service　集装箱运输

container transport　集装箱运输

containerization　集装箱化

contaminant　污染物

contaminated zone　污染地带,污染区

contamination accident　污染事故

contamination counter　污染计数器

contemporanea expositio（拉）当时的解释

contemporary international law　当代国际法

contemporary interpretation　流行解释

contempt　藐视

contempt for the law　藐视法律

contempt of congress（美）藐视国会罪

contempt of court　藐视法庭,藐视法庭罪

contempt of legislature　藐视立法机关罪

contempt of parliament（英）藐视议会罪

content of administrative legal relationship　行政法律关系的内容

content of economic legal（relations）nexus　经济法律关系内容

content of jural relation of administrative procedure　行政诉讼法律关系的内容

content of jural relation of auditing　审计法律关系内容

content of jural relation of labour　劳动法律关系内容

content of legal relationship in criminal proceedings　刑事诉讼法律关系内容

content of legal relationship of administrative procedure　行政诉讼法律关系的内容

content of legal relationship of auditing　审计法律关系内容

content of legal relationship of labour　劳动法律关系内容

content of legal relationship of revenue　税收法律关系内容

content of supervision　监督内容

contentions procedure　诉讼程序

contentious clause 有争议条款

contentious jurisdiction 诉讼管辖权

contentious matter 诉讼事件

contest 竞选

contestation of suit 辩护陈述阶段

contested election held with a large number of candidates 差额选举

contesting parties 有争议的双方

context 上下文

contexts of law 法的内容

contiguous 相邻的

contiguous obligation 随附债务

contiguous zone 毗邻区域

continental can case 大陆罐头公司案

continental European countries 欧洲大陆国家

continental law 大陆法,欧洲大陆法

continental law system 大陆法系

continental margin 大陆边

continental practice 大陆惯例

continental shelf 大陆架

contingency 意外事件,意外事故

contingency account 偶然性

contingency clause 意外条款

contingency freight 意外运费

contingency fund 应急基金

contingency risk 偶发事故险

contingent asset 或有资产

contingent beneficiary 或有受益人,第二受益人

contingent claim 附带要求

contingent debt 不确定的债务

contingent interest 不确定权益,或有权益

contingent liability 临时负债,或然负债,不确定的债务

contingent order 参考订单,或有订单

contingent remainder 附条件剩

① 余土地承受权

② contingent reserve 意外准备

③ contingent right 偶然权利

④ contingent transaction 或有交易

⑤ contingent trust 临时信托

⑥ continuance of application 连续适用

⑦

⑧ continuation clause 延续条款,延续有效条款

⑨

⑩ continuation of tenancies 续担

⑪ continue 延误

⑫ continue to employ on probation 留用察看

⑬

⑭ continued 持续的

⑮ continued insurance 继续保险

⑯ continuing agreement 持续性协议

⑰

⑱ continuing concern concept 继续经营原则

⑲

⑳ continuing contract 连续履行契约,连续契约

㉑

㉒ continuing crime 连续犯罪

㉓ continuing guarantee 继续担任,持续担保条款,持续保证,连续担保

㉔

㉕

㉖ continuing guaranty 持续担保

㉗ continuing nuisance 连续滋扰

㉘ continuing parter 继续合伙人

㉙ continuing warranty 不间断担保

㉚

㉛ continuity of law 法的连续性

㉜ continuity of operation 连续经营

㉝

㉞ continuous 连续的

㉟ continuous audit 分期继续审计

㊱ continuous bail 出庭保证书

㊲ continuous crime 继续犯

㊳ continuous offense 持续犯,持续犯

㊴

㊵ continuous possession 连续占有

㊶ continuously effective 一直有效

㊷ contra bonos mores (拉) 违反善良道德

㊸

㊹ contra credit 贷方对销

㊺ Contra veritatem lex nunquam aliquid permittit (拉) 法律绝不容忍违反真理的事情

㊻

㊼

contraband 违法交易,违禁品

contraband articles 违禁物品

contraband by analogy 类似禁制品

contraband goods 违禁品

contrabandist 违禁品买卖者

contract 协议,契约,承办,约据,订约,立约,合同

contract a loan 举债

contract administration 合同管理

contract at discretion 任意契约

contract authority 订约授权,合同授权

contract authorization 合同授权,订约授权

contract award date 合同签订日期

contract based upon the upmost good faith 最大诚信合同

contract by deed 必须使用契据形式的合同,契据

contract clause 合同条款

contract debt 合同债务,借债

contract expiry 合同期满

contract for a construction project 工程承包合同

contract for Chinese-foreign contractual joint ventures 中外合作经营合同

contract for Chinese-foreign cooperative exploitation of sea petroleum 中外合作开采海上石油合同

contract for Chinese-foreign equity joint venture 中外合资经营合同

contract for deed 契据合同

contract for delivery 供应契约,送货合约,供应合同

contract for engineering drawing 工程设计合同

contract for engineering supervision 工程监督合同

contract for future delivery 订货合同

contract for labour and material 包工包料

contract for processing work 加工合同

contract for publication 出版合同

contract for sale 契约买卖

contract for scientific and technical cooperation 科技协作合同

contract for service supply 提供服务的合同

contract for supply and installation of equipment 设备供应和安装合同

contract for the delivery of goods by installments 分批交货的买卖合同

contract for the management 承包经营合同

contract for the supply of goods 公共部门购货合同

contract for work 承揽契约

contract form 合同格式

contract goods 合同所列货物

contract implied by law 准契约,准合同

contract implied in fact 事实推定合同

contract in 保证承担义务

contract in bulk 整批售订约

contract in formula 约定受拘束方式

contract in prospect of death 死因合同

contract in restraint of trade 限制营业合同

contract in writing 书面合同

contract insurance 合同保险

contract involving foreign interests 涉外合同

contract involving gratuitous transfer of property 无偿让与财产合同

contract labour 合同工

contract law 契约法

contract law of the People's Republic of China 中华人民共

和国合同法

contract lien 契约留置权

contract market 合同市场,期货市场

contract notes 合同证明

contract novation 合同更新

contract object 合同标的

contract of adhesion 附和契约

contract of affreightment/COA 货运总合同,货运协议,运输契约

contract of association 联合合同,协作合同

contract of carriage 货运合同,运输契约

contract of carriage of passengers by sea 海上旅客运输合同

contract of carrier 运货人契约

contract of Chinese-foreign cooperative enterprise 中外合作经营企业合同

contract of combining supplies of industrial goods and purchase of farm product 购销结合合同

contract of commission agency 代理契约,代办合同

contract of consideration 有偿合同

contract of copartnership 合伙契约

contract of employment 雇佣合同,雇约

contract of engagement 雇佣契约

contract of enterprise using Chinese and foreign investments 中外合资经营企业合同

contract of exchange 交换合同

contract of future delivery 远期交货合同

contract of guarantee 担保契约

contract of guaranty 担保合同,保证合同

contract of hire of labour and service 雇工合同

contract of indemnity 索赔合同,损失赔偿合同,损失赔偿契约

contract of insurance 保险合同,保险契约

contract of international plant-engineering 国际工程承包合同

contract of labour 劳动合同

contract of lease 租售合同,租赁契约

contract of loss and compensation 损失补偿合同

contract of lump sum on firm bill of quantities 固定工程量总价合同

contract of mandate 委任合同

contract of mortgage 抵押合同

contract of on-carriage 续运合同

contract of publication 出版合同

contract of ransom 赎回合同

contract of record 记录合同,记录契约

contract of repayment 返款合同

contract of resale 再买卖契约

contract of result 提供成果合同

contract of sale 销售合同,买卖契约

contract of sale of a building 建筑物买卖合同

contract of service 雇佣契约,劳务合同

contract of split-phase engineering 工程分包合同

contract of supply 供应合同,供货合同

contract of tenancy 租赁合同,租借契约,租售合同

contract of the assumption of debts 承担债务合同

contract of total price 总价合同

contract of tourist economy 旅游经济合同

contract of transferring engineering 工程转包合同

contract of unitprice 单价合同

contract of veal right 物权契约

contract on jointly undertaking re-

search projects 技术攻关协作合同

contract out 保证不承担义务

contract out of formula 约定不受拘束方式

contract period 合同期限

contract price 承揽价格,合同价格

contract provisions 合同规定

contract purchase 合同采购,订货采购

contract purchasing 契约采购

contract regarding an interim supplement to tanker liability for oil pollution（CRISTAL）油轮油污责任暂行补充协定

contract rent 合同租金

contract sales 合同销售

contract secured by credit 信用担保合同

contract serial number 契约编号

contract supervision 合同监督,合同管理

contract system 合同制,承包制

contract system on revenue and expenditure for local government 财政包干

contract system with remuneration 联产承包责任制

contract systems of household responsibility 家庭承包责任制

contract terms 合同条款

contract theory 契约理论

contract theory of the state 国家契约论

contract to be performed by third party 由第三方履行的合同

contract to be performed to third party 第三方给付的合同

contract uberrimae fidei（拉）诚实信用合同

contract under seal 正式契约,盖印合同,依式契约

contract underwriting agreement 承包合约

contract with an absent party 非

① 对话要约合同

② contract without compensation 无偿合同

③ contract without consideration 无约因的契约,无约因合同

④ contract workers 劳务人员,合同工

⑤ contract zone 合同区

⑥ contracted field 承包田

⑦ contracted obligations 合同义务

⑧ contracted responsibility system in management 承包经营责任制

⑨ contracted rights 合同权利

⑩ contracting carrier 订约承运人

⑪ contracting enterprise 承包企业

⑫ contracting organization 合约组织

⑬ contracting parties 订约双方当事人,合同当事人

⑭ contracting parties and parties interested 保险合同的当事人与关系人

⑮ contracting parties substantially interested 有实质利害关系的缔约方

⑯ contracting party 缔约方,立约当事人

⑰ contraction in money supply 通货紧缩

⑱ contraction parties primarily concerned 主要有关缔约各方

⑲ contractions all risks insurance 建筑工程一切险

⑳ contractor 承包商,承包方,承包人,承揽人,订约人

㉑ contractor unit 承包单位

㉒ contractor's prequalification 承包资格预审

㉓ contractors agreement 承揽契约

㉔ contracts disputes 合同争议

㉕ contracts for Chinese-foreign cooperative exploration and development of n atural resources 中外合作勘探开发自然资源合同

㉖ contracts for brokerage 行纪合

同

contracts for commission 委托合同

contracts for construction projects 建设工程合同

contracts for donation 赠与合同

contracts for financial lease 融资租赁合同

contracts for inter mediation 居间合同

contracts for lease 租赁合同,借款合同

contracts for purchase and marketing of the products 购销合同

contracts for sales 买卖合同

contracts for storage 保管合同

contracts for supply and use of electricity, water, gas or heating 供用电、水、气、热力合同(注:我国"合同法"一节内容)

contracts for technology 技术合同

contracts for technology import and export 技术进出口合同

contracts for transportation 运输合同

contracts for work 承揽合同

contracts not subject to formal requirements 合同形式无要求

contracts of wife at common-law 普通法上妻的契约

contracts on the licensing of patent exploitation 专利实施许可合同

contracts take their law from agreement of the parties 合同要通过双方当事人的协议才能取得法律效力

contractual act 契约性行为

contractual agreement 契约协议

contractual claim 契约性求偿

contractual clause 契约性条款

contractual damage 由合同引起的损害,合同损害

contractual debt 契约性债务

contractual delinquency 契约性不法行为

contractual delivery 合同交货

contractual direct investment 契约性直接投资

contractual disputes 合同争议

contractual fine 违约罚金

contractual income 契约收入

contractual investment 契约性投资,合同性投资

contractual issue 合同上的争论点

contractual joint venture 契约式合营企业,契约式合营农业

contractual liability 合同规定的义务,合同责任

contractual licence 契约许可证

contractual lien 合同留置权

contractual management on household basis 家庭承包经营

contractual management responsibility system 承包经营责任制

contractual obligation 契约上的义务,约定义务,合同之债,合同债务,合同义务

contractual obligation 契约义务,合同义务

contractual obligations 合同义务

contractual period 合同期间

contractual personnel 订约承办人员

contractual practice 合同惯例

contractual product liability 合同产品责任

contractual property system 约定财产制

contractual relation 合同关系

contractual relationship 合同关系

contractual relationship of labour 劳动合同关系

contractual responsibility 契约性责任

contractual revenue 契约收益,合同上的收益**

contractual rights 合约权利,合同权利

contractual specifications 合同规定,契约规定,合同惯例

contractual system 合同制

contractual type fund 契约型基金

contractual workers 合同工

contractually specialized households 承包专业户

contractual-joint-venture 契约式联营

contractus（拉）合同,契约

contractus ad referedum（拉）尚待校准的契约

contractus assecurationis（拉）保险契约

contractus bilateralis（拉）双务契约

contractus bonae fidei（拉）善意合同

contractus civiles（罗）（拉）市民法上的契约

contractus commodati（拉）使用借贷契约

contractus conducti（拉）用益租赁契约

contractus consensualis（拉）合意契约

contractus consensu（拉）合意合同,合意契约

contractus contract 契约

contractus juris gentium（拉）万民法合同

contractus legem ex conventione accipiunt（拉）合同要通过双方当事人的协议才能取得法律效力

contractus literis（拉）书面合同,书约,书面契约

contractus locati（拉）租赁契约

contractus permutationis（拉）交换契约

contractus principalis（拉）主契约

contractus similatus（拉）假装契约,虚伪契约

contractus stict juris（拉）严法契约

contradict 反驳,抗辩

contradict the defendant's witness 反驳被告证据

contradiction 矛盾

contradictions among the people 人民内部矛盾

contradictory concept 矛盾观念

contrary 相违背的

contrary evidence 反证

contrary to architectural rule 违反建筑法规

contrary to law 违反法律

contrary to orders 违反命令

contrary to the constitution 违反宪法

contravene 触犯（法律等）,否定,违反

contravene the law 与法律相抵触

contravention 触犯（法律等）,否定

contravention to stipulations 违反规定

contravention to treaty 违反协议,违反合同

contributed capital 捐赠资本,投入资本

contribution 分配

contribution clause 责任分担条款

contribution of right 权利分摊

contributory 负连带偿还责任的人

contributory cause 附带原因

contributory fault 受害人过错

contributory mortgage 共同承押

contributory negligence 受害方的过失,与有疏忽,被害人本身的过失,促成过失,共同过失

control 监察,管制,监督,监管

control and surveillance over offender 监管人犯

control measures 控制措施

control of administration law 控权行政法

control of administration theory 控权说

control of city taxis 城市出租车管理

control of cultural and recreational places 文化娱乐场所管理

control of domicile 户籍管理

control of expenditure 监督开支

control of ground satellite receiving facilities 卫星地面接收设施管理

control of identity cards 居民身份证管理

control of interim identity cards 临时身份证管理

control of merchandise 商品管制

control of poisonous materials 毒品管制

control of pollution act 污染控制法

control of purchasing power of public organization 社会集团购买力控制

control of railroad traffic 铁路交通运输管理

control of rent increase 加租管制

control of sold and silver 金银管理

control of the cultural market 文化市场管理

control of waterways of rivers 河道管理

control office of reeducation-through-labour 劳动教养管理所

control on security finance 证券金融管理

control over living and sanitation conditions of convicts 罪犯生活卫生管理

control power 监察权,控制权

control price 管制物价

control system 监督制度

control the prices 平抑价格

controlled commodity 控制商品

controlled corporation 受控制公司,分公司

controlled drugs 管制药品

controlled economy 统制经济

controlled knife 管制刀具

controlled monopoly 控制性垄断

controlled mortgage 受控制的抵押

controlled price 管制价格,控制价格

controlled procurement and distribution 统购统销

controlled tenancy 受控制的租赁

controlled traffic 管制交通

controlled trust 受控制的信托

controller 监察员,审计师,会计监察员,审计员

controlling company 统制公司

controlling corporation 统制公司,控制公司,总公司

controlling interest 股票控制额,统制股权

controversy between the parties 当事人之间的争讼

controversy concerning a contract of guaranty 保证合同纠纷

controversy of labour contract 劳动合同争议

controversy over a borderage contract 民间合同纠纷案件

controversy over a contract of pawn 典当合同纠纷案

controversy over a loan contract 借款合同纠纷案

controversy over a technology contract 技术合同纠纷案件

controversy over a wrecking contract 打捞合同纠纷案件

controversy over an economic contract 经济合同争议案件

controversy over cargo agency contract 货运代理合同纠纷案件

controversy over cinematographic contract 电影合同纠纷案

controversy over compensation for environmental damage 环境损害赔偿纠纷案件

controversy over damage inflicted to another by environmental pollution 环境污染致人损害纠纷案件

controversy over industrial property rights 工业产权纠纷案

controversy over injuries caused by government offices or state functionaries in duty 国家机关或国家机关工作人员因执行职务致人损害纠纷案件

controversy over injuries caused in unjust enrichment 不当得利致人损害纠纷案件

controversy over mechanical and electrical equipment 机电设备争议案

controversy over ownership of grassland 草原所有权纠纷案

controversy over ownership of movables 动产所有权纠纷案

controversy over personal injuries inflicted by a medical malpractice 医疗事故致人损害纠纷案件

controversy over property ownership 财产所有权归属纠纷案

controversy over publication 出版合同纠纷案

controversy over remedy for economic damage 经济损害赔偿纠纷案件

controversy over shipping agency contract 船舶代理合同纠纷案件

controversy over tenure of grassland 草原使用权纠纷案

controversy over the right of inheritance 继承权纠纷案件

controversy over work contract 承揽合同纠纷案件

contusion 挫伤

① conular employee 领馆雇员
② convenanter 契约订约人
③ convene 召开,召集
④ convene a conference 召集会议
⑤ convenience store 杂货店
⑥ conventio omnis intelligitur rebus
⑦ sic stantibus(拉) 一切条款都
⑧ 会情势不变的条件
⑨ conventio vincit legem(拉) 约定
⑩ 优于法律
⑪ convention 会议,公约,专约,常规,协议
⑫
⑬ convention establishing the multi-
⑭ lateral investment guarantee a-
⑮ gency 建立多边投资担保机
⑯ 构公约
⑰ aonvention for legal application of
⑱ contractual obligation 关于合
⑲ 同义务法律适用的公约
⑳ convention for mutual recognition
㉑ of company and legal person
㉒ entity 关于相互承认公司和
㉓ 法人团体的公约
㉔ convention for settlement of the
㉕ conflict between domestic law
㉖ and domicile law 解决本国法
㉗ 和住所地法冲突的公约
㉘ convenion for the conservation of
㉙ antarctic seals 保护南极海豹
㉚ 公约 1972
㉛ convention for the prevention of
㉜ pollution from ships 防止船
㉝ 舶污染公约
㉞ convention for the protection of
㉟ human rights and fundamental
㊱ freedoms(Rome) 保护人权与
㊲ 基本自由公约(1950)
㊳ convention for the regulation of
㊴ aerial navigation 巴黎航空公
㊵ 约
㊶ convention for the suppression of
㊷ unlawful act against the safety
㊸ of civil aviation 关于制止危
㊹ 害民用航空安全的非法行为
㊺ 公约,蒙特利尔公约
㊻ convention for the suppression of
㊼ unlawful seizure of aircraft 海

牙(反劫机)公约

convention for the suppression of unlawful seizure of aircraft 关于制止非法劫持航空器的公约

convention for the unification of certain rules relating to maritime mortgages and liens 统一船舶抵押权与船舶留置权的若干规则的公约

convention for the unification of certain rules relating to the immunity of state-owned vessels (1926) 统一国有船舶豁免的若干规则的公约

convention for the unification of certian rules to international carriage by air 统一国际航空运输某些规则的公约

convention of international organization of legal metrology(1955) 国际法定计量组织公约

convention on a code of conduct for liner conference 班轮公会行动守则公约

convention on agency in international sales of goods 国际货物买卖代理公约

convention on certain questions relating to the conflict of nationality laws 关于国籍法冲突的若干问题的公约

convention on diplomatic relations 外交关系公约

convention on facilitation of maritime traffic 1965 便利海上运输公约(1965)

convention on fishing and conservation of the living resources of the high seas 捕鱼及养护公海生物资源公约

convention on international civil aviation 国际民用航空公约,芝加哥公约

convention on offences and concerning other acts committed on board aircraft 关于在航空器内的犯罪和犯有某些其他行为的公约

convention on protection of the mediterranean from pollution 保护地中海免受污染公约

convention on the conservation of european wildlife and natural habitats 保护欧洲野生动物和自然栖所公约 1979

convention on the high seas 公海公约

convention on the international recognization of right in aircraft 关于国际承认对航空器的权利的公约

convention on the international regime of maritime ports 关于港口国际制度公约

convention on the international regulations for preventing collisions at sea,1972 1972 年国际海上避碰规则公约

convention on the law applicable to agency 代理法律适用公约

convention on the law applicable to contracts for the international sales of goods 国际货物买卖合同法律适用公约

convention on the law applicable to contractual obligation 关于合同义务法律适用的公约

convention on the law of the sea 海洋法公约

convention on the life safety at sea 海上人命安全公约

convention on the limitation period in the international sale of goods 国际货物买卖时效期限公约

convention on the nationality of married women 已婚妇女国籍公约

convention on the prevention of maritime pollution by dumping of wastes and other matters (1972) 关于防止因倾倒废料及其他物质造成海洋污染的公约

convention on the recognition and enforcement of foreign arbitral awards 承认及执行外国仲裁裁决公约

convention on the reduction of statelessness 减少无国籍状态公约

convention on the settlement of investment disputes between states and nationals of other states 解决国家与其他国家国民之间投资争端公约(注:通称"华盛顿公约)

convention parliament 非常国会(英)

convention relating to civil liablity in the field of nuclear material 海上核材料运输民事责任公约(1971)

convention relating to the status of refugees 难民地位公约

convention relating to the status of stateless persons 关于无国籍人地位公约

convention to protect birds useful to agriculture 保护农业益鸟的公约(1902)

conventional 约定俗成的

conventional act 约定行为

conventional collateral for loans 常规贷款抵押品

conventional duty 协定关税

conventional law 协约法

conventional loan (美) 协定不动产贷款

conventional mortgage 约定抵押

conventional packing 习惯包装

conventional rights 习惯权利

conventional tariff 协定关税,协定税则,协定税率

converging accomplice 会合犯

conversion 建筑用途改变,折换,转换

conversion clause 外汇换算条款

conversion loan 转换贷款

conversion of productions 转产

conversion of property 侵占财产

conversion of the undertaking to the production of other goods 企业转产

conversion rate 汇率兑换率

convert 折换,转换

convert into 转移

convert into cash 作价

convert into money 折价

converted tenancy 被变换的租赁

convertibility (外币)可兑换性

convertible bonds 可兑换的债券

convertible currency 可兑换货币,可与黄金兑换的货币

convertible preferred stock 可转换的优先股,可兑换优先股

convey 物业转让,转让,让步

conveyance 转让,物业转让,财产转让,物权行为,运输工具,物业买卖

conveyance mark 运输工具痕迹

conveyance mark identification 运输工具痕迹鉴定

conveyance of land 土地转让

conveyance of mails act 邮递法

conveyancer 财产转让律师

conveyances on entering the country 入境交通工具

conveyancing 物业转让

conveyancing counsel 财产转让律师

conveyor 让步人

convict 囚犯,查明有罪,已决犯,既决犯,刑事罪犯,罪犯,犯人

convict (sb of a crime) 定罪

convict awaiting execution 死囚

convict establishment 罪犯自新

convict sentenced to death with a two-year reprieve 死缓犯

convict serving sentences or control outside prison 监外执行

convict undergoing reform-through-labour 劳改犯

convicted person　已决犯
convicted prisoner　既决犯
convicting magistrate　判决裁判官
conviction　刑事定罪,信仰
conviction based on testimony of three witnesses or more　众证定罪
conviction on judgement　经公诉程序的判决
convicts' communication system　罪犯通讯制度
convocation　集会
cook up charges　罗织罪名
cooking room　厨房
cooperate　合作
cooperating attorney　合作律师
cooperation　协作,合作,合作制
cooperation in production　生产协作
cooperation of others　他人的协助
cooperative　合作社
cooperative competition　合作性竞争
cooperative control　共同管理
cooperative development　合作开发
cooperative development contract　合作开发合同
cooperative enterprise　合作经营企业
cooperative exploitation or development　合作开采或开发
cooperative management　共同经营管理
cooperative ownership　合作社所有权,合作社所有制
cooperative ownership system　合作社所有制
cooperative production　合作
cooperative property　集体财产
cooperative venture　联营企业
cooperatives　合作制
cooperator　合作者
coordinate with each other and restrain each other　互相配合,互相制约
coordinating body　协调机构
coordinating committee for export control-cocom　输出管制统筹委员会
coordinating committee on multilateral export control, cocom　多边出口管制统筹委员会
coordination of tariff　协调关税
coowner common owner　共同所有人
coownership　共有权,共同所有权
cop　警察
coparties　共同当事人
copartner　合伙人,合股人
copartnership　合伙制,合伙企业
copartnery　合伙关系
compensation of employees　雇佣人员报酬
copy of a bill of complaint　起诉状副本
copy of appeal　上诉状副本
copy of the file　案卷的副本
copyright　版权
copyright action　版权诉讼
copyright bureau　版权局
copyright case　版权案件
copyright royalty　版税
copyright royalty tribunal　版权税法庭
cordon off an area　戒严
core service　核心服务
corespondent　共同答辩人
corn laws（英）谷物法
coroner　验尸官
corpnuptela(拉)　贿赂
corporate bonds and debentures　公司债券
corporal punishment　肉刑
corporal punishment　体罚
corporate　法人团体
corporate agent　代理公司
corporate body　法人团体,法人组织
corporate body　财团法人,法人

团体

corporate bonds 公司债券

corporate capacity 法人资格

corporate capital 公司资本

corporate crime 法人犯罪

corporate enterprise 法人企业

corporate entity 法人实体

corporate income 公司收益

corporate income tax 公司所得税

corporate investment 公司投资

corporate organization 法人组织

corporate ownership right 法人所有权

corporate personality 法人人格

corporate power 法人权限

corporate surety 公司担保

corporate tax fraud 法人税欺诈罪

corporate type fund 公司型基金

corporate voting 法团投票

corporatio（拉） 法人

corporation 公司,法人,社团法人,企业,法人团体

corporation aggregate 社团法人,集体法人,普通法人

corporation income tax 法人所得税

corporation law 公司法

corporation securities 证券公司

corporation sole 独资公司,单一法人

corporation tax 法人税,公司税

corporation with foreign capital 外资公司

corporeal movables 有形动产

corporeal property 有形财产,有形动产

corpse 尸体

corpus delicti（拉） 罪行构成,犯罪实质

corpus juris canonici（拉） 教会法大全

corpus juris civilis（拉） 国法大全

corpus legum（拉） 法律大全

corpus of the laws and regulations 法规汇编

correct 惩罚,加以修改,改造,改正,修正

correct handling of contradictions among the people 正确处理人民内部矛盾

correct judgment 判断正确

correction 教养,改造,修正

correction of criminal with abnormal mind 变态心理犯罪人的矫治

correction of errors 错误更正

correctional psychology 矫正心理学

corrective punishment 教养处分

corrective training 教养处分

correspond 合乎

correspond bank 代理银行

correspond to 符合

correspondence and conversation of prisoners 犯人通信接见

correspondence of prisoners 犯人通信

correspondence offense 对向犯

correspondent 代理制

correspondent agreement 代理协议

correspondent bank 关系银行,关联银行

corresponding duty 相应的义务

corresponding measures 下游,相应的措施

corresponding request 对应请求

corroborating evidence 补强证据

corrosive goods 腐蚀性物

corrupt 腐化,腐败,贿赂

corrupt element 腐化分子

corrupt officials 贪官污吏

corruption 腐败,贿赂

corruption and nonfeasance 贪污渎职罪

corruption through misuse of law 贪赃枉法

corruptionist 腐化分子

cortest 竞争,竞选

corvee 劳役

cost 代价,成本

cost and freight invoice 货价加运费发票

cost benefit analysis 成本效益分析

cost of air pollution 大气污染费用

cost of capital 资本价格

cost of construction 工程造价

cost of construction projects 工程造价

cost of erection 安装成本,安装费

cost of funds 资金成本

cost of loading and unloading 装卸费

cost of money 贷款利息

cost of overhaul 检修费用

cost of repair 修理费

cost of repairs 修理费用

cost of repairs clause 修理费用条款

cost of replacement 重置成本

cost of reproduction 重置成本

cost of storage 保管费

cost overrun 成本超支

cost principle 成本原则

cost reimbursement contract 成本补偿合同,成本加酬金合同

costs 讼费

costs for preservation of goods 保全货物费

costs of appeal 上诉费用

costs of arbitration 仲裁费用

costs of civil procedure 民事诉讼费用

costs of delay 误期费用

costs of economic litigation 经济诉讼费

costs of preservation 保全费

costs thrown way 抛弃的费用

cosurety 共同约证人

cotard syndrome 科塔德综合症

cotractor 承揽方

cottage 村舍

cottage area 平房区

① cottage industrial and commercial
② trade 家庭工商业
③ cottage industry 家庭手工业
④ cottier system (爱尔兰) 小农耕
⑤ 作制
⑥ coulisse 门厅,委员会,议会,地
⑦ 方议会,议事机构,会议
⑧ council estate 地方地产
⑨ council for mutual economic assis-
⑩ tance-CMEA coMECON 经济
⑪ 互助委员会
⑫ council of constantine 君士坦丁
⑬ 堡会议
⑭ council of judges 法官会议
⑮ council of law 法律委员会
⑯ council of legal education 法律
⑰ 教育委员会(英),法律教育协
⑱ 会
⑲ council of representatives 代表
⑳ 会议
㉑ council of state 参政院,国务会
㉒ 议
㉓ council of the United Nations envi-
㉔ ronment programme 联合国
㉕ 环境规划署规划理事会
㉖ council on environmental quality/
㉗ CEQ 环境质量委员会
㉘ council regulation No. 17/62 理
㉙ 事会 17/62 号规则
㉚ councillor 地方议员
㉛ councillorship 地方议员的职位
㉜ council-system in administration
㉝ 行政合议制
㉞ counsel 审议,律师,辩护人
㉟ counsel fees 律师费
㊱ counsel for the defense 被告律
㊲ 师,辩护律师
㊳ counseling 审议
㊴ counsellor 参赞,参事,律师
㊵ counselor-at law 律师
㊶ count 罪状
㊷ count of jail delivery (美) 监狱
㊸ 释放法庭
㊹ count the cost 权衡得失
㊺ counter execution 互相履行债
㊻ 务
㊼ counter guarantee 反担保函

counter measure　对抗措施

counter offer　反要约

counter tariff　抵消性关税,对抗关税

counteraccusation　反诉

counteracting protective duty　反保护关税

countercharge　反诉

counterclaim　反求偿,反请求,反诉

counterclaim case　反诉案件

counterdocument　抗辩书

counterfeit　冒牌,伪造,假冒

counterfeit national currency　伪造国家货币

counterfeit notes　伪钞

counterfeit of money　伪造货币

counterfeit securities　伪造有价证券

counterfeit valuable　伪造有价证券

counterfeiter　伪造者

counterfeiting currency　伪造通用货币

counterfeiting offenses　伪造货币犯罪

counterfoil　存根,票根

countermeasure　对策

countermeasure of crime　犯罪对策

counteroffer　反要约

counterpart　相对给付,相对人,对方

counterpart of an audit notice　审计通知书副本

counterplan　对策

counterplea　抗辩,反诉状

counterplead　反驳

counterplead right　抗辩权

counterplot　对抗策略

counterpurchase　反销,回购

counterrevolution　反革命

counterrevolutionary case　反革命案

counterrevolutionary clique　反革命集团

counterrevolutionary criminal　反革命犯

counterrevolutionary recidivist　反革命累犯

countersign　副署,连署

countersignature　副署,连署

counterstatement　抗辩书,反诉状

countersue　反诉

countertrade　返销贸易,抵偿贸易

countertrade transaction　返销贸易交易

countervailing duty　反贴补税,反补贴税

countervailing levy　反补贴税

countervailing tariff　抵消税,反补贴税,反倾销税,抵消关税

country　全体选民,国家

country beneficiary　受惠国

country fair　集市贸易

country market trade　农村集中贸易

country markets　集市贸易

country of dependency　附属国

country of internment　拘留国

country of origin　原籍国,原产地国

country of origin identification regulations　原产地国证明条例

country of origin mark　货源名称

country of refuge　避难国

country of residence　居住国

country quota　国家配额

country quotas　国别配额

country ruled by law　法治国家

country-man diplomacy　国民外交

county　县

county borough　自治市

county court　县法院

county court　郡法院,县法院

county people's congress　县人民代表大会

county people's court　县人民法院

county people's government　县

人民政府

county people's procuratorate
县人民检察院

coup 政变

couple family 对偶家庭

couple marriage 对偶婚

coupon 息票

coupon bond 附息票债券

coupon bonds 固定收入证券，附息票债券

coupon of bond 债券息票

coupon rate of interest 息票利率

coupon sheet 息票单

coupon tax 息票利息税

courier 外交信使

courier receipt 快邮收据

court 法院，裁判所，法庭，法官，宫廷

court acceptance fee 案件受理费

court at the habitual residence of the defendant 被告经常居住地法院

court at the place of one's convenience 便利法院，便于审理的法院

court at the place of one's inconvenience 不方便法院

court at the place of salvage 救助地法院

court at the place where a vehicle first arrives 车辆最先到达地法院

court attendance level of second instance 二审出庭水平

court attendance of second instance 二审出庭率

court attendant 法警

court bail 法庭保释

court baron 领地法院

court case 诉讼案件

court charge for real action proceedings 财产案件受理费

court clerk 法院书记员

court closed 闭庭

court costs 辩护，审理费用

court debate 法庭辩论

court decision 法院判决

court directive 法院指定

court docket 法庭备案件案件目录，法庭判决摘要

court expert-witness 法庭上的鉴定人

court for rail transportation 铁路运输法院

court hearing fee for nonproperty cases 非财产案件受理费

court identification 法庭辨认

court in the place where a ship has landed first 船舶最先到达地法院

court interrogation 法庭讯问

court judgement(s) 法院判决，法庭判决

court leet 领地刑事法院

court mediation 法院调解

court of administrative 行政法院

court of administrative litigation 行政诉讼审判庭

court of admiralty 海事法院

court of appeal 上诉法庭

court of appeal in chancery （英）大法官法院上诉法院，大法官法庭上诉庭

court of arbitration of the international chamber of commerce 国际商会仲裁院

court of assize 巡回法院

court of audience 大主教保留权法院(英)，大主教亲审法庭

court of bankruptcy 破产法庭

court of cassation(法、比等) 最高上诉法院

court of chancery （美）衡平法院，(英)大法官法院

court of chivalry 骑士法庭(英)

court of civil jurisdiction 民事审判庭

court of claims （美） 行政法院

court of common law 普通法法院

court of constitution 宪法法院

court of criminal adjudication

刑事裁判庭

court of criminal appeal　刑事上诉法庭(英国)

court of customs and patent appeals　海关及专利权上诉法院

court of equity（英）衡平法院

court of error　复审法庭(英)

court of exchequer　财政法院（棋盘法院）

court of exchequer chamber　财政大臣上诉法院(英)

court of final appeal　最终上诉法院

court of final jurisdiction　终审法院

court of first instance　初审法庭,第一审法庭

court of general sessions（美）地方刑事法庭

court of high commission　高等宗教事务法庭(英)

court of inquiry　调查法庭

court of insurance　保险法庭

court of international trade　国际贸易法院(注:指美国)

court of king's bench（美）公诉院

court of last resort　最高上诉法院,终审法院

court of law　法院

court of law suit　答辩事项

court of matrimonial causes　婚姻法院

court of medical appeal　医疗申诉法庭

court of military appeals　军事上诉法院

court of motion against rulings　抗告法院

court of policies of insurance　保单争讼法庭

court of protection（英）保护法庭

court of quarter seasons（英）季审法院

court of referee　鉴定人法庭

court of second hearing　第二审法庭

court of summary jurisdiction　即决裁判法院,简易审判庭

court of survey　船舶检查法庭

court of the Arches　坎特伯雷大主教法庭（英）

court of the lords justices　高等上诉法院(英)

court order　法庭秩序

court policeman　法警

court proceedings　法庭审理,审判程序

court prosecutor　检察官

court questioning　法庭审问

court reporter　判决发布人

court roll　法庭案卷

court room　法庭

court structure　法院系统

court system　法院系统

court system of the U.S.A.　美国法院组织

court verdict　判词,判决书

court where the defendant is kept in custody　被告被监禁地法院

courtier　朝臣

courtoise international　国际礼让(法)

courts of fairs and boroughs　定期集市法庭和自治市法庭(英)

courts of the U.S.A　美国法院

courtyard house　四合院

court-martial　军事法庭审判

court-martial appeal court　军事法庭上诉庭

cousinhood　亲属关系

cousinship　亲属关系

cousulate　领馆

covenant　契约,与合同规定相符的货物,契约里大家同意的条款,违反合同的诉讼,盟约,订立合同,合同

covenant for further assurance　再担保公司

covenant not to sue　不起诉合约

covenant of the league of nations 国际联盟约

covenant of warranty 保证书

covenant running with the land 有关土地的契约

covenanted 有合同义务

covenantee 契约受约人,合同受约人

covenanter 订立合同人

covenants 约定事项条款

cover 保证金

cover cost 期货保证金

cover loans 偿还贷款

cover note insurance slip 暂保单,承保条

cover oneself for 求偿

cover up 隐蔽,包庇

cover up a criminal 包庇罪犯

coverage 保额、保险总额,承保范围,保险金额

coverage of labour insurance 劳动保险项目

covering a project 隐蔽工程

CPA certificate 会计师查账证书

CPT (carriage paid to) 运费付至

crack the whip 采用专制政策

craft control 企业控制

craft sic clause 驳运条款

creat 产生

create a thriving market 繁荣市场

(to) creat conditions for employment 创造就业条件

create favorable conditions 创造有利条件

create legal relations 建立法律关系

create the wealth of society 创造社会财富

create 创造,创制

creating organization 创制机关

creation of administrative penalties 行政处罚的设定

creation of obligation 债务的发生

① credence 信用

② credentials 国书

③ credentials committee 代表资格审查委员会,资格审查委员会

④ credibility 证据能力,确实性

⑤ credit 抵免,贷方,信用,荣誉

⑥ credit agency 信用公司

⑦ credit agreement 信贷协定,信用协议,赊销协议

⑧ credit balance 贷方余额

⑨ credit bank 信贷银行

⑩ credit based on real property 不动产信用

⑪ credit bill 信用汇票

⑫ credit business 赊销

⑬ credit buying 赊购

⑭ credit capital 信贷资本

⑮ credit card 信用卡

⑯ credit ceiling 信贷最高额

⑰ credit commitment 信贷承诺

⑱ credit control 信贷管制

⑲ credit cooperation 信用合作,信贷合作

⑳ credit cooperative 信用合作社

㉑ credit co-operative 信用社

㉒ credit crisis 信用危机

㉓ credit economy 信用经济

㉔ credit expansion 信贷扩张,信用扩张,信贷扩大

㉕ credit for productive purposes 生产信贷

㉖ credit fraud 信用诈欺罪

㉗ credit fund(s) 信贷资金

㉘ credit gild 信贷同业公会

㉙ credit granted by supplier 卖方信贷

㉚ credit guarantee 信贷保证

㉛ credit inflation 信用膨胀

㉜ credit information 资信调查

㉝ credit institution 信贷机构

㉞ credit instrument 信用工具

㉟ credit insurance 信用保险

㊱ credit insurance agreement 信用保险协议

㊲ credit intermediary 信用中介

㊳ credit investigation 资信调查

㊴ credit lease 信贷租赁

credit limit 贷款限额,信贷额度

credit line 信贷最高限额,贷款限额,信贷业务

credit line loan 信贷额度放款

credit market 信贷市场

credit memo 付款通知单

credit money 信用货币

credit note 贷款通知,信贷清单,贷款通知书,贷方票据

credit note/CN 收款通知

credit of bankrupt 破产债权

credit of product 产品信誉

credit operations 信贷业务

credit party 借贷当事人

credit period 贷款期限

credit plan 信贷计划

credit policy 信贷政策

credit position 资信

credit price 赊销价

credit rating 信用地位,信用等级

credit receiver 受信人,受款人

credit relaxation 信贷放宽

credit restriction 信贷限制

credit risk 贷款风险

credit risk management 信贷风险管理

credit sale 信用买卖,赊账买卖,赊销,赊赁,赊卖

credit sale agreement 信贷买卖协议

credit squeeze 信贷紧缩,贷款紧缩,信用紧缩

credit squeeze measure 紧缩信用措施

credit system 学会制,信用制度,冲抵制

credit term 赊销期

credit terms 信贷条件

credit transaction 信贷交易,赊账交易

credit union 信用合作社

credit worthiness 信誉

creditable tax 可抵免的税款

credito(拉) 金钱债权

creditor 贷方,债权人,贷方

creditor asset 预付定金

creditor beneficiary 债权人受益人

creditor equity 债主权益

creditor of bankrupt 破产债权人

creditor state 债权国

creditors ledger 债权人分类账

creditors rights 债权

creed 信条

creeping expropriation 逐步征用,逐渐征收,蚕食式征用

crew 船员

crime 犯罪,罪,罪行,刑事罪

crime against copyright or right of invention 侵害著作权或发明权罪

crime against coupons 票证犯罪

crime against environment 危害环境罪

crime against humanity 危害人类罪,违反人道罪

crime against intellectual property rights 知识产权犯罪

crime against international public order 破坏国际公共秩序罪

crime against internationally protected persons 侵害受国际保护人员罪

crime against marriage and family 妨害婚姻家庭罪

crime against nature 违背自然罪,不名誉罪,反自然性交罪

crime against nature 鸡奸罪

crime against obligations in bankruptcy 违反破产义务罪

crime against peace 破坏和平罪,危害和平罪

crime against property 财产犯罪

crime against the control of financial order 破坏金融管理秩序罪

crime against the order of taxation 破坏税收秩序犯罪

crime against the safety of international aviation 危害国际航空

罪

crime against the sick and wounded 虐待战争伤病员罪

crime and noncrime 罪与非罪

crime and penalty 罪与罚

crime and punishment 罪刑

crime by deaf-mutes 聋哑人犯罪

crime by officers 军官犯罪

crime by taking advantage of credit cards 信用卡犯罪

crime committed by a drunkard 醉酒人犯罪

crime committed by taking advantage of one's position and exchanging counterfeited currencies for currencies 利用职务便利,以伪造的货币换取货币的犯罪

crime committed by the blind 盲人犯罪

crime committed out of righteous indignation 义愤动机犯罪

crime concerning invoices for the exclusive use of value added tax 增值税专用发票犯罪

crime concerning VAT invoice 增值税专用发票犯罪

crime control system 犯罪控制系统

crime culprit 主凶

crime due to abnormal psychology 变态心理犯罪

crime due to affective disturbance 情感障碍犯罪

crime due to mental disorder 精神疾病犯罪

crime in a state of passion 激情犯罪

crime in form 形式犯罪

crime index 犯罪指数

crime of a contractual dereliction of duties by a person in charge of a state-owned unit 国有单位主管人员公司渎职罪

crime of a defender or an agent ad litem hampering evidence 辩护人、诉讼代理人妨害证据罪

crime of a legal person 法人犯罪

crime of a state functionary not performing the duties of investigating the duties of investigating into the criminal act of manufacturing or marketing fake and inferior commodities 国家机关工作人员不履行追究生产、销售伪劣商品犯罪职责罪

crime of a state functionary practising favoritism for personal gains 国家机关工作人员徇私舞弊罪

crime of a state functionary's contractual dereliction of duties 国家机关工作人员合同渎职罪

crime of abducting and trafficking in people 拐卖人口罪

crime of abducting and trafficking in women and children 拐卖妇女、儿童罪

crime of abuse of office by civil servants 公务员滥用职权罪

crime of abuse of official capacity by special office holder 特别公务员滥用职权罪

crime of abusing a member of one's family 虐待罪

crime of abusing information obtained in official capacity for stock-trading purposes 滥用利用职务之便所获信息从事证券交易罪

crime of abusing the office 滥用职权罪

crime of acceptance of bribes 受贿罪

crime of accepting and sending disqualified persons to the army to be soldiers 接送不合格兵员罪

crime of active participation in a counterrevolutionary group 积极参加反革命集团罪

crime of actively participating in an organization engaged in terrorist activitites 积极参加恐怖活动组织罪

crime of adherence to sovereign's enemies 依附外敌罪

crime of administrative law enforcement personnel practising favoritism for personal gains 行政执法人员徇私舞弊

crime of advocating overthrow of government 鼓吹颠覆政府罪

crime of affray 聚众斗殴罪，互殴罪

crime of aggression 侵略罪

crime of aggressive war 侵犯战争罪

crime of aiding a client to destroy or forge evidence 帮助当事人毁灭、伪造证据罪

crime of aiding a deserter in wartime 战时资助逃兵罪

crime of aiding an escape 帮助逃脱罪

crime of aiding another to commit suicide 帮助他人自杀罪

crime of altering a bill of exchange, promissory note, or check 变造汇票、本票、支票罪

crime of altering a letter of credit or documentation attached 变造信用证或者附随的单据文件的犯罪

crime of altering currency 变造货币罪

crime of altering financial instruments and cards 变造金融证券罪

crime of altering or transferring business license for financial operations 变造、转让经营金融业务许可证罪

crime of altering the business license of a commercial bank or other financial operations 变造商业银行或其他金融机构经营许可罪

crime of an accident of teaching facilities 教学设施事故罪

crime of an environmental accident 环保事故罪

crime of an overseas mafia-style syndicate expanding its membership within the boundaries 境外黑社会组织在境内发展组织罪

crime of animal and plant quarantine personnel forging quarantine results 动植物检疫人员伪造检疫结果罪

crime of antigovernment propaganda 癫痫煽动罪

crime of apartheid 种族隔离罪

crime of armed mass rebellion 持械聚众叛乱罪

crime of armed rebellion 武装叛乱罪

crime of armed rioting 武装暴乱罪

crime of arson 纵火罪

crime of assault with intention to commit murder 故意重伤谋杀罪

crime of assembling a crowd for smuggling 聚众走私罪

crime of assembling a crowd for "beating, smashing and looting" 聚众打砸抢罪

crime of assembling a crowd to disturb order at a military control zone 聚众扰乱军事管理秩序罪

crime of assembling a crowd to disturb order at public places 聚众扰乱公共场所秩序罪

crime of assembling a crowd to disturb traffic order 聚众扰乱交通秩序罪

crime of assembling a crowd to engage in sexual promiscuity 聚众淫乱罪

crime of assembling a crowd to scramble for public or private

properties 聚众哄抢公私财物罪

crime of assembling a crowd to storm a prohibited military zone 聚众冲击军事禁区罪

crime of atrocity or persecution by special office holder 特别公务员施行暴刑、虐待罪

crime of auditors providing falsified certification 审计人员提供虚假证明罪

crime of bad check 虚假支票罪

crime of bank fraud 银行欺诈罪

crime of bearing firearms knives subject to police control, or explosives to take part in an assembly, march or demonstration 携带武器、管制刀具、爆炸物品参加集会、游行、示威罪

crime of bending the law to serve one's personal considerations for favoritism 徇私枉法罪

crime of betraying state secrets 泄露国家秘密罪

crime of bigamy 重婚罪

crime of breach of prison 突破监所罪,越狱罪

crime of breaching dikes 决水罪

crime of breaking into tombs to rob the dead 掘墓盗尸罪

crime of bribe taking by a unit 单位受贿罪

crime of bribery 贿赂罪

crime of bribing company or enterprise personnel 贿赂公司、企业人员罪

crime of buggery 反自然性交罪

crime of business embezzlement 业务侵占罪

crime of buying abducted and trafficked, kidnapped women and children 收买被拐卖、绑架的妇女、儿童罪

crime of buying counterfeit invoices for the exclusive use of value added tax 购买伪造的增值税专用发票罪

crime of careless keeping of fire arms 漫不经心收藏发火武器罪

crime of carnal knowledge of a child 奸淫幼女罪

crime of causing the spread of a Type A infectious disease or severe danger of such spread 引起甲类结染病传播或传播严重危险罪

crime of causing traffic casualties 交通肇事罪

crime of cheating and bluffing 招摇撞骗罪

crime of cheating others into taking drugs or injection 欺骗他人吸食、注射毒品罪

crime of coercion 强制罪

crime of collectively dividing up fines or confiscated properties without permission 集体瓜分罚没财物罪

crime of collectively dividing up state-owned properties without permission 集体刮分国有资产罪

crime of collusion in entering bids 串通投标罪

crime of commercial bribe-offering 商业行贿罪

crime of commission 作为犯罪

crime of common assault 普通企图伤害罪

crime of communication of information relating to munitions 非法传递军情罪

crime of compelling a woman into prostitution 强迫妇女性交罪

crime of compulsory indecency 强制猥亵罪

crime of concealing deposits abroad 隐瞒境外存款罪

crime of concealing money and goods resulting from drug offenses 窝藏毒品犯罪所得财物罪

crime of concealment of conspiracy 匿奸罪

crime of conniving by a mafia-style organization to be engaged in law-breaking and criminal activities 纵容黑社会性质的组织进行违法犯罪活动

crime of conspiracy 密谋罪,阴谋罪

crime of constructive compulsory indecency 准强制猥亵罪

crime of corruption 贪污罪,腐化罪

crime of counterfeiting 伪造罪

crime of counterfeiting a patent 假冒专利罪

crime of counterfeiting bank notes 伪造钞票罪

crime of counterfeiting currencies or trafficking, counterfeited currencies 伪造货币,贩运伪造的货币罪

crime of counterfeiting of national currency 伪造国家货币罪

crime of counterfeiting the registered trademark of another 假冒他人注册商标罪

crime of counterfeiting trademarks 假冒商标罪

crime of counterfeiting valuable bills and tickets 伪造有价票证罪

crime of counterfeiting valuable securities 伪造有价证券罪

crime of counterrevolution 反革命罪

crime of counterrevolutionary clique 反革命集团罪

crime of counterrevolutionary homicide or injury 反革命杀人伤人罪

crime of counterrevolutionary propaganda and incitement 反革命宣传煽动罪

crime of counterrevolutionary remormongering 反革命造谣罪

crime of counterrevolutionary supervision 反革命颠覆罪

crime of creating a disturbance with the weaponry 武器装备肇事罪

crime of creating disturbance in violation of regulations on the control of dangerous articles 违反险物品管理规定肇事罪

crime of creating disturbance in violation of regulations on the use of weaponry 违反武器装备使用规定肇事罪

crime of creating or proliferating computer virus 制造、传播计算机病毒罪

crime of crossing the border stealthily to flee the country 偷越国境外逃罪

crime of cruelly injuring or killing innocent residents in war zones 残害战区无辜居民罪

crime of damage to mines 损害矿井罪

crime of damage to monument 损害纪念碑罪

crime of damaging relations of identity 破坏身份关系罪

crime of damaging state owned assets 损害国有资产罪

crime of deceiving voters 欺罔投票人罪

crime of defamation 诽谤罪

crime of defamation and fallacy 诽谤妖言罪

crime of defecting to the enemy and turning traitor 投敌叛变罪

crime of defection 叛逃罪

crime of delinquent taxes 欠税罪

crime of delusional type 妄想型犯罪

crime of deprivation of rights under law 剥夺他人民权罪

crime of dereliction 玩忽职守罪

crime of dereliction of duty 渎职罪

crime of dereliction of duty by an administrative department in charge of the registration of companies and its staff members 公司登记主管部门及其工作人员玩忽职守罪

crime of dereliction of duty that leads to bankruptcy 渎职破产罪

crime of desecration of a corpse 侵害尸体罪

crime of deserting just before a battle 临阵脱逃罪

crime of destroying evidence 销毁证据罪

crime of destroying land resources 破坏土地资源罪

crime of discriminating or insulting an ethnic minority 歧视、侮辱少数民族罪

crime of disobeying orders in combat situation 战时违抗命令罪

crime of disrupting administrative duties 扰乱政务罪

crime of disrupting court order 扰乱法庭秩序罪

crime of disrupting mails and telegrams 妨害邮电通讯罪

crime of disrupting marriages of armymen 破坏军人婚姻罪

crime of disrupting money and banking 扰乱货币金融罪

crime of disrupting public service 妨害公务罪

crime of disrupting securities market 扰乱证券市场罪

crime of disrupting the managerial order of companies and enterprises 妨害对公司、企业的管理秩序罪

crime of disrupting the order of social administration 妨害社会管理秩序罪

crime of disrupting the order of supervision 破坏监管秩序罪

crime of disturbance of public as-sembly 扰乱公共集会罪

crime of disturbance of public facilities 扰乱公共事业罪

crime of disturbing order at public places 扰乱公共场所秩序罪

crime of disturbing public order 扰乱公共秩序罪,扰乱治安罪

crime of disturbing social order 扰乱社会秩序罪

crime of divulging a state secret abroad 向国外泄露国家秘密罪

crime of divulging military secrets 泄露军事机密罪

crime of divulging technological secrets 泄露技术秘密罪

crime of dodging the quarantine of animals and plants 逃避动植物检疫罪

crime of drug smuggling 走私毒品犯罪

crime of drug trafficking 贩卖毒品罪

crime of duplicating obscene articles 复制淫秽物品罪

crime of embezzlement 侵占罪

crime of embezzling private properties 侵占单位财物罪

crime of embezzling state property 侵吞国家财产罪

crime of endangering (safety of) flight 危及飞行安全罪

crime of enticing others into over-seas immigration 诱惑移民海外罪

crime of escaping from custody 脱逃罪

crime of escaping from prison 越狱逃脱罪

crime of escaping from the army 逃离部队罪

crime of evading or illegally trading in foreign exchange 逃汇、套汇罪

crime of excessively or wantonly issuing permits for logging of woods 超发、滥发林木采伐

许可罪

crime of exhumation of grave followed by damage of corpse 侵害坟墓尸体罪

crime of exposing a child to risk of being burned 置儿童于烧死危险罪

crime of extorting a confession by torture 刑讯逼供罪

crime of extorting bribes 索贿罪

crime of extorting testimony 逼取证言罪

crime of extortion 讹诈罪,敲诈勒索罪

crime of fabricating and spreading false information on securities 编造并传播虚假证券信息罪

crime of fabricating rumors to mislead people in wartime 战时造谣惑众罪

crime of failing to report 不检举罪

crime of failure in delivering a criminal case 刑事不移单罪

crime of failure to comply with an exclusion order 拒不遵守排除令罪

crime of false accusation 虚假告发罪

crime of false imprisonment 非法拘禁罪

crime of false pretenses 欺诈罪

crime of false testimony 伪供证据罪

crime of falsely making out specialized value-added-taxreceipts 虚开增值税专用发票罪

crime of falsely making out, counterfeiting or illegally selling specialized value-added-tax receipts 虚开、伪造和非法出售增值税专用发票罪

crime of falsifying certificate of assets 资产虚假证明罪

crime of feigned investment 虚假出资罪

crime of felonious entry (英) 严

重闯入罪

crime of felonious rioting 严重骚乱罪

crime of financial fraud 金融诈骗罪

crime of financial irregularities 金融舞弊罪

crime of financially aiding activities that jeopardize state security 资助危害国家安全活动罪

crime of financially aiding offenders 资助罪犯罪

crime of flight of capital contribution 抽逃出资罪

crime of fomenting rebellion 煽动叛乱罪

crime of forcible entry 闯入罪

crime of forcible seizure 抢夺罪

crime of forcing a woman into sexual intercourse 强迫妇女卖淫罪

crime of forgery of imperial document 伪造诏书罪

crime of forging invoices 伪造发票罪

crime of forging or mutilating financial instruments 伪造、变造金融票据罪

crime of forging or mutilating identity cards 伪造、变造身份证罪

crime of forming a case against another 诬告陷害罪

crime of fraud against financial instruments 金融票据诈骗罪

crime of fraud against portfolio 有价证券诈骗罪

crime of fraud in financing 集资诈骗罪

crime of fraudulent bankruptcy 诈欺破产罪

crime of fraudulent composition 诈欺和解罪

crime of fraudulent fund-raising 集资诈骗罪

crime of gaining untrue documents by fraud 骗取虚伪文书罪

crime of gathering a crowd to hinder the rescue of bought women and children 聚众阻碍解救被收买的妇女、儿童罪

crime of genocide 灭绝种族罪

crime of giving free rein to smuggling 放纵走私罪

crime of glossing over or concealing the illegality and source of money and goods gained from drug sales 掩饰、隐瞒出售毒品所得财物的非法性质和来源罪

crime of hampering the recovery of delinquent tax 妨碍追缴公款罪

crime of harboring a mafia-style syndicate 包庇、纵容黑社会性质的组织罪

crime of harboring criminal 包庇罪

crime of harboring drug criminals 包庇毒品犯罪分子罪

crime of heresy 异端罪

crime of high treason 大逆罪

crime of hijacking a ship or an automobile 劫持船只、汽车罪

crime of hindering official duties 妨碍执行公务罪

crime of hindering soldiers' execution of duty in observance of law 阻碍军人依法执行职务罪

crime of holding a huge amount of property with unidentified sources 巨额财产来源不明罪

crime of holding counterfeit currency 持有伪造货币罪

crime of hooliganism 流氓罪

crime of hostage-taking 劫持人质罪

crime of housebreaking 非法侵入罪

crime of humor-mongering and swindling by witches 巫婆造谣、诈骗罪

crime of illegal approval or registration 违法批准、登记罪

crime of illegal business operations 非法经营罪

crime of illegal capture or killing of rare and endangered spices of wild animals 非法捕杀珍贵、濒危野生动物罪

crime of illegal collecting and supplying blood 非法采集、供应血液罪

crime of illegal denudation 滥伐林木罪

crime of illegal dodgery of draft 非法规避兵役罪

crime of illegal escape from the scene of traffic accident 不法逃离交通肇事现场罪

crime of illegal felling of woods 非法采伐森林罪

crime of illegal fund-raising by fraudulent means 以诈骗方法非法集资罪

crime of illegal growing of drug plants 非法种植毒品原植物罪

crime of illegal hunting 非法狩猎罪

crime of illegal manufacturing, trading, holding, carrying firearms, ammunition or explosives 非法制造买卖、持有运输枪支、弹药、爆炸物罪

crime of illegal medical practice 非法行医罪

crime of illegal political association 非法政治结社罪

crime of illegal pooling of savings deposits 非法吸收存款罪

crime of illegal research 非法搜查罪

crime of illegal selling invoice for exclusive use of VAT 非法出售增值税专用发票罪

crime of illegal selling or presenting cultural relics of private collection 非法出售、私赠文物藏品罪

crime of illegal selling ordinary invoices 非法出售普通发票罪

crime of illegal shooting 违法射击罪

crime of illegal speculation and profiteering 投机倒把罪

crime of illegal storing firearms, ammunition or explosives 非法储存枪支、弹药、爆炸物罪

crime of illegal supply of narcotics or mental drugs 非法提供麻醉药品、精神药品罪

crime of illegally alienating the right to the use of state-owned land use right 非法低价出让国有土地使用权罪

crime of illegally approving the appropriation or occupation of land 非法批准 征用、占用土地罪

crime of illegally breaking into the computer information system of an important sector 非法侵入重要领域计算机系统罪

crime of illegally chopping down trees 盗伐林木罪

crime of illegally collecting no tax or less than due amount of tax 非法不征、少征税款罪

crime of illegally creating financial institutions 非法设立金融机构罪

crime of illegally excavating and robbing ancient cultural sites or ancient tombs 盗挖古文化遗址、古墓葬罪

crime of illegally felling trees 盗伐林木罪

crime of illegally handling the issuance of invoices, offset of tax payment, on tax rebate on exports 违法办理发售发票、抵扣税款、出口退税罪

crime of illegally holding drugs 非法持有毒品罪

crime of illegally holding or hiding a firearm or ammunition 非法持有、私藏枪支、弹药罪

crime of illegally holding state secrets 非法持有国家秘密罪

crime of illegally manufacturing or selling signs of another person's trademarks 非法制造、销售他人商标标识罪

crime of illegally obtaining military secrets 非法获取军事秘密罪

crime of illegally obtaining state secrets 非法获取国家秘密罪

crime of illegally presenting certificates of credit 非法出具资信证明罪

crime of illegally providing certification for tax rebate on exports 违法提供 出口退税凭证罪

crime of illegally purchasing invoices for the exclusive use of VAT 非法购买增值税专用发票罪

crime of illegally selling or transferring weaponry 非法出卖、转让武器装备罪

crime of impairing control of the border (boundary with a region) 妨害国(边)境 管理罪

crime of impairing official documents, certificates or seals 妨害公文、证件印章罪

crime of impairing public security 妨害公共安全罪

crime of impairing sealed, seized, or frozen properties 妨害查封、扣押、冻结的财产罪

crime of impairing telecommunications by radio 妨害无线电通讯罪

crime of impairing testifying 妨害作证罪

crime of impairing the administration of justice 妨害司法罪

crime of impairing the control of cultural relics 妨害文物管理罪

crime of impairing water conservancy 破坏水利罪

crime of imparting criminal methods 传授犯罪方法罪

crime of impeding apprehension 妨碍拘押罪

crime of impossibility 不能未遂

crime of incitement 煽动罪

crime of inciting armed rebellion 煽动武装叛乱罪

crime of inciting hatred of nationalities 煽动民族仇恨罪

crime of inciting resistance against law enforcement 煽动抗拒法律实施罪

crime of inciting split of the state 煽动分裂国家罪

crime of inciting subversion of the state's political power 煽动颠覆国家政权罪

crime of inciting to commit suicide 迫使他人自杀罪

crime of inciting war of aggression 鼓动侵略战争罪

crime of indecency in official services 公务猥亵罪

crime of indirectly taking a bribe 间接受贿罪

crime of inducing foreign aggression 诱致外患罪

crime of infanticide by drowning 溺婴罪

crime of infringement upon a citizen's right to the freedom of correspondence 侵犯公民通信自由罪

crime of infringement upon the customs and habits of minority ethnic group 侵犯少数民族风俗习惯罪

crime of infringing upon the democratic rights of citizens 侵犯公民民主权利罪

crime of injuries by explosive substances to buildings and goods therein 爆炸损害建筑物、货物罪

crime of insider trading 内幕交易罪

crime of instigating mutiny 策动叛变罪

crime of instigating rebellion 策动叛乱罪

crime of instigating the subordinates to engage in activities against the duty 指使部属进行违犯职责活动罪

crime of insulting another 侮辱罪

crime of insulting belief or religious organization 侮辱信仰及宗教团体罪

crime of insulting or slandering the head of state 侮辱诽谤国家元首罪

crime of insulting organizations or representatives of the government 侮辱政府机关、政府代表罪

crime of insulting the corpse 侮辱尸体罪

crime of insulting the national flag or the national emblem 侮辱国旗、国徽罪

crime of insulting the national flag or the national emblem of the People's Republic of China 侮辱中华人民共和国国旗、国徽罪

crime of insurance fraud 保险诈骗罪

crime of insurrection 叛乱罪,内乱罪

crime of intentional destruction or damage of properties 故意毁坏财物罪

crime of intentional homicide 故意杀人罪

crime of intentionally hindering the action of armed force in war 战时故意妨碍武装力量行动罪

crime of interests 利益罪

crime of interference in the freedom of marriage 干涉婚姻自

由罪

crime of internal disorder 内乱罪

crime of introducing a crime 介绍贿赂罪

crime of invasion of privacy 侵害私人秘密罪

crime of invasion of the privacy of speech 侵害言论隐私罪

crime of inveigling investors into securities transactions 诱骗证券交易罪

crime of inveigling minors into criminal activities 引诱未成年人参加犯罪罪

crime of involuntary manslaughter 过失杀人罪

crime of irregularities for favoritism so as to convert state-owned assets into law-priced shares or to sell off the assets at low prices 徇私舞弊将国有资产低价折股或低价出售罪

crime of irregularities for favoritism so as to result in the bankruptcy or heavy deficit of a state-owned company or enterprise 徇私舞弊造成国有公司,企业破产或严重亏损罪

crime of jeopardizing industrial secrets 妨害产业秘密罪

crime of jeopardizing interests of national defense 危害国防利益罪

crime of jeopardizing public health 危害公共卫生罪

crime of jeopardizing state security 危害国家安全罪

crime of jeopardizing the administration of tax revenue collection 危害税收征管理

crime of jeopardizing the freedom of communication 妨害通信自由罪

crime of jumping bail 逃离保释罪

crime of kidnapping for ransom 绑架勒索罪

crime of kidnapping women and children 绑架妇女儿童罪

crime of lese-majesty (拉) 大逆罪

crime of letting another cross the national border without permission 私放他人偷越国(边)境罪

crime of letting persons secretly crossing the border (boundary with a region) pass 非法放行偷越国(边)境人员罪

crime of luring another into false swearing 诱惑伪誓罪

crime of luring subordinates into offense 引诱属下犯罪罪

crime of luring, sheltering, or procuring another into prostitution 引诱、容留、介绍他人卖淫罪

crime of making false invoices of special kinds 虚开特种发票罪

crime of making false reports about military situation 谎报军情罪

crime of making false reports about military situation and passing false military orders 谎报军情和假传军令罪

crime of making vindicative attacks on a witness 打击、报复证人罪

crime of making vindicative attacks on accounting or statistical personnel 打击、报复会计、统计人员罪

crime of malfeasance 渎职罪

crime of malpractice in recruitment 招收工作舞弊罪

crime of malpractices in taxation 税务舞弊罪

crime of maltreating animals 虐待动物罪

crime of maltreating or killing prisoners of war 虐待、杀害

战俘罪

crime of maltreating or persecuting subordinate servicemen 虐待、迫害部属罪

crime of maltreating subordinate servicemen 虐待部属罪

crime of manufacturing or selling fake medicine 生产、销售假药罪,生产、销售伪劣产品罪

crime of mass disorders 聚众骚乱罪

crime of medical accident 医疗事故罪

crime of misappropriating capital of a company or enterprise 挪用公司企业资金罪

crime of misappropriating lost articles of another 侵占他人遗失物罪

crime of misappropriating public funds 挪用公款罪

crime of misappropriating specific funds and articles of the state 挪用国家特定款物罪

crime of misprison of felony 包庇重罪犯罪

crime of misprison of treason 包庇叛逆犯人罪

crime of misuse of law in adjudication 枉法裁判罪

crime of misusing marks for imperial purposes 误用御用标识罪

crime of misusing siren or sabotaging emergency facilities 滥用警报及破坏救难设备罪

crime of murder 凶杀罪

crime of negligent homicide 过失致人死亡罪

crime of negligently breaching dikes 过失决水罪

crime of negligently causing a serious accident 重大责任事故罪

crime of negligently causing another serious injury 过失重伤罪

crime of negligently causing explosions 过失爆炸罪

crime of negligently damaging gas equipment 过失毁坏煤气设备罪

crime of negligently damaging inflammable or explosive equipment 过失毁坏易爆设备罪

crime of negligently damaging means of transportation 过失毁坏交通工具罪

crime of negligently damaging power equipment 过失毁坏电力设备罪

crime of negligently damaging precious cultural relics or relics at a major historical and cultural site under protection 过失损毁珍贵文物或重点文物保护单位的文物罪

crime of negligently damaging radio and TV facilities or public telecommunication facilities 过失破坏广播电视设施、公用电信设施罪

crime of negligently damaging telecommunication equipment 过失毁坏通讯设备罪

crime of negligently damaging transportation 过失毁坏交通设备罪

crime of negligently leading to poisoning 过失引起中毒罪

crime of negligently setting things on fire 过失放火罪

crime of nonrescue 不解救罪

crime of obscene performances 淫秽表演罪

crime of obstructing the rescue of kidnapped and sold women and children by taking advantage of official capacity 利用职务阻碍解救被拐卖、绑架的妇女儿童罪

crime of obtaining a credit loan from a financial institution by fraud to engage in usurious relending 套取金融机构信贷资

金高利转贷罪

crime of obtaining border exit documents by fraud 骗取出境证件罪

crime of obtaining export tax drawback from the state 骗取国家出口退税款罪

crime of offenders 飞行肇事罪

crime of offering bribes to a unit 向单位行贿罪

crime of official encroachment 业务侵占罪

crime of opening of gambling house or assembling gamblers 开设赌场聚众赌徒罪

crime of ordinary embezzlement 普通侵占罪

crime of ordinary smuggling 普通走私罪

crime of organizing or leading an organization engaged in terrorist activities 组织、领导恐怖活动组织罪

crime of organizing a jailbreak 组织越狱罪

crime of organizing a mass prison raid 聚众劫狱罪

crime of organizing and mating use of a secret society or a heresy organization, or making use of superstition to under the enforcement of state laws and administrative regulation 组织和利用会道门、邪教组织或利用迷信破坏国家法律、行政法规罪

crime of organizing and mating use of a secret society or a heresy organization, or making use of superstition to deceive others and thus cause deaths 组织和利用会道门、邪教组织或利用迷信蒙骗他人,致人死之罪

crime of organizing or leading a counterrevolutionary group 组织、领导反革命集团罪

crime of organizing or transporting other persons to secretly cross the border (or boundary with a region) 组织、运送他人偷越国(边)境罪

crime of organizton or using superstitious sects to engage in counterrevolutionary activites 组织、利用会道门进行反革命活动罪

crime of organizing pornographic performance 组织进行淫秽表演罪

crime of organizing, coercing, inducing, permitting the stay of, or procuring others into prostitution 组织、强迫、引诱、容留、介绍卖淫罪

crime of organizing, leading, or actively participating in a mafiastyle organization 组织、领导、参加黑社会性质的组织罪

crime of ownbribing a state of organization, a state-owned company or enterprise, a government financed institution, or a people's mass association 贿赂国家机关、国有公司、企业、事业单位、人民团体罪

crime of perjury 伪证罪

crime of personnel in charge of supervision over environmental protection negligently leading to the occurrence of a serious environmental pollution accident 环保监管人员失职导致发生重大环境污染事故罪

crime of picking quarrels and provoking troubles 寻衅滋事罪

crime of pillage 掠夺罪,抢劫罪

crime of pillaging and slaughtering innocent residents in war zones 掠夺、残害战区无辜居民罪

crime of play 游戏型犯罪

crime of plotting to dismember the state 阴谋分裂国家罪

crime of plotting to subvert the

government 阴谋颠覆政府罪

crime of plunder 掠夺罪

crime of political conviction 政治信仰犯罪

crime of pooling public deposits in disguised form 变相吸收公众存款罪

crime of possessing or using drugs 持有或使用毒品罪

crime of possession of firearms while committing offenses 犯罪时持有火器罪

crime of postal staff members intentionally delaying the delivery of mails 邮政工作人员故意延误投递邮件罪

crime of posting letters threatening to murder 投寄杀人恐吓信罪

crime of practising favoritism in business operations 徇私经营罪

crime of practising favoritism in loan lending 徇私发放贷款罪

crime of preparing for and plotting inducement of foreign aggression 预备、策划诱致外患罪

crime of preparing for or plotting assistance to foreign aggression 预备、策划援助外患罪

crime of pretending to be an armyman in cheating and bluffing 冒充军人招摇撞骗罪

crime of piracy 海盗罪

crime of procuring others into prostitution 介绍他人卖淫罪

crime of producing erroneous certificate of assets 资产证明失实罪

crime of producing or selling obscene articles 制售淫秽物品罪

crime of producing, reproducing, publishing, selling, or spreading obscene articles 制作、复制、出版、贩卖、传播淫秽物品罪

crime of profiteering of government employees 公务员图利罪

crime of propagating sexually transmitted disease 传播性病罪

crime of prostitution against the youngsters 危害青少年的卖淫罪

crime of providing falsified business certificate 提供虚假业务证明文件罪

crime of providing falsified certification by assets valuers 资产评估人员提虚假证明罪

crime of providing falsified financial statements or those concealing important facts 提供虚假的或隐瞒重要事实的财务报告罪

crime of providing for false certification by personnel engaged in the assessment of capital 验资人员提供虚假证明犯罪

crime of providing forged or alternated entry/exit documents 提供伪造、变造的出入境证件罪

crime of providing licensed serial number of books for another to publish pornography 为他人提供书号出版淫秽书刊罪

crime of providing military secrets 提供军事机密罪

crime of providing premises for taking opium 提供吸食鸦片房屋罪

crime of publishing contents that discriminate or insult an ethnic minority 刊载歧视、侮辱少数民族的内容罪

crime of publishing obscene articles 出版淫秽物品罪

crime of rape 强奸妇女罪

crime of refusing or evading military service in wartime 战时拒绝或逃避服役罪

crime of refusing or delaying military orders for goods 战时拒绝或延误军事订货罪

crime of refusing or evading military obligation 拒绝、逃避军事义务罪

crime of refusing or evading recruitment or military training in wartime 战时拒绝逃避征召或军事训练罪

crime of refusing to aid officer 拒绝协助司法人员罪

crime of refusing to execute judgments or orders of the people's court 拒不执行人民法院判决、裁定罪

crime of refusing to provide evidence on espionage 拒绝提供间谍证据罪

crime of refusing to take corrective measures and resulting in serious consequences in fire control 拒不采取改正措施造成消防严重后果罪

crime of refusing to treat a sick or wounded soldier in dangerous or serious conditions 拒不救治危重伤病军人罪

crime of releasing a criminal on one's own accord 私放罪犯罪

crime of releasing a prisoner of war without authorization 私放俘虏罪

crime of relending for profiteering 转贷牟私罪

crime of relief fraud 救济津贴诈欺罪

crime of removal of articles form public places 从公共场所转移物品罪

crime of rendering economic aid to the enemy in war 战时经济资敌罪

crime of rescuing a convicted criminal, a defendant, or a criminal suspect 非法劫走罪犯、被告人或犯罪嫌疑人罪

crime of resisting lawful arrest and perpetrating 拒捕谋杀罪

crime of resorting to violence to obtain testimony 暴力取证罪

crime of retaliating upon a witness 报复证人罪

crime of rewarding or commending criminal offenses 酬劳、赞许犯罪行为罪

crime of rigging security exchange 操纵证券市场罪

crime of rigging trading prices of securites 操纵证券交易价格犯罪

crime of rioting for jailbreaks 暴力越狱罪

crime of robbery 抢劫罪,强盗罪

crime of sabotaging a computer system 破坏计算机系统罪

crime of sabotaging boundary tablets or markers along the national border 破坏国境界碑、界桩罪

crime of sabotaging collective production 破坏集体生产罪

crime of sabotaging combustible and explosive facilities 破坏易燃、易爆设备罪

crime of sabotaging communication equipment 破坏通讯设备罪

crime of sabotaging communications 破坏交通罪

crime of sabotaging computer data or programs 破坏计算机数据、程序罪

crime of sabotaging electric power, gas, or combustible and explosive facilities 破坏电力、燃气、易燃、易爆设备罪

crime of sabotaging functions of a computer information system 破坏计算机信息系统功能罪

crime of sabotaging gas facilities 破坏燃气设备罪

crime of sabotaging means of transportation 破坏交通工具罪

crime of sabotaging military facilities 破坏军事设施罪

crime of sabotaging precious cultural relics or places of historic interest and scenic beauty 破坏珍贵文物、名胜古迹罪

crime of sabotaging production and business operations 破坏生产经营罪

crime of sabotaging radio and television facilities of public telecommunication facilities 破坏广播电视设施、公用电信设施罪

crime of sabotaging transportation facilities 破坏交通设施罪

crime of sabotaging weaponry, military installations or military telecommunication 破坏武器装备、军事设施、军事通讯罪

crime of scalping relics 倒卖文物罪

crime of scalping tickets or coupons with face value 倒卖伪造的有价票证罪

crime of secret service 特务罪

crime of seduction 诱奸罪

crime of seeking avaricious profits 贪利性犯罪

crime of selling commodities carrying counterfeit registered trademarks 销售假冒注册商标的商品罪

crime of selling cosmetic products not qualified for hygiene standards 销售不符合卫生标准的化妆品罪

crime of selling counterfeit invoices 出售伪造发票罪

crime of selling counterfeit invoices for the exclusive use of value added tax 出售伪造的增值税专用发票罪

crime of selling entry 出售出入境证件罪

crime of selling fake or inferior agricultural means of production 销售伪劣农业生产资料罪

crime of selling fake or inferior articles for medical uses 销售伪劣医疗用品罪

crime of selling fake or inferior medical equipment or sanitary materials for medical purpose 销售伪劣医疗器械、医用卫生材料罪

crime of selling fake or inferior medicine 销售假药劣药罪

crime of selling foodstuffs not qualified for hygiene standards 销售不符合卫生标准的食品罪

crime of selling infringing duplicates 销售侵权复制品罪

crime of selling obscene articles 贩卖淫秽物品罪

crime of selling pirated products 销售盗版制品罪

crime of selling products not qualified for safety standards 销售不符合安全标准的产品罪

crime of setting fire to damage buildings and goods therein 纵火损害建筑物、货物罪

crime of sheltering another person in drug taking or injection 容留他人吸食、注射毒品罪

crime of sheltering another person in prostitution 容留他人卖淫罪

crime of skyjacking 劫持航空器罪,空中劫持罪

crime of slackness in combat 作战消极罪

crime of slavery 奴隶罪

crime of smuggling articles used for the purpose of manufacturing narcotics or medicine for mental disease 走私制造麻醉药品、精神药品的物品罪

crime of smuggling counterfeited

currencies　走私伪造货币罪

crime of smuggling cultural relics, gold, silver, or other precious metals　走私文物、黄金、白银及其他贵重金属罪

crime of smuggling ordinary goods or articles　走私一般货物、物品罪

crime of smuggling rare and precious animals and their products　走私珍贵动物及其制品罪

crime of smuggling rare plants and their products　走私珍稀植物及其制品罪

crime of smuggling weapons, ammunition, nuclear materials, or counterfeited currencies　走私武器、弹药、核材料或伪造的货币罪

crime of smuggling, trafficking in, transporting, or producing drugs　走私、贩卖、运输、制造毒品罪

crime of sodomy　反自然性交罪

crime of soldier cruelly injuring and slaughtering innocent residents, or pillaging innocent residents of their properties　军人残害无辜居民、掠夺无辜居民财物罪

crime of solicting another to commit suicide　教唆他人自杀罪

crime of solicting others to take or inject drugs　教唆他人吸食、注射毒品罪

crime of spreading poison　投毒罪

crime of spreading pornographic articles　传播淫秽物品罪

crime of spreading sexually transmitted disease　传染性病罪

crime of spying on military secrets　刺探军事机密罪

crime of spying on state secrets　刺探国家秘密罪

crime of stealing and exporting precious cultural relics　盗运

① 珍贵文物出口罪

② crime of stealing or insulting the corpse　盗窃、侮辱尸体罪

crime of stealing or seizing guns, ammunition, or explosives　盗窃、抢夺枪支、弹药、爆炸物罪

crime of stealing, spying out or providing military secrets　窃取、刺探、提供军事机密

crime of subjecting imprisoned persons to corporal punishment and maltreatment　体罚虐待被监管人罪

crime of subversion of the government　颠覆政府罪

crime of swindling　诈骗罪

crime of swindling a citizen of his property　诈骗公民财产罪

crime of swindling a loan　诈骗贷款罪

crime of swindling by superstitious means　借迷信诈骗罪

crime of swindling in collusion with swindlers　与诈骗分子串通共同诈骗的犯罪

crime of taking a bribe and providing falsified professional certification　受贿而提供虚假业务证明罪

crime of taking part in a mafia-style organization　参加黑社会性质的组织罪

crime of taking part in an organization engaged in terrorist activities　参加恐怖活动组织罪

crime of terrorism　恐怖活动罪

crime of torture of children　虐待儿童罪

crime of torture of the disabled　虐待残废人罪

crime of trafficking in counterfeit currency of a state　贩运伪造国家货币罪

crime of transformed robbery　转化的抢劫罪

crime of treason　叛国罪

crime of unconstitutional incitement and propagandization 违宪鼓动宣传罪

crime of unconstitutional slacking or sabotaging 违宪怠工破坏罪

crime of undermining birth control 破坏计划生育罪

crime of undermining elections 破坏选举罪

crime of undermining environmental protection 破坏环境保护罪

crime of undermining mineral resources 破坏矿产资源罪

crime of undermining survey indicators of a permanent nature 破坏永久性测量标志罪

crime of undermining the national currency and negotiable instruments 破坏国家货币及有价证券罪

crime of undermining the state financial system 破坏国家财政制度罪

crime of unlawful assembly 非法集会罪

crime of unlawful deprivation of the freedom of religion 非法剥夺宗教信仰自由罪

crime of unlawful intrusion into the residence of another person 非法侵入他人住宅罪

crime of unlawful receipt of information 非法接受信息罪

crime of unlawful supply of firearms 不法提供火器罪

crime of unlawfully raising funds 非法集资罪

crime of unreasonable restraint of trade 不合理限制贸易罪

crime of using counterfeit currencies 使用伪造货币罪

crime of uttering forged instrument 故意使用伪造文件罪

crime of violating rules on labor protection so as to cause the occurrence of a major accident or heavy losses 违反劳动保护规定发生重大事故或重大损失罪

crime of violating the citizens' rights of the person 侵犯公民人身权利罪

crime of violation against secrets of taxation 侵害赋税机密罪

crime of violation of probation or parole 违犯缓刑或假释罪

crime of violations against duties of bill recording 违反簿册记载义务罪

crime of violence 使用暴力罪,暴力犯,暴力犯罪

crime of voluntary surrender to the enemy 自动投降敌人罪

crime of willful and malicious injury 故意伤害罪

crime of willfully damaging a scenic spot or historic site 故意损毁名胜古迹罪

crime of willfully impeding military action of the armed forces 故意阻碍武装部队军事行动罪

crime of willfully making or propagating computer viruses and other destructive programs 故意制作、传播计算机病毒等破坏性程序罪

crime of withholding the illegality and source of money of and goods gained from drug sales 隐瞒出售毒品获得财物的非法性质和来源罪

crime of withholding important facts in financial statements 隐瞒重要事实的财务报告罪

crime of wounding 伤害罪

crime prediction 犯罪预测,犯罪预防

crime problem 犯罪问题

crime rate 犯罪率

crime related to booties or stolen goods 赃物罪

crime related to opium taking 吸

食鸦片烟罪

crime relating to suicides 自杀关联罪

crime scene 犯罪现场

crime scene investigation 犯罪现场勘查

crime scene protection 现场保护

crime survey 犯罪调查

crime syndicate 犯罪辛迪加

crime with amusement motives 游乐性动机犯罪

crime with curiosity motive 好奇心动机犯罪

crime with defensive motive 防卫动机犯罪

crime with friendship motive 友情动机犯罪

crime with greedy motive 贪财动机犯罪

crime with intelligence 智能犯

crime with jealous motive 嫉妒性动机犯罪

crime with retaliation motive 报复性动机犯罪

crime with sexual motive 性动机犯罪

crime with suspicious motive 猜疑性动机犯罪

crimen（拉）罪

crimes against humanity 反人道罪

crimes against peace and security of mankind 危害人类和平及安全罪

crimes against property 财产性犯罪

crimes against public security 危害公共安全罪

crimes against the state 危害国家罪

crimes committed by forging or mutilating letters of credits or documents and papers attached 伪造、变造信用证或附随的单据文件的犯罪

crimes committed by issuing loans against rules 违反规定发放贷款的犯罪

crimes in the press 出版犯罪

crimes of a soldier abusing his/her office 军人滥用职权罪

crimes of a soldier capitulating to enemy 军人投降敌人罪

crimes of a soldier causing trouble in weaponry 军人武器装备肇事罪

crimes of a soldier changing, without permission, prearranged purposes of weaponry 军人擅自改变武器装备编配用途罪

crimes of a soldier defecting to the enemy in the battlefield 军人战场投敌罪

crimes of a soldier deserting the armed forces 军人逃离部队罪

crimes of a soldier disobeying orders in combat situation 军人战时违抗命令罪

crimes of a soldier fabricating rumors to mislead people in combat situation 军人战时造谣惑众罪

crimes of a soldier illegally intentionally covering military situation 军人故意隐瞒军情罪

crimes of a soldier illegally obtaining military secrets 军人非法获取军事秘密罪

crimes of a soldier illegally releasing a prisoner of war 军人私放俘虏罪

crimes of a soldier illegally selling or transferring weaponry 军人非法出卖、转让武器装备罪

crimes of a soldier losing documents containing military secrets 军人遗失军事机密罪

crimes of a soldier losing weaponry 军人遗失武器装备罪

crimes of a soldier making a false report about a military situation 军人谎报军情罪

crimes of a soldier not coming to help others in danger in the battlefield 军人战场见危不救罪

crimes of a soldier obstructing the performance of duties 军人阻碍执行职务罪

crimes of a soldier refusing to transmit orders or transmitting false orders in military service 军人拒传、假传军令罪

crimes of a soldier refusing to treat ill and wounded soldiers 军人拒不救治伤病员罪

crimes of a soldier secretly crossing the national border (or boundary with a region) to abscond abroad 军人偷越国（边）境外逃罪

crimes of a soldier self-wounding in combat situation 军人战时自伤罪

crimes of a soldier selling or transferring, without permission, real properties of the army 军人擅自出卖、转让军队房地产罪

crimes of a soldier slacking in combat 军人作战消极罪

crimes of a soldier stealing or forcibly seizing weaponry or military goods 军人盗窃、抢夺武器装备或军用物资罪

crimes of a soldier stealing weaponry 军人盗窃武器装备罪

crimes of a soldier unwarranted abandonment of duty station 军人擅离职守罪

crimes of a soldier's abandonment of his or her unit in combat situation 军人临阵脱逃罪

crimes of a soldier's abandonment of ill and wounded soldiers 军人遗弃伤病军人罪

crimes of a soldier's maltreatment of prisoners of war 军人虐待俘虏罪

crimes of a soldier's maltreatment of subordinates 军人虐待部属罪

crimes of a soldier's neglect of duties in military service 军人玩忽职守罪

crimes of a soldier's stealing, spying, or providing military secrets to enemy 军人窃取、刺探、提供军事机密罪

crimes of abandonmentofweaponry by a soldier 军人遗弃武器装备罪

crimes of barboring and covering up a criminal 窝藏、包庇罪

crimes of concealing or disposing of plunder 窝赃、销赃罪

crimes of defection by a soldier 军人叛逃罪

crimes of misappropriating capital of one's work unit or client 挪用单位或客户资金的犯罪

crimes of soldiers violating military duties 军人违反职责罪

crimes of using a counterfeit or alternated letter of credit or such documents or papers attached 使用伪造、变造的信用证或附随的单据、文件罪

crimes ordinance 刑事罪条例

criminal 刑法上,刑事上,案犯,犯罪人,刑事,刑事罪犯,罪犯,犯人,犯罪分子

criminal abortion 犯罪性堕胎

criminal act 罪行,刑事犯罪,犯罪行为

criminal action 刑事诉讼

criminal action concerning foreign interests 涉外刑事诉讼

criminal activities of cheating 出口骗税犯罪活动

criminal activities of frauds 诈欺犯罪

criminal adjudication 刑事裁判,刑事审判

criminal anatomy 刑事解剖学,犯罪解剖学

criminal anthropology 犯罪人类学,刑事人类学

criminal appeal 刑事上诉,刑事申诉

criminal appeal law 刑事上诉法

criminal argot 犯罪隐语

criminal assault 暴力殴打,刑法上的伤害罪

criminal at large 在逃犯

criminal attempt 犯罪未遂

criminal attitude 犯罪态度

criminal attraction 犯罪吸引

criminal award and punishment 刑事奖惩

criminal biology 犯罪生物学

criminal borderline 犯罪边缘

criminal capacity 刑事责任能力,刑事能力

criminal case 刑事案件,案子

criminal case of first instance 第一审刑事案件

criminal case of second instance 二审刑事案件

criminal causation 犯罪原因学

criminal character 犯罪性质

criminal charge 刑事罪,刑事控告,刑事告诉,刑事检控

criminal circumstances 犯罪环境

criminal code 刑法,刑法典

criminal coercive measure 刑事强制措施

criminal common law 刑事普通法

criminal compensation 刑事赔偿

criminal complaint 刑事起诉书

criminal complaint filed by procuratorate against a court decision 刑事抗诉

criminal consequence 犯罪结果

criminal conspiracy 犯罪预谋

criminal contempt 藐视法庭罪

criminal court 刑事法院,刑事法庭

criminal damage 刑事损害

criminal defendant 刑事被告

criminal defense 刑事辩护

criminal demography 刑事人口统计学

criminal detection 刑事侦查

criminal disability 无犯罪能力

criminal disposal 刑事处分

criminal disposition 刑事处分

criminal division 刑事审判庭,刑事庭

criminal division of the high court 高等法院刑事庭

criminal dualism 犯罪二元论

criminal due to negligence 过失犯罪者

criminal evidence 刑事案件的证据

criminal evidence science 刑事证据学

criminal expert evaluation 刑事鉴定

criminal expert evaluation of forensic psychiatry 刑事司法精神病学鉴定

criminal facts 犯罪事实

criminal files 犯罪档案

criminal finalization 犯罪定型

criminal fine 刑事罚金

criminal for trial 候审犯人

criminal fraud 犯罪性欺诈

criminal gang 犯罪团伙,犯罪集团

criminal genetic factor 犯罪遗传因素

criminal geography school 犯罪地理学派

criminal group 犯罪集团

criminal idea 犯罪观

criminal identification 刑事鉴定

criminal immunity 刑事豁免

criminal impossibility 犯罪不能

criminal impulse 犯罪冲动

criminal in custody 在押犯

criminal indictment 刑事起诉书

criminal information 刑事控告,刑事告诉

criminal infringement 侵犯知识产权罪

criminal injuries compensation 刑事伤害赔偿

criminal injury 刑事损害,刑事伤害

criminal insanity 犯罪时正患精神病者

criminal instinct 犯罪本性

criminal intent 犯罪意图,犯罪目的,犯罪故意

criminal intent 犯意

criminal intention 犯意

criminal interrogation 刑事讯问,侦查

criminal investigation 刑事侦查

criminal investigator 刑事侦查员

criminal involved in a case 案犯

criminal judicature 刑事司法

criminal jurisdiction 刑事管辖,刑事管理,刑事管辖权,刑事审判管辖

criminal jurisprudence 刑法学

criminal jurist 刑法学家

criminal justice 刑事司法,刑事审判

criminal justice administration act 刑事司法行政法

criminal justice administration law 刑事司法法

criminal justice agency 刑事司法代行机构

criminal justice document 刑事司法文书

criminal justice professional 刑事审判人员

criminal justice research 刑事审判研究

criminal justice system 刑事司法制度,刑事司法文书

criminal knowledge 犯罪意识

criminal law 刑法

criminal law in a broad sense 广义刑法

criminal law of consequence 结果刑法

criminal law of judgment 裁判时刑法

criminal law of the Federal Republic of Germany 德意志联邦共和国刑法

criminal law of the Ming Dynasty 大明律

criminal law of will 意志刑法

criminal law system 刑法的体系

criminal laws of continental law system 大陆刑法

criminal lawsuit 刑事诉讼

criminal legal relation 刑事法律关系

criminal legal system 刑事法律制度

criminal legislation 刑事立法

criminal legislative activities 刑事立法活动

criminal liability 刑事责任

criminal libel 刑事诽谤

criminal lunatic 精神病犯

criminal matter 刑事事件

criminal mind 犯罪心理

criminal mood 犯罪情感

criminal motive 犯罪动机

criminal nature 犯罪性质

criminal negligence 犯罪过失,过失罪,刑法上的过失,过失犯罪

criminal object 犯罪客体

criminal objects 犯罪物件

criminal of losing firearms 丢失枪支罪

criminal of unlawful restraint 非法管制罪

criminal offender 刑事犯

criminal offender serving his sentence on reprieve 缓期执行的刑事犯

criminal offense 刑事罪,刑事犯罪

criminal offense against election 妨害选举罪

criminal offense against labor rights 妨害劳动权利罪

criminal offense against religion 妨害宗教罪

criminal offense against reputation

妨害名誉罪

criminal offense of fouling clean water　污秽净水罪

criminal offense of fouling water conduit　污秽水道罪

criminal offense of hooliganism　流氓活动罪

criminal offense of obscene publication　出版淫秽书刊罪

criminal offense of organizing criminal gangs　组织犯罪集团罪

criminal offense of protecting and assisting career prostitution　保护、援助职业卖淫行为罪

criminal omen　犯罪征兆

criminal omission　不作为犯,不作为犯罪,刑事疏漏

criminal organization　犯罪组织

criminal pattern　犯罪形态

criminal penalty　刑罚,刑事处罚

criminal personality　犯罪人格

criminal phenomenon　犯罪现象

criminal physiology　犯罪生理学,刑事生理学

criminal police　刑警,刑事警察

criminal policy　刑事政策

criminal policy school　刑事政策学派

criminal policy science　刑事政策学

criminal prisoner　刑事犯

criminal procedural code　刑事诉讼法典

criminal procedure　刑事诉讼程序,刑事诉讼

criminal procedure at first instance　刑事第一审程序

criminal procedure at second instance　刑事第二审程序

criminal procedure code of Germany　德国刑事诉讼法典

criminal procedure code of the Federal Republic of Germany　德意志联邦共和国刑事诉讼法典

criminal procedure concerning foreign interests　涉外刑事诉讼程序

criminal procedure law　刑事诉讼法,刑事诉讼法学

criminal procedure law in the broad sense　广义的刑事诉讼法

criminal procedure law in the narrow sense　狭义的刑事诉讼法

criminal procedure ordinance　刑事诉讼程序条例

criminal proceeding　刑事诉讼

criminal proceedings　刑事诉讼

criminal proceedings law　刑事诉讼法

criminal process　刑事程序

criminal process law　刑事程序法

criminal prosecution　刑事检控,刑事检察

criminal prosecution document　刑事检察文书

criminal prosecution office　刑事检察庭

criminal provision　刑事规定

criminal psychiatry　犯罪精神病学

criminal psychological feedback　犯罪心理反馈

criminal psychology　犯罪心理,犯罪心理学,刑事生理学

criminal psychotherapy　犯罪心理治疗

criminal punishment　刑罚处罚,刑事制裁,刑罚

criminal punishment law　刑罚法

criminal purpose　犯罪目的

criminal record　前科

criminal registration　刑事登记

criminal released on parole　被假释人的犯罪

criminal responsibility　刑事责任

criminal responsibility of state　国家的刑事责任

criminal result　犯罪结果

criminal rules　刑法规范

criminal sanction 刑事处分
criminal sentiment 犯罪情绪
criminal serving short-term imprisonment 短刑犯
criminal situation 犯罪情境
criminal social psychology 犯罪社会心理学
criminal sociology 犯罪社会学，刑事社会学
criminal somatology 刑事人体学
criminal statistics school 犯罪统计学派
criminal statute 刑法
criminal subculture 犯罪亚文化
criminal supervision and control 犯罪监护管束
criminal suspect 嫌疑犯，犯罪嫌疑
criminal technique 刑事技术，犯罪侦查技术
criminal technique expertise 刑事侦查学鉴定
criminal tendency 犯罪倾向
criminal theory of dynamics 动力学犯罪观
criminal theory of individual psychology 个性心理学犯罪犯
criminal theory of physiques and temperaments 体质性格类型说
criminal trial 刑事审判
criminal tribunal 刑事审判庭，刑事庭，刑事法庭
criminal trine 犯罪三元论
criminal's file 罪犯档案
criminalistics 刑事侦察学，犯罪侦查学
criminality 犯罪性
criminaloid 本性有犯罪倾向的人
criminals within and beyond the borders 境内外犯罪分子
criminals within the borders 境内犯罪分子
criminate 陷人于罪，归罪
crimination and recrimination 互相嫁祸罪

criminologist 犯罪学家
criminology 刑事学，犯罪学
criminous 犯了罪的
cripple 致人伤残
crippled person 残废，残废者
crisis intervention 危机干预
crisis-export 危机转嫁
criteria and methods for the economic evaluation of water resources projects 水资源项目经济评价标准与方法
criteria for interpretation 解释标准
criterion for classification 分类标准
criterion for judgement 判断标准
criterion for sentencing 量刑标准
criterion of determining economic crimes 经济犯罪认定标准
criterion of manufacturing or processing operation 制作标准或加工操作标准
criterion of punishment 刑罚标准
critical 严重
critical criminology 批判犯罪学
critical evidence 决定性证据
criticism 批评
criticism and education 批评教育
criticize 批评
criticize publicly in the printing press 登报批评
crop insurance 农作物保险
crop loss compensation 青苗赔偿费
crop seed management license 农作物种子经营许可证,农作物种子生产许可证
cross action 反诉行为
cross bill 反诉状
cross check 划线支票
cross default 交叉违约
cross defaults 串连违约

cross elasticity of demand 需求交叉弹性

cross liabilities 相互债务

cross liability 交叉责任,交叉责任制

cross licence contract 交叉许可合同,互换许可合同

cross offer 交叉报价

cross order 交叉订货

cross rate 美元标价法与套算汇率

cross trade 买空卖空

cross transaction 套汇

crossed check 划线支票

crosswise accomplice 横向共犯

cross-border supply 过境提供

cross-default clause 交叉违约条款

cross-identification 相互确认,相互证明

cross-identification method 相互确认方法

cross-offer 交错要约,交叉要约,互换要约

cross-purchase agreement 交叉购买协议

cross-subsidiazation 交叉补贴

crown court 皇室法院

crown solicitor (英) 检察官

crown 皇家,王位

crown case (英) 刑事案件

crown court 高级刑事法庭(英),皇家法院

crown law (英) 刑法

crown lawyer (英) 刑事律师

crown lease 官契

crown office in chancery 大法官法院刑事部(英)

crown prince 皇储,王储

crown privilege 政府特权

crown servant 公务人员

crown solicitor 检察官

crown witness (英) 刑事诉讼中的证人

crucial problem 决定性问题

cruel 残酷

cruel and unusual punishment 残酷惩罚,残酷刑罚,残酷和非常的刑罚

cruel punishment 大刑,酷刑

cruel torture 严刑

cruelty to animals 残害动物罪

culpa (拉) 过失

culpa in contrabendo (拉) 契约过失,缔结契约上的过失

culpa in faciendo (拉) 作为过失

culpa lata (拉) 严重过失,严重疏忽,重大过失

culpa levis (拉) 一般过失,轻微过失,轻过失

culpa levissima (拉) 轻微过失

culpability 有罪行为,罪过

culpable act 有罪行为

culpable homicide 刑事杀人

culpable negligence 重大过失

culprit 犯罪人,刑事被告,罪犯,犯人

culprit of murder 谋杀嫌疑犯

cultivated land 耕地

cultural affairs 文化事务

cultural amusement tax 文化娱乐税

cultural and ideological progress 精神文明

cultural basis of constitution 宪法的文化基础

cultural education of prisoners 罪犯文化知识教育

cultural heritage 文化遗产

cultural management 文化管理

cultural organization 文化团体

cultural property 文化财产

cultural pursuits 文化活动

cultural relics 文物

cultural relics unearthed 土地文物

cultural work 文化事业

culture 文化

cum rights 附有权利

cumul de faute 过错竞合

cumulatio (拉) 合并

cumulative convertible 累积性可兑换优先股

cumulative evidence 补充证据

cumulative offense 累罪,累犯

cumulative preferred stock 累积优先股

cumulative punishment 累加刑罚

cumulative rate 累进税率

cupboard 橱柜

cura（拉） 监督

cura absenti（拉） 失踪人的财产管理

cura bonorum（拉） 财产管理

cura generalis（拉） 全部管理

cura legitima（拉） 法定管理

cura realis（拉） 财产管理

cura specialis（拉） 特定管理

curative admissibility of evidence doctrine 证据可采性矫正原则

curator absentis（拉） 失踪人的财产管理人

curator ad hoc（拉） 特别监护人

curb 遏制

curb exchange 场外交易

curfew 戒严令,戒严

currency 通货

currency arbitrage 套汇

currency circulation 货币流通

currency control 货币管理

currency conversion 外汇汇兑

currency convertibility 货币自由兑换

currency exchange 货币兑换

currency group 货币集团

currency in a disguised form 变相货币

currency indemnity 货币补偿

currency inflation 通货膨胀

currency issue system 货币发行制度

currency liquidity 货币流通性

currency of contract 合同货币

currency of settlement 结算货币

currency option clause 货币选择条款

currency reform 币制改革

currency standards 货币本位制

currency system 币制

currency unit 货币单位

currency value 币值

current 本届,流通的,现行

current account 经常项目

current account balance sheet 流动资产负债表

current capital 流动资本

current constitution 现行宪法

current cost 流动成本

current debt 短期债券,流动负债

current decrees 现行法令

current domestic value 现行国内价值

current input 经常性投入

current interest 通行利息

current investment 流动投资

current law(s) 现行法律

current liabilities 短期债券,流动负债

current market price 当时市场价格,现时市场价格

current money 通用货币

current operations 经常性业务

current policy 现行政策

current price 时价,现价,市价

current sale 现时买卖

current standard 现行标准

current term 本届

current trend of jurisprudence 当代法学动向

current year 本年度

currently effective 现行有效

currently in effect 现行

curtail, disenfranchisement 剥夺（某人的）特权

curtain provisions 隐蔽条款

curve of criminal life 犯罪生活曲线

custodia legis（拉） 合法拘押

custodial officer 管教人员

custodial warrant 拘押证

custodian 代管人

custodian of constitution 宪法的守卫者

custodian of property 财产管理

人

custodian trustee　保管受托人

custody　关押

custody dispute　监护争执

custody house（日）拘置监

custody of goods　货物保管

custom　惯例，习惯

custom law　习惯法

custom valuation system　海员估价制度

custom(s) and usage(s)　惯例

criminal finalization　犯罪定型

customary form　惯用格式

customary freight unit　习惯运费单位

customary international law　习惯国际法

customary packing　习惯包装

customary practice　习惯做法

customary price　习惯价格

customary right　习惯权利

customary rule　惯例规则

customary tare　习惯皮重

customer　买方,顾客,客户

customer agent　顾客代理人

customhouse　海关

customhouse personnel　海关工作人员

customs　海关

customs act　海关法

customs administration act　海关行政法,海关行政管理

customs administrative organization　海关行政管理机关

customs agent　报关经纪人

customs area　关境（关税地位）

customs bonding　海关保税

customs border　海关边境

customs broker　报关行

customs certificate　海关证明书

customs charges　关税费用

customs classification　关税分类

customs clearing charges　报关费

customs code　海关法

customs confiscation　海关没收

customs convention　关税专约

customs　cooperation　council

① nomenclature　关税合作理事

② 会税则目录

③ customs court　海关法庭

④ customs declaration　海关报关

⑤ customs declaration bill of entry

⑥ 报关单

⑦ customs declaration for imports

⑧ and exports　进出口货物报关

⑨ 单

⑩ customs detention　海关扣留

⑪ customs drawback　海关退税

⑫ customs duties/tariff　关税

⑬ customs duty　税则

⑭ customs duty rate　税则税率

⑮ customs entry　海关登记

⑯ customs entry/registration　海关

⑰ 登记

⑱ customs examination　海关报关

⑲ customs examination list　海关验

⑳ 货单

㉑ customs files　海关备案

㉒ customs fine　海关罚款

㉓ customs formality　海关手续

㉔ customs franchise　关税豁免

㉕ customs fraud　海关欺诈罪

㉖ customs frontier　关税国境

㉗ customs guarantee system　海关

㉘ 担保制度

㉙ customs head office　海关总署

㉚ customs import tariff　海关进口

㉛ 税则

㉜ customs inspection　海关检验,海

㉝ 关检查

㉞ customs law　海关法

㉟ customs norms　海关准则

㊱ customs of the port　港口惯例

㊲ customs of the sea　海事惯例

㊳ customs office of the People's Republic of China　中华人民共

㊴ 和国海关

㊵ customs officer　海关工作人员,

㊶ 海关人员

㊸ customs pass　海关通行证

㊹ customs permit　海关许可证明

㊺ 书

㊻ customs police　海关警察

㊼ customs police station　海关派出

所

customs procedures　海关手续

customs quarantine control　海关检疫

customs reconsideration　海关复议

customs record　海关备案

customs registration　海关登记

customs returns　海关报表,关税收入

customs review　海关复议

customs rules　海关规章

customs sanction　海关处罚

customs supervision　海关监督

customs tariff　关税税则,海关税则,关税率

customs territories　关税领土

customs treaty　关税条约

customs union　关税同盟

customs valuation　海关估价,海员估价

customs value　海关价格

① cut　创口
② cut apart　分割
③ cut down　压缩
④ cut down expenses　压缩开支
⑤ cut down forest　砍伐林木
⑥ cut of the buyers　买方行为
⑦ cut oneself off from the outside
⑧ world　闭关自守
⑨ cut out　删除
⑩ cutting and shearing mark　剪切
⑪ 工具痕迹
⑫ cutting down and regeneration of
⑬ forest　森林的采伐更新
⑭ cutting license　采伐许可证
⑮ cut-throat　凶手
⑯ cut-throat competition　恶性竞
⑰ 争,致命竞争
⑱ CY to CFS　场到站
⑲ CY to CY　场到场
⑳ CY to door　场到门
㉑ cycle check　定期检查
㉒

D

dacoity with murder 抢劫谋杀
dactyloscopy 以指纹认明罪犯
DAF 边境交货
daily book(s) 日记账
daily price limit 日价限幅
Dali Court 大理院
Dali Temple 大理寺
damage 间接损害,损失,损毁
damage by water 水损
damage caused by crime 犯罪损失
damage caused by sweating or heating 受潮受热险
damage detention 延期损失
damage for detention 迟延损失赔偿
damage in transit 运途损耗
damage of international environment 国际环境损害
damage of non-property 非财产损害
damage of property 财产损失
damage survey 残损鉴定
damage to property 财物损失
damaged by heat and sweat 因受热受潮而损坏
damaged cargo 受损货物
damaged cargo list 受损货单
damaged cargo report 受损货物报告
damaged goods 损坏货物
damaged party 受害人
damages 损害赔偿,损失赔偿金,赔偿金,赔偿费
damages caused by the seller's fault 因出卖人过错所致违约损害赔偿
damages compensation 损害赔偿
damages for collision 船舶碰撞损害赔偿
damages for delay 延迟
damages for prospective loss 丧失预期的利益损害赔偿
damni infecti cautio(拉) 损害担保
damnification 损害
damnify 损害
damnum (拉) 损失
damnum culposum(拉) 因过失而产生的损害
damnum fatale (拉) 非人力所能预料或防止的损害
damnum hecessanium (拉) 避免不了的损害
damnum in mora (拉) 因延误产生的损害
damnum positivum(拉) 积极的损害,直接损害
damnum remotum (拉) 间接损害
danger 危险物
danger mark 危险标志
danger signal 危险信号
dangerous act 危害行为
dangerous and bad tendency 危险和恶劣的倾向
dangerous articles 危险物品
dangerous building 危房
dangerous cargo 危险货物
dangerous cargo clause 危险货物条款
dangerous driving 危险驾驶
dangerous drugs 危险药品
dangerous goods 危险货物
dangerous goods (things) 危险物品
dangerous machinery 危险机器
dangerous mark 危险品标志
dangerous object 危险物
dangerous period for commission of crime 犯罪危险期
dangerous substance 危险物品
dangerous weapon 危险武器,凶器
dangerousness 危险性

data of survey　检验日期

data of tax payment　纳税资料

date　期日

date due　到期日

date forward　预签日期

date from　追溯

date of arrival　到达日期

date of birth　出生时间,出生日期

date of complain　起诉日

date of contract　合同签订日期

date of contract service　合同送达日期

date of crime　犯罪之日

date of discharge　卸货日期

date of draft　出票日期,出票日

date of expiration　期满日

date of expiration of the obligation　债务到期日

date of grant　授予日期

date of landing　卸岸日期,卸货日期

date of loading　装船日期

date of mailing　邮戳日,邮寄日

date of mailing indicated by the postmark　邮戳日

date of manufacture　出厂日期

date of maturity　(支票、汇票)兑现日期

date of payment　付款日期

date of performance　履行日期

date of posting　邮寄日期

date of presentation　提出日期

date of production　出厂日期

date of registration　登记日期

date of service　送达日期

date of shipment　装运日期,装船日期

date of signature of the contract　合同签订日期

date of signing　签订日期

date of taking delivery　提货日期

date of the filing of the suit　起诉之日

date of transhipment　转运日期

date-telex　数据电文

① datio in solutum（拉）　代物清偿

② day dismissed from criminal service　刑事能力

④ day in court　出庭日

⑤ day of due date　满期日

⑥ day of maturity　满期日,到期日

⑦ day trade order　当日成交指令

⑧ days in transit　在途天数

⑨ days of grace　优惠期

⑩ DB　易货,约定不受拘束方式,邮电部,有担保的债权

⑫ DDP　完税后交货

⑬ DDU　未完税交货

⑭ de bonis asportatis（拉）　侵占的财产

⑯ de bonis propriis（拉）　自己负责赔偿

⑱ de facto（拉）　事实上

⑲ de facto blockade　事实上的封锁

㉑ de facto recognition　事实上的承认

㉓ de facto war　事实上的战争

㉔ De Gaule Constitution　戴高乐宪法

㉖ de homine replegiando（拉）　保释令,释放令

㉗ de jure（拉）　按照法律

㉘ de jure bankruptcy　法律上的破产

㉛ de jure corporation　依法设立

㉜ de jure domestic government　合法的本国政府

㉞ de jure government　法律上承认的政府

㊱ de jure recognition　法律上的承认

㊳ de novo（拉）　重审

㊴ de novo trial（拉）　重新审理

㊵ deacon　欺骗

㊶ dead body　尸体

㊷ dead mortgage　固定抵押品

㊸ dead rent　固定租金

㊹ dead security　固定担保物,固定抵押品

㊻ dead time　停工期间

㊼ dead weight cargo　超重货物

dead-birth 死产

deadline 最迟期限

deadline for demanding compensation 索赔期限

deadline for filing 申报所得税截止期

deadline for performance 履行期限

deadly force 致命暴力

deadweight capacity/DW 载重能力,载重量

deadweight tonnage/DWT 载重吨位

deal 交易,处理

deal in 经营

deal with 处理,处置

deal with a legal case 办案

deal with leniently 从轻处罚

dealer 证券自营商,经销商,交易商

dealer's license 经销商执照

dealing in securities 证券交易

dealing risks 交易风险

dealing without licence 无照经营罪

dealings in foreign notes and coins 外币交易

dean money 高利贷

dean of the arches 家教法院法官

dear money policy 银根紧缩政策

dearness allowance 物价津贴

death 死亡

death benefit 死亡抚恤费

death by hanging 缢死

death by misadventure 意外事故致死

death chair 电椅

death chamber 罪犯处决案

death from violence 暴力死亡

death gratuities 死亡抚恤费

death insurance 死亡保险

death of a citizen 公民死亡

death of the decedent 被继承人死亡

death rate 死亡率

death sentence 死刑判决

death sentence with a reprieve 死刑缓期执行

death sentence with a two-year reprieve 死刑缓期两年执行

death tax 遗产税

death verification of a criminal 罪犯死之鉴定

debate 辩论

debenture capital 债券本金

debenture capital 债券股本,债券本金

debenture certificate 债券

debenture certificate of indebtedness 债券

debenture holder 债券持有人

debenture issue 债券发行

debenture share 债券股

debet (拉) 债务

Debet quis juri subjacere ubi delinguit (拉) 每一个人都应当受其违反法律的地方的法律的约束

debit and credit guarantee, loan guarantee 借贷担保

debit redemption arrangement 偿债安排

debita (拉) 债务

debita passiva (拉) 应实际支付的债务

debition 债务关系

debitor (拉) 债务人

debitor assignatus (拉) 被指定的债务人

debitor chirographarius (拉) 契约债务

debitor hypothecahius (拉) 抵押债务者

debitor in solidum (拉) 连带债务人

debitor usurarius (拉) 利息债务法

debitum certum (拉) 确定债务

debitum exigibile (拉) 可要求清偿的债务

debitum illiquidum (拉) 不明确的债务

debitum incentum（拉） 不确定债务

debitum inexigibile（拉） 不可要求清偿的债务

debitum legis（拉） 合法债务

debitum liquidum（拉） 明确的债务

debitum naturae（拉） 自然债务

debitum proprium（拉） 自己的债务

deblocking of funds 资金冻结

debt 债务,债,欠款,欠债

debt capacity 借债能力

debt cciling 债务限额

debt collector 收债人

debt discount 债务折价

debt limit 债务限度,债务限额

debt management 债务管理

debt not provable in bankruptcy 不可确认的破产债务

debt of honor 信用借款,信用借款

debt ratio 债务率

debt relief 债务免除

debt secured 受担保债权

debt secured by mortgage 抵押担保债务

debt service 偿债,返本付息

debt servicing ratio（DSR） 偿债率

debtee 债权人

debtor 债务人,欠债人

debtor state 债务国

debtor's bankruptcy petition 债务人破产申请书

debtor-creditor agreement 债务人—债权人协议

debt-paying ability 偿债能力

debt-service obligation 债务偿付义务

decadent 腐朽

decasualization of labour 稳定就业政策

decedent 被继承人

decedent's last place of residence 死亡时住所地

(to) decide on questions of war and peace 决定战争与和平问题

deceit 诈欺,契纸,欺骗行为

deceition 诈欺

deceive 诈欺,欺骗,契纸

deceive as to intention 有意欺骗

deceiving propaganda 欺骗宣传

decentralism 地方分权

decentralization 地方分权,分权制,地方分权政策

decentralization of power 分权

decentralized company 分散经营的公司

decentralized management 分层管理,分权管理

deceptio（拉） 契纸

deception 欺骗,诈欺

deception as to intention 有意欺骗

deceptive business practices 不正当交易罪

deceptive mark 欺骗性标记

decern（苏格兰） 判决

decide 裁决,判定,判断,判决

decide according to law 依法处理

decide against sb. 判决某人败诉

decide by vote 表决

decide ex aequo et bono 依公平合理原则处理

decide in favor of sb 判决某人胜诉

decide jointly 共同决定

decide on the choice of 决定人选

decide on the nature of the guilt 论罪

decide that the contract is void 判决宣告合同无效

decide the issue of fact 判定事实争议

deciding factor 决定因素

decision 决议,裁定

decision by majority 过半数的表决,多数表决

decision in a case 定案

decision of a review 复审决定

decision of administrative penalties 行政处罚的决定

decision of administrative penalty 行政处罚决定

decision of administrative review 行政复议决定

decision of audit 审计决定,审计决定书

decision of bankruptcy 破产裁定

decision of compelling a drug addict to abandon one's habits 强制戒毒决定

decision of death sentence 死刑裁判

decision of majority 多数决定

decision of reconsideration 复议决定

decision on a fine 罚款决定

decision on reaffirmation 重新认定决定

decision-making power 自主权

decision-making power in operation 经营管理决策权

decision-making power in operation and management 经营管理自主权

decision-making power of enterprises 企业自主权

declarant 供人,报关人

declaration 宣言,供述

declaration by the government of the People's Republic of China on the territorial seas 中华人民共和国关于领海的声明

declaration concerning right 关于权利的声明

declaration for payment of tax 纳税申报

declaration form 申报表

declaration in course of duty 履行责任过程中的声明

declaration of adjudication 判决公告

declaration of avoidance 宣告无效

declaration of death 宣告死亡,死亡宣告

declaration of disappearance 宣告失踪

declaration of disappearance and death 失踪和死亡宣告

declaration of inability to pay 宣告无力偿债

declaration of invalidity 宣告无效

declaration of legal principles governing the activities of state in the exploration and use of outer space 外空法律原则宣言

declaration of independence 独立宣言(美)

declaration of missing people 失踪宣告

declaration of missing person 宣告失踪

declaration of one's death 撤销死亡宣告

declaration of origin form DA59 产地证明书 DA59 格式

declaration of right 权利宣告

declaration of the rights of man and of the citizen 人权宣言(法)

declaration of trust 信托声明书

declaration of will 意思表示

declaration on permanent sovereignty over natural resources 关于天然资源之永久主权宣言

declaration on principle of international law concerning friendly relations and cooperation among state in accordance with the charter of the U.N 国际法原则宣言

declaration on social progress and development 社会进步和发展宣言

declaration on the establishment of a new international economic order 建立新的国际经济秩序宣言

declaration on the granting of independence to colonial countries and peoples 给予殖民地国家和人民独立宣言

declaration on the human environment 人类环境宣言

declaration on the inadmissibility of intervention in the domestic Affairs of States and the protection of their independence and sovereignty 关于各国内政不容干涉及独立与主权之保护宣言

declaration war 宣战

declaratory statute (美) 解释性法规

declaratory theory 宣告说

declare 陈述

declare bankrupt 宣告破产

declare contract avoided 宣告合同无效,宣布合同无效

declare off 取消

declare oneself to be incompetent 自称无权

declare sb guilty 定罪

declare sth null 宣告无效

declassified document 解密文件

decline 下降

decline and fall 衰亡

decline in economic usefulness 经济效用的降低

declining industrial region 衰落中的工业区

declusion of jealousy 嫉妒妄想

deconcentration 分散权力

decontamination treatment 卫生处理

decree 处分,裁决

decree absolute (英) 判决分居令

decree in effect 现行法令

decree of general mobilization 总动员令

decree of special pardon 特赦令

decree punishment 判处刑罚

decrees and regulation 典章

decrepit house 年久失修的房子

① decretalists 教会法学家

② decretists 教会法学派

③ decretum alienandi (拉) 处分的

④ 许可

⑤ decretum de solvendo (拉) 被监

⑥ 护人支付金钱的许可

⑦ decriminalization 非犯罪化

⑧ dedicate 为建筑物举行落成仪

⑨ 式

⑩ deductable 可减税款,免赔额

⑪ (率)

⑫ deductable tax 可扣除的税额

⑬ deductible allowance 免税项目

⑭ deductible loss 可减损失

⑮ deduction 推论;扣扣,扣除

⑯ deductions and exemptions 减

⑰ 免,扣除

⑱ deductions made by the collective

⑲ 集体提

⑳ deductive value 倒扣价格

㉑ deed 依式契约,据契,契

㉒ deed mortgage on real estate 不

㉓ 动产抵押契据

㉔ deed of agreement 协议契据

㉕ deed of appropriation 使用权证

㉖ 明书

㉗ deed of arrangement 债务人与

㉘ 债权人的扣解文据,和解契据

㉙ deed of assignment 转让契,物

㉚ 业转让契据,业权转让契据

㉛ deed of covenant 契据,约据

㉜ deed of gift 赠与契据

㉝ deed of grant 财产转让契据

㉞ deed of mortgage 抵押契据

㉟ deed of mutual covenant 相互契

㊱ 据文件,公契

㊲ deed of partnership 合伙契约

㊳ deed of purchase 买契

㊴ deed of security 担保书,保证书

㊵ deed of settlement 协议契据

㊶ deed of transfer 转让契据

㊷ deed of trust 信托契约

㊸ deed of variation (英) 变更契约

㊹ deed poll 单边契据,单方执行

㊺ 的契约

㊻ deed simply 单纯契据

㊼ deed tax 契税

deed tax on pawn 典契税
deed tax on sales 买卖契税
deed to a gift 赠与书据,赠予书证
deeds of arrangement act 协议契据法例
deeds registration 契据登记
deep-rooted bad habits 劣根性
deep-sea fisheries 远洋渔业
deep-sea fishing 远洋渔业
defacement 损毁
defacement of public property 毁坏公共财产
defamation of personality 毁损人格
defame 诽谤
default 不履行义务,不履行债务,违约状令,拖欠,不到案,不履行
default clause 违约条款
default fine 违约罚金
default judgment 缺席判决
default of appearance 不到案,不出庭
default of creditor 债权人违约
default of heir 无人继承
default of payment 拒绝付款
default tax 欠税
defaulter 不出庭者
defaulter of tax 欠税人
defaulting debtor 违约债务人
defeat lawsuit 败诉案件
defeat suit 败诉案件
defeated suitor 败诉人
defect 瑕疵
defect of declaration 意思表示瑕疵
defect of form 外形瑕疵,形式瑕疵
defect of reason 缺乏理性
defect of substance 实质性的瑕疵,实质缺陷
defect of thing 物的瑕疵
defective 有瑕疵的,有缺陷的人
defective equipment 有瑕疵的设备

defective goods 有瑕疵的货物
defective packing 有缺点的包装
defective products 有瑕疵的产品
defects liability 缺陷责任
defectus(拉) 瑕疵
defend 辩护,维护
defend a case in court 出庭辩护
defend aggression 抵抗侵略
defend oneself 答辩
defend state sovereignty 维护国家主权
defendant 被告
defendant(of a civil, administrative, or criminal case) 被告,被告人
defendant case 被告的证据和争论
defendant in a civil action 民事被告
defendant in administrative proceedings 行政诉讼被告
defendant's agent 被告代理人
defendant's right 被告的权利
defendant's right to final statement(at trial) 被告人的最后陈述权
defendant's seat 被告席
defender 辩护人
defender(in scotch or canon law) 被告,被告人
defense 辩护理由,被告方
defense 防卫
defense argument 辩护论点
defense attorney 被告辩护人,被告律师,辩护律师
defense certificate 辩护证书
defense costs 辩护费用
defense ground 辩护理由
defense in court 出庭辩护
defense ministry 国防部
defense of the accused 被告人辩解
defense to civil charges 民事检控的答辩
defense witness 辩护方证人,被告证人

defense work　辩护工作
defensive act　防卫行为
defensive evidence　防御证据,辩护据
defer　期日延展
defer delivery　推迟交货
defer repayment　拖欠
defer shipment　延期装运
deferral of date　期日延展
deferral of sentence　判决延期
deferred annuity　递延年金
deferred debt　延迟债务
deferred duty　备用税率
deferred ordinance　搁置的条例
deferred payment　延期付款,延付,延迟付款
deferred payment of litigious costs　缓交诉讼费用
deferred payment sale　延期付款销售
deferred repairs　延期修理
deferred sentence　判决延期
deferred signature　延期签字
defiance　藐视,违抗
defiance of law　藐视法律
deficiency guarantee　不足额担保
deficiency in weight　重量不足
deficiency judgement　不足额判决
deficit　逆差
deficit budget, red letter budget　赤字预算
deficit financing　赤字财政
deficit of government budget　政府预算赤字
deficit spending　赤字支出
define　给…下定义
definite　确切,明确
definite advice　确切通知
definite remuneration　一定报酬
definite term　特定期限
definite undertaking　明确承诺,确定承诺
definition by example　例示定义
definition clause　定义条款
definition of terms　条文的阐释

① definition(s) of law　法的定义
② definitive bond　正式债券
③ definitive sentence　服刑期特定
④ 的判决
⑤ deflation　通货紧缩
⑥ deforcement　非法占有他人土地
⑦ deforestation　砍伐林木
⑧ deformation　变形,残废状态
⑨ deformed　残疾的
⑩ deformity　残疾
⑪ defraud　欺骗
⑫ defraud money and property　诈
⑬ 取财物
⑭ defrauding　骗取钱财
⑮ defray　扣除
⑯ defunct company　停业公司
⑰ defy　违抗
⑱ degenerate　腐朽,腐败,腐化
⑲ degree of damage　损失程度
⑳ degree of public surveillance　管
㉑ 制程度
㉒ degree of safety　安全度
㉓ degree of secrets　密级
㉔ del credere agency（拉）附保证
㉕ 的代理
㉖ delate　告发
㉗ delation　弹劾
㉘ delator　告发人
㉙ delay　推迟,延缓,延搁,延滞
㉚ delay clause　迟延条款
㉛ delay exclusion　延迟损失除外
㉜ delay in arrival　迟延到达
㉝ delay in delivery　迟延交付,延迟交货,误期交货
㉞ delay in paying rent　延付租金
㉟ delay in payment　延期支付,推迟付款,付款迟延,延期付款
㊱ delay in performance　延迟履行,给付迟延
㊲ delay in the delivery of cargo　交货迟延
㊳ delay in the execution of judgment　判决迟延执行
㊴ delay interest　延迟利息
㊵ delay of goods　货物交付延误
㊶ delay of performance　迟延履行,迟延

delay of time limit　期日耽误

delay one's work　误工

delay performance　延期履行

delay repayment　延期归还

delay shipment　迟延装运,延期装运

delay the delivery　延期交货

delay the taking delivery of the goods　迟延提货

delay time　延期时间

delayed delivery contract　延交合同

delayed payment　延期付款

delayed recognition　迟缓承认

delayed shipment　迟延装运

delegacy　代表权

delegalize　使失去法律效力

delegate　代表,委托

delegate power to the lower level　权利下放

delegate without the right to vote　列席代表

delegated authority　代理权限

delegated legislation　授权立法,授权制定法,委任立法

delegated power(s)　授予权力,委托权

delegated unit　被授权单位

delegatio（拉）　职权的委任,委托

delegatio debiti（拉）　债务的转付

delegatio nominis（拉）　债务的转付

delegation　代表团

delegation of authority　权力移交,权力委任,授权

delegation of power　权力委任

delegation of power to lower levels　权力下放

delegation to the National People's Congress　全国人民代表大会代表团

delegatus non potest delegare（拉）　代理人无权委托他人代理,代理人未经认可无权委托他人代理,代理人不能委托代理

delete　取消

delete and change　删改

deliberate　审议

deliberate intention　故意

deliberately break　明知故犯

deliberately break the law　知法犯法

deliberation　审议

deliberation in camera　秘密审议

deliberative institution　议事机构

deliberative power　审议权

delict　轻罪,不法行为,违法行为,侵权行为,犯法行为

delictual　不法的

delictual damage　侵权性损害

delictual liability　不法行为的责任

delictual responsibility　不法行为责任

delictum（拉）　侵权行为

delictum publicum（拉）　公犯

delimitation　划界

delimitation of continental shelf　大陆架划界

delineation of power　权限划分

delinquency　罪错,未成年人犯罪,实施犯罪

delinquent　违法者,违法青少年,罪犯

delinquent child　犯罪少年

delinquent juvenile　失足青年

delinquent party　违约当事人

delinquent personality disorder　悖德型人格障碍

deliver at the wrong time　误期交货

deliver the goods　交付货物

deliver the goods in advance　提前交货

deliver the goods in time　如期交货

deliver up　让与

delivered　已经交付的

delivered at frontier　边境交货

delivered duty paid　卫生处理

delivered duty paid 完税后交货,增值税未付

delivered duty unpaid 未完税交货

delivered price 到货价格

deliverer 交保者,交付人

delivery 即期交货,交付(票据),交货

delivery advice 到货通知书

delivery as per buyer's or seller's sample 凭买卖方样品交货

delivery at discharging port 卸货港交货

delivery bond 交付保证

delivery by installment 分期给付

delivery in installment 分期交货

delivery month 交割月

delivery note 提货单

delivery of goods 货物交付,交付货物

delivery of goods by installment partial delivering 分批交货

delivery of offender 引渡罪犯

delivery of security transaction 证券经纪交割

delivery of the object 标的物交付

delivery on arrival 货到交付

delivery on call 通知交货

delivery on field 就地交货

delivery on spot 即期交货,现场交货

delivery on term 定期交货

delivery order 交货证明书,交货单,提货单

delivery points 交货地点

delivery price 交割价格,到货价

delivery receipt 送货回执

delivery risk 交割风险

delivery survey 交船检验,接船检验

delivery time 交割期

deliveryman 送货人

delta of the fingerprint 指纹三角

delusion of love 钟情妄想

delusion of persecution 受害妄想,被害妄想

delusion of sin 罪恶妄想

delusional perception 妄想性知觉

demand a lower price 压价

demand back 追缴

demand bill 即期汇票

demand compensation for loss 要求赔偿损失

demand draft 票汇

demand draft rate(D/D rate) 票汇汇率

demand exceeds supply 求过于供

demand for money 货币需求

demand for payment 要求付款

demand for performance 履行催告

demand for reimbursement 索赔

demand for restitution 要求赔偿

demand loan 活期放款

demand of proof 证明要求

demand of view 被告要求查验

demand performance 催告履行义务

demand price 需求价格

demand promissory note 即期本票

demand the termination of contract 要求解除合同

demanding with menaces 以威吓向人提出要求

demarcation 定界线

demarcation claim 界线纷争

demarcation line 分界线

demarcation of outer space 外层空间的界限

demilitarization of territory 领土非军事化

demise 不动产的转让,遗赠,让与

demise charter 过户租赁合同

demise of the crown 王位让与,君权继承

demise premises 遗赠房产

democracy 民主,民主政体,民主主义,民主政治

democracy and efficiency 民主和效率

democracy and freedom 民主自由

democracy and legislation 民主与法制

democracy in the widest sense 最广泛的民主

democracy within the party 党内民主

democrat 民主人士

democrat without party affiliation 无党派民主人士

democratic 民主,民主的

democratic centralism 民主集中制

democratic constitutionalism 民主宪政

democratic consultation 民主协商

democratic election 民主选举

democratic election of one-man-one-vote 一人一票的民主选举

democratic government 民主政府

democratic law 民主的法律

democratic management 民主管理

democratic party 民主党派

democratic personage 民主人士

democratic personnel 民主人士

democratic politics 民主政治

democratic reforms 民主改革

democratic regime 民主政体

democratic republic state 民主共和国

democratic rights 民主权利,民权

democratic state 民主国家

democratic supervision 民主监督

democratic system 民主制度

democratic united front 民主统一战线

democratism 民主主义

democratization 民主化

democratize 使民主化

demokratia (希腊文) 民主

demolish 摧毁,拆毁

demolition 拆毁,取消

demolition cost 拆迁费用

demolition order (英) 诉毁令

demonstrate 显示

demonstrate repentence 悔罪表现

demonstrate with typical example 典型示范

demonstration 示威,游行示威,示威游行,游行

demonstration quarter 示范小区

demonstrative agency 指定代理

demonstrative evidence 确证

demur 抗辩

demurrage 延滞费,滞期费,延迟费,债券发行价格

demurrage charges 延迟费

demurrage lien 滞期留置权

demurrant 抗辩者

denationalization 非国有化,私有化,剥夺国籍

denial 否定

denial of a motion 驳回请求

denial of facts 否认事实

denial of justice 执法不公,司法拒绝

denominated in foreign currency 用外币标价

denomination 票面价值,面额

denouncement 退约

denouncing party 退约一方

dental jurisprudence 牙医法学

denudation of forest trees 滥伐森林

denunciation 退约,废约,契约废止

denunciation clause 废弃条款

denuntiatio (拉) 告知

deny 不予受理,不受理,驳回,否认,否定

deny a motion 驳回请求

deny one's guilt 否认罪责

depart 出境

depart from 背离

department 部门

department affiliated to 直属机构

department directly under 直属机构

department for the control of commodity prices 物价管理部门

department in charge 主管部门

department in charge of forcign cconomic cooperation and trade 对外贸易主管部门

department in charge of geology and mineral resources under the State Council (中) 国务院地质矿产主管部门

department of agricultural administration under the State Council (中) 国务院农业行政主管部门

department of commerce (DOC) 商务部

department of farming and animal husbandry 农牧业部门

department of farming and animal husbandry under the State Council 国务院农牧业部门

department of fishery administration 渔业行政主管部门

department of fishery administration under the State Council (中) 国务院渔业行政主管部门

department of international law 国际法部门

department of justice 律政司署

department of law 部门法

department of light industry (中) 轻工业部

department of petroleum industry 石油工业部

department of public works 公共工程部门

department of State Council 国务院政府部门

department of wildlife administration 野生动物行政主管部门

department protectionism 部门保护主义

department store of financial institution (美) 信托公司

departmental administrative code 部门行政法典

departmental discipline action 内部纪律处分

departmental discipline measure 内部纪律处分

departments of economy 经济部门

departure card 离境证

departure registration 出境登记

depenalization 非刑

depend on 依靠,凭借

dependability 可靠性

dependent 受抚养人

dependent agent 代理人

dependent claims 从属权利要求

dependent contract 附属合同

dependent guarantee 非独立保证

dependent personality disorder 依赖性人格障碍

dependent state 附属国

dependents of convicts 罪犯家属

depending on the circumstances on the needs of the situation 视情况需要

deport 遣送出境,驱逐出境

deportation 驱逐出境,遣送出境

deporting 驱逐出境

deposal 免职

depose 废黜

deposed from office 免职,开除公职

deposed monarch 废位君主,被废黜君主

deposed sovereign 被废黜君主

deposit 保证金,押金,定金,寄存,寄托

deposit account 存款账户
deposit at bank 银行存款
deposit bank 存款银行
deposit book 存折
deposit box 保险箱
deposit expenses 提存费用
deposit for security 保证金
deposit in foreign currency 外币存款
deposit in security 保证金,押金
deposit in trust 信托存款
deposit insurance system 存款保险制度
deposit money 随时可兑现的支票或信用证等,押金
deposit object 提存物品
deposit of ratification 交换批准书
deposit of securities 证券存款
deposit of title deeds 所有权契据存放
deposit premium 预付保险费
deposit reserves policy 存款准备金政策
deposit security 押金
deposit slip 存款单
deposit withdrawals 取款
deposita（拉）押金,寄存物
depositarius（拉）受寄人
depositary 受托人
depositary of territory 土地沉积
depositary of treaty 条约的保管
depositio debiti（拉）债务免除
deposition 宣誓作证,供状,笔录证言,听证,证人证言笔录
deposition（by witness）证据保全
deposition of a king 废黜国王
deposition procedure 证据保全的程序
deposit-loan ratio 存放比率
depository testimony 笔录证言
depositum（拉）寄托物,寄托
depositum irregule（拉）代替物寄托
depraved heart murder 极端轻率谋杀罪

depraved person 腐化分子
depravity of heart murder 极端轻率谋杀罪
depreciable assets 折旧资产
depreciation 折旧,贬值
depreciation allowance 折旧扣除额
depreciation credit 折旧优惠
depreciation fund 折旧费
depreciation of an investment 投资贬值
depreciation of the currency 货币贬值
depression 经济衰退
depression of international price 压缩国际价格
depressive insanity 抑郁性精神病
deprival 剥夺
deprival of rights 剥夺权利
deprivation 剥夺,剥夺行为
deprivation of freedom 剥夺自由权
deprivation of military rank 剥夺军衔
deprivation of nationality 丧失国籍,剥夺国籍
deprivation of personal liberty 剥夺人身自由
deprivation of political credits 剥夺政治荣誉
deprivation of political rights 剥夺政治权力
deprivation of political rights for life 剥夺政治权力终身
deprivation of right to act as administrative punishment 剥夺人身权的行政处罚
deprive 褫夺,剥夺
deprive sb of political rights 剥夺政治权力
deprive sb of political rights for life 剥夺政治权力终身
deputation 代表团
deputies to succeeding people's congress 下届人大代表
deputy 代表,代理人

deputy administrator 审计署副署长

deputy auditor-general 副审计长

deputy chief judge 副庭长

deputy chief procurator 副检察长

deputy commissioner 副局长

deputy county magistrate 副县长

deputy director 副主任,副局长

deputy director-general 副司长,副厅长,副局长

deputy governor of a province 副省长

deputy head 副职负责人

deputy head of district 副区长

deputy judge 副审判员

deputy mayor 副市长

deputy presiding judge 副庭长

deputy procurator general 副检察长

deputy provincial governor 副省长

deputy secretary of the State Council 国务院副秘书长

deputy secretary-general 副秘书长

deputy sector chief 副科长

deputy sheriff 副警长

deputy to the National People's Congress 全国人民代表大会代表

deputy to the people's congress [中]人民代表大会代表

deputy township head 副镇长

DEQ (delivered ex quay) 目的港码头交货

derelict 遗弃物

dereliction of duty 渎职,失职

dereliction of territory 领土的放弃

derivation 转承

derivative acquisition 继受取得,派生取得,转承取得

derivative action 派生诉讼

derivative deed 派生契约

① derivative demand 派生需求

② derivative suit 派生诉讼

③ derived liability 派生的责任

④ derogate 限制,废除

⑤ derogate from 违反

⑥ descend 下降

⑦ descendants who inherit in subrogation 代位继承人

⑨ describe 说明

⑩ description 说明书,货名

⑪ description clause 说明条款

⑫ description of goods 货物分类目录,货物品名,货名

⑭ descriptive constitution of a crime 叙述犯罪构成

⑯ desegregation 取消种族隔离

⑰ desert 不毛之地

⑱ deserted 被遗弃的

⑲ desertion 擅离职守罪

⑳ deserved punishment 罪有应得的惩罚

㉒ design fees 设计费

㉓ designate a representative 指定代表人

㉕ designated bounded area 指定保税区

㉗ designated guardian 指定监护人

㉙ designated price 计划价格

㉚ designation 任命

designed output 计划产量

㉜ desirable family residence 称心的家居寓所

㉞ desistance of crime 犯罪中止

㉟ desk to desk service 桌对桌服务 (注:指航空急件传送)

㊲ despatch(money) 速遣与速遣费

㊳ despot 暴君

㊴ despotic 专制

㊵ despotic political system 暴君政治

㊷ despotic rule 暴政

㊸ despotic state 专制国家

㊹ despotism 专制主义

㊺ dessein 故意

㊻ destabilize the market 扰乱市场

㊼ destabilizing factors 不安定因素

destination contracts（美）目的地合同

destroy 破坏

destroy sb's property 破坏财产

destroy the ecological environment 破坏生态环境

destruction of public property 毁坏公共财产

DES, delivered exship 目的港船上交货

detach 脱落

detached office 派出机构

detached tribunal 派出法庭

detail characteristics of fingerprints 指纹细节特征

detail estimate sheet 承包工程细目估价单

detail of contract 契约细节

detailed description 详细说明

detailed documentary investigation 逐件检查

detailed documentary search 逐件检查

detailed list of goods 货物清单

detailed provisions 详细条款

detailed regulation 详细条款

detailed regulations on rewards and penalties 奖惩细则

detailed rules and regulations 细则

detailed rules for the implementation 实施办法

details by-laws 细则

details of a case 案情

details of contract 合同细节

detain 延滞,拘留,扣留

detain for interrogation, custodial interrogation 收容审查

detained for further examination 扣留审查

detainee 被拘留人,拘留犯,非法占有

detainee awaiting trial 待决犯

detainer 扣留

detainment 收押,扣留

detect inside prison 狱内侦查

detection of a specified case inside prison 狱内专案侦查

detection of toxic chemical agents 毒剂侦检

detective packing 不良包装

detentation 暂许占有

detente 国际关系的缓和

detentio（拉）暂许占有

detention 收押,扣留,拘留,拘禁

detention by public security organizations 收容

detention center 拘留所

detention during His (Her) Majesty's pleasure 恢复神志期间的拘押

detention evidence 拘留证据

detention for interrogation 收容审查

detention for questioning 拘留查询

detention hearing（美）拘留听审

detention home of juvenile delinquents 青少年犯罪临时拘留所

detention house 拘留所,拘役所,看守所

detention of a ship 扣留船舶

detention request 拘留请求书

detention under demand 判决前的羁押

detention under demand investigative custody 判决前羁押

detention warrant 拘留证

detention with postponement 监候

détenu（拉）被监禁者

deterioration 受损失

determinate sentence 服刑期特定的判决

determinate term for security measures 保安处分定期制

determination of boundary 划定边界

determination of declaration 供述决意

determination of legal responsibili-

ty 法律责任的认定
determination of price 价格决定
determination of punishment 刑罚量定
determination of sex by blood stain 血痕性别检验
determination of terminating an action ruling of abatement of action 裁定终结诉讼
determination to dismiss a prosecution 裁定驳回起诉
determination to dismiss an appeal 裁定驳回上诉
determine 测定,判定,判断
determine power of administrative act 行政行为的确定性
determine the commission of a crime 认定犯罪
determined 确定的
deterrence policy 威慑政策
deterrent 威慑力量
deterrent force 威慑力量
dethrone 废黜
detinue 收回非法占有动产之诉
detriment 损害
detrimental 有害的
devaluate 贬值
devaluation 贬值,货币贬值
devaluation of dollar 美元贬值
develop 发展
develop at top speed 高速发展
develop production 发展生产
develop socialist democracy 发展社会主义民主
developed 发达
developed country 发达国家
developed market economic country 发达的市场经济国家
developing country 发展中国家
developing market economic country 发展中市场经济国家
developing member countries 发展中成员国
development and international economic cooperation 发展和国际经济合作

development bank 开发银行
development capital 开发资金
development expenses 开发经费
development loan 开发性贷款
development of a new product 新产品开发
development of administrative compensation 行政补偿制度的历史发展
development of administrative law 行政法学的历史发展
development of constitution 宪法的发展
development of economic law 经济法的发展
development of high technology 高技术开发
development of law 法的发展
development of natural resources 开发自然资源
development project 开发性项目
development research center under the State Council（中）国务院发展研究中心
development tax 开发税,发展税
development zone for industries using high and new technology 高新技术产业开发区
devest 褫夺
deviate from 背离,违反
deviation clause 绕航条款
deviation form the contract 违反合同
devil's advocate 诡辩律师
devise 土地遗赠,遗赠财产,遗赠
devoid of risk 无风险
devolution 授予权力
devolution agreement 案件移交协定
devolution of administrative power to lower levels 权利下放
dialectical 辩证的
dialectical logic 辩证逻辑
dialectical materialism 辩证唯

物主义

diatio tutoris（拉） 监护人的任命

dictator 独裁者

dictatorship 专政,独裁

dictatorship of bourgeoisie 资产阶级专政

dictatorship of proletariat 无产阶级专政

die of illness 病故

die out 消亡

die without issue dying without issue 死后无嗣

dies certus（拉） 确定期限

dies civilis legalis（拉） 民法上的日期

dies incentus（拉） 不确定期限

dies non（拉） 法庭休庭日

dies non juridicus（拉） 不开庭日

diet 议会

difference 区别,差别,分歧,价差

difference in price and value 价格背离价值

difference in price or value 差价

difference in principle 原则分歧

difference in regional price levels 地区差价

different cost 边际成本

different levels holding different responsibilities 分级管理

different proportional rates in different parts of the country 分地区比例税制

different treatment 差别待遇

differential between purchase and sale prices 购销差价

differential duties 差别关税

differential duty or discriminating duty 差别关税

differential election system 差别选举制

differential measures 区别对待措施

differential quota tax rate 差别定额税率

differential rates of duty 差别关税率

differential salary 差别工资

differential tariff 差别税率,差别税则

differential treatment 差别待遇,区别对待

differential voting 差额选举

differential voting system 差别投票制,差别选举制

differentiate 判别

(to)differentiate two kinds of contradictions 划分两类矛盾

digest 法律汇编

digest of a case 案例摘要

digest of cases 判决要旨

Digesta（拉） 学说汇纂

dignity of courtroom 法庭尊严

dignity of the legal system 法制的尊严

digressive taxation 递减累进税

dilapidated housing 部分破损的住房,危房

dilatio（拉） 延期

dilatio ad excipiendum（拉） 抗辩期间

dilatio conventionalis（拉） 合意的延期

dilatio legalis（拉） 法定日期

dilatio peremptoria（拉） 除权期间,提出证据期间

dilatory motion 延搁提案动议

Dillon Round 狄龙回合

diminished responsibility 减轻责任,限定责任能力

Dionysius 狄奥尼修斯

diploma 毕业文凭,学位证书,毕业证书

diplomacy 外交

diplomat 外交官

diplomatic act 外交行为

diplomatic affairs 外交事务

diplomatic agent（/representative） 外交代表

diplomatic asylum 外交庇护

diplomatic bag 外交邮袋

diplomatic channel 外交途径

diplomatic corps　外交团
diplomatic documents　外交文书
diplomatic envoy　外交使节
diplomatic immunity　外交豁免权
diplomatic institution　外交机关
diplomatic list　外交官衔名录
diplomatic matter　外交事件
diplomatic negotiation　外交谈判
diplomatic officer　外交官
diplomatic passport　外交护照
diplomatic policy　外交政策
diplomatic practice　外交惯例
diplomatic privileges　外交特权
diplomatic protection　外交保护
diplomatic protocol　外交礼节
diplomatic relations　外交关系,外交保护
diplomatic relations law　外交关系法
diplomatic visa　外交签证
direct applicability　直接适用性
direct application　直接适用
direct bill of lading　直达提单
direct business　直接买卖,直接交易
direct cause　直接原因
direct coercive enforcement　直接强制执行
direct collision　直接碰撞
direct consequence of a crime　直接犯罪结果
direct consignment　直接交货,直接运输
direct credit　直接抵免
direct damage　直接损害
direct democracy　直接民主
direct democratic system　直接民主制
direct election　直接选举
direct endorsement　直接背书
direct examination system　直接诘问,直接质证
direct exchange　直接汇兑
direct financing　直接金融
direct infringe, direct infringement　直接侵权

① direct injury　直接伤害
② direct instigator　直接教唆犯
③ direct intent　直接故意
④ direct intention　直接故意
⑤ direct investment　直接投资
⑥ direct L/C　直接信用证
⑦ direct lease　直接租赁
⑧ direct legislation　直接立法
⑨ direct liability　直接责任
⑩ direct loading　直接装运
⑪ direct loans　直接贷款
⑫ direct loss　直接损失
⑬ direct marketing by mail　邮寄销售
⑭
⑮ direct negotiation　直接洽商,直接谈判,直接协商
⑯
⑰ direct object　直接客体
⑱ direct obligation　直接责任
⑲ direct payment　直接付款
⑳ direct planning by the state　计划单列
㉑
㉒ direct price　直接价格
㉓ direct pricing　直接计价
㉔ direct principal offender　直接正犯
㉕
㉖ direct quotation　直接报价,直接标价法
㉗
㉘ direct quotation of exchanges rates　汇率直接标价法
㉙
㉚ direct rate　直接税
㉛ direct reduction mortgage　直接抵减的抵押贷款
㉜
㉝ direct representation　直接代理,狭义代理
㉞
㉟ direct responsibility　直接责任
㊱ direct sale　直接销售
㊲ direct sale clause　直接销售条款
㊳ direct sale price　直接销售价
㊴ direct securities　直接担保品
㊵ direct selling　直接销售
㊶ direct shipment　直接装运,直达货运,直达货场
㊷
㊸ direct solicitation　直接教唆
㊹ direct sth into the orbit of　纳入轨道
㊺
㊻ direct subject　直接主体
㊼ direct subsidies　直接补贴

direct tax　直接税

direct taxes and charges on persons　个人直接捐税

direct television broadcasting by satellites　卫星直接电视广播

direct trade　直接贸易

direct transaction　直接交易

directions for use　使用说明

directly applicable law　可直接适用的法律

directly subordinate agency　直属机构

director of public　检察官

director of public prosecutions　检察长

director's responsibility system　主任负责制

dirty cargo　污染货物

dirty float　受限制的汇率浮动,干预浮动

dirty industry　污染工业

disability　残废状态,残疾

disability benefits　残废利益

disability compensation　残疾赔偿金

disability of action　无行为能力

disability pension　残废抚恤金

disable　丧失能力

disabled　残疾的,丧失能力,丧失劳动能力,丧失行为能力

disabled armyman　残废军人

disabled children　残疾儿童

disabled person　残废者,残疾人

disabled soldier　残废军人

disablement　丧失能力

disablement（disability）insurance　丧失工作能力保险

disadvantages　弊端

disaffirm former judgments　撤销以往判决

disaffirmation　撤销原判,发回重审

disagree with the constitution　抵触宪法

disagreement　不一致

disagreement among the people　人民内部矛盾

disagreement and mistrial　不一致和错误审判

disallow　否决

disarrestable crime　不应逮捕罪

disaster　灾害

disavow　否认,推翻,抵赖

disavowal　抵赖

disband　解散

discern　辨认

discern between right and wrong　分清是非

discernment　辨认

discharge　排放废水,解除,清偿,撤职,开除,卸货,辞退,撤销,清偿债务

discharge a contract　履行合同,解除契约

discharge a court order　撤销法院命令

discharge capacity　排污能力

discharge fee　排污费

discharge from a post　革职

discharge in bankruptcy　破产债务之清偿

discharge licence　排放许可证

discharge of contract　合同的消灭,履行合同,取消合同,解约

discharge of contract by frustration　挫折解除契约

discharge of debt　债务清偿,清偿债务

discharge of debt performance　债的履行

discharge of duties　行使职务

discharge of duty　履行职责

discharge of noxious gases　排放有害气体

discharge of pollutants　排放污染物

discharge of responsibility　免责

discharge of sewage　排放污水

discharge of waste gas　排放废气

discharge of waste water　排放废渣

discharge pay off　偿清

discharge receipt　卸货收据

discharge sb from public employment 开除公职

discharge standard or criterion 排放标准

discharged obligation 已清偿的债务

discharged prisoner 获释犯人

discharging berth 卸货泊位

discharging expenses 卸货费用

discharging port 卸货港口,卸货港

disciplinary 惩罚性,纪律

disciplinary action 纪律处分

disciplinary action within the Party 党内处分

disciplinary authority 惩戒权

disciplinary award 纪律处分

disciplinary decision 惩戒决定

disciplinary doctrine 惩戒主义

disciplinary education 纪律教育

disciplinary law 惩戒法

disciplinary matter 惩戒事项

disciplinary measure 惩戒措施,强制处分,纪律处分

disciplinary procedure 惩戒性程序

disciplinary proceeding 惩戒性程序

disciplinary punishment 纪律处分

disciplinary punishment of public surveillance 管制处分

disciplinary sanction 纪律制裁,行政处分

disciplinary supervision of police 警纪监察

disciplinary treatment 纪律处分

disciplinary warning 警告处分

discipline 纪律,惩戒,处分

discipline inspection 纪律检查

discipline inspection committee 纪律检查委员会

discipline of the Party and the laws of the State 党纪国法

discipline relating to financial affairs 财务纪律

discipline sb as a warning 惩戒

disciplining juvenile deliquents 青少年犯管教

disclaim 权利放弃

disclaim one's right to appeal 放弃上诉权

disclaimer 放弃权利声明,否认者

disclosed defect 发现的瑕疵

disclosure risk 泄露风险

disclosure system of finance 财务公开制度

discontinuance of action limitation 诉讼时效中断

discontinuance of crime 犯罪中止

discontinuation of offense 中止犯

discontinue 停止

discontinue a counter claim 撤销反诉

discontinue an action 撤销诉讼

discontinued criminal 中止犯

discontinued operation 非连续性经营

discontinuing offense 即成犯,即时犯

discount 折扣,贴现

discount and allowances 折让

discount bank 贴现银行

discount broker 票据经纪人

discount for the sale 减价出售

discount from the price 货价折扣

discount granted 给予折扣

discount house 贴现商号

discount interest 贴现利息

discount market 贴现市场

discount of 50% 对折

discount of bills of exchange 汇票贴现

discount on capital stock 股本折价

discount on notes 票据贴现

discount on purchases 购买折扣

discount on stock 股本折价

discount rate 贴现率

discount rate policy 贴现政策

discount received 购货折扣

discountable 可贴现
discounted bills 已贴现票据
discounted cash flow 净现金量
discounted credit 贴现放款,贴现信贷
discoverer 发现人
discovery（美）先悉权
discredit 不信任
discretion 自由裁量,自由裁量权
discretion in administration 行政自由裁量权
discretion of costs 裁定诉费
discretionary act 自由裁量行为
discretionary circumstances of sentencing 酌定量刑情节
discretionary exemption from punishment 酌量免除
discretionary heavier punishment 酌从重
discretionary lesser punishment 酌从轻
discretionary principle 擅断主义
discretionary punishment 酌定刑
discretionary trust 有决定权之信托,随意信托
discriminate 歧视
discriminating duties/tariffs 差别关税
discriminating monopoly 歧视性垄断
discriminating quota tax rate 差别定额税率
discriminating tariff 差别税率,差别税则
discrimination 区别,差别对待
discrimination against women 歧视妇女
discrimination duty 差别税
discrimination treatment 歧视待遇,差别待遇
discriminatory law 歧视性法律
discriminatory legislation 歧视性法规
discriminatory measures 歧视性措施
discriminatory price 歧视性价格
discriminatory procedure 歧视性程序
discriminatory tariff 歧视性关税,差别待遇税则
discriminatory tax 差别税制,歧视性税制
discriminatory treatment 歧视性待遇
discuss 商谈
discuss and come to an agreement 商定
discuss separately 另议
discussion 审议
discussion of a case 案例讨论
discussions at the（crime）scene 临场讨论
disease 病
disease suspected to be quarantinable 疑似检疫传染病
disenfranchise 剥夺选举权
diseretionary power 自由裁量权
disestablishments 政教分离
disfranchisement 剥夺选举权,褫夺公权
disfranchisement of voters 剥夺选举权
disgrace 不名誉
disguised dumping 变相倾销
disguised increase in the prices 变相涨价
disguised price increase 变相涨价
disguised unemployment 变相失业
disguising one's nationality 隐瞒国籍
dishonest 虚假
dishonest conduct 不诚实行为
dishonest possession 恶意占有,不法占有
dishonored notes 拒付票据
dishono(u)r 拒付,奸污
dishonour by non payment 拒绝付款

dishonoured check 空头支票
dishonoured notes 拒付票据
disintegrate 解体
disintegration 解体
disinvestment 减少投资
dislocation of the economy 经济失调
disloyalty 不忠的行为
dismantlement of import tariffs 废除进口关税
dismembered body 碎尸
dismiss 不予受理,不受理,驳回,撤职,革职,辞退,罢免
dismiss a counterclaim 驳回反诉
dismiss a motion 驳回请求
dismiss a private prosecution 驳回自诉
dismiss a suit 驳回诉讼
dismiss an action 驳回诉讼
dismiss an appeal 驳回上诉
dismiss from office 罢黜
dismissal from office 开除公职
dismissal of a lawsuit 诉讼不受理
dismissal of a legal case 案件不受理
dismissal of a motion 驳回请求
dismissal of a suit 驳回诉讼
dismissal of an action 驳回诉讼
dismissal of office 免职
dismissal without prejudice 无偏袒的驳回
disobedience 违抗
disobedient party 违令者
disobey 违抗
disobey orders 违令
disobey orders and defy prohibitions 有令不行,有禁不止
disolution of contract 解约
disorderly conduct 扰乱社会治安行为,不规范行为
disorderly person 危害治安分子
disorganization of social order 社会秩序崩溃
disorganization of society 社会解体
disparity 差别
dispatch 发送,发运
dispatch advice 发货通知
dispatch note 发运单
dispel 祛除
dispensary system 中央配给制度
dispense 施行,免除
dispensing justice 执行法律
dispensing power 赦免权
dispensing with service 免除劳役,免于送达
display 显示
display window 橱窗
disponent owner "二船东"
disposable price 可支配价格
disposal 处理,处分,处置
disposal of assets 资产处置
disposal of ballast water 压舱水处理
disposal of garbage 垃圾处理
disposal of plant and equipment 厂房和设备的处理
disposal of property 处理财产
disposal of uncollected goods 未领取的货物的处理
disposal of waste gas, water and industrial residue 三废治理
dispose 处理,处分,处置
dispose of common property 分配共同财产
dispose of properties 处分财产
disposing capacity 行为能力
disposing capacity of juristic person 法人的行为能力
disposing capacity of legal person 法人的行为能力
disposing capacity of the natural person 自然人的行为能力
disposition 处分,处分权,处置权,处置
disposition handle 处理
disposition notice 处罚通知书
disposition of life time 生前处分
disposition principle 处分原则
dispositive clause 实质条款,(苏

格兰）让步条款

dispositive law 酌定法

dispositive provision 处分条款

dispositive treaty 处分性条约

disproof 反证物

dispute 纠纷、争端

dispute at law 法律争执

dispute concerning ownership of land and the right to the use of land 土地所有权和使用权争议

dispute of labour contract 劳动合同争议

dispute of power 权力争议

dispute on price 价格争议

dispute on the sea 海洋争端

dispute over boundaries of administrative areas 行政区域边界争端

dispute over claims to grassland 草原权属争议

dispute over labour insurance 劳动保险争议

dispute over ownership 所有权争议

dispute over reimbursement of damages from tort against product standard 产品标准侵权损害赔偿纠纷

dispute regarding competency 权限纠纷

dispute settlement body 争端解决机构

disputes about quantity 数量争议

disputes over administrative compensation 行政赔偿争议

disqualification 无资格,取消资格

disqualified product 不合格产品

disqualify a guardian 取消监护资格

disquality 取消资格

disregard law and discipline 目无法纪

disregard of law 不顾法律,违

反法律

disrepute 不名誉

disretionary power 自由裁量权

disrupt 破坏

disrupt public order 破坏社会秩序

disruption 妨害

disruption of civil proceedings 妨害民事诉讼行为

dissensus（拉）解除契约的含意

dissenting vote 反对票

disserting opinion 反对意见（注：指附于判决后的反对意见）

dissident 持不同意见者

dissimilation of world economy 世界经济异质化

dissolution 取消

dissolution by operation of law 依法解散

dissolution of an injunction 取消禁令

dissolution of contract 解除合同

dissolution of parliament 解散议会

dissolution of partnership 合伙解散

dissolution of responsibility 免除责任

dissolution of restitution 免除赔偿

dissolution of treaty 条约的解除

dissolve 解散,宣告无效

dissolve a law firm 撤销律师事务所

dissolve by law 依法撤销,依法解散

dissolving conditions 解除条件

distance freight 超税运费

distance water fishing 远洋捕鱼

distant bullet wound 远射枪弹创伤

distinction 区别,差别

distinctive emblem 特殊标志

distinctive mark 特殊标志

distinctive policy 特殊政策

distinctive sign 特殊记号

distinguish 分清
distinguish among different cases 区别不同情况
distinguish between right and wrong 判明是非
distinguish crime from noncrime 区别罪与非罪
distinguishing a case 区别案件
distinguishment 权利或义务的撤销
distort 曲解
distort the law for one's own purposes 曲解法律以营私利
distorting agricultural market 农产品市场紊乱
distortion of competition 扭曲竞争行为
distortion of fact 歪曲事实
distraint 扣押财物,财产扣押
distress 财产扣押
distress damage feasant 损害赔偿的留置权
distress merchandise 廉价出售的商品
distress selling 扣押物的俏售或拍卖
distressed goods 被扣押物品
distressed property 被扣押的物品,被扣押财产
distribute 分配
distribute land 分配土地
distributing agent 销售代理商
distributing syndicate 包销财团
distribution 分配
distribution in altitude 按高度分布
distribution in area 按面积分配
distribution of power(s) 权力的分配
distribution of profits 利润分配
distribution on the basis of labour 按劳分配
distribution system 分配制度
distributive channel 销货渠道
distributive justice 分配正义
distributor 经销商
distributor discount 经销商折扣

① distributorship agreement 销售协议,经销协议
③ district 区,地区
④ district attorney 地区检察官,检察官
⑥ district bank 地方银行
⑦ district council 地区议会
⑧ district court 地方初审法院
⑨ district court-martial 地区军事法庭
⑪ district government 地区政府
⑫ district head 区长
⑬ district heat supply 城市集中供热
⑮ district heat supply network 城市集中供热管网
⑰ district housing administration bureau 区房管局
⑲ district judge 联邦地区法院法官,地方初审法院法官
㉑ district jurisdiction 地域管辖权
㉒ district office 区公所
㉓ district people's congress 区人民代表大会
㉕ district people's court 区人民法院
㉗ district registries 地区法院办事处
㉙ district system of representation 区域代表制
㉛ distrust 不信任
㉜ disturb 干扰
㉝ disturb the social order 扰乱社会秩序
㉟ disturbance 动乱
㊱ disturbance in the act of will 意志行为障碍
㊳ disturbance of consciousness 意识障碍
㊵ disturbance of declaration 供述障碍
㊷ disturbance of franchise 侵犯公民权,侵犯选举权
㊸ disturbance of right 权利的侵犯
㊹ ditto 同上
㊻ divergence 分歧
㊼ divergence of views 意见分歧

diverse economic forms　多种经济形式
diverse economic sectors　多种经济成分
diverse forms of ownership　多种所有制形式
diverse sectors of the economy　多种经济成分,多种经济
diversified business　多种经济
diversified economy　多种经济
diversify the economy　多种经济
diversion　转运证书
diversion of the victim　被害人的转换
diversion payment law　转移支付法
divesting of a right　丧失权利
divestment of property rights as administrative punishment　剥夺财产权的行政处罚
divide　分配
divide out the costs　补偿诉讼费用
divide property　析产
divide responsibility for their own work, coordinate their efforts and check each other　分工负责,互相配合,互相制约
divide the spoils　分赃
divide their functions, each taking responsibility for its own work, coordinate their efforts and check each other　分工负责,互相配合,互相制约
divided country　分裂国家
divided ownership　分割的所有权
dividend　红利,股息,股票红利
dividend book　股息簿
dividend consideration　报酬
dividend coupon　股息券
dividend on shares　股利,红利
dividend rate　股息率
dividend reserve　股息准备金
dividend stock　股息股,红利股
dividend tax　股息税
dividend yield　股息收益

divine right　君权神授
divine right of kings　王权神授,君权神授
divinity　神学
divisee　被遗赠人
divisible L/C　可分割信用证
division　部门,分配,选举区
division into districts　区划
division of administrative litigation　行政诉讼审判庭
division of an enterprise　企业分立
division of business　营业部
division of common property　分割共同财产
division of constituency　选区划分
division of functions and powers　职权划分
division of labor responsibility system　分工负责制
division of labour　劳动分工
division of labour between party and government　党政分开
division of labour in society　社会分工
division of powers　权力的分配,权力划分
division of sea regions　海域的区划
divisional system　分级服刑制(英)
divisions of constitution　宪法的分类
divisions of the law　法的分类
do evil　为非作歹
do not abide by the law　有法不依
do not drop　切勿摔扔
do one's duty　尽义务
do one's duty, execution of duty　履行义务
do violence　行凶抢劫
dock　被告席,犯人栏
docket　判决摘要,(英)法院积案
doconent transaction　单据交易

doctor 博士

doctor of jurisprudence 法学博士

doctor's degree 博士学位

doctoral dissertation 博士论文

doctoral student 博士生

doctoral thesis 博士论文

doctorate ship 博士学位

doctor-in-charge 主治医师

doctrinaire 教条主义

doctrine 学说

doctrine for the defendant (in consular jurisdiction) 被告主义

doctrine of a legally prescribed punishment for a special crime 罪行法定主义

doctrine of absolute sovereignty 绝对主权论

doctrine of absorption of delict by felony 重刑吸收轻刑(原则)

doctrine of act of state 国家行为说

doctrine of asserting constitution of a crime as the criterion of consummation 既遂构成要件说

doctrine of comprehensive punishment 综合刑论

doctrine of cumulating punishments 天生犯罪人论,并科原则

doctrine of democracy 民主原则

doctrine of discetionale evaluation of evidence 自由心证制度

doctrine of educative punishment 教育刑主义

doctrine of equal litigious rights of the parties 当事人诉讼权平等原则

doctrine of equality 平等主义

doctrine of equality of men and women 男女平等原则

doctrine of equalization 平均主义

doctrine of estoppel 不可反悔的原则

doctrine of exhaustiveness (of administrative remedies) 行政救济穷尽原则

doctrine of extradiction or prosecution 引渡或起诉原则

doctrine of frustration 合同受挫原则,合同落空原则

doctrine of incorporation 合并的学说

doctrine of justiceship 法官的职权主义

doctrine of liability fixation 归责原则

doctrine of liability for wrongs 过错责任原则

doctrine of liberal construction 从宽解释说,从宽解释原则

doctrine of limited government 政府权力有限说

doctrine of national law 本国法主义

doctrine of negligence 过失主义原则

doctrine of non-intervention 不干涉主义

doctrine of non-recognition 不承认主义

doctrine of precedent 先例原则

doctrine of presumptive 过错推定原则

doctrine of primary jurisdiction 初审权原则,基本管辖原则

doctrine of protective punishment 保护刑论

doctrine of public prosecution 公诉主义

doctrine of publicity 公开原则

doctrine of punishment on party 当事人主义

doctrine of reasonableness 合理性法则

doctrine of representative character 代表性说

doctrine of retraction 不溯及主义,不溯既往原则

doctrine of retributive punishment 报应刑主义

doctrine of retroactivity 溯及既往原则

doctrine of severe punishment 重刑主义

doctrine of single nationality 单一国籍原则

doctrine of stare decisis 判例原则,(拉)判例约束主义

doctrine of strict construction 从严解释说

doctrine of supremacy of constitution 宪法至上原则

doctrine of the autonomy of the parties 当事人自治原则

doctrine of the defendant's right to defense 被告人有权获得辩护的原则

doctrine of the presumption of innocence 无罪推定原则

doctrine of the rule of administrative law 行政法治原则

doctrine of time of judgement 裁判时主义

doctrine of visual field 视野说

document 凭证书

document against acceptance 承兑交单

document against payment（D/P）付款交单

document bill 跟单票据

document for carriage 运输单据

document for claims 索赔单据

document of approval 批准文件

document of carriage 运输单据

document of obligation 债权证书

document of ratification 批准文件

document of title 物权证书,所有权凭证

document of title 所有权证

document to land 土地权利证

documental obligation 证券债务

documentary 有凭证,有单据,证书的,文件的,文据的

documentary acceptance 跟单承兑

documentary acceptance bill 跟单承兑汇票

documentary acceptance credit 跟单承兑信用证

documentary bill 跟单汇票

documentary bill for collection 跟单托收

documentary bill of exchange 跟单汇票

documentary collection 跟单托收

documentary credit 押汇信用证

documentary draft 跟单汇票

documentary evidence 书证

documentary L/C 跟单信用证

documentary letter of credit 跟单信用证

documentary materials 档案材料

documentary negotiation 书面谈判

documentary requirements 书面要求

documentation carrying the force of administrative regulation 行政法规性文件

documentation of notes and records 笔录类文书

documents 票据

documents against acceptance 承兑交单

documents against payment 付款交单

documents for claim 索赔证件,索赔单证

documents of administrative standard 行政规范性文件

documents of value 有价证书,有价证券

documents transport customary 习惯运输单据

dodge a creditor 逃债

dog keeper 养犬人

Dogger Bank Incident 多革滩事件

dogma 教义

dogmatist 教条主义

dog-keeping registration　养犬登记

doli capax（拉）有犯罪行为

doli incapax（拉）无犯罪行为，不受处罚

dollar area　美元区

dollar claim　美元债权

dollar exchange　美元外汇

dollar gap　美元短缺

dolus（拉）犯意

dolus antecedens（拉）事前犯意，事前欺诈，事前故意

dolus bonus（拉）合法的欺骗

dolus determiuatus（拉）确定的故意

dolus malus（拉）恶意

dolus manifestus（拉）明白的欺诈

dolus praesumtus（拉）推定欺诈

dolus subsequens（拉）事后犯意

domain　王国，领域，范围，领土

domestic　境内

domestic advertising　国内广告

domestic affairs　内部事务

domestic agreements　家庭协议，亲属间的协议

domestic arbitral award　国内仲裁裁决

domestic arbitration　国内仲裁

domestic bill of exchange, inland bill of exchange　国内汇票

domestic branch　国内分支机构

domestic commercial arbitration　国内商事仲裁

domestic competition　国内竞争

domestic cottage industry　家庭工业

domestic court　自治法院

domestic courts　当事人居住地的管辖法院

domestic credit condition　国内信贷情况

domestic credits　国内信贷

domestic driving permit　国内驾驶执照

domestic economic activity　国内经济活动

domestic economy　国内经济

domestic effect of treaty　条约的国内效力

domestic enterprises　当地企业

domestic exchange　国内汇兑

domestic final buyer　国内最终买主

domestic financial market　国内金融市场

domestic freight forwarder　国内货运报关商

domestic industry　国内工业，家庭工业

domestic institution　境内机构

domestic investment　国内投资

domestic judge　本国法官

domestic legislation　国内立法

domestic market price　国内价格

domestic markets　国内市场

domestic policy　对内政策

domestic proceedings　家庭诉讼

domestic producer　国内生产者

domestic production　国内生产，本国产品

domestic products of a primary commodity　国内初级产品生产者

domestic railway transport　国内铁路运输

domestic relation　亲属关系

domestic relations　内部关系

domestic remittance　国内汇兑

domestic resources　本国资源

domestic resources that may be exhausted　可能用竭的国内资源

domestic sales requirement　国内销售要求

domestic sewage　生活污水

domestic supply price　国内供给价

domestic support commitments　国内机构承诺

domestic trust　国内信托

domestic value　国内价值

domestica cautio（拉）单纯债务

证书

domesticated animal　饲养的动物

domicile　住所, 住地, 付款地, 住所地

domicile by operation of law　合法户籍, 法定住所

domicile certificate　户籍证明

domicile control　户口管制

domicile of dependency　依附住所

domicile of origin　原始住所, 出生住所

domicile of the person under guardianship　被监护人住所地

domiciled alien　有住所的外国人

domiciliary control system　户籍管理制度

domiciliary registration　户籍登记

domicilium necessanium（拉）必要的住所

dominant motive　主要动机

dominate　统治

dominatus（拉）所有权

dominion　统治, 领土

dominium biberum（拉）自由所有权

dominium dormiens（拉）停止所有权

dominium litis（拉）争议物所有权

dominium naturale（拉）自然所有权

dominium perpetuum（拉）永久所有权

dominium publism（拉）国家所有权

dominium restrictum（拉）限制的所有权

domino volente（拉）经所有人同意

dominus（拉）所有者

dominus feudi（拉）所有者, 拥有者

① dominusutilis（拉）用益权人
② don't crush　切勿挤压
③ donate　赠与
④ donated property　赠与财产
⑤ donatee　受赠人
⑥ donatio（拉）赠与
⑦ donatio inter vivos（拉）生前赠与
⑧
⑨ donatio obsoluta（拉）无条件赠与
⑩
⑪ donatio pura（拉）纯粹赠与
⑫ donatio relata（拉）基于义务的赠与
⑬
⑭ donatio simplex（拉）单纯的赠与
⑮
⑯ donator　赠与人
⑰ dono decit（拉）赠与
⑱ donor　赠与人, 遗赠人
⑲ doomsday book　末日审判书
⑳ door leaf　窗扇
㉑ door to CFS　门到站
㉒ door to CY　门到场
㉓ door to door transport　门对门运输
㉔
㉕ door way　出入口
㉖ dope　麻醉品
㉗ dormant partnership　隐名合伙
㉘ dormitory　郊外住宅区
㉙ dose a business　停业
㉚ dosed prison　封闭式监狱
㉛ dossier　案卷
㉜ dotal system　嫁资制
㉝ double adultery　已婚男女间的通奸
㉞
㉟ double criminality　双重罪行
㊱ double entry　复式记账
㊲ double fares　往返运费
㊳ double floor　带吊顶的楼板
㊴ double guarantee　双重保证
㊵ double guilty　罪上加罪
㊶ double imposition compound duties　复税
㊷
㊸ double indemnity　加倍赔偿
㊹ double leadership　双重领导
㊺ double liability　加倍责任, 双重负债
㊻
㊼ double line tariff　复关税税率

double price system　双重价格制度

double renvoi　二重反致

double round majority rule　二轮多数选举制

double round vote　二轮当选制

double rules for regulating the conflict of laws　重叠使用的冲突规范

double taxation　双重征税,复税制,重复课税

double taxation agreement　双重征税协定

double taxation relief　双重征税减免

double track directors system　双轨董事制度

double veto　两次否决,双重否决权

double-deal　欺骗

double-entry accounting　复式记账法

double-leveled legislation system　两级立法体制

double-sided accomplice　双重共犯

double-trackes system　双轨制

doubtful debts　呆账

doubtful notes and accounts　呆账

Dow Jones Index　道琼斯股票指数

Dow Jones industrials averages　道琼斯工商业股票平均价格指数

down payment　首次付款,首期付款,已付定金

down payment for transfer of technology　技术转让入门费

down payment paid　已付定金

down period　停工期

downslide　下跌

downtime　停工期

draconian law　严刑峻法

Draconian Laws　德拉古法

draft　制定,汇票,草图,征集

draft articles　条文草案

draft articles on state responsibility　关于国家责任的条文草案

draft committee　征兵委员会

draft conscription　征兵

draft constitution　宪法草案

draft declaration on the rights and duties of states　国家权利与义务宣言草案

draft dodging　逃避服兵役罪

draft law　征兵法

draft of plan　计划草案

draft of state budget　国家预算草案

draft proposal　提案草案

draft regulations　法律草案

draft resolution　决议草案,提案

draft ten articles on liability for damages　损害责任十条条文草案

draft treaty　条约草案

drafting order　征兵命令

drafting procedure　征兵程序

drag on　延误

drag out　延长

Drago Doctrine　德拉戈主义

drain of gold　黄金外流

drainage dues　排污费

draw back　退款

draw up　制定

draw...as enterprise fund　提取企业基金

drawee　付款人

drawing　提取,提款,出票,开票,草图

drawing and quartering punishment　四肢裂解刑

drawing brief　草拟案情说明书

drawing of engineering design　工程设计图纸

drawing rights　提款权

drawn clause　出票条款

dreadful punishment theory　恐惧刑理论

drive away　祛除

drive out　驱除

driver　驾驶员

driver's license　汽车驾驶执照

driving against traffic regulations 违章驾驶汽车

driving license 驾驶执照

driving permit 驾驶许可证

Drod Scott Decision 德罗特·司考特案件判决

drop 下跌,下降

drop shipment 直接装运,直达货场

droplock bond 限定下浮债券

dropped-out goods 遗漏货物

drown 溺杀

drug 药,毒品,麻醉品

drug addiction 药瘾

drug addicts under control to give up their habits 戒毒人员

drug ban 禁毒

drug control 麻醉品管制

drug crime 毒品犯罪

drug dependence 药瘾

drug offenses 贩卖毒品罪

drug prohibition 禁毒

drug rehabilitation services 戒毒脱瘾治疗业务

drug smuggling 毒品走私

drug suppression 禁毒

drumhead courtmartial 战地临时军事法庭

drug-induced mental disorder 药源性精神障碍

drug-relief reformatory 戒毒所

drug-suppression institution 禁毒机构

dry mortgage 产权抵押贷款

dual citizenship 双重公民资格

dual constitutional monarchy system 二元君主立宪制

dual leadership of prosecutorial organizations 检察机关的双重领导

dual monarchy regime 二元君主制政策

dual nationality 双重国籍

dual penalties for corporate crimes 法人犯罪的双罚原则

dual tariff 双重关税

dual test 双重检验

dual (/double) nationality 双重国籍

dualism 二元论

dualism of aim of punishment 刑罚目的二元论

dualism of end of punishment 刑罚目的二元论

dualism of punishment and security measures 刑罚与保安处分二元论

dualism of relationship between crime and punishment 罪刑关系二元论

dualist 二元论者

dualistic nature of crimes 犯罪本质二元论

duality of rights 权利重叠

duck (股票交易)破产者

due 付款日,到期

due arrival 及时到达

due authority 适当权力,适当的权限

due authorization 正式授权

due bill (美) 借约

due compensation 适当补偿,相应赔偿

due coursigence 各尽职守

due date 付款日,满期日,到期日

due office act 正当职务行为

due payment 定期付款

due procedure 正当程序

due process 正当程序,正当手续,法定诉讼程序

due process of law 正当法律程序

duel 决斗

dues and taxes 捐税

duly accviedited agent 正式委派的代理人

duly admitted 依法准许

duly authorized 经正式授权的

duly authorized representative 正式授权的代表

duly forward 及时发生

dumb bid 拍卖底价,投标底数

Dumbarton Oaks Proposals 敦

巴顿橡树园建议案

dummy tendering 假投标

dump 倾销

dump goods 倾销货物

dumping 倾销

dumping margin 倾销差价,倾销幅度,倾销差额

dumping policy 倾销政策

dumping price 倾销价格

duplicate 复制

duplicate of an audit notice 审计通知书副本

duplicate test 重复检验

duplicates of a bill of defense 答辩状副本

duplicates of pleadings 答辩状副本

duplicatio(拉) 重复抗辩

duplicity 重复

durable 持久的

dural criminality 双重犯罪

dural majority principle 双重多数原则

durante minore aetate(拉) 在未成年期间

duration 期限,期间

duration of a project 工程工期

duration of action 诉讼期间

duration of contract 契约有效期间,合同有效期

duration of election 选举期间

duration of guaranty 保证期限

duration of public summons 公示期间

duration of the agreement 协议有效期

duration of treaty 条约的有效期限

duration of trial 审判期间

duration of validity 有效期

duress 胁迫

during a criminal act 犯罪实行过程中

during preparation for a crime 犯罪预备过程中

during the review 复审期间

during the term specified in the contract 在合同约定期间

dust shaft 倒垃圾井筒

dutiable 应课税

dutiable articles 征税物品

dutiable commodities 征税品

dutiable commodity 应税商品

dutiable goods 应税货物,征税货物

dutiable price 完税价

dutiable service 应税劳务

dutiable value 完税价格

duties and responsibilities of master 船长的职责

duties of acquiescence 默许的义务

duties of humanity 人道义务

duties of the people's police 人民警察职责

duties of tow 被拖方义务

duties on imported goods 商品进口税

duty 义务,责任,职务,税,税收

duty as well as the right to receive education 受教育的权利和义务

duty assessment 估定关税

duty cabinet 责任内阁制

duty for sound goods 完好货物税

duty of abstention 不作为的义务

duty of averting or minimizing losses 防止或减轻损失的义务

duty of care 谨慎义务,谨慎责任,注意义务

duty of child to support parents 子女赡养父母的义务

duty of guardianship 监护义务,监护责任,监护职责

duty of maintenance 扶(抚)养义务,赡养义务

duty of performance 履行义务

duty of performance of contract 履行合同责任

duty of performing military service 服兵役的义务

duty of proof 证明职责

duty of super intendence 保管义务

duty of support 扶(抚)养义务，赡养义务

duty on value 增值税

duty on wine 酒类税

duty paid certificate 收税单，完税单

duty paragraph 税号

duty paying value 海关完税价格

duty paying value of imports and exports 进出口货物的关税完税价格

duty receipt 纳税收据

duty to be paid at port of import 口岸纳税

duty to convert property 变更财产的责任

duty to declare 申报义务

duty to pay tax(es) 纳税义务

duty to provide support 扶(抚)养义务，赡养义务

duty to support children 抚养子女的义务

duty to take care 注意义务

duty-free entry 免税入境

duty-free goods 免税货物，免税品

duty-paid proof 完税凭证

duty-paying value 完税价格

dwelling district 居住区

dwelling house 住宅

dying 垂死

dying evidence 临死证言

dying testimony 临死证言

dying words 遗嘱

dynamic analysis of crime 犯罪动态分析

dynamic analysis of crime of pro-rated nature 犯罪长期性动态分析

dynamic conditions 动力条件说

dynamic role 能动性

dynamic stereotype of crime 犯罪动力定型

dynasty 朝代，王朝

E

each person responsible for a particular field of work 分工负责

Each takes what he needs 各取所需

early complaint 及早控诉

early days 初期

early delivery of goods 早交货

early postmortem phenomenon 早期尸体现象

early shipment 即期装运

earmarked tax 牲口税

earned income 已获收益

earned premium 实收保险费

earnest 定金

earnest money 定金、保证金

earnest money for probation 缓刑保证金

earnings 收益,报酬

earnings before interest and tax 付息及税前利润

ease credit restrictions 放宽信贷限制

eased off 下跌

easement 地役

easier credit 放松信贷

easier money 放松银根

easing of money rate 金融市场松动

East African Economic Community (简写 EAEC) 东非共同市场

easy credit terms 扩大信贷

easy money policy 放松银根政策

easy payment 分期付款

easy to... 易于

easygoing management 松散管理

eavesdropping 窃听罪

ecclesiastical court 宗教法庭,教会法院

ecclesiastical law 天主教会法,

寺院法

eclectic action 折衷式诉讼

eclectic criminology 折衷主义犯罪学

eclecticism 混合理论

eclecticism of punishment 刑罚折衷主义

ecological balance 生态平衡

ecological benefits 生态效益

ecological disturbance 生态失调

ecological effect 生态效应

ecological environment 生态环境

ecological stress 恶劣的生态环境

ecological system 生态系统

ecological theory 生物学死亡

ecology of grassland 草原生态环境

ecology of public administration 行政生态学

economic accounting 经济核算

economic act 经济行为

economic action 经济活动,经济行为

economic activity 经济活动

economic activity in short-run 短期经济活动

economic adjudication 经济审判

economic adjudicatory power 经济审判权

economic administrative case 经济行政案件

economic advance 经济发展

economic advantage 经济优势

economic affairs 经济事务

economic agent 经济代理人

economic agreement 经济协定

economic aid 经济援助

economic ailment 经济失调

economic and financial section 财经部门

economic and technical interchange　经济和技术交流

economic and technological development zone　经济技术开发区

economic and trade contract involving foreign elements　涉外经济贸易合同

economic arbitration　经济仲裁

economic area　经济区域

economic assistance　经济援助

economic association　联营,经济联合,经济联合体

economic association affiliate　联营

economic austerity　经济紧缩

economic base　经济基础

economic basis　经济基础

economic basis of constitution　宪法的经济基础

economic behavior　经济行为

economic benefits　经济效益

economic big power　经济大国

economic bloc　经济集团

economic blockade　经济封锁

economic body　经济主体

economic boycott　经济抵制

economic bust　经济崩溃

economic calculation　经济核算

economic canon　经济法规

economic cause　经济案由

economic cause of crime　犯罪经济原因

economic clause　经济条款

economic coalition　经济联合体

economic code　经济法典

economic coercion　经济强迫

economic colonialism　经济殖民主义

economic combination (/associations)　经济联合

economic community　经济共同体

economic community of west African states　西非国家经济共同体

economic compensation　经济赔偿

economic competition　经济竞争

economic complex　经济联合体

economic condition　经济情况,经济条件

economic consequence　经济后果

economic construction bond　经济建设公债

economic contract　经济合同

economic contract law　经济合同法

economic contraction　经济萎缩,经济紧缩

economic control　经济管制

economic control law　经济管制法

economic controversy in the army　军内经济纠纷案件

economic cooperation　经济合作,经济法人

economic cooperation with foreign countries　对外经济合作

economic count　经济审判庭

economic crime　经济犯罪

economic crime by the "able people"　"能人"经济犯罪

economic criminal　经济犯罪分子

economic criminology　经济犯罪学

economic crisis　经济危机

economic criterion　经济标准

economic decline　经济衰退

economic depression　经济萧条

economic development　经济发展

economic development cycle　经济发展周期

economic development program　经济发展规划

economic development zone　经济开发区

economic disparity　经济差异

economic disproportion　经济失调

economic dispute　经济纠纷

economic dispute case　经济纠纷案件

economic division 经济庭
economic downturn 经济萎缩
economic duty 经济义务
economic effect 经济效益,经济效果
economic effectiveness 经济效益
economic effects 经济成效,经济效益
economic efficacy 经济效益
economic efficiency 经济效益
economic entity 经济实体,经济组织,经济主体
economic expension 经济扩张
economic exposure 经济风险
economic forest 经济林
economic form 经济形态
economic foundation 经济基础
economic freedom 经济自由
economic friction 经济摩擦
economic function(s) 经济职能
economic functions and power 经济职权
economic gain(s) 经济效果,经济成果
economic gap 经济差距
economic giant 经济大国
economic goal 经济目标
economic growth 经济增长
economic hardship 经济困难
economic incentive 经济鼓励
economic independence 经济独立
economic indicator 经济指标
economic infiltration 经济渗透
economic information 经济信息
economic infrastructure 经济基础设施
economic institution 经济机构,经济制度
economic integration 经济联合,经济一体化
economic integration area 经济一体化地区
economic interest 经济利益,经济权益
economic issue 经济发行
economic judgment 经济审判

economic judgment jurisdiction 经济审判管辖
economic jurisdiction 经济司法
economic jurisprudence 经济法学
economic law 经济规律,经济法
economic law regulation object 经济法调整对象
economic law system involving foreign elements in China 中国涉外经济法律制度
economic laws and regulations 经济法规
economic lawsuit 经济诉讼
economic legal relationship 经济法律关系
economic legal studies 经济法学
economic legal system 经济法制建设
economic legal system engineering 经济法治系统工程
economic legislation 经济立法
economic lever 经济杠杆
economic leverage 经济杠杆
economic lifeline 经济命脉
economic litigation prescription 经济诉讼时效
economic losses 经济损失
economic management 经济管理
economic management setup 经济管理体制
economic management system 经济管理体制
economic model 经济模式
economic nationalism 经济国家主义
economic nature of enterprise 企业经济性质
economic objective 经济目标
economic operation of the means of transport 运输工具的经济实用
economic order 经济秩序
economic ordinances 经济立法
economic organization 经济组织
economic outputs 经济产量

economic pattern 经济形态,经济结构,经济模式

economic penetration 经济渗透

economic performance 经济行为

economic plan 经济计划

economic planning 经济计划

economic planning administration 经济计划管理

economic planning and coordination authority/EPCA (美) 经济计划与协调管理局

economic policy 经济政策

economic power 经济大国

economic pressure 经济压力

economic product 经济产品

economic project 经济规划

economic prosecution 经济检察

economic prosecution division 经济检察庭

economic protectionism 经济保护主义

economic punishment 经济处罚

economic readjustment 经济调整

economic recession 经济衰退

economic reckoning 经济核算

economic reconstitution 经济重建

economic recovery 经济恢复,经济复苏

economic reform 经济改革

economic regime 经济制度,经济体制

economic region 经济区域

economic regional integration 区域性经济一体化

economic relations 经济关系

economic resource 经济资源

economic resource zone 经济资源区

economic responsibility in enterprises 企业经济责任制

economic responsibility system 经济责任制

economic results 经济效益,经济效果

① economic resurgence 经济复苏

② economic returns 经济效果

③ economic revival 经济复苏

④ economic rights 经济权利

⑤ economic rights and interests 经济权益

⑦ economic risk 经济风险

⑧ economic sanction(s) 经济制裁,经济体裁

⑩ economic sector 经济成分

⑪ economic self-determination 经济自决

⑬ economic separation 经济割据

⑭ economic situation 经济形势

⑮ economic sphere 经济领域

⑯ economic stabilization act of 1970 (美) 经济稳定法

⑱ economic stabilization policy 经济稳定政策

⑳ economic stagnation 经济停滞

㉑ economic status 经济地位,经济状况

㉓ economic statute 经济法规

㉔ economic stimulus 经济鼓励

㉕ economic strategy 经济战略

㉖ economic strength 经济实力

㉗ economic strike 经济罢工

㉘ economic structure 经济体制

㉙ economic structure reform 经济体制改革

㉛ economic suit 经济案件

㉜ economic superpower 经济超级大国

㉞ economic support 经济支持

㉟ economic system 经济制度,经济体制

㊲ economic tactic 经济战术

㊳ economic target 经济目标

㊴ economic tribunal 经济审判庭,经济庭,经济法庭

㊶ economic union 经济联盟,经济同盟

㊸ economic unit 经济单位

㊹ economic unity 经济统一

㊺ economic value 经济价值

㊻ economic viability 经济活力

㊼ economic zone 经济区

economical and functional house 经济实用型住房,低价住宅

economical jurisprudence 经济法学

economical model theory 经济模型论

economically underdeveloped areas 经济不发达地区

economics of large scale production 大规模生产经济法则

economizing energy law 节约能源法

economy 经济,经济制度,系统,组织

economy jurisdiction court（英）经济审判庭

economy of scare 规模经济

economy with different types of ownership 多种所有制

eco-equilibrium 生态平衡

ed corporation 小型公司

Edetics 折衷法学派

Edict 敕令

Edict of Lombards 伦巴德法典

Edict of Milan 米兰敕令

edifice 大建筑物

Edmondbayle fingerprint system 爱蒙培尔式指纹分类法

educate 教育

educate and reform criminals 教育改造罪犯

education 教育程度,教育

education act 教育法

education in communist morality 共产主义道德教育

education inside prison 狱内教育

education law 教育法

education of constitution 宪法教育

education of convicts on productive techniques 罪犯职业技术教育

education of legal system 法制教育

education of sexology 性教育

education on the suppression of drugs 禁毒教育

education surtax 教育附加费

Education, Science, Culture and Public Health Committee 教科文卫委员会

educational background 学历

educational function 教育功能

educational fund 教育经费

educational input 教育投入

educational institution school 学校

educational investment 教育投入

educational reform 教育改革

educational system 学制

effect 效果,影响

effect of civil ruling 民事裁定效力

effect of composition 和解效力

effect of compromise and settlement 和解效力

effect of contract 合同效力

effect of criminal law 刑法的效力

effect of criminal law in space 刑法空间效力

effect of criminal law in time 刑法时间效力

effect of evidence 证据效力

effect of mortgage 抵押的效力,抵押效果

effect of notarization 公证效力

effect of obligation 债的效力

effect of probation 缓刑效果

effect of recognition 承认的效果

effect of treaty upon third states 条约对第三国的效力

effect of withdrawing an action 撤诉效力

effect payment 履行付款

effect rational material of administrative proceedings 行政诉讼的对事效力

effect time 有效期间

effective 生效的,有效的

effective clause 有效条款

effective competition 有效竞争

effective connection 有效联系,有效联络

effective contract 有效合同,可行合同

effective control 有效控制论,有效管制

effective credit 有效信贷

effective date 生效日,生效日期

effective date of termination 有的终止期

effective demand 有效需求

effective essentials of contract 合同有效要件

effective exchange rate 有效汇率

effective guarantee 有效保证,有效担保

effective instrument 有效文件

effective interest rate 有效利率,有效利用率

effective international control 有效的国际监督

effective link 有效联系

effective measure(s) 有效措施

effective of law 法律实效

effective payment clause 实际付款条款

effective period 有效期限

effective period of the contract 合同有效期

effective price 有效价格

effective protection 有效保护

effective purchasing power 有支付能力的购买力

effective range 有效范围

effective reciprocity 有效互惠

effective recourse 有效追索

effective redemption 有效补偿

effective relief 有效的法律救济

effective remedy 有效补救方法

effective supply 有效供应

effective time period 附生效期限

effectively connected principle 实际联系原则

effectiveness 效用,有效性,可行性,有效

effectiveness of moneysier money 放松银根

efficacious 有效的

efficiency 效率,工作效率

efficiency (dwelling) unit 单室居住单元

efficiency doctrine 行政效率原则

efficiency of administration 行政效率

efficiency of supervision over administration 行政监察效率

either party 任何一方

Ejus est nolle, qui potest velle (拉) 谁可以表达意志也就有权拒绝表达意见

ekistics 城市与区域规划学

elastic clause 弹性条款

elastic constitution 弹性宪法

elastic demand 弹性要求

elastic regulation 灵活规则

elasticity of demand 需求弹性

elder brother 兄长

elder sister 姐姐

elect 推选,选举

elect sb or sth else 另行选举

elected system for relative majority 相对多数当选制

election 当选,推选,选举

election at expiration of office terms 换届选举

election at the basic 基层选举

election campaign 竞选运动

election committee 推选委员会

election criterion 当选标准

election dominated by money 金钱选举

election expenses 选举费用

election mechanism 选举机构

election mobilization 选举动员

election of deputies to the people's congress 人大代表的选举

election of majorities 多数选举制

election or appointment of liquidator 清算人的选任或指定

election results 选举结果	数据处理系统
election system 选举制	electronic fingerprinting method 电子仪器提取指纹法
election year 选举年	electrophotographic evidence 电子照相证据
electioneer 竞选	element of crime 犯罪因素
electioneering 竞选	element of the first importance 首要分子
elective franchise 选举权	elementary 基本,初级,初等
elector 合格选举人,选举人,选民	elementary education law 初等教育法
electoral action 选举诉讼	elements of crime 犯罪要素,犯罪要件
electoral boundary 选区范围,选举范围	elements of law 法的要素
electoral certificate 选民证	elements of production 生产要素
electoral college 选举团	elevate the degree of ownership 所有制升级
electoral commission 选举委员会	eligibility 合格,当选资格
electoral document 选举文件	eligible 合格的
electoral law 选举法	eligible elector 合格选举人
electoral law of the president 大总统选举法	eligible papers 银行可接受作担保的证券
electoral procedure 选举程序	eliminate 清除
electoral qualification 选民资格	eliminate effects 消除影响
electoral register 选民登记册	eliminate obstruction 消除妨碍
electoral roll 选举名册	eliminate the harmful effect 清除不良影响
electoral suit 选举诉讼	eliminate the obstruction 排除妨碍
electoral system 选举制	
electoral system for absolute majority 过多数选举制	eliminating the effects of the act 清除影响
electoral unit 选举单位	elimination of civil legal relations 民事法律关系的消灭
electorate 选民	
electra complex 恋父情结	elimination of customs barrier 废除关税壁垒
electress 女选民	elimination of dangers 消除危险
electric mark 电流斑	elimination of ill effects 消除影响
electric power 电力	
electric power law 电力法	elimination of obligation 债的消灭
electric rate schedule 电力价目表	
electrical alarm 电力警报器	elimination of quantitative restrictions 取消数量限制原则
electricity user 用电主	elimination of tariffs 取消关税
electrocution 电刑	elimination of the effects 清除影响
electronic agreement 电子协议书	
electronic banking 电子化银行经营	elimination prints 排除嫌疑印
electronic currency 电子货币	
electronic data interchange 电子数据交换	
electronic data processing 电子	

纹

emancipate the productive force 解放生产力

emancipation of women 妇女解放

emancipist 刑满释放人员

embargo 禁运

embargo on gold 禁止黄金出口

embark in an enterprise 举办企业

embarkation card 出境旅客申报表

embezzle 侵吞

embezzle public funds (money) 侵吞公款

embezzlement 侵吞

embezzlement of government funds 侵吞公款

embezzlement of public funds 侵吞公款

embezzlement of tax funds 侵吞税款

embezzler 侵吞者,贪污犯

embezzling group 贪污集团

embracery 笼络、贿赂陪审员行为

emergency 紧急状态

emergency act 紧急法令

emergency action(s) 紧急行动,避险行为,紧急避险

emergency arrest 紧急逮捕

emergency circumstances 紧急情况

emergency conference 紧急会议

emergency court of appeals 紧急上诉法庭

emergency decree 紧急状态令

emergency legislation 紧急立法

emergency measure(s) 非常措施,紧急措施,避险措施

emergency outlet 安全出口

emergency power(s) 非常时期权力,非常的权力

emergency price control act of 1942 (美) 紧急时期物价管理法

emergency procedure 紧急程

序,非常程序

emergency requisition 紧急征用

emergency session 紧急开庭

emergency situation 危急情况

emergency step 应急措施

emergency tariff 紧急关税

emigrant 出境移民,侨民

emigrant remittance 侨汇,汇入

emigrate 出境

emigrating 迁移出境

emigration 迁移出境,侨居

emigration papers 出境证件

eminent domain 征用权,国家征用

emir 元首

emirate 酋长国

emission standard 排放标准

emitio imaginamia 假装买卖

emoluments 酬金

emotion offender 激情犯

emotional intention 激情故意

emperor 帝王,皇帝

Emperor Justinian 查士丁尼安皇帝

empire 帝国

employ 雇佣

employ force 采用武力

employee's merit rating regime 考绩制度

employer 雇佣人

employer's liability 雇主责任

employer-employeerelationship 雇佣关系

employing Chinese workers and staff 雇用中国职工

employment 就业

employment agency 劳动就业服务机构,劳动介绍所

employment and indemnity clause 使用与赔偿条款

employment contract 雇用合同,雇佣合同,雇佣契约

employment credential 录用证明

employment examination 录用考试

employment exchange 劳动介绍

所

employment legislation 劳动就业立法

employment of disabled employment of persons inside houses for reeducation-through-labour 劳教人员解除教养后留所作业

employment practice 雇佣惯例

employment service institution 劳动就业服务机构

employment service system 劳动就业服务体系

employment tax 雇佣税

employment testing certificate 使用鉴定证书

empolyment inside the place for reform-through-labour after serving a sentence 留场就业

empowered organization 被授权组织

empowered person 全权代理人

empress 女皇

emptio (拉) 购买

emptor 买主

empty 搬空

empty talk 清谈

enabling act 授权法案

enabling clause 授权条款

enabling rules 授权性规范

enabling statute 授权法

enact 颁布,通过,制定,法规,规定

enact a decree 制定法令

enact a statute 制定法律

enactment 制定,条例,法例

enactment of constitution 宪法制定

enactment of criminal law 刑事立法

enactment of economic law 经济法的制定

encashment 兑现

enclave "飞地"

enclosure 圈地运动

encourage prostitution of girl under 16 years 怂恿 16 岁以下

幼女卖淫

encourage the development of foreign trade 鼓励发展对外贸易

encouragement of investment 投资鼓励

encroach 侵占

encroach on 侵夺

encroach on the interests of the people 触犯人民利益

encroach on the public interests 触犯公共利益

encroachment of right 对权利的侵犯

encumber a property with a mortgage 以财产作抵押

encumbered estate court 抵押土地法院

encumbrance 财产抵押权,财产留置权,财产留置权(或抵押权)

encyclopedia of united states supreme court reports (Ency. U.S. Sup. Ct.) 美国最高法院判例汇编百科全书

end delivery date/ED 最后交货日期

end of punishment 刑罚的目的

end user 最终用户

endanger 危害

endanger public security 危害公共安全

endanger society 危害社会

endangered species of animals 濒危动物

endangered species of wild fauna and flora 濒危野生动植物

endangering life or personal safety of others 危害他人生命或人身安全

endangering safety of railway passengers 危害铁路旅客安全

ending of partnership 合伙终止

ending price 股票卖出价格

endogenous depression 内源性抑郁

endogenous psychosis 内因性精

神病,内源性精神病

endorsable 可担保的

endorse 批准

endorse a bill 票据背书

endorse by acquiescence 默认的承认

endorsed in blank 空白背书

endorsee 被背书人,承受票据背书表

endorsement 背书,批单,签名

endorsement for collections 托收背书

endorsement in blank 无记名式背书

endorsement of bill of lading 提单的背书

endorsement to order 记名背书

endorser 背书人

endowment assurance (insurance) 养老保险,生死两全保险

ends and means 目的与手段

enemy 敌国

enemy agent (/spy) 敌国间谍

enemy alien 敌国人

enemy character 敌对身份,敌性

enemy currency 敌国货币

enemy merchant ship 敌国商船

enemy national 敌国国民

enemy occupation zone 敌军占领区

enemy property 敌产

enemy territory 敌国领土

emergency measures 紧急措施

energy and natural resources committee (美) 能源与自然资源委员会

energy conservation program 节能计划

energy conversation 能源节约

energy development 能源开发

energy law 能源法

energy needs 能源需求

energy policy and conservation act (美) 能源政策和能源保护法

energy poor 能源贫乏

energy program 能源计划

energy resources 能源资源

energy resources law 能源管理法

energy-saving investment 节能投资

enfeoff 分封土地

enfeoffment 分封制,地产授予证书

enforce 强制执行,施行,执行,强制

enforce a claim 行使债权

enforce compliance with the law 强迫服从法律

enforce martial law 戒严

enforce the law strictly 执法如山

enforceability 可执行性,强制性

enforceability of civil judgment 民事判决执行性

enforceable at law 可用法律强制执行的

enforceable contract 可强制执行的合同

enforceable effect of administrative act 行政行为执行力

enforcement 强制执行,施行

enforcement action 执行行动

enforcement at law 用法律来强制执行

enforcement in administrative proceedings 行政诉讼的执行

enforcement machinery 强制执行措施

enforcement measures 强制执行措施,强制措施

enforcement measures in administrative proceedings 行政诉讼的执行措施

enforcement of contract 合同的强制执行

enforcement of drug suppression 禁毒执法工作

enforcement of economic law 经济法的实施

enforcement of legal responsibility 法律责任的执行

enforcement of maritime decision

海事判决的执行

enforcement order issued by the court 法院发出强制执行判决的命令

enforcement organization 执行机关

enforcement power 执行权

enforcement procedure 执法程序

enforcement process 执行程序

enforcement regulations 实施法规

enforcing private rights by force 暴力行使私权罪

enforcing the law impartially 秉公执法

engage 雇佣,约定

engage in 经营

engage in industry or commercial operation 从事工商业经营

engage in pettifoggery 包揽诉讼

engage in speculation and profiteening 投机倒把

engaged salvage service 雇佣救助

engagement 约定,债务

engagement clause 保证条款

engagement in foreign exchange 经营外汇业务

engineering agreement 工程协议

engineering and designing expense 工程和设计费用

engineering contractor 工程承包商

engineering cost 工程成本

engineering data 技术数据

engineering design 工程设计

engineering design review 工程设计审查

engineering drawings 工程图样

engineering industry 机器工业

engineering instructions 技术说明书

engineering management 工程管理

engineering proposal 工程方案

engineering specifications 工程条件

engineering supervision 工程管理

engineering technology 工程技术

England 英格兰

England law 英国法

English common law 英国普通法

English doctrine of renvoi 英国反致制度

English law report 英国判例汇编

English legal system 英国法律制度

enhance the awareness of law 提高法制观念

enhance the price 提价

enhancement of environment 环境改善

enjoy a coordinate position 享有同等地位

enjoy according to law 依法享有

enjoy civil rights 享有民事权利

enjoy priority in compensation 优先受偿

enjoyment 使用权,享受权利,享有和行使

enlarged meeting 扩大会议

enlarged reproduction 扩大再生产

enlarged session 扩大会议

enlargement 权利扩展

enlargement of losses 扩大损失

enlistment age 服役年龄

enlivening the economy 搞活经济

enquiry 询问

enquiry sheet 询价单

enroll 注册,登记

enrollment 注册

enrollment of deed 契据登记

ensure 保障

ensure that existing laws are strictly observed 有法必依

ensure that law's enforcement be strict 执法必严

ensure that laws are observed 有法必依

ensure the freedom of the person 保障人身自由

ensure the quality of commodities 保证商品质量

entail 限定继承权

entail general 一般限定继承权

entailed interest 限定继承的利益

entangle 涉及

entente countries 协约国

enter 登记,备案

enter a bid 投标

enter a case in the records 备案

enter a judgment 作出判决

enter a protest against 对…提出抗议

enter into a bond 订立合同

enter into a contract 订立合同,立约

enter into a contract with 与…订立合同

enter into a debat 进行辩论

enter into agreement 达成协议

enter into an election contest 竞选

enter into bear transactions 卖空投机,看跌投机

enter into bull transaction 买空投机,看涨投机

enter into force 施行

enter the country 入境

enter upon a property 占有财产

entering judgments 判决的登录

entering to the register 注册登记

enterprise 企业单位,企业

enterprise accounting system 企业会计制度

enterprise administration 企业管理

enterprise alteration registration 企业变更登记

enterprise and institution 企事业单位

enterprise as legal person 企业法人

enterprise business 企业

enterprise contract of partnership 合伙承担

enterprise entity 企业实体

enterprise jointly managed by China and foreign countries 中外合作经营企业

enterprise law 企业法

enterprise management 企业管理

enterprise name registration application 企业名称登记申请

enterprise operating on shareholding system 股份制企业

enterprise operation 企业经营

enterprise owned by foreign capitalists 外资企业

enterprise owned by the whole people 全民所有制企业

enterprise registration 企业登记

enterprise reorganization 企业改组

enterprise run at a deficit 亏损企业

enterprise run with foreign capital 外资企业

enterprise under collective ownership 集体所有制企业

enterprise under experiment 试点企业

enterprise union 企业工会

enterprise units 企业单位

enterprise's decision-making power 企业自主权

enterprises and institutions 企事业单位

enterprises in partnership 合伙企业

enterprises or institutions 企事业单位

enterprises run by the government 公营企业

enterprises under the control of the central authorities 隶属中

央企业

enterprises under the direction administration 归口企业

enterprising businessman 企业家

enterprization 企业化

enthusiasm of the local authorities 地方的积极性

enticement 引诱物

entire contract 整体合同,不可分割,不可分合同

entire cost 一切费用

entire expense 一切费用

entire loss 一切损失

entire obligation 全部债务

entire tenancy 完整租借

entire whole 全体

entirely 全然

entirely in effect 一律有效

entirety 全部

entitle 赋予权力,使用资格

entitled to 有权要求

entitlement 权利

entitlement program 权利项目

entitlements 依法应享有的权利

entity 单位

entity without legal personality 非法人单位

entrance permit 入境许可

entrance registration 入境登记

entrap 诱骗

entrapment 执法人员诱人犯罪,诱骗

entrenched clause 刚性条款

entreport 转运港口

entrepreneur 企业家

entries of civil lawsuit 民事案由编目

entrust 委托,信托

entrusted agency 委托代理

entrusted agent 委托代理人

entrusted matter(s) 委托事务

entrusted organization 受委托的组织

entrusted task(s) 代理事项,委托事项

entrustee 受托人

entruster 信托人

entrustment 委托

entry (支票)记录,记账,入境

entry and exit authority 出境入境主管机关

entry and exit certificates 出境入境证件

entry and exit control 出境入境管制,入出境管理

entry and exit formalities 出境入境手续

entry and exit inspection 出境入境检查

entry and exit management 出境入境管理

entry and exit management department 出境入境主管机关

entry and exit management laws and regulations 出境入境管理法规

entry certificate 入境证书

entry document 入境证件

entry examination of a convict's body and thing 罪犯入监人身物品检查

entry for dutiable goods 征税货物报关单

entry healthy checkup of a convict 罪犯入监健康检查

entry into effect of treaty 条约的生效

entry into operation 施行

entry into possession 取得占有权

entry notice of a convict 罪犯入监通知书

entry passport 入境护照

entry permit 入境许可证

entry procedures 入境手续

entry registration form of a convict 罪犯入监登记表

entry under homestead 宅地登记

entry visa 入境签证

entry, exit and frontier control 出境入境和边防管理

entry-exit visa 出入境签证

entry-into-force conditions 生效条件

enumerate 列举

enumerated express power 明示权力

environment and conditions at the time of criminal act 犯罪当时的环境和条件

environment condition 环境条件

environment court 环境法庭

environment criteria 环境标准

environment law 环境保护法

environment limit 环境限制

environment of competition 竞争环境

environment of reform-through-labour 劳动改造环境

environment pollution 环境污染

environment programme 环境规划

environment protection 环境保护

environment protection zone 环境保护区

environment regulation 环境管理

environmental assessment 环境估计

environmental awareness 环境意识

environmental condition 环境条件

environmental conservation 环境保护

environmental contamination 环境污染

environmental control system 防污系统

environmental cost 环境保护费用

environmental crime 环境犯罪

environmental crisis 环境危机

environmental damage 环境损毁,环境损害

environmental damage cost 环境破坏费用

environmental decay 环境恶化

environmental defence fund/EDF 环境保护基金

environmental degradation 环境退化

environmental destruction 环境破坏

environmental development plan/EDP 环境开发规则

environmental disruption 环境破坏

environmental economics 环境经济

environmental evaluation 环境评价

environmental harm 环境危害

environmental hazard 环境危害

environmental health 环境卫生标准

environmental health criteria 环境卫生准则

environmental hygiene 环境卫生

environmental impact 环境影响

environmental impact analysis 环境影响分析

environmental impact evaluation 环境影响评价

environmental implication 环境影响

environmental improvement 环境改善

environmental injury 环境侵害

environmental law institute 环境保护法律学会

environmental management 环境管理

environmental modification technique 改变环境的技术

environmental monitoring 环境监测

environmental nuisance 环境损害

environmental parameter 环境参数

environmental planning 环境规划

environmental policy act 环境政策禁令

environmental pollution 环境污染

environmental pollution damage 环境污染危害

environmental pollution prevention 环境污染防治

environmental pollution range 环境污染区域

environmental pollution regulation 环境污染管理

environmental pollution source 环境污染源

environmental pollution survey 环境污染调查

environmental pressure 环境压力

environmental problems 环境问题

environmental proceedings 环境诉讼

environmental program 环境计划

environmental programme 环境规划

environmental protection 保护环境

environmental protection agency/EPA(美) 环境保护局

environmental protection department 环境保护部门

environmental protection law 环境保护法

environmental protection organ 环境保护机构

environmental quality 环境质量

environmental quality appraisal 环境质量评价

environmental quality assessment 环境质量评价

environmental quality control 环境质量控制

environmental quality evaluation 环境质量评价

environmental quality management 环境质量管理

environmental quality requirement 环境质量要求

environmental record 环境记录

environmental research 环境研究

environmental resource 环境资源

environmental resource protection 环境资源保护

environmental safety standard 环境安全标准

environmental science 环境科学

environmental standard 环境标准

environmental survey 环境调查

environmentalism 环境论

environmentalist 环境问题专家

envoy 公使

epidemic prevention control for keeping dogs 养犬卫生防疫管理

epidemic prevention personnel 防疫人员

epidemic prevention station 防疫站

epilepsy criminal 颠覆病犯罪人

epileptic disturbance of consciousness 癫痫性意识障碍

epileptic intellectual deterioration 癫痫性智能障碍

epileptic mental disorder 癫痫性精神障碍

epileptic personality change 癫痫性人格障碍

episcopal court 主教法院

episodic dis-control syndrome 发作性控制不良综合症

epitomize 概括

equal 对等

equal and universal electoral system 平等普选制

equal authentic 同等效力

equal binding 同等约束力

equal civil right 平等民事权利

equal conditions 同等条件

equal effect 同等效力

equal election 平等选举

equal exchange 等价交换
equal footing 同等地位
equal freedom 平等自由
equal in legal status 法律地位平等
equal in value 等价
equal installment system 等额分期付款制
equal legal status 法律地位平等
equal numbers 相等数量
equal opportunities 平等机会
equal pay act（英）同酬法
equal pay for equal work 同工同酬
equal pay for equal work for men and women alike 男女同工同酬
equal principles of party 当事人对等原则
equal protection 平等保护
equal protection of the law 法律上的平等保护
equal quality 同等品质
equal representation 平等代表
equal rights 平等权利，权利平等
equal rights for both sexes 男女平等权
equal rights with men 同男子平等的权利
equal security 平等担保
equal sharing of the burden by both sides 由双方平均分担
equal status 平等地位
equal status of women（with men）妇女的平等议位
equal suffrage 平等选举权，平等参政权
equal treatment 平等待遇
equal validity 同等效力
equal value 同等价值
equal vote 平等表决权
equality 平等
equality and mutual benifit 平等互利
equality before the law 在法律面前人人平等

equality clause 平等条款
equality in fact 事实平等，事实上平等
equality in law 法律上平等
Equality is equity 平等即公道
equality of men and women 男女平等
equality of nationality 民族平等
equality of representation 代表权平等
equality of status 地位平等
equality of the sexes 男女平等
equality of treatment 平等对待
equality under the law 法律上平等
equalization of land ownership 平均地权
equally binding 同等的约束力
equally authentic 同等效力
equal-number election between nominees and the elected-to-be 等额选举
equation price 平衡价格
equilibrium 平衡
equipment 设备
equipment importation 设备进口
equipment leasing 设备租赁
equipment supply 设备供应
equitable 合理
equitable action 衡平诉讼
equitable assignment 衡平法上的转让，债权转让
equitable assignment of debt 平衡法上债务让与
equitable burden-sharing principle 公平分担原则
equitable charge 衡平法上的负担
equitable claim 衡平法上的请求
equitable claimant 衡平法上的原告
equitable distribution of burden 合理分担
equitable doctrine of the marshalling of assets 债权清偿分

配顺序原则

equitable easement 衡平法上有效的地役权

equitable estate 衡平法上的产权,衡平法上的土地财产

equitable estoppel 衡平法的禁止翻供,衡平法上的不容翻悔

equitable execution 衡平法上的执行

equitable interests 衡平法上的权益

equitable jurisdiction 公平管辖权,衡平法的管辖权

equitable jurisprudence 衡平法学

equitable lease 衡平法租赁,衡平法上的租赁

equitable liability 衡平法上的债务,公平责任

equitable lien 衡平法留置权,衡平法上的留置权

equitable mortgage 衡平法上的抵押,平衡法有效的抵押

equitable ownership 衡平所有权

equitable plea 衡平法上有效的抗辩

equitable presumption 衡平法上有效的推定

equitable principle 公平原则

equitable remedies 衡平法上的救济

equitable set-off 对等抵消

equitable title 衡平法上的所有权

equitable waste 衡平法上的毁损

equity 衡平法,权益、产权,公平

Equity act in person 衡平法是对人的

equity and good conscience 公正原则与良心

equity and justice 公平与正义

equity capital 股本,自有资本,股东资本

equity cases 衡平法案件,衡平法上的案件

equity delights in equality 平衡法爱好平等

Equity follows the law 平衡法追随习惯法

equity interest 权益

equity investment 股本投资,投资股份

equity investment direct investment 直接投资

equity issue 证券发行

equity joint venture 股权式合营企业,合资

equity jurisdiction 衡平法管辖权

equity jurisprudence 衡平法学

Equity looks to the intent rather than the form 衡平法关注的是当事人格方的意志 而不在乎其形式

equity of redemption 衡平法上的赎回权,赎回抵押品的权利

equity ownership 业主所有权

equity power 衡平权力

equity principle of taxation 纳税公平原则

equity receiver 清算财产接管人

equity share holder equity 股东拥有的资产净值

equity stock（common stock） 普通股

equity to a settlement 衡平法授予的财产

equity to prevail 平衡法占优势

equity-debt ratio 资产负债比

equity-linked policy 股票联系保单

equivalence 等价

equivalent 同价物

equivalent commitments 当量承诺

equivalent compensation 同等补偿

equivalent exchange 等价交换

equivalent treatment 同等待遇

erection 安装

erection all risks insurance 安装

工程一切险

erection cost 安装费用

erection schedule 安装计划

erection team 安装工程队

ermine 法官制服

errancy 违背常规的

erring party 有过错一方

erroneous 错误的

erroneous and extraneous considerations 错误的和不相干的考虑

erroneous arrest 错捕

error 错误,误差,过错

error by good faith 善意过失

error facti（拉） 事实错误

error in a written judgment 判决书内容失误

error in corpore 标的物错误

error in judgment 判决错误

error in law 法律上的错误

error in management 管理过失

error in objecto（拉） 标的物错误

error in substantia（拉） 实质错误

error of culpability 有责任的错误

error of fact 事实错误

error of omission 不作为的过错

errors and omissions 错误与遗漏

errors excepted 错误不在此限

escalation lump sum contract 固值总价合同

escalation price 允许增价的合同价格

escalator clause 允许增价条款

escape 逃避

escape artist 屡次越狱的惯犯

escape clause 免责条款,免除条款,例外条款,除外条款

escaped convict 逃犯,越狱犯

escaped criminal 在逃犯

escaping justice 逃避司法执行

escheat 收归国有,收缴国库

escheat（美） 无主财产,收归国库的财产

escrow 等待条件完成的契约

escrow agreement 附条件转让协议

espionage act 惩治间谍法

essence 要素,实质

essence of a contract 合同要素

essence of evidence 证据的要素,证据本质

essence of law 法律的本质

essence of the contract 合同成立要件,契约成立要素

essential 根本

essential cause 要因

essential condition 主要条件,实质条件,必备条件,必要条件

essential condition of crime 犯罪要件

essential condition of delict 违法构成要件

essential conditions constituting an act of transgressing the administration of public security 违反治安管理行为的构成文件

essential constitution of crime 必要犯罪构成

essential goods 基本商品

essential issues 根本问题

essential offense 基本犯

essential one-crime 单纯一罪（又称本来一罪,实质一罪）,实质罪

essential stipulation 主要条件

essentialia（拉） 要素

essentialia negotii（拉） 要件

essentiality 要素

essentials 要素,实质,要件

essentials of compositing 和解要件

Essex 埃塞克斯

establish a price floor 规定最低价格

establish constitution 制定宪法

establish the mortgage of the ship 设定船舶抵押权

established principle 既定原则,确立的原则

established right 确定的权利

established rule(s) 确定性规范，成规

established rules of conduct 公认的行为准则

establishing common external tariffs 建立对外共同税率

establishing identity 同一性认定

establishment 权势集团，建置，体制

establishment 生产单位，基层单位，编制，企业

establishment in accordance with the law 依法成立

establishment of a contract 合同的成立

establishment of a withdrawal 撤诉成立

establishment of constitution 宪法制定

establishment of contract 合同成立

establishment of cooperatives 合作化

establishment of the diplomatic relations 建交

establishment of judicial person 法人设立

establishment of juristic act 法律行为的成立

establishment of mortgage of the ship 船舶抵押权的设定

establishment of nol pros（拉）撤诉成立

establishment of organizations law 机构编制法

establishment of postal enterprise 邮政企业的设置

establishment of religion 宗教机构的设置

establishment unit 基层单位

estate 财产，产业，地产

estate agent 物业经纪，不动产代理人

estate by intestacy 依法继承的房地产

estate contract 不动产契约，地产契约

estate duty 遗产税，地产税

estate in abeyance 无人继承

estate in fee-tail 有限定继承权地产

estate in gage 作抵押品的地产，已作抵押的房地产

estate in land 地产

estate in severalty 个别所有财产，单独占有的房地产

estate of freehold 不动产

estate of inheritance 被继承不动产

estate surveying 物业测量

estate tax 地产税，遗产税

estimate of expenditure 开支预算

estimate quotation sheet 报价单

estimated assessment 预算税额

estimated date of completion 预定完成日期

estimated revenue 预算收入

estimated time 预定期间

estimated time of arrival 预定到达时间

estimated time of completion of discharging 预定完成卸货时间

estimated time of completion of loading 预定完成装货时间

estimated time of delivery 预计交货时间

estimated time of finish discharging 预计卸货完毕时间

estimated time of finishing loading 预计装货完毕时间

estop 禁止翻供

estoppel 禁止翻供

estoppel by judgment 判决不容推翻

et cetera/etc（拉）以及其他

ethical 合乎道德的

ethical consideration 伦理的理由

ethics 道德，伦理

ethnic autonomous regions 民族自治地区

ethnic discrimination 民族歧视	欧洲货币协定
ethnic estrangement 民族隔阂	European monetary credit 欧洲
ethnic group 种族	货币贷款
ethnic minority 少数民族	European monetary credit agree-
ethnic minority living in compact	ment 欧洲货币借贷协议
communities 聚居民族	European monetary system 欧洲
ethnic policy 民族政策	货币体系
ethnic prejudice 种族偏见	European monetary union 欧洲
ethnic rights 民族权利	货币联盟
etiology of crime 犯罪程度	European payment union 欧洲
Eurobonds 欧洲债券	支付同盟
Euroclear 欧洲清算系统	European public law 欧洲公法
Eurocommunism 欧洲共产主义	European social charter 欧洲社
Eurodollar 欧洲美元	会宪章
European commission of human	European union（简写：EU） 欧
rights 欧洲人权委员会	洲联盟
European common market 欧洲	euthanasia 安乐死,安死术
共同市场	evade 逃避,规避
European communities 欧洲共	evade a duty 逃避职责
同体	evade debt(s) 逃债,逃避债务
European community law 欧洲	evade foreign exchange 逃汇
共同体法	evade obligations 规避义务
european convention on extradi-	evade one's responsibility 逃避
tion 欧洲引渡公约	责任
european convention on human	evade paying debts 逃债
rights 欧洲人权公约	evade repayment of debts 逃避
european convention on products	债务
liability in regard to personal	evading foreign exchange 逃汇
injury and death 关于人身伤	evading quarantine inspection 逃
亡的产品责任的欧洲公约	避检疫
European court of human rights	evaluate 作价,权衡
欧洲人权法院	evaluating function 评价功能
European currency system 欧洲	evaluation committee of academic
货币体系	degrees 学位评审委员会
European currency unit （ECU）	evaluation of convicts 罪犯考核
欧洲货币单位	evaluation of legal action 法律
European economic community	行为的评价
欧洲经济共同体	evasion of law 法律规避
European economic community	evasion of legal sanction 逃避法
law（EEC Law） 欧洲经济共	律制裁
同体法	evasion of liability by deception
European economic space 欧洲	以欺骗逃避责任
经济空间	evasion of registration 逃避登记
European free trade association	evasion of responsibility 逃避责
欧洲自由贸易联盟	任
European law 欧洲法	even bargain 公平交易
European monetary agreement	even exchange 公平交易

event of default 违约事件

eventual intent 未必故意

every (kind of) 各种

Every act is to be judged by the intention of the doer 每一个行为应当按照行为人的意图来作出判断

Every corporal punishment, even the very least, is greater than any pecuniary p unishment 每一种肉刑, 即使是最轻的, 也比罚金的刑罚为重

every industry or trade 各行各业

Every one may renounce or relinquish a right introduced for his own benefit 每个人可放弃有利于自己的权利

Every right is either made by consent, or is constituted by necessity, or is established by custom 每一项权利都是即由于得到同意又由于必须或由于惯例而产生的

everybody eating from the same big pot "吃大锅饭"

evidence 证据

evidence act 证据法

evidence at assessment 课税依据

evidence direct 直接证据

evidence for administrative proceedings 行政诉讼证据

evidence for the defense 答辩证据

evidence identification 证据辨认

evidence in support of abili 证明被告不在现场的证据

evidence law 证据法

evidence list 证据目录

evidence material 证据材料

evidence of contract 合同证明

evidence of debt 债务证据

evidence of identity 鉴别证据

evidence of innocence 无罪证据

evidence of international law 国际法证据

evidence of proof 证据的提供

evidence of title 所有权证据

evidence on appeal 上诉证据

evidence proving innocence 证明无罪的证据

evidence rules 证据法规

evidence that can be used to determine a case 定案证据

evident act 明显行为

evidentia (拉) 证据

evidential function 证据作用

evidentiary 有凭证

evidentiary document 证据文件

evidentiary fact 证据事实

evidentiary material 证据资料

evidentiary statement 口供证据

evil consequences 恶果

Evil is rewarded with evil 恶有恶报

evil law 恶法

"evil law is law" theory 恶法亦法论

evil phenomena 丑恶现象

evil practice 恶习

evil speaking 诽谤

evocation 失效

evolution of law 法律的演进

evolvement of constitution 宪法演变

ex abrupto (拉) 事前未经准备

ex abundanti cautela (拉) 由于充分注意

ex bona fide (拉) 以名誉担保, 出于至诚

ex contract 由于合同

ex contractu (拉) 因契约而引起诉讼, 契约上的, 由于合同

ex debito justitiae (拉) 应得的补救权利, 应得权利

ex delicto (拉) 由于侵权行为, 由于违法行为

ex factory 工厂交货

ex gratia (拉) 惠给金

ex leg (拉) 根据法律的

ex maker's godown 制造商仓库交货

ex maleficio non oritur contractus

（拉） 契约不能产生于不法行为

ex mero motu（拉） 出于自愿

ex mill 工场产货,工厂交货

ex more（拉） 根据习惯

ex necessitate（拉） 由于必要

ex necessitate rei（拉） 由于情况的需要

Ex nudo pacto non oritur actio（拉） 无约因之口头契约不得诉请履行

ex official principle 职权原则

ex pacto illicito non oritur actio（拉） 非法契约无起诉权

ex parte 单方面的

ex parte arbitration 仅有一方当事人在场的仲裁

ex parte divorce 仅有一方当事人在场的离婚诉讼

ex parte hearing 仅有一方当事人在场的诉讼

ex point of origin 原产地交货价,现场交货

ex post facto 有追溯力的

ex rail（拉） 铁路旁交货

ex stock 无权股票

ex store 货栈交货

ex warehouse 货栈交货

ex works 工厂交货

exact 确切

exact quantity 准确数量

exaction 强权

exam 考试

examination 考试

examination and approval 审批

examination and approval of mineral exploitation 矿产资源开采的审批

examination and approval of plans 计划的审批

examination for employment 录用考试

examination of a dismembered body 碎尸检验

examination of appeal 审查申请

examination of budget 预算审议

examination of cargo 货物检查

examination of document 检查证件

examination of evidence 证据检查

examination of final state accounts 国家决算审查

examination of seminal stain 精斑检验

examination of unknown dead body 无名尸体检验

examination report 审查报告

examinational committee （日） 检察审查会

examine 考核,审查,稽核

examine and approve 核准,审批

examine and approve a case involving death penalty 审批死刑案件

examine the matter 实质审查

examine the quality of products 检验产品质量

examine voucher(s) 审核凭证

examiner of the court 法院预审官

examining and approving organization 审批机关

examining body 考试机构

examining justice 预审法官,地方预审法官

example 范例

examplification 例证

exante savings 计划储蓄

excavation 挖坑

exceed authority 超权职权,超过权限

exceed authority and handle carbirarily on one's own 越权擅自处理

exceed one's power or authority 越权

exceed one's powers 超越职权

exceed the limits of necessity 超过必要限度

exceeding one's authority 越权

except as here in after provided 下文另有规定者除外

except with approval or by decision of a person's procuratorate 除检察机关的批准或决定

exceptio (拉) 例外

exception 例外情况,例外

exception clause 例外条款,除外条款,免责条款

exception from liability 赔偿责任的免除

exception law 例外法规

exception of Peter 彼得罗马法例案

exception of restitution 免责事项

exceptional appeal 非常上诉

exceptional circumstances 非常情况,特殊情况

exceptional measure 例外措施

exceptional remedy 特殊补救办法,特殊补救方法

exceptions exemption 免责

excess amoutization 超额偿还

excess disbursement 超额支付

excess of authority 逾越权限,越权

excess of capital 过剩资本

excess of jurisdiction 超越管辖权

excess of loss 超额赔款

excess of loss treaty 超额赔款合同

excess payment 多付,超付,超额支付

excess power 越权

excess profits tax 超额利润税

excess reserves 超额准备金

excessive 过分

excessive cutting and felling of trees 滥伐林木

excessive cutting of trees 滥砍滥伐树木

excessive damages 超额损害赔偿

excessive growth 过度增长

excessive necessity 避险过当

excessive perpetrator 实行犯过当

exchange 交易所,交易

exchange adjustments 调整汇率

exchange arrangement 外汇安排

exchange at unequal value 不等价交换

exchange broker 证券(外汇)经纪人

exchange clearing agreement 外汇清算协定

exchange control 外币管制,汇兑管理

exchange control authorities 外汇管理当局

exchange control regulation 外汇管理规定

exchange convertibility 外汇兑换

exchange customs 交易所惯例

exchange dealer 汇票交易商

exchange depreciation 汇率下降

exchange fluctuations 汇价变动,外汇变动

exchange for forward delivery 远期外汇业务,远期外汇交易

exchange for spot delivery 即期外汇业务

exchange freedom 外汇自由兑换

exchange loss 汇率损失

exchange market 外汇市场

exchange memo 外汇兑换水平

exchange of contracts 交换合同

exchange of equal value 等价交换

exchange of prisoners of war 交换战俘

exchange of ratification 互换批准书,交换批准书

exchange of securities 证券交换

exchange of shares' exchange of stocks 股份交换

exchange of skills 技术交流

exchange of unequal values 不等价交换

exchange payment 外币付款

exchange provision clause 外汇

保留条款,外汇保值条款

exchange quota 外汇配额,外汇限额

exchange quota system 外汇配额制

exchange quotations 外汇行情

exchange rate 汇率,外汇兑换率

exchange rate adjustments 汇率调整

exchange rate depreciation 汇率下跌

exchange rate quotation 外汇牌价

exchange rate system 汇率制度

exchange restriction(s) 外汇限制

exchange risk 外汇风险

exchange settlement 结汇

exchange shop 票号

exchange stabilization fund (ESF) 外汇平准基金

exchange stock 证券交易所

exchange supplementary 外汇附加税

exchange table 汇率换算表

exchange transactions 外汇交易

exchange with compensation 差价调房

excharge control regulation 外汇管理条例

excharge of notes 换文

excharge rate parity 外汇兑换的固定汇率

exchequer bond (英) 国库证券

exchequer bonds 国库券,国库债券

excise tax 货物税

excluded liability 除外责任

excluded perils 除外风险

excluded person 被拒绝入境的人

exclusion 排除在外,除外责任

exclusion act (of the U.S.A.) 美国排斥法

exclusion and restriction of contractual liability 合同责任的免除和限制

exclusion clause 排除条款,除外责任条款

exclusion of hindrance 排除妨碍

exclusion of liabilities 责任排除

exclusion of penalty 不为罪

exclusion policy 闭关政策

exclusionary rules 排除规则

exclusive 专有权

exclusive agency 总代理协议

exclusive agent 独家代理人

exclusive agent agreement 独家代理协议

exclusive authority 排他性权力

exclusive bargaining nights 独家谈判权利

exclusive bindingness 排他性的拘束力

exclusive buying agent 独家购买代理人

exclusive competence 专属职权

exclusive competencies 排他性权力

exclusive distribution 独家经销

exclusive distributorship 额外销售协议

exclusive economic zone 专属经济区

exclusive factory sale agent,sole a-gent 独家代理人

exclusive factory sales agent 独家代理商

exclusive fishery limits 专属渔区

exclusive fishing zone 专属渔区

exclusive licence 独占许可,排他许可证

exclusive license contract 独占许可合同

exclusive listing 总代理协议

exclusive patent rights 独家代理

exclusive patronage contract 独家承运契约

exclusive production licence 独家生产许可证

exclusive right 专营权,特殊权利

exclusive right of pharmaceutical 药品独占权

exclusive right to sell 专卖权

exclusive sales agreement 额外销售协议,包销协议

exclusive selling right 独家经销权,包销权

exclusive sovereignty 排他的主权

exclusive stress on material 福利主义

exclusive use 独占使用

exclusive use of firm name 企业名称专用权

exclusively foreign-owned enterprise 外商独资企业,外商独资经济

exclusiveness 排他性

exclusive-dealing agreement 专销协议

exclusivity agreement 独家经营协议

exculpable evidence 辩护证据

exculpation 免罪

excusable 可免除的

excusatio (拉) 经营

excusation (拉) 免责的理由

excuse 赦免

excuse for nonresponsibility 免责的理由

excused from a duty 免除义务

execute 使生效

execute a contract 执行合同

execute a deed 使契据生效

execute a punishment 执行刑罚,执行刑期

execute a sentence outside prison yet under surveillance 监外执行

execute an order 交付订货,欧美银行(纽约)

executed 已完成的,已生效的

executed consideration 已完成的对价,已付代价,已履行的对价

executed contract 已履行的合同

executed deed 生效的契据

executed period of a punishment 执行刑期

executed provision 已执行规定

executed sale 完成买卖

executed treaty 已执行的条约

executed trust 已生效的信托,已执行的信托

execution 强制执行,处刑,签订,执行

execution by mandate 委托执行

execution ground 刑场,法场

execution of administrative penalties 行政处罚的执行

execution of civil right 权利行使

execution of contract 执行合同,契约生效

execution of duty 履行职责

execution of judgment 判决执行

execution of power 行使权力

execution of punishment 刑罚的执行

execution of the contracts 合同的执行人

execution writ 判决执行令

executive 行政人员,管理人员

executive action 行政行动,行政措施

executive agreement 行政协定,行政性协议

executive authority 行政权

executive autonomy 行政自治

executive branch 行政部门

executive certificate 行政机关证书

executive command 行政管理,行政命令

executive committee 常务委员会

executive control 行政控制权,行政控制

executive decision 行政决定

executive declaration 行政声明

executive department 行政管理部门

executive function 行政职能

executive interpretation 行政解释

executive law 行政法

executive measure 执行措施

executive meeting 常务会议

executive meetings of the State Council 国务院常务会议

executive officer 行政官,行政官员

executive order 行政命令

executive orders of the President of the U.S. 美国总统的行政命令

executive pardon 行刑豁免

executive personnel 行政人员

executive power 行政权力,行政权,行政管理权

executive self-determination 行政自主

executive staff 行政管理人员

executor 实行犯

executory 待履行的,待生效的

executory consideration 待履行的对待,未付对价,未完成的对价

executory contract 未经履行的合同,待履行的合同,待履行之契约

executory effect 执行效力

executory interest 待生效的权益

executory trust 待执行的信托

exegetic interpretation 注释解释

exemplar 样本

exemplary 惩罚性

exempt 免除,免责

exempt from any fees or dues 免除一切捐税

exempt from customs duty 免验

exempt from inspection 免验

exempted from military service 免除服役

exempted securities 豁免的证券

exemption 免责

exemption customs duties 免征关税

exemption for dependents 抚养费免税

exemption from civil jurisdiction 民事管辖豁免

exemption from criminal jurisdiction 刑事管辖豁免

exemption from criminal penalties 免于刑事处分

exemption from customs duty 免征关税

exemption from customs examination 免验

exemption from disciplinary sanction 免于处分

exemption from double taxation 免征双重税

exemption from esxtate duty 豁免遗产税

exemption from inspection 免费检验

exemption from liability 免除责任,责任的免除

exemption from penalties 免刑

exemption from prosecution 免予起诉

exemption from punishment 免于处罚

exemption from security sanctions 免于治安处罚

exemption of punishment 刑罚免除

exequatur 领事证书

exercise 行使,实行,履行

exercise a claim 行使债权

exercise a right 运用权利

exercise collective leadership 实行集体领导

exercise dictatorship 实行专政

exercise discretion in sentencing 量刑

exercise due care 以应有的谨慎

exercise due diligence 谨慎处理

exercise ex official 运用职权

exercise of administrative power 运用行政权力

exercise of rights 权利行使,行使权力

exercise official powers 行使职

权

exercise one's functions and powers 行使职权

exercise right(s) 行使权利

exercise state power 行使国家权力

exercise strict control over 严格控制

exercise the veto 行使否决权

exert authority 行使权力

exertion 行使

exertion of power 权力的行使，行使权力

exhaust price 底线价格

exhaustion of administrative remedies 用尽行政的救济方法

exhaustion of domestic remedies 用尽国内补救方法

exhaustion of effect 有效期满

exhaustion of local remedies 用尽当地救济方法

exhaustion of local remedies rule 用尽当地救济原则

exhaustion psychosis 衰志性精神障碍

exhibit, real evidence 证物

exhibitionism 露阴癖

exhibits presented at court as material evidence 法庭上出示的物证

exhortation 催告

exigent 催告书

exigenter 催告人

exigration control 出境检查

exile 流放，流放刑

Exim 日本输出入银行

Eximbank 美国进出口银行

exist in name only 名存实亡的

existance of obligation 债权存在

existing law 存在的法律，现行法律

existing machinery 现有体制

existing price 现行价格

existing text 现行条文

existing writings 成文

exit （建筑物的）出口，出境

exit card 出境卡

① exit certificate 出境证书

② exit documentation 出售出入境

③ 证件罪

④ exit formalities 出境手续

⑤ exit passport 出境护照

⑥ exit permit 出境许可证

⑦ exit quarantine 出境检疫

⑧ exit receipt 出境回执

⑨ exit register 出境登记

⑩ exit register card 出境登记卡

⑪ exit visa 出境签证

⑫ exit-entry permit for foreigner

⑬ 外国人出入境证

⑭ exonerate 免责

⑮ exonerate from the liability for

⑯ compensation 免除赔偿责任

⑰ exoneration 免罪，解除负债，免

⑱ 责,证明无罪

⑲ exoneration clause 免责条款

⑳ exoneration from the liability for

㉑ compensation 免除赔偿责任

㉒ exoneration of international crimi-

㉓ nal responsibility 国际刑事责

㉔ 任之免除

㉕ exorbitant price 过高价格

㉖ exorbitant taxes and levies 苛捐

㉗ 杂税

㉘ expand 发展

㉙ expand enterprise autonomy 扩

㉚ 大企业自主权

㉛ expand market 扩展市场

㉜ expanded reproduction 扩大再

㉝ 生产

㉞ expansion of foreign trade 对外

㉟ 贸易扩张

㊱ expansion of the currency 通货

㊲ 膨胀

㊳ expansionary policy 扩张政策

㊴ expansionism 扩张主义

㊵ expansionist policy 扩张政策

㊶ expansive policy 扩张政策

㊷ expatriate 脱离国籍者

㊸ expatriation 出籍,脱离国籍,流

㊹ 放国外

㊺ expatriation permit 出籍许可证

㊻ 书

㊼ expectant 候补

expectant judge 候补法官,候补审判员

expectant property right 期待的财产权

expectant prosecutor 候补检察官

expectation of property 期待分得的财产

expected profit clause 期得利益条款

expected result 预期结果

expected time of arrival 预抵期

expected time of commencement of loading 预计开始装货时间

expective right 预期权

expediency 实用主义

expedit republicate ut sit finis litium（拉）从国家利益考虑

expediter 稽查员,发送人

expeditious execution of the order 迅速执行订单

expel 驱除,开除

expellee 被驱逐出境者

expenditer 发信人

expenditure tax 开支税

expense of administration 行政管理费用

expense of credit realization 实现债权的费用

expenses 费用

expenses for urban development and maintenance 城市建设和维护费

expenses of compensation 赔偿费用

expenses of performance 履行费用

expension investment 扩建投资

expent witness 鉴定证人

experience of crime 犯罪体验

experience table 死亡率统计表

experienced 有经验的

experimental enterprise 试点企业

expert 鉴定人

expert cabinet 专家内阁

expert evaluation after death 死亡后鉴定

expert evaluation of death 死亡鉴定

expert evidence 鉴定人证据

expert opinion 鉴定意见

expert testimony of juridical psychiatry 司法心理鉴定

expert valuation of sex crime 性犯罪鉴定

expert witness 鉴定证人

expertise report 鉴定书

expertise toward civil capacity 民事行为能力鉴定

expiable 可抵偿的

expiration 届满,期满,到期

expiration of contract 合同到期,合同期满

expiration of one term of imprisonment 刑期届满

expiration of one's term of office 任期届满

expiration of probation 缓刑考验期满

expiration of the agreed term 约定的期限届满

expiration of the contract period 合同期满

expiration of the period of reorganization 整顿期满

expiration of the term of guarantee 保证期限届满

expiration of the term of office of people's congress 人民代表大会任期届满

expire 届满,期满,到期

expire of the legal（苏格兰）取消期满

expired laws 失效法律

expired laws continuance act 失效法律延续法

expiree 服满刑期者,满期出狱者

expiry 期限

expiry date 失效日,期满之日,终止期限

expiry date of letter of credit 信用证有效期

expiry of charter party 租约期满

expiry of tenancy 租约期满

explain 说明

explain intent 说明意图

explanation to the letter 文字解释

explanatory notes to BTN 税目分类注释说明

explanatory statements on financial conditions 财务情况说明书

explicit 明确的

explicit interest 现付利息

explicit order 明令

explicit renewal 明示重订

explicit repudiation 明示废除

explicitly 明确地

explicitly provided 明文规定的

exploit 剥削

exploit the advantages to the full 发挥优势

exploit the patent for free 免费实施专利

exploitability 可开发性

exploitation of man by man 人剥削人

exploitation of natural resources 自然资源的开发利用

exploitation of one's unfavorable position 乘人之危

exploitation through land rent 地租剥削

exploitative system of area "区域"开发制度

exploitativeness 可实施性

exploited class 被剥削阶级

exploiting class 剥削阶级

exploiting outlook 剥削阶级思想

explorability 可勘探性

exploration project 开发性项目

exploration risks 勘探风险

explosive 易爆

explosive cargo 易爆炸货物

explosive goods 爆炸物

explosive personality disorder 暴型人格障碍

explosiveness 易爆

export administration act 出口管理法

export administration regulation 出口管理条例

export agent 出口代理

export bill 出口汇票

export bill of entry 出口报单

export bill of exchange 出口押汇

export bonus 出口奖金

export certificate 出口证明

export clause 出口条款

export commodity 出口商品

export contract 出口合同

export control 出口管制

export control act 出口管制法

export control country group 国别分组管制表

export council 出口委员会

export credit 出口信用证,出口信贷

export credit guarantee 出口信贷担保品,出口信用保险

export credit guarantee system 出口信贷国家担保制

export credit insurance 出口信贷担保

export credit rate 出口信贷利率

export declaration 出口报关

export document 出口单据

export drawback(s) 出口退税

export duties 出口税

export duty refunds 出口退税

export finance 出口融资

export gold point 黄金输出点

export inspection system 出口检验制度

export insurance 出口保险

export letter of credit 出口信用证

export licence 出口保证书,出口许可证

export market 出口市场

export of capital 资本输出

export order 出口定单

export permission 出口许可	express agreement 明示协议
export permit 出口许可证	express authority 明示权限,明示授权
export price 出口价格	
export pricing check 出口价格控制	express condition 明示条件
	express consent 明示同意,明示信托
export pricing system 出口价格制度	
	express consideration(s) 明示对价,明示约因
export processing 出口加工	
export processing zone 出口加工业	express contract 明示合同
	express declaration 明确宣告
export promotion 面向出口	express delivery 明示交付
export quarantine 出口检疫	express excusation (拉) 免责的理由
export quota(s) 出口配额制,出口限额	
	express guarantee 明示保证
export refund 出口退税	express guaranteeship 明示担保
export regulation tax 出口调节税	express in writing 作出书面表示
export regulations 出口条例	express mail 快递邮件,快件
export restrictions 出口限制	express malice 明示恶意,明显的恶意
export sales 外销	
export subsidy 出口补贴	express notification 明示通知
export surplus 出口盈余	express objection 明示异议或反对
export tariff 出口关税率	
export tax/duty 出口税	express obligation 明示债务
export techniques 出口技术	express offer and acceptance 明示要约与承诺
export trade 出口贸易	
export trade act 出口贸易法	express or implied 明示或默示
export value 出口检验	express parcel 快件
export visa 出口配额鉴证	express power 明示权力
export/bill of entry 出口报单	express proclamation 明示公告
exportation 出口物,输出货物	express prohibition 明示禁止
export-credit insurance 出口信用保险	express promise 明示诺言
	express provision 明文规定
exporter 出口商	express recognition 明示承认
exporting country 输出国	express recognition of government 对政府的明示承认
expose the executed body publicly 弃市(中国古代刑)	
	express renunciation 明文的拒绝
exposure 检举	
expound 阐明	express repeal 明显废止
expound one's views 申述自己的观点	express reservation 明示权益保留
express 明示的	express right 明示权利
express abrogation 明确废除	express term 明示条款
express acceptance 明示接受	express terms 明示条款
express act of recognition 明示承认行为	express terms of the contract 合同明文规定
express agency 明示代理	express trust 书面信托

express undertaking 明示责任
express waiver 明示放弃
express warranty 明示担保
expressed intention 意思表示
expression of apology 赔礼道歉
expression of criminal intent 犯意表示
expressly agreed terms of the contract 合同明文规定
expressly provide 明文规定
expressly stated 明文规定的
Expressum facit cessare tacitum (拉) 明示排除默示
expromission 请人代为清偿债务
expromissor 替代债务人
expropriate 征用,没收
expropriation 征用险,国家征用,征用土地,没收财产
expropriation of property 财产没收
expropriation risk 征收险
expropriator 没收人
expulsion from academic status 开除学籍
expulsion from parliament 逐出议会
expulsion from school 开除学籍
expulsion order 驱逐令
expunge one's name from a list 除名
extend 延长
extend credit to 贷款
extend of competence 权限范围
extend shipment date 延长装运日期
extend the expiration date 延长有效期
extend the time for filing claims 延长赔款期
extend the time for performance 延期履行
extend the time limit 延长期限
extended arrangement 延期安排
extended cover clause 扩展责任条款
extended custody 超期羁押

① extended fund facility 中期基金
② extended insurance 展期保险
③ extended loss 扩大的损失
④ extended of delay 延迟期
⑤ extended period 延长期
⑥ extended reproduction 扩大再生产
⑦
⑧ extended reproduction fund 扩大再生产基金
⑨
⑩ extended sentence 加刑
⑪ extendible 可延长的
⑫ extension 延长,延期还债认可书
⑬ extension agreement 延期协议
⑭ extension of apology 赔礼道歉
⑮ extension of judgment 判决的延期
⑯
⑰ extension of loan 贷款偿还期的延长
⑱
⑲ extension of maturity 延期
⑳ extension of the time limit for delivery of goods 延期交货
㉑
㉒ extension of the time limit for taking delivery of goods 延期提货
㉓
㉔ extension of time limit 顺延期限
㉕ extension of validity 有效期延长
㉖
㉗
㉘ extension project 扩建项目
㉙ extensional 外销
㉚ extensive 大规模
㉛ extensive city planing 大范围城市规划
㉜
㉝ extensive interpretation 扩充解释,扩大解释,扩张解释,广义解释
㉞
㉟
㊱ extensive order 大量采购,大批订货
㊲
㊳ extensive transaction 大批交易,巨额交易
㊴
㊵ extent for discretionary action of sentencing 量刑幅度
㊶
㊷ extent of actual control 实际控制范围
㊸
㊹ extent of authority 权限
㊺ extent of compensation 赔偿范围
㊻
㊼ extent of competence 权限范围

extent of crime 犯罪成因学
extent of damage 损害程度,损失程度
extent of danger 危险程度
extent of fault 过失程度
extent of injury 危害程度
extent of judge's power 法官的权力范围
extent of liability 责任范围
extent of power 权限
extent of protection 保护范围
extent of punishment 刑度
extent of responsibility 责任范围
extent of the damage 损坏程度
extenuate 减轻
extenuation of a crime 减轻罪行
exterior injury 外部伤害
exterior liabilities 对外负债
exterior territorial sea 外部领海
extermination of an entire family 灭族
external (/foreign) trade 对外贸易
external account 境外账户
external administrative act 外部行政行为
external administrative dispute 行部行政争议
external administrative jural relations 外部行政法律关系
external administrative law 外部行政法
external administrative laws and regulations 对外行政法规
external administrative legal supervision 外部行政法制监督
external administrative organization 外部行政机关
external affairs 外部事务
external aid 外部援助
external assets 国外资产
external control 外部控制
external debt 外债
external debt servicing 外债偿付
external evaluation 外部评价

external jurisdiction 外部管辖权
external liquidity 对外清偿能力
external mark 外部标志
external packing 外包装
external public debt 国外公债
external public law 对外公法
external purchase 外购
external relationship 外部关系
external reserve 对外储备
external security 外部安全
external short-term liabilities 对外短期负债
external solvency 对外偿付能力
external sovereignty 对外主权,对外最高权
external supervision 外部监督
external surplus 对外顺差
external trade 对外贸易
external value of currency 货币对外价值
external value of money 货币对外价值
externalization of criminal mind 犯罪心理外化
exterritorial asylum 域外保护
exterritorial jurisdiction 治外法权(领事裁判权)
exterritoriality 治外法权(领事裁判权)
exterritoriality of diplomatic envoys 外交使节的治外法权
extinction of debt 返清债务
extinction of law 法律的消亡
extinction of obligation 债的消灭
extinction of rights 权利的消灭
extinction of state 国家的消亡
extinctive prescription 诉讼时效,消灭时效
extinguish 偿清债务,使无效,偿清
extinguishment 偿清,权利的消灭,(法律关系)消灭
extinguishment fund 偿债基金
extinguishment of administrative act 行政行为的消灭
extinguishment of jural relation of

administrative procedure 行政诉讼法律关系的完全消灭

extinguishment of the mortgage of the ship 船舶抵押权的消灭

extinguishments of legal relationship of administrative procedure 行政诉讼法律关系的完全消灭

extort 敲诈勒索,索诈,强权,勒索

extort a confession 逼供

extort a confession by torture 刑讯逼供

extort bribes 索贿

extortion for confession 逼供

extortionate demand 索诈,吓诈

extortioner 敲诈勒索

extra best quality 最优等品质

extra charges 额外费用

extra discount 额外折扣

extra duty 额外税收

extra packing 特殊包装

extra premium 额外保险费

extra price 附加价格

extra tax on corporate profits 超额公司利得税

extra tax on profits increased 超额利得税

extra vires (拉) 超越法定权限

extract 判决摘录书

Extrada Doctrine 艾斯特拉达主义

extraditable crime 可引渡之罪,引渡罪

extradition 引渡

extraeconomic exploitation 超经济剥削

extrajudicial 未按法律程序,法院管辖以外的

extrajudicial confession 法院外招供

extrajudicial mediation 法院外调解

extrajudicial statement 法院外陈述

extralegal 超出法律权限的

extralegal detention 超越法律的拘留

extralegal imprisonment 违法监禁,违法拘留

extralegal search 违法搜查,超越法律的搜查

extraneous risks 额外风险,外来危险,附加险

extraordinaria judicia (拉) 非常诉讼

extraordinarily large issue of paper money 纸币发行过多

extraordinarily serious accident with casualty 特别重大伤亡事故

extraordinarily serious pollution accident 特大污染事故

extraordinarily serious safety accident 特大安全事故

extraordinarily serious traffic accident 特大交通事故

extraordinary 非常

extraordinary budget 临时预算

extraordinary case 特别案件,特殊案件

extraordinary circumstances 非常情况

extraordinary loss 特殊损失

extraordinary remedies 特别补偿

extraordinary resolution 非常决议案

extraterritorial 域外

extraterritorial asylum 域外保护

extraterritorial criminal jurisdiction 域外刑事管辖权

extraterritorial effect 域外效力

extraterritorial jurisdiction 治外法权

extraterritorial operation 域外实行,域外效力

extraterritorial protection 域外保护

extraterritoriality 法外特权,治外法权

extravagant price 过高价格

extra-atmosphere space 大气外空间

extra-budgetary funds 预算外资金

extra-budgetary investment 预算外投资

extra-contractual effect 契约外效果

extra-law 法律以外

extra-organization 编外人员

extreme limit 最大限额,最高限额

extreme measure 极端措施

① ②
③ ④
⑤ ⑥
⑦ ⑧
⑨ ⑩
⑪

extremely huge amount 数额特别巨大

extrinsic acceptance 票外承兑

extrinsic ambiguity 非契约本身固有的意义不明确

EXW 工厂交货

ex-works price 出厂价格

eyewitness 亲眼证人

eyewitness identification 目击证人辨认

eyre 巡回法庭

F

fabric 建筑物

fabricate 捏造,编造,伪造

fabricate fact 捏造事实

fabricated charge 莫须有的罪名

fabricated civil act 虚构民事行为

fabricated facts 捏造的事实

fabricated materials 装配材料

fabricating cost 安装费用

fabricating of facts 捏造事实

fabrication 伪造物,伪造

Fabrication or distortion of facts is prohibited 不得捏造或者歪曲事实

fabricator 伪造者

face amount 票据金额、面额

face par 票面价格

face value 票据金额,面额,票面价值

face(/denomination) amount 票面金额

face (/par/nominal/denomination) value 票面价值

facilitate busIness 为便于成交

facility 设备

facio ut des(拉) 双务契约

facsimile signature 印鉴样本

facsimile, telex, EDI, e-mail 传真,电传,电子数据处理,电子邮件

fact about a crime 罪状

fact and law 事实与法律

fact finding 事实调查

fact of malfeasance 违法事实

factor 代理商;因素,要素

factor agent 代办商

factor of safety 安全系数

factor service 要素服务

factor that influences the mind in crimes 影响犯罪心理的因素

factor's acts (英)代理经营法

factor's lien 代理人留置权

factorage 代理商佣金

factories act(英) 工厂法

factories and workers act(英) 工厂和车间法

factoring 代收账款,保付代理;财务代现

factoring company 代理公司

factor-price-equalization theorem 要素价格均等定理

factors of administration 行政要素

factors of production 生产要素

factory 制造厂

factory dIstrIct 工业区

factory law 工厂法

factory legislation 工厂立法

factory management 出厂价格

factory management committee 工厂管理委员会

factory price, mill price 出厂价格

factory quality terms 出厂品质条件

factory system 工厂制度

facts of a case 案件的事实,案情,案情事实

facts of procedure 程序法事实

factual basis 事实过失,事实根据

factual defects 事实瑕疵

factual negligence 事实过失

factual question 事实审

factuality 真实性

factum 个人行为

faculta jurisdictionis(拉) 裁判权

facultative insurance 临时分保

facultative reinsurance 临时再保险

faculty 权力,能力

faculty of advocates 律师联合会

faculty of law 法学院,法律系

fail in a suit 败诉

fail in an engagement 失约
fail in business 折本,歇业
fail to carry out 不履行
fail to conduct inspection and issue certificate within the limit time 延误检验出证
fail to deliver 未能交付
fail to give notice 未通知
fail to keep an appointment 失约
fail to pay an instalment 未履行分期付款义务
fail to pay the price 未履行付款义务
fail to perform a contract 未履行合同
fail to perform an obligation 未履行义务
fail to present 未提示
fail to reach an agreement 未能达成协议
fail to repay when due 延期归还,延期履行
fail to take delivery 未提货
failure 破产、倒闭
failure of appearance 拒不到场
failure of consideration 缺乏对价,不予补偿,不加考虑
failure of justice 审判不公
failure of performance of a contract 未履行合同
failure to act 未能履行
failure to appear in court 拒不到庭
failure to deliver the goods 未交货
failure to make discovery 疏于披露
failure to perform 不履行义务
fair 合理,公平,公正
fair and equitable 公允
fair and equitable treatment 公平合理的待遇
fair and free foreign trade order 公平的自由的对外贸易秩序
fair and reasonable 公平合理
fair and tear 自然磨损

① fair average quality/FAQ 平均良好品质
③ fair comtepition 公平竞争
④ fair deal 公平施政,公平交易
⑤ fair dealing 公平交易
⑥ fair ground 集市场所
⑦ fair market price 合理市价
⑧ fair market value 公平市价
⑨ fair packaging and labeling act (美)公平包装及标签法
⑪ fair play 平等对待
⑫ fair practice 合理惯例
⑬ fair pricing 合理作价
⑭ fair rent 公平租金
⑮ fair return 公平收益
⑯ fair share 合理份额
⑰ fair trade 公平交易
⑱ fair trade law 公平交易法
⑲ fair trading act 公平交易法
⑳ fair value 公平价值
㉑ fair wear and tear 自然损耗
㉒ fairness 公平
㉓ fair-trade agreement 公平贸易约定
㉕ fair-trade practices 公平交易惯例
㉗ fair-trade price 公平交易价格
㉘ faith 约定,信仰
㉙ Faith must be observed 信用必须严格遵守
㉛ faithful 忠实
㉜ fake 伪造物,冒牌
㉝ fake a real 以伪充实
㉞ fake and shoddy goods 假冒伪劣商品
㊱ fakery 伪造物
㊲ fakes 假冒商品
㊳ fall 下跌,下降
㊴ fall bar 插销
㊵ fall due 到期
㊶ fall in 到期
㊷ fall into the net of justice 落入法网
㊹ fall short of the specifications 不合规格
㊻ fall short of what is needed to cover the debts 不足以清偿

债务

fall within jurisdiction 受到法律审判

fallout 放射性微尘

false 虚假,诈欺

false act 虚假的民事行为

false arrest 假捕

false coin 伪币

false confession 假坦白

false debt 假债

false demonstration 虚伪表达,错误表达

false dernonstratio non nocet (拉) 错误的叙述不导致契据无效

false detention 错误拘留

false economic contract 假经济合同

false imprisonment 错误拘留,非法拘禁

false information with intent 有意提供假情报

false libel 不实诽谤罪

false medical testimony 不实医学确定罪

false papers 假证件

false performance 假执行

false plea 假答辩

false pretence 欺诈手段

false representation 假冒,虚伪陈述

false representation of personal names 盗用姓名

false scales 短尺少秤

false statement 虚假陈述

false trade description 虚假的商品论证,伪造商品说明书

false verdict 假裁决,不当的裁决

falsehood misstatement 虚伪陈述

falsely or wrongly charged or sentenced 冤假错案

falsely pass off 假冒

falsification of public seal 伪造公章

falsification of seal 伪造印章

falsify 编造,伪造

falsify inspection result 伪造检验结果

falsifying statistical data 伪造统计资料

family background 家庭出身,出身

family business 家族农业

family contract 家庭契约

family enterprise 家庭企业

family law 家庭法

family members of Chinese nationals residing abroad 侨眷

family members of overseas Chinese 侨眷

family of the suspect 嫌疑犯家属

family operation 家庭经营

family partnership 家庭合伙

family planning 计划生育

family planning law 计划生育法

family plot 自留地

family possessions 家庭财产

family property law 家庭财产法

family relation 亲属关系

family's property 家庭财产

famine price 高价

famous-brand product 名牌产品

farm cooperation 农业合作社

farm dwelling 农村住房

farm for reform-through-labour 劳动改造农场

farmers' market 农贸市场

farm-price method 农产品计价法

FAS (free along-side ship) 船边交货

fascism 法西斯主义

fascist 法西斯

fascist dictatorship 法西斯专政

fatal concentration 致死浓度

father right 父权

fatherland 祖国

fault 过错,罪过,过错

fault liability 过错赔偿责任,过失责任

fault of crew collision 船员过失

碰撞

fault of injuring person 加害人过错

fault of sufferer 受害人过错

fault standard of liability 责任的过失标准

faultless 没有过错,没有过失

faulty allegation of charges 罪名认定错误

faulty goods 劣质货

faulty operation and management 经营管理不善

faulty packing 包装不良,有缺点的包装

faulty prosecution 检察失实

faulty prosecutorial protest 抗诉不当

faulty ruling 裁定不当

fauna and flora 动植物

fauna and flora protection 动植物保护

favorable balance of foreign exchange earnings and outlays 外汇收支顺差

favorable balance of payments 国际收支逆差

favorable transformation of crime 犯罪良性转化

favour 赠与

favour of land 土地赠与

favour property 赠与财产

favourable 优惠

favourable balance of trade export duties 对外贸顺差

favourable conditions 有利条件

favourable economic condition 经济优势

favourable factors 有利条件

favourable price 优惠价格

favourable terms 有利条件,优惠利率

favourable treatment 优惠待遇

favoured property 赠与财产

FCA (free carrier) 货交承运人

fear motive 恐惧动机

feasibility 可行的

feasibility analysis 可行性分析

① **feasibility conditions** 可行性条件

② 件

③ **feasibility research** 可行性研究

④ **feasibility study** 可行性论证,可

⑤ 行性研究

⑥ **feasibility study reports** 可行性

⑦ 研究报告

⑧ **feasible** 可行,切实

⑨ **feasible and effective** 切实有效

⑩ **feasible program** 可行方案

⑪ **feast tax** 筵席税

⑫ **federal acts** 联邦法

⑬ **federal agency** 联邦机构

⑭ **federal anti-trust law**(美) 反垄

⑮ 断法

⑯ **federal attorney** 联邦律师

⑰ **federal boat safety act** 联邦小船

⑱ 安全法(注:指美国国会立法)

⑲ **federal citizenship** 联邦公民身

⑳ 份

㉑ **federal constitution** 联邦宪法

㉒ **federal constitutional court** 联邦

㉓ 宪法法院

㉔ **federal court**(U.S.) 美国联邦

㉕ 法院

㉖ **federal courts system** 美国联邦

㉗ 法院系统

㉘ **federal food, drug and cosmetic**

㉙ **act** 联邦食品、药品及化妆品

㉚ 法

㉛ **federal forest** 国有林

㉜ **federal government** 联邦政府

㉝ **federal instrumentality** 联邦机

㉞ 构

㉟ **federal judge**(U.S.) 美国联邦

㊱ 法官

㊲ **federal jurisdiction** 联邦管辖权

㊳ **federal law** 联邦法律

㊴ **federal police power** 联邦警察

㊵ 权

㊶ **federal question jurisdiction** 美

㊷ 国联邦问题的初审权

㊸ **federal regulations** 联邦法规

㊹ **federal regulatory commission**

㊺ 联邦管理委员会

㊻ **federal reporter** 联邦判例汇编

㊼ **federal republic** 联邦共和国

federal rules for the trial of minor offenses before United States magistrates 美国行政司法官审理青少年犯罪的联邦规则

federal state 联邦国家

federal state union 联邦

federal statutes 联邦法

federal system 联邦制

federal system (federalism) 联邦制

federal trade commission (F.T.C) 美国联邦贸易委员会

federal trade commission act 联邦贸易委员会法

federal tribunal 联邦法院

federalism 联邦制

federalist 联邦党人

federated republic 联邦共和国

federation 联邦政府,联邦

federation of states 联邦

federation of trade unions 总工会

fee 酬金

fee for a request for invalidation 无效宣告请求费

fee for excess discharge 超标准排污费

fee for sale custody 寄存费

fee for technical service 技术服务费

fee for technology transfer 技术转让费

fee for the compensation of crops 青苗赔偿费

fee for the protection and administration of wildlife resource 野生动物资源保护管理费

fee of permit 牌照税,执照税

fee simple 非限定继承的土地

fee tail 限嗣继承土地,指定继承认继承之不动产权

fee-farm rent 非限定继承土地的永久租金

fee-simple absolute in possession 绝对公有的不动产

feigned 伪造的

fell contract (苏格兰) 长期租地契约

① fellowship 共同参与

② fellow-trade price 同业价格

③ fellow-trader commission 同行折扣同行佣金

④ fellow-trader discount 同行折扣

⑤ felon 重罪犯

⑥ felonies against public moral 侵犯公德重罪

⑦ felonies against the independence and safety of the states 侵犯国家独立安全罪

⑧ felonious assault 严重暴力伤害人身罪,攻击性犯罪

⑨ felonious homicide 严重杀人罪

⑩ felony murder 重罪谋杀罪

⑪ female 妇女

⑫ female accuser 女告发人

⑬ female crime 女性犯罪

⑭ female judge 女法官,女审判员

⑮ female offender 女犯

⑯ female prisoner 女犯,女囚犯

⑰ female suffrage 妇女参政权,妇女选举权

⑱ female victim 女性被害人

⑲ feminism 女权

⑳ feminist movement 女权运动

㉑ Fenton. Johoson 牛顿·约翰逊

㉒ feoffee 不动产承受人

㉓ feoffor 不动产赠与人

㉔ ferae naturae (拉) 不属于私产的

㉕ ferm 出租的房地产

㉖ ferocious criminal 凶恶犯

㉗ ferocious criminality 凶恶犯罪

㉘ fetishism 恋物癖

㉙ fetters 镣

㉚ feudal 封建

㉛ feudal courts 采邑法院

㉜ feudal customs and habits 封建习俗

㉝ feudal dynasties 封建王朝

㉞ feudal economy 封建经济

㉟ feudal hierarchy 封建等级制度

㊱ feudal law 封建制法

㊲ feudal lord 封建主

㊳ feudal monarchy 封建帝制

feudal nobles 封建贵族

feudal privilege 封建特权

feudal republic 封建共和制

feudal separationist rule 封建割据

feudal society 封建社会

feudal state 封建制国家

feudal system 封建制度

feudalism 封建主义

feudality 封建政体,封建制度

feudal-fascist dictatorship 封建法西斯专政

fiars' price (苏格兰) 谷类法定价格

fiction theory 拟制理论

fictious plaintiff 假设原告

fictitious 买空卖空

fictitious bargain 买空卖空

fictitious bill 空头支票

fictitious capital 虚构资本

fictitious constitution 虚假宪法

fictitious price 虚价

fictitious transaction 虚构交易

Fidelcot (Philadelphia) 弗德里奇国际银行(费城)

fidelity insurance 忠诚保险,职工信用保险,忠诚保证保险

fides (拉) 忠实

fides foederum (拉) 保证契约

fides servanda est (拉) 必须守信

fiducia (拉) 信托,抵押

fiducial business 信托业务

fiduciary 受托人,信托事务,信托性

fiduciary bond 受托人保证

fiduciary contract 信托合同

fiduciary deposit 信托账户

fiduciary estates 信托财产

fiduciary investment 信托投资

fiduciary loan 信用贷款

fiduciary money 信用货币,纸币

fiduciary position 信托地位

fiduciary property 受托保管的财产

fiduciary relation 信托关系

fiduciary relationship 信托关系

fiduciary service 信托服务

fiduciary system 信用保证制度

field 领域

Field Code 菲尔德法典

field general court-martial 军内军事法庭

field survey 现场调查

field warehousing 货栈担保

fields work standards of auditing 审计现场检查标准

fight 战斗

fighting war operation 战斗

file 呈递,案卷

file a claim 提出索赔

file a claim for recovery 提出追偿

file a complaint 呈交诉状

file an application 提出申请

file an indictment 呈交诉状

file challenge 提出异议

file clerk 档案管理员

file for reexamination 报请复核

file integrity 档案的完整性

file management 档案管理

file of evidence 证据卷

file pleadings 呈递答辩状

file wag 档案工资

files 档案

filing of the award 申请仲裁

filing returns and computing and paying a tax at source 从源报税、计税、付税

filing status 申报纳税身份

fill 加以补充

fill an order 交付订货

final account 决算

final account of state revenue and expenditure 国家决策,国家收支决算

final accounts procedure 决算程序

final act 最后决议书,最后议定书

final act of the conference on the conservation of antarctic marine living resources 保护南极海

洋生物资源会议最后文件 (1980)

final administrative act 终局行政行为

final administrative ruling 终局行政裁决

final against the plaintiff 作出不利于原告的判决

final award 最后裁决

final carrier 最终承运人

final communique of the Asian-African conference 亚非会议最后公报

final date of filing 申报所得税截止期

final day of the war 战争结束日

final decision 最后裁决,终局决定,定案

final decision of reconsideration 终局复议决定

final decision rule 最后裁决规则

final decree 最后判决令,最后裁定

final destination 最后目的地,最终目的地

final evidence 结论性证据

final judg(e)ment 终审权,终局判决,最终判决

final judgment rule 最终判决规则

final order 最后订货

final port of discharge 最终卸货港

final price 最后价格,最终价格

final proceedings 终结审判

final process 最后诉讼阶段

final product price 最终产品价格

final quality certificate 最终品质证书

final rejection 最终驳回

final report 决算书

final ruling 最后裁定,终局裁决

final sale 最终销售

final sentence 最终判决

① **final shipping instruction** 最后装运通知
②
③ **final statement** 最后陈述
④ **final statement made by the defendant** 被告人最后陈述
⑤
⑥ **final supervision** 最后监督
⑦ **final user** 最终用户
⑧ **final verdict** 最终裁决,最后裁决
⑨
⑩ **finality of award** 裁决的确定性
⑪ **finalization of auditing** 审计终结
⑫
⑬ **finance** 财政、金融,提供资金
⑭ **finance act** 财政法案
⑮ **finance act/law** 财政法
⑯ **finance and economics** 财经
⑰ **finance auditing and revenue-expenditure** 财政、财务收支
⑱
⑲ **finance auditing and revenue-expenditure auditing** 财政、财务收支审计
⑳
㉑
㉒ **finance bill** 财政法案
㉓ **finance capital** 金融资本
㉔ **finance chief** 财务负责人
㉕ **finance committee** 财政委员会
㉖ **finance company** 金融公司
㉗ **finance contract** 信贷合同
㉘ **finance corporation** 金融公司
㉙ **finance house** 金融公司
㉚ **finance lease** 融资租赁,金融租赁
㉛
㉜ **finance market** 金融市场
㉝ **finance norms** 金融规范
㉞ **finance officer** 财务主管
㉟ **finance service** 金融服务
㊱ **finance subordinate relationship** 财政、财务隶属关系
㊲
㊳ **finance swap transaction** 金融期权交易
㊴
㊵ **financial** 财政的,金融的
㊶ **financial accounting** 财务会计
㊷ **financial accounting standards board** 财务会计准则委员会
㊸
㊹ **financial administration** 财务管理,财政机关
㊺
㊻ **financial affairs and accountancy** 财会
㊼

financial agent　财务代理人

financial allocations　财政拨款

financial and accounting book(s)　财务会计报告

financial and economic committee　财政经济委员会

financial and economic committee　财经委员会

financial and economic system　财经制度

financial and monetary crisis　金融货币危机

financial and monetary system　金融货币体系

financial and tax authorities　财政税务机关

financial assets　金融资产

financial attache　财务专员

financial authorities　财政机关

financial bill　金融票据

financial blockade　财政封锁

financial bond　金融债券

financial capital　金融资本

financial case　金融案件

financial center　金融中心

financial circulation　金融流通

financial claim　金融债权,债权

financial claim trust　金钱债权信托

financial clause　财政条款

financial coercion　财政强迫

financial committee　财务委员会

financial community　金融界

financial condition　财政状况

financial constraints　财政紧缩

financial control　财政监督,财务管制

financial control system　财政管理体制

financial convenant　财务约定事项

financial corporation　金融财团,金融公司

financial court　财政法庭

financial credit　财政信贷,金融信用

financial crisis　财政危机,金融危机

financial deficit　金融赤字

financial discipline　财政纪律

financial futures　金融期货

financial futures contract　金融期货契约

financial futures market　金融期货市场

financial futures trading　金融期货交易

financial group　财团

financial guarantee　财务担保

financial guaranty　财务担保

financial initiative　财政动议权

financial innovation　金融创新

financial insolvency　无力偿还

financial inspection　金融检查

financial institution　金融机构

financial instruments　金融工具

financial intermediaries　金融中介机构,金融媒介

financial interests　金融权益

financial intervention　财政干涉

financial investment　金融投资

financial issue　财政发行

financial jurisprudence　财政法学

financial law　财政法

financial laws and regulations　财政法规

financial lease　金融租赁,融资性租赁,融资租赁

financial legislation　财政立法

financial magnate　财阀

financial management　金融管理

financial market　金融市场

financial monopoly　金融垄断

financial notes　金融票据

financial obligation　财政义务

financial oligarch　金融寡头

financial organ　金融机构

financial organization　财政机构

financial overdraft　财政透支

financial policy　金融政策

financial position　金融形势,财务状况

financial power　财政权,财政议

决权

financial regulation 财政法规

financial reimbursement 经济赔偿

financial relation 财政关系

financial relationship 财政关系

financial relief 财政救济,经济救助

financial resources 财力

financial responsibility 经济责任

financial results 财务成果

financial returns 财务报告

financial revenue 财政收入

financial revenue and expenditure plan 财务收支计划

financial risk 金融风险

financial security 财政担保,经济担保

financial service 金融服务

financial services act 金融服务业法

financial settlement 财政清算

financial stability 金融稳定

financial statement 财务会计报告

financial subsidies 财政补贴

financial supervision 财政监督,财务监督,金融监督

financial syndicate 金融财团

financial system 金融体制,财政体制,金融制度

financial tariff 财政关税

financial trust 金融信托

financial trust company 金融信托公司

financial year 财政年度

financial year/FY 财政年度

financial-economic policies 财经政策

financial-economic setup 财经体制

financier 金融家,银行家,金融业者

financing 融资

financing bank 投资银行

financing body 筹资机构

① financing company 金融公司

② financing lease 融资租赁

③ financing means 融资手段

④ financing structure 金融体制

⑤ find 判决,裁决

⑥ find a market 寻找销路

⑦ find a verdict 作出裁决

⑧ find for the plaintiff 作出有利于原告的判决

⑩ find guilty 认定有罪

⑪ find innocent 裁决无罪

⑫ find not guilty 认定无罪

⑬ find out 追查,查明

⑭ find out the facts of a case 调查案件

⑯ find out the truth 查明事实真相

⑱ find sb guilty 查明有罪

⑲ find sb innocent 查明无罪

⑳ find, give a final decision 作出最后决定

㉒ finding 裁决

㉓ finding (of arbitration) 裁决结果

㉕ finding of a jury 陪审团的裁决

㉖ finding of fact 对事实的认定,对争论事实的裁决

㉘ finding of reconsideration 复议裁决

㉚ fine 罚款,罚金

㉛ fine at the discretion of the judge 法官酌处的罚金

㉝ fine for delay 误期罚款

㉞ fine on a delay 延期罚金

㉟ fine-collecting institution 收缴罚款机构

㊲ finger mark 指印

㊳ fingerprint 指印

㊴ fingerprint access 指纹存取

㊵ fingerprint registration 指纹登记

㊷ fingerprint registration of a single finger 单指指纹登记

㊹ finished product inspection 成品检验

㊻ finishing(s) 建筑装饰

㊼ finned radiator 暖气片

fire 火刑
fire and marine insurance 物产水火保险
fire brigade 消防队
fire coinsurance 火灾期保险
fire disaster 火灾
fire district 防火区
fire fighting 消防
fire fighting group 消防组织
fire insurance 火灾保险,火险
fire loss 火灾损失
fire prevention 防火
fire prevention inspection 防火安全检查
fire prevention of forest 森林防火
fire risk 火险
fire safety 防火
fire trap 易引起火灾的建筑物
firearm 枪支
firearm permit 持枪证件
firearm registration 枪支登记
firearms control 枪支管制
firearm-carrying pass 持枪通行证
firearm-carrying permit 持枪证件
fired charge 固定抵押
firefighter 消防人员
fireguard 防火员
fire-prevention rules 防火规定
fireworks control regulation 烟花爆竹管理条例
firm 企业,公司
firm contract 确定契约,约束性合同
firm for exchange and transfer of money 票号
firm lump sum contract 固定总价合同
firm offer 确定的要约,实盘,确盘
firm order 确认订单,有效订单
firm policy 既定政策
firm price 确定价格,约定价格,固定价格
firm sale contract 确定的销售合同

firmly 确信
first appeal 第一次上诉,首次上诉
first beneficiary 第一受益人,主要受益人
first carrier 第一承运人
first class disability 一等甲级伤残
first credit 第一档信贷部分贷款
first credit tranche 第一档信贷份额
first crime 初犯
first devise 优先受遗赠人
first distress 第一次扣押
first division 第一级监禁(英)
first impression case 表面上无判例的案件
first inspection 初次检验,第一次检验
first instalment 第一期分期付款
first instance 第一审,初审
first instance of civil adjudication 民事第一审程序
first instance proceedings 第一审普通程序
first lien 优先留置权,优先留权
first lien bond 优先质押债券
first lieutenant on reserve service 预备役中尉
first loss insurance 第一损失保险
first matter 第一类邮件
first mortgage 第一抵押权,首次抵押,优先抵押权
first mortgage bond 第一抵押债券
first offender 初犯
first offense 初犯,第一次犯罪
first offer 实盘
first preferred mortgage 最优抵押
first principles of law 法学通论
first quality 上等品质

first seller 原卖方

first termer 初次服刑者

first trial 初审

first trial session 第一次审理开庭期

first-class culture relics 一级文物

first-class highway 一级公路

first-class mail 第一类邮件

first-class misdemeanant 一级轻罪犯

first-class quality 头等质量

first-grade judge 一级法官

first-grade lawyer 一级律师

first-grade notary public 一级公证员

first-grade police commissioner 一级警监

first-grade police constable 一级警员

first-grade police superintendent 一级警司

first-grade police supervisor 一级警督

first-grade prosecutor 一级检察官

firsthand 原始

first-rate quality 头等质量

fiscal action 财政措施

fiscal agency agreement 代理财务协议

fiscal agent & paying agent 财务兼支付代理人

fiscal burden 财政负担

fiscal institution 财政机构

fiscal land 皇家税地

fiscal law 财政法

fiscal laws and regulations 财政法规

fiscal leverage 财税杠杆

fiscal levy 财政税收

fiscal organ 财政机关

fiscal reports and statement 会计报表

fiscal slaves 皇家奴隶

fiscal sovereignty 财政主权

fiscal subsidies 财政补贴

① fiscal year 财政年度

② fisheries jurisdiction cases 渔业管辖权案

④ fisheries law 渔业法

⑤ fishery 渔业

⑥ fishery conservation and management act(美) 渔业资源保护管理法

⑨ fishery conservation area 渔业保全区

⑪ fishery conservation zone 渔业保全区,渔业资源保护区

⑬ fishery contiguous zone 渔业毗连区

⑮ fishery control zone 渔业控制区

⑯ fishery jurisdiction 渔业管辖区

⑰ fishery law 捕鱼法,渔业法

⑱ fishery licence 渔业许可证

⑲ fishery limits 渔区

⑳ fishery production 渔业生产

㉑ fishery resources 渔业资源

㉒ fishery right 渔业权

㉓ fishery servitude 渔业地役

㉔ fishery superintendency agency 渔政监督管理机构

㉖ fishery water body 渔业水体

㉗ fishery zone 渔区

㉘ fishing 渔业,捕捞业

㉙ fishing area 渔业水域

㉚ fishing harbor 渔港

㉛ fishing licence 捕鱼执照

㉜ fishing vessel inspection agency 渔业船舶检验部门

㉞ fishing waters 渔区

㉟ fit 符合

㊱ fit in with 切合

㊲ fit in with the needs of people 满足人民的需要

㊴ fit into 纳入

㊵ fitness of law 法律适用

㊶ fitness of towage 适拖性

㊷ five principles of peaceful co-existence 和平共处五项原则

㊺ five-year plan 五年计划

㊻ fix 处罚,贿赂

㊼ fix a plot of land for each house-

hold 大包干
fix a price 定价
fix the price 规定价格
fixed 确定的
fixed amount 固定金额
fixed assets tax 固定税
fixed budget 固定预算
fixed collateral 固定抵押品
fixed date of judgment 判决确定日
fixed debts 固定债务
fixed deposit 定期存款
fixed deposit by installments 零存整取
fixed direction marketing 定向销售
fixed exchange rate system 固定汇率制
fixed exchange rates 固定汇率
fixed factors 不变因素
fixed gain 固定收益
fixed income 固定收益
fixed interest rate 固定利率
fixed investment 固定投资
fixed loan(s) secured 固定抵押贷款,定期抵押贷款
fixed maturity date 规定的到期日
fixed premium 固定保费
fixed price 固定价格
fixed price 规定价格
fixed price contract 固定价格合同
fixed property 不动产
fixed proportion 固定比例
fixed rate 固定汇率
fixed rate loan 固定利率放款
fixed rate system 固定汇率制
fixed resale price 约定转售价格
fixed royalty 固定提成
fixed savings deposits 定期储蓄存款
fixed tax 定率税
fixed term contract 定期合同
fixed term deposit 定期存款
fixed time for performance 固定履行日期

fixed trust 固定信托
fixed-asset schedule 固定资产表
fixed-date delivery 定期交货
fixed-interest bearing 固定利息
fixed-interest loan 固定利息贷款
fixed-price contract 标价合同
fixed-term imprisonment 有期徒刑
fixed-term insurance 定期保险
fixing quotas for revenues and expenditures 财务包干
flag discrimination 船旗歧视
flag of convenience 方便旗
flag state 船旗国
flagrant crime 大罪
flagrant violation 重大违反
flagrant violation of principle 公然违反原则
flagrante delicto (拉) 现行犯
flag-state jurisdiction 船旗国管辖
flash criminal 瞬间犯罪人
flat insurance 固定保险
flat price 统一价格
flat rate 比例税率
flatlet 单套间
flaw 弱点
flaw in an argument 论据的瑕疵
flaws in performance 履行缺陷
flee and hide 逃避
flee from justice 逃避审判
flemmable fabrics act 可燃性纤维法
flesh wound 皮肉之伤
Flexible constitution 柔性宪法
flexible exchange rate 浮动汇率
flexible law 酌定法
flexible measures 弹性措施
flexible monetary policy 弹性货币政策
flexible price 可变价格
flexible standard 弹性标准
flexible tariff 可变关税,灵活关税
flexible trust 灵活信托

flexible ways for investment 灵活投资方式

flight 飞行中

flight equipment 航行设备

flight of capital 资本的抽逃,抽逃资金

flight risk 飞行险

floatation of loans 举债

floating capital 流动资产

floating cargo 在途货

floating charge 浮动抵押,浮动设置

floating exchange rate 浮动汇率

floating exchange rate system 浮动汇率制

floating guarantee 浮动担保

floating interest rate 浮动利率

floating lien 浮动留置(注:指美国《统一商法典》)

floating of loan 融资

floating prices 浮动价格

floating rate bonds 浮动利率债券

floating rate loan 浮动利率放款

floating rate of tax 浮动税率

floating rate system 浮动汇率制

flog, lash 鞭笞

flood 水灾

flood control act 防洪法

flood control law 防洪法

flood control project 防洪工程

flood insurance 水灾保险

flood prevention charges 防洪费

flood-control headquarters 防汛指挥部

flood-fighting materials 防汛物资

floor 楼层

floor area (of building) 建筑面积

floor board 地板

floor drain 地漏

floor inspection 就地检验

floor leader 议会领袖

floor level 下限

floor polish 地板蜡

floor price 底价,最低限价

floor tile 地砖

flotsam 漂流物

fluctuating price contract 变动价格合同

fluctuation 价格变动

fluctuation of price 物价波动

fluctuation(s) in prices 汇率波动,价格波动

fluctuations in the rate of exchange 汇率变动

fluvial law 河川法

fly in the face of facts 违反事实

FOB 船上交货

FOB destination 目的地交货价格

FOB factory 工厂交货

foeffee in trust 不动产委托人

foenus (拉) 消费借贷

follow 遵守

follow blindly 盲从

follow the old routine 按常规办事

(to) follow the socialist road 坚持社会主义道路

follow-up investment 后续投资

Food and Agriculture Organization of the United Nations 联合国粮食及农业组织

food and drug administration (美) 食品药物管理局

food contamination 食品污染

food hygiene law 食品卫生法

food hygiene management 食品卫生管理

food hygiene standard 食品卫生标准

food poisoning 食物中毒

food processing 食品加工

food production or marketing 食品生产经营

food shortage 食品短缺

food, drug and cosmetic act of 1938 (美) 食品、药品和化妆品法

food-processing industry 食品加工工业

footprint identification 足迹鉴

定

for future reference 备查

for lucrative purpose 以营利为目的

for one's own benefits 为自己利益

for processing work 加工承揽合同

for profit 以营利为目的

for record 备案

for reference 备案

for sale abroad 外销

for the record 备案

for the third party's benefits 为第三人利益

for valuable consideration 有对价的报酬

forbear 权利的暂不行使

forbearance 宽延债务履行期

forbid 禁止

forbidden objects 违禁物品

forbidden under penalty of death 违者处以死刑

force 强制力,强行,压力,强迫,威力

force down the prices 压低价格

force into a marriage 逼婚

force majeure clause 不可抗力条款

force of attraction principle 引力原则

force of bind 约束力

force of law 法律效力

force of state 国家权力

force prices down 压价

force the bill through in the Congress 迫使议案在国会通过

force up price 抬价

force up the price 抬高价格

force's form of law 法律的效力形式

force's scale of law 法律的效力范围

forced audit 强制审计

forced conversion 强制兑换

forced discharge 强制卸货

① forced heirs 特留份继承人

② forced heirship 特留份继承权

③ forced insurance 强制保险

④ forced labor 强制劳动

⑤ forced loan 强制性贷款,强制贷款

⑦ forced sale 强制拍卖,强制性出售,强制销售

⑨ forced sale of a vessel 强制售船

⑩ forcedsale value 强制性出售价格

⑫ forced saving 强制储蓄

⑬ forced sell-off 强制变卖

⑭ forcible 强行

⑮ forcible execution 强制执行

⑯ forcible rape 强奸罪

⑰ fore closure 取消抵押的赎回权

⑱ forecasting risk 预测风险

⑲ foreclose down 赎前销后

⑳ foreclosure absolute 抵偿金

㉑ foregift 押金,押租

㉒ foregone earnings 放弃收益

㉓ foregone income 放弃收益

㉔ foreign advertising agency 外国广告代理人

㉕ foreign affairs committee 外事委员会

㉘ foreign agency 国外代理行,国外代理处

㉚ foreign agent 国外代理人

㉛ foreign aid 外部援助

㉜ foreign and commonwealth courts 域外和英联邦法庭

㉞ foreign arbitral award 外国仲裁裁决

㉟ foreign assets 外国人资产

㊱ foreign bond 国外债券,外国债券

㊴ foreign borrowing 外国借款

㊵ foreign branch 国外分支机构

㊶ foreign businessman 外商

㊷ foreign capital 外资,国外资本,外国资本

㊸ foreign capital flows 外资流量

㊹ foreign capital importation 引进外资

㊼ foreign capital inducement 吸引

外资

foreign capital inflow 外资流入

foreign capital intake 吸引外资

foreign check 外国支票

foreign citizen of Chinese origin 华裔

foreign civil aircraft 外国民用航空器

foreign commercial enterprises 外商企业

foreign contractor 外国承包商, 外国合同方

foreign corporation 外国公司

foreign court 外国法院

foreign court theory 外国法院原则

foreign currency 外币

foreign currency control 外币管制

foreign currency exchange 外币兑换

foreign currency operation 外汇业务

foreign currency regulation 外汇管理条例

foreign debt 外债

foreign economic law 涉外经济法

foreign economic policy 对外经济政策

foreign element 涉外因素, 外国因素

foreign employees 外籍职工

foreign enterprise 外国企业, 外资企业

foreign exchange 外汇

foreign exchange bank 国际汇兑银行

foreign exchange broker 外汇经济人

foreign exchange business 外汇业务

foreign exchange certificate (FEC) 外汇兑换券, 外汇证明

foreign exchange control 外汇管制, 外汇管理

foreign exchange control board 外汇管理局

foreign exchange control law 外汇管理法

foreign exchange crisis 外汇危机

foreign exchange dumping 外汇倾销

foreign exchange fluctuation 汇兑波动, 汇率波动, 外汇波动

foreign exchange fluctuation insurance 汇率波动保险

foreign exchange free market 外汇自由市场

foreign exchange fund 外汇基金

foreign exchange gain or loss 汇兑损益

foreign exchange guarantee 外汇担保

foreign exchange instrument 外汇票据

foreign exchange liabilities 外汇负债

foreign exchange license 外汇许可证

foreign exchange loans 外汇贷款

foreign exchange market 外汇市场

foreign exchange of account 记账外汇

foreign exchange option 外汇期权

foreign exchange policy 外汇政策

foreign exchange quota accounts 外汇额度账号

foreign exchange quotation 外汇价目表, 外汇行情

foreign exchange rate 外汇汇率

foreign exchange receipt 外汇收入

foreign exchange receipt and disbursement 外汇收支

foreign exchange regulating (/readjustment) market 外汇调制市场

foreign exchange regulations 外汇条例

foreign exchange reserves 外汇储备

foreign exchange retention system 外汇留成制度

foreign exchange transaction audit 外汇业务稽核

foreign exchange transactions 外汇事宜,外汇交易

foreign exchange control regulation 外汇管制规定

foreign exchange futures 外汇期货

foreign exchange transaction center 外汇交易中心

foreign goods 外货,外国货,外国产品

foreign government 外国政府

foreign guardians 外国人的监护人

foreign household 外侨户

foreign immigrant 外国侨民

foreign immunity 外国人豁免权

foreign interference 外国干预

foreign intervention 外国干涉

foreign investment 外资,外商投资,外国投资,国外投资

foreign investment law 外资法,外国投资法

foreign investment management commission 外国投资管委会

foreign investment screening and monitoring agency 外资审查机构

foreign investment screening and monitoring system 外资审批制度

foreign investments in China 外商对华投资

foreign investor 外国投资者

foreign joint venturer 外国合营者

foreign juristic person 外国法人

foreign law 外国法,外国法律

foreign law investment 涉外投资法

foreign legal history 外国法制史

foreign legal persons 外国法人

foreign legislation 外国立法

foreign loan 外债,外国贷款

foreign loan issue 外债发行

foreign market 国外市场

foreign market price 国外市场价格

foreign market value 国外市场价

foreign merchant 外商

foreign nationals 外国公民,外国侨民

foreign offender 外国罪犯,外籍罪犯

foreign office certificate 外交证明书

foreign organization 外国组织

foreign partner 外国合伙人

foreign people 外国人

foreign plant-engineering contract 涉外工程承包

foreign policy 对外政策

foreign price 国外价格

foreign products 外国产品

foreign public law 外国公法

foreign resident 外国居民

foreign revenue 外国税收

foreign sales 国外销售

foreign secretary 外交大臣(英)

foreign securities 外国证券

foreign settlement 外国人成留区,租界

foreign settler (/immigrant) 外侨

foreign short-term assets 国外短期资产

foreign sovereign immunities 外国主权豁免

foreign tax law 涉外税收

foreign trade 对外贸易

foreign trade commodities 对外贸易商品

foreign trade law 对外贸易法律制度

foreign trade order　对外贸易秩序

foreign trade policy　对外贸易政策

foreign trade work　对外贸易工作

foreign tradesman　外商

foreigner　外国人

foreigner treatment　外国人待遇

forensic anthropology　法医人类学

forensic argument　法庭辩论

forensic chemistry　法医化学

forensic doctor　法医

forensic histology　法医组织学

forensic immunology　法医免疫学

forensic medicine　法医学

forensic medicine in appraisal of material evidence　法医物证学

forensic pathology　法医病理学

forensic pharmacy　法医牙科学，法医制药学

forensic psychiatry　法医心理分析学,司法精神医学

forensic psychology　法律精神病学

forensic serology　法医血清学

forensic surgery　法医外科学

forensic thanatology　法医死因学

forensic toxicology　法医毒物学，法医鉴定学

forensic traumatology　法医损伤学

foresee　预见

foreseeability of breach　违约的可预见性

foreseeability of law　法的可预测性

foreseeable　可预见的

foreseeable loss　可预见损失

foreseen loss　可预见损失

foresight　预见

forest　森林

forest conservancy　森林保护

forest court　森林法院

forest fire　森林火灾

forest for special use　特种用途林

forest management and administration　森林经营管理

forest procuratorate　森林检察院

forest protection　森林保护

forest ranger　林警

forest reserve　保留林

forest resources　森林资源

forest tree cutting　森林采伐

forestry act　森林法

forestry administration departments　林木主管部门

forestry administrative agency　林业管理机构

forestry center　林场

forestry department at all levels　各级林业主管部门

forestry law　森林法

forestry management right　森林经营权

forestry reserve　森林保护区

Forfaiting　福弗廷

forfeit　没收,没收物,丧失

forfeit of civil right　丧失公民权

forfeit one's property　没收财产

forfeiter　没收人

forfeiture　罚没物,没收财产

forfeiture formalities　没收手续

forfeiture of deposit　没收融资

forfeiture proceeding　没收程序

forge　伪造

forge a signature　伪造签名

forge official document　伪造公文

forge or alter accounting book(s)　伪造、变造会计资料

forged　伪造的

forged contract　伪造合同

forged document　伪造单据,伪造证件

forged seal　伪造印章

forged signature　伪造的签字,伪造签名,假冒签名

forger 伪造者

forgery 伪造

forgery and illegal imitation of brandname products 假冒伪造名优产品,假造名优产品

forgery of a document 伪造文件

forgery of household registry certificate 伪造户口证件

forgery of inspection conclusion 伪造检验结论

forgery of seals 伪造印章罪

forgery of valuable securities 伪造有价证券

forgetful offender 忘却犯

forging or altering a certificate of origin 伪造,变造原产地证

form 样式,格式

form a judgment 断定

form for the ratification of rewards and punishments of convicts 罪犯奖惩审批表

form of action 诉讼方式

form of business 企业类型

form of complicity 共同犯罪的形式

form of crime 犯罪形式

form of general use 通用表格

form of government 政体

form of judicial review 司法审查的形式

form of organization 组织形式

form of state 国家形式

form of state administration 国家管理形式

form of taxation 征税形式

form of the state structure 国家结构形式

form of thing 物的形状

form of treaty 条约方式

form of trial of administrative cases 行政诉讼的审理方式

formal 合乎格式的

formal act 正式行为,要式法律行为

formal administrative act 要式行政行为

formal administrative measure 要式的行政措施

formal agreement 正式协议

formal answer 正式答复

formal constitution of crime 形式犯罪构成

formal contract 要式合同,正式合同

formal crime 形式犯罪

formal criminal law 形式刑法

formal defect 形式上的瑕疵,手续上的漏洞

formal fallacy 形成错误

formal insult 形式侮辱罪,形式侮辱罪

formal juristic act 要式法律行为

formal justice 形式上的公正

formal logic 形式逻辑

formal negotiation 正式谈判

formal notice 正式通知

formal notification 正式通知

formal provision 正式规定

formal rule-making act 正式制定规章行为

formal schooling documents 学历证书

formal source 正式渊源

formal source of law 法的形式渊源

formal summons 传票

formal treaty 正式条约

formal truth 形式真实

formal ultra vires 形成越权

formalism 形式主义

formalist jurisprudence 形式主义法学

formalities 法律手续,正当手续

formalities for capture into custody 捕押手续

formalities for defense 辩护手续

formalities of contract 契约格式

formality 手续,要式,程式

formality of contract 合同格式

format 格式

formation of constitution 宪法的产生

formation of criminal mind 犯罪

心理形成

formed action 措辞方式固定的诉讼

formed design 故意

former 前者,前任

former crime 原罪,原犯

former offense 原犯

former office 前任职务

former post 原职

former premier 前任总理

former president 前任主席

former prime minister 前任首相

former prison where one was kept 原关押监狱

former scope 原有范围

formidable 威力

formidable natural conditions 恶劣的自然条件

formless contract 不定型合同,非正式合同

forms and formulas of official documents 公文程式

forms of law 法律形式

formula of criminal behavior 犯罪行为公式

formulate 制定,创制

formulating organization 创制机关

formulation 制定

Forsta Sparbanken (Stockholm) 佛斯诺储蓄银行(斯德哥尔摩)

forswear 发誓否认

fortuitous accident 意外事故

fortuitous causal relationship 偶然因果关系

fortuitous causalty 意外损失

fortuitous event 偶然事件,意外事件

fortuitous intent 偶然故意

fortuitous joint principal offender 偶然共同犯罪

fortuitousness 意外事件

fortuity 意外事故

fortuna 埋藏物

fortune 财产

forum contractus(拉) 契约缔结地法院

forum conveniens(拉) 方便法院,便利法院,便于审理的法院

forum delicti commissi(拉) 侵权行为地法院

forum domicilii(拉) 被告住所地

forum domicilii jurisdiction(拉) 被告住所地管辖

forum non conveniens(拉) 不方便法院

forum rei(拉) 被告住所地

forum shopping 法院选择,诉讼地选择,择地制度

forum vei(拉) 物所在地法院

forum vei sitae(拉) 物所在地法院

forward 序言

forward contract 远期合同,预约,期货合同

forward delivery 定期交货,远期交货

forward exchange 远期外汇

forward exchange deals 远期外汇交易

forward exchange market 外汇期货市场

forward exchange transaction 外汇期货交易

forward foreign exchange 远期外汇

forward order 远期订货

forward price 远期价格,期货价格

forward purchase 购进期货

forward purchase agreement 先期购买协议

forward purchasing agreement of project financing 项目贷款先期购买协议

forward purchasing contract 预购合同

forward rate 远期汇率

forward transaction(s) 期货交易,期汇交易,远期交易

forwarder 转运人,货运承揽业,交付人

forwarder's cargo receipt 货运承揽商收据

forwarder's certificate of receipt 货运承揽商收据

forwarder's certificate of transport 货运承揽商证明

forwarder's receipt 货运承揽商收据

forwarding 转运

forwarding agent 货运承揽业,运输商,运输代理行,运输代理人

forwarding agent's certificate of transport 货运承揽商证明

forwarding agent's commission 运输代理佣金

forwarding commission 运输代理佣金

forwarding order 运输委托书,托送单

forwards 期货

foster 抚养

foster home for delinquent children 违法儿童管教所

fosterage 抚养

foundation 地基

foundation of criminal responsibility 刑事责任基础

four basic principles 四项基本原则(中)

four conventions of the law of the sea 海法四公约

fourth market of stocks 股票第四市场

fractional currency 辅币

fractional money 辅币

fracture of the base of the skull 颅底骨折

fragile 易碎的

fragile article 易损品

fragmentation of group property rights 集团产权分割

frame 捏造

frame a case against sb 罗织罪名

framework 体制

framing of issues 草拟诉讼纲要

franc area 法朗区

franchise 免赔额(率),特许专营

franchising 特许专营

franchising system 特许制度

franco rendu(拉) 指定地点交货

Frank 法兰克

frank tenement 自由保有之不动产

Franks 法兰克人

frans(拉) 契纸

fraternal insurance 互助性保险

fraud 欺诈,诈欺

fraud at common law 普通法上的欺诈行为

fraud in advance 事前欺诈

fraud in insurance fraud 保险诈骗

fraud on a power 以权诈欺,诈欺用权

fraudulence 欺诈

fraudulence on commercial instruments 票据欺诈行为

fraudulent 欺诈的,欺骗的

fraudulent act 欺骗行为

fraudulent alienation 欺诈让与

fraudulent alience 欺诈让与的受让人

fraudulent assignment 欺诈性转让

fraudulent bankruptcy 欺诈破产

fraudulent bankruptcy by a third party 第三人诈欺破产罪

fraudulent claim 欺诈性索赔

fraudulent conduct 欺诈行为

fraudulent conveyance 欺诈性财产转让,欺诈性交付,诈欺性让与

fraudulent evasion of law 诈欺规避

fraudulent intention 欺诈意图

fraudulent means 欺诈手段

fraudulent misrepresentation 欺

诈性之逃避,欺诈性误述,虚伪陈述

fraudulent preference 欺诈性优惠,特惠欺诈

fraudulent representation 欺诈陈述

free 免除

free and equal 自由与平等

free and open market 自由与公开市场

free at factory 工厂交货

free capital 自由资本

free carrier 货物交付承运人价

free choice of goods 选购商品

free choice of law 自由选择法律

free choice of occupation 自由择业

free choice of partners 婚姻自由

free competition 自由竞争

free credit 无条件信用

free delivery 任意交货,指定地点交货

free delivery price 目的地交货价格

free delivery unconditional delivery 无条件交货

free education 免费教育

free enterprise 自由企业

free exchange market 自由外汇市场

free exchange rate 自由汇率

free foreign exchange 自由外汇

free from commitment 不承担义务

free from contamination 无污染

free from liability of negligence 不负过失责任

free from particular average 平安险

free hold estate 世袭领地

free import and export 自由进出口

free interpretation 自由解释

free loan 无息贷款

free market 自由市场

free market exchange rates 自由汇率

free market rate 自由市场利率

free of damage 损害不赔,残损不赔

free of general average 不赔偿的共同海损

free of turn 不计顺序的

free on board 船上交货

free on board mill 工厂交货

free on rail/FOR 铁路交货

free or board factory 工厂交货

free pardon 特赦

free particular average 平安险

free perimeter 外商通过检疫

free port 自由港

free port foreign investments in China 外商通过检疫

free price 自由价格

free rates 自由汇兑率

free reserve 自由储备金

free speech 言论自由

free state 自由邦

free tenement 自由保有之不动产

free time 免费使用期

free trade 自由贸易,自由经营,商业自由

free trade area 自由贸易区

free trading 自由买卖

free transit 自由过境

free use 无偿使用

free voting 自由投票

free world 自由世界

free world trade 世界自由贸易

freed assets 不受拘束的资产

freed security interest 不受约束的担保物权

freedom 自由

freedom and equality 自由与平等

freedom from being exploited 不受剥削的自由

freedom from encumbrance 不受负担约束

freedom from fear 免于恐惧的自由

freedom from want 免于匮乏的自由

freedom of action 行动自由

freedom of assembly 集会自由

freedom of assembly and association 集会结社自由

freedom of association 结社自由

freedom of belief 信仰自由

freedom of choice of residence 居住自由

freedom of communication 交往自由

freedom of conscience 良心自由,信仰自由

freedom of contract 订约自由,契约自由

freedom of correspondence 通信自由,通讯自由

freedom of demonstration 示威自由

freedom of expatriation 出籍自由,放弃国籍自由

freedom of expression 表达自由

freedom of fishing 捕鱼自由

Freedom of fishing on the high seas 公海捕鱼自由

freedom of information 情报自由,新闻自由

freedom of judicial discretion 自由裁量权

freedom of learning knowledge 学问自由

freedom of marriage 婚姻自由

freedom of migration 迁徙自由

Freedom of navigation on the high seas 公海航行自由

freedom of not believe in religion 不信仰宗教的自由

freedom of opinion 意见自由,发表意见自由

freedom of parading 游行自由

freedom of passage 通行自由

freedom of person 人身自由

freedom of political conviction 政治信仰自由

freedom of procession 游行自由

freedom of religion 宗教信仰自由

freedom of religious belief 宗教信仰自由

freedom of silence 沉默自由

freedom of speech 言论自由

freedom of the city 城市自治

freedom of the open sea 公海自由

freedom of the press 出版自由

freedom of the will 意志自由

freedom of thought 思想自由

freedom to change one's residence 迁徙自由

freedom to engage in cultural pursuits 进行文化活动的自由

freedom to engage in literary and artistic creation 进行文学艺术创造的自由

freedom to engage in scientific research 进行科学研究的自由

freedom to strike 罢工自由

freedom to use one's own spoken and written languages 使用自己的语言文字的自由

freedom to work 工作自由

freehold 不动产的所有权,自由保有不动产权,土地完全保有权

freehold of office 终身职务

freehold property 自由保有的财产

freely convertible currency 自由兑换货币

freely floating exchange rate 自由浮动汇率

freely negotiable 自由议付

freeman 自由民

freeze 冻结

free-spending management 浪费经营

freight 货运,运费,货物,运费

freight absorption 运费免收

freight advice 运费通知

freight agent 货运代理人,运输代理人

freight and miscellaneous charges 运杂费

freight at destination 到达运费

freight at destination bill of lading 运费到付提单

freight bill 运费单

freight broker 货运经纪人

freight carriage 运费

freight charge 运费

freight clause 运费条款

freight collect 到付运费

freight contract 货运合同

freight forward 到付运费,运费到付

freight forwarder 货运承揽业,运输代理人,货运转运商

freight in full 全包运费

freight insurance 运费保险

freight limitation 运费限额

freight list 运费清单,运价表

freight market 运费市场,货运市场

freight note(s) 运费单,运送单

freight notice 运费通知书

freight paid 运费已付

freight paid in advance 预付运费

freight paid to 运费付至

freight paid to...terms 运费付至…条件

freight payable at destination 到达目的地付运费

freight prepaid 运费预付,预付运费,运费已付

freight prepaid bill of lading 运费预付提单

freight prepayable 运费可预付

freight rate 运费率

freight rebate 运费回扣,运费折扣

freight retention clause 运费扣留条款

freight service 货运

freight tariff 运费率表,运价表

freight to be prepaid 应预付的运费

freight to collect 到付运费

freight to prepaid 运费预付

freight transport 货运

freight unit 运费单位

freight volume 运输量

freightage 货运,运费

freighter 托运人

freight-out 销货运费

French civil code 法国民法典

French community 法兰西共同体

French constitution 法国宪法

French law 法国法

fresco 壁画

fresh and difficult to keep 鲜活不易保管

fresh goods 鲜活商品

friendly treaty 友好条约

fringe beneficium 附带利益

fringe benefit 额外利益

frisk pick-pocketing 扒窃

from above 自上而下

from among 从中

from below 自下而上

from bottom to top 自下而上

from each according to his ability, to each according to his needs 各尽所能,按需分配

from each according to his ability, to each according to his work 各尽所能,按劳分配

from ignorance 出于无知

from ignorance of law 出于对法律的无知

from top to bottom 自上而下

front bencher 前座议员

front door 正门

frontier 边界,国境,边境

frontier defense 边防

frontier duty 边界关税

frontier health and quarantine inspection 国境卫生检疫

frontier health and quarantine law 国境卫生检疫法

frontier health and quarantine organization 国境卫生检疫机关

frontier health and quarantine organization of the People's Republic of China 中华人民共和国国境卫生检疫机关

frontier health and quarantine work 国境卫生检疫工作
frontier inspection 边防检查
frontier inspection organization 边防检查机关
frontier inspection station 边防站
frontier inspection system 边防检查制度
frontier pass 边防通行证
frontier port health supervisor 国境口岸卫生监督员
frontier ports 国境口岸
frontier system 边境制度
front-end fee 一次性手续费
frozen assets 冻结资产
frozen fund 冻结资金
fructus（拉）收益
fructus civiles（拉）法定孳息
fructus industriales（拉）劳动成果
fruits 孳息
fruits of labour 劳动成果
frustrate 使无效
frustrate a contract 使合同落空
frustrated aggression 挫折攻击
frustrated contract 受挫失效的契约,受阻之契约
frustrated reaction 挫折反应
frustrating event 合同落空事件
frustration 契约落空
frustration of contract 合同落空,合同受挫,合同受阻,履行受挫
frustration-aggression theory of crime 挫折-攻击论犯罪观
fugitive clause 刑事逃犯
fugitive criminal 刑事逃犯
fugitive slave act 逃奴追缉法
fulfil a former agreement 履行预约
fulfil one's duty 尽职,履行义务
fulfil one's duty of guardianship 履行监护义务
fulfil one's obligation(s) 履行义务,尽义务

fulfil one's promise 遵守诺言
fulfil the obligation 履行债务
fulfill a contract 执行合同
fulfill quality requirements 达到质量要求
fulfillment in good faith of international obligations 忠实履行国际义务
fulfilment date 履行日期
fulfilment of plan 完成计划
fulfilment of treaty 条约的履行
full 充分
full age 成年
full amount 金额
full and clear 详明
full and clear annotations 详明的注解
full authority 全权
full capacity for civil conduct 完全民事行为能力
full capacity of conduct 完全民事行为能力
full compensation 充分补偿
full consultation 完全磋商,全部磋商
full court 合议庭
full credit 金额抵免
full defense 全面辩护
full discharge 全部履行
full employment 充分就业
full exemption 全部免税法
full faith and credit clauses（美）充分诚意与信任条款
full freight 全部运费
full hearing 充分审理
full insurance 全额保险
full liability 完全责任,全部责任
full name 全名
full payment 全部付清,全部付额
full power 全权证书,全权,全权委任
full price 足价
full proof 充分的证明
full qualification 完全资格
full registered 完全注册登记

full right(s) 全权,全部权利,完全权利

full set 全套

full signature 完全签字

full tax credit 税收金额抵免

full tax exemption 税收全部豁免

full terms 全部条件

full text 全文

full time attorney 专职律师

full time layer 专职律师

full value insurance 全值保险

full, timely and effective compensation 充分、及时、有效地补偿

fully 定额地

fully account for 完全解释

fully utilize 充分利用

full-disclosure principle 充分反映原则

full-scale operation 全面实施

full-time labour 全劳动力

function and office 职权

function and powers 职权

function building 专用建筑

function of constitution 宪法的功能

function of defense 辩护职能

function of environmental protection organ 环境保护机构的职责

function of guarantee of criminal law 刑法的保障机能

function of punishment 刑罚的功能

function of the agency for food hygiene supervision 食品卫生监督机构的职责

function of the dictatorship 专政职能

function(s) of the state 国家职能

functional administrative organization 行政职能机关

functional approach 功能论

functional architecture 实用建筑

functional authority 职能权限

functional department 职能部门

functional department of an enterprise 法人职能机关

functional interpretation 职能解释

functional machinery 职能机构

functional organization 职能机构

functional pricing 职能定价

functionary of administrative organizations 行政机关工作人员

functioning machinery 职能机构

functions and duties of administrative bodies 行政机关的职责

functions and power reference 职能范围

functions and powers of state civil servants 国家公务员的职权

functions and powers of supervision over administration 行政监察职权

functions of a diplomatic mission 使馆职务

functions of criminal proceedings 刑事诉讼职能

functions of the dictatorship 专政职能

fund 基金,奖金,经费

fund accounts 预算科目

fund for economic growth 经济增长基金

fund for prevention and control of pollution source 污染源治理基金

fund holder 证券持有人

fund in trust 信托基金

fund manager 基金管理人

fund of capital 资本基金

fund of negotiable instrument 票据资金

fund of self-insurance 自身保险储备金

fund pool 基金联合投资

fund raising institution 融资机构

fundamental 根本,基本

fundamental breach 基本违约,

根本违反合同,重大违约

fundamental breach of contract
根本违约

fundamental categories of jurisprudence 法学的基石范畴

fundamental change of circumstances 情势基本变迁

fundamental duties of citizens 公民的基本义务

fundamental duties of states 国家的基本义务

fundamental duty 基本义务

fundamental freedom 基本自由

fundamental human rights 基本人权

fundamental interest 根本利益

fundamental law 根本大法,根本法,基本法

fundamental law of the state 国家的根本法

fundamental policy 基本政策

fundamental principle 基本原则

fundamental principle of criminal law 刑法基本原则

fundamental principle of international law 国际法基本原则

fundamental principles of administrative law 行政法基本原则

fundamental principles of civil procedural law 民事诉讼法基本原则

fundamental right(s) 基本权利

fundamental rights and duties of citizens 公民的基本权利与义务

fundamental rights of states 国家的基本权利

funded debt 固定债务,长期借款

funded income 长期收益

funded liability 长期借款,长期负债

fund-holder 公债持有人

funding loan 固定贷款,基金贷款

funding mortgage bond 偿还抵押债券

funding system 公债制度

fund-in-trust 信托基金

funds for construction 建设资金

funds for extending credit 信贷资金

funds for handling cases 办案经费

funds for state compensation 国家赔偿经费

funds statement 资金表

funeral expenses 丧葬费

funeral home 殡仪馆

fungible 可替代,代替物

fungible things 代替物

furnish consideration 付出对价

furnish evidence 提供证据

furnish proofs 提供证据

furnish reference material 提交参考资料

furnished (rooming) house 备有家具的出租住房

furnishing false information 提供假情报

further postponement 继续展期

furtum (拉) 盗窃法

furtum conceptum (拉) 赃物

furtum manifestum (拉) 人赃并获的盗窃犯

furtum nec manifestum (拉) 暗盗

furtum oblatum (拉) 窝赃

future delivery 远期交货

future freight 将来运费

future goods 期货

future goods contract 期货合同

future interests 未来权益

future lease 未来租赁

future property 将有财产

future trading 远期交易

futures 期货

futures business 期货交易

futures contract 期房合同

futures market 期货市场

futures price 期货价格

futures transaction 股票期货交易

G

gag 言论自由的压制

gag law 言论箝制法,限制主论自由的法令

gag rule 言论禁止令

gage 抵押物,抵押品

gage registration 抵押物登记

gain 收益

gain an enormous personal profit, seek exorbitant profits 牟取暴利

gain on conversion of investments 投资变换收益

gain or income tax 收益税

gale 地租、年金

gallery 长廊

gambler 投机商

gambling 赌博罪

gambling contract 赌博契约

gang crime 结伙犯罪,团伙犯罪

gang fighting 结伙斗殴

gang of larceny 盗窃团伙

gang of terrorists 恐怖分子集团

gang robbery 结伙抢劫

gang stealing 集团盗窃,结伙盗窃

ganged crime 纠合性犯罪

ganged crime with characteristics of underworld 带黑社会性质的集团犯罪

ganger 工长,领班,工头,监工

gangland crimes 黑社会犯罪

gangland criminal syndicate 黑社会性质的犯罪集团

gangway 出入通道

gaps in supervisory of banks at the international level 国际监控空白区域

garconniere 单身男子公寓

garnish 传唤

garnishee 第三债务人

garret 顶层阁楼

garrote 绞刑

garroting 绞杀

gate 大门

gathering 集会

GATT(general agreement on tariffs and trade) 关贸总协定

gauntlet 夹笞刑

Gautama Smiti 乔达摩法经

gazette 政府公报

GBH 严重身体伤害

GENCON 金康合同

general 普遍

general acceptance 一般性承兑

general accepted rules 公认的规则

general accomplice 一般共犯

general act 总决议书,总议定书

general administration for industry and commerce 工商行政管理总局

general administrative rules 普通行政规章

general agency 总代理,总代理权,一般代理

general agency system 总代理制度

general agent 一般代理人

general agreement 一般协定

general agreement on tariffs and trade 关税与贸易总协定

general agreement on trade in service(简写:GATS) 服务贸易总协定

general alliance 一般性同盟

general amnesty 大赦

general and special damages 一般及特殊的损害赔偿金

general and specific policy 方针政策

general approximate amount 概率

general articles 一般条款

general articles of contract 合同的一般条款

general assembly of the United Nations 联合国大会

general attorney 一般代理人

general average 共同海损

general average adjustment 共同海损理算

general average contribution 共同海损分摊金额

general average expenses insurance 共同海损费用保险

general average guarantee 共同海损担保函

general average interest 共同海损利息

general average loss 共同海损损失

general average measures 共同海损措施

general average sacrifice 共同海损牺牲

general average security 共同海损担保

general average statement 共同海损理算书

general bonds 一般债券

general calumny 一般诽谤罪

general certificate of origin 一般原产地证

general clause 一般条款,概括条款

general colitigants 普通共同诉讼人

general colitigation 普通共同诉讼

general condition 通用条件,共同条件

general conditions applicable to loan and guarantee agreements 贷款协议和担保协议通则

general conditions of delivery 一般交货条件

general conditions of sale 一般销售条件

general conference 全体大会,全体会议

general congress 全体大会

general constitution of crime 一般犯罪构成

general constitutive elements of crime 犯罪构成一般要件

general contract 普通合同,一般合同

general contractor 总承包人

general contributory values 共同海损分摊价值

general convention 一般公约

general council of the bar 律师联合委员会

general count 一般罪项

general creditor 一般债权人

general custom 一般惯例,普遍习惯

general damage 一般损害赔偿

general defect 一般瑕疵

general demurrer 概括抗辩

general deposit 普通保证金

general duty 普通关税

general education 普通教育

general election 普遍选举,大选

general election day 普选日期

general entail 一般限定继承权

general exceptions 一般例外

general form 一般格式

general functions 一般职能

general fund trust 普通资金信托

general guarantee 全面保证

general guaranty 一般保证,一般担保

general indorsement 无记名背书

general industry 普通工业

general inspection on commodity prices 物价大检查

general instructions to tenders 投标须知

general intent 一般故意

general intent of crime 一般犯意

general interests 全局利益

general international convention 一般性国际公约

general international law 一般国际法

general international organization 一般性国际组织

general international standards 国际通用标准

general internment 普遍拘禁

general introduction of economic law 经济法通论

general jurisprudence 普通法学

general law 一般法律

general ledger(s) 总账

general legal capacity 一般权利能力

general legal point of view 一般法律观点

general letter of hypothecation 一般抵押书,一般值押书

general license 一般性许可证,普通许可,普通许可协议

general licensing system 一般许可制度

general lien 概括留置权,总留置权,总括留置权

general management 综合管理

general meeting 全体大会

general meeting of shareholders 股东大会

general merchandise 一般产品

general MFN treatment 一般最惠国待遇

general mobilization 总动员

general monopoly contract 总承包合同

general mortgage 一般抵押

general most-favoured-nation clause 一般性最惠国条款

general most-favoured-nation treatment 一般最惠国待遇

general multilateral convention 国际公约

general multilateral treaty 一般性多边条约

general name 一般名称

general negligence 一般过失

general normative treaty 一般规范性条约

general object 一般客体

general offer 一般发价

① general office 办公厅

② general office of the State Council 国务院办公厅

④ general pardon 大赦

⑤ general part of administrative jurisprudence 行政法学总论

⑦ general partner 普通合伙人

⑧ general partnership 普通合伙

⑨ general power of attorney 全权委托书

⑪ general preferential duties 关税普遍优惠制

⑬ general preferential duties system 一般优惠关税制

⑮ general prescription 普通诉讼时效

⑰ general price level 总物价水平

⑱ general principle of justice and equity 公正与公平的一般原则

㉑ general principles 总纲,一般原则

㉓ general principles of administrative action 行政诉讼基本原则

㉖ general principles of justice and equity 公正与公平一般原则

㉘ general principles of law 一般法律原则

㉚ general procedure 普通程序

㉛ general procedure for administrative penalties 行政处罚的一般程序

㉞ general program(es) 总纲

㉟ general protection 全面保护

㊱ general provisions 通则,总则,一般规定,一般条款

㊳ general provisions of criminal law 刑法总论

㊵ general proxy 一般代理人

㊶ general public 公众

㊷ general responsibilities 一般责任

㊹ general responsibility 一般义务

㊺ general right 一般权利

㊻ general right of action 普通诉权

㊼ general risk contingencies 一般

意外风险

general rule(s) 总则,概括法则,一般规则

general rules of administrative law 行政法总论

general rules of agreement between client and consulting engineer 咨询协议基本条款

general rules of interpretation 一般性解释规则

general sanction 全面制裁

general saving clause 一般性保留条款

general secretary 总书记

general situation 概况

general standard 一般准则

general statute 普通成文法规

general stipulations 一般规定

general strike 总罢工

general subject 一般主体

general substantive administrative law 一般行政实体法

general succession 概括继承

general suffrage bill 普选法案

general supervision 一般监督,全面监督

general tariff system 固定税率制

general tax law in a narrow sese 狭义税法

general taxpayer 一般纳税人

general terms 一般用语

general terms and conditions 一般交易条件

general theories of constitutional law 宪法总论

general theory 一般原则

general trade 总贸易

general trend 总趋势

general understanding 通常解释

general validing concerns 一般有效关系

general verdict 概括裁决,关于事实上和法律上的裁决

general violations against law 一般违法行为

general warranty 一般保证,一

① 般担保

② general welfare 公共福利

③ general will 公意,共同意志

④ Generale Bank (Brussels) 通用银行(布鲁塞尔)

⑤ generalia(拉) 一般原则,一般规定

⑥ generalia verba sunt 一般性用语应作一般的解释

⑩ generality 概括性

⑪ generalization doctrine 概括主义

⑬ generalize 概括

⑭ generalized accounting law 广义会计法

⑯ generalized auditing law 广义审计法

⑱ generalized interest 一般利益

⑲ generalized norm 概括性规范

⑳ generalized system of preference 普遍优惠制

㉒ generalized tariff preferences 普通关税优惠

㉔ generally accepted 普遍接受的,公认的

㉖ generally accepted rule 公认规则

㉘ generally acknowledged truth 公理

㉚ generally held standards 通用标准

㉜ general " liberty " option clause 自由选择条款

㉞ generic name of the goods 商品通用名称

㊱ genetic variability of criminals 罪犯遗传上的变异

㊳ Geneva conventions 日内瓦公约

㊴ Geneva protocol 日内瓦议定书

㊵ Genoa 基罗亚

㊶ genocide 灭绝种族,种族灭绝

㊷ gentleman of the rode 律师

㊸ gentlemen's agreement 绅士(君子)协定,君子协定

㊺ gentlemen's agreement of export credit 出口信贷君子协定

㊼ genuine belief 真实相信

genuine link 与船旗国无真正联系

genuine rule of law 以法治国

geographic division 区域划分

geographical distribution of the different sectors of the economy 经济布局

geographical evidence 地理证据

geographical factors and crime 地理因素与犯罪

geographical monopoly 地区垄断

geographical representation 地区代表制

geopolitical factor 地缘政治因素

geostationary orbit 地球静止轨道

geosynchronous orbit 地球同步轨道

German civil code 德国民法典

German commercial code 德国商法典

German school 德国学派

Germanic law 日尔曼法

gerrymander 不公正地划分选区

get a discount off a price 折价

get elected by bribery 贿选

get into debt 借债

get into trouble with the law 吃官司

get legal redness 得到法律上补救

get off 不受处罚

get out of debt 还债

get rid of 排除,驱除,革除

get sb to post bail 取保

gibbet 绞刑台

gift 赠与物

gift causa montis (拉) 死因赠与

gift in prospect of death 死因赠与

gift of land 土地赠与

gift of property 财产赠与

gift tax 赠与税

gilt-edged securities 金边证券,

① 优良证券

② gilt-edged shares 金边股

③ gist of an offense 犯罪要点

④ give 给付,给予

⑤ give a discount on 打折扣

⑥ give a fair trial 给予公正裁判

⑦ give a final ruling 作出最后裁定

⑨ give a heavier and quicker punishment 从重从快处罚

⑪ give a heavier punishment 从重处罚

⑬ give a judgment 作出判决

⑭ give a lesser punishment 从轻处罚

⑯ give a ruling 作出裁决

⑰ give a severer punishment 从重处罚

⑲ give an aggravated punishment beyond the maximum prescribed 加重处罚

㉒ give an immediate reply 立即答复

㉔ give an instruction 发出指示

㉕ give appropriate compensation 给予适当补偿

㉗ give appropriate security 提供适当担保

㉙ give away 下跌

㉚ give credit 赊账,赊欠

㉛ give effect to 使生效

㉜ give evidence 提供证据

㉝ give full play to 充分发挥

㉞ give full scope to the role of the judicial organs 发挥司法机关的职能作用

㊲ give official recognition to 给予正式承认

㊳ give one's pledge 作出保证

㊵ give sb disciplinary warning 予以警告处分

㊷ give security 提供保证,提供担保

㊹ give something by way of payment for 抵偿

㊻ give tacit consent to 默认

㊼ give tick 赊购

give time 给予一个期限
give up 让步
give up a business 停业
give up evil and return to good 改邪归正
give up the throne 退位
give-and-take equally 平等交换
giver 赠与人
giving examination for approval without delay 及时审批
glass curtain 玻璃幕墙
glazed cladding 玻璃幕墙
global quota(s) 绝对配额,全球配额
glory 荣誉
gloss 法律原本注释
glove money 贿赂金
go against 违背
go against one's superior 犯上
go against the laws of social development 违反社会发展规律
go against the people's interests 触犯人民利益
go against the will of the people 违背人民的意愿
go bankrupt 致破产
go beyond 超越
go beyond one's authority 越权
go beyond one's commission 越权
go beyond one's terms of reference 超越职权范围
go beyond the limit 超过限度
go down 下跌
go into business 开业
go into liquidation 停业清理
go into operation 投产,开业
go on strike 罢工
go or come down 下降
go out of business 歇业
go partners 共同出资
go slow 怠工
go straight 改过自新
go to court 打官司
go to law 诉诸法律
go to the chair (美) 被处死刑
go up 上涨

going (concern) value 继续经营价值
going abroad for the purpose of study at ones own expense 自费出国学习
going price 通行价格,现行价格
going short 卖空
gold agreement 黄金协议(指英国海上运输赔偿限额规定)
gold and dollar reserves 黄金美元储备
gold and foreign exchange reserve 黄金外汇储备
gold and silver act (英) 金银输出管理法
gold bar 金条
gold bloc 金本位
gold bullion standard 金块本位制
gold bullion system 金块本位制
gold clause 黄金条款
gold coin standard 金币本位制度,金铸币本位制
gold currency 金本位货币
gold exchange standard 金汇兑本位制
gold exchange standard system 金汇兑本位制
gold guarantee (发行纸币)黄金保证
gold market 黄金市场
gold parity 黄金平价
gold point 黄金输送点
gold pool 黄金总库
gold reserve 黄金储备
gold standard system 金本位制
gold standard(s) 金本位,金本位币,金本位制
gold tranche 黄金份额
good administration and stability 安邦治国
good and lawful 善良守法
good consideration 合适的对价
good faith 诚实信用,善意
good faith accord 诚意协议
good intention 善意

good merchantable quality/GUQ 上好可销品质

good money 优良货币

good offices 斡旋

good performance contract 忠诚履行合同

good product 合格产品

good till canceled 长期有效委托书,撤销前有效

good title 有效所有权

good will 善意

good will partner 商誉合伙人

goods 有形动产,物,商品,动产,鲜货,货物

goods and chattels 私人财产

goods and services 货物与劳务

goods averum（拉） 物品

goods carriage 货物运输合同

goods credit 货物抵押贷款

goods exchange and payments agreement 换货和付款协定

goods forbidden to be exported 禁止出口货物

goods freight 货物运输,货物运费

goods in bad order 残损货物

goods in stock 现货

goods in transit 运输途中的货物,转口货品

goods insured 保了险的商品

goods marks 商品商标

goods of the contract description 与合同规定相符的货物

goods on consignment 寄售货物,寄售品

goods on consignment-out 寄售货物

goods on hand 存货

goods on order 订购货物

goods on the spot 现货

goods receipt 货物收据

goods rejected 退货

goods returned 退货

goods tax 货物税

goods to be carried 待运货物

goods to be transhipped 中转货物

goods traffic 货运

goods train 铁路货车

goods transport 货运

goods under lien 被留置货物

goodwill 商誉,信誉

good-time credit system 善时折减制度

good-will 信誉

Gospel, according to Matthew 马太福音

Gospel, according to St. John 约翰福音

govern 统治

governing a country by law 依法治国

governing law 适用法律条款

government 政府

government activity 政府活动

government agency 政府机关,国家机关

government apparatus 政府机构

government attorney 官方律师,检察员

government bill 政府法案

government bonds 政府债券,政府公债

government budget deficit 政府预算赤字

government business enterprise 公营企业

government by law 法治

government by the people 民治

government capital 国有资本

government concerned 有关政府

government contract 政府合同

government control over enterprises 政府对企业的管理

government controlled corporation 政府控制的企业

government decree 政令,政府法令

government department 政府部门

government department in charge of earthquake and relief work 防震减灾工作主管部门

government department in charge of radio and television administration 广播电视行政主管部门

government deposit 政府存款，财政存款

government discipline 政纪

government document 政府公文

government enterprise 官办企业

government establishments law 编制法

government finance 政府财政

government for the people 民享

government functionary 公务人员

government guarantee 政府保证，政府担保

government interference 政府干预

government intervention 政府干预

government land 公有土地

government license 政府许可证

government loan 政府贷款

government loan agreement 政府借贷协议

government man 官员

government monopoly 政府垄断

government of laws and not of men 要法治，不要人治

government of the people, by the people, and for the people 民有、民治、民享

government office in feudal China 衙门

government official 政府官员

government operated enterprise 公营企业

government owned corporation 国有公司

government ownership 国有制

government post 政府职务，公职

government procurement 政府采购政策

government procurement policy 政府采购政策

government property 公用财产，公有财产，政府财产

government purchase law 政府采购法

government receipts 财政收入

government regulation 政府法规

government representative 政府代表

government revenue and expenditure 财政收支

government rules and regulations 政府规章

government ship 政府船舶

government succession 政府继承

government tort 政府侵权行为，行政侵权

government tort immunity 政府侵权豁免

government tort responsibility 政府侵权责任

government unit 机关

government utility 国营公用事业

government work report 政府工作报告

governmental agency 政府机关

governmental agent 官员

governmental apparatus 政府机构

governmental arbitrator 国家仲裁人

governmental body of industry and commerce administration 工商行政管理机关

governmental debt 政府公债

governmental duties 政府职责

governmental functions 政府职能

governmental instrumentality 政府机构

governmental interests 政府利益

governmental intervention 政府干预

governmental intervention princi-ple 国家干预原则

governmental power(s) 政府权力,治权

governmental purpose 政府目的

governmental tort immunity 行政侵权责任豁免

governmental tort liability 行政侵权责任

government-directed price 政府指导价

government-fixed price 政府定价

government-operated 政府经营的

government-owned deposits 政府存款

government-planned price 国家计划价格

governor 总督

governor-general 总督

go-slow 消极怠工

grace 赦免,仁慈

grace of payment 付款宽限

grace period （债务的）宽限期,优惠期

gradation of crime 罪的等差

grade 1 accountant 一级会计师

grade 2 judge 二级法官

grade 2 procurator 二级检察官

grade 3 culture relics 三级文物

grade 3 judge 三级法官

grade 3 police commissioner 三级警监

grade 3 police superintendent 三级警司

grade 3 police supervisor 三级警督

grade 3 procurator 三级检察官

grade 4 judge 四级法官

grade 5 judge 五级法官

grade 5 prosecutor 五级检察官

grade B wound and disability 乙级伤残

grade jurisdiction 级别管辖

grade labelling 分级标签

grade mark 等级标志

graded examination and approval 分级审批

graded system 等级制度

grades of judges 法官的级别

grades of military posts for officers on reserve service 预备役军官职务等级

grade-one national enterprise 国家一级企业

grading of legal effect of adminis-trative law 行政法律效力层级

grading of medical malpractices 医疗事故等级

grading of the wounded and dis-abled 伤残等级

gradually reach perfection 趋向完善

graduated income tax 累进所得税

graduated tax rates 分级税率

graduated taxation 分级课税

graduation certificate 毕业证书

graduation clause 毕业条款

graft 贿赂

graft and embezzlement 贪污盗罪

grafter 受贿者

grain standard act （美）谷物标准化

grain tax 粮食税

grammatical interpretation 文法解释,语法解释

grand administrative region 大行政区

grand constituency system 大选区制

grand counseil （法）法国大法院

grand court （日）大法庭

grand criminal tribunal （德）大刑事庭

grand duchy 大公国

grand duke 大公爵

grand entrance 正门

grand jury 大陪审团

grand jury witness 大陪审团的证人

grand justice conference 大法官会议

grand larceny 大盗窃犯

grand procurator 大检察官

grand prosecutor（中）大检察官

grand remonstrance 大抗议书

grand sergeant 大警官

grand sergeanty 大服役土地保有

grands droits 大权利

grant 赠与,授予,出让,让步,承认,授权,给予

grant a credit 给予贷款

grant a loan 给予贷款,贷款

grant a special amnesty 特赦

grant back clause 回授条款

grant back might 技术反馈权

grant component 赠与组成部分

grant in aid for housing 住房支出财政补贴

grant in perpetuity 永久赠与

grant of land 土地赠与

grant of probate 通过遗嘱的认证

grant political asylum 给予政治庇护

grant property 赠与财产

granted property 赠与财产

grantee 受让人、被授予者,受让方

grantor 授予人,让步人

grant-in-aid 财政补贴

graphology 笔录

grass root 基层

grassland 草原

grassland law 草原法

grassland office 草原管理机构

grassland resources 草原资源

grassroots 基层

grassroots court 基层法院

grassroots public security station 公安派出所

grassroots unit 基层单位

gratuitous 无偿的,免费的

gratuitous act 无偿民事法律行为,无对价民事法律行为

gratuitous bailment 无报酬之货物寄托,义务货物寄托

gratuitous contract 单方受益的合同,无偿合同

gratuitous legacy 无偿遗赠

gratuitous loan 无债借贷

gratuitous requisition 无偿征用

gratuitous voluntary 无偿的

grave 严重

grave breach of contract 严重违约

grave breaches 严重违约行为,严重破坏行为

grave consequences 严重后果

grave negligence 严重疏忽,严重过失

gravity of the circumstances 情节严重

Gray's Inn 格雷法律学院

grease one's hand 贿赂

grease the hand of 暗中行贿

grease the palm of 暗中行贿

great depression 大萧条

great inquest 大陪审团,大审判

great power 大国

great reform 大化改新

great seal 国玺

great society 大社会

greater military region 大军区

great-power chauvinism 大国沙文主义

great-power politics 大国外交

Greece 希腊

greedily seek exorbitant profit 牟取暴利

Greek church 东正教会

greensward 草地,草坪

gregorian calendar 公历年

grey area measures 灰色区域措施(注：指绕过 GATT 的贸易保护措施)

grievous bodily harm 严重身体伤害

grievous bodily harm 严重人体伤害,严重之身体侵害

grievous faulty 重大过失

grievous injury 严重损害,严重伤害

gross 总额
gross amount 总额
gross case 重大案件
gross crime 重大犯罪
gross criminal case 重大刑事案件
gross disparity 重大失衡
gross export value 出口总值
gross fault 重大过失
gross floor(s) area(GFA) 建筑面积
gross foreign currency position 毛外币头寸
gross injustice 大冤案
gross interference 粗暴
gross investment 总投资,投资总额
gross lease 金额租赁
gross misbehavior 严重不法行为
gross national product/GNP 国民生产总值
gross neglect of duty 严重失职
gross negligence 重大疏忽,严重疏忽,重大过失
Gross negligence is equivalent to fraud 重大过失等于诈骗
gross pay 工资总额
gross position 毛头寸
gross premium 保险费总额
gross price 总价格
gross salary 工资总额
gross sales 销售定额
gross sum 总额
gross supply 总供给
gross tonnage 总吨位
gross weight 毛重
grossly interfere 粗暴干涉
ground floor 底层
ground of punishment 刑罚根据
ground traffic control 地面交通管制
groundless 没有理由,无理由的,无根据的,莫须有
grounds for avoidance 宣告无效的理由
grounds of decision 判决理由

① grounds of judgment 判决根据
② grounds of opposition 抗辩理由
③ group action 集团诉讼
④ group agreement 集团协定
⑤ group decision 集体决策
⑥ group home 教养院
⑦ group insurance 团体保险
⑧ group life accident insurance 团体人身意外伤害保险
⑨ group of first offense 初犯群体
⑩ group of ten(G/10) 十国集团
⑫ group order 集体订货
⑬ group participation 集体参与
⑭ group product 集体产品
⑮ group purchase 组合购买
⑯ group sale(美) 集体销售
⑰ group veto 集团否决
⑱ grouping of contacts 关系聚集地
⑲
⑳ grouping of the economy 经济集团化
㉑
㉒ grow 发展
㉓ grown lease 官契
㉔ grown ownership(港) 官方所有权
㉕
㉖ grown privilege 王室特权
㉗ grown servant 王室官员
㉘ grown-up 成年人
㉙ grown up children 成年子女
㉚ grueling trial 车轮式审讯
㉛ guarantee 保证,担保、保证书,作保证人,受保人,保障,保证书
㉜
㉝
㉞ guarantee against double jeopardy 一事不再理的保证
㉟
㊱ guarantee agreement 担保协议
㊲ guarantee by aval 第三人对票据的付款保证
㊳
㊴ guarantee by third party payment 第三人付款保证
㊶ guarantee company 担保公司
㊷ guarantee contract 立即参与保证合同,担保合同
㊸ guarantee deposit 押金,保证金
㊹
㊺ guarantee freedom of speech for the people 保障人民言论自由
㊻

guarantee fund 保证基金

guarantee law of the People's Republic of China 中华人民共和国担保法

guarantee limitation 担保限度

guarantee money 押金,保证金

guarantee of a bill 票据的保证

guarantee of acceptance 承兑保证

guarantee of delivery 交货保证

guarantee of insurance 保险担保书

guarantee of payment 付款保证

guarantee of performance 履行担保

guarantee of quantity 数量保证

guarantee payment 保证款项

guarantee performance of contract 保证合同的履行

guarantee price 担保价格

guarantee sum 保证金额

guarantee the freedom of speech 保障言论自由

guarantee trust 保证信托

guarantee with one's property 以财产担保

guaranteed 被保证的,被担保的

guaranteed bill 有担保的票据

guaranteed bond 担保债券

guaranteed by endorsement 背书担保

guaranteed credit 有保证的贷款

guaranteed letter of credit 担保信用证

guaranteed loan 担保借款

guaranteed mortgage 担保抵押

guaranteed price 保证价格

guaranteed qualities 品质保证

guaranteed suitable 保证适当

guarantees 抵押品

guarantor 保证人、担保人

guarantor enterprise 担保企业

guaranty 保证,抵押品,保证书

guaranty funds 保证金

guaranty insurance 担保风险

guaranty mode 保证方式

guaranty of trustworthiness 可靠的担保,有信用的担保

guaranty period 担保期间,保证期间

guaranty trust company 担保信托公司

guard 监狱看守

guard against 预防

guard state secrets 保护国家秘密

guardian 保护人、监护人

guardian by election 选择监护人

guardian by nature 自然监护人

guardian of person 人身监护人

guardianship 监护关系,监护职责

guardianship measure 监护处分

guardianship of infants act 未成年人的监护人法例

guardianship proceedings 监护权诉讼

guerrilla 游击队

guest house 宾馆

guest prosecutor 特约检察员

guest supervisor 特约监察员

guide consumption 引导消费

guidelines of reform-through-labour 劳动改造方针

guiding ideology 指导思想

guiding ideology of criminal law 刑法指导思想

guiding principle 方针

guild 行会

guild system 行会制度

guillotine 断头台

guilt 罪行

guiltless 无罪的

guilty belief 犯罪信念

guilty consciences 犯罪意识

guilty deed 犯罪行为

guilty intent 犯罪故意

guilty intention 犯意

guilty knowledge 犯罪意识,自知有罪

guilty mind 犯意

guilty of victim 被害人有罪

gulf state 海湾国家

gullibly believe it possible to avoid 轻信能够避免

gullibly believe it possible to avoid these consequences 轻信能够避免这种结果

gun robber 持枪抢劫犯

gun robbery 持枪抢劫

gunboat diplomacy 炮舰外交

gun-related crime 涉枪犯罪

guns 枪支

Gupta Dynasty 笈多王朝

H

habeas corpus（拉） 人身保护令,人身保护状

habeas corpus act（英） 人身保护法

habeas corpus writ 人身权利状

habendum（拉） 契据的物权条款

habitant 居民区

habitation of crime 犯罪习癖化

habitual board 惯常住所

habitual business office 经常营业所

habitual criminal 惯犯

habitual offender 常习犯

habitual recidivist 常习累犯

habitual residence 经常居住地,习惯居所,惯常住所

habitual robber 惯盗

habitual swindler 惯骗

Hachijuni Bank（Nagano） 八十二银行（长野）

hagard 危险因素

hague convention for the peaceful settlement of peaceful settlement of international disputes 海牙和平解决国际争端公约

Hague convention system 海牙公约系统

Hague peace conferences 海牙和平会议

Hague rules 海牙规则(注:全称为统一提单若干法律规定的国际公约

hajj 朝觐

Halare agreement 哈拉雷议定书

half-day 半日制

half-insane offender 半疯癫罪犯

half-mast 半旗

half-proof 部分证据,初步证明

halfway house 重返社会训练所

hall 大厅

hall mark 品质证明

Hallmote 佃户法庭(英)

hallucinogenic 迷幻药

halter 绞索

Hamburg rules 1978 汉堡规则（Hamburg）

hamlet 村庄

Hammurabi 汉穆拉比

Han chauvinism 大汉族主义

Hanabilah 罕百里派

Hanafiyah 哈奈斐派

hand expert 笔迹鉴定人

hand grain 手纹

hand in one's resignation 辞职

handcuffs 手铐

handicapped 残疾的

handicapped person 残疾人

handicraft industry 手工业

handle 处理,处置

handle a legal case 办案

handle cases in conformity with legal provisions 依法办案

handle contradictions among the people 处理人民内部矛盾

handle with care 小心搬运

handling 处理方法,装卸

handling facilities 装卸设备

handling method 处理方法

handling of convict's complaint 罪犯申诉处理

handling of land 土地开发

handling of the indictment of a convict 罪犯控告处理

handprint identification, thumb print identification 手印鉴定

handsel 定金

handwriting 笔迹

handwriting authentication 笔迹鉴定

handwriting verification 笔迹检验,字迹检验

hang 搁置;(被)绞死,吊死

hanger 绞刑执行人

hanging 绞刑

hanging matter 绞刑案件

hangman 绞刑执行人

harassment 困扰罪

harbor 包庇

hard-and-fast 不可能犯的,不可触犯的

hard cash 硬币-现金

hard currency 硬通货,硬货币

hard drug 麻醉品

hard money 可兑现货币,可与黄金兑换的货币

hardened criminal 不知悔改的罪犯

hardened offender 惯行犯

hardened thief 惯窃犯

hardship clause 艰难情势条款

harm 危害,损害

harm the country's military interest 危害国家军事利益

harm the public interest 危害公共利益

harmful 有害的

harmful act 有害行为

harmful substance 有害物质

harmfulness 危害性

harmfulness of crime 犯罪危害

harmless 无害的

harmonization of laws 法律的协调

harmonized commodity description and coding system 协调商品名称与编码制度

harsh 严厉的

harsh government 苛政

Harter act 哈特法(注:美国制订于1893年)

hasten the dispatch of the order 迅速发送订货

haulage 托运费

haulier 承运人

(to)have a better education 有文化

have a brush with law 吃官司

(to)have a strong sense of discipline 有纪律

have a lien on the goods 有权留

置货物

have a right to compensation 享有补偿权

have already started to perpetrate a crime 已经着手实行犯罪

have an analytical and critical eye 有分析,有批判

have an impact on 影响

(to)have high ideals 有理想

(to)have moral integrity 有道德

have no effect 无效

have no faith in 不信任

have no objection 无反对意见

have no power of agency 无代理权

have no precedent to go by 无先例可援引

have no remedy at law 法律上无任何补救办法

have power to abrogate 有权撤销

have power to nullify 有权撤销

have priority in compensation 优先受偿

have recourse to law 诉诸法律

have right to charge against 有控告…的权利

have standing 有资格

have the effect of 权能

have the right 有权

(to)have the right as well as the duty to work 有劳动的权利和义务

(to)have the right to compensation in accordance with the law 有依照法律取得赔偿的权利

(to)have the right to material assistance 有获得物质帮助的权利

(to)hold the nationality of 具有…国籍

have to do with 涉及

having joint operation based on specific technology 技术联营

having the right to establish public organizations in conformity with the law 有权依法组织社会

团体

hawker 摊贩

hazard 公害

hazard beacon 警告灯标

hazard to public 公害

hazardous articles (goods, cargo) 危险物品

hazardous goods 危险货物

hazardous substance 危险物品

dangerous articles 危险物品

He who can will has a right to refuse to will 谁可以表达意志也就有权拒绝表达意见

He who seeks equity must do equity 要求公平者必须公平待人

head 首长

head charter 原租船合同

head charter party 原租船合同

head charterer 原租船人,原船舶承担人

head downward 倒吊刑

head money 人头税

head nurse 护士长

head of a state 元首

head of government 政府首脑

head of household 户主

head of the state 国家元首

head of the town 镇长

head of township 乡长

head tax 人头税

heads of a charge 控告要点

head-note 判词提要

heal estate mortgage 不动产抵押

health 卫生

health administration 卫生管理

health and sanitary regulation 卫生检疫规定

health certificate 健康证明

health checkup of convicts 罪犯健康检查表

health declaration form 健康申明卡

health insurance 疾病保险

health law 卫生法

health measure 卫生措施

health quarantine 卫生检疫

health quarantine organization 卫生检疫机关

health regulation and rules 卫生法规、规章

health standards 卫生标准

health supervision 卫生监督

health supervisor 卫生监督员

healthy development of the socialist market economy 社会主义市场经济的健康发展

hear both sides of the question 兼听双方意见

hear in private session 不公开审理

hearing 听审,听证会,听证

hearing in camera 秘密审讯

hearing in the public 公审

hearing proceeding of price irregularity case 价格违法案件审理程序

hearing system 听证制度

hearing time 开审日期

heart land 中心地带

heating radiator 暖气片

heavier punishment 从重

heavier punishment in public security 从重治安处罚

heavy cargo 重货

heavy economic losses 重大经济损失

heavy industry 重工业

heavy lift additional 超重附加费

heavy lift cargo 超重货物

heavy loss 重大损失,严重亏损

heavy price 高价

heavy sentence 重刑

heavy sentencing 量刑畸重

heavy speculation 严重投机倒把

heavy tax 重税

Hebrew 希伯来人

hecessani a cautio (拉) 法定抵押

hedge clause 避免条款

hedge fund 对冲基金

hedging 套期保值,套头交易,

套期保值

hegatire right of claim 相请求权

hegemonism 霸权主义

hegemonists 霸权主义者

hegemony 霸权

heinous crime 十恶不赦的大罪,十恶不赦的罪行,弥天大罪

heir 继承人

heir in tail 限嗣继承人

heirless 无继承人

heirolovm 相传动产

held cover 暂予负责

held in trust 委托保管

helical stair 螺旋楼梯

Hellenes 古希腊人

help and education for one released on bail 保外帮教

help production 有利生产

help sb to change 感化

help to bring the initiative of the localities into full play 发挥地方的积极性

Henry's analysis of fingerprints 享利式指纹分析法

hereditament 可继承的不动产

hereditary 世袭

hereditary determinism of crime 犯罪遗传决定论

hereditary property 世袭财产

hereditary system 世袭制度

heresy 异端

heritablity 被继承

hestero-demonopathy syndrome 癔病性附体综合症

heterogeneous cargo 异质货物

hexi(罗) 合同的双方当事人

hidden 隐蔽的

hidden danger 隐患

hidden dumping 隐蔽倾销

hidden inflation 隐蔽性通货膨胀

hidden injury 内伤

hidden resources 地下资源

hide 隐蔽

hide property 隐匿财产

hide the facts 隐瞒事实

hiding property 隐匿财产

hierarchical conference 等级会议

hierarchical organization 等级制组织

hierarchy 等级制度,统治集团

high 高级

high and new-technology industry 高新技术产业

high commissioner 高级专员

high court 高等法院

high court and crown court centre(英) 高等法院和刑事法院中心

high court of admiralty 高等海事法院(英)

high court of delegates 高级特派法庭(英)

high court of errors and appeals 高等上诉和复审法院(英)

high court of errors and appeals(美) 高等上诉和复审法院

high court of justice 高等法院

high degree 高度

high degree of autonomy 高度自治权

high degree of centralized and unified management 高度集中的统一管理

high level of democracy 高度民主

high price 重价,高价

high seas 公海

high street 大街

high technology industry 高技术产业

high treason 重叛逆罪,杀君

high voltage operations 高电压作业

higher authorities 上级

higher authority 上级主管

higher court 上级法院

higher credit 高档信贷部分贷款

higher education 高等教育

higher law 高级法

higher level 上级

higher people's court 高级人民法院

higher people's procuratorate 高级人民检察院

higher procuratorate 上级检察院

highest 最高

highest administrative organization 最高行政机关

highest bid 投标最高价

highest discount 最大抵扣

highest organ of state administration 最高国家行政机关

highest organ of state power 最高国家权力机关

highest supervisory office 最高监督机关

highest supervisory organization within state administration 最高监察机关

highly 高度

highly centralize 高度集中

highly centralized policy-making setup of the state 高度集中的国家决策体系

highly demanded commodities 紧缺商品

highly industrialized state 高度工业化国家

highly toxic 剧毒

hightech industry 高技术产业

highway 公路

highway acts 公路法规

highway administrative organization 公路行政管理机关

highway authority 公路管理机构

highway laws 公路法规

highway maintenance act 公路行政管理行为

highway maintenance department 公路养护部门

highway man 拦路强盗,拦路抢劫犯

highway regulations 公路法规

highway safety 公路安全

highway toll station 公路收费站

highway traffic accident 公路交通事故

highway traffic law 公路交通法

highway-user tax 公路使用税

high-handed 专横的

high-handed policy 高压政策

high-interest loans 高利贷

high-level 高级

high-speed means of transport 高速运输工具

high-tech products 高技术产品

Higo Bank (Kumamoto) 肥俊银行(熊本)

hike prices regardless of government regulations 随意涨价

hill forest 山林

hilly land alloted for private use 自留山

hilly land allotted for private use 自留山

hinder official duties 妨碍执行公务

Hinduism 印度教

hire 雇佣,租赁,租金

hire labour 雇工

hire of processing work 加工承揽

hire out 罪犯放风

hire purchase 分期付款买卖

hirer 雇用人,租借人

hire-purchase 租入买卖

hire-purchase agreement 分期付款买卖协议

hire-purchase price 分期付款价格

hiring of thing 物件租赁

hiring standards 雇佣标准

historic bay 历史性海湾

historic right 历史性权利

historic title 历史性权利

historical 历史性

historical and cultural sites under government protection 文物保护单位

historical evolution of constitution 宪法的历史发展

historical interpretation 历史解释	① hold the shipment 停止装运
historical jurisprudence 历史法学	② holder 占有人
	③ holder in bad faith 恶意占有人
historical jurist 历史法学家	④ holder in due course 合法持有人
historical materialism 历史唯物主义	⑤
	⑥ holder in good faith 善意占有人
historical offender 历史犯	⑦ holder on trust 受托人
historical origin of law 法的历史渊源	⑧ holder's meeting 股东大会
	⑨ holdover tenant 延期承担人
historical relics 文物	⑩ holy 神圣
historical school of law 历史法学派	⑪ holy office 宗教法庭
	⑫ home 私人寓所
historical water 历史性水域	⑬ home affair 民政,内务
history of crime 犯罪史	⑭ home branch 国内分支机构
history of economic law 经济法学的历史发展	⑮ home building 住房建设
	⑯ home constituency 原选区
history of legal system 法制史	⑰ home country 祖国
hitting time 到达时间	⑱ home delivery service 送货上门服务
hitting tool mark 打击工具痕迹	⑲
hive 租赁	⑳ home department 内政部
HK and Macao 港澳	㉑ home improvement 住房改善
hoc titulo (拉) 根据这种权限	㉒ home industry 家庭工业
Hohenstaufen 霍亨斯陶芬	㉓ home market 国内市场
hoist the price 提价	㉔ home ownership flat 拥有产权的自住套房
hold 扣留,约束	㉕
hold a coordinate position 享有同等地位	㉖ home policy 国内政策
	㉗ home price 国内价格
hold a demonstration 示威	㉘ home production 国内生产
hold back 隐瞒	㉙ home products 本国产品
hold brief for 承办案件	㉚ home rule 地方自治,自治
hold contract 抵押合同	㉛ home value declaration 国内价格申报
hold court from behind a screen 垂帘听政	㉜
	㉝ homestead 宅基地
hold covered/HC 继续承担	㉞ homogeneous goods 同质货物
hold equal status 享有同等地位	㉟ homologate 批准
hold exhibitions 举办展览,提供信息	㊱ homosexual act 同性恋行为
	㊲ honest and clean government 廉政
hold in custody 拘留	㊳
hold in one's own possession 个人持有	㊴ honest and upright official 清官
	㊵ honest belief 真实相信
hold in pledge 持作抵押品,抵押	㊶ honest possession 合法占有
	㊷ honest wrong belief 诚实错误信念
hold lethal weapons 持凶器	㊸
hold office 任职	㊹ honesty and credibility 诚实信用
hold sb to ransom 绑票	㊺
hold the line 稳定价格	㊻ Hong Kong 香港
	㊼ Hong Kong and Macao 港澳

Hong Kong and Macao regions 港澳地区

Hong Kong SAR passport 香港特区护照

Hong Kong Special Administrative Region 香港特别行政区

Hong Kong, China 中国香港

hono(u)r 承兑远期票据,信用,荣誉

hono(u)r policy 信用保险单

honor a check 承兑支票

honorary chairman 名誉主席

honorary consul 名誉领事

honorary duty 名誉职务

honorary feuds 名誉封地

honorary office 名誉职务

honorary post 名誉职位

honorary president 名誉主席

honorary titles 荣誉称号

honour agreement 履行协议

honour clause 不受法律约束的条款,不受法律约束的条约

honour of motherland 祖国荣誉

honour one's liability 承担赔偿责任

honourable duty 光荣义务

hood 窗遮篷

hook damage 钩损险

horizonal integration 水平一体化

horizontal association 横向联合,横向结合

horizontal audit 横向审计

horizontal cartel 横向组合

horizontal combination 同业合并,横向合并

horizontal competition 同业竞争

horizontal consolidation 横向合并

horizontal economic union 横向经济联合

horizontal integration 横向联合

horizontal international division labour 水平型国际分工

horizontal linkage 横向联合

horizontal merger 横向合并

horizontal separation of powers 横向分权

hospital discharge certificate 出院证明

host country 东道国

host country tax reimbursement 东道国税务补偿

hostage 人质,抵押物

hostage murder 杀害人质

hostile 敌对

hostile class 敌对阶级

hostile country 敌对国

hostile embargo 敌国船只的扣留

hostile international law 战时国际法

hostile nationality 敌国国籍

hostile policy 敌对政策

hostile relations 敌对关系

hot 违禁的

hot money 游资

hot on the trial 紧急追捕

hot pursuit 紧急追捕

hotchpotch 财产混同

hot-water ordeal 浸开水神判法

house 收容

house agent 房地产经纪人

house allowance 住房津贴

house and rehabilitate 收容教养

house counsel 企业法律顾问

house duty 房产税

house for rent 房屋出租

house hunter 寻找出租房屋者

jouse of commons 平民院

house of correction 教养院

house of detention 拘留所,看守所

house of lords 贵族院(英),上议院

house of peers 贵族院

house of representative 众议院

house property mortgage 房产抵押

house sites 宅基地

house tax 房产税

household contracted responsibility system with remuneration 家

庭联产承包责任制

household contractual system 家庭承包责任制

household head 户主

household industry 家庭工业

household management 家庭经营

household manufacture 家庭工业

household operation 家庭经营

household production 家庭生产

household register 户籍

household register act 户籍法

household register certificate 户籍证明

household registration 户口登记

household registration book 户口本

household registration office 户口登记机关

household registration system 户口登记制度

household registry certificate 户口证件

household registry jurisdictional area 户口管辖区

household sideline production 家庭副业

householder 户主

households engaged in individual enterprises 个体户

household-based contract system 家庭承包责任制

housing commercialization 住房商品化

housing conditions 住房状况

housing construction 住宅建设

housing court 房屋法庭

housing dispute 房屋纠纷

housing estate 居住小区

housing funds 住宅建设基金

housing guarantee program 住宅担保项目

housing industrialization 住宅产业化

housing loan 住宅贷款

housing management 住房管理

housing need 住房要求

housing preference 住房选择

housing supply 住房供应量

huff 提高价格

huge amount 数额巨大

huge organization 机构雍肿

hull insurance 船舶保险

hull insurance clause 船舶保险条款

hull policy 船舶保险单

hull war and strikes risk 船舶战争、罢工险

human 人道的,人的,人类的

Human are equal before the law 法律面前人人平等

human being 人类,自然人

human dignity 人的尊严

human ecology 人类生态学

human law 人定法

human remains 人文痕迹

human resources 劳动力资源

human right act 人权法

human right(s) 人性,人仅

human rights diplomacy 人权外交

human rights report 人权报告

human rights situation 人权状况

human rule 人道规则

human testimony and material evidence 人证物证

human treatment 人道待遇

humanism 人道主义,人文主义,人本主义

humanist 人本主义者

humanistic 人本主义

humanistic psychological view of crime 人本主义犯罪心理观

humanitarian intervention 人道主义的干涉

humanitarian law 人道主义法

humanitarian rule 人道规则

humanity 人性

humiliate the nation and forfeit its sovereignty 丧权辱国

hundred court (港) 百户法庭

hybrid class action 混合性群体诉讼

hybrid offense 混合罪

hygiene 卫生

hygienic license 卫生许可证

Hyogo Sogo Bank（Hyogo） 兵库相互银行(兵库)

hypotaxis 从属关系

hypothec bank 不动产抵押银行

hypothec(a) 抵押数,担保数

hypotheca generalis（拉） 全部财产抵押权

hypotheca specialis（拉） 特定抵押权

hypotheca tacita（拉） 默示抵押权

hypothecarius（拉） 抵押权人

① hypothecary action 关于抵押财产索赔权的诉讼,抵押权诉讼

③ hypothecary value 抵押价值

④ hypothecate 质押

⑤ hypothecated asset 抵押资产

⑥ hypothecation 抵押权,质押契据,质押,抵押,质契

⑧ hysteric personality disorder 癔病型人格障碍

⑩ hysterical disturbance of consciousness 癔病性意识障碍

⑫ hysterical disturbance of sensation 癔病性感觉障碍

⑭ hysterical emotional out burst 癔病性情感爆发

I

ibid/id（拉）同一章节

ibidem（拉）同一章节

icc arbitration　国际商会仲裁

ice clause　冰冻条款

icebox　单人牢房

ID card for permanent resident of
Hong Kong　香港永久性居民
身份证

idea of criminality　犯罪观

idea of law　法律的理想

idea of pacific economic
sphere　PECC 太平洋经济圈
设想

ideal　理想

ideal element of law　法律的理
想成分

idelogical coincident crime　观念
充分犯

idem（拉）同上

identical goods　相同货物

identifiability　可识别性

identification　鉴定，确认，辨认

identification by palm print　掌
纹鉴定

identification capacity　辨认能力

identification card　身份证

identification evidence　辨认证
据，鉴定证据

identification eyewitness　辨认证
人

identification mark　识别标记

identification marking　识别标记

identification of bullet　弹头鉴定

identification of corpse　尸体辨
认

identification of goods　物的辨认

identification of images　形象辨
认

identification of law　法律的确
认

identification of materials　实物
辨认

identification of poison　毒物鉴
定

identification of tool marks　工具
痕迹鉴定

identification of vehicle traces　车
辆痕迹鉴定

identification record　辨认笔录

identified object　被认定同一客
体

identifier　鉴定人

identify　认同，辨认

identify the problem　确定问题
之所在

identify to the contract　确定在
合同项下

identifying the object　物品辨认

identity　鉴别，同一性

identity card of residents　居民身
份证

identity discipline　同一原则

identity of carrier clause　确认承
运人条款

identity of state　国家的同一性

identity of views　观点一致

ideological　意识形态的

ideological and political education
of prisoners　罪犯思想政治教
育

ideological and political work　思
想政治工作

ideological offense　思想犯罪

ideological system　思想体系

ideology　思想，思想体系

idle　无根据的，闲散，无效

idle capacity　闲置生产能力

idle capital　闲置资本

idle cost　停工损失

idle exercise　无意义的行为

idle fund(s)　闲置资金

idle labor　闲散劳动力

idle money　闲散资金

idle talk　清谈

idle time　停工期间

idle time lost　停工费用

idling period　停产期,停工期
ignis judicium（拉）　火判法
ignoramus（拉）　不予起诉
ignorance　无知
ignorance(mistake) of fact　事实错误
ignorantia（拉）　无知
ignore　不受理
ignore a complaint　拒绝无理起诉
ill　疾病
ill founded accusation　罪名不成立
ill founded charge　罪名不成立
ill will　恶意
illegal　非法的,不法的,不合法的
illegal act　不法行为,违法行为,犯法行为
illegal act in taxation　税收违法行为
illegal action　非法行为
illegal activities　非法活动,不法活动,违法活动
illegal association　非法结社
illegal carrying of controlled knives　非法携带管制刀具
illegal consideration　违法对价
illegal contract　违法合同,非法合同
illegal disposition　违法处分
illegal economic act　经济违法行为
illegal entry into and exit from the border of China　非法入出中国国境
illegal felling of trees　滥伐树木
illegal gains　违法所得
illegal immigrant　非法入境者
illegal income　非法所得,不法收益
illegal interest　不法收益
illegal interference or obstruction　非法干预和阻挠
illegal intervention　非法干涉
illegal means　非法手段
illegal offense　非法侵犯

illegal organization　非法组织
illegal pawning（港）　非法典估
illegal possession　不法占有,非法占有
illegal practices　不法行为
illegal profit　不当得利
illegal publication　非法出版物
illegal regime　非法政府
illegal search and seizure　非法搜查与扣押
illegal speculator　投机倒把分子
illegal structure　不合法建筑物
illegal transaction　非法交易
illegal transfer　非法转让
illegal vote　非法表决
illegality　违法性,不法
illegality clause　非法条款
illegally cross the border　非法越境
illegally obtained evidence　非法获得的证据
illegitimacy　不合理
illegitimate　非法,不法的,不合法的
illegitimate purpose　非法目的
illicit　违禁的,非法,不法的,不合法的,违章
illicit activity　违法活动
illicit sale　私卖
illicit sexual intercourse　奸淫
illiquid holdings　不动产
illness　病
illogical　不合逻辑的推论
illustrated catalogue　售房图解说明
illustration　例证
ill-founded　无事实根据的
ill-timed necessity　避险不适时
ill-treat　虐待
ill-use　虐待,滥用
ILO（International Labour Organization）　劳工组织
imaginative defense　假想防卫
imaginative joiner of offense　想象竞合犯,想像数罪
imaginative plural crimes of the same kind　同种想像数罪

imaginatively several crime 假想数罪

imbecile 禁治产人

IMF 国际货币基金组织

imitate 假冒

imitation 假冒

imitative commodities 假冒商品

Immanuel. Kant 伊曼纽尔·康德

immaterial 非实质的

immaterial product 无形产品

immature 未成年的

immeasurable 无法计量的

immediate 即时的,即期交货

immediate annuity 即时年金

immediate at sight 即期

immediate cash（payment） 立即付现,即付

immediate cause 近因,直接原因

immediate compensation 立即赔偿

immediate complaint 即时控告

immediate consequence 直接后果

immediate consultation 直接磋商

immediate delivery 立即交付,立即交货

immediate fund 即期资金

immediate interest 切身利益

immediate liabilities 流动负债

immediate notice clause 立即通知条款

immediate order 即时订货单

immediate packing 直接包装

immediate participation 立即参与保证合同

immediate payment 立即付额,立即支付,即期付款,即时付款

immediate recourse 立即向保证人追索

immediate reply 即时答辩

immediate shipment 即期装运

immediate will of the people 人民的迫切愿望

immemorial possession（美） 自古占有,远占占有

immigrant 移民

immigrant visa 移民签证

immigration 移居入境

immigration law 移民法

immigration office（/service） 移民局

immobile property 不动产

immobilized capital 固定化的资本

immoral act 不道德行为

immoral consideration 不道德的对价

immoral contract 不道德契约,不道德的合同

immoral obligation 不道德义务

immoral trade 不道德交易

immovable estate 不动产

immovable mortgage loan 不动产抵押放款

immovable property 不动产

immovables 不动产

immune from liability 免责

immunity 豁免权,免疫,安全

immunity clauses 免责条款

immunity from administrative order 行政管理豁免

immunity from arrest 不受逮捕

immunity from attachment 诉讼保全豁免

immunity from criminal responsibility 刑事责任豁免

immunity from diseases 免疫

immunity from duties 关税豁免

immunity from prosecution 免于公诉

immunity from punishment 免受惩罚

immunity from taxation 捐税豁免

immunity from trial 不受审判

immunity of warships on the high sea 军舰在公海上的豁免

immunity warships on the high sea 军舰在公海上的豁免

impact 影响

impact mark 弹着痕迹

impair 损害

impair relations 损害关系

impair the health of citizens 损害公民身体健康

impairment 损害,妨害

impairment of a law 减低法律的效力

impairment of public security 妨害公共安全行为

impartial 公正的

impartial taxation 公平税

impartiality 公正性

impartible 不可分的,不可分割的

impartible right 不可分割的权利

impeach 弹劾,检举

impeached for treason 被指控犯有叛国罪

impeachment 弹劾

impeachment case 检察案件

impeachment of waste 制止土地荒芜

impeachment power 弹劾权

impediment to practice of law 实施法律的障碍

impel 促使

impel sb to rehabilitation 促使某人改过自新

imperative 必须履行的,强行

imperative necessity 迫切必要

imperative obligation 必须履行的责任

imperfect 不能履行的

imperfect acceptance 不完全接受

imperfect act 不完全行为

imperfect competition 不完全竞争

imperfect gift 不完全赠与,不完善赠与

imperfect obligation 不受法律约束的责任,不完全的义务

imperfect ratification 不完全批准

imperfect real right 不完全物权

imperfert obligations 不完全的义务

imperial authority 皇权

imperial court 王朝,王室

imperial household 皇室

imperial kinsmen 皇族

imperial power 皇权

imperial royal 皇家

imperialism 帝国主义

imperium 帝权

impersonal assets 非个人的资产

impersonal entity 法人单位

impersonal security 非个人担保

impersonal tax 对物税

impleader 起诉人

implement 完全履行,施行,执行

implement a contract 履行合同

implement a policy 实施政策

implementary provisions 施行细则

implementation 施行

implementation and revision of plans 计划的执行和修改

implementation of constitution 宪法实施

implementation of the contract 合同的执行人

implicate 牵连

implicated offender 牵连犯,连累犯

implied 默示的

implied abrogation 默示废除

implied acceptance of risk 默示承担风险

implied authority 默示授权

implied condition 默许的条件

implied confession 默示认罪

implied consent 默许,默示同意

implied contract 隐含的契约,准合同,默示合同,准契约

implied contract in fact 事实上的默示合同

implied duty 默示义务

implied exception 默示例外

implied malice 隐含的恶意

implied objection 默示异议或反

对

implied obligation(s) 默示义务，默示债务

implied partnership 默示合伙

implied power 默示权力

implied powers of congress 国会的默示权力

implied promise 默示承诺

implied ratification 默示批准

implied recognition 默示承认

implied renunciation 默示放弃

implied repeal 默示规定

implicd representation 默示代理

implied repudiation 默示废弃

implied reservation 默示保留，默示权益保留

implied revocation 默示取消

implied term 默示条款，默示条件

implied termination 默示终止

implied terms 默示条款

implied trust 默示信托

implied use 默示使用权

implied warrant 默示保证

implied warranty 默示担保，默示保证

implied warranty of fitness for a particular purpose 适合特别目的的默示担保

implied warranty of merchantability 商销性的默示担保

imply 默示

import and export 进出口

import and export corporation 进出口公司

import and export credits 进出口信贷

import and export declaration 进出口申报

import and export of goods 货物进出口

import and export of technologies 技术进出口

import and export tariffs 进出口税则

import authorization 进口许可证

import bill 进口汇票

import cargo 进口货物

import certificate 进口执照

import control 进口管制

import credit 进口信用证

import declaration 进口报关单，进口申报单

import direct lease 进口直接租赁

import duty 进口税

import duty memo 海关进口税缴纳证

import exchange 进口外汇

import licence system 进口许可证制

import of advanced technology 引进先进技术

import quantum 进口量

import quota(s) 进口配额，进口限额

import quotas system 进口配额制

import substituting industry 进口替代工业

import substitution 进口替代

import surplus 入超

import surtaxes 进口附加税

import tariff 进口税则

import techniques 进口技术

import trade 进口贸易

import trade bill 进口贸易票据

importance conditions of effective administrative act 行政行为成立要件

important and complicated case 案情重大、复杂

important condition 要件

importam conditions constituting a crime 构成犯罪要件

important criminal 要犯

importation 进口(货)

imported patent 引进专利

importer 进口商

impose 征收，强迫

impose a curfew 戒严

impose a fine 罚款

impose a fine in accordance with the rules　照章罚款

impose a penalty　处以罚金

impose a punishment　处刑

impose a sentence　判处

impose a strict ban on　严格禁止

impose fines　执行罚款

impose sanctions　实行制裁

impose sanctions against　处分

imposition of penalty　判处刑罚

imposition of surcharge　征收附加税

imposition of tax　课税

impossibilis conditio（拉）不可能的条件,不能完成的条件

impossibility　不能犯

impossibility of instruments　工具不能犯

impossibility of means　方法不能犯,手段不能犯

impossibility of performance　不可能履行,不能履行,无法履行

impossible attempt　不能未遂

impossible condition　不能履行的条件

impossible event　不可能事件

impotentia（拉）无能力

impound　没收

impoverishment　贫困化

imprecise term　意图不明确的条文

imprescriptibility　不受时效限制者

imprescriptible　不可剥夺的,不可侵犯的,不受法律约束的

imprescriptible right　不可剥夺的权利,不受时效限制的权利,不因时效而丧失的权利

imprevision　不可预见

imprimatur（拉）出版许可

imprison　囚禁

imprisonment　关押,徒刑

imprisonment for debt　债务监禁

imprisonment in the second division　轻罪拘禁

improper　不合理,不当

improper act　不当行为

improper act of rescue　紧急避险不当

improper arrest　不当的逮捕,错捕

improper motion　不合程序的动议

improper necessity　紧急避险不当

improper packing　包装不当

improper performance　不适当的履行

improper purpose　不正当的目的

improper storage　保管不当

improper trading practice　不正当交易行为

improve　改良,加以修改

improve after-sale services　完善售后服务

improve the living environment and the ecological environment　改善生活环境和生态环境

improve the price　提价

improve the quality of products　提高产品质量

improve the socialist legal system　健全社会主义法制

(to) improve working conditions　改善劳动条件

improvement　技术改进条款

improvement in progress　在建房屋修缮改良工程

impulse behavior　冲动行为

impulsive insanity　冲动性精神病

impunity　免罪,免刑,免于处罚

imputable causation　归罪因果关系

imputatio（拉）归责

imputation　归责

imputation of legal responsibility　法律责任的归结

impute　归罪

imputed notice　责任通知

in a manner prescribed by law

依法定方式,依法定程序

in accordance with 符合,依照

in accordance with contract 根据合同

in accordance with practice 按照惯例

in accordance with procedures prescribed by law 依照法律规定的程序

in accordance with specific conditions 根据具体情况

in accordance with the law 依照法律规定,依法

in accordance with the policy of combining punishment with leniency 依照惩办与宽大相结合的政策

in advance 提前

in all charge 负全部责任

in any case 在任何情况下

in any event 在任何情况下

in any instance 在任何情况下

in bad faith 以恶意

in batches 分批次地

in breach of 违反

in breach of contract 违约

(hear a case)in camera 不公开审判

in cash 用现金

in circumstances of urgent need 在紧急需要的情况下

in commendam (拉) 代为保管,委托

in company savings trust 公司内存款信托

in compensation for 作为赔偿

in complete action 法律上完全生效行为

in compliance with 遵守

in conformity with 符合

in conformity with the law of nature 合乎自然规律

in consideration of 鉴于

in consideration of 以…作对价

in consimili casu (拉) 在同样的情况下

in continuous effect 一直有效

① in contradiction to 违反
② in contravention of 违反
③ in correspondence 在信函中
④ in court 当庭
⑤ in custody 被监禁
⑥ in delict 有过失
⑦ in delicto (拉) 有责任
⑧ in disregard of law 不顾法律
⑨ in dubio (拉) 在不确定状态中
⑩ in duplicate 一式两份
⑪ in effect all along 一直有效
⑫ in emergency circumstances 紧
⑬ 急情况下
⑭ in equity 依衡平法
⑮ in essence 实质上
⑯ in extenso (拉) 全部
⑰ in extremis (拉) 在最后的时刻
⑱ in fact 事实上
⑲ in fault 有过错
⑳ in favour of 以…为受益人
㉑ in fraud of 为欺骗
㉒ in fraud of law 规避法律
㉓ in full accord 完全一致
㉔ in full agreement 完全同意
㉕ in full charge 负全部责任
㉖ in full operation 全面实施
㉗ in full settlement 全部偿还
㉘ in fully 定额地
㉙ in general manner 通用方式
㉚ in good faith 出于诚意
㉛ in good order 完整无损
㉜ in good shape 完整无损
㉝ in good time 及时
㉞ in gremio legis (拉) 在法律保护
㉟ 下
㊱ in hoods pennyworth 廉价出凭
㊲ In irons 被监禁
㊳ in jure (拉) 法律上的
㊴ in justice and fairness 按良心和
㊵ 公平原则
㊶ in kind 实物
㊷ in law 依法
㊸ in legal form 以法律的形式
㊹ in line with 根据
㊺ in loco (拉) 在适当的地方
㊻ in omnibus (拉) 在所有问题上
㊼ in one's favour 以…为受益人

in one's name 以某人名义

in pari delicto（拉）同等罪犯

in passing 附带

in personal effect of administrative procedure law 行政诉讼的对人效力

in pledge 在抵押中

in point of law 依法律观点

in present-day conditions 在目前条件下

in principle 在原则上

in quadruplicate 一式四份

in quintuplicate 一式五份

in re（拉）案由

in reference to 有关

in regard to 有关

in respect of 有关

in right of 凭…权利

in septuplicate 一式七份

in service 使用中

in stock 有存货

in surplus 顺差

in tempore 及时

in the absence of any other agreement 如无其他约定

in the absence of fault 没有过错

in the absence of other provisions in the law or contract 法律或合同并无另外规定时

in the act 当场

in the capacity of 以…身份，以…资格

in the custody of 代管

in the eye of（the）law 依法律观点

in the form of an omission 以不作为的形式

in the interests of 为…的利益（立法、判决等）

in the light of 依据，依照，根据

in the light of actual conditions 参照具体情况

in the name of 以…名义

in the person of 以…资格

in the presence of justifiable reasons 如有正当理由

in the present circumstances 在目前情况下

in the principals name 以被代理人名义

in the process of manufacture 在生产过程中

in the process of production 在生产过程中

in the short time 在短期内

in the spirit of mutual assistance 互相帮助原则

in time 及时

in toto（拉）全部

in transit 运输途中，在途中

in transitu（拉）在途中

in triplicate 一式三份

in use 在使用中

in vain 无效

in vem on property interest 物权

inactive 闲散

inactive intent 相故意

inactive negligence 相过失

inadequate damages 不当损害赔偿，不足承担赔偿金

inadequate personality disorder 不适当人格障碍

inadequate sentencing 量刑不当

inadmissible 不可接受的

inadmissible evidence 不可接受的证据

inadvertent negligence 无认识的过失

inalienability of sovereignty 主权的不可分割性

inalienable 不可让与的

inalienable action 不可分离之诉，不可分之诉

inalienable right 不可让与的权利，天赋权利

inappropriate 不当

inappropriate decision 不适当的决定

inappropriate sentencing 量刑不当

inappropriate wording 措辞不当

inaugural speech 就职演说

inaugurate 就职

inauguration　就职
inauguration day　就职日
inauguration speech　就职演说
incapability　丧失能力
incapability of consent　无承诺能力
incapable　丧失能力
incapacitate　丧失能力
incapacitated　丧失能力
incapacity　丧失能力,无资格
incapacity for criminal responsibility　无责任能力
incapacity of disposition　无民事行为能力,无行为能力
incarcerated individual　被禁闭的人
incentive mechanism　激励机制
incentive price　奖励价格
incest　亲属相奸罪
incest taboo　乱伦禁异
incestuous adultery　乱伦通奸
Inchmaree clause　殷其玛利条款
inchoate　不完全的
inchoate crime　初始罪,犯罪未遂
inchoate subordination　不完全从属之债
inchoate title　不完全权利,未完成权利
incidence of taxation　纳税负担
incident　附带的条件
incidental appeal　附带上诉
incidental claim　附带请求
incidental crime　附带犯罪
incidental judgement　附带判决
incidental legal relationship　附随法律关系
incidental loss　意外损失
incline to　趋向
inclosure　私有土地
including price　价内税
including war risks　包括战争险
inclusive offense　吸收犯
incognito（拉）隐名
income　收益,没收违法所得
income before tax　纳税前收入
income beneficiary　收益受益人

① income from capital　资本收益
② income from foreign sources　外国来源所得
③
④ income from immorable property　不动产所得
⑤
⑥ income from inside China　中国境内所得
⑦
⑧ income from investment(s)　投资收益
⑨
⑩ income from labour　劳动收入
⑪ income from labour remuneration　劳务报酬所得
⑫
⑬ income from outside China　中国境外所得
⑭
⑮ income from remittance sent by overseas Chinese　侨汇收入
⑯
⑰ income fund　收益基金
⑱ income on investment　投资收益
⑲ income stock　收益股份
⑳ income tax　所得税,收益税/收益额课税
㉑
㉒ income tax allocation　分摊所得税
㉓
㉔ income tax collected at source　从源课征所得税
㉕
㉖ income tax credit　所得税的抵免
㉗ income tax law　所得税法
㉘ Income tax on personal property replacement　动产重置所得税
㉙
㉚ income tax surcharge　所得附加税
㉛
㉜ income tax withholding　代扣所得税
㉝
㉞ incomparable factors　不可比因素
㉟
㊱ incompetent　法律上无效的
㊲ incompetent evidence　法律上无效的证据
㊳
㊴ incompetent judge　被回避的法官
㊵
㊶ incompetent person　无行为能力人
㊷
㊸ incompetent plaintiff　不符合的原告
㊹
㊺ incomplete　不完全批准
㊻ incomplete action　不完全行为
㊼ incomplete attempt　着手未遂

incomplete form of socialist ownership by the whole people 不完全的社会主义全民所有制形式

incomplete performance 不完全履行

incomplete transaction 不完全交易

incompletely constituted trust 未完全成立的信托,未完全设定的信托

incompleteness of a crime 犯罪未完成

incongruity 不一致

inconsistency 不一致

inconsistency with good morals 违背善良道德

inconsistent with 与…不符

incontestable clause 不可抗辩条款

incontrovertible proof 无可争议的条款

inconvertability 不自由兑换风险

inconvertible notes 不兑现纸币

inconvertible paper money 不兑现纸币

incorporate crime 吸收犯

incorporated association 法人团体

incorporation 组成法人团体

incorporeal chattel 无形动产

incorporeal property 无形财产

incorporeal property right 无体物权,无体财产权

incorrect 错误的

incorrect ruling 错误裁决

increase and protection of fishery resources 渔业资源的增殖和保护

increase duties and obligations 增加责任和义务

increase of duties and obligations 增加责任和义务

increase of penalty 加刑

increase of risk 危险增加

(to) increase remuneration for work 提高劳动报酬

(to) increase social benefits 提高社会福利

increase the interest rate 提高利率

increased amount 增加金额

increased cost clause 增值条款

increased value insurance 增值保险

increment amount on land value 土地增值额

increment tax on land value 土地增值税

incriminating evidence 控诉证据,证明有罪的证据

incubatio (拉) 瑕疵占有

incubation period 潜伏期

incubator (拉) 瑕疵解者

inculpate 归罪

inculpatory evidence 定罪证据

incumbency functions and powers 职权

incumbent 负有责任的

incumbent president 在职总统

incur a loss 遭受损失

incur debt 借债

incur obligation 负有义务

incurable or hardly curable 对人身或健康有不治或难治的伤害

incurred obligation 承担债务

incutpatory evidence 控告证据,攻击证据

indebitatus (拉) 法律上有义务偿还的

indebitatus assumpsit (拉) 被告承认负担债务之诉,承担所欠的债务

indebiti condictio (拉) 非债务的偿还请求

indebiti solutio (拉) 非债务的错误偿还

indebtedness 负债,债务

indecent publications 淫秽出版物

indefinite 不确定的,不明确的

indefinite duration 无限期

indefinite limitation of time 不确定期限

indefinite right 没有限定的权利

indefinite term 不确定期限

indemnification 补偿,赔偿金

indemnification for loss 损失赔偿,损失赔偿金

indemnification recompense 赔偿金

indemnification satisfaction 赔偿物

indemnification 赔偿

indemnify 补偿,补偿损失,偿付

indemnify for damage 赔偿损失

indemnify for losses 赔偿损失

indemnify sb from damage 保护某人不受伤害

indemnify sb from damage 保护某人不受伤害

indemnifying measure 赔偿办法

indemnifying obligation 赔偿义务

indemnitor 赔偿人

indemnity 赔偿金,赔偿金,赔偿物,偿付,赔款,补偿损失,赦免

indemnity bond 补偿保证

indemnity claim 赔偿请求

indemnity claimant 赔偿请求人

indemnity clause 赔偿条款

indemnity decision 补偿决定

indemnity for requisition of grass-land 草原征用补偿

indemnity for risk 危险赔偿

indemnity for the loss incurred 赔偿所受损失

indemnity neurosis 索赔性神经官能症

indemnity of loss 损失赔偿

indemnity recoverable 可获得的赔偿

indemnity subrogation receipt 代位求偿权收据

indent 订货单,契约

indent agent 订货代理人

indent contract 委托代购契约

indent obligations pact 合同

indenter 委托代购人

indenture obligation 契约

indenture of lease 租赁契约,租借契约,租售合同

indenture trustee 合同受托人

independence 独立性

independence of auditing 审计的独立性

independence of countersuit claims 反诉请求的独立性

independence of judges 法官独立

independence of judicature 司法独立

independence of state 国家的独立

independence of trial and decision 审判独立

independent 独立

independent accountability 独立核算

independent accounting 独立核算

independent accounting agency 独立核算单位

independent adjudication 独立审判

independent adjudicatory power 独立审判权

independent administrative measure 独立的行政措施

independent administrative regulation 独立的行政法规

independent agency 单独代理

Independent by bear civil liability 独立承担民事责任

independent contraction 独立承包人,独立承揽人,独立订约人,独立承包商

independent defense 自主辩护

independent economic entity 独立的经济实体

independent evidence 独立证据

independent exercise of powers within the framework of the law

依法独立行使职权

independent guarantee 独立保证,单独担保

independent inspection certificate 独立检验证明书

independent instigator 独立教唆犯

independent judgment 独立判决

independent judicial power 独立司法权

independent judiciary system 独立司法制度

independent kingdom 独立王国

independent labour 独立劳动

independent regulatory agency 独立管理机构

independent regulatory agency of the United States 美国独立管制机构

independent regulatory commission 独立管制委员会

independent regulatory organization 独立管制机构

independent right 独立权利

independent source rule 独立取证原则

independent state 独立国家

indeterminacy 不确定性

indeterminate 不明确的

indeterminate intent 不确定故意

indeterminate judgment 不定期判决

indeterminate sentence 不确定判决,不特定判决,不定期刑

indeterminate sentence system 不定期刑制度

index clause 指数条款

index number of all commodities 总物价指数

index of crime 犯罪指数

index of crime movement 犯罪动态指标

index of taxation 税收指标

indicative plan 指示性计划

indicator of economic development 经济发展指标

indicators for performance check 考核指标

indicators for plan 计划指标

indicia 邮戳

indictable 可以起诉

indictable misdemeanor 可予起罪的轻罪

indictable offender 刑事犯

indictable offense 可以起诉的罪行,公诉罪

indictee 被控方,被控犯罪人

indictment 公诉,控告书

indifference 放任

indigenization 本地化

indigenous policy 土政策

indirect 间接损害

indirect accessory 间接从犯

indirect appeal 间接上诉

indirect bill 间接汇票

indirect collision 间接碰撞

indirect competitor 间接竞争者

indirect confession 间接供述

indirect contract 间接合同

indirect control 间接管制

indirect credit 间接抵免

indirect delivery 间接交货

indirect democracy 间接民主政治,代表民主制

indirect effect 间接效果

indirect expropriation 间接征收

indirect finance 间接融资

indirect financing 间接金融

indirect foreign lease 间接对外租赁

indirect guilt 间接正犯

indirect infringement 间接侵害

indirect instigation 间接教唆

indirect intent 间接故意

indirect intention 间接故意

indirect interpretation 间接解释

indirect investment 间接投资

indirect lease 间接租赁

indirect legislation 间接立法

indirect liabilities 间接责任

indirect loss 间接损失

indirect principal 间接正犯

indirect quotation 间接报价

indirect responsibility 间接责任

indirect review 间接检查

indirect sales 间接销售

indirect subsidies 间接补贴

indirect trade 间接贸易

indiscriminate collection of contributions 乱收费

indiscriminate lawsuit(s) 滥诉

indispensable condition 必要条件

indispensable co-offender 必要共犯

indispensable evidence 必要证据

indispensable joint action 必要共同诉讼

indispensable joint crime 任意共同犯罪,必要共同犯罪

indispensable joint criminal 必要共犯

indispensable joint offense 任意共犯,必要共犯

indispensable parties 必要共同诉讼人

indisputable 无可争议

indisputable fact 无可争议的事实

individed right 不可接受权利

individual 个别,个体

individual act 个人行为

individual advantage 个人利益

individual bargaining 个别议价

individual business 个体企业,个体工商户

individual businesses 个体工商户

individual capital 个人资本

individual check 个人支票

Individual codification 个别法典化

individual criminal responsibility 个人刑事责任

individual debt 个人债务

individual diagnosis of criminals 罪犯个别诊断

individual economic unit 个体户

individual economy 个体经济,个体经济

individual economy private economy private sector 个体经济

individual enterprise 私营企业,个人企业,个体企业

individual environmental right 公民环境权

individual farmer 个体农户

individual guarantee 个别保证

individual households with specialized lines of work 个体专业户

individual human rights 个人人权

individual income adjustment 个人收入调节税

individual income tax 个人所得税

individual industrial and commercial entity 个体工商户

individual instigator 单独教唆犯

individual interrogation 个别讯问

individual investment 个人投资

individual investor 个人投资者

individual liability 个人责任,个别责任

individual license 个体营业执照

individual name 个别名称

individual naturalization 个别入籍

individual negotiation 个人诉讼

individual norm 个别规范

individual obligation 个人债务

individual operation 个体经营

individual operator 个体经营者

individual ownership 个体所有制

individual ownership of citizen 公民个人所有权

individual partnership 个人合伙

individual person 个人

individual prediction of crime 犯罪分体预测

individual private ownership 个体所有制

individual property 个人财产

individual proprietorship 个人企业,个体经营

individual relief 个别救济

individual responsibility 个别责任,单独责任,个人责任

individual retailers 个体商贩

individual retirement account 个人退休账户

individual rights 个人权利,个体权利

individual rule 例外法规

individual self-defence 单独自卫

individual subject theory 个人主体说

individual trader and pedlar 个体商贩

individual unit of industry and commerce 个体工商户

individual value 个别价值

individual workers 个体劳动者

individual working people 个体劳动者

individualism 个人主义,自由放任主义

individualist 个人主义

individualistic 个人主义的

individualistic government 个人主义的政府

individualistic theory 个人主义学说

individualization of parole 假释个别制

individually defined thing 物定物

individually owned capital 个人资本

individually owned enterprise 个人企业

indivisibilities 不可分性

indivisibility of charge 告诉不可分

indivisibility of complaint 告诉不可分

indivisibility of public prosecution 公诉不可分原则

indivisible 不可分割的,不可分的

indivisible contract 不可分合同

indivisible credit 不可分割债权

indivisible obligation 不可分之债,不可分割债务

indivisible thing 不可分物

indoctrinate 教育

indoctrination 教育

indoctrination center 教养所

indolent in making a notice 怠于通知

indorse 签名,批准

indorsee 被背书人,受让方

indorsement 签名

indorser 背书人,转让人

indubitable proof 确证

induced consumption 劝诱消费

induced inflation 诱发性通货膨胀

induced investment 劝诱投资

inducement 诱骗

inducing breach of contract 劝诱违约

induction of evidences 提供证据

inductive questioning 诱导性发问

industrial act 工业法,劳工法

industrial an mining establishments 工矿企业

industrial and commercial bureau 工商局

industrial and commercial consolidated tax 工商统一税

industrial and commercial operation 工商业经营

industrial and commercial taxes 工商税,工商业税

industrial and commercial units 工商户

industrial and mineral products 工矿产品

industrial arbitration 劳资仲裁

industrial bank 工业银行

Industrial Bank of Japan (Tokyo) 日本兴业银行(东京)

Industrial Bank of Korea (Seoul) 朝鲜工业银行(汉城)

industrial code 工业法规

industrial conflict　劳务冲突

industrial contract　工业合同

industrial convention for the unification of certain rules of law relating to bills of lading, signed at brussels on august 25, 1924　关于统一提单若干法律规定的国际公约(1924)

industrial convention on the establishment of an industrial fund for compensation for oil pollution damage, 1971　关于设立油污损害赔偿基金的国际公约

industrial corporation　工业公司

industrial country　工业国家

industrial court　劳资法庭

industrial credit　工业信贷

industrial custom　工业惯例

industrial democracy　工业民主

industrial designs　工业品外观设计

industrial disease　工业病

industrial dispute　工业纠纷

industrial district　工业区

industrial enterprise　工业企业

industrial enterprise act（law）工业企业法

industrial enterprise law　工业企业法

industrial espionage　工业间谍活动

industrial estate　工业区

industrial goods　工业用品,工业产品

industrial human rights　个人人权

industrial insurance　工业保险

industrial investment　工业投资

industrial life assurance　简易人身保险

industrial loan　工业贷款

industrial market　工业市场

industrial nation　工业国家

industrial noise　工业噪声

industrial nuisance　工业污染

industrial park　工业区

① industrial policy　产业政策

② industrial pollution　工业污染

③ industrial pollution source　工业污染源

⑤ industrial power　工业大国

⑥ industrial product　工业品,工业产品,工业制成品

⑧ industrial production　工业生产

⑨ industrial property right　工业产权

⑪ industrial refuse　工业废物

⑫ industrial relations　劳资关系

⑬ industrial sector　工业部门

⑭ industrial sewage　工业污水,工业废水

⑯ industrial standard　工业标准

⑰ industrial state　工业国家

⑱ industrial stock　工业股票

⑲ industrial structure　产业结构

⑳ industrial waste disposal　工业废物

㉒ industrial waste residue　工业废渣

㉔ industrial waste water　工业废水,工业污水

㉖ industrial waste water, gas and residue　工业"三废"

㉘ industrial wastes　工业废物

㉙ industrial worker　产业工人

㉚ Industrialcredit Bank（Duesseldorf）工业信贷银行(杜塞尔道夫）

㉝ industrialist　企业家

㉞ industrialists and businessmen　工商业者

㊱ industrialization of the country　国家工业化

㊳ industrialized country　工业化国家

㊵ industries　行业管理

㊶ industry　产业,工业

㊷ industry and agriculture　工农

㊸ industry and commerce administration　工商行政管理

㊺ industry and commerce administration authorities　工商行政管理机关

industry and commerce administrative rules 工商行政管理法规

industry in the coastal regions 沿海工业

industry in the interior 内地工业

industry law 产业法

industry property 工业产权

industry segment 工业部门

industry tax 产业税

ineffective 无效

ineffective contract 无效合同

ineffectiveness of administrative act 行政行为的无效

inefficacy 无效力

inequitable 不公平的

inequitable exchange 不等价交换

inequity 不平等

inevitable 无法避免的,不可避免的

inevitable accident 不可避免的意外事件,无可避免之意外

inevitable mistake 不可避免的错误

inevitable trend 势在必行

inexorable law 必然规律

inexorable trend 必然趋势

infamous crime 丑行罪

infamous punishment 不名誉刑罚

infancy 未成年

infant 未成年人,未成年的

infant delinquent 幼年犯

infant industry 新生工业,幼稚工业

infant partner 未成年合伙人

infanticide 杀婴罪

infanticide by drowning 溺婴

infantry 步兵

infect 传染

infection 传染

infectious vector 传染媒介

infectious victim 传染病人

inference 推理

inference of law 法律上的结论

① inferior 劣等品,劣质货

② inferior as superior 以次充好

③ inferior civil court 初等民事法庭

④

⑤ inferior court 低级法院,初级法院

⑥

⑦ inferior court of record 初级记录法庭

⑧

⑨ inferior medicines 劣药

⑩ inferior quality 质量低劣,劣等品质

⑪

⑫ infeudate 分封土地

⑬ infill site 需动迁后才能腾出的地块

⑭

⑮ infirmative consideration 无效对价,无效约因

⑯

⑰ inflammability 易燃

⑱ inflammable 易燃

⑲ inflammable cargo 易燃品

⑳ inflammable goods 易燃物品,可燃物

㉑

㉒ inflammableness 易燃

㉓ inflation 通货膨胀

㉔ inflation control 通货膨胀控制

㉕ inflation of credit 信用膨胀

㉖ inflation of currency 通货膨胀

㉗ inflationary gap 通货膨胀缺口

㉘ inflationary pressures 通货膨胀压力

㉙

㉚ inflationism 通货膨胀主义

㉛ inflict a punishment on a criminal 惩处罪犯

㉜

㉝ inflict punishment 处以刑罚

㉞ inflict punishment on sb 给予惩罚

㉟

㊱ inflict the death 处以死刑

㊲ inflicter 加害人

㊳ infliction 加刑,处罚

㊴ inflow of capital 资本流入

㊵ inflow of funds 资金流入

㊶ influence 影响

㊷ info quote 参考报价

㊸ inform 报告,告知

㊹ inform against 告发

㊺ inform authorities of 检举

㊻ inform of an offense 举报

㊼ informal 缺乏法定形式的,非

正式的

informal act 非正式行为,不正式法律行为,不要式行为

informal administrative act 不正式行政行为

informal administrative measure 不正式的行政措施

informal agreement 非正式协定

informal contract 不正式契约,简式契约,不要式合同

informal interpretation 非正式解释

informality 不正式

informant 报案人

informant-witnesses 提供信息的证人

information 控告书,情报

information memorandum 情况备忘录,信息备忘录

information pollution 信息污染

informative system 告知制度

informed defect 已告之瑕疵

informer 告发人

informing 告知

infra metas (拉) 在范围内

infraction 违法

infraction of regulations 违反规章

infrangible 不可违背的,不可侵犯的

infrared photography of material evidence 红外线物证照相

infrastructural investment 基础设施投资

infrastructure 基础结构,基础设施

infrastructure project 基础设施项目

infringe 侵犯,侵犯法律,违犯,违反

infringe a right 侵犯权利

infringe right 侵犯权利,侵权

infringe the provisions 违反规定

infringe upon human rights 侵犯人权

infringe upon sb's right 侵犯某人的权利

① **infringement disputes** 侵权纠纷

② **infringement of civil right** 侵犯
③ 公民权利

④ **infringement of customs regula-**
⑤   **tions** 违反海关规章

⑥ **infringement of freedom** 侵犯自
⑦ 由

⑧ **infringement of right** 侵犯权利

⑨ **infringement of title** 侵犯所有
⑩ 权

⑪ **infringement of trade mark** 商
⑫ 标权侵权

⑬ **infringement on storage** 侵害保
⑭ 管罪

⑮ **infringement upon one's manage**
⑯   **real decision-making power**
⑰ 侵犯法律规定的经营自主权

⑱ **infringer** 侵害人,侵权人

⑲ **infringing act** 侵权行为

⑳ **infringing entity** 侵权单位

㉑ **infringing party** 侵害方

㉒ **ingress** 入境

㉓ **inhabitant** 常住居民

㉔ **inherent cause** 附带原因

㉕ **inherent impossibility** 固有不能

㉖ **inherent nationality** 固有国籍

㉗ **inherent power** 固有的权力

㉘ **inherent right** 固有权利,原属
㉙ 权利

㉚ **inherent vice** 固有缺陷,固有瑕
㉛ 疵,内在缺陷

㉜ **inherent vice of the goods** 潜在
㉝ 缺陷

㉞ **inherit in subrogation** 代位继承

㉟ **inheritable** 有权继承

㊱ **inheritance** 遗赠

㊲ **inheritance tax** 遗产税

㊳ **Inherited right** 固有权利

㊴ **inhuman act** 非人道行为,不人
㊵ 道行为

㊶ **initial an agreement** 草签协定

㊷ **initial capital tax** 股本税

㊸ **initial carrier** 最初承运人

㊹ **initial day of lease** 超租日

㊺ **initial design** 初步设计

㊻ **initial fee** 入门费

㊼ **initial impossibility** 自始不能

initial inspection　预检验

initial installment paid for the purchase of　定金

initial investment　最初投资

initial loss　开办期损失

initial lump sum　初付费

initial payment　入门费,初付费,首期付款

initial premium　初期保险费

initial screening survey　初步审查

initial shipment　首批装运

initial situation　初期状况

initial stage　初期

initial transaction　首次交易

initial treaty　初级契约

initialed statement　草签声明

initialed text　草签文本

initialling　缩写的签名,草签

initiate　倡导,创议,创制

initiate a crime　犯罪着手

initiative　创制权,能动性,积极性

initiative constitution　创制性宪法

initaitive of local authorities　地方的主动性

initiative testifying motive of a witness　证人主动作证动机

injection gun　注射枪

injunction　禁令

injured party　受害人,受害者

injured person　受害人

injurer　加害人

injurious　有害的

injurious act　侵害行为

injustice　不公平的

inland bay　内海湾,内河湾

inland check　国内支票

inland duty　内地税

inland navigation　内河航行

inland sea　内海海域

inland strait　内海峡

inland trade　内地贸易

inland waters　国内水域,内河

inland(/enclosed)sea　内海

innate need of　内在需要

① inner cabinet　核心内阁,内内阁

② inner contradictions　内在矛盾

③ inner temple　内寺法律学院(四

④ 大学院之一)

⑤ innocent　清白无辜

⑥ innocent character　无害性质

⑦ innocent homicide　无辜杀人

⑧ innocent infringement　善意侵权

⑨ innocent merchant　无害商人

⑩ innocent misrepresentation　善意

⑪ 误述,无辜性误述,无心误述,

⑫ 非故意的错误陈述

⑬ innocent omission　无意遗漏

⑭ innocent passage　无害通过

⑮ innocent passage on strait　海峡

⑯ 的无害通过

⑰ innocent purchaser(美)　善意购

⑱ 买人

⑲ innocent third party　无辜的第

⑳ 三人

㉑ innominate contract　无名合同

㉒ innovate　创新,改革

㉓ innovatio(拉)　更改

㉔ innovation　技术革新

㉕ innovational investment　技术革

㉖ 新投资

㉗ inoffensive　无害的

㉘ inofficiosum(拉)　违反道德义务

㉙ inofficiosum testamentum（拉）

㉚ 违法的遗嘱

㉛ inoperative　不能实行的

㉜ inproper behaviour　出轨行为

㉝ input in cash　现金投放,现金投

㉞ 入

㉟ input in kind　实物投入

㊱ inquire　询价,质问,询问

㊲ inquire into　审查

㊳ inquire of sb about sth　询问

㊴ inquiry　询问,审查,询盘

㊵ inquiry for merchandise　商品询

㊶ 价

㊷ inquiry procedure　调查程序

㊸ inquisition　异端裁判所,宗教裁

㊹ 判所

㊺ inquisition by torture　刑讯

㊻ inquisitional proceedings　纠问式

㊼ 诉讼,审问式诉讼

inquisitional system 纠问制度

inquisitional trial 纠问式审判

inquisitive hearing 调查讯问式审理

inquisitive trial 纠问式审判

insane delusion 精神虚狂症

inscribed securities 记名证券

inscribed stock 记名股票

inscriptions 记名证券

insects which are carriers of disease 病媒昆虫

inseparable 不可分的

inside jurisdiction 内部管辖权

insider dealing 内幕交易

insider trading 内幕人士交易

insofar as the contract gives no indication 如合同上无约定时

insolvency 无力偿债,无偿债能力,无力支付,破产,无偿付能力,无力支付

insolvency clause 破产条款

insolvency proceedings 破产程序

insolvent debtor 破产债务人,无偿债能务的债务人

inspect 监察

inspection 检验条款,监察

inspection for food hygiene 食品卫生检验

inspection free 免费检验

inspection method 检验方式

inspection of cargo 检验货物

inspection of cargoes with respect to general or particular average 海损鉴定

inspection of container cargoes 集装箱检验

inspection of evidence 证据检查

inspection of finished product 成品检验

inspection of firearms system 枪支查验制

inspection of food hygiene 食品卫生检查

inspection of goods by the buyer 买方检货

inspection of packing of goods for export 出口商品的包装检验

inspection of quality 质量检验

inspection of quantity 数量检验

inspection of saliva spots 唾液斑检验

inspection of traces 痕迹检验

inspection of weight 重量检验

inspection on damaged cargo 货物残损检验

inspection organizations 检验机构

inspection period 检验期间

inspection personal 检验人员

inspection personnel 检验人员

inspection result 检验结果

inspection standards 检验标准

inspection system 审查制度

inspection ticket 检验单

installation 设备,安装,就职

installation height 安装高度

installation works 安装工程

installment 就职

installment buying 分期付款购买

installment contract 分期付款合同,分期分批履行的合同,分期合同,分期履行的合同

installment delivery 分期交货

installment guarantee 分期付款保证

installment in full 金额分期付款

installment insurance 分期保险

installment mortgage 分期付款的抵押

installment payment 分期付款

installment payment of tax 分期缴税

installment sale 分期付款买卖

installment sales contract 分期付款销售合同

installment shipment 分批装运,分批装船

instance of court 法院审级

instant dismissal 即时解雇

instantaneous crime 即时犯

instate 任命

instigation of defense 防卫挑拨

instigator 违意犯

institute 学校,创制

institute a complaint up aginst court rulings 提起抗诉

institute a countersuit 提起反诉

institute an appeal 提起上诉

institute of international law 国际法学会

institute of London underwriters 伦敦保险协会

institute of political science and law 政法学院

institute proceeding for annulment 提起合同无效的诉讼

institute public prosecution 提起公诉

institute the procedure for prosecutorial supervision over adjudication 提起审判监督程序

institute warranties 公会保证条款

institution 制度,事业单位,条例,体制

institution as legal person 事业单位法人

institution for the inspection of pharmaceuticals 药品检验机构

institution of civil law 民事立法活动

institution of public prosecution 提起公诉

institution of regulations 制定条例

institution unit 事业单位

institutional advertising 厂商广告

institutional arbitration 机构仲裁

institutional change 体制变化

institutional household 集体户

institutional investor 机构投资人

institutional purchasing 集团购买

institutional purchasing power 集团购买力

institutional sector 机构部门

institutional smuggling 单位走私

institutional structure 体制结构

institutionalization and legalization of socialist democracy 社会主义民主制度化、法律化

institutions 典章

institutions of executing punishment 行刑设施

institutions of higher learning 大专院校

instruct 责令,教育,通知

instruction 教育

instructor 讲听

instrument of adherence 加入文件

instrument of credit 信用工具

instrument of crime 犯罪工具

instrument of dictatorship 专政工具

instrument of interpretation 解释文件

instrument of law 法律文件

instrument of monetary regulation 货币客观手段

instrument of national policy 国家政策工具

instrument of pledge 抵押契据

instrument of ratification 批准书

instrument of succession 遗嘱

insufficiency of consideration 对价不充分,代价不充分

insufficiency of evidence 证据不足

insufficiency of will 意思表示瑕疵

insufficient 数额不定

insufficient evidence 不充分证据

insufficient insurance to value 保险价值不足

insufficient quorum 不足法定人数

insult 冒犯

insurable risks 可保风险

insurable value 可保险价值

insurance 保险

insurance against all risks 应保一切险

insurance against breakage 破碎保险

insurance agent 保险代理人

insurance applicant 申请保险人,投保人

insurance application 投保申请

insurance broker 保险经纪人

insurance business 保险企业

insurance canvasser 保险推销员

insurance certificate 分保单,保险证明书,保险凭证

insurance claim 保险索赔

insurance clause 保险条款

insurance company 保险公司

insurance conditions 保险条件

insurance contract 保险合同

insurance expense 保险费

insurance for life 终生保险,人寿保险

insurance fraud 保险诈骗活动

insurance fund 保险基金

insurance fund reserve 保险基金

insurance indemnity 保险赔偿

insurance industry 保险业

insurance instruction 投保通知

insurance law 保险法

insurance market 保险市场

insurance obligation 保险义务

insurance on goods 货物保险

insurance period 保险期限

insurance policy 保单,保险单

insurance premiums 保险费

insurance proceeds 保险赔偿金

insurance reserve fund 保险准备基金

insurance slip 投保单

insurance subject 保险标的

insurance system of the victim 被害人保险制度

insurance till death 人寿保险

insurant 被保险人

insured 被保险人,受保人

insured amount 保险金额,投保金额

insured interest 保险利益,可保利益

insured property 投保财产

insured risks 承保的危险

insured subject matter 保险

insurer 保险人,承保人,保险商

insurer of goods 货物保险人

insurer's interest 保险人利益

insurgent community 叛乱团体

insuring clause 承保条款

insurmountable 不能克服的

intake weight 装船重量

intangible 无形的

intangible chattels 无形动产

intangible damage 无形损害

intangible goods 无形商品

intangible goods trade 无形商品贸易

intangible movable, intangible movables 无形动产

intangible property 无形财产,无形产权

intangible property right 无体物权,无体财产权

intangible right 无形权利

intangible value 无形价值

integral case study 综合案例分析

integral restitution 全部归还

integrate programme for commodities 商品综合方案

integrated development 全面发展

integrated management 综合管理

integrated offense 结合犯

integrated plan 综合计划,综合计划,综合项目

integrated project(s) 统筹计划

integrated regional co-operation 一体化区域合作

integration 一体化,取消种族隔离

integration of religion and politics

政教合一

integration of theory with practice
理论联系实际

integration process 一体化进程

integration to the society 重返社会

integrative jurisprudence 整体法学

integrative typical theory of crime
统一综合犯罪类型论

integrity of law 法律的完整性

intellectual 知识分子

intellectual insanity 智能精神病

intellectual property 无体财产权,无形物权

intellectual property rights 知识产权

intellectual structure of a crime
犯罪智能结构

intelligence 情报

intelligence agency 情报机关

intendant 地方行政长官

intended saving 计划储蓄

intended use of the loan 贷款用途

intense passion of crime 犯罪激情

intensification of criminal mind
犯罪心理强化

intensity 集约化

intensive management 集约化经营,集约经营

intent and motive 目的和动机

intent before the fact 事前故意

intent to kill 故意杀人意图

intention 意向,用意,故意,内涵

intention agreement 意向协议

intention of an abettor 教唆故意

intention of criminal punishment doctrine 目的刑主义

intention of parties 当事人意图

Intention to contract 契约目的,意向书

intentional 有意的

intentional bombing 故意毁损

① **intentional concealment** 故意隐瞒

③ **intentional conduct** 有意的行为

④ **intentional crime** 故意犯罪,预谋犯罪

⑥ **intentional crime in complicity**
共同故意犯罪

⑧ **intentional flooding** 故意决水

⑨ **intentional offense** 故意犯

⑩ **intentional offering of falsified certification** 故意提供虚假证明文件

⑬ **intentional tort** 故意侵权行为

⑭ **intentionally** 有意

⑮ **intent-to-kill murder** 目的谋杀罪

⑰ **inter** 扣留

⑱ **inter partes**（拉） 当事方之间

⑲ **interaction** 制约性

⑳ **interagency committee on export expansion** 跨部门和出口扩张委员会

㉓ **interbank rate** 同业汇率

㉔ **intercessio**（拉） 承担债务

㉕ **intercession** 调解

㉖ **intercountry substitution** 国与国替代

㉘ **interdicted person** 禁治产人

㉙ **interdictum**（拉） 占有手段

㉚ **interdictum utrubi**（拉） 关于保护占有动产的诉讼

㉜ **interdisciplinary cooperation** 多学科性合作

㉞ **interest** 利息,利率,权益,（英美）权利

㊱ **interest arbitrage** 套利

㊲ **interest coupon** 息票

㊳ **interest data** 计息日期

㊴ **interest free loan** 无息贷款

㊵ **interest group** 利益集团

㊶ **interest in expectancy** 期得权益,期望的利益,期待的权益

㊸ **interest in red** 应付利息

㊹ **interest of adhesion** 附延缓条件（民事）法律行为,附意合同

㊻ **interest of criminal law** 刑法利益

interest of the whole 全局利益
interest on arrears 延期利息
interest on calls 通知借款利息
interest on capital 资本利息
interest on condition 附条件的权益
interest on deposit 存款利息
interest on investment 投资利息
interest on loans 借贷利息
interest on loans, loan interest 贷款利息
interest on national debt 国债利息
interest on overdraft 透支利息
interest payments 付息
interest period 利息期限,计息期间
interest policy 利息政策
interest prepaid 预付利息
interest rate 利率
interest rate futures 利息期货
interest rate liberalization 利率市场化
interest rate policy 利率政策
interest tax 利息税
interested government 有关政府
interested motive 不纯动机
interested party 利害关系当事人
interested party 利害关系当事人,当事人
interested person 利害关系当事人,利害关系人
interested relate to 涉及
interests 利害
interests of collective 集体利益
interests of motherland 祖国利益
interests of society 社会利益
interests of the state 国家利益
interest-bearing loan 贷款付息
interest-free credit 无息贷款
interest-free loan 无息贷款
interfere 干涉,干预,干扰
interfere with 加以干涉
interfere with the educational system of the state 妨碍国家教育制度

interfere with the freedom of marriage by violence 暴力干涉婚姻自由行为
interference 干涉
interference with course of justice 干扰司法公正
interference with submarine cables 干扰海底电缆罪
interference with the right of privacy 妨害私人秘密
interfering with subsisting contract 干涉履行现存的合同
intergovernment council of copper exporting countries-ICC-EC 铜出口国政府间委员会
intergovernment international organization 政府间的国际组织
intergovernmental maritime consultative organization (IMCO) 政府间海事协商组织
interim 暂行
interim agreement for a project 建设项目施工临时协议书
interim attachment 临时扣押
interim budget 临时预算
interim cabinet 过渡内阁
interim constitution 临时约法
interim credit 临时信贷
interim deed 临时契约
interim government 过渡政府,临时政府
interim identity card 临时身份证
interim measure 过度措施,暂行办法
interlm order 暂行法令
interim plan 临时计划
interim president 临时人总统
interim price 暂时价格,临时价格
interim procedure(s) 暂行办法
interim procedures for the developing and managing of land in stretches by foreign investment 外方投资经营成片土地暂行

管理办法

interim regulation(s) 暂行条例

interim relief 临时救济

interim rules 临时规则

interim senate 临时参议院

interior liability 对内负责

interlocutory 暂时性

interlocutory proceeding 中间程序

interlope 无照营业，侵占他人权利，侵占他人权益

interloper 无照营业者

intermediary constituency system 中选区制

intermediate 中级

intermediate agency 中间代理人

intermediate credit 中期信贷

intermediate discharge 中间港卸货

intermediate links of taxation 纳税环节

intermediate order of civil action 民事决定

intermediate people's court 中级人民法院

intermediate service 居间服务

intermediation contract 居间合同

intermediator 居间人

intermittent explosive disorder 间歇性暴发障碍

intermittent imprisonment 间歇监禁刑

intermittent or predatory dumping 间歇性或掠夺性倾销

intermodel transport operator 联运经营人

internal act 内部行为

internal administration 内部事务

internal administrative act 内部行政行为

internal administrative dispute 内部行政争议

internal administrative law 内部行政法

internal administrative laws and regulations 对内行政法规

internal administrative organization 内部行政机关

internal administrative regulation 内部行政法规

internal affairs 内政,内部事务

internal audit 内部审计

internal audit procedure 内部审计程序

internal auditing setup 内部审计结构

internal auditing system 会计稽核制度

internal check 内部检查

internal check system 内部牵制制度

internal commerce 国内商业

internal connecting link 内在联系

internal constitutional organization 内部宪法组织

internal contradictions 内部矛盾

internal control 内部控制

internal debt 内债

internal decision-making 内部决定

internal discipline 内部纪律

internal disturbance 内乱

internal economy 内部经济

internal factor 内在因素

internal injury 内伤

internal interpretation 内部解释

internal law and order 国内法律、法令

internal legislation 国内立法

internal loan 内债

internal policy 国内政策

internal regulation 内部规章,内部条例

internal relationship 内部关系

internal reorganization 内部改组

internal rules 内部规则

internal security 国内治安

internal sovereignty 对内主权

internal supremacy 对内最高权

internal supervision 内部监督

internal supervisory system 内部监督制度

internal supervisory system of government 政府内部监督体制

internal taxes 各种国内税

internal transportation, domestic carriage 国内运输

internal value of money 货币对内价值

internal war 内战

internal waters 内水

internalization of criminal mind 犯罪心理内化

international air law 国际航空法

international administrative tribunal 国际行政法庭

international administrative union 国际行政组合

international agriculture adjustment 国际农业调整

international air services transit agreement 国际航班过境协定

international air traffic 国际航空运输

international air transport agreement 国际航空运输协定

international associated enterprises 国际联属企业

international association for the protection of industrial property (AIPPI) 国家保护工业产权协会

international atomic energy agency 国际原子能机构

international bank credit 国际银行信贷

international bank group 国际集团银行

international banking 国际银行业务

international bankruptcy case 国际破产案件

international bauxite association 国际铝土协会

international bill of exchange 国际汇票

international bill of human rights 国际人权宪章

international bonds 国际债券

international bonds market 国际债券市场

international bonds rating 国际债券评估

international borrowing 国际借贷

international broker 国际经纪人

international bureau of weights and measures 国际计量局

international bureau of weights and measures/BIPM 国际度量衡局

international canals 国际运河

international capital market 国际资本市场

international case 国际判例

international centre for settlement of investment disputes 解决投资争端国际中心

international chamber of commerce 国际商会

international characteristic crime 国际性质的罪行,国际性质之刑罚

international civil and commercial arbitration 国际民商事仲裁

international civil aviation organization (ICAO) 国际民用航空组织

international civil jurisdiction 国际民事管辖权

international civil legal relation 国际民事法律关系

international civil procedural laws 国际民事诉讼程序法

international civil procedural norms 国际民事诉讼程序规范

international civil relations 国际民事关系

international clearing 国际清算

international code of conduct on the transfer of technology 联合国国际技术转让行动守则

international commercial arbitration 国际商事仲裁

international commitments 国际承诺

international committee of the red cross（ICRC）红十字国际委员会

international commodity agreement 国际商品协定

international commodity price index 国际商品价格指数

international commodity stock 国际商品储存

international commodity trade 国际商品贸易

international community 国际社会

international competitive bidding/ZCB 国际竞争性招标

international conference 国际会议

international conflict of laws 国际法律冲突

international consultation 国际协商

international convention 国际公约

international convention against taking hostages 反对劫持人质国际公约

international convention for safe container（CSC）国际集装箱安全公约

international convention for the prevention of pollution from ships,1973 防止船舶造成污染的国际公约

international convention for the prevention of pollution of the sea by oil,1954 （1954 年）防止洋油污染国际公约

international convention for the protection of new varieties of plants 保护植物新品种用国际公约（1961）

international convention for the regulation of whaling 国际捕鲸管理公约

international convention for the safety of life at sea 国际海上人命安全公约

international convention for the unification of certain rules of law in regard to collisions 统一船舶碰撞若干法律规定的国际公约

international convention for the unification of certain rules relating to penal jurisdiction in matters of collision or other incidents of navigation 统一船舶碰撞或其他航行事故中刑事管辖权若干规定的国际公约

international convention for the unification of certain rules relating to the carriage of passengers by sea,1961 统一海上客运若干规则的国际公约

international convention on certain rules concerning civil jurisdiction in matters of collision, 1952 统一船舶碰撞民事管辖权若干规定的国际公约（1952）

international convention on civil liability for oil pollution damage-CLC 国际油污损害民事责任公约

international convention on economic,social and cultural rights 经济、社会和文化权利国际公约

international convention on load lines 国际船舶载重线公约

international convention on salvage, 1989 国际救助公约（1989）

international convention on standards of training, certification and watchkeeping,（1978）海员培训、发证和值班标准国际

公约(1978)

international convention on tonnage measurement of ships 国际吨位大量公约

international convention relating to intervention on the high seas in case of oil pollution casualties 干预公海油污事件的国际公约

international convention relating to the arrest of seagoing ship 关于扣留运船的国际公约

international convention relating to the arrest of seagoing ship 扣船公约 (1952)

international convention relating to the arrest of seagoing ship 1952 (1952年)扣押海运船舶的国际公约

international conventions 国际条约

international counterfeiting crimes 国际伪造货币犯罪

international court of justice 国际法院

international covenant on civil and political rights 公民权利和政治权利国际公约

international credit 国际信贷

international crime(s) 国际犯罪,国际罪行

international criminal assistance in jurisdiction 国际刑事司法协助

international criminal clique 国际犯罪集团

international criminal cooperation 国际刑事合作

international criminal law 国际刑法

international criminal responsibility 国际刑事责任

international currency 国际货币

international custom 国际习惯

international decision 国际判决

international delict 国际违法行为

① international development assistance 国际发展援助

③ international development association(IDA) 国际货币开发协会

⑤ international development authority(IDA) 瑞典国际开发局

⑧ international direct investment 国际直接投资

⑩ international direct lease 国际直接租赁

⑫ international dispute 国际争端

⑬ international double tax imposition 国际重叠征税

⑮ international double taxation 国际重复征税,国际双重征税

⑰ international drainage basin 国际河流流域

⑲ International economic aid 国际经济援助

㉑ international economic connections 国际经济联系

㉓ international economic contract 国际经济合同

㉕ international economic co-operation 国际经济合作

㉗ international economic exchanges 国际经济交流

㉙ international economic integration 国际经济一体化

㉛ international economic intercourse 国际经济交流

㉝ international economic interflow 国际经济交流

㉟ international economic law 国际经济法

㊲ international economic order 国际经济秩序

㊴ international economic organization law 国际经济组织法

㊶ international economic organizations 国际经济组织

㊸ international economic relations 国际经济关系

㊺ international economic zone 国际经济区

㊼ international environment 国际

环境

international environmental protection 国际环境保护

international equal exchange 国际平均交换

international equity tribunal 国际平衡法院

international exchange 国际汇兑

international federation of industrial property attorney 工业产权律师国际联合会

international finance corporation（简写：IFC）国际金融公司

international finance law 国际金融法

international financial aid 国际财政援助

international financial center 国际金融中心

international financial credit 国际金融借贷

international financial crisis 国际金融危机

international financial leasing 国际金融租赁

international financial market 国际金融市场

international financial position of the State 国家国际金融地位

international fiscal association/IFA 国际财政协会

international flight 国际飞行

international guarantee 国际担保

international human rights law 国际人权法

international illegal act 国际不法行为

international income deficit 国际收支赤字

international indebtedness 国际债务

international indirect investment 国际间接投资

international institute for the unification of private law 国际统一私法协会

international intermediary trade 国际居间贸易

international investers 国际投资者

international investment 国际投资,海外投资

international investment dispute 国际投资争议

international investment trust 国际信托投资

international joint venture 国际合营企业

international judicial assistance 国际司法协助

international judicial enforcement 国际司法执行

international judicial settlement 国际司法解决

international jurisprudence 国际法学

international labour organization 国际劳工组织

international law 国际法

international law association 国际法协会

international law commission 国际法委员会

international law of contract 国际合同法

International law of peace 平时国际法

international law on environment 国际环境法

international lease 国际租赁

international lease contract 国际租赁合同

international leasing 国际租赁

international leasing company 国际租赁公司

international legal act 国际法律行为

international legal order 国际法律秩序

international legal relation 国际法律关系

international legal responsibility

国际法律责任

international lever lease 国际杠杆租赁

international license contract 国际许可合同

international licensing agreement 国际许可证协议

international liquidity 国际流通手段,国际债偿能力

international litigation 国际诉讼

international loan 国际贷款

international loan agreement 国际借贷协议

international loan and credit 国际信贷

international mandatory conciliation 国际强制调解

international maritime committee (IMC) 国际海事委员会

international maritime organization 国际海事组织

international market 国际市场

international market price 国际市场价格

international market value 国际市场价值

international marketing 国际市场营销

international monetary and foreign exchange 国际货币与外汇

international monetary crisis 国际货币危机

international monetary fund agreement 国际货币基金协定

international monetary law 国际货币法

international monetary order 国际货币秩序

international monetary system 国际货币体系,国际货币制度

international monitoring measures 国际监测措施

international monopoly combines 国际垄断同盟

international monopoly organization 国际垄断组织

international monopoly price 国际垄断价格

international multimodal transport 国际多式联合运输

international navigable waterway 国际可航水道

international navigational route 国际航道

international obligations 国际义务

international offense 国际犯罪行为

international payment agreement 国际支付协定

international payment currency 国际支付货币

international payments 国际支付

international payments deficit 国际收支赤字

international payments situation 国际收支状况

international peace 国际和平

international penal law 国际刑法

international personality 国际人格

international plant-engineering contract 国际工程承包合同

international practice 国际惯例

international price level 国际价格水平

international private investment 国际私人投资

international protection of human rights 人权的国际保护

international public order 国际公共政策

international public policy 国际公共政策

international recognition 国家承认,国际承认

international red cross 国际红十字

international relations 国际关系

international remedy 国际补救方法

international reserve 国际储存

international river 国际河流

international river community 国际河流共同体

international rules for the internation of trade terms 国际贸易术语解释通则

international safeguards 国际保障措施

international sanctions 国际制裁

international sea area 国际海域

international sea commission 国际海洋委员会

international sea-bed area 国际海底区域

international sea-bed authority 国际海底管理商,国际海底管理局

international securities 国际证券

international service cooperation 国际服务合作

international service trade 国际服务贸易

international service trade enterprises 国际服务贸易企业

international servitude 国际地役,国际地级

international settlements 国际结算

international social justice 国际社会正义

international social law 国际社会法

international standard organization/ISO 国际标准化组织

international standards 国际标准规格

international stock 国际股票,国际储存

international sublease 国际转租赁

international supply contract 国际借贷合同

international tax haven 国际避税港

international tax law 国际税法

international taxation agreement 国际税收协定

international technical consultation 国际技术咨询

international technological cooperation 国际技术合作

international technological exchange 国际技术交流

international technology transfer 国际技术转让

international technology transfer law 国际技术转让法

international telecommunication union 国际电信联盟

international terrorism 国际恐怖主义

international tort 国际侵权行为

international trade administration (ITA) 国际贸易署

international trade agreement 国际贸易协定

international trade charter 国际贸易宪章

international trade commission (ITC) 国际贸易委员会(注:指美国)

international trade customs 国际贸易惯例

international trade deficit between imports and exports 进出口差额

international trade policy 国际贸易政策

international treaties 国际条约

international treaty and convention 国际公约

international tribunal for the law of the sea 国际海洋法法庭

international trust 国际信托法

international trusteeship system 国际托管制度

international uniform legal regime 国际统一法律体制

international waterway pollution 国际水道污染

internationalisation of crime 犯罪国际化

internationalism 国际主义

internationalization of economic life 经济生活国际化

interned alien 被拘禁外国人

interned person 被拘禁人

internee 被拘留人,拘留犯

internment 拘禁

interpersonal conflict of laws 人际法律冲突

interplead 互诉

interpleader 互诉人

interpleader cause 确权之诉

interpleader issue 互争权利诉讼的系争点

interpol 国际刑警

interposition 采取法律上的救偿手段

interpret 解释

interpretatio authentica(拉) 有权解释

interpretatio extensiva(拉) 广义解释

interpretatio legislative(拉) 立法解释

interpretatio restrictiva(拉) 狭义解释

interpretation 说明解释,注释

interpretation act 解释法

interpretation and review of the judgement of ICJ 国际法院的解释与复核

interpretation by history of legislation 立法史解释

interpretation by history of the law 法律史解释

interpretation by way of comparative law 比较法方法解释

interpretation clause 释义条款,解释条款

interpretation of constitution 宪法的解释

interpretation of judgement 判词的解释,判决书解释

interpretation of law and statute 法律法规的解释

interpretation of statutes 法规的解释

interpretation of statutory language 法律文字的解释

interpretation of supreme people's court 最高人民法院的解释

interpretation of the supreme people's procuratorate 最高人民检察院的解释

interpretation of treaty 条约的解释

interpretation section 条文解释,注释条款

interpretation to criminal law 刑法解释

interpretative provisions 解释性规定

interpretative rules 解释性规章

interpretative statement 解释性说明

interregional cooperation 区域间合作

interrelating analysis of crime 犯罪相关分析

interrelation 相互关系

interrogate 讯问,质问

interrogating by hypnotism 催眠术讯问方法

interrogation 书面质询,质问

interrogation record 讯问笔录

interrogatory 询问

interrogatory answer 书面质询答复

interrupt 中断

interrupt the running of the statute of limitation 中断时效,中断法令时效

interruption of a right 中断权利,权利的中断

intertemporal conflict of laws 时际法律冲突

interunit pricing 单位间定价

interunit transfer 单位间转让

interurban 城市之间

interval 停止期间

intervene 干预,参加诉讼

intervener 干涉者

intervening act 干预行为

intervening action 参加诉讼

intervening party 介入诉讼当事人,参加诉讼方

intervening psychology 参诉心态

intervening third party with independent claims 参加诉讼而有独立请求权的第三人

intervening third party with no independent claims 参加诉讼而无独立请求权的第三人

intervenor in administrative proceedings 行政诉讼第三人

intervenor in an administrative review 行政复议第三人

intervention 干涉

intervention by right 依权干涉,依据权利的干涉

intervention capability 干预能力

intervention price 干预价格

intimidate 威吓

intimidate sb into doing sb 胁迫某人做某事

intimidation 恐吓罪

into bankrupt 致破产

intoxicating liquor 酒类

intra fidem (拉) 可信赖的

intra vires (拉) 在正当的权限之内

intradermal hemorrhage 皮内出血

intra-enterprise 内部企业之间

intra-enterprise conspiracy doctrine 企业内部合谋原则

intra-family lease 集团内部租赁

intra-family pricing 集团内部定价

intra-family services 集团内部票务提供

intra-family transaction 集团内部交易

intra-family transfer pricing 集团内部转让定价

intricate 错综交杂

intrinsic value 固有价值

introducing foreign investment 利用外资

introducing of technology from abroad 技术引进

introduction of advanced technology 引进先进技术

introduction of economic law 经济法概论

introduction of foreign capital 引进外国资本

introduction of foreign credit 引进国外信贷

introduction of foreign investment 引进外国投资

introduction of foreign technology 引起国外技术

introduction of patent 引进专利

introductory part of judgment 判决序言部分

intrusion 侵入

inundation 水灾

invade to grab 侵夺

invalid 无效

invalid ballot 无效选票

invalid ballot 无效票

invalid clause 无效条款

invalid contract 无效合同

invalid contract of technology 无效技术合同

invalid if altered 涂改无效

invalidate 使无效

invalidating judgment (for negotiable instrument) 除权判决

invalidity of treaty 条约的无效

invasion of privacy 侵犯私人秘密权罪

invention to contract 缔约目的

invention-creation 发明创造

inventory on seizure 没收清册

invest 投资

invest with full powers 授予全权

invested capital 投入资本

investee 接受投资者

investigate 侦讯,追查

investigate and accordingly deals with major and important cases 查办大案要案

investigate and ascertain 查明
investigate inspect 稽查
investigate into a case 调查案件
investigate the evidence of a case 案验
investigation 调查
investigation and statistics of victims 被害人调查统计
investigation and study 调查研究
investigation and taking of evidence 调查取证
investigation certificate 稽查证
investigation into an arson case 放火案件的侦查
investigation into criminal offences 追查刑事犯罪
investigation judgment 侦查判断
investigation method 调查方法
investigation of cadres 干部审查
investigation of crime 犯罪调查
investigation of infectious agent 传染源调查
investigation personnel 侦查人员
investigation plan 侦查计划
investigation reasoning 侦查推理
investigation test 侦查实验
investigational assumption 侦查假设
investigational hypothesis 侦查假定
investigative measures 侦查措施
investigative organization 侦查机关
investigative record 调查笔录
investigative tactics 侦查策略
investigative target 侦查对象
investigator 侦查员
investiture 授权
investment 投资
investment abroad 国外投资
investment account 投资账户
investment adviser 投资顾问
investment agreement of project financing 项目贷款投资协议
investment analysis 投资分析
investment appraisal 投资评估
investment bank 投资银行
investment banker 投资银行家
investment banking 投资银行业务
investment bond 投资债券
investment capital 投资资本
investment climate 投资环境
investment company 投资公司
investment counselor 投资顾问
investment credit 投资信贷,投资信用
investment decision 投资决策
investment effect 投资效应
investment fund 投资基金
investment goods 投资货物
investment grants 投资转让
investment guarantee 投资保证
investment house 投资公司
investment in bonds 债券投资
investment in breadth 扩张投资
investment in capital constructure 基本建设投资
investment in default 有拖欠的投资
investment in depth 集约投资
investment in education 教育投入
investment in foreign countries 国外投资
investment in land 土地投资
investment in real estates 房地产投资
investment in securities 有价证券投资
investment in stocks 股票投资
investment in technology 技术投资
investment in the business 投资总额
investment incentives 投资刺激,投资鼓励
investment income 投资收益
investment market 投资市场
investment of foreign capital 外

资输入,外资资本

investment of money 货币投放

investment opportunity 投资机会

investment orientation 投资方向

investment portfolio 投资证券

investment program 投资计划、投资方案

investment project proposal 投资项目建议书

investment protection 投资保护

investment rate 投资率

investment risk 投资风险

investment securities 投资证券

investment situation 投资情况

investment stock 投资股票

investment trust 投资信贷,投资信托

investment trust company 投资信托公司

investment under the plan 计划内投资

investment value 投资价值

investor 投资者

inveterate criminal 屡教不改犯

inviolability 神圣,不可侵犯性

inviolability of diplomatic envoys 外交使节的不可侵犯权

inviolability of personal freedom 人身自由不可侵犯

inviolability of private property 私有财产神圣不可侵犯

inviolability of property 财产不可侵犯,财产不受侵犯

inviolability of residence 居所不可侵犯性

inviolability of the person 人身不可侵犯

inviolability of the residence 住宅不受侵犯

inviolable 不可能犯的,不可侵犯的,不受侵犯的,神圣

inviolate 神圣

invisible earnings 无形收益

invisible gain 无形收益

invisible loss 无形损失

invisible trade 无形贸易

invisible transaction 无形交易

invitation for offer 要约邀请,要约引诱

invitation to tender 招标

invitation to treat 邀请要约

invite tenders 招标

invited tendering 邀请招标

invitee 被邀请方

inviting bids 招标

invito (拉) 违背意愿,未经同意

invocational statutory sentence 援引法定刑

invoice 发票,发货单

invoice dispatch list 发货单

invoice for customs purpose 报关发票

invoke 援引

invoke a legal provision 援引法律条文

invoke a precedent 援引先例

involuntary 非出于自愿的

involuntary abandonment 非自愿中止

involuntary abatement of action 被迫中止诉讼

involuntary conduct 非自愿的行为

involuntary crime 过失犯罪

involuntary dissolution 强制解散

involuntary manslaughter 意外杀人罪

involuntary servitude 强制劳役

involve 涉及,牵连

involve the interests of the state and the people 关系计民生

involved offender 连累犯

inward cash remittance (transfer) 现金转入

inward documentary bill 进口押汇单

inward manifest 进口货清单

IOU (I owe you) 欠条

ipso facto (拉) 依照事实

ipso jure (拉) 依照法律,依法

ipso jure avoidance (拉) 依法宣布无效

ipso jure termination of a contract
依法终止合同

iron law 铁的法律

iron out difference 消除分歧

iron rule 苛政

iron rule（against prisoners）（美）
严格处罚规则

irrebuttable legal presumption
不容置疑的法律推定

irredeemable bank note 不能兑
现的银行票据

irredeemable bonds 不可兑现债
券,不能赎还的债券

irredeemable currency 不可兑
现的货币

irregular 非正式的,不合法的

irregular air service flight 不定
期航班飞行

irregular audit 不定期审计

irregular conduct 不正当行为

irregular interpretation 非正式
解释

irregular term of sentence 不定
期刑

irregularity 不正式手续;形成
上的瑕疵,不符司法程序

irregularity of judgments 判决
不当

irrelevant consideration 考虑不
相关因素

irremediable 无可被救的,不可
挽回的,不可约补的

irreparable 无可被救的,不可
挽回的,不可约补的

irreplaceable 不能恢复原状的

irresistibility 不可抗拒力

irresistible 不可抗拒的

irresistible clause 不可抗拒的原
因

irresistible force 不可抗力

irresistible impulse 不可抑制的
冲动

irresistible impulse rule 不能控
制规则

irresistible incident 不可抗拒的
事件

irresistible reasons 不可抗拒的

① 原因

② irresponsibility 不负责任

③ irresponsible conduct 不负责任
④ 的行为

⑤ irretrievable 不可挽回的,不可
⑥ 约补的,不能恢复的

⑦ irretrievable loss 不可弥补的损
⑧ 失

⑨ irreversible 不可撤销的

⑩ irrevocable 不可撤销的,无可
⑪ 挽回的

⑫ irrevocable beneficiary 不能复
⑬ 原的受益人

⑭ irrevocable condition 不可撤销
⑮ 条件,不可取消的条件

⑯ irrevocable credit 不可撤销的
⑰ 信用证

⑱ irrevocable documentary accep-
⑲ tance credit 不可撤销跟单承
⑳ 兑信回证

㉑ irrevocable indictment 不可撤
㉒ 回的诉状

㉓ irrevocable L/C 不可撤销信用
㉔ 证

㉕ irrevocable letter of credit 不可
㉖ 撤销的信用证

㉗ irrevocable title deed 死契

㉘ irrevocable trust 不可撤销信托

㉙ irritancy 权利废置,无效条款

㉚ Islam 伊斯兰教

㉛ isolated case 孤立案件

㉜ isolated explosive disorder 单次
㉝ 暴发障碍

㉞ issue 出票,纠纷

㉟ issue a check 开出支票

㊱ issue a decree 颁布法令

㊲ issue a directive 发出指示

㊳ issue amount 发行额

㊴ issue an order 发布命令

㊵ issue bank 发行银行

㊶ issue bonds 发行债券

㊷ issue debentures 发行债券

㊸ issue for enforcement 颁行

㊹ issue house 证券发行公司

㊺ issue price 发行价格

㊻ issue price of bonds 债券发行价
㊼ 格

issue tax　发行税
issuer　证券发行人,债券收行人
issues　公债券,政府债券
issuing authority　签发机构
issuing credit　信贷发行
Italian criminal school　意大利
　刑事学派

item of internal audit　内部审计
　事项
items of audit　审计事项
Itinerant ambassador　巡回大使
ITO(international trade organiza-
　tion)　国际贸易组织
iurisprudentia (拉)　罗马法理学

J

jab 戳伤

jack up the price 提高价格

jackal 帮凶

jacking-up 抬高市价

Jacob's constitution 雅各宾宪法

jail 看守所,牢狱,拘役所

jail delivery 监狱大出空

jailcress 监狱女看守

Jainism 耆那教

Jamaica Agreement 牙买加协定

jamb 侧柱

Japanese civil code 日本民法典

Jason clause 杰森条款

jeopardize 危害

jeopardize national security 危害国家安全

jeopardize the social order 妨害社会秩序

jerry-building 偷工减料的工程,偷工减料商

Jiusan society 九三学社

job 职务

job action 临时性罢工示威

job age 劳动年龄

job classification 职位分类

job discipline 劳动纪律

job lot 成批出售

job order 分批订货

job schedule 工程进度

job specifications 工作规范

job vacancy 职位空缺

job work 包工

jobber share broker 股票经纪人

job-related technological achievement 职务技术成果

Johnan Shinkin Bank (Tokyo) 城南信用金库(东京)

John·Locke 约翰·洛克

join in partnership 入伙

joinder 联合诉讼

joinder of actions 诉讼合并

joinder of crimes 数罪并合

joinder of criminal punishments 合并处刑

joinder of defendants 被告的合并

joinder of indictments 合并诉状

joinder of information 合并诉状

joinder of offenses 并合论罪,合并罪

joinder of penalties 合并处罚

joinder of punishments for plural crimes 数罪并罚

joinder of recidivist 混合累犯制

joined efforts in developing 共同开发

joiner of offenses 一般共犯

joint act of tort 共同侵权行为

joint administration 共同管理

joint adventure 共同投资

joint agency 共同代理

joint and several 连带

joint and several debtor 连带债务人

joint and several guarantee(s) 连带并按份保证,连带保证责任

joint and several liability 连带责任

joint and several obligation 连带债务,连带责任

joint and several responsibility 共同连带责任

joint authority 联合权力

joint bid 联合要价

joint business 合伙企业

Joint communique 联合公报

joint contribution 共同出资

joint control 共同控制权,共同管理

joint credit 共同债权,连带债权

joint creditor 连带债权人,共同债权人

joint debt 共同债务,连带债务

joint debtor 共同债务人,连带债务人

joint defendant 共同被告人

joint defense 共同辩护

joint defense for public security 治安联防

joint delict 共同侵权行为

joint doers 共同行为人

joint endorsement 联合背书

joint enterprise 合办企业,联合企业

joint estate 共有财产,共同资产

joint fault 共同过错

joint financing 联合融资

joint float 联合浮动

joint guarantee 连带保证,联合保证,共同担保

joint guarantor 连带保证人

joint guaranty 共同证

joint illegal act 共同不法行为

joint indictment 联合诉状

joint infringement 共同侵权

joint inspection of ships 船舶联合检查

joint intent 共同故意

joint interest 共同利害关系

joint interpretation 共同解释

joint investment 共同投资,联合投资,合资

joint invitation to tender 联合招标

joint legal relations 连带法律关系

joint liability 连带负责,连带责任,共同债务,共同责任

joint loan 联合放款,共同贷款

joint management 共同管理,联合经营

joint management in contract type 合同型联营

joint management in partnership 合伙型联营

joint mortgage 联合担保

joint negligence 共同过错

joint obligation 连带责任,连带债务

joint obligation in debt 连带债务

joint offender 共同犯罪人

joint operation of factories and export corporations 工贸联营

joint owner 共有人,共同所有人

joint ownership 共同所有权,共用权,共同共有,共有权

joint processing 联合加工

joint product 关联产品

joint production 联合生产

joint products offer 搭配出售产品

joint property 共有财产

joint provisions 共同规定

joint purchasing and marketing 联购联销

joint registration 联合登记

joint resolution of the congress 两院联合决议

joint responsibility 连带责任

joint responsibility for profits and losses 共负盈亏

joint shareholding management 合股经营

joint signature 合签,联署,连署

joint social relations 社会连带关系

joint solicitor 共同教唆

joint sovereignty 联合主权

joint statement 共同声明

Joint state-private operations 公私合营

joint stock 合资

joint stock association 股份组合,股份公司

joint stock bank 股份银行,合资银行

joint sureties 共同担保人

joint suretyship 共同担保,连带担保

joint survey 联合检验

joint tenancy 共有不动产权,共同共有,共同租赁

joint tenant 共同租赁人,不动产共有人

joint tort 共同侵权行为

joint tortfeasors 共同侵权人

joint transaction 联合交易

joint trial 会审

joint trustee 共同受托人

joint undertaking by industrial and commercial departments 工商联营

joint venture 合资经营企业,合营企业,共同投资,联合企业

joint venture account 合伙账户

joint venture investment 共同投资,联合投资,合伙投资

joint venture with Chinese and foreign investment 中外合资经营企业

joint venturer 合营者

joint verdict 共同裁决

joint victims of a crime 共同被害人

jointly and severally 连带

jointly and severally bound 连带责任

jointly and severally liable 连带责任,负连带责任

jointly and severally pay 连带支付

jointly owned and operated 合营

jointly sign 合签

joint-stock association 合股公司

joint-stock banks 合股银行

joint-stock company 股份公司,合股公司

joint-stock enterprise 股份制企业

Judex aequitatem semper spectare debet (拉) 法官应当始终考虑公平原则

Judex non potest esse testis in propria causa (拉) 法官在自己的案件中不得当证人

judge 法官,裁判,判定,判断,审判,副庭长,判决,审判员,权衡

judge advocate (英) 军事审判员

judge advocate general 代理检察长

judge between right and wrong 评断是非

judge from the fact 根据事实判断

judge in chambers 内庭法官

judge in reserve 候补法官,候补审判员

judge law 法官法

judge of the high court 高等法院法官

judge of the trial bench 审判员

judge rules 法官规则(英 1964)

judge what is right and what is wrong 判断是非

judge's comment 法官的评价

judge's direction to a jury 法官给予陪审团的指示

judge's mental impression 法官心证

judge's note 法官笔录

judge's oath 法官的宣誓

judge's power of discretion 法官的自由裁量权

judge's rules 法官规程(1912年)

judge's statement on decision 法官的判决陈词

judge's summons 法官传票

judgement 审判,判决,判断

judgement by confession 根据招供作出的判决

judgement creditor 判决确定的债权人,胜诉债权人

Judgement is to be given according to the laws, not according to examples or precedents 判决应当根据法律而不应当根据判例作出

judgement lien 判定留置

judgement of first instance 初审判决

judgement of God 神意判决

judgement of international court of justice 国际法院判决

judgement on merits 实质问题的判决

judgement seat　法官席

judges of international court of justice　国际法院法官

judges sitting together　合议法官

judging the law　评断法律

judicatory　法院

judicature　司法制度,法官的管辖权,司法权,法院

judicature act　法院组织法,司法组织法

judicial act　司法行为,司法活动

judicial administration　司法行政

judicial aid　司法协助

judicial apparatus　司法机关

judicial arbitration　法院仲裁

judicial assistance　司法协助

judicial assistance in civil proceedings　民事司法

judicial assistance in criminal cases　刑事司法协助

judicial attachment　法院扣押

judicial authorities　司法机关

judicial body　司法机关

judicial branch　司法部门

judicial cadre　司法干部

judicial capacity　司法权,司法职能

judicial clause　司法条款

judicial committee　审判委员会

judicial committee of people's court　人民法院审判委员会

judicial committee of the privy council　枢密院司法委员会

judicial committee of the same court　本院审判委员会

judicial committee of the supreme people's court　最高人民法院审判委员会

judicial damages　司法损害赔偿

judicial day　法庭开庭日

judicial decision　司法判决

judicial department　司法部门

judicial detention　司法拘留

judicial discretion　法官自由裁量权

judicial divorce　判决离婚,呈诉离婚,法院判定的离婚

judicial document　司法文件

judicial documents of civil action　民事司法文书

judicial evidence　法院认定的证据

judicial function　司法职能

judicial guarantee　法律保证

judicial immunity　法官豁免权,司法豁免权

judicial independence　司法独立

judicial interpretation　司法解释

judicial investigation　法院调查

judicial justice　司法公正

judicial legislation　司法法规

judicial lien　法律上的管置权

judicial mortgage　法院判定的抵押

judicial negligence　违法过失

judicial notice　司法认知,审判知识

judicial office　司法机关

judicial officer　承审员,法官

judicial official　司法人员

judicial organization　司法机关

judicial organs　审判机关,司法机构

judicial partition of inheritance　法院判定的遗产分割

judicial penalty　司法刑罚

judicial person　法人

judicial personnel　司法工作人员

judicial police　司法警察,法警

judicial power　司法权

judicial power of the state　国家审判权

judicial practice　司法惯例,司法程序

judicial pragmaticism　实用主义法学

judicial precedent　司法判例,成案,判例

judicial principle　司法原则

judicial probation　司法制缓刑

judicial procedure　司法程序,审

判程序

judicial pronouncement 司法裁决

judicial psychology 司法心理学

judicial redress 司法赔偿

judicial redress procedure 司法赔偿程序

judicial reform 司法改革

judicial remedy 司法补救方法

judicial review （英、美）行政审查，司法审查

judicial review act 司法审查权条例

judicial review of administrative act 行政行为的司法审查

judicial review system 违宪审查制度

judicial safeguard 司法保障

judicial sale 司法拍卖

judicial supervision 司法监督

judicial system 司法制度

judicial tribunal 裁判庭

judicial tyranny 司法专横

judiciary 司法机关,法官

judiciary act 司法条例

judiciary court 刑事法院

judicium（拉） 裁决,法庭

judicium capitale（拉） 判处死刑

juggle 欺骗

juggle with the law 歪曲法律

jump bail 保释中逃跑

jungle law 弱肉强食法则

junion security 非优先抵押权债券

junior 未成年人,初级律师,初级

junior counsel 初级律师

junior interest 从属权益

junior judge 初任审判员,低级法官

junior lien 后序留置权

junior magistrate 低级法官

junior police officer 初级警官

junior procurator 初任检查员,初任检查员

"junk" a contract 撕毁合同

jura in personam（拉） 对人权

jura in re aliena（拉） 限制物权

jura in rem（拉） 对世权

jura regalia 君主权

jural postulates 法律假定

jural relation of accounting 会计法律关系

jural relation of administrative procedure 行政诉讼法律关系

jural relation of auditing 审计法律关系

jural relation of education 教育法律关系

jural relation of labour 劳动法律关系

jural relation of labour administration 劳动行政法律关系

jural relation of public security administration 公安行政法律关系

jural relations in slant administration 斜式行政法律关系

jural relations in the administration of culture 文化行政法律关系

jural relations in the administration of finance 财政行政法律关系

jural relations in the administration of health 卫生行政法律关系

jural relations of civil litigation 民事诉讼法律关系

jural relations of internal administration 内部行政法律关系

jural relations of procedure 诉讼法律关系

jural relations of tax revenue collection 税收征收法律关系

jural relationship in criminal action 刑事诉讼法律关系

juramentum dolo（拉） 诈欺的宣誓

juridical 司法的

juridical association 社团法人

juridical person 财团法人

juridical person of making profit 营利法人

juridical person of public welfare

公益法人

juridical personality 法律人

Juries are the judges of fact 陪审员是事实的裁判者

Juris affectus in executione consistit (拉) 法律的效力在于执行

juris civilis doctor/JCD (拉) 民法学博士

juris possessor (拉) 权利的占有人

juridical person 法人

jurisdiction 审判权,司法

jurisdiction by law 法律管辖

jurisdiction by order 裁定管辖

jurisdiction clause 管辖权条款

jurisdiction from agreement 协定管辖

jurisdiction in matter of prize 捕获管辖权

jurisdiction in person 对人的管辖权

jurisdiction in rem (拉) 对物管辖说,对物的管辖权

jurisdiction/judicial power 审判权

jurisdiction of administrative penalties 行政处罚的管辖

jurisdiction of administrative punishment 行政处罚的管辖

jurisdiction of civil adjudication 民事审判管辖

jurisdiction of civil cases 民事案件审判权

jurisdiction of investigation 侦查管辖

jurisdiction of notarization 公证管辖

jurisdiction of tax revenue 税收管辖权

jurisdiction of taxation 税收管辖权

jurisdiction of trial instance 审级管辖

jurisdiction over administrative action 行政诉讼管辖

jurisdiction over aerial hijacking offense 对空中劫持的管辖权

jurisdiction over criminal action 刑事诉讼的管辖

jurisdiction over placing cases on file 立案管辖

jurisdiction over property 对财产的管辖权

jurisdiction over reconsideration 复议管辖

jurisdiction rationae materiae (拉) 对事管辖,对事的管辖权

jurisdiction rationae personae 对人管辖

jurisdiction theory 司法权理论

jurisdiction to determinate its own jurisdiction 对管辖权的管辖权

jurisdiction within territorial space 领空管辖权

jurisdiction within territorial waters 领海管辖权

jurisdiction within territories 领土管辖权

jurisdictional 管辖范围的

jurisdictional interpretation 司法解释

jurisdictional limit of auditing 审计管辖范围

jurisprudence 法学、法理学

jurisprudence of administrative procedure 行政诉讼法学

jurisprudence of reform-through-labour 劳动改造法学

jurisprudent 法理学家

jurist 法学家

juristic act of veal right 物权行为

juristic act subject to a conditional precedent 附意合同,附停止条件法律行为

juristic act subject to a time 附期限民事法律行为

juristic person 法律人格体,法人

juristic writing 法律文献

juror 陪审员

jury system 陪审制

jury witness 证人陪审制

jus abutendi（拉） 随意处分财产权

jus abutendi aut obusus（拉） 处分权

jus ad bellum（拉） 诉诸战争权

jus civile（拉） 市民法

jus cogens（拉） 强行法

jus criminale（拉） 刑法

jus dispensandi（拉） 免除义务权,处分权

jus dispositivum（拉） 酌定法

jus dominii（拉） 所有权

jus ex injuria non oritur（拉） 侵权不得产生权利

jus fruendi（拉） 收益权

jus gentium（拉） 万民法

jus honorarium（拉） 最高裁判官法（罗马法）,(罗)大法官法

jus in personam（拉） 债权,对人权（英）

jus in re propria（拉） 自物权

jus in rem（拉） 对物权

jus in ve aliena（拉） 他物权

jus legitimum（拉） 合法权利

jus mariti（拉） 夫权

jus publicum privatorum pactis mutari non potest（拉） 私人契约不得变更公共权利

jus reprasentationis omnimodae（拉） 全权代表权

jus retentionis（拉） 留置权

Jus romanum（拉） 罗马法

Jus sanguinis（拉） 血统主义

jus sanguinis doctrine 血统主义

jus soli（拉） 出生地主义

jus tertii（拉） 第三方权利,第三者权利

jus utendi（拉） 使用权

just 正义

just and sound 公允

just authority 合法权利

just before execution 临刑

just compensation 合理赔偿,合理补偿

just debt 合法债务

just demands 正当要求

just price 公平价格

just punishment 应得的惩罚

just title 合法所有权

justa possessio（拉） 合法占有

justic 公正的

justice 正义,公正原则,法官,公正,(中) 大法官

justice ministry 司法部

Justice of assize 巡回法官

justice of procedural law 程序法公正

justice of the peace 治安法官

justice of the supreme court（日） 最高裁判所判事

justice proccdurc 公正的程序

justicer 法官

justiceship 法官的职位

justiciable dispute 可由法院裁判的争执

justiciary 法官的裁判权

justifiable defence 正当防卫

justifiable homicide 正当杀人

justification of detention 正当拘留,合法拘留

justification of punishment 处罚正当

justified 有理由,合理

justified expectat joint stock assties 当事人的正当期待

justIfled price 合理价格

justified races 合理上涨

justify 正当

justifying bail 适当担保

juvenile 未成年人

juvenile adult 青少年

juvenile court 少年法院,儿童法庭(香港)

juvenile criminal law of the Federal Republic of Germany 德意志联邦共和国青少年刑法

juvenile criminology 青少年犯罪学

juvenile delinquency 少年犯罪

juvenile delinquent 触法少年

juvenile law 青少年保护法

juvenile offender 少年犯

juvenile prison 少管所

Jydske code 裘特法典

K

keep a contract 遵守合同

keep a record 备案

keep a secret 为保密

keep accounts 记账

keep down prices 平抑价格

keep effective 继续有效

keep from 预防

keep guard 保守

keep idle 闲置

keep intact the scene of a crime
保护犯罪现场

keep one's identity hidden 隐名

keep one's words, act up to one's
promise 遵守诺言

keep secrets 保密

keep social order 维持社会秩序

keep state secrets 保护国家秘密

keep the law 守法

keep the left 靠左行驶

keep the peace 维持治安

keep under strict supervision 严
格监管

keep under temporary detention
看押

keep up 继续,支持,保存

keep upright 切勿倒置

keep within the four corners of the
law 在法律范围内

keep your quotation 维持你方
报价

Kennedy round 肯尼迪回合

Kennedy round of multilateral
tariff negotiations 肯尼迪回
合多边关税谈判

Kennedy round of tariff negotiations 肯尼迪回合关税谈判

Kennedy round of tariff reduction
肯尼迪回合削减关税谈判

kerb stone broker 场外经纪人

keresy 异端

key contract 关键契约

key country group 强国集团

key enterprises 骨干企业

key industry 基础工业,关键工
业,基本工业

key industry investment fund 基
础工业投资基础

key money 额外租金,额外小费

key risk 关键风险

key sector 关键部门

key technology 关键技术

Keyneianism 凯恩斯主义

Keynes plan 凯恩斯计划

keypoint project 重点工程

Khalife 哈里发

kick-back 贿赂,回扣,佣金,酬
金

kidnap 绑架

kidnap for ransom 绑票

kidnapper 绑架者

kidnapping for ransom 掳人勒
赎罪

Kiel canal 基尔运河

kind of currencies 货币种类

kind of punishment(s) 刑种,刑
罚种类

kindred 亲属关系

kindred circumstances 同样情况

kinds of taxes 税种

king 王

king in name only 虚位君主

king's (queen's) serjeant 国王
高级律师

king's counsel 皇家律师

kingdom 王国

kingly way 王道

kingship 王权

kinship 家族关系,亲属关系

kinship relations 亲属关系

kitchen 厨房

kitchen cabinet 厨房用长橱,厨
房用碗柜

kitchen stove 厨灶

kite bill 空头票据

knight 骑士

knight fee 骑士采邑制

Knights of St. John 圣·约翰骑士团

knock for knock agreement 各自负责协议

knockout drops 蒙汗药

knock-out agreement 勾结折卖协议

know the laws and abide by them 知法守法

knowingly 明知

knowledge intensive product 知识密集型产品

known loss 已知损失

know-how 专有技术

know-how license contract 专有技术许可合同

Ksatriya 刹帝利

Ku Klux Klan 三K党

Kur'an 古兰经

L

label clause　标签条款

label coupon　息票

labeling regulation　标签条例

labeling theory of crime　犯罪标签论

labor education and rehabilitation　劳动教养

labor force　劳动力

labor protection for women　妇女劳动保护

labor reform team　劳动改造管教队

labour　劳动,劳动力,劳动者

labour (/labor) insurance　劳动保险

labour (/labor) protection　劳动保护

labour act　劳工法

labour administration department　劳动行政部门,劳动管理部门

labour administration law　劳动行政法

labour age　劳动年龄

labour agreement　劳动协议,劳资协议

labour and management　劳资双方

labour and personnel management　劳动人事管理

labour appraisal committee　劳动鉴定委员会

labour arbitration　劳动仲裁

labour arbitration law　劳动仲裁法

labour behaviour　劳动行为

labour charter　劳动宪章

labour compensation　劳动赔偿

labour conflict　劳动争议行为

labour contract　劳动契约,劳务合同

labour contract law　劳动合同法

labour contract system　劳动合同制

labour contractor　包工头

labour convention　劳动公约

labour cooperation agreement　劳务合作协议

labour court　劳资法庭,劳资争议法庭

labour discipline　劳动纪律,劳动法律

labour dispute　劳动争议

labour dispute arbitration　劳动争议仲裁

labour dispute arbitration organization　劳动争议仲裁机关

labour dispute arbitration system　劳动争议仲裁制度

labour dispute litigation　劳动争议诉讼

labour dispute mediation committee　劳动争议调解委员会

labour education and rehabilitation　劳动教养

labour education and rehabilitation school　劳动改造感化院

labour federation　劳工联盟

labour force　劳动力

labour income　劳动收入

labour indemnity　劳动赔偿

labour inspection law　劳动监察法

labour insurance　劳动保险

labour insurance administration　劳动保险管理

labour insurance benefits　劳动保险待遇

labour insurance committee　劳动保险委员会

labour insurance dispute　劳动保险争议

labour insurance management　劳动保险管理

labour intensity　劳动强度

labour jurisprudence　劳动法学

labour law　劳动法

labour law system 劳动法律制度

labour legislation 劳动立法,劳动法规

labour market 劳务市场

labour norms 劳动规范

labour organization 劳动组织,工人组织

labour outside prison 监外劳动

labour pact 劳动公约

labour plan 劳动计划

labour power 人力

labour protection 劳动保护

labour protection inspector 劳动保护检查员

labour protection law 劳动保护法

labour protection measures 劳动保护措施

labour protection regulation 劳动保护法规

labour psychology 劳动心理学

labour reform camp 劳动改造营

labour regulation 劳动法规,劳工条例

labour relation(s) 劳务关系,劳动关系

labour relationship 劳动关系

labour remuneration income 劳务报酬所得

labour rent 劳役地租

labour resources 劳动力资源

labour safety dispute 劳动安全争议

labour service charge 劳动服务费

labour service tax 劳务税

labour service trademark 劳务商标

labour standards 劳动规范

labour supervision system 劳动监察制度

labour supervisor 劳动监察员

labour system 劳动制度

labour tribunal 劳资审裁处

labour trouble 劳资纠纷

labour union organization 工会组织

labourer working on his own 个体劳动者

labour-intensive industry 劳动密集型工业

labour-intensive product 劳动密集型产品

labour-management dispute(s) 劳资纠纷

labour-management relations act (Taft-Hartley Act; US) 劳资关系法

labour-management relationship 劳资关系

lacerated wound 碎裂伤

laceration 挫裂创

lack 缺乏,缺少

lack experience 缺乏经验

lack legal formality 缺乏法定形式

lack of competence 无权限

lack of evidence 证据不足

lack of foreign exchange 外汇短缺

lack of maturity 未成年

lack of repayment 缺乏偿还能力

lack of value 缺乏对价

lack the competence 缺乏能力

lactation period 哺乳期

laden weight 装载重量

lady judge 女审判员

laesio(拉) 损害

laggard 滞销汇券

laissez-passer 免验证,通行证

lake 湖泊

Lamaism 喇嘛教

land 国家,卸货

land acquisition 土地征用

land administration 地产管理,土地管理

land administration department 土地管理部门

land agency 地产管理处,地产经纪行,地产公司

land agent 地产管理人,地产经

纪人,土地管理人
land allotment 土地分配
land and building 房地产
land and water 水陆
land appraisal 地产评估,土地评估
land board 土地局
land certificate 地契
land clearance 清理场地,拆平房屋
land collectivation 土地集体化
land compensation 土地补偿费
land conservation 土地保护
land contract 土地承包
land contracts 土地契约
land control measures 土地管理措施
land costs 地价
land deed 土地使用证书
land developer 土地开发者
land development 土地开发
land disputes 土地纠纷
land domain 领陆
land dues 地皮税
land expropriation 土地征收,土地征用
land expropriation right 土地征用权
land fixtures 地上定着物
land frontiers 陆地边境
land grab 强占土地
land grant 土地出让
land holder 土地所有人,土地租用人
land holding tax (城镇)土地使用税
land improvements 土地改良
land in abeyance 所有权未定的土地
land in the cites 城市的土地
land in the rural and suburban areas 农村和城市郊区的土地
land intensive product 土地密集型产品
land investment corporation 地产公司
land law 土地法

① land lease 土地租契
② land legislation 土地立法
③ land locked state 内陆国
④ land lot 地段
⑤ land management 土地管理
⑥ land management law 土地管理法
⑦
⑧ land needed 用地
⑨ land occupancy charge 土地使用费
⑩
⑪ land of uncertain ownership 所有权不明的土地
⑫
⑬ land office 土地管理局
⑭ land owner 土地的所有者,土地所有人
⑮
⑯ land ownership 地权
⑰ land policy 土地政策
⑱ land price 土地价格
⑲ land price tax 地价税
⑳ land property right 地产产权
㉑ land proprietor 地产所有人,土地所有人,地主
㉒
㉓ land ratio 土地利用率
㉔ land reclamation 土地复垦
㉕ land reform 土地改革
㉖ land registration 土地登记
㉗ land registry 土地登记处
㉘ land rentals 土地租赁费
㉙ land requisition 土地征用
㉚ land resources 陆地资源
㉛ land revenue 土地收益
㉜ land right 地产权,土地权
㉝ land sale 土地出售,土地买卖
㉞ land steward 土地管理人
㉟ land survey and statistics system 土地调查统计制度
㊱ land surveyor 土地测量员
㊲ land system 土地制度
㊳ land tenancy 土地租佃
㊴ land tenure 土地租赁期
㊵ land transaction 土地交易
㊶ land transfer 土地转让
㊷ land trust 土地信托投资
㊸ land use 用地,土地利用,土地用途
㊹
㊺ land use assessment 城市用地评估

land use balance 用地平衡

land use capability 土地利用率

land use certificate 土地使用证书

land use plan 土地使用规划

land use right granting 土地使用权出让

land use right transfer 土地使用权转让

land use rights 土地使用权

land use tax (城镇)土地使用税

land utilization 土地利用

land value 地价

land value tax 地价税

land warrant 土地转让证书

landed estate 不动产,地产

landed estate court 地产法院

landed price 卸岸价格

landed property 不动产,地产

landed proprietor 土地所有人

landing charges 卸货费用

landing account 仓储单

landing agent 卸货代理人

landing certificate 卸货证明

landing order 卸货单

landing place 卸货地点

landing tax 入境税

landing weight 卸货重量

landlord 地主

landlordism 地主所有制

landmark 地界

landowner 地主,土地所有人

landowner's royalty 土地开采权使用费

land-grabber 侵占土地

land-locked sea 内陆海

land-ownership 土地所有制

lange sized complete sets of equipment 大型成套设备

language authenticity 文字效力

language of the court 法庭用语

language of treaty 条约的语文

lapse 遗赠失效,失效

lapse of law 法律的失效

lapse of offer 要约失效

lapsed gift 因失效而转归他人的赠与

① lapsed insurance 过期保险

② larcener 盗窃公共财产罪

③ larcenist 盗窃公共财产罪,窃贼

④ larceny 盗窃罪

⑤ larceny case 盗窃案件

⑥ larceny of auto 盗用汽车罪

⑦ larceny of defalcation 盗用公款罪

⑨ larceny of fraudulent use of official seals 盗用公章罪

⑪ larceny of military equipment 盗窃军用物资罪

⑬ larceny of nuclear materials 盗窃核原料罪

⑮ larceny of property lost, misdealt, or delivered by mistake 盗取丢失、错放或误送财物罪

⑱ larceny of technical know-how 盗窃技术秘密罪

⑳ larceny of weaponry 盗窃武器装备罪

㉒ larceny suspect 盗窃嫌疑犯

㉓ large borrower 大额借款人

㉔ large city 较大的市

㉕ large deposit 大笔存款

㉖ large estate 大地产

㉗ large loans 大额贷款

㉘ large order 大量采购,大批订货

㉚ large-scale 大规模

㉛ large-scale capital investment project 大规模投资项目

㉝ large-scale land holdings 大土地占有

㉟ large-scale production 大规模生产

㊲ large-scale retailing 大规模销售

㊳ large-scale socialized production 社会化大生产

㊵ large-volumed commodities in bulk 大宗散袋商品

㊷ last clear chance rule 最后明显机会原则

㊹ last frontier port of departure 最后离开的国境口岸

㊻ last judgment 末日审判

㊼ lasting 持久的

lasting law and order　长治久安

lasting peace and stability　长治久安

lasting political stability　长治久安

lata culpa（拉）重大过失

lata culpa dolo aequiparatur（拉）重大过失等于诈骗

late acceptance　迟到的承诺

late postmortem phenomena　晚期尸体现象

late presentation　迟延提示

late shipment　延迟装运,迟延装运

latent conflict　隐存冲突

latent criminal　潜伏的罪犯

latent defect　潜在瑕疵,潜在缺陷,隐蔽的瑕疵,隐蔽的缺陷

latent defect clause　潜在瑕疵条款

latent defects of goods clause　货物潜在缺陷条款

latent natural law　隐秘自然人

latent power　潜在力量

later laws prevail over those which preceded them　后法优于前法

lateral delimitation　横侧划界

lateral economic ties　横向经济联合

lateral integration　横向合并

lateral judge　副审判员

latest shipment date　最后装船日期

latifundist　拥有大量地产者,大地产商

latifundium　大地产

latifundium system　大庄园制

Latin America free trade association（简写：LAFTA）拉丁美洲自由贸易协会

launching state　发射国

Lauterpacht Hersch　劳特派特

law　法,规律,法律,规律性

law against unfair competition　反不正当竞争法

law agent　诉讼代理人

law and discipline　法纪

law and economics　经济分析法学

law and order　社会治安

law and regulation　法规

law applicable in the state　现行法律

law breakers　违法分子

law case　法律案件,案子

law circle　法律界

law committee　法律委员会

law department　法律系

law dictionary　法律词典

law enforcement　法律的实施

law enforcement agency　执法机关

law enforcement identity certification　执法身份证

law enforcement level　执法水平

law enforcement officer　执法人员

law enforcement officials　执法人员

law fallen into desuetude　已废除的法律

law firm　律师事务所

law for people to lodge complaints against officials　"民告官的法律"

law for the preservation of cultural relics　文物保护法

law governing application　实施法

law governing the control of aliens entering and leaving China　外国人入境出境管理法

law in action　行动中的法

law in force　现行法律

law in operation　现行法律,实施中的法律

law in which noting is made　拒绝证书作成地法

law in which unjustified enrichment occurs　不当得利事实发生地法

law less person　不法之徒

law lords　上议院高等法官

law making stipulations　造法规

定

law of administration of merchandise imports and exports 进出口商品管理法律制度

law of administration of technology imports and exports 技术进出口管理法律制度

law of administrative establishment 行政编制法

law of administrative supervision 行政监督法

law of agency 代理法

law of application 适用法,施行法

law of attorneys 律师法

law of aviation 航空法

law of bankruptcy 破产法

law of bill 票据法

law of bills of exchange and cheques 汇票支票法

law of business organization 企业组织法

law of carriage by sea 海上运输法

Law of carriage of goods 货物运输法

law of carriage of goods by sea 海上货物运输法

law of China's mainland 中国大陆的法律

law of coal 煤炭法

law of company (/corporation) 公司法

law of compensation for wrong detention and conviction 错捕错判赔偿法

Law of competition 竞争法则

law of conscription 兵役法

law of contract 契约法,合约法

law of counter-unfair competition 反不正当竞争法

law of co-ordination 对等关系的法律

law of criminal execution 刑事执行法

law of damages 损害赔偿法

law of distress 财产扣押法

① law of economic contract 经济合
② 同法
③ law of economic control 经济统
④ 治法
⑤ law of education 教育法
⑥ law of electric power 电力法
⑦ law of enterprise(s) 企业法
⑧ law of environment protection
⑨ 环境保护法
⑩ Law of foreign capital 外资法
⑪ law of forestry 森林法
⑫ law of guarantee 保证法
⑬ law of household register 户籍
⑭ 法
⑮ law of incidence 负担法则
⑯ law of insurance 保险法
⑰ law of international bills 国际票
⑱ 据法
⑲ law of international civil procedure 国际民事程序法
⑳ dure 国际民事程序法
㉑ law of judge 法官法
㉒ law of jungle 弱肉强食法则
㉓ law of labour administration 劳
㉔ 动行政法
㉕ law of labour contract 劳动合同
㉖ 法
㉗ law of labour safety and hygiene
㉘ 劳动安全卫生法
㉙ law of labour supervision 劳动
㉚ 监察法
㉛ law of labour supervision and inspection 劳动监督检查法
㉜ spection 劳动监督检查法
㉝ law of labour-management relations 劳资关系法
㉞ tions 劳资关系法
㉟ law of large numbers 大数法则
㊱ law of lawyers 律师法
㊲ law of liabilities for administrative damage 行政损害责任法
㊳ damage 行政损害责任法
㊴ law of market control 市场管理
㊵ 法
㊶ law of market economy 市场经
㊷ 济法
㊸ law of mass production 大量生
㊹ 产法则
㊺ law of morality 道德法则
㊻ law of nationality 国籍法
㊼ law of nations 万国公法

law of nature 自然法

law of nature reserve management 自然保护区管理法

law of navigation 航运法

law of negotiable instrument 票据法

law of obligation 债法

law of officers on reserve service 预备役军官法

law of physical culture and sports 体育法

law of planning 计划法

law of plans 计划法

law of post 邮政法

law of press 新闻出版法

law of procedure 诉讼程序法,程序法

law of prosecutors 检察官法

law of public prosecutors 检察官法

law of publication 出版法

law of railway nationalization 铁路国有化法

law of real property（港）物业法

law of regional national autonomy 民族区域自治法

law of responsibility and authority 权责法

law of restitution 赔偿法

law of retaliation 同态复仇法

law of rights over things 物权法

law of society 社会法

law of the place where the property is situated 财产所在地法

law of the road 公路法规

law of the sea 海洋法

law of the stronger 强权法则

law of the unity of opposite 对立统一规律

law of torts 民事侵权法

law of trade 美(1974) 贸易法

law of treaties 条约法

law of trusts（港）信托法

law of unfair competition 不正当竞争防治法

law of value 价值规律

law of war 战争法,战时国际法

law office 律师事务所

law officer 司法人员

law officers of the crown 政府法律官员

law on administrative functionaries 行政工作人员法

law on authorized sizes of government organization 行政编制法

law on compulsory primary education 初等义务教育法

law on foreign capital enterprises 外资企业法

law on forestry 森林法

law on international securities 国际证券法

law on sales 买卖法

law on technological contract 技术合同法

law on the management of government establishments 编制管理法

law on the protection of the rights and interests of returned overseas chinese and the family members of overseas Chinese 归侨、侨眷权益保护法

law on the set number of personnel in administrative establishment 行政机关编制法

law presumption 法律推定

law price 廉价

Law Quarterly Review 《法律评论季刊》

law reform 法律改革

law reform committee 法律改革委员会

law relating to public order 有关公共秩序的法律

law report 法律报告

law reports 判例汇编

law school 法律学院,法学院

law society 法律学会,法协会,法学会

law spiritual 宗教法

law term 法律术语

law textbooks 法学教科书

law theory 法律理学

law to the status of aliens 外国人地位法

law year book 法律年鉴

law's enforcement must be strict 执法必严

lawful 合法的,法定

lawful act 合法行为

lawful age 法定年龄

lawful arrest 合法逮捕,合法拘捕

lawful at act 合法行为

lawful authority 合法权利,合法权限

lawful basis 合法依据

lawful civil rights 合法民事权利

lawful condition 法定条件

lawful damages 法定损害赔偿额

lawful day 开庭日期,有效日期,法定日期

lawful duties 法定职责,法定义务

lawful goods 合法货物

lawful holder bearer 合法持票人

lawful impediment 合法延误

lawful interest of property 合法财产收益

lawful interest(s) 合法利益

lawful means 合法手段

lawful merchandise 合法货物

lawful money 法定货币

lawful operation 合法经营

lawful possession 合法占有

lawful property 合法的财产

lawful property owned by a citizen personally 个人合法财产

lawful reserve 法定准备金

lawful rights 合法权益,合法权利

lawful rights and interests 合法权益,合法的权利和利益

lawful sovereign 合法君主

lawfully 依法

lawfully-earned income 合法收入

lawfulness of administration doctrine 行政合法性原则

lawless 没有法律依据的,不法的

lawlessness 无法可依

lawn 草坪

laws and decrees 法令

laws and regulations 法律、法规

laws and regulations of Ming Dynasty 明代法规

laws and regulations on protection of cultural relics 保护文物法规

laws and regulations on the protection of farmland 农田保护法规

laws of edward the confessor 忏悔者爱德华法律汇编

laws of the lombards 伦巴帝法

laws outside the basic laws 基本法律以外的法律

laws, regulations, and rules 法律、法规、规章

lawsuit 案件

lawsuit filed in a protest by a prosecutorial office 检察院抗诉的案件

lawyer 律师

lawyer's competence certificate 律师资格证书

lawyer's fee(s) 律师费

lawyer's license 律师执照

lawyer's qualification certificate 律师资格证书

lawyers' association 律师协会

lawyers' discipline 律师纪律

lawyers' law 律师法

lawyers' office 律师事务所

lawyers' qualification test 律师资格考试

lawyers' system 律师制度

lay 世俗

lay aside 搁置

lay corporation 非营利法人

lay day(s) 装卸期,装卸时间

lay judge 非职业法官
lay off 辞退
lay stress on economic results 注重经济效益
lay time 装卸时间,装卸期限
laytime 债券发行价格
lay-off 停工期间
ld 质量差价,自留地,质量低劣
lead manager 牵头经理人,牵头银行
leader manager 证券牵头经理人
leader of the opposition 反对党领袖
leadership 领导权
leadership from different quarters 多头领导
leading administrative official 行政领导干部
leading body 领导机关
leading cadre 首长
leading cadres' responsibility system 首长负责制
leading case 判例案件
leading firm 主要厂商
leading interrogation 诱导性讯问
leading official 负责人
leading organization 领导机关
leading position 领导职务,领导地位
leading position of the state economy 国民经济主导地位
leading position of worker class 工人阶级的领导地位
leading post 领导职务
leading principles of law 法学导论
leading question 诱导性询问
leaf tobacco purchasing contract 烟叶收购合同
leaf tobacco purchasing plan 烟叶收购计划
league of Arab states 阿拉伯国家联盟
league of nations 国际联盟
leaking secret 泄密

learn from past mistakes to avoid future ones, and cure the sickness to save the patient 惩前毖后,治病救人
learning among prisoners 狱内学习
leasable 可出租的
leasable area 出租面积
lease 租借,租赁,出租,租约
lease agreement 租约,租赁协议,租赁合同
lease back 回租
lease broker 租赁经纪人
lease charge 租赁手续费
lease contract 租赁合同
lease finance company 租赁财务公司
lease financing 租赁融资,租赁筹资
lease fixed assets 租赁固定资产
lease in perpetuity 永久租借,永租权,永租
lease of land 土地租赁
lease of land use right 土地使用权出租
lease of property 财产租赁
lease period 租期,租赁期限
lease purchase(/installations) 租借购买
lease rent 租赁金
lease term 租期,租赁期
lease terms 租借条件
leaseback 租回已售出的产业,回租租赁
leased immovables 租借不动产,租赁不动产
leased land 租赁土地
leased property 出租财产,租赁财产
leased territory 租借地
leasee 租借人
leasehold 租赁权,租赁期,租期
leasehold ground rent 租赁土地租费
leasehold interest 租赁权益
leasehold interest insurance 租赁权益保险

leasehold relationship 租赁关系
leaseholder 租借人,租户
leaseholder hirer 租借人
leaseholding farm households 农村承包经营
leasement 地役权
leash license 养犬许可证
leasing company 租赁公司
leasing condition 租赁条件
leasing contract 租赁合同,租售合同
leasing funds 金融租赁,融资租赁
leasing industry 租赁业
leasing land 土地出租
leasing market 租赁市场
leasing of machines and tools 机器租赁
least development country 最不发达国家
leave 闲置
leave a deposit 给付定金
leave sb uncontroled in the society 弃于社会
leave the country 出境
leave the country and settle abroad 出境定居
leave the country for employment abroad 出境就业
leave the country for studies 出境留学
leave the country on tour abroad 出境旅游
leave the country to inherit properties abroad 出境继承财产
leave the country to visit families 出境探亲访友
leaving certificate 毕业证书
leaving the country and settling down abroad 出境定居
leaving the country for the purposes of visiting ones relatives 出境探亲
lecture 讲听
legacy 遗赠动产
legacy duty 分遗产税,动产继承税

legacy tax 动产继承税
legal 依法,法定的,法定
legal action 法律行为
legal address 法定地址
legal administrator 法定财产管理人
legal adult age 法定成年年龄
legal advantage 合法利益
legal advice 法律意见,法律咨询
legal affairs 法律事务
legal age 法定成年人的年龄,法定年龄
legal agency 法定代理
legal agent 法定代理
legal aid 法律援助
legal and disciplinary education 法纪教育
Legal arbitration 法律仲裁
legal assignment 法律上的物证,法定转让
legal attachment 依法扣押
legal authority 合法权力,法定权限
legal basis 法律根据,法律依据
legal basis for the trial of administrative cases 行政诉讼的审理依据
legal bibliograph 法律书目文献
legal binding 法律约束
legal body 法人
legal capacity 法律行为能力
legal capacity of juristic person 法人的权利能力
legal capacity to make contracts 立约的权利能力
legal case 案件,(古)词讼
legal case for quashing the declaration of a citizen's death 撤销公民死亡宣告案
legal case for quashing the guardianship 撤销监护案件
legal cause 法律原因
legal character 法律性质
legal character of contract 合同的法律物证
legal claim 合法要求

legal compensation 合法赔偿,法律补偿

legal competency 合法权利

legal competition 合法竞争

legal competition, legitimate competition 合法竞争

legal concept 法律概念,法制观念

legal condition 法定条件

Legal consequence 法律后果

legal consideration 合法对价

legal constituted authority 法统

legal construction of supervision over administration 行政监察法制建设

legal contract 合法契约

legal counsel 法律指导,法律顾问

legal credence of detainment 收押法律凭证

legal culture 法律文化

legal currency 法定货币

legal custody 合法拘留,法律的语法

legal custody of property of a denton 依法扣留债务人财产

legal death 宣告死亡

legal debt 合法债务

legal debt limit 法定债务限额

legal debt margin 法定债务限额,法定债务差额

legal decision 法律判决

legal defects 法律瑕疵

legal defense 正当防卫,合法辩护,合法防卫

legal definition 法律定义

legal delay 法定延迟

legal demand 合法要求

legal department 法律部门

legal detention 合法拘留,合法扣留

legal disputes 法律性质的争端,法律手端

legal doctrines 法律原理

legal document 法律文件,法律文书

legal domicile 法定住所

legal duty 法定义务

legal education 法制教育

legal education and training 法律教育与培训

legal education and training of the U.S.A. 美国法律教育及培训

legal effect of contract 合同的法律效力

legal effect of planning permission 计划许可法律效力

legal effection 法律效力

legal encyclopaedias 法律百科全书

legal entity 法律实体,法人实体,法人

legal environment 法律环境

legal estate 普通法上的财产权益,法定财产

legal ethics 法律职业道德

legal evidence 法定证据

legal expert 法律专家

legal fact 法律事实

legal fact in civil law 民事法律事实

legal fiction 法律上的拟制,法律上的假定

legal for quashing the declaration of a missing citizen 撤销公民失踪宣告案

legal force of contract 合同的法律效力

legal form 法定形式

legal formalities 法律形式

legal fruits 法定孳息

legal ground 法律上的依据

legal history 法制史

legal holiday 法定假日,法定休息日

legal humanism 人文主义法学派

legal impedim, law of insurance 保险法

legal information 法律信息

legal inspection of imported and exported commodities 进出口商品法定检验

legal institution 法制
legal interest 法定权益
legal interest rate 法定利率
legal investigation 法律侦查
legal investment 合法投资
legal jurisdiction 合法管辖
legal keeping 合法持有
legal language 法律用语,法庭用语
legal lending limit 法定贷款限额
legal liabilities on violating pricing law 违反价格法的法律责任
legal liabilities of subjects in economic law 经济法主体的法律责任
legal liabilities on violating product quality law 违反产品质量法的法律责任
legal liability 法律责任
legal liability insurance 法定责任险
legal liability of audit 审计法律责任
legal liquidated damages 法定违约金
legal literature 法律著述
legal litigious right 法定诉讼权利
legal logic 法律逻辑
legal maxims 法律格言
legal means 法律手段,合法手段
legal means of settlement of international disputes 国际争端的法律解决方法
legal measure 法律措施
legal measuring instruments 法定测量器具
legal medicine 法医学
legal memory 法律记忆
legal methodology 法律方法
legal minimum wage 法定最低工资
legal monopoly 合法垄断
legal mortgage 法定抵押,法定垄断,合法抵押

legal negligence 法律上的过失
legal net weight 法定净重
legal nihilism 法律虚无主义
legal norms in administrative supervision 行政监督法律规范
legal obligation 法定义务
legal opinion 律师意见书,法律意见书
legal order 法律秩序
legal organization 合法组织
legal owner 合法所有人
legal ownership 合法所有权
legal period of hearing 法定审理期限
legal person 法人
legal person of the cooperative enterprise 中外合作经营企业法人
legal person of the enterprise owned by the foreigner 外资企业法人
legal person trust 法人信托
legal personality 法律上的人格,法人资格,法律人,合法的个人财产
legal persons 法人
legal phenomenon 法的现象,法律现象
legal portion 特留份,物财产
legal possession 合法占有
legal possessor 合法占有人
legal possibility and factual impossibility 法定不能犯与事实不能犯
legal practitioner 开业律师,执业律师资格
legal precedent 判例
legal precedent establish a case upon report by informants 成案
legal prescription 法定起诉期限
legal price 法定价格
legal procedure 法定程序
legal procedure of indictment 法定起诉程序
legal proceedings 法定诉讼程序,法定程序

legal process 法律程序
legal property 合法财产
legal proposal 法律提案
legal protection 法律保护
legal protection of know-how 专有技术的法律保护
legal provisions 法律规定,法律条款,法律条文
legal provisions on foreign trade order 对外贸易秩序法律制度
legal psychology 法律心理学
legal punishment 合法处罚,依法惩处
legal quality 法律性质
legal rate of interest 法定利率
legal real estate 合法不动产
legal redress 法律补救,法律上的赔偿
legal regime of the socialist market economy 社会主义市场经济法律体系
legal relation 法律关系
legal relation of civil adjudication 民事审判法律关系
legal relationship of customs administration 海关行政法律关系
legal relations of finance 金融法律关系
legal relationship in criminal action 刑事诉讼法律关系
legal relationship in criminal proceedings 刑事诉讼法律关系
legal relationship in the administrative of finance 财政行政法律关系
legal relationship of accounting 会计法律关系
legal relationship of administrative procedure 行政诉讼法律关系
legal relationship of auditing 审计法律关系
legal relationship of education 教育法律关系
legal relationship of industry and commerce administration 工商行政法律关系
legal relationship of internal administration 内部行政法律关系
legal relationship of labour 劳动法律关系
legal relationship of labour administration 劳动行政法律关系
legal relationship of revenue 税收法律关系
legal relationship of tax revenue collection 税收征收法律关系
legal relationship of taxation 税收法律关系
legal relationships in planning 计划法律关系
legal remedy 法律救济,法律补偿
legal representative 法定代表人
legal representative in civil action 民事诉讼代理人
legal requirement 法律要件
legal research 法律研究
legal reserve ratio 法定准备金率
legal residence 依法登记的住所,法定住所
legal responsibility 法律责任
legal responsibility of archives management 档案管理法律责任
legal responsibility of file management 档案管理法律责任
legal restraint 法律约束,法律上的限制
legal result 法律后果
legal right 法律权利,法定权利
legal right of action 法定诉讼权利
legal sanction 法律制裁
legal sanctity 法律的尊严
legal scholarship 法律学术
legal security 法定担保
legal sense 法律意义
legal sentence 法定刑期
legal sequestration 合法扣留

legal standard value 法定价格

legal standards 法律标准

legal state 法治国家

legal status 合法地位,法律地位

legal status of the vessel 船舶的法律地位

legal subject 法律主体

legal supervision 法律监督

legal supervision department 法律监督机关

legal supervision of civil litigation 民事诉讼法法律监督

legal supervision on future trade 期货贸易的管理法律制度

legal supervision on stock exchange 股票交易的监管法律制度

legal supervision organization 法律监督机关

legal supervision over economic litigation 经济诉讼法律监督

legal supervision over internal administration 内部行政法制监督

legal system 法律体系,法律体制,法律系统

legal system international service trade 国际服务贸易法律制度

legal system of accounting 会计法律制度

legal system of administration of classified state-owned property 国有资产分类管理的法律制度

legal system of foreign investment 外商投资的法律制度

legal system of inspection on imports and exports 进出口商品检验法律制度

legal system of revenue 税收法律制度

legal system of tax revenue 税收法律制度

legal technicalities of a case 案件的法律细节

legal tender 法定货币

legal tender note 法定货币

legal term(s) 法定期限

legal terminology 法律术语

legal theory 法学理论

legal time 法定日期,法定时间

legal time limit 法定期限

legal time limit of indictment 法定起诉期限

legal title 合法所有权

legal toxicology 法医毒理学

legal treatise and textbook 法律专著和教科书

legal unit of measurement 法定计量单位

legal validity 合法性

legal warranty 合法担保

legal worker 法律工作者

legal working day 法定工作

legal working time 法定工作时间

legalism 条文主义

legality 法制,合法性

legality doctrine 合法性原则

legality of purpose 合法目的

legalization 合法化

legalize 使有法律效力

legally 依法,法律上的

legally binding 有法律约束力

legally binding force 法律约束力

legally binding instrument 具有法律约束力的文件

legally competent to contract 有法定缔约资格

legally named contract 具名合同

legally prescribed circumstances of sentencing 法定量刑情节

legally sufficient evidence 法律上充分的证据

legally-prescribed punishment 法定刑

legally-prescribed time periods prescribed time 法定期间,法定期限

legate 遗赠

legator 遗赠人

legatum（拉）遗赠

legatum conditionatum（拉）附条件遗赠

legatum liberationis（拉）债务免除的遗赠

legatum purum（拉）无条件遗赠

legatum usus fructus（拉）用益权遗赠

leges barbarorum（拉）蛮族法

leges figendi et refigendi consuetudo est periculosissima（拉）惯于制定和修改法规是最有害的作法

legis actio（拉）口头诉讼制度（罗马）

legislation 立法，法例

legislation for criminal injuries compensation 被害人补偿立法

legislation mandate 立法委任权

legislation of euthanasia 安乐死立法

legislation of supervision over administration 行政监察立法

legislation on government establishments 编制立法

legislation under delegation 委任立法

legislations of environmental protection 环境保护法规

legislative 立法权

legislative branch 立法机构

legislative competence 立法权限

legislative desire 立法愿望

legislative effect 立法效力

legislative explanation 立法机关的解释，立法解释

legislative initiative 立法创制权

legislative institution 立法机构

legislative intent 立法旨意，立法意图

legislative interpretation 立法解释

legislative jurisdiction 法律管辖

legislative power 立法权

legislative power of the state 国家立法权

legislative procedure 立法程序

legislative spirit 立法精神

legislative system 立法体制

legislative thinking 立法思想

legislative trend 立法趋势

legislative veto 立法否决

legislator 立法者，议员

legitim（拉）遗留份

legitimacy 合法性

legitimacy of evidence 证据的合法性

legitimate 给…合法地位，使合法，使合法

legitimate act 合法行为

legitimate authority 法定职权

legitimate claim 合法要求

legitimate commercial interest 正当商业利益

legitimate conditions of administrative act 行政行为的合法要件

legitimate freedoms and rights 正当的自由和权利

legitimate government 正统政府

legitimate interest(s) 正当利益，合法权益，正当权益

legitimate loan 合法借贷

legitimate power 合法权利

legitimate private property 合法私有财产

legitimate religious activities 合法的宗教活动

legitimate right(s) 合法权益，合法权利

legitimate rights and interest of Chinese nationals residing abroad 华侨的正当权利和利益

legitimate rights and interests 合法权益

legitimate rights and interests outside the country 在境外的正当权益

legitimate social activity 合法社会活动

legitimate sovereign 合法君主

lend money at usurious rates 重利盘剥

lender 出借人,贷方,出借者,出租人

lending activities 贷款业务活动

lending institution 放款机构

lending limit 贷款限额

lending money on interest 附息贷款

lending office 贷款地点

lending operations 放款业务

lending priorities 贷款方向

lending rate 贷款利率

lending rate of interest 贷款利率

lend-lease 租借

length of limitation period 时效期限

length of maturity 贷款期限

length of residence 居住时间,居住期限

length of service 工作年限

length of the limitation period 时效期

lengthy cargo 超长货物,长件货物

leniency 仁慈

leniency to those who confess their crimes and severity to those who refuse to 坦白从宽、抗拒从严

leniency toward those who acknowledge their crimes and severe punishment of tho se who refuse to confess 坦白从宽,抗拒从严

less developed country/ LDC 欠发达国家

lessee 承租人,租户

lessee company 租赁公司

lession of property 财产转让

lessor 出租方,出租人,租户

let contract 发包

let out 罪犯放风

let prisoners out to relieve themselves 罪犯放风

lethal weapon 凶器

letter 许可证

letter of attorney 授权书,授权委托书

letter of authorization 委托书,授权委托书

letter of confirmation 确认书

letter of delegation 授权书

letter of guarantee 保证书

letter of hypothecation 抵押权证书

letter of indemnity 赔偿保证书,损害赔偿约定书,保函

letter of intent 合同草约,意向书

letter of lien 财产留置权书

letter of pledge 抵押权证书

letter of proposal for prosecution 起诉意见书

letter of recommendation 介绍书

letter of representation 代理证书

letter of request 证据要求书

letter of subrogation 权益转让书

letter of trust 信托书

letter of understanding 担保书

letter of undertaking 承诺书

lettre de rappel 召回国书[法]

level jural relations of administration 平行行政法律关系

level of capacity 能力水平

level of one's understanding 认识水平

level of operation and management 经营管理水平

levissima cupla (拉) 轻微过失

levy 征收,税额

levy taxes 征税

lex (拉) 法律

lex cause (拉) 准据法

lex delicti commisi (拉) 侵权行为地质法,犯罪地法

lex domicilli debitoris (拉) 债务人住所地法

lex fori (拉) 法院地法,诉讼地

法

lex frumentanis（拉）谷物法

lex fundamentalis（拉）基础法

lex incerta（拉）不确定法

lex local actus（拉）行为地法

lex loci（拉）本地法

lex loci celebrationis（拉）婚姻举行地法

lex loci contractus（拉）合同履行地法，合同缔结地法，契约订立地法，立契约地方的法律

lex loci delicti（拉）侵权行为地

lex loci delictus（拉）侵权行为地质法

lex loci rei sitae（拉）财产所在地法

lex loci sitae（拉）物主所在地法

lex loci solutionis（拉）合同履行地法，债务履行地法，债务清偿地法

lex naturale（拉）自然法

lex non scripa（拉）非成文法

lex partriae（拉）当事人本国法

lex personalis（拉）属人法

lex posterior derogat priori（拉）后法优于前法

lex rei sitae（拉）物之所在地法

lex situs（拉）物主所在地法，物所在地法，所在地法

lex specialis derogat generali（拉）特别法优先一般法

lex voluntatis（拉）当事人自主选择的法律

Lexington 列克星敦

liabilities 负债，债务

liabilities for administrative compensation 行政赔偿责任

liabilities for infringement 侵权责任

liabilities of tower and tow 承拖方责任

liability 责任，责任

liability between partners 合伙人间的责任

liability certificate 负债证明书

liability clause 责任条款

liability for breach contract 违约责任

liability for breach of contracts 违约责任

liability for compensation for government tort 行政侵权赔偿责任

liability for compensation for infringement of right 侵权赔偿责任

liability for damage 损害责任，损失所负责任，损失赔偿责任

liability for delay 误期责任，延迟责任，延误责任

liability for detective equipment 提供有缺陷设备的责任

liability for fault 过错赔偿责任，过失责任

liability for government 行政侵权责任

liability for guarantee 保证责任

liability for loss 损失赔偿责任，对损失所负责任

liability for product quality 生产产品质量责任

liability for restitution 赔偿责任

liability for satisfaction 清偿责任

liability for the risk of loss 损失风险责任

liability for tort 侵权民事责任，侵权责任

liability for wrongs 过错责任

liability insurance 责任保险

liability limits 责任范围

liability of guaranty 保证责任

liability of indemnity 补偿责任

liability of infant for tort 未成年人对侵权行为的责任

liability of the multimodal transport operator 多式联运经营人的赔偿责任

liability on guaranties 保证责任

liability to give evidence 提供证据的责任

liability to pay compensation 补偿责任

liability to third party 对第三人的责任

liability with negligence 过失责任

liability without fault 无过失责任,无过错责任

liability without negligence 无过失责任

liable for compensation 负责赔偿

liable jointly and severally 负共同连带责任

liable on conviction upon indictment 被检控罪名成立

libellee (in maritime or canon cases) 被控方

libelous action 诽谤行为

liber (拉) 契约登记簿

libera batella (拉) 渔区,渔业权

liberal construction 扩大解释,任意解释

liberal criminal law 自由刑法

liberal interpretation 自由解释,从宽解释,扩大解释,任意解释

liberalization of economy 经济自由化

liberalization of international trade 国际贸易自由化

liberalization of trade 贸易自由化

liberalize 自由

liberticide 扼杀自由

liberty 自由

liberty of commerce 商业自由

liberty of contract 契约自由

liberty of the press 出版自由

liberty on promise 诺issue约释放

liberum arbitrium (拉) 任意

liberum veto (拉) 自由否决权

libor 同业折放利率

license/licence 许可,许可证,普通许可协议,牌照

license duty 执照税

license for business enterprise of radioactive drugs 放射性药品经营企业许可证

license for circulation of audiovisual products 音像制品发行许可证

license for duplicating business of audiovisual products 音像制品复制经营许可证

license for import and export of cultural relics 文物进出境许可证

license for manufacturing enterprise of radioactive drugs 放射性药品生产企业许可证

license for operating stage performance 演出经营许可证

license for pharmaceutical trading 药品经营许可证

license for practicing 执业许可证

license for the safe production of explosives 爆炸物品安全生产许可证

license for the use of radioactive drugs 放射性药品使用许可证

license for tobacco monopoly manufacturing enterprise 烟草专卖生产企业许可证

license management 许可证管理

license number 批准文号

license system 许可证制度

license tag 牌照

license trade 许可证贸易

licensed premises 已注册的房地产

licensee 被许可受让方,受让方,被许可方

licensing 国际许可贸易工作者协会

licensing system 许可证制度

licensor 许可方,出让方

licentious criminal 淫乱性犯罪人

lie always safely afloat "始终安全浮泊"条款

lie in grant 要式转让

lie in livery 非要式转证

lie safely aground clause "完全

搁浅"条款

lien 留置,留置权

lien clause 留置权条款

lien for freight 运费留置权

lien for taxes 纳税留置

lien holder 留置权享有人

lien letter 留置权证书

lien of covenant 合同留置权

lien of ship 船舶留置权

lien on goods 货物留置权

lien on ship 船舶留置权

lien-creditor 典主

lien-holder 典权人

lienee 典主,留置权人

liense securing claims in respect of collision 保护碰撞产生的债权的管置权

lieutenant colonel on reserve service 预备役中校,预备役少将

life accident insurance 人身意外伤害保险

life insurance 人寿保险

life insurance premium 人寿保险费

life insurance reserve 人寿保险责任壮准备令

life of contract 合同有效期

life of writ 令状有效期

life peerages 非世袭贵族

life salvage 人命救助

life style 生活方式

life table 生命表

life tenure at leading posts 领导职务终身制

lifelong-tenure system 终身制

lift a ban 取消禁令

light fixtures 灯具

light industrial products 轻工产品

light industry 轻工业

light punishment 轻刑

light sentencing 量刑畸轻

lighter punishment in public security 从轻治安处罚

like product 相同产品

limit 限制,限定

limit down （交易所）跌停板

limit of competency 权限限制

limit of debate 辩论范围

limit of defense 防卫限度

limit of liability 责任限度,责任限额

limit of necessity 避险限度

limit of time 时效

limit on unit liability 单位责任限制

limit one's liability 限制赔偿责任

limit order 限制性订单,限价指令

limit the growth of the money supply 紧缩银根

limit the liability 限制赔偿责任

limit up （交易所的）涨停板

limitation 时效,除斥期间,期限

limitation bill "限定王位继承法案"（英 1861）

limitation clause 责任范围条款

limitation for security measures 保安处分期间

limitation for the power to execute punishment 行刑权时效

limitation in law 法律时效

limitation of action 诉讼时效

limitation of administrative action 行政诉讼起诉期限

limitation of arbitration 仲裁时效

limitation of credibility 证据能力的限制

limitation of debate 辩论范围

limitation of liability 责任限度,责任限制,赔偿责任限制,责任范围

limitation of liability rule 限责规则,限制责任的规则

limitation of liability system 责任限额制

limitation of prosecution 追诉时效

limitation of public prosecution 公诉时效

limitation of punishment 刑罚时

效

limitation of sovereignty 限制主权

limitation of territorial sovereignty 领土主权的限制

limitation of the crown act 限制王位继承法(英 1701 年)

limitation of time 时效,期限

limitation on credit 抵免限额

limitation on foreign investment 外资限制

limitation period 时效期限,时效期,时效期间

limitation rules 时效规则

limitations 局限性

limitations of liability of shipowner 船舶所有人责任限制

limitation-of-damages 损害赔偿限制

limited administration 有限管理

limited amount guarantee 限额保证

limited breakdown insurance 有限破损险

limited by guarantee company 担保有限公司

limited capacity for civil conduct 限制民事行为能力,限制行为能力

limited capacity for criminal responsibility 限制责任能力

limited civil capacity of conduct 限制民事行为能力

limited course project financing 有追索权的项目贷款

limited disposing capacity 限制行为能力,不完全行为能力

limited duration guarantee 定期保证

limited entry certificate 有限入境证

limited flexibility 有限浮动

limited floating rate 有限浮动汇率

limited government 有限政府

limited guarantee 限额担保函

limited guaranty 有限担保

limited in private rights 民事权利的限制

limited legacy administration 有限定的遗产管理

limited liability 有限责任

limited market 有限市场

limited merchantable thing 限制流转物,限制流通物

limited monarchism 有限君主制

limited monarchy 君主立宪政体

limited offer 限定报价

limited on disposal 资产处分限制条款

limited order 有限指令,有限订单

limited owner 有限制的所有人

limited partner 有限责任合伙人

limited partnership 有限责任合伙,有限合伙企业

limited partnership act(英) 有限责任合伙法

limited recognition 有限承认

limited recourse project financing 有限追索权项目贷款

limited responsibility clause 责任范围条款

limited right of things 限定物权,限制物权

limited succession 有限继承,限定继承

limited trust 有限信托

limiting government institution's purchase of consumer goods 压缩机关团体购买力

limits for examinity and approving authority 审批权限

limits of authority 权限

limits of jurisdiction 管辖范围

limits of one's functions and powers 职权范围

limits of power prescribed by law 法定权限

limits of the review of constitutionality 违宪审查的范围

line department 生产部门	① liquidation of the debt 清偿债务
line executive 生产经理	② liquidation organization 清算组
line of actual control on the border 边界实际控制线	③ 织
line of business 行业、营业范围	④ liquidation procedure 清算程序
line of credit 信贷额度,信用额度,信用放款,信贷限额	⑤ liquidation sale 停业清理大拍
line of duty 公务	⑥ 卖
lineal warranty 被继承人担保人	⑦ liquidation statement 清算表
liner 班轮	⑧ liquidation tax 清算所得税
liner conference 班轮公会	⑨ liquidation team 清算组
liner negligence clause 班轮疏忽条款	⑩ liquidator 清算人
liner terms 班轮条款	⑪ liquidity 清偿力,清偿能力,偿债能力
lineup 人身辨认	⑫ 债能力
linguistic interpretation 语言解释	⑬ liquidity basis 清偿基础
linked industry 关联产品	⑭ liquidity reserve 流动公积金
linked-purchasing 连锁购买	⑮ lis pendens in the relations between jurisdiction of different states 不同国家的裁判管辖关系中的诉讼系属
lip print 口唇印痕	⑯
liquid investment 流动投资	⑰
liquidate 清偿债务,清算	⑱
liquidate a debt 偿清债务	⑲ lis sub judice(拉) 争议物
liquidated 已付清的,已清偿,已清算的	⑳ list 列举
liquidated damage of delay 误期罚款	㉑ list of candidates 候选人名单
	㉒ list of charges 主要罪状
	㉓ list of commodities 商品种类表
liquidated damage(s) 清算性损害赔偿,预定损害赔偿金,违约金	㉔ list of contraband articles 违禁商品单
	㉕
	㉖ list of delegates 代表名单
liquidated debt 已清偿的债务	㉗ list of eligible voters 选民榜
liquidated obligation 已清偿的债务	㉘ list of shareholders 股东名单
	㉙ list price 厂价,定价
liquidating value 清算价值	㉚ listed security 上市证券
liquidation 清算,清产核资,清理	㉛ listing 上市
	㉜ literal contract 成交契约
liquidation account 清算账户	㉝ literal interpretation 字面解释,文字解释
liquidation arrangement 清算安排	㉞
	㉟ literarum obligatio(拉) 书面义务
liquidation balance sheet 清算资产负债表	㊱
	㊲ literary and artistic creation 文学和艺术创造
liquidation committee 清算组	㊳
liquidation company 清算公司	㊴ Liti 半自由人
liquidation group 清算组织	㊵ litigant 好争诉的,当事人
liquidation holdings 清算债券	㊶ litigant neurosis 诉讼性神经官能症
liquidation income 清算收益	㊷
	㊸ litigant parties 诉讼双方当事人
	㊹ litigant representative of a certain number of participants 人数确定的诉讼代表人
	㊺
	㊻
	㊼ litigant representative of an uncer-

tain number of participants 人数不确定的诉讼代表人

litigant's admission 当事人承认

litigant's statement 当事人的陈述

litigants of the lawsuit 本案当事人

litigation 诉讼

litigation of administrative compensation 行政赔偿诉讼

litigation of labour dispute 劳动争议诉讼

litigation or lawsuit 仲裁和诉讼

litigious claims of partial alteration 部分变更诉讼请求

litigious expense of first instance 一审案件诉讼费用

litigious fee for new trial 重审案件诉讼费用

litigious party 案件当事人

litigious relation 诉讼关系

litigious right 诉权,诉讼权利

litigious right and obligations 诉讼权利义务

litigious right of the parties 当事人的诉讼权利

litigious rights of an individual 个人诉讼权

litis contestatio (拉) 辩护陈述阶段

litis pendentia (拉) 权利的约束

litterae credentiales(拉) 认证证书

littoral 沿海地区

lity 外国国籍

live abroad 侨居

livery of seisin (英) 占有转移

livestock farming 牧业

livestock for personal needs 自留畜

livestock trade tax 牲畜交易税

livestock trading tax 牲畜交易税

living body of a human being 人身

living conditions 生活条件

living constitution 现行宪法

living environment 居住环境

living expenses of a convict 罪犯生活费

living floor area 居住面积

living law 话的法律

living marine resources 海洋生物资源

living resources 生物资源

living resources of the high seas 公海生物资源

living space 居住面积

living standard 生活水平

living subsidies 生活补助

load a ship 装船

loading and discharging 装卸

loading and unloading 装卸

loading broker 装船代理人,装货代理

loading capacity 载重能力

loading charges 装船费,装货费用

loading days 装货天数

loading expenses 装货费用

loading hire 装货费

loading list 装船单,装货清单

loading manifest 装货清单

loading port 装船港,装运港,装货港

loading surplus 附加利益

loading warranty 装货保证

load-line 载货吃水线

loadline mark 载重线标志

loadline survey 载重线检验

loan 贷款

loan account 贷款账户

loan agreement 贷款合约,贷款协定,贷款协议

loan applicant 申请货款人,申请借款人

loan application 申请货款,贷款申请书

loan authority 贷款权力机构

loan bank 放款银行

loan capital 贷款资本,借入资本

loan ceiling 贷款总额

loan commitment 贷款承诺

loan contract 贷款合同	loan-deposit ratio 贷款与存款比率
loan creditor 贷款债权人	
loan delinquency 贷款拖欠	loan-participant 贷款参加人
loan for consumption 消费借贷	lobby 第三院,门厅
loan from foreign powers 外债	local 地方性(的)
loan funds 贷入资金	local action 当地诉讼
loan in trust 贷款信托	local administration 地方行政
loan interest rate 贷款利率	local administration budget 地方预算
loan market 借贷市场	
loan office 当铺	local administrative department 地方行政机关
loan on bills 票据抵押贷款	
loan on credit 信用贷款	local administrative law 地方行政法
loan on deed 契据抵押贷款	
loan on favourable terms 优惠贷款	local affairs 地方事务
	local allocation tax 地方分配税
loan on guarantee 保证贷款	local auditing offices 地方各级审计机关
loan on real estate 不动产抵押放款	
	local auditing organizations 地方各级审计机关
loan or personal guarantee 个人保证贷款	
	local authorities in charge 地方主管当局
loan raised on the security of the vessel 以船舶为担保的贷款	
	local authority 地方当局
loan rate 贷款利率	local autonomous government 地方自治政府
loan relationship debtor-creditor relationship 借贷关系	
	local autonomy 地方自治
loan request 贷款要求	local autonomy law 地方自治法
loan restriction 贷款限制	local bill 同城票据
loan risk 放款风险	local clearing 同城交换
loan secured by credit 以信用担保贷款,信用担保贷款,用信用担保的贷款	local court 地方法院,当地法院
	local credit 本地信用证,国内信用证
loan secured by real estate 不动产抵押放款	local criminal court 地方刑事法庭
loan secured by things 以物担保的贷款,物品担保贷款	
	local custom 地方习惯
loan shank 高利贷者	local economic construction 地方经济建设
loan societies (美) 贷款协会	
loan trust 贷款信托	local education surcharge 地方教育附加费
loan without security 无担保贷款	
	local effect 局部效应
loaning rate 贷款利率	local enterprises 当地企业
loans extended to enterprises loans to enterprises with foreign investment 外商投资贷款	local freight 局部运费
	local government 地方政府,地方自治
loans to enterprises with foreign investment 外商投资企业贷款	Local government act 地方政府规章
	local government body 地方政府机构

local income tax　地方所得税

local industry　地方工业

local law　本地法,地方法

local law theory　本地法说

local lawsuit　当地诉讼

local lawyer　本地律师

local legislation　地方立法

local legislature　地方性法规

local levy　地税

local market　本地市场

local measure　当地措施

local obligation　地方义务

local organization of state power　地方国家权力机关

local people's congress　地方人民代表大会

local people's congress of the People's Republic of China at various levels　中华人民共和国地方各级人民代表大会

local people's congresses at different levels　地方各级人大,地方各级人民代表大会

local people's court　地方人民法院

local people's courts at different levels　地方各级人民法院

local people's government　地方人民政府

local people's government of the People's Republic of China at various levels　中华人民共和国地方各级人民政府

local people's governments at different levels　地方各级人民政府,地方各级人民 法院

local people's procuratorate　地方人民检察院

local people's procuratorates at different levels　地方各级人民检察院

local People's Prosecutors' offices at different levels　地方各级人民检察院

local people's prosecutors' office　地方人民检察院

local people's, government at various levels　地方各级人民政府

local police station　当地警察派出所,派出所

local popular court　地方普通法院

local price　当地价格,地方价

local prices　国内价格

local privilege tax　地方优惠税

local product　本地产品

local property tax　地方财产税

local protection　当地保护,地方重点保护野生动物

local public security force　地方公安部队

local regulation(s)　地方性法规,地方法规,地方性规章

local remedies　当地救济,当地救济方法

local restriction　局部限制

local road tax　地方公路税

local rules and regulations valid for the whole village　乡规民约

local state organs　地方国家机构

local supervision　就地监督

local surtax　地方附加税

local surtax, additional local tax　地方附加税

local tax　地税,地方税

local taxation authorities　地税局

local tribunal（日）地方裁判所

local union　基层工会

localism　地方主义

locality of a crime　犯罪地

localization　地方化

locally administered state enterprises　地方国营企业

locally administered state-owned enterprise　地方国有企业

locally administered state-run enterprise　地方国营企业

locatio conductio（拉）雇佣

locatio conductio operarum（拉）雇佣

locatio conductio rei（拉）租赁

locatio operis faciendi（拉）定作

locatio rei（拉）财产租偿

location　场所,所在地,地段

location and position photography of a crime scene　现场方位照相

location of factory　厂址

location of the people's government　人民政府所在地

loci celebrationis（拉）合同缔结地

locked market　封锁市场

lockerroom　存物间

lockup　拘留所

locus（拉）场所

locus contractus（拉）合同地

locus criminis（拉）罪行发生地,犯罪地

locus delicti（拉）侵权行为地

locus delicti commissi（拉）侵权行为地

locus sigilli（拉）盖印处

locus standi（拉）出庭

lodge a claim　索赔

lodge a protest against a sentence/judgment or ruling　抗诉

lodge claims　提出索赔

lodger　寄宿人

lodgings　临时住所

logic　逻辑

logic in legal contexts　法律中的逻辑

logical　合乎逻辑

logical interpretation　逻辑解释,论理解释

logical reasoning　逻辑推理

logical structure of legal rule　法律规范的逻辑结构

logistic officer on reserve service　预备役后勤军官

Lombrosian theory on crimes　龙伯罗梭犯罪论

Lome convention　洛美协定

Lonbard rate　伦巴德利率

London convention　伦敦公约

London court of bankruptcy　伦敦破产法院

London court of international ar-bitration　伦敦国际仲裁院

long arm jurisdiction　长臂管辖权

long arm statute　长臂管辖法案

long credit　长期信贷

long date paper　远期票据

long-distance transport　长期运输

long-duration employment　经常性失业

long-haul traffic　长期运输

long-pending case　积案

long-range agreement　长期协议

long-range fishing　远洋捕鱼

long-range plan　长期计划

long-run dumping　长期性倾销

long-short haul clause　长短途运输条款

long-standing case　陈案

long-term　长期,长期徒刑犯

long-term annuity　长期年金

long-term bonds　长期债券

long-term borrowings　长期借贷

long-term capital　长期资本

long-term construction contracts　长期工程承包

long-term contract　长期合同

long-term credit　长期贷款,长期信贷

long-term creditor　长期债权人

long-term deposits　长期存款

long-term deprivation of freedom　长期自由刑

long-term dumping　长期性倾销

long-term forward contract　长期期货合同

long-term imprisonment　长期徒刑

long-term insurance　长期保险

long-term interest　长远利益

long-term interest free loan　长期无息贷款

long-term investments　长期投资

long-term lease　长期租约,长期租赁

long-term liabilities　长期负债

long-term loan　长期贷款

long-term prediction of crime 犯罪长期预测

long-term prisoner 长刑犯

long-term rate (of interest) 长期利率

long-term storage 长期储存

long-term trust 长期信托

loop 箕型纹

loose interpretation 任意解释

lopsided view 片面的观点

lord advocate 总检察长

lord chief justice 高等大法官 (英)

lord commissioners of justiciary (苏格兰) 高等法院法官

lord high chancellor 大法官

lord justice-general (英) 最高刑事法官

lord of the manor 采邑领主

lords temporal 世俗贵族

lordship 地主身份

lose 丧失,遗失

lose a lawsuit 败诉

lose an action 败诉

lose more than what one gains 得不偿失

lose the right 丧失权利

lose the right to limit liability 丧失限制责任的权利

lose time 延误时日

losing effect 失效

losing one's nationality 丧失国籍

losing one's nationality automatically 自动丧失国籍

losing party 败诉当事人,败诉方

loss 损失

loss and damage caused by breakage of packing 包装破损险

loss apportionment 损失分摊

loss apportionment doctrine 损失分担论

loss clause 损失条款

loss from bad debt 坏账损失

loss from suspension 停业损失

loss in income 收入损失

① loss in price 价格损失

② loss in weight 重量损失

③ loss in weight clause 重量损失条款

⑤ loss maker 亏损企业

⑥ loss of capacity to work 劳动能力丧失

⑧ loss of control at the macroscopic level 宏观失控

⑩ loss of delay 延误损失

⑪ loss of freight 运费损失

⑫ loss of goods 货物的灭失

⑬ loss of life 人身伤亡

⑭ loss of macroeconomic control 宏观失控

⑯ loss of market 市价损失

⑰ loss of ownership 所有权的丧失

⑱ loss of right 丧失权利

⑲ loss of time 时间损失

⑳ loss of weight 重量损失

㉑ loss of working time 误工

㉒ loss on bad debt 坏账损失

㉓ loss on exchange 汇兑损失

㉔ loss on fire 火灾损失

㉕ loss on foreign exchange transactions 外汇交易损失

㉗ loss rate 损失比率

㉘ loss ratio 损失率

㉙ loss sustained 所受损失

㉚ loss value 受损价值

㉛ losses 物质损失

㉜ losses caused by idling of the labour force 窝工损失

㉞ losses directly caused by 由…所致的损失

㊱ losses due to policy 政策性补贴

㊲ losses from 由…所致的损失

㊳ losses of a management nature 经营性亏损

㊵ losses on bad account, bad debts losses 呆账损失

㊷ losses on devaluatiorn 货币贬值损失

㊹ losses permitted by policy 政策性补贴

㊻ loss-incurring enterprise 亏损企业

loss-payable clause 赔偿支付条款

loss-spreading 损害分担

lost bill 遗失票据

lost certificate 遗失证券

lost check 遗失支票

lost note 遗失票据

lost or not lost clause 不论得失与否条款

lost property 遗失物

lost-and-found object 遗失物,拾得物

lost-plus contract 加费合同

lot and block system 不动产登记制

lot cargo 大批货物

lot line 地界

lot number 批号

low cost housing project 低成本住房计划

low currency dumping 低汇率倾销

low grade goods 劣质货

low level 低水平

low price policy 低物价政策

low rent house 低租金房屋

low tax rate 低税率

lower chamber 下议院,下院

lower court 低级法院,初级法院

lower house 下院,下议院

lower limit 下限

lower management 基层管理

lower price 降价

lower stage 低级阶段

lower-class people's court 下级人民法院

lowering ages of criminal offenders 犯罪低龄化

lowest price 最低价

low-hazard industrial building 低危险工业建筑物

low-income housing 低收入者的住房

low-priced sale 廉价出凭

low-productivity 低生产力的

low-rent welfare type housing system 低租金福利房体制

low-rise building 低层建筑

low-water line 低潮线

loyalty examination 忠诚调查

lucrative investment 有利投资

lucrum (拉) 收益

lucrum cessans (拉) 相得益,(法) 所失利益

lump price 包干价格

lump sum 总额

lump-sum appropriation 一次拨款

lump sum contract 总包价格合同,总价合同

lump sum payment 总付,一次总全付

lump sum price 总括价

lumpsum award 一次总付损害赔偿会

lump-sum purchase 一揽子购买

lunatic criminal 神经错乱罪犯,精神病罪犯

lus privatum (拉) 罗马私法,罗马公法

lust murder 淫乐杀人

Luxembourg declaration 卢森堡宣言

luxury duty 奢侈品关税

luxury tariff 奢侈品关税率

luxury tax 奢侈品税

luxury turnover tax 奢侈品销售税

lynch 处以私刑

lynching 使用私刑

M

Macarran act 麦卡伦法

machine 机器保养

machine attendance 机器保养

machine breakdown 机器损坏

machine building 机器制造

machine building industry 机器制造业,机器工业

machine error 机械误差

machine fault machine 机器故障

machine maintenance 机器保养

machine work 机械加工

machinery and plant 机器和厂房

machinery breakdown insurance 机器损坏保险

machinery clause 机器系数

machinery equipment 机器设备

machinery parts 机械零件

machine-building industry 机械制造工业

machining 机械加工

Macpherson V. Buick Motor Co. 麦克弗森诉别克汽车公司案

macro prediction of crime 犯罪宏观预测

macroadjustment 宏观调节

macrocontract 总合同

macrocontrol 宏观控制,宏观治理

macroeconomic control 宏观调控

macroeconomic plan 总体经济计划

macroeconomic policy 宏观经济政策

macroeconomic regulation and control 宏观经济调控

macroforecast 宏观预测

macroperformance 宏观效益

macropolicy 宏观政策

macroscopic 宏观的

macroscopic cause of crime 犯罪宏观原因

macroscopic equilibrium 宏观平衡

macroscopic readjustment and control 宏观调控

mactator (拉) 谋杀犯

madrid agreement concerning the international registration of marks 商标国际注册马德里协定

mafia 秘密犯罪组织

mafia-style crime 带黑社会性质的集团犯罪

mafia-style criminal gang 黑社会性质的犯罪集团

magistrate 地方法官,治安法官

magistrates' courts (港) 裁判署法庭

magna culpa (拉) 重大过失

mail 邮件,邮寄

mail box rule (美) 邮筒规则

mail carring charges 邮递费

mail certificate 邮件执照

mail contractor 邮递物品递送承揽人

mail day 邮件截止日

mail days 邮寄日数

mail fraud 邮件欺诈

mail handing 邮递

mail letter of credit 邮递信用证

mail matters 邮件

mail of prisoners 犯人邮汇

mail transfer 信汇

mail transfer rate (M/T rate) 信汇汇率

mail-box rule 发信主义,投邮生效规则,投邮主义

mailer 邮寄人

main administrative office 主要办事机构

main articles of contract 合同的主要条款

main body 主体

main business lines 主要营业项目

main circumstance 主要情节

main clause 主要条款

main contract 主要合同

main criminal facts 主要犯罪事实

main entrance 正门

main hall 正厅

main loin/note/money 主币

main office 主营业地

main or principal clause 总条款

main points of a case 案由

main risks of cargo insurance 货物保险主要险别

main schools of administrative jurisprudence 行政法学的主要流派

main street 大街

main technical parameter 主要技术

main terms of contract 合同主要条款

main war criminal 主要战犯

maintain 保持,维修,抚养,维持

maintain an administrative decision 维持行政决定

maintain confidentiality 保守秘密

maintain independence and keep the initiative in one's own hands 独立自主

maintain market 维持市场

maintain prices at a stable level 稳定物价

maintain public order 维护公共秩序

maintain resale price 维持再售价格

maintain secrecy 保密

maintain social stability 维持社会安定

maintain the law 维护法律

maintain the original price 维持原价

maintenance 维修,赡养,抚养,

包揽诉讼

maintenance contract 维修合同

maintenance fund 维修资金

maintenance management 维修管理

maintenance margin 维修范围

maintenance of actions 包揽诉讼

maintenance of justice 维护正义

maintenance of order 维持秩序

maintenance of peace 维持治安

maintenance of possession 继续占有

maintenance of social order 维护社会秩序

maintenance of social stability 维持社会安定

maintenance price 维持价格

major breakdown 大事故

major case 重大案件

major case of smuggling 重大走私案

major crime 恶性犯罪

major criminal 重犯

major criminal case 重大刑事案件

major criminal offender 重刑犯

major deficiency 主要缺陷

major factual circumstances remain in doubt 重大事实情节分清

major industry 主要产业

major issues of principle 大是大非

major meritorious performance (of a suspect, convict, or prisoner) 重大主动表现

major on reserve service 预备役少校

major power 大国

major premise 大前提

major proposition 大前提

major repairs 大型修葺工程

major safety accident 重大安全事故

major serious case 重大恶性案件

major suspect　重大嫌疑分子

major trend　主要趋势

majoritariarism　多数表决制

majority　成年,多数

majority ballot　多数票

majority interest　多数权益

majority leader　多党领袖

majority party　多数党

majority representation　多数代表制

majority rule　多数裁定原则,多数当选制,多数规则

majority verdict　多数裁决

majority vote　多数票,多数票决

majority voting　多数表决

make a contract with　与…订立合同

make a discount　打折扣

make a discount off a price, allow a discount off a price　折价

make a gift to another　赠与他人

make a judgement according to the law　依法判决

make a law　制定法律

make a price　定价

make a random inspection　抽查

make a ruling　作出裁决

make a spot check　抽查

make a statement of repentance　具结悔过

make a thorough investigation of　查清

make an agreement　签订协议

make an appointment　预约

make an exorbitant profit　牟取暴利

make appropriate compensation　适当赔偿,给予适当补偿

make claim　提出权利主张,索赔

make compensation for losses　赔偿损失

make compensation for the economic loss　赔偿经济损失

make delivery of the goods　提交货物

make exposure of　检举

make good　抵偿

make good a loss　弥补损失,赔偿损失,赔偿

make innovation　创新

make known　报告,表明

make loans　贷款

make necessary corrections　作必要的更正

make no commitment　不承担义务

make no discrimination　同等对待

make out in Chinese and English　以中英文书写

make overall plans and take all factors into consideration　统筹兼顾

make prompt delivery　迅速交货

make public the administration of finance　财政公开

make rational use of resources　合理利用资源

put resources to rational use　合理利用资源

make replacements and technical innovations　更新改造

make restitution　退赔,返还

make sure of fact　弄清事实

make tenders　投标

make the best of the bad business　尽力减少损失

make the investment inefficient　无效投资

make up　弥补,补偿,捏造

make up for a loss　弥补损失

make use of foreign investment　利用外资

make vindictive attacks on sb　打击报复

making a public apology　公开赔礼道歉

making compensation for equal value　等价有偿

making of international law　国际法的制定

making of law by judges　法官立法

making of plan 计划编制

making to order 定作

mala（拉） 不法的

mala fides 恶意

Mala grammatica non vitiat chartam（拉） 语法不通不影响合同效力

mala in se（拉） 本质罪恶的犯罪

mala praxis（拉） 医疗事故

maladministration 管理不善

malefaction 罪行，犯罪行为

malfeasance 违法行为，渎职，不法的行为，违反职责行为

malice 恶意

malice aforethought 谋杀罪中的恶意预谋，预谋不轨

malice in law 法律上的恶意

malicious abuse of civil proceedings 恶意滥用民事诉讼程序

malicious abuse of legal process 恶意滥用法定程序

malicious act 恶意行为

malicious arrest 非法扣押

malicious collusion 恶意串通

malicious damage 恶意损害

malicious damage clause 恶意损害条款

malicious falsehood 蓄意欺骗

malicious injury 恶意伤害

malicious killing 恶意杀害

malicious motive 恶意动机

malicious omission 蓄意遗漏

malicious prepense 预谋不轨

malignance 恶意行为

malignant act 恶意行为

malignantly 恶意行为

malo animo（拉） 不法意图

maltreat misuse 虐待

Maltreatment of children is prohibited 禁止虐待儿童

Maltreatment of old people is prohibited 禁止虐待老人

Maltreatment of women is prohibited 禁止虐待妇女

malum（拉） 不法的，错误的

malum prohibitum（拉） 法律禁止的犯罪

man 成年男子

man's natural right 天赋人权

manacles 手铐

manage 处置，经营

managed price 管制价格

management 经营

management agency on the protection of scientific and technological secrets 科技保密管理机构

management agent 经营代理商

management and administrative rights 经营管理权

management and education house of juvenile delinquents 少年犯管教所

management behavior 管理行为

management by grouping of enterprises 集团化经营

management by personal supervision 监督管理

management by various levels 分级管理

management committee 管理委员会

management committee of prison production 监狱作业委员会

management committee of prisoners' food 犯人伙食管理委员会

management committee of the people's commune 人民公社管理委员会

management consultant 经营顾问

management contract 管理合同，经营承包责任制

management contract responsibility system 经营承包责任制

management contract system 经营承包制

management control 经营管理

management council 管理委员会

management efficiency 经营管理效率

management fee lump sum contract 管理费总价合同

management function 管理职能

management game 经营的策略

management mechanism of the people's police 人民警察管理体制

management objcctive 经营目标

management of colleges and universities 普通高校管理

management of economic plans 计划管理

management of economy 经济管理

management of farm produce markets 农贸市场管理

management of fire-fighting equipment 消防设备管理

management of food hygiene 食品卫生管理

management of freight transportation 货运管理

management of grassland 草原管理

management of overseas Chinese affairs 华侨事务管理

management of power grid 电网管理

management of prisoners' living schedule 犯人作息时间管理

management of prisoners' property 犯人财物管理

management of production quota 劳动定额管理

management of public health 公共卫生管理

management of public safety 公共安全管理

management of public security 治安管理

management of science and technology 科技管理

management of state assets 国有资产管理

management of taxation 征税管理

management of the recreation industry 游乐业管理

management of tobacco monopoly commodity 烟草专卖品的经营

management of tools 工具痕迹

management of trades 行业管理

management of trust 信托管理

management of various 行业管理

management operating system/MOS 经营管理制度

management participation 参与管理

management performancc 经营管理成绩

management power 经营权

management responsibility system 经营责任制

management right 经营权

management rules of dynamites 炸药管理规定

management rules of hotels 旅游业管理规定

management rules on satellite telecommunication 卫星通信管理规定

management skills 管理技术

management system 管理制度,管理体制

management system for lawyering 律师工作管理体制

management through planning 计划管理

management through quantificatlons 计量管理

management-investment company 管理投资公司

manager 管理人员

manager (appointed by the court) (英) 财务管理人

manager agent 代管人

manager group 经理团

managerial act in the administration of railroad traffic 铁路交通行政管理行为

managerial activity 管理活动

managerial and administrative expertise 经营管理水平

managerial contract system 经理承包制

managerial control 管理监督

managerial decision-making power 经营自主权

managerial department 管理部门

managerial employees 管理人员

managerial force 经营管理人员

managerial setup 经营权构

managerial supervision 管理监督

managing board 管理委员会

mancipatio（拉）买卖式让与，拟制买卖（罗马法）

mancipium（拉）要式买卖

mandatarius（拉）受任者

mandatory 受托人，强行

mandatory application 强制适用

mandatory clause 法定条款

mandatory detention 强制扣留，强制拘留

mandatory dismantling 强制拆除

mandatory enforcement 强制执行

mandatory injunction 指令性强制令或禁止令

mandatory investigation 委托调查

mandatory law 强制性法律

mandatory order 强制命令

mandatory plan 指令性计划

mandatory provision 强制性规定，约束性条款，强制规定

mandatory redemption 定期偿还

mandatory restrictions on exports 强制出口管制

mandatory rule of law 强制性法规

mandatory rule(s) 强行法，强制性规则

mandatory rules of law 强制性法规

mandatory sanction 强制制裁

mandatory summons 强制传唤

mandatory term 强制条款，强制性条款

mandatory withholding 强制扣缴

mandatum（拉）委任合同

mandatum generale（拉）一般委任

mandatum solvendi（拉）偿付委任

mandatum speciale（拉）特定委任

manhood suffrage 男公民选举权

manhunt 搜索逃犯

mania 躁狂症

manic psychosis 狂躁性精神病

manic-depressive insanity 躁狂抑郁性精神病

manic-depressive psychosis 躁狂抑郁性精神病，躁郁症

manifest 载货单，货物清单

manifest injustice 明显不公平

manifest intent 明显意图

manifest of cargo 货物清单

manifesta probatione non indigent（拉）明显的事情无需我证据

manifestation 现象，示威

manifesto issued on assumption of office 就职宣言

manifold directions of crime 犯罪多向性

mankind 人类

manner of payment 付款方法

manor 领地

manpower 人力

manshalling of securities 抵押品的分配

mansion 大厦，大楼

manslaughter 非正常死亡

manrfacture 制造业

manufacture in a rough and slip-shod way 粗制滥造

manufacture's liability 产品责任

manufactured goods 工业制成

品,工业品

manufactured housing 预制住房

manufactured product 工业制成品,工业产品

manufacturer 制造商,制造者

manufacturer's agent 厂商代理人

manufacturer's export agent 制造商代理人

manufactures' obligation concerning product quality 生产者的产品质量义务

manufacturing and processing work 制造和加工过程

manufacturing another person's registered trademark symbol without authorization 擅自制造他人注册商标标识

manufacturing defect 制造缺陷

manufacturing district 加工区,工业区

manufacturing enterprise 生产企业

manufacturing establishment 工业公司

manufacturing industry 制造业

manufacturing inspection 制造检验

manufacturing license 制造许可证

manufacturing management 生产管理

manufacturing production 工业生产

manufacturing requirement 制造方面要求

Mao Tse-tung Thought 毛泽东思想

map out 规划

marble 大理石

march 游行

mare clausum 闭海论

mare liberum (拉) 海洋自由论

Marevan injunction 玛瑞禁制令

margin 保证金,附加利率,利息率,差额

margin of dumping 倾销差额

margin of preference 优惠幅度

margin requirement 额定保证金

margin transaction 保证金交易、信用交易

marginal case 边缘案件

marginal efficiency of investment 投资边际效率

marginal land 边角地

marginal rate of tax 边际税率

marine dumping 海洋倾倒

marine environment 海洋环境

marine extension clauses 延期条款

marine insurance 海上保险

marine pollution 海洋污染

marine pollution zone 海洋污染区

marine resources 海洋资源

marital violator 破坏、妨碍他人婚姻者

maritime arbitration 海事仲裁

maritime arbitration court 海事仲裁庭

maritime arbitration procedure 海事仲裁程序

maritime belt 领海带

maritime ceremonials 海上礼节

maritime claim 海事索赔

maritime coasting trade 海洋沿海贸易

maritime convention 海洋公约

maritime customs 海关

maritime dispute 海事纠纷

maritime domain 领海权

maritime environment 海洋环境

maritime environment pollution 海域污染

maritime flag 海上公用国旗

maritime international law 国际海洋法

maritime jurisdiction 海事司法管辖权

maritime law 海商法,海事法

maritime law committee 海洋法委员会

maritime lawsuit 海事诉讼

maritime lien 海上留置权

maritime mortgage 海事抵押权

maritime negligence 海上过失

maritime ports 海港

maritime sovereignty 海洋主权

maritime state 海洋国家

maritime supremacy 海上霸权

maritime territory 海洋领土

maritime tort 海上侵权行为

maritime transportation 海上运输

maritime waters 海洋水域

maritime(/marine)insurance 海上保险

mark down 减价

mark of manual strangulation 扼痕

mark price 标明价目

markable bonds 可售债券

markdown 降价

markdown cancellation 降价取消

marked improvement 显著进步

marked man 被监视的人

marked price 价目,标志价格

market 集市,集市贸易,市场

market a product 推销产品

market aboard 海外市场

market access 市场准入

market administration 市场管理

market analysis 市场分析

market at home 国内市场

market capacities 市场容量

market control department 市场管理部门

market demand 市场需求

market difference 市场价差

market disaster clause 市场紊乱条款,市场动乱条款

market disruption 市场扰乱

market economy 市场经济

market economy country 市场经济国家

market exchange rate 市场汇率

market fixed price 市场定价

market fluctuation 市场波动

① market for monetary funds 货币
② 资金市场
③ market information 市场信息
④ market interest rate 市场利率
⑤ market lease 市场摊位租约
⑥ market makers 市场交易人
⑦ market mechanism 市场机制
⑧ market method 按市价计价法
⑨ market movements 市价变动
⑩ market of equities 产权市场
⑪ market order(s) 市场指令,市
⑫ 场扫托,市场定购单
⑬ market orientation 市场导向
⑭ market overseas 海外市场
⑮ market permit 市场准入
⑯ market price 标价,市价,市场
⑰ 价格,市场价格,价金
⑱ market price method 按市价计
⑲ 价法
⑳ market prospective 市场前景
㉑ market prospects 市场前景
㉒ market rate 市场汇率
㉓ market readjustment 市场调节
㉔ market risk 市场风险
㉕ market sales promotion 推销
㉖ market stability 市场稳定
㉗ market supervision law 市场管
㉘ 理法
㉙ market supply and demand 市场
㉚ 供求
㉛ market system 市场制度
㉜ market town 集镇
㉝ market value 市价
㉞ marketable commodity 适销品
㉟ marketable goods 易销货物
㊱ marketable securities 有价证券
㊲ marketing 推销,营销
㊳ marketing another person's regis-
㊴ tered trademark symobl without
㊵ authority 擅自销售他人注册
㊶ 商标标识
㊷ marketing information 市场信
㊸ 息
㊹ marketing packing 销货包装
㊺ marketing research by sampling
㊻ 市场抽样调查
㊼ marketing system 市场体系

marking of fired cartridge case
弹壳发射痕迹

markup　标高价格,加价

marriage at common-law　普通
法上的婚姻

marriage broker　媒妁

marriage by capture　抢婚

marriage by cheating　骗婚

marriage in feudal law　采邑法
中的结婚

marriage upon arbitrary decision
by any third party　包办婚姻

married allowance　夫妇免税额

married women property act　已
婚女子财产法

marshal of court　法院执行官

marshal the assets　排列债权人
的顺序

Martens clauses　马尔顿斯条款

martial law　戒严法

Marxian value theory　马克思的
价值理论

Marxism　马克思主义

Marxism-Leninism　马克思列宁
主义

Marxist　马克思主义者

Marxist jurisprudence　马克思主
义法学

Marxist jurist　马克思主义法学
家

Marxist legal theory　马克思主
义法律理论

masochism　受虐狂

masonry　砖石建筑

mass control　群管制

mass group　群众团体

mass management　集体管理

mass marketing　大量销售,大规
模销售

mass media　大众媒介

mass meeting　群众集会

mass migration　大规模迁移

mass observation　大量观察,民
意调查

mass organization　群众团体,社
会团体,人民团体

mass organization as legal person

社会团体法人

mass organization of self-government　群众性自治组织

mass organization of self-management at the grass-roots level
基层群众性的组织

mass production　大量生产,大
规模生产

mass sales　大量销售

mass selling　大量销售

mass sports　群众体育

mass sports activities　群众性体
育活动

massive　大规模

massive retaliation　大规模报复

master　硕士

master contract　主合同,主契约

master of the high court　高等法
院主事官

master's degree　硕士学位

master's report of marine accident　海事报告

masters in chancery　大法官法
庭主事官

masters of the bench　法律学院
院监(英)

masterwork of modern architecture　现代建筑杰作

mastery　控制权,统治权

matching principle　配比原则

mate's receipt　大副收据

material　决定性的;实质性的,
重大的,重要的

material alteration(s)　实质性改
变

material benefits　福利

material breach　实质性违约,实
质违反

material carrier　物质载体

material circumstances　重要情
况

material circumstances of a crime
犯罪具体情节

material civilization　物质文明

material compensation　物资补
偿

material condition　物质条件

material contract　重要合同

material control　原材料控制

material damage　物质损害,严重损害,物质损害,物质损失

material date　实施日期

material deprivation syndrome　母爱剥夺综合征

material error　实质错误

material fact　合同中规定的对等给付物

material facts in the pleadings　答辩状中的重要事实

material goods　有形商品

material incentives　物质刺激,物质鼓励

material injury　重大损害,实质损害

material injury test　重大损害标准

material interest　物质利益

material interpretation　实质性解释

material law　实体法

material object　实物

material omission　重要遗漏

material prerequisite　物质条件

material purchase　原材料采购

material remains of a crime　犯罪遗留物

material representation　重要陈述

material resource(s)　物质条件,物力,物力资源,物质资源

material reward　物质鼓励,物资奖励

material sphere of treaties　条约效力范围

material stimulants　物质刺激

material stimulation　物质刺激

material stipulation　重要关系的条款,实质条款

material wealth　物质财富

materials　物力

materials for processing　加工材料

materials in the case　案卷材料

maternal grandparent　外祖父母

① maternity benefit　产妇分娩津贴

② maternity leave　产假

③ maternity pay　产假工资

④ matriarchal　母权的

⑤ matricide　杀母罪,弑母罪

⑥ matrilineal society　母系社会

⑦ matrimonial action　婚姻诉讼

⑧ matrimonial proceedings　婚姻诉讼程序

⑩ matrimonial tort　婚姻过失罪

⑪ matron　女看守,护士长

⑫ matter civil　民事事件

⑬ matter entrusted　被委托代理事项

⑮ matter in deed　有契据事项

⑯ matter of priority　优先事项

⑰ matter of record　备案事项

⑱ matter(s) of law　法律上的问题

⑲ matters of domestic jurisdiction　国内管辖事项

㉑ matured principal　到期本金

㉒ matured repayment　到期应偿付金额

㉔ maturing liability　即将到期的负债

㉖ maturity　偿还期,到期日,到期,期限

㉘ maturity date　偿还日,到期日,期满之日

㉚ maturity of period of parole　假释期满

㉜ Maurya Dynasty　孔雀王朝

㉝ maxims of equity　衡平法的格言

㉞ maximum　劳动所得最高税额,最高限额

㊱ maximum amount　最高额

㊲ maximum and minimum tariff　最高和最低税则

㊳ maximum liability　最高责任,最大责任

㊶ maximum limitation of action　最长诉讼时效

㊸ maximum occupancy　最多居住人数

㊺ maximum price　最高价格

㊻ maximum sentence　最高刑罚

㊼ maximum statutory penalty　法

定最高刑

maximum statutory sentence 法
定最高刑

mayhem 伤害人的肢体罪,重伤
罪

mayor 市长

MCorp(**Dallas**) 乐山银行(达拉
斯)

meager profit 薄利

meaningful 有意义的

means 财产

means of adducing evidence 举
证方法

means of bribery 贿赂手段

means of communications 交通
工具

means of crime 犯罪工具

means of criminal segregation 刑
事隔离手段

means of defense 防卫手段,辩
护方式

means of financing 融资手段

means of interpretation 解释方
法

means of massive reprisal 大规
模报复手段

means of mortgage 抵押方式

means of performance 履行方法

means of perpetuating testimony
证据保全的方法

means of production 生产手段,
生产资料

means of proof 证据方法

means of public administrative
行政管理手段

means of transport 运输工具

means of transportation 交通工
具

means of voting 表决方法

measure 管理措施,措施

measure of damage(s) 确定损害
赔偿金,损失赔偿估量,损失
程度

measure of indemnity 赔偿限度

measure of protection 保护措施

measure of safeguard 保障措施

measure of security 保安处分

measure of supervision 监督方
法

measure penalty 量刑

measure to protect the right 保
障权利的办法

measurement 计量,测量

measurement dimension 计量尺
寸

measurement error 计量误差

measurement of crime 犯罪测量

measures provided by law 法律
规定的措施

**measuring examination and deter-
mination organization** 计量鉴
定机构

measuring instrument 计量器具

mechanical accident 机械事故

mechanical budget 固定预算

mechanical character 机械性能

mechanical description 机械说
明

mechanical error 机械误差

mechanical injury 机械性损伤

mechanical loss 机械损失

mechanical treatment 机械加工

mechanism 机制,体制

**mechanism of mental transforma-
tion of prisoners undergoing reformation** 罪犯改造心理转化
机制

**mechanism of selection through
competition** 竞争淘汰机制

**mechanized manufacturing indus-
try** 机器工业

medal of honor 荣誉勋章

meddle 干预

mediate an issue 调解纠纷

mediate between 从中调解

mediate evidence 第二手证据,
间接证据

mediate possession 委托占有

mediation 调解,调停,调解人,
调停国

mediation by the court 法院调
解

mediation committee 居民调解
委员会

mediation documents 调解书

mediation in civil litigation 民事调解

mediation out of court 法庭外调解

medical aircraft 医务航空器

medical and sanitary management for prisoners 犯人医疗卫生管理

medical certificate 医疗证

medical convenience card 就诊方便卡

medical evidence 医学证据

medical examiner 验尸官

medical examiner's death certificate 法医死亡证明书

medical expenses 医疗费用

medical expert testimony 医疗鉴定,医学鉴定

medical expertise 医疗鉴定,医学鉴定

medical jurisprudence 医学法理学

medical malpractice 医疗事故

medical negligence 医疗事故

medical personnel 医疗人员,医务人员

medical practitioner 开业医生

medical prison 医疗监狱

medical rules 医疗规章

medical ship 医疗船

medical unit 医疗单位

medical witness 医学证人

medicare prison 医疗监狱

medicine 药

medicolegal appraisal of documents 法医文证审查

medicolegal autopsy 法医尸体解剖

medicolegal examination of the living 法医学活体检查

medicolegal expertise 法医鉴定

medicolegal investigation of crime scene 法医现场勘查

medieval 中世纪

medieval European law 欧洲中世纪法律

mediu/medium of circulat, medium of circulatan 中期计划

medium enterprise 中型企业

medium grade 中级

medium quality 中等品质

medium-grade professional title 中级职称

medium-leveled professional and technical position 中级专业技术职务

meet 满足

meet a need 满足需要

meet engagements 还债

meet one's engagement(s) 偿清债务,履行约定

meet the need(s) 满足需要,适应需要

meet the needs of the people's everyday life 满足人民的生活需要

meet the requirement 满足需要

meet the specifications 合规格

meet the time limit of 逾期

meeting 会议,集会

meeting and sending abducted women and children 接送被拐卖妇女、儿童行为

meeting for the placement of orders 订货会

meeting in camera 秘密会议

meeting of directors 董事会议

melt down 变卖财产

member 成员,会员

member of a committee 委员

member of a delegation 代表团成员

member of a legislature assembly 议员

member of congress 众议员

member of parliament 下议院议员

member of standing committee 常委

member of the chamber of deputies 众议员

member of the Chinese people's political consultative conference

全国政协委员

member of the house of representative 众议员

member of the mission 代表团成员

member of the party committee 党委委员

member of the people's mediation committee 人民调解委员

member of the political bureau 政治局委员

member of the prosecutorial committee 检察委员会委员

member of the standing committee of the political bureau 政治局常委

member states of the federal state 联邦成员国

members of the diplomatic staff 外交职员

members of the mission 使馆人员

members of the United Nations 联合国会员国

membership function 隶属关系

memoradum of appearance 出庭通知

memorandum clause 附注条款

memorandum in uniting 合同书,书面契据

memorandum of understanding 谅解备忘录

memorandum sale 试销

memorial 地契摘要,请愿书

memory ability of witness 证人的记忆能力

memory factors of negligent offender 过失犯罪者的记忆因素

mend one's way 改过自新

mental basis of reforming convicts 罪犯改造的心理依据

mental characteristics of convicts 罪犯心理特征

mental deficiency 精神不健全,智力缺陷

mental disorder 精神障碍,精神错乱

mental factors influencing reformation of prisoners 影响罪犯改造的心理因素

mental health 精神健康状况

mental health conditions 精神健康状况

mental plasticity of a convict 罪犯心理的可塑性

mental tests 精神测验

mental transformation of a criminal 罪犯心理转化

mentality in sexual motive 性犯罪心理

mentality of sexual reverse 性逆变心理

mentally defective person 智力有缺陷的人

mentally ill person 精神病人

mentor 教师

mercenary 雇佣

mercenary marriage 买卖婚姻

merchandise 货物,商品

merchandise marks 商品标记

merchandise on hand 现货

merchandise policy 商品政策

merchandise resource 货源

merchandise valuation 商品估价

merchandising business 商业企业

merchant 商贩

merchant rate 商人汇率

merchant shipper 托运人

merchant shipping act 商船法

merchantability 适销性,商销性

merchantable quality 适合商销品质,商销品质,可销售的质量,可销售品质

merchantable things 融通物,不限制流通的物

merchantile contract 商业合同

mercantile law 商法

mercilessly punish 严惩不贷

mercy killing 安乐死,安死术

mere equity 单纯分单权利

merge 兼并,合并

mergence of compound objects of

litigation　并列诉讼客体合并

merger clause　合并条款

merger of obligee and obligor　债权人与债务人混同

merger of states　国家的合并

merit system of the civil service　文官的考绩制度

meritorious consideration　有价值的约因

mess　大锅饭

messages on the epidemic situation of infectious diseases　传染病疫情通报

messages tax　电信税

messenger-at-arms　高等法院执行官

metaphysics　形而上学

mete out unjustified fines　乱罚款

method impossibility　手段不能犯

method of adjustment　调整方法

method of administrative law　行政法方法

method of comparative analysis　比较分析法

method of converting currencies　货币折合办法

method of crime prediction　犯罪预测方法

method of deduction　扣除法

method of determining testimony reliability　判断证言可靠性的方法

method of discount　利息先付法,贴现法

method of doing business　营业方法

method of exemption　免税法

method of intersecting circles　交圆法

method of jurisprudence　法学方法

method of operation　经营方法

method of performance　履行方式

method of reimbursement　索偿办法

method of residues　剩余法

method of thinking　思想方法

method of voting　表决方法

methodology　方法论

methodology of jurisprudence　法学方法论

methods of bearing civil liability　承担民事责任的方式

methods of investigation　侦查方法

methods of the study of economic law　研究经济法的方法

metrological administrative department　计量行政部门

metrological administrative department of the State Council (中)　国务院计量行政部门

metrological appliance　计量器具

metrological certification　计量认证

metrological legislation　计量法规

metrological regulation　计量规章

metrological service　计量部门

metrological supervision　计量监督

metrological supervision and administration　计量监督管理

metrological supervisor　计量监督员

metrological verification　计量检定

metrological verification organ　计量检定机构

metrology　计量

metropolitan board of works (英)　大都市工作委员会

metropolitan territory　本国领土

micro prediction of crime　犯罪微观预测

microcontrol　微观治理

middle and small industrialists and merchants　中小工商业者

middle delimination　中间划界

middle price 中间价

middle rank 中级

middle rate 中间汇率

mid-term election 中期选举

mid-term prediction of crime 犯罪中期预测

might 强权,能力

Might is right 强权即公理

migrate 迁徙

migration 迁户口,迁居

military adjudicatory committee 军事审判委员会

military administrative action 军事行政诉讼

military age 兵役年龄

military attache 武官

military attorney 军队律师

military blockade 军事封锁

military crime 军事犯罪

military criminal law 军事刑法

military criminal litigation 军事刑事诉讼

military establishment 部队编制

military judge 军事审判员

military law 军法

military laws of the United States (MLUS) 美国军事法规

military laws of the United States annotated 美国注释军事法规

military lawyer 军队律师

military leadership 兵权

military malfeasance 违犯军法的行为

military observers of the United Nations 联合国军事观察员

military offense 触犯军法罪

military penal law 军事刑法

military personnel in active service 现役军人

military power 兵权

military prosecutor 军事公诉人

military ranks for officers on reserve service 预备役军官军衔

military service law 兵役法

military service register 兵役登记

military tenure 军役领地

militia 民兵,民兵组织

mill's certificate 工厂证明书

mind of habitual criminal 惯犯心理

mind of negligent offense 过失犯罪心理

mind of preparation for a crime 犯罪预备心理

mind of the accused for first offense 初犯被告人心理

mind of the professional criminal 职业犯罪心理

mine 矿藏

mine accident 矿山事故

mine safety supervision 矿山安全监督

miner and collieries act (英) 矿工与矿山法

mineral 矿藏

mineral exploration 矿产资源的勘查,矿藏勘探

mineral exploration result 矿产资源勘查成果

mineral properties 矿业权

mineral prospection 矿藏勘探

mineral resources 矿物资源,矿藏资源

mineral resources conservation 矿产资源保护

mineral right 开采权

mine-shaft safety 矿井安全

minimum amount 最低额

minimum cash balance for checking account 支票户最低存款

minimum floor area requirement 最小的楼板面积要求

minimum freight 最低运费

minimum housing standard 最低住房标准

minimum international standard treatment 最低国际标准待遇

minimum lethal dose 最小致死量

minimum obligation 最低限度义务

minimum of hearing 低度听审

minimum price 最低限价,最低价

minimum quantity 最低数量

minimum reserve requirement 最低准备金要求

minimum statutory penalty 法定最低刑

minimum statutory sentence 法定最低刑

minimum term 最低期限

minimum term limit of statutory sentence 法定刑的最低期

minimum value 最低限价

mining industry act (英) 矿业法

mining license 采矿许可证

mining resource management system 矿产资源管理制度

mining rights 采矿权

mining tax (英) 采矿税

minister 部长,公使,大臣

minister plenipotentiary and envoy extraordinary 特命全权公使

minister prosecuting system 大臣追诉制度

minister responsibility system 部长负责制

minister without portfolio 不管部部长

ministerial act 行政行为

ministerial responsibility 大臣责任制(英)

ministers in charge of commissions 各委员会主任

ministers in charge of ministries 各部部长

ministries and commissions 部委

ministry of defense 国防部

ministry of metallurgical industry (中) 冶金工业部

ministry of posts and telecommunications (中) 邮电部

ministry of supervision 监察部

ministry of water conservation (中) 水利部

minor criminal case 轻微刑事案件

minor criminal offender 轻刑犯

minor offender 轻罪犯

minor wound 轻伤

minority leader 少数党领袖

minority nationality 少数民族

minority partners 少数合伙人

minority right 少数者权利

mint of exchange 法定平价

mint par 铸币平价

mint price 法定价

Miranda hearing 米兰达检验

misadventure 意外事故

misapplication of law 法律的误用

misappropriate 滥用

misappropriate public articles peculate public articles 挪用公物

misappropriation 营私

miscalculate 误算

miscalculation 误算

miscarriage of justice 审判不当

miscellaneous 各种

miscellaneous provisions 其他规定

miscellaneous tax 杂税

mischarge 错定罪名

mischief 不明确的文字

mischief of statute 条文晦涩

mischief rule 缺陷规则

misconduct 过错

misconstruction 误解

misconstrue 误解,曲解

misfeasance 过失,不适当履行

misfeed 误传

misinterpret the meaning of a passage 曲解一段文章的含义

misjoiner 错误共同诉讼人,错误的合并

misjoiner of causes 不同诉案的错误合并

misjudge 判断错误

misjudged case 错案

misjudgment 判决失当

mismanage 处置不当

mismanagement 管理失当

misplaced confidence 误信

mispleading 不当的辩护

mispresent 错误陈述

misprision of felony 藏匿重罪犯的罪行

misreport 隐匿谎报销毁会计资料

misrepresent facts 曲解事实

mlsrepresentation 误述,错误表示,错误说明,错误陈述,虚伪陈述

misrepresentation act 1967（英）误述法

misrepresentation of law 曲解法律

missed working time 误工

missend 误发

missing 下落不明

missing cargo 下落不明货物

missing person 失踪人

missing term 失踪期间

missing-person status 失踪人身份

mission 使馆,代表团

missionary salesman 推销员

missionary system 代表团制

misstate 错误陈述

mistake 误认,错误

mistake as to the victim 受害者错误

mistake in judgment 判断错误

mistake of fact 事实错误

mistake offender 错误犯

mistaken belief 误信

mistaken detention 错羁

mistaken recognition 误认

mistreat 滥用

misunderstanding 误解

misuse 滥用

mis-shipped cargo 误装货物

mis-statement 错误陈述

mitigate a punishment 减轻处罚

mitigated injury 轻度伤害

mitigated offense 减轻犯

mitigated offense by circumstances 情节减轻犯

mitigating constitution of crime 减轻犯罪构成

mitigation of penalty below the minimum statutory prescript 减轻处罚

mitigation of punishment 减轻刑罚

mitigation of the original sentence 减轻原判刑罚

mittimus 案犯监押令,羁押令,徒刑执行令,收监令

mix in the inferion or fake 掺杂使假

mixed action 混合式诉讼

mixed agent 兼营代理

mixed arbitration 混合仲裁

mixed baseline 混合基线

mixed constitution of crime 混合犯罪构成

mixed duties 复合关税

mixed government 混合政府

mixed jurisdiction 混合管辖

mixed larceny 混合盗窃罪

mixed or compound duties 混合税

mixed or compound duty 混合税

mixed proceedings 混合式讼诉程序,混合诉讼

mixed system 混合制

mixed tribunal 混合法庭

mob law 暴民法

mobile residence 移动住房

mobilization 动员

mobilization order 动员令

mobilize 动员

mobilize the initiative of all groups 调动各方面积极性

mobocracy 暴民政治

mock auction 假拍卖

modal survey 典型调查

mode for the review of institutionality 违宪审查的方式

mode law on international commercial arbitration 国际商事仲裁示范法

mode of business operation 经营方式

mode of guaranty 保证方式

mode of living　生活方式
mode of payment　付款方法
mode of proof　证明方式
mode of transport　运输方式
model agreement　示范协定
model code　示范法典
model contract　合同范本,示范合同,标准合同
model law　示范法律
model law for developing countries on invention（Patent）发展中国家专利示范法
model law for developing countries on registration of contracts on transfer of technology　技术转让合同管理示范法
model of build-operate-transfer contract/BOT　建设—经营—移交发包模式
model of commencement　起诉方式
model of competitive contract　竞争性发包模式
model of the economy　经济模式
model regulations　示范规章
model statute　示范法规
model text of each kind of contract　合同示范文本
model unit　样板单元
models of recognition　承认的方式
moderate quantity　中等数量
moderator　议长
modern administrative law　现代行政法
modern architecture style　现代建筑式样
modern barter trade　现代易货贸易
modern building　现代建筑
modern constitution　现代宪法,近代宪法
modern information technology　现代信息技术
modern international law　近代国际法
modernization　现代化,维新

modernization of legal system　法制现代化
modernize　现代化
modes and procedures of quota allocation　配额的分配方式和办法
modes of administrative act　行政行为的模式
modes of international liability　国际法律责任的承担方式
modes of payment　支付方式
modes of recognitions　承认的方式
Modestinus　莫迪斯蒂努斯
modification and assignment of contracts　合同的变更和转让
modification of contracts　合同的修改,变更
modification to treaty　条约的修改
modified uniform system of liability　修正的统一责任制
modify　变更,改变,修改
modify administrative decisions　变更行政决定
modify contents licensed　变更许可内容
modify one's registration　变更登记
Mohammedan　穆罕默德
Mohammedan law　穆罕默德法
Mohism　墨家学说
Mohist school　墨家（中）
monarch　君主,国君,帝王
monarch sovereign　君主
monarchical　国君
monarchical parliamentary system　议会君主制
monarchical power　君权,王权
monarchical sovereignty　君主主权
monarchy　帝制,君主政体,君主制度,君立制
monetary　货币
monetary action　金融措施
monetary and securities market　金融证券市场

monetary assets 金融资产

monetary authorities 金融主管当局

monetary clause 货币条款

monetary compensation clause 货币补偿条款

monetary compensatory amount/MCA 货币补偿金额

monetary correction 价格修正

monetary crisis 金融危机

monetary facilities 金融机构

monetary funds market 货币资金市场

monetary inflation 通货膨胀

monetary integration 货币一体化

monetary interests 金钱上的利益

monetary law 货币法

monetary limit of liability 责任的金额限制

monetary market 金融市场

monetary market rate 金融市场利率

monetary obligation 金钱债务

monetary penalty 罚款处分

monetary policy 货币政策

monetary reform 币制改革

monetary sovereignty 货币自主权

monetary standard 货币本位

monetary system 金融制度,货币制度

monetary term 以货币值表示的期限

monetization of debt 国债货币化

money bill 金融法案,财政法案

money consideration 金钱对价

money corporation 金融机构

money damages 金钱赔偿

money desk 金融市场

money loan 货币放款

money manager 货币经营

money marker deposit account 货币市场存款账户

money market 金融市场

money of account 记账货币

money order 汇票

money rate 金融利率

money rent 货币地租

money stock 金融股票

money supply 货币供给,货币供应量,货币发行量

money trust 金钱信托,资金信托

money worship and crime 拜金主义与犯罪

money-back 退款

monism 一元论

monism of punishment and security measures 刑罚与保安处分一元论

monitoring for food hygiene 食品卫生监测

monitoring of environment 环境监测

monitoring of infections diseases 传染病监测

monitoring system 监测系统

monocracy 独裁政治

monoculture 单一经营

monopolize lawsuits 包揽诉讼

monopoly 独占权,专利权

monopoly contract 独立承包合同

monopoly in foreign trade 外贸垄断,对外贸易垄断

monopoly price 独占价格,垄断价格

monopoly profits 垄断利润

monopsony 买方独家垄断

monstrous crime 弥天大罪,暴行

monthly instalments 按月摊付的款项

moot 进行辩论

moot court 观摩庭

mora creditoris(拉) 债权者的迟延

mora debitoris(拉) 债务者的迟延

mora restituendi(拉) 返还的迟延

moral　道德上的

moral action　道德诉讼

moral basic of legal obligation　法律责任的道义基础

moral code　道德原则

moral consideration　道德上的对价,无物质价值之报偿

moral culture　德育

moral damage　精神损害赔偿

moral duty　道德义务

moral education　道德教育,德育

moral evidence　道德证据

moral fraud　有意欺诈,实际诈欺,事实上诈欺

moral insanity　悖德狂,道德狂乱症

moral law　道德法律,道德法则

moral mania criminal　悖德狂犯罪人

moral obligation　道德义务,道义上的责任

moral principle　道德原则

moral reparation　精神赔偿

moral rights　精神权利

morality　道德

morality and justice　道义

morals　道德

moratorial　延期偿付

moratorium　暂停期,延缓履行权,延缓履行,延期偿付权

moratorium contingency　延期偿付风险

moratory　延期偿付

morbid personality　病态人格,变态人格

morbid psychology　病态心理

more controls to power　加强权力控制

more or less clause　超过或不足条款

more pay for more work　多劳多得

more than half　半数以上

morganatic marriage　贵贱通婚

moribund　垂死

morphine addiction　吗啡瘾

morphinism　吗啡瘾

mortgage　抵押,抵押契据,抵押权,质权,抵契

mortgage action　抵押权诉讼

mortgage agreement　抵押协议

mortgage banking　银行抵押业务

mortgage bond　抵押公司债券

mortgage clause　抵押条款

mortgage condition　抵押条件

mortgage contract　抵押合同,质权合同

mortgage debt　抵押负债

mortgage deeds　抵押契据,质权契据

mortgage for record　制作抵押记录

mortgage instrument　质权证书

mortgage liability　抵押负债

mortgage loan　抵押合同,抵押借款,抵押放款

mortgage of chose in action（美、英）可依法占有而实际占有的动产抵押

mortgage of land use right　土地使用权抵押

mortgage of ship　船舶抵押权

mortgage registry tax　抵押登记税

mortgage rights　抵押权

mortgage term　抵押期

mortgage terms　抵押条款

mortgaged contract with risks　风险抵押承包

mortgaged property　抵押财产

mortgagee　承受抵押人,抵押权人,质权人

mortgagee following next　次抵押权人,次债权人

mortgagee of the ship　船舶抵押权人

mortgagee's rights　受抵押人权利

mortgagor　抵押人

mortgagor's rights　抵押人权利,出债人权利

mortuary　验尸所,殡仪馆

Moslem 穆斯林

most-favoured-nation 最惠国

most-favoured-nation clause 最惠国条款

most-favoured-nation treatment 最惠国待遇

most-nation-treatment 最惠国待遇

mot motive of witness de motive of witness de 证人否定前证的动机

mother company 母公司

mother right 母权

mother tongue 本民族语言

motherland 祖国

motion 议会动议,提案,动议

motion (of defense) 被告的请求

motion for a ruling 请求裁决

motion for amendment 修改动议

motion for debate 请求辩论动议

motion for quashing a case 撤销案件动议

motion in error 提请复审

motion of deputies 委员提案

motion of non-confidence 不信任案

motion of urgent necessity 紧急动议

motions examination committee 提案审查委员会

motions sponsor 提案人

motivation psychology 动机心理学

motive force 推动力

motive of a prisoner undergoing reformation 罪犯改造动机

motive of witness refusing to testify 证人拒绝作证动机

motor vehicle tonnage tax 汽车吨位税

mount the scaffold 被处绞刑

mount the guillotine 上断头台

mountain for personal needs 自留山

mountains 山岭

mouthpiece 代言人

movable mortgage loan 动产抵押放款

movable property 动产

movable property tax 动产税

movable trust 动产信托

movables 动产

move 提议

movement 迁户口,迁居

movement of personnel 自然人流动

moving state track 动态痕迹

moving tool mark 动态工具痕迹

MT B/L 多式联运提单

mulct 罚金刑

mulification on impairment of interest 利益的丧失成损害

multieconomic operation 多国经济合作

multifactory enterprise 多厂企业

multilateral agreement 多边协议

multilateral agreement on investment(注:简写为 MAI) 多边投资协议(注:经合组织 成员国制订)

multilateral clearing 多边清算

multilateral commitment 多边承诺

multilateral consultations 多边协商

multilateral contracts 多边合同

multilateral force 多边力量

multilateral guarantee 多边保证

multilateral investment guarantee agency 多边投资担保机构

multilateral investment treaty 多边投资协定

multilateral trade negotiation 多边贸易谈判

multilateral treaty 多边条约

multilevel policy decision 多层决策

multimember district system 多数选区制

multimodal transport operator 多式联运经营人

multinational area 民族杂居区

multinational company 多国公司

multinational country 多民族国家

multinational economic organization 多国经济组织

multinational enterprise, transnational 跨国企业

multinational enterprises 多国企业

multinational firm 多国企业

multinational river 多国河流

multiparties international legal act 多方国际法律行为

multiparty election 多党选举

multiparty system 多党制

multiple degrees of freedom 多自由度

multiple economic sectors 多种经济成分

multiple election 多级选举

multiple exchange rate 复式汇率

multiple forms of ownership 多种所有制形式

multiple insurance 重复保险

multiple leading 多头领导

multiple management 多头管理

multiple patterns of management 多种经营形式

multiple-business monopoly corporation 综合性垄断公司

multiple-factor theory of crime 犯罪多因素论

multiple-schedule tariff 复式税率

multiplicity of an action 缠讼

multiplicity of economic sectors 多种经济成分

multiplicity of legal proceedings 繁多的法律程序

multipurpose economic undertakings 综合经营

multiquota constituency system 大选区制

multiracial election 多种族选举

multisectoral operation 跨行业经营

multivalued decision 多种价值性决策

municipal administration 市政管理

municipal bond 地方债券

municipal courts 国内法院

municipal district 市辖区

municipal law 国内法

municipal legislation 国内立法

municipal people's court 市人民法院

municipal people's government 市人民政府

municipal people's procuratorates' office 市人民检察院

municipality 自治城市,市

municipality directly controlled by a provincial government 省辖市

municipality directly under the central authority 直辖市

muniments 土地所有权证明文件,档案

munitions industry 军火工业

munitions of war act（英） 军需法

mural fair price 集市交易价格

murder 秘密杀人罪,凶杀罪

murder case 凶杀案

murder during a robbery 抢劫杀人

murder of the first degree 一等谋杀罪

murder suspect 凶杀嫌疑犯,谋杀嫌疑犯

murderer 谋杀犯,杀人犯

murderess 女谋杀犯

murdrum（拉） 秘密杀人罪

museum 博物馆

Mushgannu 穆什钦努

muster 货样

mutability 易变性

muteness system 沉默制

mutilation 变造

mutual agency 相互代理

mutual agreement 相互协议,双方协议,共同协议

mutual and equitable benefit 平等互利

mutual assistance 互助

mutual benefit 互利,相互利益

mutual concealment 互相包庇

mutual confidence 相互信任

mutual consent 相互同意,双方同意,协议

mutual contradiction 相互抵触

mutual covenants 共同契约,互相赔偿损失的协约

mutual efforts 双方努力

mutual fund 共同基金

mutual guarantee treaty 互相保证条约

mutual indemnification 相互补偿

mutual interest 相互利益,双方利益

mutual mistake 相互误解

mutual mutual non-aggression treaty 互不侵犯条约

mutual noninterference 互不干涉

mutual non-aggression 互不侵犯

mutual pension trust 互助养老信托

mutual promise 相互约定

mutual recognition 相互承认

mutual relations 相互关系

mutual respect for sovereignty 互相尊重主权

mutual respect of sovereignty and territorial integrity 互相尊重主权和领土完整

mutual security act（MSA） 美国共同安全法

mutual supervision 互相监督

mutual termination 相互终止

mutual transformation 互相转化

mutuality of assent 双方同意

mutuality of contract 契约上的相互关系

mutually agree 双方同意

mutually conditional 互为条件

mutuum（拉） 无偿经费借贷,用物品还债契约

My Lord 法官阁下

N

n doubtful cases 疑则不罚

nail down 确定合同等

naked agreement 无偿合约,无偿合同

naked bailment 无偿寄存

naked contract 无保证合同,无担保合同,无担保契约,无偿契约,无偿合同

naked possession 无担保占有

naked transfer of technology 无偿技术转让

naked trust 无偿信托,无担保信托

name and symbol of the national legal unit of measurement 国家法定计量单位的名约符号

name of commodity 商品名称条款

name of judicial person 法人名称

name of (the) punishment 刑名

name of treaty 条约的名义

named consignee 指定收货人,指名收货人

named departure point 指定发货地点,指定启运地点

named person 记名人

named place of destination 指定目的地

named port of shipment 指定装运港

named principal 指名授权人

nameless 无合法名义的

nameless dead registration 无名尸体登记

nant and senior captain 预备役尉官

narcissistic personality disorder 自我恋型人格障碍

narcoanalysis 麻醉分析讯问法

narcomanic 麻醉剂犯

narcotic drug 麻醉品

narcotics 毒品,麻醉品

narcotics control 麻醉品管制

narcotism 麻醉药物依赖

narrative constitution of a crime 叙明犯罪构成

narrative facts about a crime 叙明罪状

narrow definition 狭义解释

narrow interpretation 狭义解释

narrow margin 薄利

narrow market 呆滞市场

narrow outlet 稍有销路

narrow rigid way of thinking 本本主义

narrowing of spread 缩小差幅

nation 民族

nation heritage 民族遗产

nation's economic budget 国家经济预算

national 国民

national affairs 国家事务

national anthem 国歌

national anthem of the People's Republic of China 中华人民共和国国歌

national appropriation 国家占有

national architecture 民族建筑

national armed forces 国家武装力量

national assembly 国民大会

national assets 国有资产

national assimilation 民族同化

National Assistance Board (美)国家济贫局

national autonomous area(s) 民族自治地方,民族自治区

national autonomous region 民族自治区

national autonomy 民族自治,民族自治权

national awareness 民族意识

national bourgeoisie 民族资产阶级

national budget 国家预算

national bureau of economic research（美）国民经济调查局

national capital 民族资本,国都

national capital market 国内资本市场

national capitalist 民族资本家

national cargo bureau/NCB（美）国家货物局

national center for air pollution control/NCAPC（美）全国大气污染控制中心

national committee 民族委员会

national committee of the Chinese People's Political Consultative Conference 中央人民政治协商会议全国委员会

national company 国营公司

national conditions 国情

national conservation bureau（英）国家资源保护局

national conservation commission（美）自然资源调查委员会

national convention on maritime search and rescue, 1979 国际海上搜寻救助公约(1979)

national corporation 国营公司

national courts 国内法院

national customs 民族风俗

national customs territory 国家海关辖区

national day of the People's Republic of China 中华人民共和国国庆节

national debt 国家债务

national debt management 国债管理

national defence capability 国防力量

national development plan 国家发展计划

national dignity 民族尊严

national discord 民族纠纷

national economic plan 国民经济计划

national economic planning 国民经济规划

national economic recovery period 国民经济恢复时期

national economy 国民经济

national emblem 国徽

national emblem of the People's Republic of China 中华人民共和国国徽

national enterprise 国营企业

national environmental policy act（美）国家环境政策法

national equality 民族平等

national flag of the People's Republic of China 中华人民共和国国旗

national good quality product mark 国家优质产品标志

national good quality products 国家优质产品

national goods 本国产品

national habits 民族习惯,民族风俗

national honour 民族尊严

national hunt rules 全国狩猎法规（英）

national hygiene standard for drinking-water 国家饮用水卫生标准

national income 国民收入

national independence 国家独立

national independent state 民族独立

national industrial recovery act（美）国家工业振兴法

national industrial relations court 全国工业关系法院（英）

national industry 民族工业

national investment company 国家投资公司

national judge 当事国法官,本国法官

national labor relation's act（Wagner Act）全国劳工关系法（华格纳法）

national legal unit of measurement 国家法定计量单位

national legislation 国内立法,国家立法

national legislative council 全国立法委员会（美）

national liberation 民族解放

national liberation movement 民族解放运动

national liberation organization 民族解放组织

national liberation war 民族解放战争

national market 全国市场

national metrological verification regulations 国家计量检定规程

national metrological verification system 国家计量检定系统

national metrology bureau 国家计量局

national minority 少数民族

national ocean space 国家海洋空间

national ownership 国家所有制

national personality 国家人格，民族性格

national policy 国策，国家政策

national prize court 国内捕获法院

national protection 本国保护

national quota 国家配额

national relation 民族关系

national religion 国教

national residing abroad 侨民

national resource industries 国家资源产业

national river 国内河流，国有系统

national scum 民族败类

national secessionism 民族分裂主义

national security 国家安全

national security act 国家安全法

national self-determination 民族自决

national sentiment 民族感情

national solidarity 民族团结

national sovereignty 国家主权，国家主权，民族主义

national state 民族国家

national state assets administration bureau 国家国家资产管理局

national statistical investigation 国家统一调查

national strength 国力

national system of unit of measurement 国家计量单位制度

national tariff 法定税率

national tax 国税

national territory 国境

national township 民族乡

national traffic and motor vehicle safety act 交通及汽车安全法

national treatment 国民待遇，国民待遇原则，国民待遇条款

national united front 民族统一战线

national unity 民族团结，国家统一

national value 国民价值

national way(s) 民族习惯民族风俗

nationalism 民族主义，民权主义

nationalities affairs 民族事务

nationality 民族，国籍

nationality areas 民族聚居地

nationality by birth 出生国籍

nationality by domicile 依居住地取得的国籍

nationality by parenthood 依父母取得的国籍

nationality certificate of ship 船舶国籍证书

nationality continueness 国籍继续原则

nationality decrees in Tunis and Morocco case 突尼斯摩洛哥国籍法令案

nationality law 国籍法

nationality law of China 中国国籍法

nationality of aircraft 航空器的国籍

nationality of origin 原国籍

nationalization 国有化，民族化，

收归国有

nationalization act（英） 国有民法

nationalization decree 国有化法令

nationalization of banks 银行国有化

nationalization of enterprise 企业国有化

nationalization of land 土地国有,土地国有化

nationalize 收归国有

nationalized citizen 已归化公民

nationalized industry 国有化工业

nationalized land 公有土地

nationalizing state 国有化国家

nationals of both parties 双方公民

national-born citizen 本国出生的公民

nationhood 民族主义

native court 本地法院

native industry 本地工业,地方工业

native land 祖国

native language 本民族语言

native product 本地产品

native spoken and written language 本民族语言文字

native subject 本国人民

natural accretion 自然添附

natural body 自然人

natural calamities 自然灾害

natural causes 自然原因

natural crime 自然犯

natural death 自然的死亡,生理死亡

natural destruction 自然毁损

natural disaster 自然灾害

natural environment 自然环境

natural fruits 天然孳息

natural guardian 自然的监视人,自然监护人

natural heritage 自然遗产

natural heritage protection 自然遗产保护

natural interpretation 当然解释

natural joint offense 当然从犯

natural jurisprudence 自然法学

natural justice 自然公正

natural law 自然法规,自然规律

natural liberty 天赋自由权

natural life 自然的生命

natural loss 途耗,自然损耗

natural loss or normal loss 途耗或自然损耗

natural man 自然人

natural monopoly 自然垄断

natural obligation 自然债务

natural occuring articles 天然存在物

natural person 自然人（注:在我国也可译为 citizen）

natural phenomena 自然现象

natural possession 自然占有

natural protection zone（中） 自然保护区

natural reserves 自然保护区

natural resources 资源,自然资源

natural resources law 自然资源法

natural resources protection 自然资源保护

natural rights 天赋权利

naturalia negotii（拉） 一般要件

naturalis possessio（拉） 自然占有人

naturalists 自然法学派

naturalization 入籍,归化

naturalization act 入籍法

naturalization person 入籍者

naturalization proceedings 入籍程序

naturalization right 入籍权

naturalize 归化

naturalized national 归化国民

natural-born by birth 本生国民

natural-born subject 生来籍民

nature of business 营业性质

nature of constitution 宪法本质

nature of criminal law 刑法本质

nature of danger 危险性质

nature of law 法律的性质

nature of tort 侵权行为的性质

nature preservation zone 自然保护区

nature resources administration law 自然资源管理法

naval blockade 海上封锁

naval bombardment 海军轰击

navigable river 通航河流

navigable waterway 通航水道

navigation 航行

navigation accidents (/casualty) 航行事故

navigation of submarine 潜艇航行

navigation right 航运权

near delivery 近期交货

near relatives 近亲属

near-term target 近期目标

necessary conditions 必需文件

necessarily prudent attitude 应有的谨慎态度

necessary and proper clause 必要和适当条款

necessary and reasonable measures 必要的合理措施

necessary colitigation 必要共同诉讼

necessary damages 必要的损失赔偿

necessary formality 必要手续，必要程序

necessary living expenses 必要的生活费

necessary parties 必要当事人

necessary portion 必要金额

necessary probation 必要缓刑

necessary repair 必要补偿

necessary share 必要金额

necessitas（拉） 不可避免的原因

necessity 必要性

necessity in defense 防卫必要

necessity outside law 超法规紧急避险

necessity, inevitability 必然性

necrophilia 恋尸癖，奸尸

negate 否定

negation 否定

negative 否定,净欠,抵消

negative act 不行为,不作为,相反行为

negative assurance clause in an auditor's report 审计报告中的消极保证条款

negative conflict of jurisdiction over administrative action 行政诉讼管辖消极冲突

negative crime 不作为犯

negative duty 消极义务

negative easement 不作为的地役权

negative evidence 反面证据

negative income tax 负债所得税,倒付所得税

negative list 限制进口商品表

negative omission 不作为犯罪

negative pledge clause 消极担保条款

negative pledge covenant 否定质押条款

negative prescription 失去时效,消灭时效

negative resolution 否定决议

negative statute 消极法规

negative tax 负赋税

negative view on causation of omission 不作为因果关系否定说

negative vote 反对票,否定票

neglect or default of the management of the ship 管理船舶过失

neglect or default of the navigation of the ship 驾驶船舶过失

neglect to provide food for infants 未向婴儿供食罪

negligence 过失

negligence clause 疏忽条款

negligence with undue assumption 过于自信的过失

negligent act 过失行为

negligent crime 过失犯,过失犯罪

negligent homicide　过失杀人罪, 过失致死

negligent injury　过失伤害

negligent liability　过失责任原则

negligent offender　过失犯

negotiability　可流通性

negotiable　可转让的

negotiable certificates of deposit　可转让存单, 可转让定期存单

negotiable deposit certificates of large denomination　大额可转让存单市场

negotiable instrument　票据

negotiable securities　有价证券

negotiate　谈判, 商谈

negotiate price　议价

negotiate separately　另议

negotiated agreeme damage　损害不负责

negotiated price　议价, 协商价格

negotiated tendering　谈判招标

negotiating bank　议付行

negotiation　磋商, 谈判

negotiation L/C　议付信用证

negotiation of contract　磋商合约条款

negotiorum gestio（拉）无因管理

negotiorum gestor（拉）无权代理

negro slaves　黑奴

neighborhood administrative system　保甲制度

neighborhood committee　街道居民委员会

neighboring　邻近的, 附近的

neighbourhood committee　居民委员会

neighbouring real estate　相邻不动产

neofascism　新法西斯主义

neo-federalism　新联邦主义

neo-natural school of law　新自然法学派

neo-theory of negligence　新过失论

net assets　净资产

net back price　厂价

net bonded debt　债券负债净额

net estate　纯地产

net external position　净对外头寸

net foreign currency position　净外币头寸

net income　净收入

net interest　净利

net loss　净亏损

net of tax　纳税后净额

net position　净头寸

net profit　净利润

net profit after taxation　付税后纯利

net receipt　净收入

net weight　净重

neutral alien　中立国侨民

neutral asylum　中立国庇护

neutral duty　中立义务

neutral inhabitants　中立国居民

neutral port　中立港

neutral ship　中立国船只

neutral state　中立国

neutral subjects　中立国国民

neutral waters　中立领海

neutral zone　中立地带

neutralism　中立政策

neutralist　中立政府

neutrality　中立

neutrality law　中立法

neutrality pact　中立公约

neutrality proclamation　中立宣告

neutrality regulations　中立条例

neutralization of territory　领土中立化

neutralized zone　中立化地带

new adjudication　更审

new analytical jurisprudence　新分析法学

new analytical school of law　新分析法学派

new deal　新成交

new democracy　新民主主义

new economic policy　新经济政策

new for old 新换旧

new introduction of economic law 经济法新论

new investment 新投资

new Jason clause 新杰森条款

new law 新法

new market 新销路

new material 新材料

new obligor 新债务人

new or fresh consideration 新对价

new order 新订价

new order of international economy 国际经济新秩序

new packing 新包装

new procedures 新程序

new process 新工艺

new product 新产品

new technology 新技术

new three principles of the people 新三民主义

new world order 国际新秩序

new york produce exchange NYPE 纽约物产交易所

new york foreign exchange market 纽约外汇市场

newly built construction 新工程

newly developed industry 新兴工业

newly industrializing countries-NICS 新兴工业化国家

newly-increased value 新增价值

new-deal "新政"(美)

new-democratic revolution 新民主主义革命

New-Hegelianism 新黑格尔主义

nexum (罗) (拉) 以人身偿债的契约

nihil (拉) 不切合的

nihility 虚无

NK clause 不负责条款

no appeal resulting in additional punishment 上诉不加刑

no change in conditions 情势不变

no compensation 不予补偿

no consideration 无对价

no discount 无折扣

no double taxation 免征双重税

no dumping 切勿投掷

no exchange surrendered 不结汇

no fault 无过失

no guilt due to psychosis 有病无罪论

no lawyer 不懂法律的人

no longer bear 不再承担

no mark/N/M 无标记

no one is punished twice for the same offense 一罪不二罚

no penalty without law making it so 法无明文者不罚

no protest forl unit of measurement 国家法定计量单位

no right 无权

no risk 无风险

no risk after discharge 卸货后一般方不再负担责任

no separate legal entity 无独立法人地位

no state's land 无主地

no trial of an adjudicated case 定案不再理

no trial without complaint 告诉才处理

Noahide laws 诺亚律法

noasthenia 精神幼稚症

nocure-nopay 无效果—无报酬

noise pollution 噪音污染

noises of aircraft 航空器噪音

nolpros (拉) 不起诉,撤回告诉

nol pros application (拉) 撤诉申请

nol pros decision (拉) 不起诉决定

nol pros decision in writing (拉) 不起诉决定书

nol pros effect (拉) 撤诉效力

nol pros procedure 撤诉程序

nolens volens (拉) 不论是否同意

nolo contendere (拉) 不拟答辩

nomenclature 税则目录

nominal amount 名义金额

nominal constitution 名义宪法

nominal contract price 名义合同价格

nominal customs duties 名义关税

nominal damages 名义赔偿,象征性赔偿

nominal distributive contractor 名义分包商

nominal exchange 名义交易

nominal expulsion for further examination 开除留用察看

nominal liabilities 名义负债

nominal monarch 虚权元首

nominal owners 名义所有人

nominal partner 名义合伙人

nominal party 名义当事人

nominal protection 名义保护

nominal quotation 名义报价

nominal shipper 名义托运人

nominal sovereignty 名义主权

nominal tariff 名义关税

nominal value of shares 股票票面价值

nominate 任命

nominating procedure 提名程序

nomination 提名,任命,任命权

nomination of representative candidates 代表候选人的提名

nomination procedures 任命程序

nominator 提名者

nominee 被提名的候选人

nominee buyer 指定买主

non-acceptance 不接受

non-aggression 不侵犯

non-aggression treaty 互不侵犯条约

non-aligned country 不结盟国家

non-aligned movement 不结盟运动

non-antagonistic contradiction 非对抗性矛盾

non-appearance before the court 不出庭

non-appearance certificate 不出庭证书

non-arbitral dispute 不可仲裁的争端

non-assignable duty 不可转让的义务

non-authenticity criminal 非预谋的杀人罪

non-belligerency 非交战地位

non-binding agreement 非拘束性协定

non-causal juristic act 不要因的法律行为

non-coercive form of administrative action 非强制性行政行为

non-combatant 非战斗员

non-combatant of enemy 敌国的非战斗人员

non-commercial risks 非商业性风险

non-competing group 非竞争集团

non-compliance 违约行为,不遵守

non-compliance to law 不遵守法律

non-compulsory means of dispute settlement 解决争端的非强制方法

non-contest clause 不争议条款

non-contracting parties 非缔约国

non-contractual 非合同的

non-contractual document 非契约性文件

non-contractual liability 非合同性责任

non-contractual obligation 非合同性义务,非合同性责任

non-convertible preferred stock 不可转换的优先股

non-corporal punishment 非体罚

non-cumulative preferred stock 非累积优先股

non-delivery 未能送达,未交货

non-delivery of the entire package

整包提货不着

non-dirscriminatory treatment 无差别待遇

non-discretionary power 非自由裁量权

non-discrimination 非歧视原则,非歧视

non-discriminatory preference 无歧视优惠

non-essential provision 非主要规定

non-essential stipulation 非主要条款,非主要条件

non-execution 不执行,不履行

non-exercise of entitlements 不行使应享权利

non-existence 不存在

non-extradition of political offenders(/prisoners) 政治犯不引渡

non-factor service 非要素服务

non-fault collision 无过失碰撞

non-fault condition 无过失情形

non-fault liability 无过失责任

non-firm offer 虚盘

non-fulfilment 不履行

non-full sovereign state 非完全主权国

non-fundamental breach 非重大违约

non-fungible thing 不可代替之物,不可替代性

non-governmental organization 非政府机关

non-gratuitous 有偿合同

non-gratuitous storage contract 有偿的保管合同

non-hearing hearing 不同陪审团的庭审

non-hostile relation 非敌对关系

non-inland bay 非内海湾

non-interference 不干predicate

non-interposition 不干预

non-intervention 不干涉

non-intervention policy 不干涉政策

non-lien 无留置权

non-markable bonds 不可售债券

non-material loss 无形损失

non-military objective to enemy 敌国的非军事目标

non-military personnel 文职人员

non-military personnel of enemy 敌国的非军事人员

non-national rivers 非内河

non-navigable river 不通航河流

non-nuclear state 非核国家

non-obligatory act 非责任行为

non-observance 不遵守

non-open port 未开放港口

non-participating preferred stock 非参与优先股

non-party personages 党外人士

non-payment 不支付,无力支付

non-performance 不践约,不给付,不履行

non-performance fail to carry out 不履行

non-performance of duty 不履行义务

non-performance of legal obligation 不履行法律义务

non-performance of obligation 不履行义务,债的不履行

non-permanent members of the security council 安理会非常任理事国

non-physical loss 无形损失

non-prescriptive nature 无时效性质

non-price 非价格竞争

non-price competition 非价格竞争

non-productive goods 非生产物品

non-professional 非专业的

non-profit 非营利的

non-project type assistance 无项目贷款

non-ratification 不批准

non-reciprocal terms 非互惠条件

non-recourse project financing 无追索权的项目贷款
房

non-recoverable preferred stock 不可收回的优先股

normal inspection 一般检验

non-regular armed forces 非正规军

normal interest rate 一般利率

normal legal safeguards 正常法律保障

non-resident account 境外账户

normal loss 正常亏损,自然损耗

non-resident alien 过境侨民

non-resident taxpayer 非居民纳税人

normal management activities 正常管理活动

non-restricted preference 无限制优惠

normal meaning 通常意义

normal price 正常价格

non-returnable container 一次性包装

normal regious activitis 正常的宗教活动

non-risk asset 无风险资产

normal sale 正常销售

non-scheduled flight 非航班飞行

normal value 正常价值

normalization 规范性,规范化

non-self-executing treaty 非自执行条约

normalization of law 法律的规范性

non-self-governing territories 非自治领土

normalization of normative legal document 规范性法律文件的规范化

non-standard economic contract 非标准经济合同

normalizative document of law 规范性法律文件

non-state entity 非国家实体

normalizative usage of law 法的规范作用

non-tariff barrier/wall 非关税壁垒

Normandy 诺曼底

non-tariff barriers (NTBS) 非关税壁垒

Norman-sicilian law 诺曼底-西西里法典

non-tariff device 非关税手段

normative 规范化

non-tax objective 非税目的

normative connection 规范关系

non-tax payment 税外负担

normative constitution 规范宪法

non-territorial strait 非领峡

non-user 不行使权利

normative decrees 规性法令

non-vessel operation carrier 无船承运人

normative function of criminal law 刑法的规制机能

non-war pact 非战公约

normative jurisprudence 规范法学

norm of the civil law 民法规范

norm 规范

normative order 规范性秩序

norm in principle 原则性规范

normative rule of law 规范的法律规则

norm international law 国际法规范

normativist 规范法学家

norm of criminal law 刑法规范

norminal partner 挂名全伙人

norm of law 法律规范

norminal rate 名义汇率

norm of lending 贷款标准

norms 规范,规格

norm of morality 道德规范

norms of international criminal law 国际刑法规范

normal competition 正常竞争

normal house for sale 标准商品

Norris-La Guardia act 诺里斯-

拉瓜第法

north American free trade area （简写：NAFTA） 北美自由贸易区

north Atlantic treaty organization 北大西洋公约组织

Norwegian law 挪威法

not applicable（NA） 不可适用

not claimed 无人领取

not forbidden by law 法律所不禁止的

not go into past misdeeds 不咎既往

not held order 全权委托，自行处理委托

not in session 休会期间

not inquire into the cause 不予追究

not later than 至迟

not liable for indemnity 不负赔偿责任

not placing a case on file for investigation or trial 不立案

not responsible clause 不负责条款，免责条款

not satisfied 未签署

not to approve 不批准

not to be called to legal account 不受法律追究

not to be heard in public 不公开审理

not to be laid flat 切勿平放

not to investigate criminal responsibility 不追究刑事责任

not to ratify 不批准

not tolerated by law 为法律所不容

not tolerated by the law 法律所不容许

not trial without complaint 不告不理

not up to the standard 不合标准

notable 显著

notarial act 公证行为

notarial attestation 公证证明

notarial centificate 公证证书

notarial certification 公证证明，公证证

notarial deed 公证证书，公证文书

notarial department 公证机关

notarial document 公证证书

notarial fee 公证费

notarial instrument 公证文件

notarial office 公证处

notarial procedure 公证程序

notarial protest certificate 拒付证书

notarial supervision 公证监督

notarial survey 公证鉴定

notarial verification 公证认证

notarially certified transaction 由公证人证明的法律行为

notaries 司法人员，录事

notarization 公证人的证实，公证书，公证

notarization by mandate 委托公证

notarization law 公证法

notarization of contract 合同的公证

notarize 公证

notarized 由公证人证实的

notarized contract 经公证的合同

notary 公证人，公证员

notary activities 公证活动

notary department 公证部门

notary office 公证处

notary organization 公证机关

notary organs or agencies 公证机关

notary public 公证人，公证员

notary system 公证制度

note 照会，票据

note issuance facilities，NIFS 票据发行便利

note of acceptance 承诺书

note of arrival 到货通知

note of protest 海事声明，抗议照会

note on demand 即付票据

note rate 钞票汇率

notes　笔录供词

Nothing that is against reason is lawful　不合理的事不会合法

notice　通知

notice day　通知日

notice for defense in court　出庭辩护通知书

notice for rewards and punishments of convicts　罪犯奖惩通知书

notice in writing　书面通知

notice of a call　催款通知

notice of a convict's death　罪犯死亡通知书

notice of a penalty decision　处罚决定书

notice of abandonment　委付通知

notice of acceptance of a case　受理案件通知书

notice of action　诉讼通知书

notice of an audit　审计通知书

notice of appeal　上诉通知

notice of appearance　出庭通知

notice of assessment of tax　征税通知

notice of criminal execution　刑事执行通知书

notice of delay　延迟通知

notice of detention　拘留通知书

notice of discharging　卸货通知书

notice of dismissal　驳回通知书

notice of dismissal of accusation by the court　不予受理起诉通知书

notice of disposition　处分通知

notice of hearing　开审通知书

notice of trial　开审通知书

notice of judgment　判决通知书

notice of loss or damage　过失或损害通知

notice of mailing　邮寄通知

notice of no case-filing　不立案通知书

notice of payment　付款通知

notice of payment of tax revenue　交付税收通知书

notice of penalties　处罚通知书

notice of protection（美）知悉保护

notice of quashing a case　撤销案件通知书

notice of rescission　解约通知

notice of resignation　辞职通知书

notice of settlement　协议通知书

notice of shipment goods　发货通知

notice of supervision over administration　行政监察通知书

notice of tax assessment　征税通知

notice of tax payment　纳税通知书

notice of termination　终止通知

notice of violation　违法通知

notice on canceling the decision of living at home under surveillance　撤销监视居住通知书

notice on quashing a written notarization　撤销公证书通知书

notice period　通知期限

notice to produce　提出证件之通知

notification　通知,告知

notification of arrival　到货通知

notification of assent　同意通知

notification of continuance　延续通知

notification of payment of taxes　纳税通知书

notification of rejection of export license application　拒收出口许可通知

notify　通知,告知

notifying party　通知方

notional planning　国家计划

Nottebohm case　诺特包姆案

Nova constitutio futuris formam imponere debet, non praetritis（拉）法不溯既往

novatio（拉）债务更新

novatio voluntaria（拉）任意的

更改
novation 债务更新
novation of contract 合同更新
novation of debt 债务转承
novation of obligation 债的变更
novellae (拉) 新律
NPC standing committee 全国人大常委会
nuclear state 有核国家
nuclear test cases 核试验案
nuclear war 核战争
nuclear weapon test ban treaty 核武器禁试条约
nude contract 无对价合同,无偿合同
nude pact 无偿契约
nudum jus quiritium (拉) 市民法上的虚名权
nudum pactum (拉) 无对价合同,无对价的单纯合意,无偿合同
nuisance 公害
nuisance value 超付价值
nulity of juristic act 无效法律行为
null 宣告无效,无效
null and void 依法无效,无效,失效

① nullification 无效
② nullify 废弃,使无效
③ nullify a contract 宣布合同无效
④ nullify an agreement according to law 依法解约
⑤
⑥ nullify one's registration 注销登记
⑦
⑧ nullity 无效
⑨ nullity and voidness 无效
⑩ nullity of contract 契约无效,无效合同
⑪
⑫ nullity suit 合同无效的诉讼
⑬ number of cases accepted at second instance 二审收案数
⑭
⑮ number of deputies 代表名额
⑯ number of patent application 专利申请号
⑰
⑱ number of people due to be elected 应选人数
⑲
⑳ number of people to be elected or sent 代表名额
㉑
㉒ number of voters 投票人数
㉓ numerical strength of police 警力
㉔
㉕ Nürenberg trial 纽伦堡审判
㉖ nurse 护士
㉗ nursing woman 哺乳妇女
㉘ nymphomania 女性色情狂

O

oath against bribery（英）不进行贿赂活动的宣誓

obey 服从

obey orders 服从命令

obiter dictum（拉）判决中的附带意见

object 客体,标的物,赔偿主体

object enroute of carriage 在途货物

object impossibility 对象不能犯,客体不能犯

object in the relations of ownership 所有制关系客体

object of a crime 犯罪客体

object of a legal right 合法权利的客体

object of action 诉讼标的

object of adjudication 审判对象

object of administrative legal relationship 行政法律关系的客体

object of application of punishment 刑罚适用对象

object of assessment 课征对象

object of civil jural relations 民事法律关系客体

object of civil relation 民事法律关系客体

object of crime 犯罪对象

object of criminal proceedings 刑事诉讼客体

object of dictatorship 专政对象

object of economic legal（relation）nexus 经济法律关系客体

object of international delinquency 国际不当行为的客体

object of international law 国际法客体

object of jural relation of administrative procedure 行政诉讼法律关系的客体

object of jural relation of auditing 审计法律关系客体

object of jural relation of labour 劳动法律关系客体

object of legal relation 法律关系客体

object of legal relationship in criminal proceedings 刑事诉讼法律关系客体

object of legal relationship of administrative procedure 行政诉讼法律关系的客体

object of legal relationship of auditing 审计法律关系客体

object of legal relationship of labour 劳动法律关系客体

object of legal relationship of revenue 税收法律关系客体

object of legal responsibility 法律责任客体

object of malfeasance 违法客体

object of obligation 债的标的,债的客体

object of performance 履行标的

object of pledge 抵押物

object of prevention 预防对象

object of proof 证明对象

object of punishment 刑罚对象

object of regulation of economic law 经济法调整对象

object of right 权利客体

object of supervision 监察对象

object of supervision over administration 行政监察对象

object of taxation 纳税对象,征税客体,课税对象,征税对象,税收客体,课税品

object of the right 权利客体

object of the right of ownership 所有权客体

object of treaty 条约的客体

object punishment doctrine 目的刑主义

object quantity 标的物数量

object to which inquiries are addressed　质询对象

objection　异议

objective aspect of malfeasance　违法客观方面

objective cause　客观原因

objective circumstances　客观情况

objective circumstances of a crime　犯罪客观要件

objective condition　客观条件

objective criminal psychology　客观犯罪心理学

objective fact　客观事实

objective factor　客观因素

objective interpretation　客观解释

objective law　客观规律

objective neutrality　客观中立

objective reality　客观实际

objective responsibility　客观责任

objective responsibility system during director's term of office　厂长任期目标责任制

objective tax　特定目的税

objectivism　客观主义

objectivism of punishment　刑罚客观主义

objectivist theory of criminal law　客观主义刑法理论

objectivity　客观性

objectivity of auditing　审计的客观性

objectivity of evidence　证据的客观性

objectivity principle　客观原则

objects clause　目的条款

oblatio（拉）　付款偿债

oblatio debiti（拉）　偿还债务的提供

oblatio verbalis（拉）　口头的偿还承诺

oblatio verbalis nuda（拉）　单纯偿还的承诺

obligate　负有义务

obligatio（拉）　债务关系

obligatio accessonia（拉）　附随债

务,从属债务

obligatio bonae fidei（拉）　善意债务

obligatio certa（拉）　确定债务

obligatio civilis（拉）　民法上的债务

obligatio communis（拉）　共同债务

obligatio conditionalis（拉）　附有条件的债务

obligatio consensualis（拉）　合意上的义务

obligatio correalis（拉）　全部的共同债务

obligatio divisibilis（拉）　可分债务

obligatio ex contractu（拉）　契约债务

obligatio ex delicto（拉）　侵权行为债务

obligatio ex maleficio（拉）　由于侵权行为而产生的债务

obligatio generalis（拉）　全部债务

obligatio in solidum　（拉）连带债务

obligatio indivisibilis（拉）　不可分的债务

obligatio limitata（拉）　有限义务

obligatio naturalis（拉）　自然债务

obligatio personalis（拉）　人的义务,人的债务

obligatio principalis（拉）　主债务

obligatio quasi ex contractu（拉）　准契约债务

obligation　负有义务,债,义务,责任

obligation assumed　负担的义务

obligation created by administrative orders　行政命令之债

obligation financial obligations　债务

obligation for payment　支付责任

obligation in administrative law　行政法律责任

obligation of compensation 赔偿义务

obligation of compensation for damage 损害赔偿之债

obligation of compensation for loss 赔偿损失义务

obligation of conscription 兵役义务

obligation of contract 合同义务

obligation of crew 船员的义务

obligation of personal service 劳务之债

obligation of giving claim notice 索赔通知义务

obligation of giving notice 通知义务

obligation of maintaining confidentiality 保密义务

obligation of maintenance 维修义务

obligation of military service 兵役义务

obligation of non-recognition 不承担义务

obligation of notice 协助义务

obligation of tax 纳税义务

obligation outstanding 待付义务

obligation pledge 债权质

obligation principle 责任原则

obligation relating to civil law 民事责任

obligation to give information and advice 提供资料和告知的义务

obligation to pay tax 纳税义务

obligation under bond 担保责任

obligation with an option 选择之债

obligation with several creditors or several debtors 多数之债,多数人之债

obligational authority 责任权限

obligationes ex lege (拉) 依法律规定产生的债务,法定债务

obligations incurred 已发生责任

obligations of administrative bod-ies 行政机关的义务

obligations of subjects in economic law 经济法主体的义务

obligations of the judge 法官的职责

obligations outstanding 未清偿责任

obligations under the contract 合同义务

obligatory 有约束力的,必须履行的

obligatory arrest 必须逮捕

obligatory norm 义务规范

obligatory organization for juridical redress 司法赔偿义务机关

obligatory provisions 强制性规定

obligatory registration 强制登记

obligatory right 债权

obligatory rights 应然权利

obligatory rule 义务性规范,强制性规则

obligee 债权人,权利人

obligor in the maintenance 负抚养义务人

obliterate signature 涂改签名

obode 常住地

obscene object 淫秽物品

obscene publication, pornogragphic publications 淫秽出版物

obsente reo 被告缺席情况下

observance of treaties 条约的遵守

observant party 守约方

observative evidence 观察性证据

observe 遵守

observe discipline and abide by the law 遵纪守法

observe labour discipline 遵守劳动纪律

observe law and discipline 遵守法纪

observe public order 遵守公共秩序

observer 观察员

obtain a surety and conditional release　取保假释

obtain evidence　取证,调取证据

obtain evidence to determine guilty　取证定罪

obtain remuneration　获得报酬

obtain the consent　取得同意

obtain unreasonably high profits　牟取暴利

obtaining citizenship　获得国籍

obtaining evidence from abroad in civil and commercial matters　民商条件国外调取证据

obtaining pecuniary advantage by deception　以欺骗获得金钱利益

obvious　显而易见

obvious defect　明显的瑕疵

obvious party　明显当事人

obviously unfair juristic act　显失公平民事行为

occasional contraband　偶然禁制品

occasional dumping　偶然性倾销

occult crime　秘密犯罪

occupancy　占有期间,先占,占有

occupancy change　调换房屋类型

occupancy right　占有权

occupant　实际占有人

occupation　侵占,先占,职业

occupation tax　开业税

occupier　占用人,占有人

occupier's liability　占用人责任

occupying power　占领国

occupying tenant　占用承租人

occur prior to shipment　在装运前发生

ocean environment protection　海洋环境保护

ocean marine cargo insurance　海洋运输货物保险

ocean marine cargo transportation insurance　海洋货物运输保险

ocean pollution　海洋污染

ocean space　海域

odd man　投决定性一票的人

odentification of the parties　当事人各方

odious debt　恶债

Odious debts are not to be succeeded to　恶债不予继承

odle capacity loss　闲置能力损失

odontological examination　牙齿痕迹检验

oedipux complex　恋母情结

of a vile nature　性质恶劣

of accession clause of adhesion　加入条款

of all cabinet members　内阁一致原则

of good faith　信誉良好的

of one's own accord　自愿,自愿的

of the same class　同等

of the same kind　同类的

of the same of on an equal basis　同等

of the same rank　同等

off board market　交易所场外市场

off hire clause　停租条款

off shore　离岸

offend　触犯,冒犯

offender　罪犯,犯罪分子,犯罪人,营业犯

offender moving form place to place to commit crimes　流窜犯

offender on a medical treatment　保外就医的刑事犯

offense/offence　罪行,罪过

offense against privacy　窥探隐私罪

offense against property　侵犯财产罪

offense against state　国事犯

offense against the law　犯法行为

offense against the traffic laws　交通事故罪

offense against uniform of a friendly nation　穿着友好国家

制服罪

offense against willing victims 自愿被害人犯罪

offense by nontypical status 不纯正身份犯

offense by standard status 纯正身份犯

offense committed by young students 青年学生犯罪

offense for profits 利欲犯

offense in essence 本犯

offense in form 刑式犯

offense in substance 实质犯

offense involving interference with course of justice 涉及干扰司法公证罪

offense of abusing the right of guardianship or upbringing 滥用监护或教养权罪

offense of accepting or offering dowry 收受或给付嫁娶财礼罪

offense of accepting stolen goods 接受赃物罪

offense of act 行为犯,表现犯

offense of bait and switch 欺骗买主罪

offense of burglary 夜盗罪,夜入私宅罪

offense of concealment of birth 隐瞒出生罪

offense of consequence 侵害犯

offense of custodial indecency 管束猥亵罪

offense of damage to corn trees, and vegetable products 损害谷物、树木和蔬菜产品罪

offense of deceptive business practice 不正当交易罪

offense of detaining and delaying mail 扣押和延误邮件罪

offense of detention of official documents 扣押公文罪

offense of disclosing personal secrets 散布个人秘密罪

offense of disregard of victim 置被害人于不顾罪

offense of disrupting justice 扰乱司法罪

offense of driving under the influence of alcohol 酒后驾驶罪

offense of environmental pollution 污染环境罪

offense of failure to aid 怠于救助罪

offense of failure to report on illicit sexual relations 不告奸罪

offense of general abandonment 一般遗弃罪

offense of handling stolen goods 处置赃物罪

offense of harassing life 扰乱生活罪

offense of harassing the work of the legislative organization 侵扰立法机关工作罪

offense of hiding books 藏书罪

offense of illegal construction 无权建筑罪

offense of infringement on the dignity of human personality 侵害人性尊严罪

offense of joint negligence 共同过失犯罪

offense of mistreatment of corpse 凌辱尸体罪

offense of misusing credit cards 滥用信用卡罪

offense of misusing radioaction 滥用放射线罪

offense of neglect of one's duty to supervise 未尽监管义务罪

offense of no consequence 欠效犯

offense of nontypical omission 不纯正不作为犯

offense of obstructing or intimidating witness 阻拦或恫吓证人罪

offense of outraging public decency 凌辱公德罪

offense of overcharging public expense 超收公费罪

offense of poaching 偷猎罪

offense of possessing housebreaking implements 拥有破门工具罪

offense of rape 奸淫罪,强奸罪

offense of rigging publicly exhibited contest 不正当公开竞技

offense of riot 暴乱罪

offense of segregation by location 隔地犯

offense of segregation by time 隔时犯

offense of sending indecent articles 传送淫秽物罪

offense of sex temptation 性诱惑罪

offense of sheltering creditors 庇护债权人罪

offense of suppression 压制罪

offense of suppression of evidence 湮灭证据罪

offense of throwing stones 掷石罪

offense of unauthorized use of certificates 滥用证明书罪

offense of unlawful oaths 违法立誓罪

offense of unlawful strike 罢工罪

offense of vagrancy 流浪罪

offense of vocational negligence 业务过失犯罪

offense pfandstelle 自空位制度

offense related to drinking 酗酒犯罪

offense stayed in the process of starting to commit a crime 着手中止犯

offense suspended after commission 实行中止犯

offense under illusion 幻觉犯

offense with motives for money and properties 领财动机犯罪

offenses against honour 侵犯名誉罪

offenses against the crown and government 危害国王和政府罪

offenses against the person 侵犯人身罪

offenses due to neurosis 神经症犯罪

offenses of public hazards 公害犯罪

offensive cargo 违禁货物

offer 发价,发盘,报盘,要约

offer a bid 递盘

offer a proposal 提出建议

offer and acceptance by post 通过邮政发价和接受

offer by description 附说明书的要约

offer by post 邮寄报价

offer by tender 投标报价

offer facilities 提供方便

offer for sale 出卖

offer in the market 在市场上出售

offer make an offer 出价

offer sheet 报价单

offer subject to being unsold 以货未售出为有效的报价

offer subject to buyer's approval 以买方检骗或接受的报价

offer subject to buyer's inspection 以买方检骗或接受的报价

offer subject to immediate reply 以立即答复为有效的报价

offer subject to prior sale 先售有效的发价

offer under seal 签字蜡封要约

offer with engagement 有约束力的报价

offer without engagement 不受约束的要约,不受约束发价

offer without engagement 虚盘

offered rate 贷款利率

offeree 相对人

offering a bribe 以财请求

offering circular 债券发行说明书

offeror 要约人,发价人

offers for sale 公开让售

offhire survey 交还船检验

office 职位,机关,办事处

office building 办公楼

office in charge 主管部门

office of administrative body 行政机关的职责

office of advisers 参事室

office of entry 入境地海关

office of fair trading/OFT（英）公平交易局

office of price administration/OPA(美) 物价管理局

office of the commanding officer 幕府

office of the United Nations high commissioner for refugees 联合国难民事务高级事务署

officer 官员

officer on reserve dutynant 预备役军官

officer on reserve service with a general's rank 预备役将官

officer on reserve service with military ranks between the lieutenant colonel to senior colonel 预备役校官

officer on reserve service with military ranks between the second lieute 预备役尉官

official 法定,官员

official act 官方行为

official as subject to the king 臣子

official authorized 正式授权

official capacity 官方权力

official competence 法定权限

official confirmation 正式确认

official counsel 公设律师

official court 行政法院

official deed 正式契据

official documents requesting approval for reeducation through labour 呈清劳动教养审批表

official exchange rate 官定汇率,外汇官价

official fixed price 法定价格,官方价格

official holiday 法定休息日,法定假期

official inspection 官方检查

official interpretation 官方解释,正式解释

official letter 行政公函

official license to do business 开业证书

official liquidator 清理人

official market 官方市场

official misconduct 不良职务行为犯

official negotiation 正式谈判

official notification 正式通知

official organ as legal person 机关法人

official parity 法定平价

official petitioner 正式破产申请人

official price 官方价格,法定价格

official quality standard 法定质量标准

official rate 官方汇率

official receiver 破产事务官

official sanction 正式认可

official seal 公章

official statistics 官方统计,官方统计资料

official transaction 官方交易

officiency of management 经营管理效率

officious copy 非正式文本

offset 冲销,补偿,抵消

offset guilt by merit 立功赎罪

offset of obligation 债的抵消

offset prison term by converting into sentence the custodial period till the announcement of sentence 刑期折抵

offset statement 补偿报表

offset to the loss 对损失的补偿

offset transaction 抵消交易

offsetting transaction 抵消交易

offshore 境外

offshore fund 海外投资

oil contract 石油合同

oil embargo 石油禁运

oil exploration 石油勘探
oil facility 石油贷款
oil industry 石油工业
oil law 石油法
oil pollution 石油污染
oil pollution damage 油污损害
oil pollution liability 油污损害在事责任
oil pollution occurrence 油污事故
oil pollution risk 船舶油污责任险
old 年老
old international economic order 旧国际经济秩序
old way of thinking 旧思想
older estate awaiting redevelopment 需改造的旧(住宅)小区
oligarchy 寡头政治
oligopoly 少数制造商对市场的控制
oligopoly and oligopsony prices 寡头垄断售价与购价
oligopsony 少数买主垄断
oligopsony price 少数买主垄断价格
OLYLONG code of laws 奥里朗法典
Ombudsman 议会督察专员制度
omestic middleman 国内中间商
omission 遗漏,不作为
omissive 遗漏
omit 遗漏
omittance 遗漏
omnia praesumuntur legitime facta donec probetur in contrarium (拉) 一切行为在没有相反证明之前均应推定为合法
omnibearing 全方位
omnibus clause 总括条款
omnibus hearing 混合审理
omnis regula suas partitur exceptiones (拉) 一切规则皆有其例外
on 关于

① on a parity basis 在平等的基础上
③ on account payment 预付款项
④ on all fours 完全一致
⑤ on an equal footing 在平等的基础上
⑦ on any ground 以任何理由
⑧ on approval 看货和试用后决定
⑨ on arrival terms 到货条件
⑩ on behalf of 代表
⑪ on board 已装船
⑫ on board B/L 已装船提单
⑬ on board bill of lading 已装船提单
⑮ on contract terms 以承包方式
⑯ on default 如有过失,有疏忽
⑰ on demand 凭要求即付
⑱ on demand rate (O/D rate) 即期票汇汇率
⑳ on equal conditions 同等条件下
㉑ on equal footing 在平等的基础上
㉓ on hire survey 交船检验,接船检验
㉕ on lease 在出租中
㉖ on mortgage 作抵押
㉗ on one's own account 自行负责
㉘ on one's own responsibility 责任自负
㉚ on reasonable terms 以合理条件
㉜ on return 允许退货的交易
㉝ on sale 出售,允许退货的交易
㉞ on sale or return 准许退还剩货
㉟ on the barrelhead 用现金
㊱ on the basis 依据
㊲ on the basis of 根据
㊳ on the basis of law 按照法律
㊴ on the same term 以同样条件
㊵ on the spot 当场
㊶ on these grounds 据此
㊷ once on demurrage, always on demurrage "一旦滞期,永远滞期"条款
㊺ one central task, two basic points 一个中心,两个基本点
㊼ one contracting party 合同当事

人一方,缔约方

one country, two systems　一国两制

one crime　一罪

one crime in nature　实质罪

one crime in sentence　科刑一罪

one majority alliance system　一轮多数联盟制

one man, one vote　一人一票

one nation, two systems　一国两制

One ought to be subject to the law of the place where he offends　每一个人都应当受其违反法律的地方的法律的约束

one party　一方当事人

one price policy　定价统一政策

one room system　大开间房型,大房型

one side to blame collision　单方过失的碰撞

one signer　缔约方

one time payment　一次总付法

one's immediate or vital interests　切身利益

one's own fault　自己的过错

one's unit　单位

one's ward　被监护人

one-bedroom unit　单卧室单元

one-man-one-bankruptcy　一人一破产

one-party system　一党制

one-price　单一价格

one-room apartment　单间(公寓)套房

one-room flat　单间套间

one-round election system　一轮当选制

onerous act　有偿民事法律行为,有对价民事法律行为

onerous contract　有偿合同,有偿契约

onerous loan　有偿贷款

onerous requisition　有偿征用

one-side accomplice　片面共犯

one-sided　片面

one-sided test　单侧检验

one-storey building　单层建筑物

one-tailed test　单侧检验

one-way　单向,单行

one-way joint crime　单向共犯

on-site circuit trial　就地巡回审理

on-site trial　就地审判

onstream　中游

on-the-open order　开盘订单

on-the-spot inspection　现场检查

onus neale(拉)　不动产上的负担

onus of proof　举证责任

onus of proving evidence in administrative cases　行政诉讼的举证责任

open　未完成的,公开

open (/blank/Bearer) bill of lading　不记名提单

open a business　开业

open a court session　开庭

open air space　公空

open arbitration　公开仲裁

open bond　无限额抵押

open charge　公开指控

open coastal city　沿海港口开放城市

open coastal economic area　沿海经济开放区

open competition　公开竞争,开放竞争

open contract　简略合同,未订明条件的合同,不订明条件的合同

open credit　无担保信贷

open crossed check　无记名划线支票

open diplomacy　公开外交

open door policy　对外开放政策

open door to the outside world　对外开放

open economy　开放经济

open election　公开选举

open general licence　公开一般许可证

open insurance contract　预约保险合同

open insurance policy 预约保险
单

open market 自由市场,公开市
场

open market policy 公开市场政
策,公开市场业务

open market price 公开市场价
格

open market purchase 公开市场
采购

open mortgage 开放抵押,开口
抵押,未定额之按揭,无限额
抵押

open order 延续定单

open outcry 公开喊价

open policy 开放政策

open price agreement 公开价格
协定

open question 没有理决的问题

open registry 开放登记制度

open registry system 公开登记
制度

open sea 公海

open tender 公开招标

open tendering 公开招标

open to buy 允购定额

open to the outside world 对外
开放

open trade 未完结交易

open treaty 开放性条约

open trial 审判公开

open trial system 公开审判制度

opening of a wound 创口

opening price 开盘价格

opening quotation 开盘

opening statement 开庭陈述

opening to the outside world 对
外开放

operate 营业,经营

**operate a machine contrary to in-
struction** 违章操作

operate independently 自主经营

operate jointly in different ways
多种形式的联合经营

operating activities 经营活动

operating autonomy 经营的独
立性

operating budget 业务预算

operating capability 经营能力

operating cost 经营成本

operating cycle 经营周期

operating decision 营业决策

operating decision making 营业
决策

operating deficit 营业亏损

operating fund 经营资金

operating lease 经营性租赁

operating leverage 营业杠杆

operating loss 经营损失

operating method 经营方法

operating personnel 经营人员,
管理人员

operating plan 营业计划

operating risk 经营风险

operating rules 操作规程

operating statement 营业报表

operation 营业,经营

operation activities 经营活动

**operation and management of
reservoirs** 水库管理

operation cost 业务费用

operation lease 经营租赁

operation manual 使用说明书

operation of constitution 宪法实
施

operation of enterprise 企业经
营

operation of funds 资金调度

operation of law 法的生效

operation of treaty 条约的实施

operation of war 战斗

operation on borrowing 负债经
营

operation period 经营期

operation sheet 说明书

operational activities 经营活动

operational characteristics 使用
性能

operational cost 经营成本

operational expenditure 业务费
用

**operations conducted high above-
ground** 高空作业

operations involving high pressure

高压作业

operative clause 生效条款,实施条款

operative instrument 施行文件

operative mistake 有效之错误

operative part 履行部分

operative part of a deed 契据实施之主要部分,契据的履行部分

opinio(拉) 确信

opinion 法官意见书,判决意见

opinion of title 产权审查书

opponent 抗辩人

opportunity criminal 机会犯

oppose 对立

opposite 相对

opposite faction 反对派

opposite party 对方当事人

opposition party 在野党,反对党

oppress 压迫

oppression 压力

oppressive government 苛政

optimal land utilization 最大限度用地

optimum production base 最佳生产基地

optimum standard of care 最高注意标准

option 选择权,买卖权,期权

option agreement 选择权协议

option dealing 选择权合同

option of nationality 选择国籍

option of reconsideration doctrine 复议选择原则

option trading 选择权买卖

option transaction 期权交易,股票选择交易

optional clause 任择条款,任意条款

optional compulsory jurisdiction 任意强制管辖

optional contract 有选择权的合同

optional early redemption 任意偿还

optional instalment payment 有

选择权的分期付款

optional nature 任意性,选择性

optional obligation 选择之债

optional port of discharge 选择卸货港

optional statutory sentence 选择法定刑

optional stipulation 可选择的合同条款

optional trust 任意信托

options on futures 期货期权

options on physicals 现货期权

or destroy accounting book(s) 隐匿谎报销毁会计资料

oral agreement 口头协议,口头协定

oral argument 口头辩论

oral civil decision 口头民事决定

oral civil findings/order 口头民事裁决

oral complaint 口头起诉

oral confession 被告口供,被告人口供,口供

oral contract 口头契约

oral defense 口头答辩

oral evidence 证言

oral evidence of the victim 被害人的口供

oral findings 口头裁定

oral form 口头形式

oral hearing 口头审理

oral negotiation 口头谈判

oral order 口头裁定

oral purchasing 口头采购

oral reply 口头答辩

oralscript of oral complaint 口诉笔录

ordain 规定

ordeal 神审

ordeal of fire 火审

ordeal of water 水审

ordeal system 神示制度

order for goods 订单

order 订货单,判令,责令,裁定,法令,秩序,定作,责令,裁定书,订购,预约

order about 驱使

order B/L 指示提单

order bill of lading 指示提单

order by sample 凭样品订货

order check 记名支票

order for ejectment (/of expulsion) 驱逐令

order for goods 订货单

order for the suspension of business for rectification 责令停业整顿

order form 订货单,订单

order in foreign trade activities 对外贸易秩序

order into a contract 订购合同

order note 订货单,订单

order of acquittal 清偿令

order of adducing 引证程序

order of business 议事程序

order of international economy 国际经济秩序

order of motions 动议次序

order of planing permission 计划许可的命令

order of priority 优先次序

order of procedure 进行程序

order of severity 严重程度

order of society 社会秩序

order of suspension of business 停止营业令

order of the bank 银行指示

order price 订货价格

order quantity 订货数量

order sb to leave the country within a time limit 限期出境

order sheet 订货单,订单

order size 订货数量

order the return of 责令退还

order to discontinue production or business operation 责令停产停业

order to dissolve 责令解散

order to guarantee 通知担保

order to make a formal apology 责令赔礼道歉

order to make compensation for losses 责令赔偿损失

order to make public correction and criticism 责令公开改正批评

order to restore vegetation 责令恢复植被

order to sign a pledge of repentance 责令具结悔过

order to stop business for rectification 责令停业整顿

order to stop irregularities 责令停止违法行为

order to stop the use 责令停业使用

order to suspend business 责令停产停业

order to suspend production 责令停产停业

order under reference 参考订单

ordered goods 定作物

ordered market arrangement 有秩序的市场安排

ordering party 定作人

ordering to make compensation for an injury 责令赔偿损害

ordering to pay compensation for it 责令退赔

order-placing meeting 订货会

orders of knighthood 骑士等级

ordinance 法令

ordinance of Alcale 亚加拉敕令

ordinance of forest (英) 森林法

ordinary accident 一般责任事故

ordinary affinity 普通姻亲

ordinary agent 普通代理人

ordinary breakage 通常踊得

ordinary business practice 通常业务

ordinary cargo 一般货物

ordinary circumstances 一般情况

ordinary civil disputes 一般民事纠纷

ordinary civil service examination 普通文职官员考核

ordinary constitution of crime 普通犯罪构成

ordinary courses of business 一般商业过程

ordinary court 普通法庭

ordinary credit 限额抵免,一般抵免

ordinary criminal 普通刑事犯

ordinary criminal law 普通刑法

ordinary criminal offense 一般刑事犯罪

ordinary customs duty 普通关税

ordinary drawing right 普通提款权

ordinary fault 一般过失

ordinary interest 通常利息

ordinary law 普通法律

ordinary license 普通许可

ordinary loan 普通贷款,一般贷款

ordinary mail 平信

ordinary majority 普遍多数

ordinary meaning 通常意义

ordinary offense 普通罪,常事犯

ordinary offense against official capacity 普通职务犯罪

ordinary passport 普通护照

ordinary postal materials 平常邮件

ordinary procedure 普通程序,普通诉讼程序

ordinary procedure of first instance 第一审普通程序

ordinary quality 中等品质,一般估量

ordinary recidivism 普通累犯

ordinary residence 通常居所

ordinary violation 一般违法行为

ordinary war crime 普通战争罪行

ordinary wear and tear 自然损耗

ordinary written law 一般成文法

ordinis beneficium（拉） 保证人先诉抗辩的恩典或特权

① ordre public（法） 公共秩序

② ordre public international（法） 国际公共政策,国际公共秩序

④ ordre public interne（法） 国内公共秩序

⑥ ore resource law 矿产资源法

⑦ organ 机关

⑧ organ concerned 有关机关

⑨ organ for pharmaceutical administration 药政机关

⑪ organ for the inspection of pharmaceutical 药品检验机关

⑬ organ of authority 权力机关

⑭ organ of judicial person 法人机关

⑯ organ of legal supervision 法律监督机关

⑱ organ of the state 国家机关

⑲ organ of violence 暴力机关

⑳ organic act 组织法

㉑ organic law of administrative establishments 行政机关组织法

㉔ organic law of the NPC 人民代表大会组织法

㉖ organic law of the people's court 人民法院组织法

㉘ organic law of the people's procuratorates 人民检察院组织法

㉚ organic rules 组织条例

㉛ organization 机关

㉜ organization delegated of powers by laws and regulations 法律、法规授权的组织

㉟ organization for administrative review 行政复议机关

㊲ organization for economic cooperation 经济合作组织

㊴ organization for economic cooperation and development 经济合作与发展组织

㊷ organization for execution of punishment 刑罚执行机关

㊸ organization for proceedings by a sole arbitrator 独立审理

㊻ organization for reeducation-through-labor 劳动教养机关

organization for the implementation of administrative penalties 行政处罚的实施机关

organization in charge of government establishments 编制管理机关

organization liable for administrative compensation 行政赔偿义务机关

organization of administration adjudication 行政审判机关

organization of administrative legislation 行政立法机关

organization of administrative trial 行政审判机关

organization of African unity 非洲统一组织

organization of American states (OAS) 美国国家组织,美洲国家组织

organization of Arab petroleum exporting countries (OAPEC) 阿拉伯石油输出国组织

organization of consultation 协商机关

organization of dictatorship 专政机关

organization of highway administration 公路行政管理机关

organization of justice 司法机关

organization of powers 权力机关

organization of road traffic control 道路交通管理机关

organization of state power 国家权力机关

organization of supreme power 最高权力机关

organization of supreme state power 国家最高权力机关

organization of the petroleum exporting countries-OPEC 石油输出国组织

organization of the socialized sector 社会化部门

organization of the united front 统一战线组织

organization of truck transport 汽车运输组织

organization of violence 暴力机关

organization responsible for the review of constitutionality 违宪审查的机关

organization tax 开办税

organization with indemnifying obligation 赔偿义务机关

organizational form of political power 政权组织形式

organizational setup 组织机构

organization-owned housing 单位住房

organized crime 群集犯罪,组织犯罪,集团犯

organized market 有组织的市场

organs of political power 政权机关

origin 出身,原产地,渊源

origin certificate 原产地证书

origin criterion 原产地标准

origin of state 国家起源

origin rules 原产地规则

original 原始

original administrative act 原行政行为

original administrative organization 原行政机关

original agreement 原始协议

original area quarantine inspection 原产地检疫

original assigner 原有让与人

original constitution 原始宪法

original contract 原合同

original copy of the dead 正契

original copy script 原件

original cost 原价

original credit 税收普通抵免

original damaged cargo 原残货物

original data 原始数据

original debtor 原债务人

original description 原说明书

original domicile 原住所

original electoral unit 原选举单位

original form or appearance 原状

original inspection organizations 原检验机构

original investment 原始投资,原投资额

original item(s) 原物

original jurisdiction 初审管辖数,原始管辖数

original language 原来文字

original letter of credit 信用证正本

original member 创始会员国

original mortgage 原抵押

original nationality 原始国籍

original obligor 原债务人

original of constitution 宪法的起源

original offer 原要约,原发价

original order 原订货

original organization for approval 原批准机关,原审批机关

original packing 原包装

original party 原始当事方

original price 原价

original responsibility 原始责任

original sentence of reprieve 原缓刑判决

original sentence on probation 原缓刑判决

original specification 原说明书

original state 原状

original title 原始所有权

original undertaking 原企业

original voucher(s) 原始凭证

originality 独创性

originate from one of the clients 由客户提出

originate with one of the clients 由客户提出

ostensible agency 名义代理

ostensible authority 名义代理权

ostensible partner 名义合伙人,挂名全伙人,(港) 外表合伙人

other contracting parties 其他缔约方,订约的另一方当事人

other goods within the same class 同类的其他商品

other legitimate reason 其他正当理由

other side 对方当事人

our time 我方时间

out lay for advertisement 广告费

out let store 代销店

out of 出于

out of a base (illegal, or immoral) consideration, an action does (can) not arise 对非法或不道德的对价不能诉诸履行

out of control 不受控制

out of habit 出于习惯

out of malevolence 出于恶意

out of tax rebates in export 出口骗税犯罪活动

out put to be retained by the collective 集体提

out rage 严重违法行为

outbuilding 车库外房

outcast 被遗弃者

outer bar 外席法庭(英)

outer barrister 外席律师(英)

outer limit of the territorial sea 领海外部界限

outer packing 外包装

outer region 边远地区

outer space 外层空间

outer space law 外空法

outfall 出水口

outgoing quality 出厂质量

outlaw 剥夺权益

outlaw government 非法政府

outlawry 剥夺权益,不受法律保护

outlawry of treaty 条约的失效

outlay (/out-of-pocket) cost 付现成本

outlays for facilities relating to prison administration 狱政设施经费

outlet (建筑物的)出口,出水口

outlet for investment 投资场所
outline 大纲,草图
outline on world natural resources protection 世界自然资源保护大纲
outmoded conventions 陈规
outmoded conventions and bad customs 陈规陋习
outpacking 外包装
outpost 派出机构,派驻机构
output tax 产出税
outrage 严重违法行为
outright purchase 买断交易
outside finance 外部资金
outside of law 超出法律范围的
outside service prisoner 外役犯
outside the competence 在权限以外
outside the law 超出法律范围
outstanding 未清偿的
outstanding amount 未付金额
outstanding capital 未偿资本的
outstanding contract 尚待执行的合同
outstanding debt 未偿债务
outstanding government securities 未偿公债
outstanding interest 未付利息
outstanding loan 未偿贷款
outstanding loss 未决赔款
outstanding loss reserve 未决赔款准备金
outstanding obligations 未偿债务
outstanding price 优价
outturn clause 卸货数量条款
outturn weight 到货重量
outward blockade 外向封锁
over insurance 超额保险
over lapping debt 重复债务
over loan 超额贷款
over par 溢价发行
over standard 超标准
overall 大局
overall balance 综合平衡
overall calculation 一次总算法
overall consideration 综合考虑

① overall control 领导权
② overall development planning 全面发展规则
④ overall floorage 总建筑面积
⑤ overall integration 全盘一体化
⑥ overall limit 全部限额
⑦ overall limitation, comprehensive limitation 综合限额
⑨ overall plan 总体规划
⑩ overall plan for land utilization 土地利用总体规划
⑫ overall planning 全面计划
⑬ overall planning and all-round consideration 统筹兼顾
⑮ overall program 全面规划
⑯ overall remuneration 全部报酬
⑰ overall supervision 全面监督
⑱ overbought position 抢购
⑲ overcome 推翻
⑳ overcompensation 过分补偿
㉑ overconsuming 超前消费
㉒ overdraft 透支
㉓ overdrafts on current account secured 往来抵押透支
㉕ overdraw 透支
㉖ overdue 误期
㉗ overdue credit 过期债权
㉘ overdue debt 过期债务
㉙ overdue delivery 逾期交货
㉚ overdue interest 逾期利息
㉛ overdue loan 逾期贷款
㉜ overdue payment 延付款项
㉝ overdue ship 误期船只
㉞ overdue tax 积欠的税款
㉟ overdue vessel 误期船只
㊱ overestimate 高估
㊲ overhead price 全价
㊳ overlapping leadership 多头领导
㊴ overlord 最高统治者,封建君主,大地主
㊷ overpay 多付,超额偿付
㊸ overpayment 多付,超付
㊹ overprice 作价过分
㊺ overproduction 生产过剩
㊻ overreach 超越
㊼ overrule 驳回,否决

overseas 海外的,境外,侨民

overseas agent 国外代理人

overseas bank 国外银行

overseas branch 国外分支机构

overseas Chinese 华侨

overseas Chinese affairs office 侨办

overseas contract 海外契约

overseas debt 外债

overseas economic cooperation Fund 日本海外经济协作基金

overseas investment 海外投资

overseas market 国外市场,海外市场

overseas private direct investment 海外私人直接投资

overseas private investment corporation(注:简写为 OPIC) 海外私人投资公司(注:指美国)

overstate 高估

overstep 超越,越权

overstep authority of approval 超越批准权限

overstep one's authority 超越权限,逾越权限

overstep one's power of agency 越权代理

overstep the bounds 出轨

overstep the power of agency 越权代理

overstock of commodity houses 商品房积压

overstocking of goods 积压商品

overstocking of materials 材料积压

oversupply 过度供给

overt 公开

overt act 明显的行为

overt constitution of a crime 开放犯罪构成

overt market 公开市场

overtax 超额征税,征税过重

overtaxation 征税过重

overthrow a confession 翻供

overthrow the reactionary rule 推翻反动统治

overture 提案,动议

overvaluation 过高估价

owe 欠债

own jointly 共有

own option 我方有选择权

own risk 自己承担风险

owner 所有人,所有者,物主

owner lessor 物主出租人

owner of property 财产所有人

owner of the exclusive right of pharmaceutical 药品独占人

owner of the goods 货物所有人,货主

owner trustee 物主受托人

owner's equity 业主权益,所有者权益

owner's option 由船主选择

owner's responsibility system for a project under construction 建设项目业主责任制

owner's risk 货主风险

owner-farmed land 自耕地

owner-in-common 共同所有人

ownerless 无主的,无主

ownerless articles 无主物

ownerless land 无主土地

owner-occupier 所有人,占用人

owners of collective property 集体财产所有人

ownership 物主身份,所有权,所有制

ownership by the entire people 全民所有制

ownership by the whole people 全民所有制

ownership of land 地权,土地所有权

ownership of mining resource 矿产资源所有权

ownership of mountain forest 山林所有权

ownership of mountains and forests 山林所有权

ownership of private houses 私有房屋所有权

ownership of property 财产所有权

ownership of ship 船舶所有权

ownership of territorial sea 领海所有权

ownership of the means of production by the whole people 生产资料全民所有制

ownership relation 所有制关系

ownership system 所有制

ownership system of land 土地所有制

ownership-in-common 共同所有权

ozone layer 臭氧层

P

pacific basin economic cooperation committee 太平洋地区经济合作委员会

pacific blockade 平时封锁

pacific economic cooperation conference 太平洋经济合作会议

pacification 绥靖

package 合同上的利益,一揽子许可

package bid 组合投标

package deal 整批交易,一揽子交易,一揽子交易条款

package license 一揽子许可

package licensing 一揽子许可,一揽子许可证交易

package manner 包装方式

package mortgage 包括家用设备在内的住房抵押贷款

package price 组合价格

package program 一揽子计划

packaged mortgage plan 一揽子抵押方案

packaging and labelling regulation 商品包装及标签规定,包装和标签规定

packaging standard 包装标准

packer guarantee clause 卖方保证条款

packing 包装条款

packing cargo 包装货物

packing list 装箱单,装箱清单

packing mark 包装标记

pact 契约

pacta conventa (拉) 约定条款

pacta dant legem contractui (拉) 协议构成合约的法则,当事人协议构成共有法律效力的合同

pacta sunt servanda (拉) 契约必须遵守约定必须信守原则,条约必须遵守原则(法),当事人的协议必须信条执行(拉),约定必须遵守(拉)

pacta tertiis nec nocent nec prosunt (拉) 契约对第三方无损害

paction 契约,合同

pactional 契约的,合同的

pactum (拉) 无方式契约

pactum acquisitionis (拉) 取得契约

pactum acquisitivum (拉) 取得契约

pactum adjectum (拉) 附属合同,附属契约

pactum de non cedendo (拉) 不转让的合同

pactum de non petendo (拉) 不起诉的契约

pactum illicitum (拉) 非法协定,非法合同

pactum juris (拉) 质物契约

pactum legitimum (拉) 适法契约

pactum reservati dominii (拉) 保留所有权的含意

pactum vestitum (拉) 有效契约

paddy wagon 囚车

paid (/cancelled) check 付讫支票

paid out of capital 人资本纳税

paid rent 已付租金

paid-in portion 已缴部分

paid-up loan 已清偿贷款

pair price 公平价格

Paisache 毕舍遮婚

palace 宫廷

palace coup 宫廷政变

palliate 辩解,辩解

palliation of a crime 减轻罪行

palming off another person's registered trademark 假冒他人注册商标

Panama canal 巴拿马运河

pani causa (拉) 地位平等

panic 经济大恐慌

panic buying of goods 抢购物资

panic reaction 惊恐反应

pannor 典出人

panol contract (英) 无盖章契约

panopticon 圆形监狱

pans quanta (拉) 必要的继承份额

pant owners 共有人

partnership business 合伙企业

papal muncios 教廷大使

paper blockade 纸上封锁

paper currency standard 纸币本位判

paper money 纸币

paper of civil court directive 民事决定书

paper of civil judgment collateral to criminal proceedings 刑事附带民事上诉状

paper of civil mediation 民事调解书

paper of confiscation decision 没收决定书

paper of decision for placing a case on file 立案决定书

paper of determining the responsibility in a road traffic accident 道路交通事故责任认定书

paper of expert evaluation of death 死亡鉴定书

paper of forfeiture decision 没收决定书

paper of identification in science and technology 刑事科学技术鉴定书

paper of judgment 判决书

paper of sentence 刑事判决书

paper of the decision of civil sanctions 民事制裁决定书

par of exchange 外汇比价

par value of stock(s) 股票面值, 股票票面价值

parade 游行, 示威游行

parade and demonstration 游行示威

paragraph 段

Parallel exploitation system 平行开发制度

parallel loan 平行贷款

paramount clause 首要条款

paramount lien 优先留置权

paramount ownership 最高所有权

paramount responsibility 首要责任

paramount right 首要权利

paranoid disorder 偏执狂精神病

paranoid schizophrenia 妄想性精神分裂症

parastatal 半国营

para-state enterprise 半国营企业

parcel 邮包

parcel post 包裹邮件, 邮政包裹业务, 邮包

parcel receipt 包裹收据

parcenary 土地共同继承

parcener 土地共同继承人

parde evidence 证言

pardon 赦免

pardon for execution of punishment 行刑豁免

parenchyma homosexuality 实质性同性恋

parent of the country 政府监督

parental liability 父母的责任

parental rights and duties 父母的权利和义务

parental support 抚养

parenticide 杀亲罪

pari causa (拉) 权利平等

pari passu clause 平等条款

pari passu covenant 比例平等条款

paris convention for the protection of industrial property 保护工业产权巴黎公约

Paris coordinating committee 巴黎统筹委员会

Paris foreign exchange market 巴黎外汇市场

Paris peace conference 巴黎和约

Paris union 巴黎联盟

parity of treatment 同等待遇

parity price 对等价格

parking ordinance 停车规则

parlementaire 军使

parliament 议会,国会

parliament act 议会法,国会法案

parliament of Great Britain 大不列颠议会(英)

parliament rolls 议会案卷

parliamentarian 国会议员

parliamentarianism 议会制,代议制政体

parliamentarism 议会制度,国会制

parliamentary act 议会法

parliamentary committee 议会委员会

parliamentary debate 议会辩论实录

parliamentary dissolution 议会解散

parliamentary election 国会选举

parliamentary government 议会内阁制,议会政体,议会制政府,代议政府

parliamentary immunity 议员豁免

parliamentary law 国会法案

parliamentary legislation 国会立法

parliamentary privilege 议员特权

parliamentary republic 议会制共和国

parliamentary sovereignty 议会主权

parmanent 常驻

parol promise 口头允诺

parole 假释

parole certificate 假释证明

parole officer 保释官

parole revocation hearing 假释撤销审查

parricide 杀害父母罪

① pars (拉) 当事人

② pars adversa (拉) 对方

③ pars gravata (拉) 受害者

④ pars pro toto (拉) 以部分代整体

⑤

⑥ part 篇

⑦ part disorder 部分精神障碍

⑧ part installment 部分分期付款

⑨ part of the criminal facts are untrue 部分犯罪事实失实

⑩

⑪ part of the litigants 部分当事人

⑫ part owner 共同所有人

⑬ part payment 部分付款,部分支付

⑭

⑮ part performance 局部管制,局部清理,部分履行

⑯

⑰ part revocation 部分撤销

⑱ part sovereign state 部分主权国家

⑲

⑳ particulars of a charge 控告要点

㉑

㉒ partial acceptance 部分接受

㉓ partial adjustment 部分调整方案

㉔

㉕ partial alteration 部分变更

㉖ partial annulment 部分废止

㉗ partial armistice 局部休战

㉘ partial cash transaction 部分现金交物

㉙

㉚ partial cession 部分割让

㉛ partial compensation 部分补偿

㉜ partial delay 局部延误

㉝ partial delivery 部分交付,部分交货

㉞

㉟ partial disablity 部分残废

㊱ partial evidence 部分证据

㊲ partial failure 部分失败

㊳ partial guarantee 部分担保

㊴ partial incapacity 局部丧失行为能力

㊵

㊶ partial invalidity 部分无效

㊷ partial judgment 部分判决

㊸ partial loss 部分损失

㊹ partial monopoly 不完全竞争,部分垄断

㊺

㊻ partial neutrality 局部中立

㊼ partial nonperformance of obligation 债的部分不履行

partial payment 部分付款,部分支付

partial performance 部分履行

partial ratification 部分批准

partial relief 部分诉讼救济

partial renvoi 部分反致

partial shipment allowed 允许分批装运

partial succession 部分继承

partial transfer 部分转让

partial war 局部战争

partially exempt obligations 部分免除责任

partially secured creditors 部分担保的债权人

partially secured liabilities 部分担保责任

partibility of chattel 动产的可分割性

particeps criminis(拉) 帮助犯,共犯,伙同犯

participant 合营者

participant in reconsideration 复议参加人

participants in administrative reconsideration 行政复议参加人

participants in civil proceedings 民事诉讼参加人

participants in criminal action 刑事诉讼参与人

participate in 参与

participate in action 参与诉讼

participate in and discuss government and political affairs 参政议政

participate in decision-making 参与决策

participate in evaluation and election 参选

participate in government and political affairs 参政

participating in the loan 参与贷款权

participating preferred stock 参与优先股

① participation in homicide 参与杀人

③ participation in mobbing 参与聚众闹事罪

⑤ participation in reconsideration 复议参加人

⑦ participation in self-injury(日) 加工自伤罪

⑨ participation in suicide(日) 加工自杀罪,得承诺杀人

⑪ participation loan 银团贷款

⑫ participative management 参与管理

⑬ participatory democracy 参与民主制

⑯ particular article 特殊条文

⑰ particular average 单独海损

⑱ particular cargo 特定货物

⑲ particular case 特殊案件

⑳ particular charges 单独费用

㉑ particular custom 特有习惯

㉒ particular form 特定形式

㉓ particular industry 特定工业

㉔ particular lien 特定留置权,特别留置权

㉖ particular packing 特种包装

㉗ particular period 特定阶段

㉘ particular risk 特定危险

㉙ particular rules 特定规章

㉚ particular torts 特别民事侵权

㉛ particularity of human rights 人权的特殊性

㉝ particularized interest 个别利益

㉞ parties 当事人

㉟ parties according to season 季节差价

㊱ parties to a contract 契约当事人

㊳ parties to a labour dispute 劳动争议当事人

㊶ parties to administrative jural relations 行政法律关系当事人

㊸ parties to an economic lawsuit 经济诉讼当事人

㊺ parties to civil action 民事诉讼当事人

㊼ parties to international court of

Justice 国际法院的当事者

parties to joint venture 合营多方

parties to the case 本案当事人

partisan 同党

partition 分割土地房屋

partition property 析产

partner 合伙人,合股人

partner operation 合伙经营

partner's personally solvent 合伙人个人偿债能力

partnership 合伙,合伙契约,合伙企业,合伙关系

partnership act（美）合伙法

partnership assets 合伙资产

partnership at will 随意合伙企业,随意合伙

partnership certificate 合伙证明

partnership characteristics 合伙性质

partnership contract 合伙合同,合伙契约

partnership income 合伙收入

partnership instrument 合伙文据

partnership's debts 合伙债务

partnership's property 合伙财产

parts of the infrastructure 基础设施

party 当事人,集会,关系人

party and government organizations 党政机关

party cabinet 政党内阁

party committee 党委

party concerned 当事人一方,有关当事方,有关方

party conduct 党风

party constitution 党章

party discipline 党纪

party discipline and the law of the country 党纪国法

party in breach 违约当事人

party in conflict 冲突一方

party in default 违约当事人

party in delay 延迟方

party in interest 利害关系当事

① 人

② party injured 受害方

③ party interested 利害关系当事

④ 人

⑤ party issuing contract 发包人

⑥ party jointly liable with the debtor

⑦ 与债务人负连带责任的人

⑧ party losing a lawsuit 败诉方

⑨ party member 党员

⑩ party membership 党籍

⑪ party politics 政党政治

⑫ party secondarily liable 第二债

⑬ 务关系人

⑭ party severally liable with the

⑮ debtor 与债务人负连带责任

⑯ 的人

⑰ party subject to administration

⑱ 行政管理相对一方当事人

⑲ party to a case 案件当事人

⑳ party to a contract 合同当事

㉑ 人,立约当事人

㉒ party to a treaty 缔约当事国

㉓ party to arbitration 仲裁当事人

㉔ party to the conflict 冲突一方

㉕ pass 批准

㉖ pass a judgment or sentence at

㉗ fixed time, render judgment at

㉘ fixed time 定期宣判

㉙ pass a judgment or sentence in

㉚ court 当庭宣判

㉛ pass a law 通过法律

㉜ pass a sentence 宣判

㉝ pass through the territory of a

㉞ country 过境

㉟ passage 航行权

㊱ passage ticket 通行证

㊲ passage ticket clause 船票条款

㊳ passageway 通道

㊴ passenger 乘客,旅客

㊵ passing of title 所有权转移

㊶ passing off 假冒

㊷ passion and crime 激情与犯罪

㊸ passive act 消极行为

㊹ passive administrative measure

㊺ 消极的行政措施

㊻ passive citizen 消极公民

㊼ passive crime 被动犯罪,被动性

犯罪

passive criminal 被动性犯罪人

passive duty 消极义务

passive homosexuality 被动性同性恋

passive means 消极方法

passive personality 消极人格

passive personality disorder 被动型人格障碍

passive policeman 被动的警察（指自由贸易论中的国家）

passive testimony motive of witness 证人被迫作证的动机

passive title 消极所有权

passport 护照

passport of the People's Republic of China 中华人民共和国护照

passport visa 护照登记

past remedy 无法补救

patent 专利

patent ambiguit 明显的意见含糊

patent applicant 专利申请人

patent cooperation treaty 专利合作条约

patent defect 明显

patent for invention 发明专利

patent for utility models 实用新型专利

patent license contract 专利许可合同

patent number 专利号

patent of importation 引进专利

patent rights 专利权

patentee 专利权人

paternal grandparent 祖父母

paternal power 父权

paternity exclusion 父权否定

pathological drunkeness 病理性醉酒

pathological motive 病理性动机

pathological passion 病理性激情

patient 病人

patria potestas（拉） 家父权（罗马）

patriarch system 宗法制度

patriarchal clan commune 父系氏族公社

patriarchal society 宗法社会

patriarchal system 家长制

patriarchy 父权制度,家长制

patricide 杀父罪,弑杀罪

patrimonial sea 继承袭海

patrimony 世袭财产

patriot who stands for reunification of the motherland 拥护祖国统一的爱国者

patriot who supports socialism 拥护社会主义的爱国者

patriotic personage without party affiliation 无党派爱国人士

patriotic united front 爱国统一战线

patta sunt servanda（拉） 合同必需履行

pattern 样式,格式

pattern of investment 投资结构

pattern of ownership 所有制结构

patterns of administrative compensation 行政补偿的方式

patterns of administrative indemnity 行政赔偿方式

patterns of enterprises 企业结构

pavol agreement verbal 口头协议

pawn 当押,典押,抵押品,质契,抵押

pawn pledge 典当

pawn ticket 抵押凭据

pawnbroker 当押商

pawnee 受当人,质权人

pawner 出租人,典出人

pawning and auctioning house 典当拍卖行

pawnship 当铺

pawnticket 当票

pay 报酬,给付

pay agent 付款代理人

pay by installments 分期付款

pay compensation 退赔

pay date of bond interest 债券

付息日

pay day 交割日

pay down 用现金支付,即时支付,即时付款

pay earnest money 付定金

pay for a loss 赔偿损失

pay in cash 付现款,现金支付

pay in full 全部支付

pay in full (/off) 付清

pay in indemnification 支付赔偿

pay in kind 以实物支付

pay in money 以现金支付

pay installment 分期付款

pay money down 现款支付

pay off 清偿债务,贿赂,暗中行贿

pay off a debt 还债

pay off a score 还债

pay off in dump-sum 一次付清

pay off the mortgage 归还抵押货物

pay on account 先行支付

pay on delivery 货到付款

pay on time 准时付款

pay one's debt 还债

pay respects to 朝拜

pay taxes 纳税

pay the freight 支付运费

pay the hire 支付租金

pay tribute 朝贡

pay up 按时付款

pay up in time 及时付清

payable at a definite time 定期付款

payable at a fixed date 定期付款

payable at maturity 到期付款

payable at usance 远期付款

payable by installment 分期支付

payable on receipt/POR 收货付款

payable on the installment 分期付款

payback period 返本期间,返款期限

① payee 受款人,付款人

② payer 交付人

③ paying ability 支付能力

④ paying agency agreement 代理付款协议

⑤

⑥ paying agent 付款代理人,支付代理人

⑦

⑧ paying bank 汇入行,付款行

⑨ paying compensation for damage 赔偿损失

⑩

⑪ paying in advance 预付

⑫ payment 支付条款,付款,追缴,清偿

⑬

⑭ payment ability 偿还能力

⑮ payment after delivery 交货后付款

⑯

⑰ payment after inspection clause 验付条款

⑱

⑲ payment against delivery 交货停担

⑳

㉑ payment agreement 支付协定,支付协议

㉒

㉓ payment apportionment 摊派

㉔ payment at regular fixed time 定期付款

㉕

㉖ payment by acceptance 承兑付款

㉗

㉘ payment by banker 银行交付

㉙ payment by cash 现款支付

㉚ payment by installments 分期付款

㉛

㉜ payment by mistake 误付

㉝ payment by mistake of fact 误付

㉞ payment by post 邮寄付款,邮寄支付

㉟

㊱ payment for goods 货款

㊲ payment forward 预付货款

㊳ payment in advance 预付货款,预付提前付款

㊴

㊵ payment in arrears 拖欠款项

㊶ payment in cash 现金付款

㊷ payment in full 全部付款

㊸ payment in installments 分期支付

㊹

㊺ payment in kind 实物支付

㊻ payment in lien 以付款代替

㊼ payment in part 部分支付,部

分付款

payment insufficient 付款不足

payment into court 交存法院的押金

payment of breach of contract damages 支付违约金,违约金

payment of damages 支付损害赔偿,支付损害赔偿金

payment of hire 租金支付

payment of postage 邮件资费

payment on account 暂付

payment on delivery 交货停担,货到付款

payment on demand 见票即付

payment on terms 定期付款

payment order 付款通知

payment respite 延期付款

payment schedule 付款日程表

payment separation 离职补助费

payment terms 付款条件

payment undertaker 付款承担人

payment upon arrival of documents 单到付款

payment upon arrival of shopping documents 单到付款

pay-off 报酬

peace and order 治安

peace keeping 维护和平

peace treaty 和约

peace treaty of Westphalia 威斯特伐里亚和约

peaceful coexistence 和平共处

peaceful demonstration 和平示威

peaceful evolution 和平演变

peaceful settlement 和平解决

peacetime administrative law 平时行政法

peach against an accomplice 告发同案犯

peccatum（拉）错误行为

peculate 侵吞

peculation 外汇投机

peculiar property 特有财产

peculium（拉）特有财产

pecunia（拉）现金

pecunia credita（拉）债权金额

pecunia numerata（拉）现金

pecuniary benefits 金钱上的受益

pecuniary claim 金钱赔偿

pecuniary claim 金钱术语

pecuniary damage 金钱损害

pecuniary loss 金钱损失

pecuniary offense 应课罚金的罪

pecuniary penalty 罚金刑

pecuniary punishment 科以罚款的处分

pecuniary reparation(s) 金钱赔偿

pecuniary sanction for specific performance 执行罚

peeler 警察

peeling of the skull 颅骨削平

pegged price 控制价格

pelagic fishing 远洋渔业

pelagic whaling 远洋捕鲸

per package 每件

penal 刑事

penal action 刑事诉讼

penal clause 刑事条款,罚则

penal code 刑法典

penal colony 流放地

penal companion 刑事伙伴

penal damages 惩罚性损害赔偿

penal institution 刑罚执行机关,刑罚机构

penal jurisdiction 刑事啼辖权

penal jurist 刑法学家

penal law 刑法

penal procedure 刑事诉讼程序

penal proceedings 刑事诉讼

penal process 刑罚程序,刑事追诉

penal provision 刑事规定,刑法条文规定

penal psychology 刑则心理学

penal rate 极不利价格

penal section 刑罚条文部分

penal sentence 刑事判决,徒刑

penal servitude 劳役监督,(英)监禁和劳役合并的惩罚

penal stipulation 刑法规定

penal sum 罚金总额

penal tribunal 刑事法庭

penalbond 违约金

penalize 惩处,惩罚,处以刑事惩罚,处罚

penalties in financial administration 财政处罚

penalties in financial management 财政金融管理处罚

penalty 刑罚,违约罚金,违约金,刑,处罚

penalty decision 处罚决定

penalty for breach of contracts 违约罚金

penalty for delay 误期罚款

penalty for non performance of contract 未履行合同罚金,违约罚金

penalty on delayed delivery 延迟交货罚金

penalty provision(s) 罚则

penance 宗教法上的刑罚

pendens(拉) 待决

pendens lis(拉) 待决案件

pending 待决

pending action 待决诉讼

pending application 待审批的申请

pending case 待决案件

pending negotiations 在谈判期间

pending trial 待审

penetration 侵入

penetration pricing 渗透价格

penitential committee 刑务委员会

penitentials 忏悔录

penitentiary 罪犯忏悔所,应予惩罚的,(美)联邦监狱,拘留所,教养所,看守所

penitentiary committee 刑务委员会

penological principle 狱政管理原则

penological system 狱政制度

penologist 刑罚学家

penology 刑罚学,狱政管理学,监狱学

pension fund 养老基金

pension trust 养老金信托

penthouse 顶层高级套房

Pentoville prison 本顿维尔监狱

peonage 劳役偿债

people 国民

people under control to give up their drug habits 戒毒人员

people undergoing reeducation through labour 被劳教人员

people's armed forces department 人民武装部

people's assessor 人民陪审员

people's charter 人民宪章

people's commune 人民公社

people's congress 全国人大常委会,人民代表大会

people's congress at the basic level 基层人民代表大会

people's congress at the corresponding level 本级人大

people's congress at the next higher level 上一级人大

people's congress of a higher level 上级人大

people's council 人民委员会

people's court 人民法院

people's court at the corresponding level 本级人民法院

people's court at the county level 县级人民法院

people's court at the domicile of the defendant 被告住所地人民法院

people's court at the next higher level 上一级人民法院

people's court at the original domicile of the defendant 被告原住所地人民法院

people's court at the place of the licensee 被许可方所在地人民法院

people's court of first instance 第一审人民法院

people's court of second instance

第二审人民法院

people's court where the accused enters registration　被告注册登记地人民法院

people's court where the accused is under reform through education　被告被劳动教养地法院

people's court where the domicile of the representative agency is seated　代表机构所在地人民法院

people's democracy　人民民主

people's democratic constitutionality　人民民主宪政

people's democratic dictatorship　人民民主专政

People's democratic state　人民民主国家

people's democratic system　人民民主制度

people's democratic united front　人民民主统一战线

people's deputies　人民代表

people's deputy from the army　军队人民代表

people's government　人民政府

people's government at the corresponding level　本级人民政府

people's government at the county level　县级人民政府

people's government at the next higher level　上一级人民政府

people's government at the provincial level　省级人民政府

people's government of higher levels　上级人民政府

people's judge　人民审判员

people's livelihood　民生,民生主义

people's mediation commission　人民调解委员会

people's organization　人民团体

people's police　人民警察

people's procuratorate　人民检察院

people's procuratorate at the ba-sic level　基层人民检察院

people's procuratorate at the corresponding level　各级人民检察院

people's procuratorate at the county level　县级人民检察院

people's procuratorate at the next higher level　上一级人民检察院

people's procuratorate at the provincial level　省级人民检察院

people's prosecutor's office　人民检察院

people's public security　人民公安

people's republic　人民共和国

people's revolutionary military committee　人民革命军事委员会

people's supervision　人民监督

people's tribunal　人民法庭

peppercorn rent　名义上租金,象征性租金

per auter vie　在他人生存期间享有的不动产物权

per country limitation　分国限额

per formulas(拉)　程式诉讼

per incuriam(拉)　由于不慎

per infortunium(拉)　由于不幸的事故

per se doctrine(拉)　本身违法原则

per se rules(拉)　本身违法原则

percentage agreement　按百分比收费协议

percentage of forest cover　森林覆盖率

percentage of voter turnout　投票率

percentage rent　按百分比计的租金

perceptibility of witness　证人的感知能力

perceptio(拉)　受领

perceptual knowledge　感性认识

peregrine　寄居外国的人

peremptory 强行,不能上诉

peremptory judgment 不能上诉

peremptory mandamus 强制履行金

peremptory norm 强制规则,强制性规范

peremptory norm of general international law 一般国际法强制规律

peremptory provision 强制性规定

peremptory reservation 强制性保留

peremptory rule 强制性规则,强制规定

perfect 健全

perfect act 完全行为

perfect and imperfect rights 完全权利和不完全权利

perfect competition 完全竞争

perfect instrument 有效证件

perfect neutrality 完全中立

perfect obligation 合法债务

perfect sovereign state 完全主权国家

perfect substitute 完全代替品

perfect title 完全所有权

perfect trust 完全信托

perforated signature 打孔签字

perforating bullet wound 贯通枪弹创

perform 履行,行使

perform a contract 履行合同,执解合同

perform military service 服兵役

perform obligations 履行权利,履行义务

perform one's duty 履行职责

perform the debt 履行债务

perform the obligation 履行义务

performance 给付

performance bond 履行保证书,履行保证函,履行担保书,履行保函,履行保证金

performance budget 经营成绩预算

performance by accord and satisfaction 代物清偿

performance by the third party 第三人清偿

performance criteria 履行标准

performance expenses 履行费用

performance guarantee 履行保证书,履行担保人,履约担保,履行保证

performance in part or on installment 部分履行

performance of a contract 契约之履行

performance of a definite act 特定行为的履行

performance of an obligation 履行债务

performance of debt 债务清偿

performance of obligation 债的履行

performance of official business 执行公务

performances in reforming oneself 改造表现

performative role 履行作用

performer 执行公务

performing one's duties 执行公务

Pericles 伯里克利

peril 危险事故

perils clause 危险条款

perils of the sea 水上灾害

period 期间

period depreciation charge 当期折旧费

period for presenting claim 提出请求的期限,索赔期限

period for probation of execution 暂缓执行期间

period for reporting claims 债权申报期限

period for the repayment of the debt 债权受偿期限

period of absolute criminal responsibility 完全刑事责任时期

period of accounting practice 会

计核算期间

period of commonwealth 共和时期

period of commutation of criminal responsibility 减轻刑事责任时期

period of constitutional government 宪政时期

period of custodial investigation 侦查羁押期间

period of death 死亡期

period of delay 延迟期

period of detention 扣留时间

period of insurance 保险期限

period of limitation 时效期限

period of limitation time bar 时效

period of prescription 时效期

period of recovery （国民经济）恢复时期（中国）

period of residence 居住期间

period of service （送达回执）送达期间

period of shipment 装船期限

period of validity 有效期,有效期限

period stipulated for delivery 约定交货期

periodic charges 定期购买费

periodic check 定期检查

periodic examination 定期检查

periodical publication 定期刊物

Perioeci 皮里阿西

perishable 鲜活不易保管,易腐

perishable article 易腐品

perishable cargo 鲜货,易腐货物

perishable food 易腐烂变质食品

perishable goods 易腐货物

perjuries 伪证

permanent 常设

permanent administrative organization 常设行政机关

permanent agreement 永久性协议

permanent assets 永久性资产

permanent body 常设机构,常设机关

permanent committee 常设委员会

permanent connection 经常性联系

permanent court of arbitration 常设公断法院,常设仲裁法院

permanent court of international justice 国际常设法院

permanent deprivation of one's political right 剥夺政治权力终身

permanent domicile 永久住所

permanent establishment 常设机构

permanent house 常住房屋

permanent identity card 永久性居民身份证

permanent investments 永久投资

permanent means of transport 永久运输工具

permanent members of the security council 安理会常任理事国

permanent mission 常驻使团

permanent neutrality 永久中立

permanent neutralized state 永久中立国

permanent organization 常设机构

permanent population 常住人口

permanent property 永久性财产

permanent repair 永久修理

permanent residence 永久居留,永久居所

permanent resident 永久居民,永久性居民

permanent resident of Hong Kong 香港永久性居民

permanent right of defence 永久抗辩权

permanent saving 长期储蓄

permanent sovereignty of every state over its natural resources 国家对自然资源的救主权

permanent sovereignty over natural resources 自然资源的承文主权(1962,联大决议)

permanent surveying market 永久性测量标志

permanently acting body 常设机构

permission 同意

permissive joinder 任意合并

permissive legislation 任意法规

permissive provisions 任选条款,任意条款,非约束性条款

permissive regulation 任意性规范

permissive waste 通常损耗

permit 批准,许可

permit for carring and transporting firearms 枪支携运许可证

permit for presale 预售许可证

perniciousness 危害性

perpetration 作为犯罪,实施犯罪

perpetrator 犯罪人,实行犯,执行犯

perpetrator of unjustifiable self-defense 防卫过当者

perpetual allegiance 永远效忠的义务

perpetual annuity 永久年金

perpetual debate 长期辩诉

perpetual injunction 永久性止制令,永久止制令

perpetual lease 永久租赁,永租权,永租

perpetual lease 永租权

perpetual license 永远许可证

perpetual loan 无期贷款

perpetual right 永久性权利

perpetual statute 永久性法规

perpetuity 永久不得转让的房地产,永久拥有的房地产,永久所有权

persecution mania 被迫害妄想狂

persecution of victimization 被害预测,被害原因

persistent criminal 固执性犯罪人

persistent dumping 持久性倾销

persistent offender 常习犯

person 自然人

person against who a judgment or order is being executed 被执行人

person against whom an application for execution is filed 被申请执行人

person being reported against 被举报人

person bound to furnish support 负抚养义务人

person capable of disposing 有行为能力的人

person chiefly held responsible 主要负责人

person concerned 有关的人,当事人

person declared dead 被宣告死亡的人

person declared missing 被宣告失踪的人

person declared missing or dead 被宣告失踪或死亡的人

person directly responsible 直接责任人

person entirely incapable of legal transaction 完全丧失行为能力,完全丧失行为能力的人

person excused from prosecution 被免诉人员

person having a quarantinable infectious disease 检疫传染病染疫人

person having no capacity for civil conduct 无民事行为能力人

person holding deputy posts 副职负责人

person in charge 负责人

person in charge of a public security organization 公安机关负责人

person in charge of administrative organization 行政负责人

person in charge of finance 财务

负责人

person in custody 被拘留人

person in necessary colitigation 必要共同诉讼人

person in power 当权者

person liable 责任人

person limited in disposing capacity 限制行为能力人

person other than involved in the case 案外人

person released upon completion of a sentence 刑满释放人员

person required in action 被吸收加入诉讼的人

person sanctioned 受处罚人

person serving a document 送达人

person subject to administration 行政管理相对人

person summoned to court with force 被拘传人

person suspected of having quarantinable infectious diseases 检疫传染病染疫嫌疑人

person under a legal disability 法律上无行为能力的人

person under age 未成年人

person under guardianship 被监护人

person under surveillance 被监管人员

person undergoing reeducation-through-labour 被劳教人员, 劳动教养人员

person under a legal disability 法律上无行为能力的人

person who prepares a written accusation 具状人

person who resorts to necessity 紧急避险人

person who takes an act of rescue 紧急避险人

person with capacity for civil conduct 有民事行为能力人

person with full capacity for civil conduct 完全民事行为能力人

person with incompetent responsibility 无责任能力人

person with limited capacity for civil conduct 限制民事行为能力人

person with no capacity 无行为能力人

person without capacity of civil conduct 无民事行为能力人

person worthy of merit in reporting crimes 举报有功人员

persona（拉）自然人

persona certa（拉）特定人

persona non grate（拉）不受欢迎的人

personal abuse 人身攻击

personal act 个人法

personal act of law 法律对人的效力

personal action 人的诉讼

personal benefit 个人利益

personal capital 个人资本

personal contract 动产契约

personal credit 个人信贷

personal debt 个人债务

personal dignity 人格尊严, 人身尊严

personal disability 无民事行为能力, 诱骗, 无行为能力

personal dues and taxes 对人捐税

personal effect of criminal law 刑法的对人效力

personal effects 私人财产

personal estate 私人财产

personal freedom 人身自由, 个人自由

personal guarantee 个人担保, 私人担保, 个人保证

personal identification 本人身份证明

personal injury 人身伤害, 人身伤亡

personal insult 人身侮辱

personal insurance 人身保险

personal inviolability 人身的不可侵犯性, 人身不可侵犯性

personal jurisdiction 属人管辖权

personal law 属人法

personal law of legal person 法人属人法,个人负债

personal liberty 个人责任个人自由,人身自由权

personal liberty of citizens 公民的人身自由

personal non-property relations 人身非财产关系

personal pension annuities 退休年金保险

personal property 个人财产,私人财产

personal property replacement income tax 动产重置所得税

personal property right 个人财产权

personal property tax 动产税

personal protection order 人身保护令

personal punishment 人身罚

personal relation 人身关系,人身非财产关系

personal relationship 人身关系

personal remedies 债权救济

personal reputation 个人名誉

personal responsibility 个人责任

personal right 人权,人身权,人格权,人身权利,对人权

personal right over body 人身权

personal rights and interests 人身权益

personal safety 人身安全

personal seal 私章

personal security 人身安全

personal service 个人服务,送达当事人本人

personal sphere of validity 属人效力范围

personal status 个人身份

personal status relationship 身份关系

personal surety 个人担保

personal taxes 对人税

personal trust 个人信托

personal union 君合国,人合国

personal warranty 个人担保

personalities of laws 法律属人原则

personality 人格尊严,法律人,人格

personality cult 个人迷信

personality disorder 病态人格

personality disorder of passive aggression 被动攻击型人格障碍

personality of women 妇女人格

personate security 人身安全

personification of the vessel 船舶的人格化

personnel administration 人事管理,人事行政

personnel concerned 有关人员

personnel dossier management 人事档案管理

personnel handling a case 办案人员

personnel management rules 干部管理办法

personnel system 人事制度

persons deprived of political rights 被剥夺政治权利的人

persons entering the country 入境人员

persons serving sentences 服刑人员

persons undergoing reeducation-through-labor 劳动教养人员

persuasive precedent 具有说明力的判例

pertain to 涉及

pertinent certificate 有关证件

pervert 滥用

pervert justice for a bribe 贪赃枉法

pervert the law 枉法

perverting the course of justice 败坏司法审判

pesticide control law 农药管理法

pesticide producing license 农药生产许可证**

petition 请愿,请愿书,申请

petition another to write a document 请求代书

petition for asylum 请求庇护

petition for judgment of the case 本案判决请求权

petition for requestration 请求查封状

petition for retrial 请求复审

petition for revision 请求复审状

petition of right 权利请愿书（1860 年）

petition of right 1628 民权宣言（1628）

petition of right act 权利请愿书

petition of service 送达请求书

petitioner 上诉人（注：指二审中）

petitioning creditor 出具请求书的债权人

petrol-dollar 石油美元

pettifog 包揽诉讼

pettifogger 包揽诉讼人

petty bourgeoisie 小资产阶级

petty crime 轻微罪行

petty criminality 微罪

petty jury 小陪审团

petty loan 小额贷款

petty loss 轻度损失

petty private owners 小私有者

petty seasonal court 简易季审法庭

petty sessions 小治安裁判法庭，即决法院

pexport quarantine 出口检疫

pharaoh 暴君,法老

pharmaceutical administration 药品管理,药品行政,药政

pharmaceutical administration law 药品管理法

pharmaceutical inspection institution 药品检验机构

pharmaceutical inspector 药品监督员

pharmaceutical management law 药品管理法

pharmaceutical packaging 药品的包装

pharmaceutical producer licence 药品生产企业许可证

pharmaceutical producing enterprise 药品生产企业

pharmaceutical standard 药品标准

pharmaceutical supervision and control 药品监督管理工作

pharmaceutical trading enterprise 药品经营企业

pharmaceutical trading enterprise licence 药品经营企业许可证

pharmacist's license 药师执照

pharmacodynamics effect 药理效应

pharmacological testing 药理试验

phenemenon 现象

phenonmenology of law 法的现象学

philanthropism 仁爱

philosophy of law 法律哲学,法哲学

phobia neurosis 恐怖性神经官能症

phonomania 嗜杀狂

phoposed regulation(s) 试行条例

photography for identification 辨认照相

photography on criminal inspection 刑事检验照相

photography related to criminal investigation 刑事照相

photoreconnaissance 空中照相侦察

phrenology 颅相学

physical 人身伤害

physical assault 行凶抢劫

physical assets 有形资产

physical capital 有形资本

physical damage 物质损失

physical delivery 实际交货

physical delivery terms 实际交货条件

physical disability 劳动能力丧

失

physical distribution 实物运销

physical feature of a place 地势

physical goods 实物

physical injury 身体伤害,肉体伤害

physical loss 物质损失

physical loss or damage 有形灭失或损坏

physical makeup 物质补偿

physical market 现货市场

physical motives of crime 生理性犯罪动机

physical person 自然人

physical protection 人身保护

physical resource 物质资源

physical setting of a crime 犯罪环境

physical traces of a crime 犯罪痕迹

physiological factors of crime 犯罪生理因素

pick up goods 提货

pick-test 抽样检查

piece ratewage 计件工资

piece wages 计件工资

piecework payment 计件工资

piecework wage 计件工资

pigeonholk 搁置

pignus (拉) 契约

pile building 岸边房屋(半水半陆的)

pile dwelling 岸边住房

pilgrimage 朝圣

pillager 抢劫犯

pilot 驾驶员,新产品试制

pilot agreement 试行协议

pilot enterprise 试点企业

pilotage 领港权

pioneering work 创举

piracy 海盗行为,海上掠夺

pirate 盗版

pistol wound 手枪弹创伤

place 地方,场所,任命

place a case on file 立案

place a case on file for investigation, prosecution or trial 立案受理

place an offer 发出订价

place an order for 订购

place an order with 向…订货

place and date of issue 签发地点与日期

place money in 投资

place of a crime 犯罪地

place of arbitration 仲裁地点

place of business 营业地点

place of contracting 合同缔结地

place of custody 羁押场所

place of delivery 交付地,交货地点

place of domicile 户籍所在地,户籍地

place of drawing 汇票发票地点

place of execution 刑场

place of injure 损害发生地

place of labour service performance 劳务实施地

place of loading 装船地,装货处,装货地

place of origin 原产地

place of performance 履行地点

place of performance of a labour contract 劳动合同履行地

place of receipt 接货地点

place of reform-through-labour 劳动改造场所

place of registered permanent residence 户籍地

place of residence 住所地

place of shipment 装运地点

place of signing 签订地点

place of survey 检验地点

place of the court session 开庭地点

place of the defendant's action 加害行为地

place of the defendant's principal establishment 被告主营业所所在地

place on record 记录在案

place prior to arrest 捕前所在地

place under house arrest 软禁

place where a criminal act is discovered 犯罪发现地

place where a criminal involed in a case is locked up 案犯关押地

place where a labour contract is performed 劳动合同履行地

place where a malfeasance is committed 违法行为发生地

place where an exposed case has occurred 发案地

place where property targeted for execution is situated 被执行的财产所在地

placement of industry 工业布局

places where there are relatively large numbers of returned overseas Chinese 归侨人数较多地区

placing immovable 抵押不动产

placing movable 抵押动产

placing of state orders with private enterprises for the manufacture of goods 计划订货

placita coronae (拉) 刑事审判

plagiarism 剽窃

plain 简单

plain arch 弧形纹

plain meaning 明显意义

plaint 控告式诉讼程序

plaintiff 原告(注:指一审中)

plaintiff in administrative proceedings 行政诉讼原告

plaintiff in civil 原告

plan 计划

plan for development of science and technology 科技发展规划

plan for economic and social development 经济和社会发展计划

plan for gold and silver earning and expenditure 金银收支计划

plan for statistical investigation 统计调查计划

plan formulation 计划编制

① plan period 计划期

② plan target 计划指标

③ planing power 计划权

④ planned allocation 计划调拨

⑤ planned board 计划委员会

⑥ planned change 计划变动

⑦ planned committee 计划委员会

⑧ planned cycle 计划周期

⑨ planned economy 计划经济

⑩ planned expenditure 计划内支出,计划支出

⑫ planned indicators 计划指标

⑬ planned industrial district 计划工业区

⑮ planned investment 计划内投资

⑯ planned limit 计划限额

⑰ planned loan 计划贷款

⑱ planned management 计划管理

⑲ planned management structure 计划管理体制

㉑ planned managerial system 计划管理体制

㉓ planned norm 计划定额,计划限额

㉕ planned output 计划产量

㉖ planned parenthood 计划生育

㉗ planned price 计划价格

㉘ planned product 计划产品

㉙ planned production 计划生产

㉚ planned profit 计划利润

㉛ planned project 规划项目

㉜ planned purchase 计划收购

㉝ planned quota 计划定额,计划限额

㉟ planned readjustment 计划调市

㊱ planned regulation 计划调市

㊲ planned saving 计划储蓄

㊳ planned spacing of birth 计划生育间隔

㊵ planned supply 计划供应

㊶ planned supply coupons 计划供应票证

㊸ planning 规划

㊹ planning authorities 计划管理部门

㊻ planning by objective 按目标制定规划

planning cycle 计划周期
planning data 计划资料
planning estimate 计划概算
planning function 计划职能
planning law 计划法
planning mechanism 计划机制
planning of auditing items 审计项目计划
planning period 计划期
planning permission 规划许可证
planning planned 计划
planning settlement 计划结算
planning superior 计划主管人
planning system 计划管理体制
planning unit 计划单位
planning-programming-budgeting 计划预算
plans as binding instructions 指令性计划
plans with a mandatory nature 指令性计划
plant bargaining 工厂谈判
plant national economy and social development 国民经济和社会发展计划
plant quarantine certificate 植物检疫证明书
plant-engineering contract 工程承包合同
Plato 柏拉图
play the market 投机倒把
plea 第一次答辩
plea against a criminal accusation 刑事答辩状
plea agreement 答辩交易（又辩诉交易）
plea bargaining 答辩交易（又辩诉交易）
plea based on prescription 根据时效的抗辩
plea in abatement 妨诉抗辩
plea in bar 被告抗辩,法庭上的答辩
plea in mitigation of damages 请求减轻损失
plea of defense 答辩陈述

plea of general issue 总括性之抗辩
plea of military necessity 出于军事上需要的答辩
plea of non est factum（拉）非其行为之抗辩
plea of non-discrimination 无歧视抗辩
plea of non guilty 不认罪答辩,无罪答辩
plea of public policy 公共秩序抗辩
plea of self-defense 出于自卫的抗辩
plea of tender 提存抗辩,准备给付之抗辩
plea of "act of state" 国家行为抗辩
plea to jurisdiction 对管辖权的抗辩
plead 抗辩,答辩,辩护
plead guilty 领罪,服罪
pleader 答辩人,辩护人,抗辩者
pleadings 辩护词
pleas of the crown 刑事诉讼,（英）公诉
please confirm/PLSCONFM 请确认
pledge 抵押,质物,质押,出值,典当品,发誓,质权,质契,抵押物,抵押品
pledge assets 抵押资产
pledge of bill of lading 提单抵押
pledge of immovables 不动产抵押
pledge of movables 动产质权,动产质押,动产抵押
pledge of obligation 债权质押,债权质权
pledge of rights 权利质押
pledge of secrecy 保密宣誓
pledged assets 押出资产
pledged securities 抵押有价证券
pledgeholder 抵押品持有人

pledgor 出质人

pleding 诉辩状

plena jure（拉） 全权

plena potestas（拉） 全权委任

plena probatio（拉） 充分证据

plena proprietas（拉） 全部所有权

plenary 充分

plenary conference 全体会议

plenary confession 彻底坦白

plenary meeting 全体会议

plenary power 全权

plenipotentiary 有全权的,全权代表

plenitude 权限的完整

plenum dominium（拉） 完全所有权,绝对所有权

plot of land for personal needs 自留地

plots of cropland allotted for private use 自留地

plough back 利润再投资

plural crimes in reality 实际数罪

plural crimes of a kind 同种数罪

plural nationality 多重国籍

plural punishments 数刑

plural represention 复数代表制

plural vote 一人多选票制,一人多选区投票

plural vote system 复数投票制

pluralism 多元论,多元主义

plurality 多元制,未超过半数的最多票数,多数

plurality of votes 相对多数票

plurality system 相对多票制

plurality votes 相对多数票,较多票数

plus or minus clause 增减条款

pocket money for prisoners 犯人零用钱

pocket veto 搁置否决权,议案搁置否决权,袋中否决

pocket veto right 口袋否决权

poenae stipulatio（拉） 违约罚金

point block 点式房屋

① point of contract 合同要点

② point of defense 辩护要点

③ point of entry 入境地点

④ point of exit 出境地点

⑤ point of law 法律要点

⑥ point of plea 抗辩要点,答辩要点

⑧ point of pleadings 答辩要点

⑨ point of rejoinder 第二次答辩论点

⑪ point of transhipment 转运地点

⑫ pointing of the ground 地上财产扣押之诉

⑭ points of claim 请求要点

⑮ point-of-purchase advertising 店面广告

⑰ poke 戳伤

⑱ polarization between the rich and the poor 贫富分化

⑳ police 警察

㉑ police act 警察法

㉒ police agency 警察机构,公安派驻机构

㉔ police agent 警察

㉕ police apparatus 警察机构

㉖ police authority 警察权

㉗ police bureau 警察局

㉘ police court 警察法院

㉙ police in disguise 便衣警察

㉚ police law 警察法

㉛ police lock-up 警察局拘留所

㉜ police management system 警察管理体制

㉞ police offence 违警罪

㉟ police office 警察局

㊱ police officer 警察

㊲ police organization 警察组织

㊳ police patrol 警察巡逻

㊴ police power 警察权

㊵ police preservation of public peace 维持治安

㊷ police rank 警察衔级

㊸ police rank system 警衔制

㊹ police station 警察局

㊺ police strength 警力

㊻ police substation 公安派出所,派出所

police substation at the habitual residence 常驻公安派出所

police weapon 警械

policeman 警察

policeman in charge of household registration 户籍警

policeman on point duty 岗警

policemen engaged in reform- and reeducation-through-labour 劳改劳教干警

policewoman 女警察

policy 政策

policy character of administrative act 行政行为的政策性

policy depreciation 政策性折价

policy going against the law 与法律相抵触的政策

Policy of Appeasement 绥靖政策

policy of benevolence 仁政

policy of civil trial 民事审判工作方针

policy of containment 遏制政策

policy of economic control 经济管制政策

policy of education, reform through persuasion and exemplary deeds and redemption 教养、感化、挽救的方针

policy of force 实力政策

policy of grab 掠夺政策

policy of laying equal stress on 并重方针

policy of no perversion of the law for the innocent or the guilty 不枉不罪方针

policy of opening up to the outside world 对外开放政策

policy of premiums for sale 奖售政策

policy of protective tariff 保护关税政策

policy of redemption 赎买政策

policy of reforming criminals 改造罪犯的政策

policy of reforming quality criminals 改造罪犯的政策

policy of reward for sale 奖售政策

policy of the law 法律政策

policy on locality 地方分权政策

policy protective trade policy 保护贸易政策

policy science of law 政策法学

policy surveillance 政策监督

policy towards nationalities 民族政策

policymaker 决策者

policymaking 决策,制定政策

policymaking body 决策机构

policy-oriented approach 政策定向说

polis 城邦

political 政治性,党派政治

political appearance 政治面目,政治表现

political assassination 政治性暗杀

political association 政治性结社

political asylum 政治避难,政治庇护,政治庇护权

political authority 政治权力

political basis 政治基础

political basis of constitution 宪法的政治基础

political bureau 政治局

political bureau of the general committee of the communist party of china 中共中央政治局

political consultation 政治协商

political consultation system 政治协商制度

political consultative conference 政协,政治协商会议

political crime 政治犯罪

political crisis 政治危机

political democracy 政治民主

political democracy supervision 政治民主监督

political duty 政治责任

political entity 政治实体

political equality 政治平等

political fugitive 政治逃犯

political functionary　政务类公务员

political independence　政治独立

political institutions　政治体制

political interpretation　政治解释

political intrigue　政治阴谋

political jurisdiction　政治管辖权

political jurisprudence　政治管辖,政治法学

political jurist　政治法学家,政治法学

political liberty　政治自由

political means of settlement of international disputes　国际争端政治解决方法

political offender　政治犯

political officer on reserve service　预备役政治军官

political opponent　政敌

political order　政治秩序

political organization　政治组织

political party　政党

political party system　政党制度

political persecution　政治迫害

political philosophy　政治哲学

political power　政权,政治权力

political prerogative　政治特权

political programme　政纲

political purposes　政治目的

political reasons　政治原因

political reform　政治体制改革

political relation　政治关系

political rights　参政权,政治权利

political rights of women　妇女政治权利

political risks　政治风险

political sanction　政治制裁

political science　政治学

political self-determination　政治自决

political situation　政局,政治局势

political solution　政治解决

political sovereignty　政治主权

political standing　政治地位

political status　政治地位

political strategy　政治策略

political structure of state　国家政体

political supervision　政治监督

political suspicion　政治嫌疑犯罪

political system　政治体系,政治制度

political thought　政治思想

political trickery　权术

political turmoil　政治动乱

political view　政见

political work　政治工作

political-legal cadre school　政法干部学校

political-legal circle　政法界

political-legal committee　政法委

political-legal department　政法部门

political-legal functionaries　政法干部

politician　政客,政治家

politicking　政治活动

politics　政治,政治生活

politics strike　政治罢工

poll　投票结果,投票人的名册,选举投票,民意测验,投票

pollbook　选举人名册

poll-clerk　选举投票工作人员

polling agent　投票代理人

polling booth　投票站

polling day　投票人,选举日

polling place　选举地点

polltaker　民意测验者

pollutant　污染物,污染物质

pollutant discharging unit　排污单位

pollute the environment　污染环境

pollution　污染,环境污染

pollution abatement cost　环境保护费用

pollution control　污染控制

pollution control zone　污染控制区

pollution damage to the environment　环境污染损害

pollution discharge standard　污染物排放标准

pollution indicating organism　污染指示物

pollution monitoring　污染监测

pollution of air　空气污染

pollution of atmosphere　大气层污染

pollution of environment　环境污染

pollution of sea　海洋污染

pollution of water　水污染

pollution source　污染源

pollution zone　污染区

polyarchy　多党政治,多头政治

polycentrism　多中心主义

polygamy　多配偶制

polytheism　多神教

pooling funds　集中资金

pooling funds in share form　股票集资

pooling of interest　共同经营,联合经营

pooling of land as shares　土地入股

poor criminal　贫困性犯罪人

poor efficiency　低效率

poor law(s)　济贫法

poor lawyer　不懂法律的人

poor management　经营管理不善

poor operation and management　经营管理不善

popular　人民的

popular action　民众诉讼

popular feelings　民心

popular sense　常识

popular sovereignty　人民主权

popular will　民意

populated country　居民区

population census　人口普查

population quality　人口质量

porn trafficking gang　贩黄集团

port　港口

port facilities　港口设施

port of call　停泊港

port of debarkation　卸货港

port of departure　发货地

port of delivery　交船港

port of discharge　卸货港口,卸货港

port of dispatch　发货地

port of embarkation　装货港,出境港

port of loading　装货港,装运港

port of refuge expenses　避难港费用

port of shipment　装运港,装船港,装货港

port of transshipment　转运单,转运港口

port of unloading　卸货港口

port superintendency agencies of the People's Republic of China　中华人民共和国港务监督机构

port tax　港口税

Portalis　波塔利斯

portent of crime　犯罪征兆

portfolio　阁员职务

portfolio acquisition　全部购买

portfolio investment　证券投资

portio（拉）　一部分

portionless　无继承份

pose　提出

position　职位,地位

position foreign exchange　外汇头寸

position of bleeding　血痕出血部位测定

position of brigade commander　副旅职

position of criminal law　刑法地位

position of deputy army commander　副军职

position of deputy battalion commander　副营职

position of deputy company commander　副连职

position of deputy division commander　副师职

position of deputy platoon commander 副排职

position of deputy regimental commander 副团职

position of law 法律的地位

position sheet 头寸表

positive 确定的,明确的,绝对的

positive act 积极行为

positive administrative law 积极行政法

positive administrative measure 积极的行政措施

positive causal relationship 必然因果关系

positive clause 实质条款

positive condition 积极条件

positive conditionality 积极制约原则

positive conditions of an action 积极诉讼要件

positive conflict of jurisdiction over administrative action 行政诉讼管辖积极冲突

positive connection 必然联系

positive control 积极管制

positive damage 积极的损害

positive duty 积极义务

positive effect 积极效果

positive guarantee 积极保证,积极担保

positive jurisprudence 实在法学,实证法学

positive law 实在法,实证法,实定法

positive law of nations 实在万国法

positive obligation 积极义务

positive prescription 确定的时效

positive representation 积极代理,主动代理

positive results 积极效果

positive servitude 积极地段

positivist 实在法学派

positivist jurisprudence 实在主义法学

possess 占有

possessio bonorum（拉） 财产占有

possessio corporis（拉） 有体的占有

possessio injusta（拉） 不合法占有

possessio juris（拉） 权利的占有

possessio naturalis（拉） 自然占有

possessio publica（拉） 公然占有

possession 占有权

possession by entireties 共同占有

possession of counterfeit currency 持有伪造货币罪

possession of house-breaking instruments 持有入屋行窃的工具

possession of land 土地占有

possession of nonowner 非所有人占有

possession of owner 所有人占有

possession of property 财产占有

possession through management 经营中的占有

possessions 财产

possessor 占有人

possessor corporis（拉） 有体物占有人

possessor juris（拉） 权利占有人

possessor of estate 财产占有人

possessory lien 船舶留置权,占有留置权

possessory right 占有权

possessory title 占有性所有权

possessory title to land 土地占有权

possibility 可能性

possible debt 或有债务

post 职位,邮件

post a bail and await trial with stricted liberty of moving 取保候审

post and communication industry 邮电通信业

post and telecommunication office

邮电局

post and telecommunications branch office 邮电支局

post and telecommunications office 邮电局

post and telegraph 邮电

post audit 事后审计

post calculated contract price 后算的合同价格

post censorship 事后新闻检查

post cerebral traumatic dementia 颅脑损伤后痴呆

post cerebral traumatic epilepsy 颅脑损伤性癫痫

post cerebral traumatic syndrome 颅脑损伤后人格改变

post check 邮政支票

post date-marks 邮政日戳

post mark 邮戳

post matters 邮件

post office 邮局,邮政局

post receipt 邮局收据

post responsibility system 岗位责任制

post supervision 事后监督

post telegraph and telephone office 邮电局

postage 邮费

postage certificate 邮资凭证

postage due letter 欠资信件

postage due mail 欠资邮件

postage paid 邮资已付,邮费已付

postage paid by license 邮资总付

postage stamp pattern 邮票图案

postal 邮费

postal administrative organization 邮政管理机关

postal advertising 邮政广告

postal and telecommunication personnel 邮电工作人员

postal and telephone 邮电

postal articles 邮递物品

postal code 邮政编码

postal convention 邮政公约

postal correspondence 邮政函件

① postal enterprise 邮政企业
② postal facility 邮政设施
③ postal forbidden articles 邮政禁寄品
⑤ postal item 邮件
⑥ postal law 邮政法
⑦ postal management 邮政管理
⑧ postal material 邮件
⑨ postal matter 邮件
⑩ postal money order 邮政汇票
⑪ postal note 邮政汇票
⑫ postal order 邮政汇票
⑬ postal parcel 邮政包裹
⑭ postal relation 邮政关系
⑮ postal remittance 邮政汇款
⑯ postal service 邮政,邮政事业
⑰ postal tariff 邮费表
⑱ postal territory 邮区
⑲ postbag 邮袋
⑳ postdate 迟填日期
㉑ postdoctor 博士后
㉒ posting 职务
㉓ posting and delivery of postal material 邮件的寄递
㉕ postliminium 权利恢复
㉖ postman 送信人
㉗ postmark 邮戳
㉘ postmark date 邮戳日
㉙ postmaster 邮政局长
㉚ postmortem 验尸
㉛ postmortem dismemberment 死后分尸
㉝ postmortem examination of a criminal 罪犯尸体检验
㉟ postmortem fingerprinting 死后指纹捺印
㊲ postmortem injury 死后伤,死后碎尸
㊳ postmortem interval 死后间隔时间
㊴ postpone 推迟,延缓
㊶ postpone payment 延付
㊷ postpone the shipment 推迟装船
㊸ postpone without day 无限延期
㊹ postponement of imprisonment 暂缓执行监禁
㊼ posts and telecommunications 邮

电

posts of state civil service 国家公务员职务

posttraumatic neurosis 创伤后神经官能症

potential competition 潜在竞争

potential crime 潜在性犯罪

potential criminal 潜在罪犯,可能犯罪者

potential demand 潜在需要

potential resources 潜在资源

potential victim 潜在被害人

potential wealth 潜在财富

potestas 主权

power 威力,强权,权限,权力

power and benefits 责权利

power and functions 权能

power and influence 权势

power games 权术

power in trust 信托权利

power interruption 供电中断

power of administration trial 行政审判权

power of administrative adjudication 行政审判权,行政裁决权

power of administrative bodies 行政机关的权力

power of administrative control 行政控制权

power of administrative law enforcement 行政执法权力

power of administrative law system 行政法制监督权

power of administrative penalty 行政处罚权

power of administrative review 行政复议权

power of administrative sanction 行政处分权

power of agency, agent's right 代理权限,代理权期间

power of alienation 财产转让权

power of appointment 任命权

power of appointment and removal 任免权

power of arbitrary administrative execution 行政强制执行权

power of attorney 代理人之权能,代理证书,委任代理权,委托授权,委托书

power of attorney for civil agency 民事代理授权委托书

power of civil adjudication 民事审判权

power of construction 解释权

power of contracting a treaty 约权

power of criminal adjudication 刑事审判权

power of eminent domain 国家征用权

power of executive control 行政控制权

power of final instance 终审权

power of financial supervision 财政监督权

power of interpretation 解释权

power of investigation 侦查权

power of issuing administrative orders 行政命令权

power of making administrative decisions 行政决定权

power of punishment 刑罚权,惩罚权

power of punishment with respect to public security 治安处罚裁决权

power of review of constitutionality 违宪审查权

power of sale 变卖权,出售权

power of self-management 自主权

power of state 国家权力

power of statistics supervision 统计监督权

power of supervision over administration 行政监察权

power of taxation 征税权

power of the sword of justice 司法权

power of veto 否决权

power over business practices 对经营活动管理权

power politics 强权政治
power structure 权力结构
power struggle 权力斗争
power to adjudicate 审判权
power to create administrative penalties 行政处罚设定权
power to engage in import and export trade 进出口经营权
power to impose penalties 处罚权
power to institute administrative punishment 行政处罚的设定权
power to interpret the constitution 解释宪法权
power to make decisions 决定权
power to make statistics report 统计报告权
power to promulgate law 颁布法律权
power to remove another from office 免职权
power to sign 签字权
power to statistics survey 统计调查权
power to supervise through auditing 审计监督权
power treading law 权大于法
power veto 否决权
power-holder 实权派
power-on time 供电时间
powers and functions 权能
powers and responsibilities 职权和责任
powers of audit office 审计部门的权力
practicability 可行的
practicable 切实
practical capacity 实际生产能力
practical owner 事实上的所有人
practical results prescribed 规定的实绩
practical step 实际措施
practice 惯例诉讼规程
practice bribery at election 贿选

practice direction 程序指示,程序指令
practice master's rules 程序主事官规则
practicing certificate 开业证书,营业证书
practicing certificate of a law office 律师事务所执业证书
practicing doctor 执业医师
practicing physician 执业医师
practicing physicians law 执业医师法
practicing requirements 执业资格
practise democracy 实行民主
practise usury 盘剥
pragmatism 实用主义
pragmatist 实用主义者
preamble 制定法的序文,序言
preamble of constitution 宪法序言
preambular part 序言部分
prearranged sales contract 预定买卖契约
precapitalist criminal law 前资本主刑法
precarious possession 不稳定的占有
precarious right 不确定的权利
precaution 预防措施,预防
precautionary measures 预防危害措施
precautions to be taken 预防危害措施,预防措施
precedence 优先地区
precedence of diplomatic officer 外交官位次
precedence of states 国家的位次
precedent 先例,判例,前项
precedent administrative case 行政判例
precedent condition 先决条件
precedent of international jurisprudence 国际判例
precedented 有先例的
precedented to go by 有先例的
preceding 前任

preceding article　前条

preceding claims　在前的权利要求

preceding clause　前款,前罪

preceding paragraph　前款,前项

preceding president　前任总统

precensor　预先审查

precious cultural relics　珍贵文物

precipitate recognition　过急承认

precision of auditing　审计的精确性

preclude disputes　预防纠纷

preclusive buying　阻止性购买

precondition　先决条件

preconsideration　优先权

precontract　预约

precursor　前任

predate　提前日期

predatory dumping　恶意倾销

predatory price cutting　竞争性削价,掠夺性削价

predatory pricing　掠夺性定价

predecessor　前任

predelinquent　虞犯少年

predial　不动产的

predictability　可预测性

prediction of first offense　初犯预测

prediction of subject of crime　犯罪主体预测

prediction of the means of crime　犯罪手段预测

preelect　预先选举

preelection　预先选举

preemption　优先购买权,先买权

preemptive audit　事前审计

preemptive right　先买权

prefabricated building　预制装配式房屋

preface　序言

prefecture　地区

prefer　申请

prefer efficiency　优先效力

preference　优先项目

preference prices　优惠价格

preferential　优惠的

preferential clause　优惠条款

preferential debts　优先清偿的债务

preferential debts in bankruptcy　优先破产债权

preferential duties　特惠税,优惠关税

preferential interest rate　优惠利率

preferential margin　优惠幅度

preferential measure　优惠方法

preferential payment(s)　优先偿付,优先付给

preferential period　优惠期

preferential price(s)　优惠价格

preferential rate　优惠汇率

preferential right　优惠权

preferential right to renew the contract　更新合同的优先权

preferential tariff　优惠税则,特惠关税

preferential tariff system　关税特惠制

preferential trade arrangement　优惠贸易安排

preferential treatment　优惠待遇

preferred debt　优先债务

preferred house　优先选择的房屋

preferred mortgage　优先抵押

preferred stock　累积性可兑换优先股

prejudgment report　判决前报告书

prejudice　受损害,影响

prejudicial act　侵害行为

preliminary agreement　初步协定,初步协议

preliminary clause　初步条款

preliminary conference　预备会议

preliminary consultation　初步协商,事先磋商

preliminary criminal proceedings　刑事预备程序

preliminary detention 候审羁押
preliminary enquirty 初步调查
preliminary evidence 初步证据
preliminary examination 预先审查
preliminary inquiry 初步调查
preliminary inspection 初步勘验
preliminary negotiation 初步谈判,预备谈判
preliminary objection 初步异议
preliminary plan of a capital construction project 基本建设项目计划任务书
preliminary proof 初步证明
preliminary question of first degree 一级附随问题
preliminary question of second degree 二级附随问题
preliminary report 初步裁定
preliminary round of election 首轮选举
preliminary sketch 初步设计
preliminary survey 初步调查
preliminary treaty 初步和约
premier 总理,首相
premier of the People's Republic of China 中华人民共和国国总理
premier of the State Council 国务院总理
premier responsibility system 总理负责制
premiership 首相职权
premise 前提
premises 场所
premises to let 出租房屋
premium 保险费,加价,酬金
premium deposit 保险存款,预付定金
premium discount 升水与贴水
premium on bond 债券溢价
premium rate 保险费率
premium sale 有奖销售
premium-priced 高价
prepaid expense 预付费用
prepaid income 预收收益

prepaid interest 预付利息
prepaid transportation charge 预付运费
preparation 作成(票据)
preparation for (a) crime 犯罪预备
preparation for solicitation 教唆预备
preparation of oneself 自我预备行为
preparatory behavior for a crime 犯罪预备行为
preparatory crime 预备犯
prepare a written accusation 具状
prepay 提前偿付,预付
prepayment 提前偿付,预付款
prepayment method 预付款退还担保
preposition of composition doctrine 和解前置主义
preposition of reconsideration doctrine 复议前置原则
prepossession 先占
prerequisite 先决条件,前提条件,必要前提
prerogative court (英) 大主教法庭
prerogative law 特权法
prerogative of mercy 特赦权,赦免特权
prerogative of the grown 皇室特权
prerogative writs 君主特权令
presale 楼花
preschool education 学前教育
prescribe 规定
prescribed by 由…规定
prescribed examination 法定检查
prescribed form 规定格式
prescribed minimum 下限
prescribed penalty 法定刑罚
prescribed requirement 规定的要求
prescribed time 法定期间,法定期限

prescribed time-limit 规定的期限

prescription 时效,占有

prescription for execution of punishment 刑罚执行的时效

prescription in criminal law 刑法上的时效,刑法时效

prescription of execution of judgment 判决执行时效

prescription of execution of sentence 行刑时效

prescription of parole by law 必要假释,假释法定制

prescription term 规定的期限

prescriptive right 因时效而取得的权利,时效权

presence 到庭

present 赠与,呈递

present a petition 请愿

present documents 颁证

present estate 现有房地产

present price 市价,现行价格

present sale 即时买卖

present section 本节,本条

presentation 控告书

presentence investigation 判决前调查

presenter 赠与人

presenter donor 赠送人

presenting claims for administrative indemnity 行政赔偿请求的提出

presentment 提示,公诉

present-in-area 当时当地

preservation and notarization of evidence 保全公证证据

preservation measures 保全措施

preservation of assets 保持资产条款

preservation of environment 环境保护

preservation of evidence 证据保全

preservation of good order 维持秩序

preservation of goods 保全货物

preservation of public peace 维

① 持治安

② preservation of rights 保留权利

③ preservative measure 保全措施

④ preservative measures for property in litigation 诉讼财产保全措施

⑤ preservative measures in litigation 诉讼保全措施

⑥ preservative postmortem phenomenon 保存型尸体现象

⑦ preserve 保全,维持

⑧ preserve goods 保全货物

⑨ preserved building 保留建筑,被保护的建筑

⑩ preserving procedure 保全程序

⑪ preshipment inspection 装船前检验

⑫ preshipment inspection activities 装船前检验活动

⑬ preshipment inspection entity 装船前检验机构

⑭ preshipment survey 装船前检验

⑮ president 国家主席,总统,大总统,议长,主席

⑯ president agreement 总统协定

⑰ (the) president elect 当选总统

⑱ (the) president elected 当选的下届议长

⑲ president elector 总统选举人

⑳ president of law court 法院院长

㉑ president of supreme people's court(中) 最高人民法院院长

㉒ President of the People's Republic of China 中华人民共和国主席

㉓ president of the supreme court (日) 最高裁判所长官

㉔ president of the supreme people's court 最高人民法院院长

㉕ president's responsibility system 校长负责制

㉖ presidential 国家主席的

㉗ presidential candidate 总统候选人

㉘ presidential election 总统选举

㉙ presidential electoral college (美)

总统选举团

presidential executive agreement
总统行政协定

presidential government 总统制
政府

presidential primary 预备选举

presidential republic 总统制共
和国,总统咨文

presidential system 总统制

presidential tenure 总统任期

presidential year (美) 总统选举
年

presidential's assistant for national security (美) 总统国家安
全事务特别助理

presiding chairman 执行主席

presiding judge 首席法官

presiding officer 主席

presidium 主席团

presidium of the National People's
Congress 全国人民代表大会
主席团

press 出版社

press attache 新闻专员

press censor 新闻检查官

press censorship 新闻检查

press for rent 催租

press law 出版法

pressure 压力

pressure group 压力集团,第三
院

prestige 信誉

presume 推定

presume on one's position 滥用
职权

presume upon one's position 滥
用职权

presumption 推定

presumption great 明显证据

presumption of corruption 推定
腐犯罪

presumption of death 死亡推
定,推定死亡

presumption of fact 事实的推定

presumption of fault 过失推定

presumption of good faith 善意
推定

① presumption of guilt 有罪推定
② presumption of innocence 无罪
③ 推定
④ presumption of law 法律的推定
⑤ presumption of law by estoppel
⑥ 不可推翻的法律上推定
⑦ presumption of legality 推定合
⑧ 法
⑨ presumption of loss 损失推定
⑩ presumption of negligence 推定
⑪ 过失
⑫ presumptive evidence 推定性证
⑬ 据,推定证据
⑭ pretax income 纳税前收入
⑮ pretax profits 纳税前利润
⑯ pretended transaction 虚假行为
⑰ preterlegal 无法律根据的
⑱ pretrial of complaint 起诉预审
⑲ pretrial psychology 预审心理学
⑳ prevailing party 胜诉方当事人
㉑ prevailing price 通行价格,现行
㉒ 价格
㉓ prevailing rate 现行价格
㉔ prevent or control industrial pollu-
㉕ tion 工业污染源综合防治
㉖ prevent pollution damage to the
㉗ environment 防止环境污染
㉘ 损害
㉙ prevent the recurrence of similar
㉚ incidents 防止类似事件重演
㉛ prevention 预防
㉜ prevention after committing a
㉝ crime 犯罪预防
㉞ prevention after criminality 罪
㉟ 后预防
㊱ prevention and control of air pol-
㊲ lution 大气污染防治
㊳ prevention and control of industri-
㊴ al pollution 工业污染防治
㊵ prevention and control of pollution
㊶ source 污染源治理
㊷ prevention and control of water
㊸ pollution 水污染防治
㊹ prevention and elimination of pol-
㊺ lution and other hazards to the
㊻ environment 防治污染和其
㊼ 他公害

prevention before a crime 罪前预防

prevention during criminality 罪中预防

prevention during the crime 犯罪中预防

prevention measures 预防性措施

prevention of crime(s) 防止犯罪,预防犯罪

prevention of danger 防险

prevention of fraud investments act 防止诈骗投资法例

prevention of groundwater pollution 防止地下水污染

prevention of juvenile delinquency 防止青少年犯罪

prevention of negligent offense 过失犯罪的预防

prevention of pollution 防止污染

prevention of sexual crime 性犯罪预防

prevention of surface water pollution 防止地表水污染

prevention of youth crime 青少年犯罪预防

prevention on performance 履行受阻

prevention system 预防体系

prevention theory 预防说

preventive detention 预防监禁

preventive maintenance 预防性维护

preventive measure 预防措施

preventive review 预防性审查

preventive measures 预防措施

previous conviction 以前判的罪

previous crime 前科罪,以前犯的罪

previous notice 预先通告

previous question 先决问题

previous shipment(goods) 前批货

price 代价,售价,基价,物价

price a money 贷款利息

price actually paid or payable 实付或应付价格

price adjustment 价格调整

price agreed upon 约定价金

price at factory 出厂价格

price at the time of order 订货时价格

price auctions 价格拍卖法

price band 价格幅度

price benefit 价格补贴

price card 标价

price cartel 价格卡特尔

price catalog 价目表

price ceiling 价格上限

price change clause 价格变动条款

price changer 价格变动

price check 物价检查,价格检查

price check group 物价检查小组

price clause 价格条款

price competition 价格竞争

price condition 价格条件

price contract 价格合同

price control 价格管理,价格管制,物价管制,物价控制

price control authority 物价管理部门

price control law 价格管理法

price correction 价格修正

price decision 价格决定

price determination 价格决定

price differences 价格差别

price directed by the state 国家指导价格

price discipline 价格规则

price discrimination 价格歧视,价格差别

price downward 物价趋跌

price duty paid 已付税价格

price elasticity of demand 需求价格弹性

price evaluation 价格评估

price fixing 确定价格,定价

price fluctuation 价格浮动,物价波动

price for premium sale 奖售价

格

price form　价目表

price freeze　价格冻结,物价冻结

price gap　价差

price gauging　价格欺骗

price guarantee　价格保证

price guideline　价格指标

price in money　价金

price index　价格指标,价格指数,物价指数

price indexation　价格指标化

price inflation　物价膨胀

price inversion　价格倒挂

price law　价格法

price leader　吸引价格,先导价格,诱买价格

price level　物价水平,价格水平

price limit　价格极限

price list　价目表

price loco　购买地价格

price maintenance　价格维持

price maintenance agreement　价格维持协定

price management pricc margin　价格差

price margin　价格差额

price markup　加价

price mechanism　价格结构

price negotiation　价格谈判

price not including tariff　不含税价格

price of factory　厂价

price of floating goods　在途货物价格

price of goods　货款

prlce of money　贷款利率

price of rule of law　法治的代价

price of share　股票价格

price of technology transfer　技术转让价格

price of trade conducted at rural fairs　集市交易价格

price offence　价格违法行为

price on a uniform basis　统一定价

price on quality　按质论价

① price on spot　现售价格

② price or cost difference　差价

③ price parity index　比价指数

④ price per unit　单价

⑤ price policy　物价政策

⑥ price range　价格幅度,物价幅度

⑧ price ratio　比价

⑨ price readjustment　价格调整

⑩ price redetermination clause　价格重订条款

⑫ price regulations　定价法规

⑬ price ring　价格集团

⑭ price rise　涨价

⑮ price risk　价格风险

⑯ price set uniformly by the state　国家规定的统一价格

⑱ price setter　价格制定者

⑲ price setting　价格制定

price setting and regulating agency　物价机构

㉒ price spread　价格差距

㉓ price spread arbitrage　价格差距套利

㉔ price stabilization　价格稳定,稳定物价

㉗ price stabilization cartel　稳定价格卡特尔

㉙ prlce standard　价格标准

㉚ price strays from value　价格背离价值

㉜ price structure　价格结构,物结构

㉞ price subsidy　价格补贴

㉟ price supervision　价格监督

price supervision and inspection　价格监督检查

price supervision group　物价监督小组

price support　价格补贴,价格支持

㊷ price system　价格体系

㊸ price tag　物价标签

㊹ price term　价格条件

㊺ price theory　代价论

㊻ price ticket　物价标签

㊼ price variance　价格差异

price variation 价格变动
priced by piece 计价
priced themselves out of the market 因抬高价格以至于没有销路
price-earning ratio 市盈率,价格收益比率
price-fixing agreement 价格统一协定,固定价格协议
price-support scheme 价格支持计划
pricing methods 定价方法
pricing policy 定价政策
pricing power 定价数
pricing problem 定价问题
pricing regime 定价制度
pricing strategy 定价策略
pricing structure 价格体系
priestess 女祭司
primage 运费折扣
primary 初级,初等
primary affinity 主姻亲
primary agent 首位代理人
primary cause 主因
primary cause of injury 损害的主要原因
primary characterization 一级识别
primary commodities 初收货物
primary deposit 原始存款
primary education law 初等教育法
primary election 首轮选举
primary fact 主要事实
primary factor 主要因素
primary goods 初级货物
primary industry 基本工业
primary interests 基本利益
primary jurisdiction 初步管辖权
primary liability 主要责任,直接责任,第一位责任,首要责任
primary market 初级市场,发行市场,一级市场
primary obligation 首要义务,初级义务

primary or principal obligor 主债务人
primary pollution source 主要污染源
primary principles of macrocontrol law 宏观调控法的基本原则
primary production 基本生产
primary professional posts 初级职务
primary professional ranks 初级职务
primary reconsideration 一次复议
primary review 一次复议
primary review system 一次复议制
primary rule 主要规则
primary scene 第一现场
primary standard of measurement 计量基准器具
primary system of industry law 产业法的基本制度
primary system of planning law 计划法的基本制度
primary system of pricing law 价格法的基本制度
primary transaction 初级交易
prime contract 基本合同
prime contractor 主要缔约人
prime cost 原价
prime interest rare 优惠利率
prime minister 内阁总理,内阁总理大臣,首相
prime mover industry 主导工业
prime quality 上好品质
prime rate 优惠利率
primitive law 原始法
primogeniture 长子继承权
prince 亲王
prince regent 摄政王
principal 委托人(指托收业务),主债务人,被代理人,本金,正犯,当事人,委托方
principal act 主行为
principal bank 中央银行
principal channel 主航道

principal clause 主要条款

principal contract 主契约,主合同

principal contradiction 主要矛盾

principal creditor 主债权人

principal crime 本罪

principal culprit 主凶,首犯

principal debt 主债务

principal debtee 主债权人

principal debtor 主债务人

principal in the second degree 第二主犯

principal legal system 主要法律体系

principal murderer 谋杀主犯

principal obligation 主要义务,主债务

principal offender 主犯,从犯,胁从犯,正犯

principal office 主营业地

principal penalty 主刑

principal person in charge 主要负责人

principal place of business 主营业所,主要营业地

principal punishment 主刑,基本刑

principal right 主要权利

principal staff member 主任科员

principalis（拉）当事人,主债务人

principle 原理

principle concerning evaluation 作价原则

principle of administration by law 依法行政原则

principle of administrative democracy 行政民主原则

principle of administrative openness 行政公开原则

principle of advocacy of civil procedure law 民事诉讼法的辩论原则

principle of arm's length 独立竞争原则

principle of bearing responsibility solely for one's own crime 罪责自负原则

principle of combining punishment with education 惩罚与教育相结合原则,处罚与教育相结合的原则

principle of comparability 可比性原则

principle of compensation 补偿原则

principle of conciliation of civil procedure law 民事诉讼法的调解原则

principle of consistence 内阁一致原则

principle of consultation 协商原则

principle of contractual freedom 契约自由原则

principle of culpability for state compensation 国家赔偿的归责原则

principle of dealing with each case on its merits 区别对待原则

principle of delegation 授权原则

principle of democratic centralism 民主集中制原则

principle of discretion of security measures 保安处分量定原则

principle of discretionary action of sentencing 量刑原则

principle of disposition 处分原则

principle of disposition in civil procedure law 民事诉讼法的处分原则

principle of dual faults for state compensation 国家赔偿的双重过错原则

principle of economy and rationality 经济合理原则

principle of effective control 有效控制原则

principle of effectiveness 有效统治原则,有效原则

principle of equality 平等原则

principle of equality and mutual benefit 平等互利原则

principle of equality of nationality 民族平等原则

principle of equidistance-medium-line 等距离中间线原则

principle of equitable burden-sharing 公平分担原则

principle of exercising the powers of investigation, prosecution and adjudication by specialized organizations 侦查权、检察权、审判权由专门机关行使的原则

principle of fairness 公平原则

principle of family planning 计划生育原则

principle of faults in official duties for state compensation 国家赔偿的公务过错原则

principle of faults of the subject plus actual breach of law for state compensation 国家赔偿的主体过错加行为违法的原则

principle of free intention 自由心证原则

principle of good faith 诚实信用原则，诚信原则

principle of head-office control 总部管制原则

principle of honesty and credibility 诚实信用原则

principle of honesty and good faith 诚实信用原则

principle of humanitarianism 人道原则

principle of identity 相同原则（即同一原则）

principle of independence or separation 独立或分离原则

principle of international cooperation for development 国际合作以谋发展原则

principle of interpretation 解释原则

principle of justice and equality 公正平等原则，公正、公开原则

principle of law 法理

principle of least sacrifice 最小牺牲原则

principle of legal equality of parties 当事人诉讼法律地位平等原则

principle of legality 法律原则

principle of liability for fault 过错责任原则

principle of liability with fault 过错责任原则

principle of liability without fault 无过错责任原则

principle of making compensation for equal value 等价有偿原则

principle of malfeasance 违法原则

principle of mirror image 映象原则

principle of morality 道德准则

principle of more pay for more work 多劳多得原则

principle of mutual benefit 互利原则

principle of mutual benefit and reciprocity 互惠对等原则

principle of mutual non-aggression 互不侵犯原则

principle of national treatment 国民待遇原则

principle of nationality independence of married women 已婚妇女国籍独立原则

principle of natural justice 自然公正原则

principle of natural prolongation 自然延伸原则

principle of new law 从新原则

principle of nonalteration 不更易原则

principle of non-extradition of nationals 本国国民不引渡原则

principle of non-extradition of political offenders 政治犯不引

渡原则

principle of non-intervention in domestic matter 不干涉国内事务之原则

principle of non-intervention in each other's internal affairs 互不干涉内政原则

principle of not using mediation in administrative procedure 不适宜调解原则

principle of now-extradition of political offenders 政治犯不引渡原则

principle of parent bank control 总部管制原则

principle of peaceful settlement of international disputes 和平解决国际争端原则

principle of people to self-determination 民族自决原则

principle of people's mediation 人民调解原则

principle of permanent residence 永久居所原则

principle of presentation of order before arrest 令状有效出示原则

principle of proportionality 比例原则

principle of public administration 行政原理

principle of public summons 公示原则

principle of punishing the few and reforming the many 惩办少数,改造多数的原则

principle of punishment as stipulate(d) 处罚法定原则

principle of rationalization 合理原则

principle of reasonableness 合理性原则

principle of reciprocity 互惠原则,对等原则

principle of restituting actual losses 赔偿实际损失原则

principle of rule of law 法治原则

principle of safeguarding the fundamental human rights 保障基本人权原则

principle of safeguarding the fundamental rights of citizens 保障公民基本权利原则

principle of safeguarding the litigious rights of litigation participants 保障诉讼参与人诉讼权利的原则

principle of safeguarding the rights of the party interested (to an administrative punishment) 保障当事人人权利原则

principle of self-determination 民族自决原则

principle of sentencing 量刑原则

principle of simple and efficient administration 精简的原则

principle of single nationality 单一国籍原则

principle of specialify 特定罪名原则,专一原则

principle of state recourse prosecution 国家追诉主义

principle of state sovereignty 国家主权原则

principle of strict interpretation 严格解释原则

principle of suitability 适当性原则

principle of suiting punishment to crime 罪刑相适应原则

principle of supervision and check 监督制约的原则

principle of supporting accusation of civil procedure law 民事诉讼法的支持起诉原则

principle of taxpayer's residence 纳税人居住地原则

principle of territorial jurisdiction 属地管辖原则

principle of territoriality of criminal law 刑法的属地原则

principle of territory 属地原则

principle of the law 法律的原理

principle of transparency 透明度原则

principle of unified leadership and decentralized administration 统一领导分级管理原则

principle of uninterrupted trial 不间断原则

principle of universality 普遍原则,普遍性原则

principle of using native language 使用本民族语言原则

principle of utmost good faith 最大诚信原则

principle of validity 有效原则

principle of violations of law or violations of legal duties for state compensation 国家赔偿的违法或违反法定义务的原则

principle of voluntariness and mutual benefit 自愿互利原则

principle of voluntary nationality 国籍自愿原则

principles of administrative law 行政法原理

principles of democratic centralism 民主集中制的原则

principles of equity 平衡法原则

principles of international law 国际法原则

printed clause 印戳条款

prior to the expiration of the term 期限届满前

prior 优先的

prior art 已有技术

prior consent 事先同意

prior consultation 事先协商

prior limitation 预定限额

prior notice 事先通知

prior study 先行研究

prior to loading onto and after discharging from the ship 装船前和卸货后

prior to shipment 在装运以前

prior to the date due 到期前

priorendorsor 前手

priorities of capital construction 基本建设重点

priority 优先,优先权,优先项目

priority caution 优先告诫权

priority claim to seagoing ships 船舶优先请求权

priority date 优先权日

priority in consultation and treatment 优先诊治

priority in government procurement 政府采购的优先原则

priority in rearing 优先托养权

priority inhibition 优先禁止权

priority notice 优先权通知书

priority of assignment 优先转让

priority of contract 契约的相互关系

priority of mortgage 优先抵押权

priority period 优先权期限

priority principle 优先权原则

priority processing 优先处理

priority project 重点工程

priority right 先用权

priority right to be repaid 优先受偿权

priority system 优先权制度

primary system of state-owned property administration law 国有资产管理法的基本制度

prison 看守所,牢狱

prison at the bar 刑事被告

prison discharge certificate 出狱证明

prison factory 监狱工厂

prison guard 狱警

prison hostel scheme 监狱寄宿舍方案

prison inmate 犯人

prison labor 狱中劳役

prison law 监狱法

prison of punitive servitude 惩役监

prison of state 国事犯

prison official 狱政官员,监狱工作人员,管教人员

prison outlay 监狱经费

prison psychology 监狱心理学
prison raid 劫狱罪
prison reform 监狱改革
prison regulation 监狱规则
prison riot 罪犯暴狱
prison staff 监狱工作人员
prison term 刑期
prison violence 监狱暴乱
prisoner 羁押犯,在押犯人,犯人
prisoner detainees 被监管人员
prisoner in knowing a secret 知密犯
prisoner of war 战俘
prisoner under sentence of death 死刑犯
privacy of correspondence 通信秘密,通讯秘密
privacy right 私生活权
private 私有,私营
private agreement 私人协定
private building 私人房屋
private carriage 私人运输
private carrier 私人承运人,私人运输行,私营承运人
private claim 私人求偿
private company 封闭式公司
private contract 私人契约
private debt 私人债务
private defense 个人防卫
private direct investment 私人直接投资
private economy 私营经济,私有经济
private employee 私人雇员
private enemy property 敌国私有财料
private enterprise 私营企业,私人企业,民间企业
private enterprise law 私营企业法
private hearing 不开庭审理
private hill land 自留山
private house 私人住宅
private immovable property 私有不动产
private industry and commerce 个体工商业

private institutions 私营机构
private international law 国际私法
private investment 私人投资
private juridical person 私法人
private labourer 个体劳动者
private land 私有土地
private law 私法
private lot 宅基地
private meeting 秘密会议
private members' bill 个人议员法案(英)
private nuisances 私人妨碍
private ownership 个体所有制,私有,私有制,个体所有制
private ownership mentality 私有观念
private ownership of the means of production 生产资料私有制,生产资料私有制
private ownership system 私有制
private partnership enterprise 私营合伙
private plot(s) of cropland 自留地
private plot(s) of hilly land 自留山
private powers 私人权限
private practice 民间惯例
private property 私有财产,私人财产
private property right 私人财产权
private residence 私人住宅
private sale 私人销售
private sector 私营部门
private sector of economy 私有经济
private sector of the economy 私营经济
private servant 私人仆役
private ship 私有船舶
private treaty 私人协议,财产出让契约
private trust 私益信托
private vessel 私有船舶

privateer 私掠船

privately farmed hilly land 自留山

privately farmed plots of cropland 自留地

privately operated 私营,民营

privately owned 私有

privately owned industrial and commercial enterprises 私营工商业

privately owned livestock 自留畜

privately secretly 私自

privately-farmed plots of cropland 自留地

privately-operated 私营

privately-operated business 私营企业

privately-owned industrial and commercial enterprises 私营工商业

privately-owned livestock 自留畜

privatization 私有化

privatorum conventio juri publico non derogat (拉) 私人契约不损害公共权利

privilege 特权,特殊权利

privilege from arrest 不受拘捕的特权

privilege of being above the constitution and law 超越宪法和法律的特权

privilege of inviolability 不可侵犯特权

privilege of non-appeal 不上诉之特权

privileged claim 优先索赔权

privileged debt(s) 优先债权,特权债务

privileged position 特权地位

privileged will 特权遗嘱

privileges and immunities of the United Nations 联合国特权与豁免

privilegium 特别权利

privity 由契约规定的对同一权利的有关当事人的相互关系,相互关系

privity of contract 合同的相互关系,合同有关当事人的相互关系,契约之相互关系,与合同当事人一方有关系而产生的非合同当事人的权益

privity of estate 土地权利的相互关系

privy 关系人

privy council (英) 枢密院

prize action 捕获诉令

prize case 捕获案

prize court 捕获法院,捕获物法庭

prize jurisdiction 捕获判决,捕获管辖权

prize procedure 捕获程序

pro forma 形式上的

pro indiviso (拉) 不可分开的

pro interesse suo (拉) 根据本身利益,在本身利益范围内

pro memoria (拉) 数额待定

pro se (拉) 代表自己

probate (美) 遗嘱

probate, divorce and admiralty court 继承、离婚和海事法庭

probation 缓执行

probation classification 缓刑分类

probation for fixed-term imprisonment 有期徒刑缓刑

probation home 缓刑犯教养所

probation hostel 缓刑犯收容所

probation in a broad sense 广义的缓刑

probation of execution 暂缓执行

probation officer 监视缓刑犯的官员

probation period for parole 假释考验期

probational period 缓刑考验期,缓刑期间

probational review 缓刑的考察

probational sentence 缓刑判决

probational system 缓刑制度

probationary cabinet 预备内阁

probationer 缓刑犯人

probative effect 证明效力

probative force 证明力

probe into the essence of things 探索事物的本质

procedendo（拉）发还再审令

procedural action 程序意义上的诉讼

procedural administrative regulation 程序的行政法规

procedural auditing 程序审计

procedural clause 程序条款

procedural due process 程序性正当法律程序

procedural justice 程序公正

procedural law 程序法

procedural law of taxation 程序税法

procedural matter 程序事项

procedural military law 程序军事法

procedural motion 程序动议

procedural natural law 程序自然法

procedural party 程序意义当事人

procedure 诉讼程序，程序，手续

procedure clause of mutual consult 相互的差异程序条款

procedure for commencement of action 起诉程序

procedure for concluding a contract 签订合同的程序，签约程序

procedure for deciding on administrative penalties 行政处罚决定程序

procedure for judicial review of death sentences 死刑复核程序

procedure for making plans 计划编制程序

procedure for penalties in financial administration 财政处罚程序

procedure for perpetuating testimony 证据保全的程序

procedure for resumption of execution 恢复执行程序

procedure for single administrative act 单一行政行为的程序

procedure for supervision upon adjudication 审判监督程序

procedure for the handling of medical malpractices 医疗事故处理办法

procedure for the making of administrative norms 行政规范制定程序

procedure for the recognition and enforcement of foreign arbitral awards 承认与执行外国仲裁裁决的程序

procedure for the recognition and enforcement of foreign judgment 承认与执行外国法院判决的程序

procedure for withdrawing an action 撤诉程序

procedure of a criminal case 刑事案件的诉讼程序

procedure of administrative compensation 行政补偿的程序

procedure of administrative indemnity 行政赔偿程序

procedure of administrative punishment 行政处罚程序

procedure of administrative review 行政复议程序

procedure of amendment 修改程序

procedure of arbitrary administrative execution 行政强制执行程序

procedure of bankruptcy 破产程序

procedure of certification 鉴证程序

procedure of commutation 减刑程序

procedure of compensation 赔偿程序

procedure of conclusion of treaties 条约的缔结程序

procedure of consultation 协商程序

procedure of customs 报关程序

procedure of first instance 第一审程序,一审程序

procedure of hearing on administrative penalties 行政处罚的听证程序

procedure of indemnity 赔偿程序

procedure of interpretation 解释程序

procedure of investigation 侦查程序

procedure of parole 假释程序

procedure of punishment 处罚程序

procedure of second instance 第二审程序

procedure of sentencing 判决程序

procedure principle 程序原则

procedure verdict 程序裁决

procedures for alien entry into and exit from the People's Republic of China 中华人民共和国外国人入境出境管理法

procedures for making and promulgating administrative regulations 行政法规制定、发布程序

procedures of plan formulation 计划编制程序

procedures of registration 登记程序

proceed with compulsory execution according to law 依法强制执行

proceeding 程序

proceeding of enforcement of administrative punishment over security 治安管理处罚执行程序

proceeding sub-paragraph 前项

proceedings for revision 复核程序

proceedings for supervising and urging the clearance of debt 督促程序

proceedings for the application of compulsory measures of a medical character 采用医药性强制方法的诉讼程序

proceedings in error 复审程序(英)

proceedings of international court of justice 国际法院的诉讼程序

proceeds 收益

proceeds of the auction sale of the ship 船舶拍卖所得价格

process 加工

process criterion 加工标准(指确认原场地)

process cycle 加工周期

process of commission of crime 犯罪过程

process of legal action 法律行为的过程

process of legal relation 法律关系的运行

process of proof 证明过程

process of public surveillance 管制程序

process server 送达人

process service 传票送达

processing and ordering goods 加工订货

processing industry 加工工业

processing plant 加工厂

procession 游行队伍

processors 加工企业

proclaim 公布

proclaim in court 当庭宣告

proclamation 宣言书,宣言,公布

proclamation of martial law 戒严令

proclamator (英) 高等民事法庭官员

proconsul 领事代理,地方总督

procontract 前约

procrastinate 延搁

proctor (英) 代诉人

procuration 代理处,代理权

procuration by the attorney 律师代理

procuration by the lawyer 律师代理

procuration endorsement 代签

procuration of women 介绍妇女卖淫

procurator 代诉人,皇家总督,代理人,检察官,检察员

procurator general 检察长

procurator in reserve 候补检察官

procuratorate 检察院

procuratorate of a higher level 上级检察院

procuratorial action 代理人诉讼

procuratorial committee 检察委员会

procuratorial committee of people's procuratorate 人民检察院检察委员会

procuratorial department 检察部门

procuratorial organization 检察机关

procuratorial supervision 检察监督

procuratorial work 检察工作

procuratorial work on law and discipline 法纪检察

procuratorship 代诉人职位

procurator-general of people's procuratorate 人民检察院检察长

procurator-general of the supreme people's procuratorate 最高人民检察院检察长

procurement conference 订货会

procurement contract 采购合同

procurement price 采购价格

procutor of administrative proceedings 行政诉讼代理人

produce evidence 提出证据

produce exchange 物产交易所

produce proof to the contrary 提供相反证据

produce reason 提出理由

produced goods 生产资料

producer capital 生产资料

producer or marketer of food 食品生产经营者

producer price 出厂价格

producer's cooperative 生产合作社

producer's goods 生产资料

producers' sovereignty 生产者主权

product 创造

product advertising 商品广告

product buyback 产品返销

product defect 产品缺陷

product description 有关产品的文字说明

product design 产品设计

product identification 产品识别

product in short supply 紧缺商品

product liability 产品责任,产品赔偿责任,产品责任

product liability insurance 产品责任保险

product liability law 产品责任法,产品质量责任法

product of the same category 同类产品

product quality 产品质量

product quality dispute 产品质量纠纷

product quality inspection organ 产品质量检验机构

product quality standard 产品质量标准

product standard 产品标准

product tax 产品税

product test 产品试验

product warranty 产品保证书

production and construction funds 生产建设资金

production and marketing 生产与销售

production and operating plans 生产经营情况

production and operation activities 生产经营活动

production brigade 生产大队

production control 生产控制

production department 生产部门

production effect of growth 经济增长的生产效果

production facility 生产设施

production factor market 生产要素市场

production factors 生产要素

production for merchandise 商品生产

production fund 生产资金

production inputs 生产投入

production management 生产管理

production mark 生产标志

production of goods for civilian use 民用产品

production of tobacco monopoly commodity 烟草专卖品的生产

production of tobacco product 烟草制品的生产

production payment agreement of project financing 项目贷款产品支付协议

production personnel 生产人员

production plan 生产计划

production price 生产价格

production programme 生产规划

production quality test 产品质量检验

production scale 生产规模

production skill 生产技能

production subsidies 生产补贴

production team 生产队

production technique 生产技术

production unit 生产单位

production-related contracting 联产承包

production-related household contract system 联产到户

production-related individual con-

tract system 联产到人

productive forces 生产力

productive power 生产能力

productivity 生产效率

products for export 外销产品

product-in-hand 产品到手

professional fraud 技术诈欺

professional functionary 业务类公务员

professional liability insurance 职业责任保险

professional misconduct 失职罪

professional morality 职业道德

professional offender 职业犯

professional standard 专业标准

professor 教授

profit 营利

profiteer 牟取暴利者,投机倒把分子,投机商

profiteering 投机活动,不当剥削行为

profits after tax 纳税后利润

profit-making enterprise 获利

profit-seeking 营利

program 程序

program appropriation 计划拨款

program lending 计划货款

program of legislation 立法规划

program outline 计划纲要

program result audit 事后审计

programmatic document 纲领性文件

programme of action on the establishment of a new international esonomic order 建立新的国际经济秩序的行动纲领

programme result audit 事后审计

programming 规划

programming phase 策划阶段

progressive development 逐渐发展

progressive income tax 累进所得税

progressive income tax system 累计所得税制

progressive interpretation 渐进的解释

progressive tax 递增税，累进税

progressive tax exemption 税收累进豁免

progressive tax rate in excess of specific amount 超额累进税率

progressive tax rates 递增税率

progressive rate 累进税率

prohibit 禁止，查禁

prohibit by official order 明令禁止

prohibited articles 违禁品

prohibited by official order 明令禁止

prohibited flight area 禁止飞行区

prohibited products 违禁品

prohibition 禁令

prohibition of business strife 竞业禁止

prohibition of the payment apportionment toward enterprise 禁止向企业摊派

prohibitive import 禁止进口

prohibitive import duty 禁止性进口税

prohibitive price 过高价格

prohibitory duty 禁止性关税

project agreement 项目协议

project bid 工程投标

project contract 工程管理

project contracting 工程承包

project expenditure 计划项目支出

project financing 计划性融资，项目贷款

project for which the loan is intended 贷款项目

project implementation order 计划执行书

project in preparation 筹建项目

project line 计划额度

project loan 计划贷款

project management 计划管理

project notes 计划性债券

project supervision 工程监理

project under construction 在建项目，在建工程

projects for basic facilities 基础设施

projects where equipment and technology are introduced from abroad 国外引进项目

proletarian dictatorship 无产阶级专政

prolocutor 议长

prolong 延长

prolongation of bill 汇票展期

prominent features 突出特征

promise 许诺，允诺，作出保证，预约，约定，订约，立约

promise pay 约定报酬

promise to pay 付款承诺

promise to undertake 承诺

promisee 受要约人，要约人，订约者

promissory 订约，约定

promissory estoppel 不得自食诺言的原则

promissory note 期票，本票

promissory warranty 承诺保证

promote 促进

promote sales 推销

promote the reform of economic system 促进经济体制改革

promote the sale of product 推销产品

promoter （企业）发起人，创办人，煽动者，带头者

promotion of foreign trade 对外贸易促进，推进对外贸易

promotion of political objects 促进政治目标

promotion of state civil servants 国家公务员的晋级

promotion worker 推销员

promp shipment 即期装运

prompt 立即行动的，迅速的，当场交付的

prompt cash 即付现金

prompt day 交割日

prompt delivery 即期交货，即时

加工

prompt execution by agency 即时代执行

prompt goods 现货

prompt payment 立即付额

promptness 及时性

promulgate 公布

promulgate a constitution 颁布宪法

promulgate a decree 公布法令

pronographic magazine 色情刊物

pronounce sb guilty 判决有罪

proof 依据,证据,(苏格兰)法官单独审理证据

proof evident 明显证据

proof of death 死亡验证

proof of delivery 发货证明

proof of handwriting 笔迹证据

proof of innocence 证明无罪

proof of loss 损失证明

proof of service 送达回证,送达证书

propaganda 假宣传

propel the society forward 推动社会前进

proper 正当

proper law in foreign insurance 涉外保险关系准据法

proper law in foreign product liability 涉外产品责任准据法

proper means 正当手续

proper measures appropriate measure 适当措施

proper punishment 适当处罚

proper share of the responsibility 相应责任

properly pack 妥善包装

propert of the state 国有财产

properties of products 产品性能

property 物（权），财产权，财物,财产

property accessory to immovable property 不动产附属财产

property assets 不动产

property attached 被扣押的物品,被扣押财产

property bond（英）财产债务

property claim 产权要求

property collectively owned 集体财产

property controversy 财产纠纷

property damages 财产损失

property dispute 财产纠纷

property in common 共有财产

property in goods 货物所有权

property in mortgage 抵押不动产,抵押动产

property insurance 财产保险

property investment management 物业投资管理

property law 财产法律

property loss 财产损失

property management 物业管理

property of all the people 全民财产

property other than involved in the case 案外财产

property outside the country 境外财产

property owned by the whole people 全民所有的财产

property owner 财产所有人

property ownership 所有制

property ownership right 财产所有权

property preservation 财产保全

property relation 财产关系

property relationship 财产关系

property right and interests 财产权益

property right(s) 产权,财产权

property settlement agreement 财产授与协议

property status 财产状况

property suit 财产诉讼

property tax 财产税

property title 财产契约

property torts 侵犯财产权

property transfer deed 授产契据

property trust 财产信托

property without owner 无主财产

property, possessions　财产

property-oriented penalties　财产刑

prophylactic reprisals　预防性报复

proponent　提出证据的人,提出认证遗属者,提议人

proportion　比例

proportional election system　比例选举制

proportional flat rate　比例税率

proportional punitive punishment system　比较罚金制

proportional representation　比例代表,比例代表制

proportional representation system　比例代表制

proportional tax　比例税

proportional tax rate　比例税率

proportional taxation system　比例税制

proportionate payment　提成支付

proportionate payment plus an advance payment of entrance fee　提成支付附加预付入门费法

proportionate relationships　比例关系

proposal　意思表示,提案,动议,提议

proposal for parole　假释建议

proposal of closing account　决算案

proposal of recall　罢免案

propose　提议

proposed contract　建议契约,草约

proposed enforcement provisions　试行细则

proposed regulations　试行条例

proposer　提议人

proposition　创议

proposition of law　法律主张

propound　提出建议

propounder　提出遗嘱者

proprietary equity　业主产权

proprietary interest　业主权益

proprietary name　专利商标名

proprietary remiedy　所有权救济

proprietary right　财产权利,所有权

proprietary technology　专有技术

proprietors' obligations　经营者的义务

proprietorship　业主所有权,所有权

proprietorship register　所有人登记

propriety articles　专卖品

prorogated jurisdiction　合同管辖

prorogation　休会

prorogue　休会

prory statement　代理委托书

proscribed by formal decree　明令取缔

prosecuratorial function　检察职能

prosecute　追究,检察

prosecuting agency of civil administration　民事行政检察机构

prosecuting attorney　检察官,公诉律师

prosecuting witness　控方证人

prosecution　检举

prosecution committee of the same prosecutors' office　本院检察委员会

prosecutor　检察员

prosecutor general（日）　检察总长

prosecutor's complaint in the procedure for prosecutorial supervision over adjudication　审判监督程序抗诉

prosecutor's complaint to a court during appellate proceedings　上诉程序抗议

prosecutorial committee　检察委员会

prosecutorial committee of the supreme people's procuratorate

最高人民检察院检察委员会

prosecutorial division of law and discipline　法纪检察庭

prosecutorial function　检察职能

prosecutorial interpretation　检察解释

prosecutorial investigation　检察侦查

prosecutorial office　检察院

prosecutorial organization　检察机关

prosecutorial power　检察权

prosecutorial supervision　检察监督

prosecutorial system　检察制度

prosecutorial work　检察工作

prosecutorial work at prisons and reformatories　监听检察

prosecutorial work for civil adjudication　民事审判检察工作

prosecutorial work in respect of administrative action　行政诉讼检察工作

prosecutorial work on law and discipline　法纪检察

prosecutors law　检察官法

prosecutors' office　检察院

prosecutors' office for rail transportation　铁路运输检察院

prosecutor-protested case　抗诉案件

prosecutrix　女起诉人

prospect interest　可得利益

prospective borrower　贷款对象

prospective damages　未来之损害赔偿,预期性赔偿,预期之损害赔偿

prospective earnings　预期收益

prospective home buyer　有意购房自住者

prospective liabilities　预期之债务

prospective yield　预期收益

prospectus　发行说明书,证券销售书

prostituting gang　卖淫团伙

protasis　前项

① protect　保全,包庇
② protect public property　爱护公
③ 共财产
④ protect the commercial secrets
⑤ 保守商业秘密
⑥ protect the lawful rights and inter-
⑦ ests of citizens　保护公民的合
⑧ 法权益
⑨ protect the lawful rights and inter-
⑩ ests of legal persons　保护法人
⑪ 的合法权益
⑫ protect the lawful rights and inter-
⑬ ests of other organizations　保
⑭ 护其他组织的合法权益
⑮ protect the life and property of the
⑯ people　保护人民的生命财产
⑰ protect wildlife　野生动物保护
⑱ protected goods　受保护的货物
⑲ protected occupier　受保护的公
⑳ 用人
㉑ protected prisoner of war　受保
㉒ 护的战俘
㉓ protected shorthold tenancy　受
㉔ 保护的短期租赁
㉕ protected tenancy　受保护的租
㉖ 赁
㉗ protecting state　保护国
㉘ protection & indemnity association
㉙ 保障赔偿协会
㉚ protection (of women) of breast-
㉛ feeing period　哺乳期保护
㉜ protection and indemnity clause
㉝ 保障与赔偿条款
㉞ protection and indemnity insur-
㉟ ance　保赔保险。保障与赔偿
㊱ 保险
㊲ protection and management of
㊳ wild medicinal herb resource
㊴ 野生药材资源保护管理
㊵ protection forest　防护林
㊶ protection of civil right　保护民
㊷ 事权利
㊸ protection of cultural property in
㊹ war　战时文物保护
㊺ protection of electric power facility
㊻ 电力设施保护
㊼ protection of environment　环境

保护

protection of grassland 草原的防护

protection of human rights and basic freedom 保护人权与基本自由

protection of land 土地保护,土地的保护

protection of legal rights and interests of overseas Chinese 华侨合法权益保护

protection of mineral resource 矿产资源保护

protection of ownership 所有权保护

protection of rare animals 珍稀动物保护

protection of rare plants 珍稀植物保护

protection of terrestrial wildlife 陆生野生动物保护

protection of the interest of minor 保护未成年人的利益

protection of trading interests property 保护贸易利益法

protection of wages on insolvency fund 保护破产工资基金

protection of wildlife 野生动物保护

protection of women's rights and interests 保护妇女权益

protection policy 保护政策

protectionism 保护主义

protective barrier 保护性壁垒

protective clause 保护性条款

protective custody 保护性拘留

protective design 防护设计

protective device 安全装置

protective duty 保护义务,保护关税

protective emblem 保护标志

protective export duty 保护性出口税

protective function of criminal law 刑法的保护机能

protective import duty 保护性进口税

protective jurisdiction 保护性管辖

protective law 保护法

protective legislation 保护立法,保护法律

protective measure(s) 保护处分,保护性措施,保护性措施,保全措施,保护措施

protective prevention 保护性预防

protective price 保护价格

protective principle 保护原则

protective sanction 保护性制裁

protective tariff 保护关税,保护性税则

protective trade 保护贸易

protective zone 保护区

protectorate 摄政时期

protest 提出异议,抗诉

protest (/dishonor/rejected) check 拒付支票

protest for non-payment 拒绝支付的抗议书

protestant reformation 宗教改革

protocol 议定书,草约

protocolar clause 形成条款

protool relating to the status of refugees 难民地位议定书

protract a debate 延长辩论

protracted 持久的

provable debt 确认的债务,实债

provide 规定

provide a banker's guarantee 提供银行保证

provide a complete set of service 提供成套服务

provide a guaranty 提供担保

provide a loan 贷款

provide a surety 提供担保

provide an evidence 提出证据

provide for 抚养

provide funds 出资

provide legal advisory paper 出具法律意见书

provide material base 提供物质

基础

provide security 提交抵押物

provide them with consulting ser-vices 提供咨询服务

provided by 由…规定

provided by economic law 按经济法律规定

province 地方，

provincial 省，地方性(的)

provincial committee of the com-munist party of China 省委

provincial constitutions 大主教教令

provincial court(s) 大主教辖区法庭(英)

provincial governor 省长

provincial people's congress 省级人民代表大会

Provinsbanken (Arhus) 丹麦省会银行(奥尔胡斯)

provision 条文，措施，条款

provision for income tax 预付所得税

provision of law 法律条文

provisional 暂行，暂时

provisional agenda 临时议程

provisional agreement 临时协定

provisional assessment 临时评税

provisional certificate 临时执照

provisional charter 临时执照

provisional clause 临时条款

provisional constitution 临时约法，临时宪法

provisional constitution-making 预备立宪

provisional contract 临时合同，暂时合同，临时契约

provisional detention 暂行扣留

provisional estimate 暂估计

provisional government 临时政府

provisional price 临时价格

provisional quarantine inspection 临时检疫

provisional recognition 暂时承认

provisional regulation 暂行条例

① provisional regulations for the in-spection of imported and ex-ported commodities 进出口商品检验暂行条例

⑤ provisional regulations on state civil servants 国家公务员暂行条例

⑧ provisional remedy 立即补偿，临时补偿

⑩ provisional rule 暂行规定

⑪ provisional seizure 临时扣押

⑫ provisions 若干规定

⑬ provisions for pesticide registra-tion 农药登记规定

⑮ provisions of law 法律规定

⑯ proviso 但书,合同的附件

⑰ proviso clause 限制性条款

⑱ provisory 附带条件

⑲ provisory clause 除外条款

⑳ provocation of defense 防卫挑拨

㉑ provost 市长,监督者,院长

㉒ proximate cause 近因

㉓ proximate damage 直接损害

㉔ proxy 委托书,代表权,委托代表,代理人,代理权

㉖ Prussian constitution 普鲁士宪法

㉘ pseudo-guarantee 假保证,假担保

㉚ psychiatric syndrome 精神疾病综合征

㉜ psychic homosexuality 精神性同性恋

㉞ psychoanalysis 精神分析

㉟ psychoanalytic method of interro-gation 精神分析讯问法

㊲ psychological characteristics of the defense 辩护人心理品质

㊳ psychological effect of punishment 刑罚的心理效果

㊶ psychological entanglement of the victim and the criminal 被害人与犯罪人心理纠葛

㊹ psychological mechanism of the defense 被告人的防御心理机制

㊼ psychological statistics of crime

犯罪心理统计

psychology after crime 犯后心理

psychology before crime 犯前心理

psychology in defense 辩护心理

psychology of abnormal offense 变态犯罪心理学

psychology of civil action 民事诉讼心理学

psychology of civil adjudication 民事审判心理学

psychology of convicts 罪犯心理学

psychology of criminal adjudication 刑事审判心理学

psychology of group crime 群体犯罪心理学

psychology of imprisonment 监禁心理学

psychology of influence on convicts 罪犯感化心理学

psychology of influence through labour 劳动感化心理学

psychology of investigation 侦查心理学

psychology of negligent offense 过失犯罪心理学

psychology of preliminary hearing 预审心理学

psychology of principal criminals 主犯心理

psychology of testimony 证言心理学

psychology of the accused for felony 重罪被告人心理

psychology of the accused for misdemeanor 轻罪被告人心理

psychology of victims 被害人心理学

psychology of witness 证人心理学

psychology of youth 青少年心态

psychomotor excitement 精神运动性兴奋

psychopathia 精神变态

psychopathic offender 精神病犯罪人

psychopathy 精神变态,变态心理

psychosexual abnormality 性心理变态

psychosexual disorder 性心理障碍

psychosis criminal 精神病犯罪人

psychotic symptomatology 精神病症状学

psychotic symptoms 精神病症状

psycho-diagnostics of crime 犯罪心理诊断方法

public 公开

public accumulation funds for housing 住宅公积金

public act 公益法令

public activities 社会活动

public administration 公共行政,行政

public administrative 行政管理

public advantage 公共利益

public attorney 公律师,检察总长

public auction 公开拍卖

public benefit 公益

public good 公益

public bidding 公开投标

public bill(s) 公共法案,公益性质的议案

public body 公安团体,民意机关,公共团体

public carrier 公共运输商

public coercion 公开胁迫

public company 开放式公司

public contract 官方合同

public corporation 公营法人团体,国有公司

public debate 公开辩论

public debt law 国债法

public defender 公设辩护人,公设律师

public delicts 公犯

public discussion 公议

public domain 公有土地,(美)国有土地

public duty 公共义务

public economy 公营经济,国营经济

public election 公开选举

public enemy number one 第一号罪犯

public enterprise 公共企业,公营企业,国营企业

public establishment 公共企业

public figures outside the party 党外人士

public finance 财政

public finance law 财政法律制度

public functionary 公务人员

public functions 公共职能

public harm 公害

public hazard 公害

public indecency 公开文字诽谤

public information act (美) 公共信息法案

public institution 事业单位

public interest groups/PLGS 公共利益集团

public interest trust 公益信托

public interest(s) 社会公共利益,公众利益,公共利益

public intervention principle 社会干预原则

public investment 公共投资,官方投资

public jurisprudence 公法学

public juristic person 公法人

public land 公共土地

public law 公法

public law and order 公共法律和秩序

public law claim 公法求偿

public law clause 公法条款

public law of nations 万国公法

public lawyer 公设律师

public liability insurance 公众责任保险

public market 公开市场

public meeting 公共集会

public monopoly 公共垄断

public morality 公共道德

public nuisance 公害

public offense 公罪

public opinion poll 民意调查

public opinion 舆论

public or general rights 公权或一般的权利

public order 公共秩序,治安,社会治安

public order detainee 违反治安规定而受拘留者

public order theory of law 法律的公共秩序论

public order violator 违反治安管理的人

public ownership 公有制,公共所有权

public ownership of means of production 公有制

public ownership of the means of production 生产资料公有制

public ownership of the raw material for production 生产资料公有制

public ownership system of socialism 社会主义公有制

public peace 公共安全

public placement 公募发行

public policy 公共政策

public postal facility 邮政公用设施

public procurement contract 公共部门购货合同

public project 公共事业工程项目

public property 公共财产,公有财产,公用财产

public property is sacred and inviolable 社会公有财产神圣不可侵犯

public prosecution 检察,公诉

public prosecution in court 出庭分析

public prosecution system 检察制度

public prosecutor 检察员

public relief 社会救济

public right 公共权利

public safety 公安

public sale 拍卖

public seal 公章

public security 公安,社会治安

public security administration 公安行政

public security administration law 公安行政法

public security administration regulation 治安管理条例

public security body 保卫部门

public security bureau 公安局

public security bureau at the place of immigration 迁入地公安局

public security department under the provincial government 公安厅

public security departments 公安部门

public security management 公安管理

public security officers 公安干警,公安人员

public security organization 公安机关

public security organization in charge of traffic control 公安交通管理机关

public security penalties 治安处罚

public security sector 公安部门

public security subbureau 公安分局

public security system 公安体制

public security unit 公安机关

public service 公共事业

public services and facilities 公共事业

public session 公开开庭期

public sittings 公开审讯

public standard of measurement 公用计量标准器具

public surveillance 群众监督

public tender 公开投标

public trial 公开审理,公审

public trustee 公共受托人

public utilities 公共事业

public utility expenditure 公共事业支出

public utility of city 城市公用事业

public verdict 公开裁决

public virtue 公德

public wealth 社会财富

public welfare 社会公益,社会福利

public welfare measure 公众福利措施

public will 公意

public works 公共建筑工程

publication 出版物,公示送达

publication contract 出版合同

publication of statistical data 统计资料的公布

publicist 公法学家

publicity 推广

publicity of democracy 民主公开性

publicize 推广

publicly elected body 民选机构

publicly-owned 公共所有,公有

publicness 公开性

public-owned economy 公有制经济

public-private joint management 公私合营

public-private joint operation 公私合营

publisher 出版人,出版商

publishing and circulating institution 出版发行机构

publishing firm 出版社

publishing house 出版社

puctum illicitum 非法契约

puisne mortgage 普通抵押

punish 惩办,处分,惩罚,惩处,处罚,制裁

punish according to the law 依法惩处

punish by law 依法惩处

punish in accordance with the law 依法惩处

punish in the act 当场处罚

punish on the spot 当场处罚

punish sb 治罪

punish sb with severity 严厉惩罚某人

punish with severity 从严处罚

punish without mercy 严惩不贷

punishment 刑罚,刑,制裁,处罚

punishment against freedom 自由刑

punishment against liberty 自由刑

punishment against the person 身体刑

punishment as a means of education 刑事教育手段

punishment by labour force 罚役

punishment by labour service 处以劳役

punishment condition 处罚条件

Punishment does not fit the crime 罚不当罪

Punishment fit the crime 以罪定刑

punishment for audit 审计处罚

punishment in measure of safety 保安刑

punishment in respect to management of public security 治安管理处罚

punishment in the original judgment 原判刑罚

punishment law 刑罚法

punishment not in keeping with the crime 罚不当罪

punishment of absolute announcement 绝对宣告刑

punishment of control 管制处罚

punishment of depriving freedom 剥夺自由刑

punishment of depriving rights 权利刑

punishment of detention 拘留处罚

punishment of honor 名誉刑

punishment of spanking buttocks 打屁股刑

punitive 惩罚性的

punitive damages 惩罚性的损害赔偿,惩罚性赔偿,惩罚性损害赔偿费

punitive function 惩罚功能

punitive measure 惩罚措施

punitive power 惩罚权

punitive prevention 惩戒性预防

punitive prison (日) 惩治监

punitive sanction 惩罚性制裁

pupil 未成年人

puppet regime 伪政权

pur autre vie (法) 在他人生存期间享有的不动产物权

purchase 购买

purchase allowance 购买折扣

purchase and sale by trademark 凭商标买卖

purchase by agreement 协议购买

purchase by luring 诱购

purchase commission 代购租金

purchase commitment 购货承诺

purchase contract 购货合同

purchase discount 购货折扣,购买折扣

purchase in the market 买入注销

purchase money mortgage 买入财产抵押

purchase order 购货订单

purchase price 购买价格

purchase rebates and allowances 购货回扣和折汇

purchase tax 购置税

purchase with a quota 定购

purchaser 买方

purchaser for value without notice 善意第三人

purchases and sales contract 购销合同

purchase-money obligation 买入财产债务

purchasing agreement of project financing 项目贷款购买协议

Q

quadrangle 四合院

quadripartite agreement 四方协定

quaestio(拉) 严刑拷问

qualification 品质证书,条件,附加条件,限制条件

qualification characterization 识别

qualification credentials of a representative 代表资格的审查

qualification for accredited status 认可的资格

qualification for election 当选资格

qualification for intervention 参诉资格

qualification of a deputy 代表资格

qualification of a legal person 法人资格

qualification of a representative 代表资格

qualification of lawyers 律师资格

qualifications 资格

qualifications for defense in court 出庭辩护资格

qualifications for standing for election 候选人的资格

qualified 合格的,有资格的

qualified acceptance 有条件接受

qualified election 合格选举人

qualified endorsement 附条件的背书

qualified majority 特定多数

qualified notary 有资格的公证人

qualified ownership 限制性所有权

qualified privilege 特有权

qualified product 合格产品

qualified property 有限制的物权

qualified property right 限制财产权

qualified title 有限制的所有权,有限度之产权,有限制的所有权

qualified voter 合格投票人

qualify 限制

qualifying clause 限制条款

qualitative changes of criminal mind 犯罪心理质变

quality 品质

quality as per buyer's sample 品质凭买方样品

quality as per seller's sample 品质凭卖方样品

quality assurance 品质保证

quality assurance system 质量体系

quality certificate 品质证书

quality certification 质量认证

quality characteristic 品质特点

quality control 质量管理,质量控制

quality control of pharmaceutical production 药品生产质量管理

quality differential 品质差别

quality goods 优质品

quality guarantee period 质量保证期

quality guaranty period 质量保证期

quality inspection 品质检验,质量检验

quality inspection of export commodities 出口商品的品质检验

quality landed 卸岸品质

quality licence system 质量许可证制度

quality of commodity 商品品质

quality of construction and installation　工程质量

quality of measuring instrument
　计量器具的质量

quality of medicine　药品质量

quality of reception　接收质量

quality of the work　工程质量

quality of tobacco product　烟草
　专卖品的质量

quality of work　工作质量

quality price difference　质量差
　价

quality rating　资信等级

quality requirements　质量要求

quality responsibility　质量责任

quality restriction　质量检验

quality review　质量检查

quality sample　品质样品

quality shipped　装船品质

quality specifications　质量规格，
　质量说明书

quality standard　质量标准

quality test　质量检验

quality variation from sample　品
　质与样品不符

quantification　计量

quantification management　计量
　管理

quantified system analysis　定量
　系统分析

quantitative changes of criminal
　mind　犯罪心理量变

quantitative control　数量控制

quantitative criteria　数量标准

quantitative limit　数量界限

quantitative limitation　数量限制

quantitative management　计量
　管理

quantitative restriction　数量限
　制

quantity　数量

quantity allowance　允许短装数
　量

quantity delivered　交付数量

quantity discount　大宗交易折
　扣，数量折扣

quantity index　数量指标

quantity of crime　罪数

quantity of pollutant discharge
　排放污染物数量

quantity ordered　订货数量

quantity term　数量条件

quantity variance　数量差异

quantum contract　数量合同

quantum meruit（拉）　合理价
　格，支付合理价格原则

quantum valebat（拉）　支付合理
　价格原则

quarantinable infectious diseases
　检疫传染病

quarantine certificate　入境检疫
　证

quarantine doctor　检疫医师

quarantine of animals and plants
　动植物检疫

quarter　地区

quarter sessions　四季法院

quarterage　每季付款

quash　撤销

quash a case　撤销案件

quash a court judgment　撤销法
　庭判决

quash a parole　撤销假释

quash a ruling　撤销裁定

quash an indictment　撤销起诉

quash an order　撤销裁定

quash the original judgment　撤
　销原判

quash the original judgment and
　send back the suit（to court of
　first instance）for retrial　撤销
　原判，发回重审

quash the written decision to bail
　out for further trial　撤销取保
　后审决定书

quasi-active criminal　准现行犯

quasi-administrative act　准行政
　行为

quasi-confiscation　追征

quasi-contract　准契约，准合同

quasi-contractual　准契约的

quasi-contractual obligation　准
　合同义务，准契约性义务

quasi-delict　准不法行为

quasi-delictum（拉）　准私犯（罗

马法）

quasi-flagrant offense 准现行犯

quasi-guardian 准监护人

quasi-judicial 准司法

quasi-judicial jurisdiction 准司法裁判权

quasi-legislative act 准立法行为

quasi-legislative power 准立法权

quasi-liquidation 准清算

quasi-negotiable 准可流通

quasi-official bribery 准公务贿赂罪

quasi-personality 准动产

quasi-possessor 准占有人

quasi-proportional representation 准比例代表制

quasi-proprietary right 准所有权

quasi-real rig 准物权

quasi-realty 准不动产

quasi-security transaction 准担保交易

quasi-state 半独立国

quasi-tort 准侵权行为

queen 王后,女王

Queen can do no wrong 女王无过失

queen consort 王后

queen's consent 女王同意

queen's proctor 女王代诉人

queen's recommendation 女王建议

queen's regent 摄政女王

queen's regulations 女王条例（英）

question 普通质询,询问,质问

question of constitution 宪法问题

question of law 法律问题

① question of procedure 程序问题

② question of reality 现实问题

③ question time 质询时间

④ questioning 质问

⑤ qui facit per alium facif per se 代理人的行为由委托人负责

⑦ qui sentit commodum sentire debet et onus（拉）获取利益者应负有责任

⑩ quibble 狡辩

⑪ quick return on an investment 迅速地发挥投资效果

⑬ quickly develop a return on an investment 迅速地发挥投资效果

⑯ quid pro quo（拉）交换条件

⑰ quiet enjoyment right 安宁享有权

⑲ quietus 收据

⑳ quittance 免除债务证书,收据

㉑ quoad hoc（拉）在这点上

㉒ quorum（拉）法定人数

㉓ quota clause 限额条款

㉔ quota control 配额管制

㉕ quota international association 国际配额协会

㉗ quota level 配额水平

㉘ quota limit 限额范围

㉙ quota management 配额管理

㉚ quota of taxation 税收指标

㉛ quota system 配额制

㉜ quota tax rate 定额税率

㉝ quotas administered 配额管理

㉞ quotation 报价,报价单

㉟ quotation of price(s) 报价单

㊱ quotation sheet 报价单

㊲ quotation table 价目表

㊳ quote 援引,报价

㊴ quoted price 报价

R

race　种族，民族

race relation　种族关系

racial conflict　种族冲突

racial differentiation　种族差别

racial discrimination　种族歧视

racial equality　种族平等

racial minorities　少数民族

racial segregation　种族隔离

racism　种族主义

racist regime　种族主义政权

rack　拉肢刑具

rack-rent　最高额租金，最高年租

radical criminology　激进犯罪学

radio and television administration　广播电视行政

radioactive dust　放射性微尘

radioactive material　放射性物质

radioactive poisoning　放射性中毒

radioactive pollution　放射性污染

radioactive substances　放射物质

raid the market　扰乱市场

raiding (/disrupting) finance　扰乱金融

rail traffic regulations　列车运行规章

rail-carrier　铁路承运人

railroad interline traffic　铁路联运

railroad police station　铁路公安派出所

railroad safety management　铁路安全管理

railroad through transport　铁路联运

railroad transit　铁路转送

railroading law　铁路法

railway advice　铁路到货通知

railway and steamship combination ticket　铁路轮船联运票

railway bill　铁路运单

railway consignment note　铁路托运单

railway management　铁路经营

railway passenger transport　铁路客运

railway police　路警，乘警

railway policeman　乘警

railway statute　铁路运输条例

railway traffic department　铁路运输局

railway traffic quarantine　铁路交通检疫

railway transportation　铁路运输

railway warehouse　铁路仓库

rain fresh water damage　淡水雨淋险

raise　抚养，提出

raise a claim　提出索赔等的要求，提出要求

raise a plea　提出抗辩

raise a presumption　提出假定

raise an objection　提出异议

raise price in a disguised form　变相涨价

raise taxes　征税

raise the current price　抬高时价

raise the price　提价

rally　价格迭后复升

rally in price　物价回升

ramshackle house　草率建成的房子

random fee collection　乱收费

random fines　乱罚款

range　范围

range of punishment　刑度

ranking of creditors　排列债权人的顺序，债权排列顺序

ranks of judges　法官的等级

ransom　赎金，赎价，赎买金，赎回

ransom money　赎金，赎买金

ransom price　赎价

ransom statute 赎罪法
rapacity 强权
rape 强奸罪,奸污
rape by compulsion 逼奸
rape by fraud 骗奸
rape or seduce 奸污
raper 强奸犯
rapist 强奸犯
rare animal 珍兽
rare aquatic animal 珍贵水生动物
rare bird 珍禽
rate clause 比率条款
rate of classification of product 等级品率
rate of dividend 股息率
rate of duty 关税率,税率
rate of duty on imports 进口税率
rate of escapees among persons undergoing reeducation-through-labour 劳改人员逃跑率
rate of established case 成案率
rate of exposed cases 发案率
rate of freight 运费率
rate of income tax 所得税税率
rate of inflation 通货膨胀率
rate of occurrence of criminal cases 刑事案件发案率
rate of qualified products 合格品率
rate of recidivism 重新犯罪率
rate of reported cases inside prison 狱内发案率
rate of return on investment 投资回收率
rate of second-instance cases settled with modified sentences 二审改判率
rate of second-instance cases settled with rate of cases settledat second instance 二审结案率
rate war 减价竞争
rateable property 该纳税的财产
rated tax 额定税金

ratemaking power 定价数
ratepayer (B.E) 纳税人
ratification 批准,追认
ratification of contract 合同的追认
ratification of treaty 条约的批准
ratify 批准
rating 信用等级
ratio 比率,比例
ratio between investments 投资比例
ratio decidendi (拉) 判决理由
ratio of exchange 交易比例
ratio of first-grade product 一级品率
rational 合理
rational act 合理的行为
rational decision 合理决策
rational delegation of power 合理授权
rational development and utilization of mineral resources 矿产资源的合理开发利用
rational distribution 合理布局
rational division of labor 合理分工
rational kernels 合理的内核
rational man 有理性的人
rational price 合理价格
rational principle 合理原则
rational transport 合理运输
rationalism 理性主义
rationalization 合理化
rationalization of crime 犯罪合理化
rationalization scheme of fine 罚金刑合理化方案
rationalized explanation 合理化解释
rationed purchase 定购
rationed shaves 配股
rationing of exchange 外汇配给
ravage the market 扰乱市场
ravisher 强奸犯
raw and processed materials 原材料

raw and semifinished materials 原材料

raw materials 原材料

raze 拆毁

reach 达到

reach an agreement 达成协议

reach man's estate 达到成年

reaction 反动,反应仅作用

reactionary 反动,反动分子,反动派

reactionary class 反动阶级

reactionary element 反动分子

reactionary organization 反动组织

reactionary secret societies 反动会道门

reactive insanity 反应性精神病

reactive psychosis 反应性精神病

readjudicate 更市

readjudication 更市

ready delivery 即期交货

ready house 现房

ready money 现金

ready shipment 即期装运

ready-money price 现金价格

reaffirm 再次确认,重申

real 真实,领域

real act 实践性法律行为,要物行为

real action 对物诉讼,产权诉讼,财产案件

real and personal 人权物权混合诉讼

real consideration 真正对价,有价值的对价

real contract 实践合同,实践契约,要物行为;物权合同

real defense 基于物权的抗辩

real estate 房地产,物业不动产,不动产

real estate agent 不动产代理人

real estate bond 不动产担保债券

real estate business 不动产业务

real estate investment 不动产投资

real estate law 不动产法

real estate management regulations 物业管理条例

real estate mortgage bonds 不动产抵押债券

real estate right 地产产权

real estate tax 不动产税

real estate title 不动产产权

real estate trust 不动产信托

real evidence 实证

real income 实际所得

real injury 实际伤害

real intention 本意,真正意思

real investment 直接投资

real litigation (joined by a third party) 本诉讼

real net weight 实际净重法

real obligation 真正义务

real owner 真正的所有人

real party 真正当事人

real power 实权

real price 真实价格,实际价格

real property 不动产

real property act (英) 不动产法

real property limitation act 不动产诉权限制法

real property things real 不动产

real remedies 物权救济

real representative 不动产代理人

real right of pledge 担保物权

real right 对物权(对世权)

real securities 不动产作保证物

real servitude 对物地役

real union 政合国

realism 现实主义

realism jurisprudence 现实主义法学

realist school of law 现实法学派

realistic system 现实制度

reality 实在性,现实

reality of law 法律的现实

reality transfer tax 房地产转移税

realization and liquidation 变产清算

realization concept 实现原则

realization of law 法的实现

realization of mortgage 抵押权的实现

realization of property 变卖财产

realize 变卖

realized price 实际价格

realm 王国

realty 不动产

reap colossal profit 牟取暴利

reaping usurious profits 暴利罪

reapplication for inspection 重新报验

reappoint 重新约定

reappointment 重新约定

reappraise the stocks and assets 清产核资

rear and educate 抚养

rear land 不临街的土地

reason 理性,原因

reason for finding 裁决理由

reason for judgement 判决理由

reason of rejection 不接受理由

reason of findings 裁决理由

reason of no case-filing 不立案理由

reasonable 合理

reasonable act 正当行为

reasonable and lawful 合理合法

reasonable and probable cause 合理及可能的理由

reasonable basis 合理的根据

reasonable belief 合理相信

reasonable but unlawful 合理不合法

reasonable calculation 合理计算

reasonable care 合理的注意

reasonable compensation 合理补偿

reasonable comtemplation 合理期待

reasonable consideration 合理约因

reasonable construction 合理解释

reasonable departure clause 合理背离条

reasonable excuse 合理的解释

reasonable ground 合理的理由,正当的理由

reasonable inference rule 合理推定规则

reasonable interpretation 合理解释

reasonable judgement 公正的判决

reasonable length of time 合理期间

reasonable maintenance 合理

reasonable man doctrine or standard 有理性的人的原则或标准

reasonable means 合理法

reasonable measure 合理措施

reasonable notice 合理期限通知

reasonable packing 合理包装

reasonable price 合理价格

reasonable punishment 合理处罚

reasonable request 合理要求

reasonable restraint 合理限制

reasonable terms 合理条件

reasonable time 合理时间内,合理的时间,合理时间,合理期间

reasonable time limit 合理期限

reasonable utilization of fishery resources 渔业资源的合理利用

reasonableness check 合理性检验

reasonableness of administration doctrine 行政合理性原则

reasonableness principle 合理原则

reasonableness test 合理性检验,合理标准的验证

reasoning from anology 类推

reassessment 再估价

reassure 重要保证

rebal 辩驳

rebale 付款总额的减少

rebate 折扣,回扣

rebel 反叛

rebuild 整修,重建

rebus sic stantibus（拉） 情势变迁原则,情势不变

rebut 反驳

rebut a claim 反驳诉讼请求

rebuttable presumption of law 可予驳回的法律推定

rebuttal 辩驳

rebuttal evidence 反驳证据

recall 罢免权,召回,撤回,罢免,撤销,取消

recall a decision 取消决定

recall by popular vote 投票罢免

recall on order 撤销订货单

recapture 取回

recede from promise 取消允诺

receipt 收据

receipt for a convict's articles 罪犯物品收据

receipt of business license 领取营业执照

receipt of cargo 货物收据

receipt of goods 收到货物

receipt of tax payment 纳税凭证

receive 收到

receive a bribe 受贿

receive legal protection 受法律保护

receive or accept any stolen or unlawfully obtained property 收受赃物或非法所得财产

received for shipment 收货待运

received for shipment B/L 收货特运提单

received for shipment bill of loading 收讫待运提单,待运提单,备运提单

received letter of acceptance 到达生效

received letter of acceptance rule 受信主义

received of the letter of acceptance rule 到达生效原则(注:指大陆法合同生效时间规则)

receiver 清算人

receiver of bribes 受贿者

receiver's certificate 清算人债务证书

receiving delivery system 交接方式

receiving party 收货方

receiving quotation 接受报价

recently emergent industries 新兴产业

reception and delivery of cargo clause 货物收交条款

recess 休庭,休会

recession 撤回,经济衰退

recession by agreement 协议撤销

recession clause 经济衰退条款

recheck 复查

recidivism 更犯,重新犯罪,累犯,再犯

recidivist of different crimes 异种累犯

recidivist rate 重新犯罪率

recipient 收件人,被许可方

reciprocal 对等

reciprocal buying 相互购买

reciprocal causation 互为因果

reciprocal contract 互惠合同

reciprocal currency agreement 货币互换协定

reciprocal exemption 相互免除

reciprocal L/C 对开信用证

reciprocal representation 相互表示

reciprocal trade 互惠贸易

reciprocal treatment 对等待遇

reciprocity 对等权利

reciprocity clause 互惠条款

reciprocity in trade 贸易互惠,贸易上的互惠

reciprocity principle 对等原则

recission 撤销

recital 契约等中陈述或证明事实的部分

reckless 轻率的

reckless conduct 轻率的行为

reclassify 再分类

reclusion 单独监禁

recognition 承认

recognition and enforcement of

foreign judgments in civil and commercial matters 民商事外判决的承认和执行

recognition of government 政府承认,政治承认

recognition of state 国家承认

recognizance 保释金,保证金

recognized principle 公认的原则

recognized right 公认的权利

recompense 补偿,报酬,酬劳,赔偿

reconcilliation 修好

recondition 整修

recondition expense 检修费用

reconditioning fee 整理费

reconsider 复议

reconsideration 复议

reconsideration body 复议机构

reconsideration concerning administration of communications 交通行政复议

reconsideration of a case 复议案件

reconsideration proceedings 复议程序

reconsideration system 复议制

reconstruction 重建

recontract 重订契约

record 档案,备案,笔录供词,案卷,登记

record commission 法律文献委员会(英)

record of a case 案情记录

record of a collegiate bench 合议庭评议笔录

record of births 出生登记

record of deaths 死亡登记

record of examination 检查笔录

record of inspection 检验笔录

record of investigation test 侦查实验笔录

record of means of crime 犯罪手段登记

record of sale 销售记录

record of settlement 结案记录

record of wildlife resource 野生动物资源档案

record of witness' testimony 证人证言笔录

record office 档案局

record to execute death sentence 执行死刑笔录

recorder 法官,(英)地方首席法官

recording of change of name 变更姓名登记

recording voucher(s) 记账凭证

records evidence 记录性证据

records made on the scene 现场笔录

records of a hearing 听证笔录

records of conciliation 词解笔录

recoup 补偿

recoup a loss 补偿损失

recoup the capital outlay 收回投资

recoupment 求偿权

recoupment compensation for loss or damage 补偿损失

recourse 追索,追索权,偿还请求权,追偿权

recourse against the responsible third panty 向责任第三方追偿

recourse of administrative compensation 行政追偿

recover 追缴

recover damages 取得赔偿,补偿损失

recover funds in full 追回全部款项

recover losses 追偿损失

recover of original property 返还原物

recover the goods 要求退货

recoverable preferred stock 可收回的优先股

recovery 重新获得

recovery action 要求偿还的诉讼

recovery of one's reputation 恢复某人名誉

recovery of original state 恢复原

状

recovery of premises 收回房产

recovery of right 恢复权利

recovery of three wastes 治理"三废"

recovery of undue payment 索回不应付之款

recreational offense 游戏性犯罪

recriminate 互控

recruit 征集

recruitment of civil servants 公务员的录用

recruitment of state civil servants 国家公务员的录用

rectification 更正

rectitude 公正

recuperatio（拉） 恢复财产

recur 重演

recycling 重新利用

red cargo 红标签货物

red cross society 红十字会

red live clause 特别声明条款

red political authority 红色政权

redecoration 重新装饰

redeem 赎买，赎回

redeem a mortgage 赎回抵押品

redeem a note 赎单

redeem one's obligation 履行义务

redeem sth pawned 赎当

redeem up 赎前销后

redelivery bond 发还考核证

redelivery survey 交还船检验

redemption 赎买，偿还方式，债券偿还方式，买回

redemption action 清偿债务之诉，赎回抵押品之诉

redemption date 偿还日

redemption of a promise 允诺的履行

redemption of bonds 债券偿还

redemption price 赎回价格

redevelopment 再开发，重建

redevelopment area 再开发区，重建区

red-handed 当场

redhibition 由于发现货物有瑕疵以至不能使用而取消购货合同

redhibitory action 因货物有瑕疵要求取消合同的诉讼

redict of innocence 裁决无罪

rediscount 再贴现

redistribution 再分配

redistribution of land 重新分配土地

redress 补偿

redress a misjudged case 改正错案

redress damage 赔偿损失

redress of wrongs 损失赔偿，补偿损失

reduce 精简，折抵，压缩

reduce expenses 压缩开支

reduce investment outlay 节省投资

reduce legal capital 减少法定资本

reduce price 降价

reduce stocks 压缩库存

reduce the limitation of liability 降低责任限额

reduce the price 减少价款，减价

reduced payment of litigious costs 减交诉讼费用

reduced responsibility 限定责任能力

reducing instalment 分期递减折旧

reducing or exempting customs duty 减免关税

reducing or remitting taxes 减免税收

reduction after combine sentence 先并后减

reduction and exemption of income tax 减免所得税

reduction of administrative 精简机构

reduction of capital 减少资本

reduction of sentence 减刑

reduction of sentence at judicial discretion 酌量减轻

reduction or remission of taxes 减免税收

reeducation-through-labor 劳动教养

reeducation-through-labor agency 劳动教养机关

reelect 改选

reexam 复审

reexamination 再检查,复查

reexamine 复查

refer to arbitration 提请仲裁

refer to in application 比照适用

referee 鉴定人

reference 保证人

reference material 参考资料

reference price 参考价格

reference standard 参考标准

reference to contract or statement as a whole 合同陈述的整体进行考虑(原则)

reference to the law 适用法律

referendum 请示书,复决制,全民投票

referential rules 参照规章

refine 再制

reflation 通过再膨胀

reform 维新,改造,改革,改良

reform and education 教育改造

reform and opening 改革开放

reform and opening policies 改革开放政策

reform and opening to the outside world 改革开放

reform irrational rules and regulations 改革不合理的规章制度

reform of higher education 高等教育改革

reform of organization system 体制改革

reform of personnel system 人事制度改革

reform of the economic structure 经济体制改革

reform of the structure of economic management 改革经济管理体制

reform school 感化院,教养院

reform society 改良社会

reformation 改造,合同的改正

reformation of a delinquent through education 对罪犯的教育改造

reformation of convicts 罪犯改造

reformation of juvenile delinquents 教养

reformation of prisoners 罪犯改造

reformation of prisoners through labor 对罪犯的劳动改造

reformatory 感化院

reformatory education 感化教育

reformatory education of convicts 罪犯教育改造

reforming economic setup 经济体制改革

reformism 改良主义,改良派

reformist 改良主义者

reform-through-labour 劳动改造

reform-through-labour bureau 劳改局

reform-through-labour organ 劳动改造机关

reform-through-labour policy 劳动改造政策

reform-through-labourprosecution 劳改检察

reform-through-labour sites for study, work, and living 劳改工作三大现场

reformulate 改订

refractory prisoner 顽固犯

refrain from punishing law-breakers 违法不究

refresher fee 额外诉讼费用

refrigeration industry 冷藏工业

refuge 避难处,安全地带

refugee 难民

refugee government 流亡政府

refund 退还,偿还,退款

refund for any over payment or a supplemental payment for any deficiency　多退少补

refundment bond　偿还保证书

refundment guarantee　偿还保证书

refunds and rebates　回扣

refusal　拒绝,取舍权,先买权

refusal of payment　拒绝付款

refusal of ratification　拒绝追认

refusal of recognition　拒绝承认

refusal to implement effective judgments of a court　拒不履行法院生效判决

refuse　不予受理

refuse to give a notarization　拒绝公证

refuse to own up　拒不交代

refuse to pay　拒绝支付

refuse to perform　拒不履行

refuser to the removal　钉子户

refute　辩驳,驳斥,反驳

refute a fallacy　驳斥谬论

regain of lost territory　收复失地

regal power　王权

regality　地方管辖权

regard as agreed upon　视为同意

regency　摄政权,摄政时期,摄政,统治

regency acts　摄政法

regenerative energy　可再生能源

regent　摄政

regicide　杀君

regime　政权

regime of centralism　集权制

regime of law　法律制度

regime of maritime ports　港口制度

regina　女王

region　地区

region of attraction　吸引地区

region of war　战区

regional　地方性(的)

regional administrative regulation　地区的行政法规

regional arrangement　区域办法

regional autonomy　地区自治,区域自治

regional autonomy of minority nationalities　少数民族区域自治,民族区域自治

regional blockade　地区封锁

regional body　地方机构

regional committee of the Chinese People's Political Consultative Conference　中国人民政治协商会议地方委员会

regional condification　区域性法典编纂

regional control of noise　城市噪声分区控制制度

regional cooperation　地区性合作

regional co-operator organization for development/ RCOD　区域合作发展组织

regional crime　区域性犯罪

regional development grants　地区开发补助金

regional distribution of the economy　地区经济

regional economic integration　区域经济一体化,区域性经济一体化

regional economic union　区域性经济组合

regional economics　区域经济

regional economy　地方经济

regional election system　区域一体化

regional emblem　区徽

regional flag　区旗

regional group　区域集团,区域性集团

regional international law　区域国际法

regional international organization　区域性国际组织

regional law　地方法

regional national autonomy　民族区域自治

regional plan　区域性计划

regional policy　地区政策

regional price difference　地区价

差

regional price differentials 地区差价

regional rules 区域性规则

regional system 地方系统

regional system of law 区域性法律体系

regional trust fund for the protection of the Mediterranean sea against pollution 保护地中海免受污染区域信托基金

regionalism 属地主义

register 立条,备案,注册,登记

register according to law 依法登记

register of judgment 判决登记册

register the charges 变更登记

registered (/inscribed) stock 记名股票

registered accountant 注册会计师

registered bonds 记名债券

registered capital 已注册资本,注册资本

registered letter 挂号信

registered mail 挂号信

registered number of approval 批准文号

registered permanent residence 户口

registered post 挂号邮件

registered symbol of aircraft 航空器的登记标志

registered voter 已登记的投票人

registrant 登记人

registrar police 户籍警

registration 所有权登记,登记,注册

registration accepted 已接受登记

registration and administration of corporate entity 企业法人登记管理

registration and management of exploring mineral resources 矿产资源勘查登记管理

registration at immigration 迁入登记

registration authority 登机机关

registration certificate 注册证书

registration certificate for household relocation 户口迁移证

registration certificate for newspaper 报纸登记证

registration for mineral exploration 矿产资源勘查的登记

registration for the missing person 失踪人登记

registration law of industrial and commercial enterprises 工商企业登证法

registration of arrests 逮捕登记

registration of birth 出生登记

registration of business 商业企业登记

registration of commons 共用地登记

registration of death 死亡登记

registration of death penalty 死刑登记

registration of encumbrances 土地负担登记

registration of enterprise legal person 企业法人登记

registration of juristic persons 法人登记

registration of movement 迁移登记

registration of permanent residence 常住户口登记

registration of real right 物权的登记

registration of residence 居住登记

registration of securities 证券上市登记

registration of ships 船舶登记

registration of temporary stay 暂住登记

registration of the mortgage of ship 船舶抵押权登记

registration of title 产权登记

registration of transient residence 暂住登记

registration of treaty 条约的登记

registration of voters 投票人登记

registration of votes 选民登记

registration of writs 令状登记

registration on a voluntary basis 自愿登记

registration system 登记制度

registration tax 注册税

registry 注册

regrate 倒卖

regressive rate 累退利率

regressive taxation 递减累进税

regular air service flight 定期航班飞行

regular armed forces 正规军

regular audit 定期审计

regular donation 定期给付的赠与

regular education 正规化教育

regular inspection 定期检查

regular internal auditing 定期内部审计

regular meeting 例行会议

regular order 常规出货

regular pattern 规律

regular practitioner 挂牌律师

regular price 固定价格

regularity 规律性

regularization 正规化

regulate 规定,管制

regulate price 规定价格

regulated price 规定价格

regulated tenancy 定限租赁

regulation 规则,部门规章(行政规章),规章,管制,行政法规

regulation for the safety and supervision in the mines 矿山安全监察条例

regulation for the safety in the mines 矿山安全条例

regulation going against the law 与宪法相抵触的规定

regulation in force 现行规则

regulation of academic degrees 学位条例

regulation of environmental pollution 环境污染管理

regulation of road traffic control 道路交通管理条例

regulation on the education of the disabled 残疾人教育条例

regulation on the management of government establishments 编制管理条例

regulation through the market 市场调节

regulations 条例,规程

regulations concerning rewards and disciplinary sanctions 奖惩条例

regulations for suppression of corruption 惩治贪污条例

regulations for suppression of counterrevolution 惩治反革命条例

regulations for technical operations 技术操作规程

regulations for the management of salt industry 盐业管理条例

regulations governing conscription 征兵工作条例

regulations governing the management of mass organizations 社会团体管理条例

regulations of administrative review 行政复议条例

regulations of state civil service 国家公务员条例

regulations of the European Community 欧洲共同体章程

regulations of the People's Republic of China on consular privileges and immunities 中华人民共和国领事特权与豁免条例

regulations on the control of firearms 枪支管理条例

regulations on the exercise of autonomy 自治法规,自治条例

regulations on the protection and management of wild medicinal herb resources 野生药材资源保护管理条例

regulations on the protection of power facilities 电力设施保护条例

regulation-making power 制定规章权

regulatory act 制定规章的行为

regulatory agency 管理机构

regulatory board of management 管理委员会

regulatory power 制定规章的权利

regulatory regime 管理制度

regulatory rules 规范性规则

rehabilitate 修复,恢复

rehabilitate one's reputation 恢复名誉

rehabilitation 修复

rehabilitation of reputation 恢复名誉

rehabilitation-through-labor 劳动教养

rehear 重审,重新审理

rehear a case to pass a new judgment or sentence 重新审判

rehouse 重新安置住房

rei vindicatio(拉) 对物之诉

reign 统治,王权

reimbursable 可补偿的,可补偿

reimbursable expenses 赔偿费用

reimburse 偿还,偿付,索款,求偿,退款,索偿

reimburse one's estimated price 折价格偿

reimbursement 补偿,求偿,索偿

reimbursement agreement 偿付协议

reimbursement clause 偿付条款

reimbursement of capital 退还资本

reimbursement solve 偿付

reimbursing agent 偿付银行

reimbursing bank 偿付银行

reinforcing evidence 补强证据

reinstate 恢复

reinstatement 恢复生效,恢复原状

reinstatoment value insurance 重置价值保险

reinsurance 再保险

reinvest 再投资

reinvestment 再投资

reject 不受理,驳回

reject a counterclaim 驳回反诉

reject a private prosecution 驳回自诉

reject an appeal 驳回上诉

reject an offer 拒绝要约

reject denial from count 不予受理

rejection of offer 拒绝要约

rejoin 第二次答辩,答辩

rejoinder 答辩状,第二次答辩,被告第二轮答辩

rejury motive of witness 证人的伪证动机

rejuvenation of plant 厂房设备更新

relate to 关于

related 有关的,连带

related departments 有关部门

related enterprises 关系企业,关联企业

related interest parties 有利害关系当事方

related property rights 与财产所有权有关的财产权

relation arising from the employment of labour 因雇佣劳动所产生的关系

relation between sellers and buyers 买卖双方关系

relation in public 公法关系

relation of administrative procedure 行政诉讼关系

relation of equality 平等关系

relation of private right 私权关系

relation of production 生产关系

relations 性行为

relations on an equal footing　平等关系

relationship of administrative procedure　行政诉讼关系

relationship of administrative subordinateness　行政隶属关系

relationship of administrative subordination　隶属关系

relative advantage　相对利益

relative comparative　相对

relative duties　相对的义务

relative immunity　相对豁免

relative invalidity　相对无效

relative majority　相对多数

relative price　相对价格,比价

relative price difference　相对价格差别

relative right　对人权,相对权

relative title　相对所有权

relatively definite statutory sentence　相对确定法定刑

relatively large amount　数额较大

relatively stable　相对稳定

relatives and friends abroad　出境探亲访友

relatives or friends outside the country　境外亲友

relativism　相对主义

relativist jurisprudence　相对主义法学

relativity　相对性

release　抵押解除,刑满释放,弃权

release certificate　释放证明书

release from an obligation　不再承担义务

release from nationality　国籍解除

release from reeducation-through-labour　解除劳动教养

release from the contract　免除合同义务

release mortgage　解除抵押

release of bank accounts　银行存款解冻

release of custody　解除扣押

release of debt　债务免除

release of distress　解除扣押

release on bail　交保释放,保释

release on bail for medical treatment　保外就医

release on probation　缓刑释放

release procedure　释放手续

release upon completion of one's term of imprisonment　刑满释放

release vessel　释船

released prisoner　获释犯人

releasor　让步人

relegate　委托

relevance　关联性

relevance of evidence　证据的关联性

relevancy of auditing evidence　审计证据的相关性

relevant　有关的

relevant competent department　有关主管部门

relevant departments　归口部门

relevant document　有关证件

relevant documents and materials　相关单证和资料

relevant economic market　有关的经济市场

relevant quality certificates　相关质量证明

relevant regulations　有关条例

relevant supporting document　有关证明文件

relevant to　涉及

relevant units at home and abroad　国内外有关单位

reliability　可靠性,可信赖性

reliable　可信赖的

reliable guaranty　可靠保证,可靠的担保

relief　免责,救济,信仰

relief from criminal responsibility　交付担保

relief from detention before the due date　提前解除拘留

relief from double taxation　双重课税宽免

relief in the form of money 金钱赔偿

relief materials and equipment 赈灾物资

relievable 可解除,可免除

relieve from obligation 免除义务

relieve one's obligation under the contract 解除合同义务

religion 宗教,信仰

religious 宗教的

religious affairs 宗教事务

religious belief 宗教信仰

religious bodies 宗教团体

religious court 宗教法庭

religious customs 宗教习惯

religious discrimination 宗教歧视

religious faith 宗教信仰

religious organization 宗教组织

relinquish 撤回,弃权

reliquatio (拉) 残额的债务

reliquator (拉) 残额债务者

relocated units or households 搬迁户

relocation 搬迁,重新安置,迁户口

relocation certificate 迁移证

relocation household 拆迁户

relocation housing 周转房

relocation payment 搬迁费

relocation settlement cost 搬迁安置费用

rely on 依据,凭借,依靠

rem (拉) 不切合的

Remain is force 继续有效

remain out of custody to obtain medical treatment 保外就医

remain with in the four corners of the law 在法律范围内

remainder 剩余财产权

remaindership 残留权

remaining crime undiscovered 余罪

remaining forces 残余势力

remake 再制

remand 还押,羁押候审

remand (to a low court) 案件发回

remand a case back for a new trial 发回重审

remand a lawsuit (of an appelate court to the original) for a new trial 发回重审

remand for new trial 发回重审

remand home 未成年犯管教所

remanufacture 再制

remarkable result 显著效果

remedial action 救济诉讼

remedial measure(s) 补救措施,补救办法

remedial step 补救措施

remedy 救济,补救,弥补,

remedy a defect 弥补缺陷

remedy by public force 公力救济

remedy by someoneself 自力救济

remedy for breach of contract 因违反合同而要求补偿,违约救济

remedy means of redress 补救方法

reminder of the samples after the inspection 验余的样品

remiss and benlghted crimInal 怠性与愚昧性犯罪人

remission 案件的移交,反致

remission (of a case) 案件发回

remission from disciplinary sanction 免于处分

remission from punishment 免于处罚

remission of punishment 免除刑罚

remission of the term of imprisonment 刑期减免

remit 免除,赦免

remit a case 案件发回

remit (a) punishment 免除处罚

remittance 汇付,汇款

remittance against documents 凭单付款

remittance by check 支票汇款

remittance check 汇款支票

remittance instruction (/slip) 汇款通知书

remitter 汇款人

remitter (of a case to a low court) 案件的移交

remitting bank 汇出行,托收行,托收银行

remittitur(拉) 减免损害赔偿

remore the impediment 清除障碍

remortgage 再抵押

remote border district 边远地区

remote cause 间接原因

remote damage 间接损害,间接损失

remote districts 偏远地位

remote sensing of the earth by satellite 卫星遥感地球

remoteness of damage 间接损失

removal 免职

removal certificate 迁移证

removal cost 拆迁成本

removal of action 诉讼转移

removal of obstacles 排除妨碍

removal order 案件移送令

removal power 免职权

remove 祛除,排除

remove an obstacle 排除障碍

remove from office 撤职,革职

remove outside interference 排除外来干扰

remove sb from office 免职

remuneration 报酬,酬金

remuneration for workers 劳动者报酬

remuneration from land 土地报酬

remunerative price 报酬性价格

render 给予,呈递,给付,报告

render a default judgment 处以缺席裁判

rendition 卖

rendition of judgment 判决的宣读

rendor 卖主

renegotiation 再议价

renew a contract 使合同展期,续订合同,准予合同展期,续约

renewable lease 可续期租约

renewable resources 可再生资源,再生资源,可更新资源

renewable sources of energy 再生能源,可更新能源

renewal 合同的展期,重建

renewal notice 到期通知书

renewal of contract 续约

renewal of lease 续订租约

renewal of negotiation 恢复谈判

renewed order 重新裁判

renewed ruling 重新裁决

Renminbi rate (RMB rate) 人民币汇率

renounce one's litigious claim 放弃诉讼请求

renounce one's litigious right 放弃诉讼权利

renounce one's right to appeal 放弃上诉权

renounce one's substantial rights 放弃实体权利

renounce right 抛弃权利

renouncing one's nationality 退出国籍

renovate 整修

renovation of production techniques 技术创新

rent 租金,承担,地租,租赁,租借

rent act 租金法例

rent charge 地租

rent deposit 押租

rent in kind 实物地租

rent to cover maintenance 以租养房

rental 罪犯放风

rental receipts (/income) 租金收入

rental value 租赁价格

renter 出租人

renunciation act 权利放弃法(英 1783)

renunciation of nationality 国籍

的放弃

reorganization plan of the enterprise　企业整顿方案

repair　补救,修缮,补偿,维修

repair cost　修理费

repair reworking or replacement　修理,重作,更换

reparable　可补偿,可赔偿

reparable loss　可补偿损失

reparation by equivalence　同等赔偿

reparation committee　赔偿委员会

reparation for injuries suffered in the service of the V. N.　损害赔偿案

reparation in kind　实物赔偿

Reparation is cash　现金赔偿

reparations　赔偿

reparations for damage　损害赔偿

repatriate　遣送回国

repatriation　遣送回国

repatriation of prisoners of war　战俘遣返

repay　报偿,赔偿

repay a debt　还债

repay by instalments　分期偿还

repay economic losses　赔偿经济损失

repay one's debt　偿还债务

repaying ability　还债能力

repaying capability　偿还能力

repayment　赔偿

repayment conditions　偿还条件

repayment guarantee　偿还保证书,预付款担保,预付款退还担保

repayment of advances　归还预付款

repayment of bank loans　归还贷款

repayment terms　偿还条件

repeal　撤销,废除

repeal a complaint　撤销起诉

repeal a court order　撤销法院命令

repeal a decree　撤销的法令

repeal a ruling　撤销裁定

repeal an order　撤销命令

repeal by implication　默示作废

repeat an error or offense　重犯

repeat offender　累犯

repeated auditing　查账

repeated crime　重新犯罪

repeatedly commit crimes　多次作案

repent and make a fresh start　悔过自新

repent and turn over a new leaf　悔过自新

repentance right　收回权

repetition　要求归还不当给付的金钱财物的诉讼

replace　退还,更替,替代

replacement　替换

replacement housing　拆迁户住房

replacement investment　更新投资

replacement value　重置价值

replacing law by power　权大于法

repleader　第二次申诉答辩

replenish　补充

replevin　排除妨碍

reply　答辩,答辩状

reply brief　答辩书

report　报告

report a case (to security authorities)　报案

report about placing a case on file　立案报告

report of birth　申报出生

report of epidemic diseases　疫情报告

report of escapes from inside prison　狱内脱逃报告

report on concluding the adjudication of a criminal case　刑事案件审理终结报告

report on placing a case that has occurred inside a prision on file for investigation　狱内案件立

案报告

report on sentence 判刑报告

report on the adjudication of a criminal case 刑事案件审理报告

report upon conclusion of investigation 侦查终结报告

reporter 报案人

reporting the loss of check 支票挂失

reports 判例汇编,报表

reports of judgements 判例汇编

repossessed goods 重新占有的货物

repossession 重新占有,返还占有

representation 代位继承,代表权

representation and warranties 陈述与担保条款

representation heir 代位继承人

representative 代表,代位继承人,代表大会

representative action 代表人诉讼,代理诉讼,集团诉讼

representative agency 代表机构

representative business agency 派驻机构

representative capacity 代表能力,代表资格

representative democracy 代议民主政治,代议民主制,间接民主政治,代议制民主

representative democratic system 代表民主制,代议制

representative government 代议政府,代议制政府

representative institution 代议制机构

representative of action 诉讼代表人

representative office of banks 银行代表处

representative organ of the people 人民代表机关

representative system 代表制,代议制

① representativeness 代表性
② representor 表意人
③ repress 压迫
④ reprieve of detention 拘役缓刑
⑤ reprieve system 缓刑执行制
⑥ reprimand 惩戒
⑦ reprint 转载
⑧ reprisal(s) 报复行为,报复
⑨ reprises 地租
⑩ reprocess 重作
⑪ reprocessing 再加工
⑫ reproduce 再生产
⑬ reproduction 再生产
⑭ reproduction on an enlarged 扩大再生产
⑯ republic 共和国,共和
⑰ republican form of government 共和政体
⑲ republican government 共和制政体
㉑ republican party 共和党
㉒ republicanism 共和,共和制
㉓ repudiate 拒绝履行,废弃
㉔ repudiate contract 否认合同有效
㉖ repudiation 拒绝履行,拒付债务
㉘ repudiatory breach 实质性毁约
㉙ repulsive 丑恶
㉚ repurchase 赎买,重购买,买回
㉛ repurchase agreement 回购协议
㉜ reputation 信誉
㉝ reputed owner 挂名所有人,共知的所有人
㉟ reputed ownership 挂名所有权
㊱ request according to law 依法申请
㊳ request for compensation 赔偿请求
㊵ request for invalidation 无效宣告请求书
㊷ request for payment 要求付款
㊸ request for permission 请求批准
㊹ request satisfaction 请求清偿
㊺ request the cancellation of contract 要求解除合同
㊼ request the return of 要求退还

request to extend time-limit of claim 要求延长索赔期

requested organization 被请求机关

require performance of an obligation 要求履行义务

require united exertion 同心协力

required by law 合法的

required majority 法定多数

requirement 必要条件,要件

requirement contract 有限制条款的合同

requirement of form 形成要件

requirement of technology transfer 技术转让要求

requirements and potentialities 需要与可能

requirements of administrative procedure 行政程序要求

requisites to constitute an offense 违法要件

requisition 申请书,征收,征用

requisition for payment 付款申请书

requisition of grassland 草原征用

requisition of land 征用土地

rcs accessoria（拉）从属物

res communis（拉）共有物

res communis omnium（拉）共有财产

res contraversa（拉）争议物

res fungibiles（拉）可替代物

res ipsa loquitur（拉）事实本身说明问题

res litigiosa（拉）争议物

res nullius（拉）无主地

res sic stantibus（拉）保护

resale 转卖

resale contract 转卖合同

resale price 转卖价格

resale price agreement 转售价格协议

resale price maintenance 转售价格控制,维持转售价格,维持再售价格

rescheduling of payment 重要安排付款期

rescind 撤回,撤销,取消,废除,宣告无效

rescind a contract 撤销契约,取消合同

rescind a judgment 取消判决

rescind an agreement 取消协议

rescind one's right 权利的撤除

rescind the entrustment 取消委托

rescinded civil acts 被撤销民事行为

rescission 解约,撤销

rescission of a contract 合同废纸,契约的撤销

rescission of concessions for a disposition 和解让步的撤销

rescission of contract 撤销合同

rescous（拉）劫夺犯人

rescript 上谕

research and development management 科技开发管理系统

research methods of criminology 犯罪学研究方法

research paper 学术论文

research work 调查工作

resell 倒卖

resell goods 转卖货物

reservatio dominii（拉）所有权的保留

reservation 附加条件,预定,保留

reservation clause 保留条款

reservation of public order 公共秩序保留

reservation of right 保留权利,权利的保留

reservation of right and interest 保留权益

reservation of treaty 条约的保留

reservation price 保留价格

reserve 预定

reserve duty 预备役

reserve for taxes 纳税储备

reserve forces 预备役部队

reserve fund 银行准备金,公积金,准备金

reserve liability 保留责任

reserve on deposit 存款准备金

reserve price 最低价格,开拍价格

reserve requirements on deposit 法定存款准备金

reserve servicemen 预备役军人

reserve the right of disposal 保留处分权

reserve the right to do sth 保留…的权利

reserve tranche 储备份额

reserve tranche facility 储备部分贷款

reserve zone 保留区

reserved authority 保留权限

reserved power 保留权力

reserved right 保留权利

reserved shipments 保留质载

resettlement 重新定居

reshipment 转载

reshuffle of cabinet 内阁改组

residence 居所

residence permit 居留证

residence permit for foreigners 外国人居留证

residence zone 居住区

resident 常住,境内

resident aliens 外籍居民

resident auditor 常住审计师

resident population 常住人口

resident taxpayer 居民纳税人

residenter 常住人口

residential allotment 住房分配

residential district 居民区

residential quarter 居住区

residential standard 居住标准

residents' committee 街道居民委员会

residual competence 剩余权限

residual estate 剩余财产

residual liability 剩余赔偿责任

residual property 剩余财产

residual right 剩余权利

residue 剩余财产

resign 辞职

resign from office 辞职

resignation 辞职

resignation en bloc 全体辞职

resignation from office 辞职

resistance 对抗

resisting 抗拒

resistive psychology of a convict 罪犯抗衡心理

resocialization 再社会化

resolution 议案,议决案,决议

resolution of majority 多数决议案

resolution of the creditors' meeting 债权人会议的决议

resolution on definition of aggression 关于侵略定义的决议

resolution passed 已通过的议案

resolutive condition 解除条件

resolutory condition 解除条件

resort to arms 采用武力

resort to sophistry 狡辩

resort to violence 采用暴力,诉诸暴力

resource compensation 资源补偿费

resource tax 资源税

resource utilization rate 资源利用率

resources distributed by state in a unified way 国家统配资料

respect 遵守

respect intellectuals 尊重知识分子

respect one's words 遵守诺言

respect social ethics 尊重社会公德

respect the law 尊重法律

respect to one's promise 遵守诺言

respective contributions to the investment 各自的出资比例

respectively 分别

respond in damages 承担赔偿费用,对损失负责

respondent 被上诉人,被上诉人(注二指二审中),答辩人,被

告,被告人

response in response 法庭反应

response to judgment 判决反应

responsibilities and interests of an enterprise 权责利

responsibilities for product quality 产品质量责任

responsibilities of management 管理责任

responsibility 能力,责权利,责任

responsibility cabinet 责任内阁制

responsibility contracts on specialties 专业承包

responsibility for administrative contract 行政合同责任

responsibility for administrative malfeasance 行政违法责任

responsibility for administrative violations of law 行政违法责任

responsibility for debt 债务承担

responsibility for default 不履行责任

responsibility for jointly and severally bound 连带责任

responsibility for result 结果责任

responsibility for risk 危险责任

responsibility for violation of discipline 行政违纪责任

responsibility in administrative law 行政法律责任

responsibility of breach 违约责任

responsibility of guardianship 监护责任

responsibility of international organization 国际组织的责任

responsibility of state 国家责任

responsibility of state for the act of individuals 国家对个人行为的责任

responsibility of state for the act of its organs 国家对其机关行为的责任

responsibility of the multimodal transport operator 多式联运经营人的责任

responsibility system 经营承包责任制,责任制

responsibility system for operation 经营责任制

responsibility system for production 生产责任制

responsibility system of manager 经理负责制

responsibility system of the chief prosecutor 检察长负责制

responsible for compensation 负责赔偿

responsible for rehabilitation 负责修复

responsible government 责任政府

responsible institution 主管机关

responsible party 责任方

responsible person 负责人

responsible tenant 按期交租的承租人

restate 重申

rested estate 即约财产

resting order 长期有效订单

restitute 赔偿

restitutio in integrum (拉) 回复原状

restitution 退还,赔偿,返还

restitution in integrum 恢复原状

restitution in kind 恢复实物原状

restitution interest 恢复原状利益

restitution of advance payment 退还预付款

restitution of property 返还财产

restitution of unjust enrichment 返还不当得利

restitution/restoration of the original conditions 恢复原状

restoration for the reputation 恢复名誉

restoration of facial features 颜

骨面貌复原

restoration of nationality 恢复国籍

restoration of original condition 恢复原状

restoration of right 权利恢复

restoration to the original state 恢复原状

restore 恢复

restore to original status 恢复原状

restrain 制约

restrain the liberty 限制自由

restraining statute 限制性法律

restraint effect of administrative act 行政行为的拘束力

restraint on liberty 限制自由

restraint on alienation 限制让步

restransit cum suo onere (拉) 债务随财产一并转移

restrict 制约,限制,约束

restrict sale 限制销售

restrict the import or export 限制进口或者出口

restricted 限定

restricted air space 空中禁区

restricted competition 有限竞争

restricted contract 受制合同

restricted negotiable 限制议付

restriction measures 限制措施

restriction of import 进口限制

restriction of liabilities 责任限制

restriction of powers 权力限制,权力制约

restriction of transfer 转让限制,限制转让

restriction on the expiration of industrial property 工业产权期满后的限制

restriction on the improvement and development of technology 对技术改进与发展的限制

restrictive 限制性的,自制的

restrictive application 限制性适用

restrictive business practice 限制

性商业惯例,限制性商业做法

restrictive business practices or restrictive clauses 限制性的商业做法

restrictive business practices/RBP 限制性商业惯例

restrictive clauses 限制性条款

restrictive condition 限制条件

restrictive corenant 限制性契约

restrictive function 制约作用

restrictive interpretation 缩小解释,限制解释

restrictive license 限制性许可证

restrictive measure 限制措施

restrictive practices court 限制贸易实施法庭(英)

restrictive prevention 限制性预防

restrictive provision 限制性规定

restrictive trade practices act 限制贸易实施法(英 1956)

restructuring 重新组织

restructuring economy 经济体制改革

restructuring the economy 经济体制改革

result 决议,效果

result of conviction 定罪结果

result of judgment 判决结果

result of sentence 判决结果

resulting powers 派生权力

resulting use 归复使用权

results of inspection 检验结果

resume 恢复

resume sovereignty over HongKong 恢复对香港行使主权

resumption of citizenship 公民资格的恢复

resumption of nationality 国籍恢复

retail loan 零售放款

retail price 零售价格

retail trade of tobacco product 烟草制品零售业务

retain 保留

retained property 留置财产

retainer（of legacy） 保留权

retaining citizenship（/nationali-ty） 保留国籍

retaliate 报复,打击报复

retaliation 报复,打击报复

retaliatory act 报复行为

retaliatory duty 报复关税

retention money bond 保留金担保

retention of ownership 所有权保留

retire a bill 赎单,赎票

retiree 退休人员

retirement 赎回

retirement of stock 股票回收

retirement of trustees 受托人终止受托

retirement system of judges 法官的退休制度

retiring partner 退伙人

retortion 反报

retract a confession 翻供

retract one's promise 取消诺言

retreat 收容所

retreat rule 撤退原则

retrench 精简

retrial 复审,再审

retrial by the same count of its own accord 自行再审

retributive justice 报应性司法

retributive punishment 报复性惩罚

retributivism 报应主义

retrieve the funds in full 追回全部款项

retroact 追溯既往

retroactive application 追溯适用

retroactive effect 追溯力

retroactive effective 追溯效力

retroactive force 追溯力

retroactive force of treaty 条约的追溯力

retroactive interpretation 追溯解释

retroactivity 追溯性

retroactivity of criminal law 刑法溯及力

retroactivity of law 法律的追溯力

retrocession 权利交还

retrospect 溯及力

retrospective 可追溯的

retrospective effect 溯及力

retrospective law 追溯法

retrospective legislation 有追溯效力的立法

retry 重审,重新审理

return 退还,选举,退货,返还,追缴

return and compensate 退赔

return cargo 回运货物

return day 传票退还日

return for no claim 无赔偿退货

return freight 运回运费

return of down-payment 退还押金

return of foreign trade 对外贸易收入

return of goods 退货

return of one's property 归还财产

return of property 返还财产

return property to the rightful owner 物归原主

return the goods 退货

return the property 返还财产

（of a convict）return to society 重返社会

returned goods 退还货物

returned overseas Chinese 归侨,归国华侨

returned purchase 退货

returning officer 选举监察官员

revelation 天启

revelation before committing crime 罪前表露

revendication 退缴

revenge murder 报复杀人

revenue 税收,收益

revenue agent 税务员

revenue duty 财政关税,关税收入

revenue from tax 税收

revenue officer 税务稽查员
revenue paper 税单
revenue ruling 税则
revenue stamp 税章
revenue tax 财政税收,财政税
revenue(s) tariff 财政关税,收入关税
reversal 翻案,变更判决
reversal of judgment 判决的推翻
reversal original judgment 变更原判
reverse a court decision 撤销法庭判决
reverse a judgment 撤销原判
reverse a judgment cassation 翻案
reverse dumping 逆倾销
reverse engineering 反向工程
reverse preference 反向优惠
review 复议,复审
review a case in which a death sentence has been passed 复核死刑案件
review a case in which a death sentence has been passed on probation 复核死缓案件
review for the second time 二次复议
review of a criminal's case 罪犯案件复查
review of constitutionality 违宪审查
review of taxation 征税复查
reviewable administrative act 可受司法审查的行政行为
revise 修订,修正,修改
revise a constitution 修改宪法
revise a contract 修改合同
revise price 调整价格
revised American foreign trade definition 美国对外贸易定义修订本·(1941)
revised statutes 经修订的成文法,修订的制定法
revision 修正
revision clause 修改条款

revision of constitution 宪法修改
revision of judgment 判决复核
revision of treaties 条约的修改
revision procedure 修改
revision procedure of the Charter of the United Nations 联合国宪章的修改程序
revival of treaties 条约的恢复
revive 使再生效
revocable 可撤销的
revocable L/C 可撤销信用社
revocation 撤回,撤销,取消
revocation of a testament 遗嘱撤销
revocation of offer 撤销要约
revocation of order of planning permission 计划许可命令的撤销
revocation of probation 缓刑的撤销
revocation of will 撤销遗赠
revoke 撤回,撤销
revoke a parole 撤销假释
revoke an application for review 撤销复审申请书
revoke an offer 撤销要约
revoke the declaration of one's missing-person status 撤销失踪宣告
revoke the sale 撤回出卖
revoke will 撤销遗赠
revoked 取消的
revolt 反叛
revolution 革命
revolutionary 革命
revolutionization 革命化
revolving L/C 循环信用证
revolving loan 循环放款
reward 酬金,报酬,酬劳
rewards and punishments for state civil service 国家公务员的奖惩
rework 重做
Rhine river 莱茵河
ribbon development 带形开发
ride herd on 监督

right 法权,权利,权责利

right against all the world 对世权

right against double jeopardy 一罪不受两次审判的权利

right against particular person 相对权,对人权

right and true delivery 切实交付

right arising from defects of goods 由货物瑕疵而产生的权利

right barred by reason of time limitation 因时效完成不能行使的权利

right entitled by law 法定权利

right every wrong 有错必纠

right for lodging a claim 索赔权

right in dispute 有争议的权利

right in personal 债务

right in personam 对人权

right in vem （拉）物权

right of accusation 控告权

right of action 起诉权,诉讼权

right of action for alteration 变更诉权

right of action for the recovery of damages 损害赔偿请求权

right of action in chief 本诉权

right of action of prestation 给付诉权

right of adjacent 相邻权

right of administration 治权

right of air cabotage 国内两地间空运权

right of amnesty 大赦权

right of anticipation 提前偿付权

right of appeal 上诉权

right of archipelagic sea lanes passage 群岛海道的通行权

right of assembly 集会权

right of association 结社权

right of asylum 庇护权

right of attribution 归属权

right of autonomy 自治权

right of autonomy for enterprise 企业自主权

right of boycott 抵制权

right of cancellation 解除权,撤销权

right of citizenship 公民权

right of claim 求偿权,请求权,索赔权

right of common 共有权利,共用权

right of communication 传播权

right of complaint 控告权

right of confrontation 对质权

right of contribution 权利分摊,请求分担权,补偿权

right of correspondence 通信权

right of creditor 债权

right of cross action 反诉权

right of defense 辩护权

right of development 发展权

right of diplomatic protection 外交保护权

right of discovery 发现权

right of discreation 自由裁量权

right of disposal of the goods during transit 运输途中处理货物的权利

right of disposition 处分权

right of drainage 排水权

right of education 教育权

right of election 选举权

right of equality 平等权

right of equity 对等权利

right of establishment 建立企业的权利

right of existence 生存权

right of exoneration 衡平免责权,探矿权

right of exploitation 使用权

right of general detention 普通扣押权

right of hire 出租权

right of honor 荣誉权

right of hot pursuit 紧追权

right of independence 独立权

right of independence and self-determination 独立自主权

right of information 获得信息权

right of initiative 创制权

right of innocent passage 无害通过权

right of inviolability 不可侵犯权

right of jurisdiction 管辖权

right of labour 劳动权利

right of lien 留置权

right of life and health 生命健康权

right of life and health protection 生命健康权

right of lighting 采光权

right of litigation jurisdiction 诉讼管辖权

right of making motions 提案权

right of management 经营权

right of marriage by choice 婚姻自主权

right of monopoly 专卖权

right of mortgage with respect to a ship 船舶抵押权

right of name 名权

right of national autonomy 民族自治权

right of necessity 紧急避险权

right of negotiable instrument 票据权利

right of nol pros（拉） 撤诉权

right of objection 抗诉权

right of offset 抵消权

right of ownership 所有权

right of ownership in immovables 不动产所有权

right of ownership of grassland 草原所有权

right of pardon 赦免权

right of passageway 通行权

right of patent application 专利申请权

right of peoples to self-determination 民族自决权

right of personal freedom 人身自由权

right of personal liberties 人身自由权

right of personal name 姓名权

right of personal security 人身安全权

right of personality 人格权

right of petition 申诉权

right of pleadings 抗辩权

right of pledge 典质权, 质权

right of pocket veto 搁置权

right of portrait 肖像权

right of preemption 优先购买权

right of prior 优先权

right of priority 优先权

right of privacy 隐私权

right of prize 捕获权

right of property 财产权

right of public prosecution 公诉权

right of recourse 追偿权利

right of redemption 赎回权

right of redrers 索赔权

right of relief 获得补偿权

right of remuneration 报酬权

right of reply 答辩权

right of representation 代表权, 代理权

right of reputation 名誉权

right of resale 再卖权, 转卖权, 转售权

right of rescission 撤销权, 解约权

right of resistance 抵抗权利

right of respect 尊荣权

right of rest 休息权

right of retention 保留权, 留置权

right of retirees to ensure livelihood 退休人员的生活保障权

right of revocation 撤销权

right of sanctuary 庇护权

right of second claim 第二次请求取

right of self-defence 自卫权

right of self-determination of (the) peoples 人民自决权

right of self-preservation 自保权

right of silence 沉默权

right of state 国家权利

right of stoppage in transit（英）

中途停运权

right of subrogation 代位求偿权,代位权

right of supervision 监督权

right of taxation 征税权

right of the accused 被告的权利

right of the owner of copy 用户的权利

right of the person 人身权利

right of the third party 第三人权利

right of thing 物权

right of trademark 商标权

right of transit 过境权

right of use 使用权

right of ventilation 通风权

right of visit 登临检查权

right of withdrawal 撤回权

right of withdrawing an action 撤诉权

right on lack of conformity 因货物不符合合同而主张的权利

right over movables 动产权

right over the property of another 他物权

right possession 占有权

right quality and well-known products 名优产品

right relating to civil law 民事权利

right to a fair trial and public hearing by an independent and impartial tribunal 由独立而无偏倚的法庭进行公正和公开审判的权利

right to a view into the distance from a high 眺望权

right to acquire compensation according to law 依法获得赔偿的权利

right to action of procedure 程序意义上的诉权

right to address question 质询权,质问权

right to adduce evidence 举证权

right to administer properties 财产管理权

right to advocacy 律师辩护权

right to an effective judicial remedy 有效的司法救济权

right to bail 保释权

right to be elected 被选举权

right to be heard 听证权

right to be left alone 不被干扰的权利

right to be protected by laws 受法律保护权

right to be recognized as a person before the law 被承认在法律面前的人格的权利

right to claim 求偿权,请求权,要求赔偿的权利

right to claim damages 要求损害赔偿的权利

right to claim for damages 要求赔偿损失权

right to claim indemnity 赔偿请求权

right to compensation 获得赔偿权,赔偿请求权,取得赔偿权

right to contract for management 承包经营权

right to counsel 获得律师辩护的权利

right to criticize and make suggestions 批评建议权

right to defend oneself 申辩权

right to defense 答辩权,抗辩权

right to defense by attorney 律师辩护权

right to demand administrative compensation 要求行政赔偿权

right to demand compensation 要求赔偿的权利

right to develop resources 资源的开发权

right to district jurisdiction 地区管辖权

right to education 受教育权

right to enjoy equal treatment with other citizens after release upon completion of one's sentence terms 刑满释放后享受

与其他公民平等待遇权

right to equal and fair treatment 享受平等和公正待遇的权利

right to equal pay for equal work 同工同酬权

right to exclude all others 排他的权利

right to exist 生存权

right to existence 生存权

right to fair and impartial trial 公平而公正的审判权

right to fair trial 要求公正审判的权利

right to fix service charges 劳务定价权

right to free down in buying and selling 买卖自由权

right to habeas corpus 人身保护权

right to impeach 弹劾权,检举权

right to impose punishments for public security 治安行政处罚权

right to indemnification 受偿权利

right to information 取得情报的权利

right to initiate bills of administrative regulations 行政法规提案权

right to intervene 干预权

right to inviolability of residence 居所不可侵犯权

right to issue paper money 货币发行权

right to just and favourable remuneration 获得公平优裕报酬的权利

right to know 知道权

right to land 地权

right to learn the truth 知情权

right to limit liability 限制赔偿责任权

right to maintain and develop existence 生存权

right to material assistance 获得物质帮助权

right to muteness 沉默权

right to participate in government and political affairs 参政权

right to payment 请求赔偿权

right to personal safety 人身保护

right to petition 请愿权

right to protection of laws 受法律保护权

right to protest 抗议权

right to recall 罢免权

right to recourse 求偿权

right to recover a debt 债权

right to remuneration 获得报酬权

right to report 检举权

right to request compensation 请求赔偿权

right to rescind the contract 解除合同的权利

right to self-determination 自决权

right to silence 沉默权

right to slow down 怠工权

right to speak 发言权

right to speak out 发表言论权

right to stand for selection 被选举权

right to tranquillity 宁静权

right to use grassland 草原使用权

right to vote 表决权,投票权,选举权

right to vote and stand for suffrage 选举和被选举权

right to watercourse 水道通行权

right to work 劳动权利,工作权,劳动权

righteous 正义

righteous action 正义的行为

rightful owner 失主,合法所有人

right-of-way 地役权

rights and duties 权利与义务

rights and duties of both parties

双方当事人的权利和义务

rights and duties of relatives 亲属间权利义务

rights and interests 权益

rights and obligations 权利与义务

rights and remedies 权利和救济方法

rights and wrongs 曲直

Rights depend upon remedies 权利依赖于救济

rights of administrative bodies 行政机关的权利

rights of citizens 公民的权利

rights of crew 船员的权利

rights of invention 发明权

rights of judges 法官权利

rights of life and health 生命健康权

rights of mankind 人类权利

rights of maritime claim 海事请求权

rights of subjects in economic law 经济法主体的权利

rights reserved 保留权利,保留的权利

rights under the contract 合同权利

rigid and absolute enforcement 强制施行

rigid constitution 刚性宪法

rigorous 严格

rigorous performance of contract 严格执行合同

ring green 城市周围绿地

ring trading 垄断交易

ringleader 首要分子

ring-dropping 欺诈盗窃罪

riot police 防暴警察

rip off 盗窃

rise 上涨

rise and fall clause 价格升降条款

risk 危险

risk asset 风险资产

risk funds 风险基金

risk in transit 运输风险,运输途中的风险

risk management 风险管理

risk of carriage 运输风险

risk of clashing and breakage 碰损破碎险

risk of contamination 玷污险

risk of damage 毁损风险

risk of leakage 渗漏险

risk of liability 责任风险

risk of missing 丢失风险

risk of odour 串味险

risk of rusting 锈损险

risk of shortage 短量险

risk responsibility 危险责任

risk transfer 风险转移

risk unit 危险单位

river law 河流法

river pollution 河流污染

road accident 公路交通事故,交通事故

road administration 路政

road agent 拦路强盗,拦路抢劫犯

road capacity 道路通车量,道路运输能力

road safety act 公路安全法

road signal 道路信号

road traffic accident 道路交通事故

road traffic control 道路交通管理

road traffic control organization 道路交通管理机关

road traffic law 公路交通法

rob with murder 抢劫谋杀

robber 抢劫犯,拦路强盗,拦路抢劫犯

robbery after the event 事后强盗罪

Roberspierre 罗伯斯庇尔

Robinson-patman act 鲁宾逊—帕特曼法

rock bottom price 最低价格

rogatory letters (美) 委托书

roguery 流氓团伙

role of law 法的作用

role of subjective intentions 主观

作用

roll 档案,盗窃

roll back 压平物价,压价

roll call 唱名

rollback policy 压价政策

rolls 案卷

rolls court 案卷法庭

Roman digest 罗马法律汇编

Roman law 罗马法

Rome convention for the protection of performers, producers of phonograms and broadcasting organizations 保护表演者、录音制作者和广播组织的罗马公约

Rome international institute for the unification of private law 罗马统一私法国际协会

root 根本

root cause 根本原因

Roscoe Pound 罗斯科·庞德

Roosevelt's new deal 罗斯福新政

roster of candidates 候选人名单

rotten clause 损坏条款

roughhouse 室内殴斗与喧闹行为

rough-wrought product 半助加工制品

round table conference 圆桌会议

roundsman 推销员

round-table conference 圆桌会议

route 航线

route of a parade 游行路线

routine court 常规法院

routine examination 常规检查

routine inspection 常规检查,例行检查

routine session 例行会议

routine test 定期检查

royal assent 恩准

royal cabinet 皇位继承

royal colonies 英王直辖殖民地

royal court 王朝

royal court of justice 皇室法院

royal decree 圣旨

royal edict 圣旨

royal family 王室

royal household 皇室

royal instructions 皇家训令(英)

royal power 王权

royal prerogative 君主特权,王室特权,君权

royal veto 君主否决权

royal writ 王室令状

royalties for transfer of technology 技术转让提成费

royalty 提成支付,提成费,版税

rubber cheque 空头支票

rubber stamp 橡皮图章

ruffianism 暴徒行为

rule 常规,规律,统治,规章

rule by constitutional government 宪政之治

rule by law 法治

rule by man 人治

rule by special privilege 特权统治

rule for measures to preserve property 裁定采取诉讼保全措施

rule for practice 工作规范

rule imposing duty 设定义务的规则

rule imposing obligation 设定义务的规则

rule of adjudication 审判规则

rule of administrative law 行政法治

rule of advance execution 裁定先予执行

rule of conferring right 授予权利的规则

rule of conflict 冲突原则,冲突规则

rule of direct consignment 直接运输规则

rule of effectiveness 实效规则

rule of equity 衡平法规则

rule of evidence 证据规则

rule of fair trade 公平贸易原则

rule of general elimination of quantitative restrictions 一切取消数量限制原则

rule of general exceptions 一般负责条款

rule of imposing duty 设定义务的规则

rule of injunction 禁止性规范

rule of justice 正义规则

rule of law 法治

rule of man 人治

rule of morality 道德规则

rule of morals 德治

rule of order 命令性规范

rule of origin 原产地规则

rule of protecting infant industry 幼稚产业保护原则

rule of reason 合理的准则,合理规则

rulership 统治权

rules 规程

rules of conflict 冲突法

rules of construction 解释法律之规则

rules of court 法庭规则

rules of debate 辩论规则,议事规则

rules of evidence for administrative proceedings 行政诉讼证据规则

rules of international civil jurisdiction 国际民事裁制管辖权规则

rules of international civil procedure 国际民事诉讼程序规范

rules of jus commune 普通法规则

rules of law 法律规程

rules of local governments 地方政府规章

rules of natural justice 自然公正规则

rules of operation 操作规程

rules of order 程序规则,议事规程

rules of practice 习惯做法

rules of prison 监狱规则

rules of private international law 国际私法规范

rules of procedure 议事规则,程序规则,程序法

rules of procedure for international mandatory conciliation 国际强制调解程序规则

rules of the air 空中规则

rules of the enterprises with foreign investment 外商投资企业章程

rules of the law merchant 商法通例

rules of the management of tour guides 导游人员管理规定

rules of uniform substance 统一实体规范

rules on air warfare 空战法规

rules on the control of dangerous goods 危险物品管理规定

rules on the management of cable TV 有线电视管理规定

rules on the management of wired broadcasting network 有限广播网管理规定

rules on the protection of scientific and technological secrets 科技保密规章

ruling 裁定

ruling against acceptance of a case 裁定不予受理

ruling against execution (of arbitration awards and notarized claims of credit) 裁定不予执行

ruling against voluntary dismissal 裁定不准撤诉

ruling class 统治阶级

ruling clique 统治集团

ruling in force 发生法律效力的裁定

ruling in writing 裁定书

ruling of a criminal action 刑事裁决书

ruling of compensation 赔偿裁决

ruling of first instance 初审裁

决,第一审裁定

ruling of parole　假释裁定

ruling of release　释放裁定书

ruling of restitution　赔偿裁决

ruling party　执政党

ruling price　现价

rummage　海关检查

rummaged　已经海关检查

rumming agreement　续合约

run　经营,营业

run counter to　违背,违反

run counter to the policy　违反政策

run for office　竞选职位

run into debt　借债

runaway inflation　失控通货膨胀

runner　竞选人

running characteristics　使用性能

running days or consecutive days　连续日

running maintenance　经常性维修

running the country according to law　以法治国

running with the land　有关土地的

runoff primary　第二次预选

rural collective economic organization　农村集体经济组织

rural constable　乡警

rural contracting entity　农村承包经营产

rural fair trade　集市贸易

rural market　集镇

rural political power organization　农村政权组织

rush for goods　抢购物资

rush to purchase　抢购

Russian federation　俄罗斯联邦

Russian revolution　俄国革命

S

sabotage 从事破坏活动,怠工

saboteur 怠工者

sacral punishment 圣训

sacral swamp 圣坛

sacred 神圣

sacred duty 神圣职责

sacred obligation 神圣职责

sacred territory 神圣领土

sacrificial punishment 牺牲刑

sacrilege 渎圣罪

sadism 虐待淫乱症,虐待狂,性虐待狂

sadistic rape 淫狂强奸

safe altitude 安全高度

safe bearing capacity 安全承载能力

safe berth clause "安全泊位"条款

safe broad side 安全范围

safe custody charges 寄存费

safe location 安全场所

safe parking distance 安全停车距离

safe port clause "安全港口"条款

safe reliability 安全可靠性

safe retreat 收容所

safe service life 安全使用年限

safe-deposit trust 保管信托

safeguard 保护措施,维护,保证条款,保卫,保障

safeguard clause 保护条款,保证条款

safeguard provision 安全保障条款

safeguard rights and interests 维护权益

safeguard state sovereignty and territorial integrity 保卫国家主权和领土完整

safeguard the autonomy of foreign trade operators in their operations 保障对外贸易经营者的经营自主权

safeguard the people's interests 维护人民利益

safeguard the security of motherland 维护祖国安全

safeguard the unity of the country 维护祖国统一

safeguarding duties 保护性关税

safeguarding of industry act（英）工业保护法

safe-keeping 妥善保管

safety 安全

safety and hygiene of labour 劳动安全卫生

safety and protection against dust in mines 矿山安全和防尘

safety bearing power 安全承载力

safety certification 安全认证

safety colour 安全标志色

safety device 安全设备

safety distance 安全距离

safety door 安全门

safety factor 安全系数

safety gate 安全门

safety measure 安全措施

safety precautions 安全保障措施

safety regulation(s) 安全规章,安全规程,保安规程

safety specification 安全规程

safety switch 安全开关

sag 经济萧条

salaries/wages adjustment tax 工资调节税

sale 出售,卖,变卖

sale and leaseback 出售和租回,回租租赁,售后回租

sale and repurchase 出租和购回

sale based on documents 凭单出售,单据买卖

sale by auction 拍卖

sale by bulk 成批出售

sale by cash　现金买卖
sale by description　凭证明销售，凭证明书出售
sale by documents　凭单据销售，单据买卖
sale by grade　凭规格买卖
sale by installments　分期出售
sale by proxy　代销
sale by sample　凭样品买卖，照样品出售，货样买卖
sale by specification　凭规格，凭证明书买卖
sale by trade mark　凭商标买卖
sale for cash　现金交易
sale lease　销售租赁
sale marketing　销售
sale of collateral　变卖抵押物
sale of collateral in order to foreclose on a debt　变卖抵押物抵偿债务
sale of goods ordinate　货物买卖条例
sale of property　财产出售
sale of securities　出售担保品
sale of specific goods　特定货物的买卖，特定物的买卖
sale of tobacco product　烟草制品的销售
sale of unascertained goods　非种类物的买卖
sale on account　赊卖
sale on approval　试验买卖，试销
sale on consignment　代销，委托销售
sale on credit　信用买卖
sale on type　照种类出售
sale or return　可退货经销
sale price　成交价
sale promotion　推销
sales account　售货清单
sales agent　销售代理商
sales agreement　销售协议
sales as per specifications　照规格出售
sales by brand or trademark　凭商号或商标买卖

① sales by description　凭说明书的买卖
③ sales by inspection　看货买卖
④ sales by sample　凭样品买卖，按样品买卖
⑥ sales by specification, grade or standard　凭商品规格、等级或标准的买卖
⑨ sales channels　销售渠道
⑩ sales commission　回扣
⑪ sales confirmation　售货确认书，销售确认书
⑬ sales contract　售货合同，销售合同
⑮ sales department　销售部门
⑯ sales force　推销员
⑰ sales law　买卖法
⑱ sales load　销售费用
⑲ sales on commission　承销，委托销售
㉑ sales order　销售订单
㉒ sales organization　销售机构
㉓ sales price　销售价
㉔ sales quota　销货定额，销货限额
㉕ sales records　销售记录
㉖ sales representative　销售代表
㉗ sales slip　销货单
㉘ sales tax　零售税
㉙ sales terms　售货条件
㉚ sales territory　销货区域
㉛ sales transaction　销售交易
㉜ sales transaction on trial　试用买卖
㉞ sales value　销售价值
㉟ sales volume　销货量
㊱ sales warrant　销售保证
㊲ salesman　推销员
㊳ Salique law　撒利克法
㊴ salt duty　盐税
㊵ salvage action　救助诉讼
㊶ salvage agreement　救助协议
㊷ salvage at sea　海上救助
㊸ salvage awards (/remuneration)　救助报酬
㊹ salvage charge　救助费用
㊻ salvage contract　救助合同
㊼ Salvage convention (1910)　救助

公约(1910)

salvage expenses 救助费用

salvage of property 财产救助

salvage value 残值

salvo 保全手段

salvor's expenses 救助人所花费用

same recidivist 同种累犯

sample 样品,样本,货样

sample charge 样品费

sample drawn by owner 由货主自抽货样

sample for reference 参考样品

sample for test 化验样品

sample of buyers 买方样品

sample of sellers 卖方样品

sample survey 样品检验,抽样调查

sample trade 货样买卖

samples of goods 货样

sampling 抽样调查

sampling computation 抽样计算

sampling for a test 采样检验

sampling inspection 抽样检查

sampling survey of crime 犯罪抽样调查

San Francisco conference 旧金山会议

sanction 制裁,约束力,同意,批准

sanction of expulsion 开除处分

sanction of forfeiture 没收处分

sanction of treaty 条约的核准

sanctioning authority 处分机关

sanctionist 制裁国

sanctions 制裁

sanctities 神圣的权利,神圣的义务

sanctity 神圣不可侵犯性

sane person 神智健全的人

sanitary and antiepidemic station 卫生防疫站

sanitary code 卫生法规

sanitary conditions 卫生状况

sanitary custom-house regulation 海关检疫条例

sanitary inspection 卫生检验

sanitary inspection certificate 卫生检验证书

sanitary measure 卫生措施

sanitary supervision and inspection institution 卫生监督检验机构

sanitation 卫生

sanitation measures 卫生处理

sanity 神智健全,公正

sapphism 女性同性恋

sash 窗框

sash pocket 窗框

sate interest 国家利益

satellite state 卫星国

satisdatio (拉) 保证,

satisfaction 补偿,履行义务,赔偿

satisfaction of judgment 判决执行书

satisfactory 充分

satisfactory evidence 充分证据

satisfactory product 合格产品

satisfactory security 满意的担保

satisfied term 完成的期间

satisfy 满足,赔偿

satisfy a creditor 返清债务

satisfy a debt 返清债务

satisfy the conditions for a loan 具备贷款条件

satisfy the prescriptive period 完成时效期

saturation of crime 犯罪饱和率

saturation point 市场饱和点

savage 野蛮

save from damage 保全

save one's bail 保释后如期出庭

saving 保全

saving bonds 储蓄债券,储蓄国债

saving clause 但书

saving of energy 节约能源

savings and loan association 信用合作社

Saxon code 撒克逊法典

Saxon law 撒克逊人法律

scale 比例,尺度

scale of business 经营规模
scale of operation 经营规模
scale of punishment 刑罚等级
scaling of physical disability 劳动能力丧失程度鉴定
scalp 投机倒把
scalper 投机倒把分子
scamp work and stint material 偷工减料
scarcity 短缺
scattered funds 闲散资(主)
scattered plots of unutilized land 闲散土地
scene of death 尸体现场
scepter 君权
schedular system of taxation 分类税制
schedule of duty rates 税率表
schedule of fees for arbitrators of international cases 国际案件仲裁员收费表
schedule of payment 付款日期
scheduled airline 班机运输
scheduled cost 计划成本
scheduled flight 航班飞行
scheduled offense 表列罪
scheduled output 计划产量
scheduled period 预定期间
scheduled production 计划产量
scheduled purchasing 计划采购
scheme 计划，体制
scheme for private gain 营私
scheme of arrangement 还债协议
scheme of operation 经营计划
schizophrenia 精神分裂症
scholastic theories of law 经验法学
school 学校
school education 学校教育
school graduates waiting for employment in urban area 城镇待业人员
school of comparative jurisprudence 比较法学派
school of continental jurists 大陆法学派

school of criminal anthropology 刑事人类学派
school of criminal psychology 犯罪心理学派
school of criminal sociology 刑事社会学派
school of experimentation 实证学派
school of judicial realism 实在主义法学派,实证主义法学派
school of natural law 自然法学派
school of positive crime 犯罪实证学派
school of romanists 罗马法学派
school of science of handwriting verification 笔相学派
school of social utilitarianism 社会功利派
school system 学制
schooling 学校教育
school teacher 教师
science and technology 科技
science and technology committee (美) 科学技术委员会
science and technology concerning criminal matters 刑事科学技术
science and technology planning 科技规划
science and technology system 科技体制
science of administrative 行政学
science of administrative procedural law 行政诉讼法学
science of case study 案件学
science of civil law 民法学
science of civil procedure law/ 民事诉讼法学
science of comparative civil law 比较民法学
science of comparative constitutional law 比较宪法学
science of constitutional law 宪法学
science of countermeasures of crime 犯罪对策学

science of criminal evidence 刑事证据学

science of criminal investigation 刑事侦查学

science of criminal investigation 犯罪侦查学

science of criminal law 刑法学

science of criminal policies 刑事政策学

science of criminal procedural law 刑事诉讼法学

science of economic adjudication 经济审判学

science of evolution of criminal law 沿革刑法学

science of executing punishment 行刑学

science of gunshot verification 验枪学

science of historical criminal law 刑法史学

science of in-prison investigation 狱内侦查学

science of public administrative 行政学

science of reeducation-through-labour 劳动教养学

science of reformatory education 教育改造学

science of reform-through-labour economy 劳改经济管理学

scientific and technical structural reform 科技体制改革

scientific and technical structure 科技体制

scientific and technological advance 科技进步

scientific and technological agreement 科技协定

scientific and technological management system 科技管理体制

scientific and technological power 科技大国

scientific and technological productive forces 科技生产力

scientific and technological progress 科技进步

scientific and technological system 科技体制

scientific and technological talents market 科技人才市场

scientific committee on Antarctic research 南极考察科学委员会

scientific method 科学方法

scientific research 科学研究

scientific research management 科研管理

scientific research of seas 海洋科学研究

scissors gap between international prices 国际价格剪刀差

scissors movement of world market price 国际价格剪刀差

scope 范围

scope of administrative cases to be accepted by the court 行政诉讼的受案范围

scope of administrative compensation 行政补偿的范围

scope of administrative indemnity 行政赔偿范围

scope of administrative procedure 行政诉讼范围

scope of administrative proceedings 行政诉讼的范围

scope of administrative reconsideration 行政复议范围

scope of agency 受委托范围

scope of application of criminal law 刑法的适用范围,刑法适用范围

scope of authority 授权范围,委托权限,授权范围

scope of authorization 委托的范围

scope of business 经营范围

scope of business of auditor's firm 审计事务所的业务范围

scope of cover 责任范围

scope of foreign trade operations 对外贸易经营范围

scope of judicial review 司法审

查的范围

scope of official duty 职责范围

scope of operation 经营范围

scope of prosecutorial protest 抗诉范围

scope of protection 保护范围

scope of repair 检修范围

scope of service 业务范围

scope of the power entrusted 委托权限

scope of tortious acts for administrative indemnity 行政赔偿的侵权行为范围

scope of tortious damages for administrative indemnity 行政赔偿的侵权损害范围

scope of validity 效力范围

Scotland 苏格兰

scotoma of the victim 被害人盲点症

scout inside prisons 狱内侦查

scrap certificate 拆毁许可证

scrap handling 废料处理

scrap value 残值

scrape 勉强通过,擦伤

scratch 擦伤,划痕

scratch mark 插划痕迹

scratch marks of tools 插划工具痕迹

screen a criminal 包庇罪犯

screening of a case 案件的筛选

scrip 股票临时收据

script 笔迹

scrivener 公证员

scrupulous 严格的

scrutineer 选票检查人

scrutinize 审查

sea laws 海洋法

sea perils 海上风险

sea power 海军强国

sea right 领海权

sea-bottom beyond continental shelf 大陆架以外的海底

sea-going freedom of land locked states 内陆国出海自由

seal 署押,印章,图章

seal of the court 法庭印鉴

seal of the state 国玺

seal up 查封

sealed bid 非公开招标

sealed contract 有法律效力的合同,有签署或盖章的合同,正式契约,盖印契约,正式合同

sealed contract 盖印合同,依式契约

sealed off 加封

sealed offer 盖印要约

sealed property 被查封的财产

sealer 盖章人

sealing of contracts 合同的签署

sealing of criminal records 罪犯案卷的密封

sealing up 对财产的查封、扣押、冻结

seaport 海港

seaport quarantine 海港检疫

search for violations of a ban 查禁

searching enquiry 深入调查

season and crimes 季节与犯罪

seasonal adjustment 季节性调整

seasonal deposit 季节性存款

seasonal discount 季节折扣

seasonal duty 季节性关税

seasonal goods 季节性商品

seasonal industry 季节性产业

seasonal price differences 季节差价

seasonal restrictions 季节性限制

seasonal risk 季节性风险

seasonal tariff 季节性税率

seasonal variation 季节性变动

seasonally adjusted/SA 季节性调整

seat 所在地,席位

seaworthiness 适航

secession of state 国家的分离

seclusion, seclude a nation from the outside world 闭关锁国

second arrest 第二次拘捕

second beneficiary 第二受益人,

受让人

second best theory 次佳原理	second-hand evidence 第二手证据
second brief 第二次辩护状	secrecy agreement 保密协议
second hand 转手	secrecy classification 保密级别
second hearing 第二审	secrecy regulation 保密条例
second instance 第二审	secret 秘密警察,机密
second lien 二等留置权,第二管置权	secret ballot 无记名投票,秘密投票
second lieutenant on reserve service 预备役少尉	secret clause 秘密条款
second mortgage 第二抵押权	secret election 秘密选举
second mortgage bonds 第二抵债券	secret judgment 秘密审判
second offense 再犯	secret lien 秘密留置权
second preferred mortgage 次优抵押	secret partner 隐名合伙人
second public procurator 副检察长	secret poll 秘密投票
second trial 第二次审判	secret reservation 秘密保留权利
secondary aspect of a contradiction 矛盾的次要方面	secret sentencing 秘密审判
secondary cause 次要原因	secret session 秘密会议
secondary characterization 二级识别	secret sitting 秘密会议
secondary contradiction 次要矛盾	secret societies 秘密社团
secondary energy 二次能源	secret voting 秘密投票
secondary energy sources 二次能源	secretary 秘书
secondary evidence 次要证据,间接证据	secretary of state 国务卿
secondary liability 从属负债,间接责任	secretary of the party committee 党委书记
secondary market 次级市场,流通市场,二级市场	secretary-general 秘书长
secondary mortgage market 二级抵押市场	secretary-general of the Standing Committee of the National People's Congress 全国人大常委会秘书长
secondary offender 次要实行犯	secretary-general of the State Council 国务院秘书长
secondary party 次当事人	secretary-general of the United Nations 联合国秘书长
secondary perpetrator 次要实行犯	secretly withdrawing funds 抽逃资金
secondary pollutants 二次污染物	section 条
secondary pollution 二次污染	sectional management 行业管理
secondary question 次要问题	sectionalized house 装配式住房
secondary reading 第二读	sector of economy 经济部门
secondary rule 次要规则	sector of the economy 经济成分
	sector standard 行业标准
	sectoral integration 部分一体化
	sectors of national econom 国民经济部门
	secular 世俗
	secular court 非宗教法院

secular law　世俗法律
secular price　长期价格
secular society　世俗社会
secular trend　长期趋势
secure the debt　承担债务
secured　有保证的,有担保,被担保的
secured claim　有担保的债权
secured creditor　享有担保的债权人,持有担保的债权人
secured liability　担保欠债,无担保债务
secured loan　担保贷款
secured tenancy　有保障的租赁
secured time loan　定期担保贷款
secured transaction　担保交易
securities　有价证券
securities analysis　证券投资分析
securities company　证券公司
securities disclosing system　证券披露制度
securities exchange act　证券交易法
securities investment　证券投资
securities investment trust　证券投资信托
securities market　有价证券市场,证券市场
securities transfer tax　证券交易税
securities trust　证券投资信托
security　(不动产)抵押,担保,担保物,安全,抵押品,保全
security administration　治安管理
security analysis　证券分配
security arrangements　保安措施
security body　保卫机关
security classification　保密级别
security committee　保密委员会
security company　证券公司
security cost　担保费用
security dealer　证券商
security departments　保卫部门
security deposit　保金

security documents　担保文件
security exchange　证券交易所
security fee　保安费
security for a loan　贷款抵押品,贷款担保,贷款抵押
security for costs　费用担保,讼费保证
security for debt　债务保证,债务担保品
security in maritime litigation　海事诉讼保全
security interest　担保物权,担保权益
security measure(s)　保安措施,保安处分
security of a maritime claim　海事请求保全
security of costs　诉讼费用担保
security of obligation　债的担保
security of society　社会保安
security of tax payment　纳税担保
security of tenure　租地使用权的保障
security personnel　保安人员
security police　秘密警察
security regulation(s)　治安条例
security system　保安系统,证券,抵押物,担保
sedition　煽动罪
sedition act　镇压叛乱法
seditious meetings act　危及治安集会处置法
seducement　笼络手段
see a doctor outside houses for reeducation-through-labour　劳教人员所外就医
seed amelioration　种子改良
seed business license　种子经营许可证
seed capital　原始资本
seed law　种子法
seed-breeding license　种子生产许可证
seek a new market　寻找新市场
seek graft　营私
seek profits　牟利

seek redress 要求赔偿

seek truth 探索真理

seeking truth from facts 实事求是

segment of the economy 经济部门

seismic stability 抗震稳定性

seize 抢占,没收

seize and deliver to the police 扭送

seize illegal income 没收违法所得

seize unlawful property 没收非法财物

seizer 查封者

seizin 依法占有的不动产

seizing on freezing of property 对财产的查封、扣押、冻结

seizure 查封

seizure of illegal income 没收违法所得

seizure of property on default of payment 因不付款而扣押财产

seizure under legal process 司法扣押

(to) select cadres from among women 选拔妇女干部

selective bidding 选择性投标

selective claim 选择式权利要求

selective purchase 选购商品

selective safeguards clause 选择性保障条款

selective selling 选择销售

selective tender 选择性招标

selective tendering 选择性投标

selectman (美) 行政委员

self salvage clause 船东自救条款

self-contradictory 自相矛盾

self-declarant taxpayer 自行申报纳税人

self-defender 防卫人

self-defense 防卫

self-determination 自决

self-determination of arbitration and court proceedings 裁审自决

self-determination of people 人民自决

self-employed 个体经营的,自营

self-employed individual 个体户

self-employed labourer 个体劳动者

self-employed silversmith 个体银匠

self-employed small business 个体户

self-employed workers 个体劳动者

self-employment 自营职业

self-evident 显而易见

self-evident truth 公理

self-executing administrative measures 不须受领的行政措施

self-executing treaty 自动执行条约

self-governing mass organization 群众自治组织

self-government 自治

self-help 自助救助

self-help housing 自建住房

self-incriminating criminal complaint in writing 刑事自约状

self-induced frustration 自己行为引起的履约受偿

self-liquidating 自动清偿,自动偿付

self-liquidating loan 自偿性放款

self-liquidation 自动偿付

self-managed construction 自营

self-mortgage 自身抵押

self-prevention of crime 自我预防犯罪

self-reliance, hard struggle 自力更生,艰苦奋斗

self-restraint agreement 自限协定

self-seclusion 闭关自守

self-sufficient natural economy 自给自足的自然经济

self-withdrawal 自行回避

sell 出让,销售,出售,卖,卖出

sell ... at the going rate 变价出售

sell and leaseback agreement 售后租回协议

sell at a bargain price 廉价出售

sell at a loss 廉价出售

sell at marked price 明码销售

sell at premium 高价出售

sell by auction 拍卖

sell by wholesale 整批出售

sell long 做多头

sell mineral resources 买卖矿产资源

sell off 变卖

sell on a commission basis 代销

sell on account 赊销

sell on consignment 寄销

sell on credit 赊卖,赊销,赊赁

sell on trust 赊卖

sell out the interests 出卖利益

sell short 做空头,卖空

sell up 变卖债务人的财产的抵债

sell wholesale 趸卖

sell-and-lease-back agreement 回租协议

seller 销售者,出卖人,卖主

seller of land 土地出卖人

seller's failure to perform a contract 卖方不履行合同

seller's guarantee 卖方担保

seller's option 卖方选择权,由卖方选择交割日期的选期合同

sellers market 卖方市场

sellers' obligation concerning product quality 销售者的产品质量义务

selling agency 售货代理

selling agent 销售代理,销售代理商

selling commission 销货佣金

selling expense 销售费用

selling group 推销集团

selling operation 销售业务

selling price 卖价,售价

selling rate 卖出汇率

selling sample 销售货样

selling-out 卖出

semantic ambiguity 语义含混

semantic constitution 语义宪法

semantic extension 语义扩展

semi turn-key contract 半统包合同

semi-bankruptcy 半破产

semi-colonial and semi-feudal country 半殖民地、半封建的国家

semi-colonial, semi-feudal society 半封建半殖民地社会

semi-colony 半殖民地

semidetached house 半独立式住宅

semifeudal 半封建

semifinished room 粗装修的房间

semigross weight 半毛重

semiliterate 半文盲

semi-president system 半总统制

semi-turn-key 半统包

senate 元老院（古罗马）,上议院

senate conservator 护宪元老院

senate of the inns of court and the bar 法律学院和律师业评议会(英)

senator 参议员

send by mail 邮寄

send by mistake 误发

send by post 邮寄

sender 发送人,发信人,高级

senior judge 高级法官

senior lien 优先留置权

senior officer 首长

senior partner 主要合伙人

senior procurator 首席检察院

senior security 主要担保

seniority 资格

sense of guiltiness 罪恶感

sense of hierarchy 等级观念

sense of participation 参与意识

sensitive personality disorder 易感型人格障碍

sensitive product 敏感性产品

sentence 处刑,判决,刑期,刑事判决

sentence by balancing the criminal motives 原心论罪

sentence in force 发生法律效力的判决

sentence in writing 刑事判决书

sentence independently to the deprivation of political rights 单处剥夺政治权利

sentence of bankruptcy 宣告破产

sentence of conviction and criminal punishment 定罪处刑判决

sentence of conviction and exemption from criminal punishment 定罪免刑判决

sentence of "not guilty" 无罪判决

sentence sb to death with a reprieve 判处死刑缓期执行

sentence to fixed-term imprisonment 处以有期徒刑

sentence to imprisonment 判处监禁

sentence under an erroneous charge 错定罪名

sentencing council 量刑委员会

sentencing criterion 量刑标准

sentencing policy 判决政策

(to) separate the functions 政企分开

separable obligation 可分债务

separable thing 可分物

separate 独立

separate action 单独诉讼

separate action for indemnity 单独式赔偿诉讼

separate arbitration agreement 单独仲裁协议

separate claim to indemnity 单独式赔偿请求

separate code 特别法典

separate contract 分项合同

separate control and custody 分管分押

separate entity concept 独立实体概念

separate examination 分别检验,单独讯问

separate flat 成套住房,独立单元

separate government functions from commune management 政社分开

separate jurisdiction 分别管辖权

separate part of administrative jurisprudence 行政法学分论

separate payment 单独支付

separate provision 分别规定

separate regulation 单行条例

separate rules of administrative law 行政法分则

separate the family and divide the property 分家财产

separate the functions of the party from those of the government 党政分工

separately 分别

separation of composition doctrine 和解分离主义

separation of functions 职能的分工

separation of judicial and executive branches 审执分立

separation of judicial person 法人分立

separation of juridical and prosecutorial branches 审检分立/审检分署

separation of nationalities 民族分裂

separation of ownership and management 所有权与经营权分离

separation of ownership and use 产权与使用权分离

separation of powers 分权,权力的分立,权力分离,权力划分

separation of powers and functions 权能分立

separation of property regime 分别财产制

separation of religion and politics 政教分离

separation of the function of the party and the government 党政分工

separation of three powers 三权分立

seperation of the right of management from the right of ownership 经营权与所有权分离

sequelae of the victim 被害人的后遗症

sequential sampling method 按序抽样法

sequester 没收,查封

sequestrate 查封,没收

sequestrator 查封者,假扣押财产保管人

serf system 农奴制度

serfdom 农奴制度

series of resales 一系列转卖

serious 严重

serious and complex case 重大复杂案件

serious breach of law 严重违法行为

serious crime 重大犯罪

serious criminal 重罪犯

serious criminal activities 严重违法犯罪

serious illegal act 严重违法行为

serious losses 严重亏损

serious misunderstanding 重大误解

serious prejudice 严重损害

serious warring 严重警告

seriously hamper 严重妨碍

seriously misunderstanding 重大误解

serjeant-at-law (英) 高级撰状律师

serous criminal activities 重大犯罪活动

servant of the carrier 承运人的受雇人

serve 送达

serve (a sentence) on bail 保外执行

serve a sentence 服刑

serve a sentence on bail 保外执行判决

serve admonitions 训诫

serve as a record 备案

serve as a witness at court 出庭作证

(to) serve no more than two consecutive terms 连续任职不超过两届

serve sentence outside prison under surveillance 监外服刑

serve the people 为人民服务

service 送达

service abroad of judicial and extrajudicial documents in civil and commercial matters 民商事司法和司法外文件的国外送达和通知

service by publication 公示送达

service charge 劳务费

service charge fixing right 劳务定价权

service credit 劳务信贷

service date 送达日

service fees 酬金

service for foreign court 法院委托

service lease 服务租赁

service life 使用年限

service market 劳务市场

service of a notice 送达通知书

service of a written judgment 判决书

service of litigious documents 送达诉讼文书

service of notice 送达通知书

service passport 公务护照

service relations 劳务关系

service secret police 秘密警察

service trade 服务贸易

service wholesaler 中间批发商

serviced by post 邮寄送达

session 开会期,秘密会议,会议

session of parliament 议会会期

session of territory 领地割让

session of the standing committee 常委会会议

set a deadline 规定期限

set a price 作价,定价

set about a crime 着手实行犯罪

set aside 宣告无效,搁置

set aside an arbitral award revoke an arbitral award 撤销仲裁裁决

set down one's position on the question 阐述对某一问题的立场

set forth 阐述

set off 抵消

set off a claim 抵消债务

set off against each other 相互抵消

set one's hand seal to 签名盖章

set price 固定价格

set quota 规定的指标

set term imprisonment 有期徒刑

set up a business 开业

set up and perfect financial organizations in the service of foreign trade 建立和完善为对外贸易服务的金融机构

setting 安装

setting day 交割日

setting things right 拨乱反正

setting up account books in China 在中国境内设置会计账簿

setting up public welfare establishments 兴办公益事业

settle a bargain 达成协议

settle a claim 了结债权

settle a debt by payment 偿清债务

settle a lawsuit 结案

settle accounts immediately 即时清洁

settle claims and debts 清理债权债务

settle disputes and terminate litigation 解纷息纷

① settle estates 处理财产

② settlement day 到期日

③ settle on (or with) 商订

④ settle up 清偿

⑤ settlement 授予财产,移民点,⑥ 清算

⑦ settlement by transferring ac-⑧ counts 转账结算

⑨ settlement clauses 结算条款

⑩ settlement cost 成交费用

⑪ settlement day 清算日,交割日

⑫ settlement in spot exchange 现汇⑬ 结算

⑭ settlement of accounts 清算账目

⑮ settlement of disputes 争端的解⑯ 决

⑰ settlement of international pay-⑱ ment 国际支付清算

⑲ settlement of labour dispute 劳⑳ 动争议处理

㉑ settlement of loss 损失处理

㉒ settlement price 清算价格

㉓ settling day 清算日

㉔ settlor 财产授予人

㉕ setup for economic administration ㉖ 管理机构

㉗ set-up 安置

㉘ several 个别的

㉙ several bankruptcies by one man ㉚ 一人数破产

㉛ several liability 分别责任

㉜ several obligation 分别承担之 义务

㉞ several offenses in different kinds ㉟ 异种数罪

㊱ several part of administrative ju-㊲ risprudence 行政法学分论

㊳ several sentences 数刑

㊴ severally liable 分别的责任

㊵ severance of diplomatic relations ㊶ 断交

㊷ severance tax 采掘税

㊸ severe 严厉的

㊹ severe damage 严重损失

㊺ severe law 严刑峻法

㊻ severely punish 严惩

㊼ sewage disposal 污水处理

sewage farm 污水处理场

sewage outfall 排污口

sewage purification 污水净化

sewage system 污水系统

sewage treatment (／disposal) 污水处理

sewage treatment facility 污水处理设施

sex act 性行为

sex characteristics of the criminal 犯罪人性别特征

sex crime 性犯罪

sex education 性教育

sex equality rule 男女平等原则

sexual abnormality 性反常行为

sexual behavior 性行为

sexual crime 性犯罪

sexual harassment 性骚扰

sexual perversion 性反常行为

sexual psychopathy 性心理变态

sexually promiscuous criminal 淫乱性犯罪人

sex-abnormal crime 性畸变犯罪人

shackles 镣铐

shadow cabinet 影子内阁

shall hereafter be renewable accordingly 依此法顺延

sham and shoddy commodities 假冒伪劣商品

sham democracy 假民主

sham pleading 假答辩

shameful secret 隐私

Shantou Special Economic Zone 汕头经济特区

shape of product 产品形状

share bonus 股票红利

share circular market 股票流通市场

share consolidation 股份合并

share dividend 股份分红

share economy 股份经济

share funds 股份基金

share price 股票价格

share register 股份登记

share responsibility for 分担责任

share risks 共担风险

share the loot 分赃

share the responsibility 分担责任

share transfer 股票过户, 股份转让

share warrant 股份证书

shared natural resources 共有自然资源

shared tax 分成的税收

shareholder equity 股东产权

shareholder loan 股东贷款

shareholding 股份持有

share-issuing enterprise 股份制企业

shares worth 股票值

sharing profits and losses 共负盈亏

shark of high finance 金融寡头

sheikhdom 酋长国

shelter and rehabilitate 收容教养

shelter belts 防护林带

shelterbelt 防护林

shelve 搁置

sheriff substitute (苏格兰) 行政司法官助理

sheriff's court 郡长法院

Sherman act 谢尔曼法

Sherman anti-trust act of 1890 谢尔曼反托拉斯法 (1890)

shield 包庇

shift a crisis on to 转嫁危机

shift of power to the grassroots 权利下放

shift rate 替换率

shift the responsibility upon 转嫁责任

shifting of customs duties 关税转嫁

shifts in technology 技术的转变

ship 装运, 装船

ship collision 船舶碰撞

ship in batches 分批装运

ship loading 装船

ship mortgage 船舶抵押权

ship out 发运

ship the goods 装运货物
ship's certificate 船舶文书
ship's protest 海事声明
ship's warrant 船舶保证书
shipment 装运,装船,载运
shipment advice 装运通知书
shipment and delivery 交货条款
shipment clause 装运条款
shipment contract 装运契约
shipment deadline 最后装船日期
shipment from point of origin 由原产地运出
shipment price 发运价格,交运价格
shipment state 装运状况
shipments for crosstrade 第三国货款
shipowner under charter party 船舶出租人
shipped B/L 已装船提单
shipped bill of lading 已装船提单
shipped on board 已装船
shipped quality term 装运品质条件
shipped quantity 装载数量
shipper 托运人,发货人
shipper's liabilities in through shipment 联运托运人责任
shipping 装船
shipping advice 装运通知
shipping agent 货运代理商,货运代理人
shipping bills 装运单据
shipping business 航运业
shipping charge 运输价格,装船费,装运费
shipping clause 装运条款
shipping country 海运国家
shipping date 装运日期,装船日期
shipping document(s) 装运单据
shipping exchange 航运交易所
shipping interest 装运利益
shipping law 海运法,航运法,船舶法

shipping list 货单,装货单
shipping mark 货物标志
shipping note/S.N. 装船通知单
shipping notes 装运单据
shipping notice 装船通知单
shipping offenses 妨害船运罪
shipping order 发货通知,发运单
shipping order/S.O. 装货单
shipping port 装货港
shipping quality 装船品质,装船质量
shipping receipt 装货收据
shipping sample 发货样品
shipping tag 货运标签
shipping ton 吨税
shipping value 装运价值
shipping weight 装船重量
shipping weight term 装船重量条件
shirk one's responsibility 逃避责任
shogunate politics 幕府政治
shop chairman 工人代表
shop deputy 工人代表
shop instructions 工厂守则
shop management 出厂价格
shop order 工厂订单
shop steward 工人代表,工会代表
shopname 字号
shopping goods 挑选性商品
shopping rush 抢购
shops commissioned to sell certain goods 代销店
short 短缺,买空
short cause 简易诉案
short contract 卖空契约
short delivery 交货短少
short form 简易格式
short from acceptance 简式承兑
short in entire package 整件短少
short in quantity on weight 数量或重量短缺
short of foreign exchange 外汇短缺

short on the catty and the ounce 缺斤少两

short sale 卖空

short selling 卖空

short shipped claim 未装卸货物索赔权

short supply at home 国内供应短缺

short weight 重量不足,缺量

shortage 短缺,缺量,缺额

shortage in weight 重量不足

shortened constitution of a crime 截短犯罪构成

shortfall(s) 不足部分费用,缺少,缺额

short-period price 短期价格

short-period value 短期价值

short-term act 短期行为

short-term dumping 短期性倾销

short-term economic policy 短期经济政策

short-term effect 短期效应

short-term funds solvency 短期资金清偿能力

short-term prediction of crime 犯罪短期预测

short-term price agreement 短期价格协议

shoulder 负担

show 表示,显示,告知

show contempt for law 有法不依

show one's intention 意思表示

showing no difference 一致

show-how 技术示范

shut evil and do good 弃恶从善

shut up business 停止营业

shutdown inspection 停工检查

shuttlecock letters 往来书信

sick leave 病假

sickness 病

side agreement 附属协定

side door 侧门

side issue 次要问题

side-bar lawyer 兼职律师

sigh of the registered trademarks ① 商标标识

② sigh or issue a visa 加签

③ sight 即期

④ sight L/C 即期信用证

⑤ sight payment 即期付款

⑥ sign 署名,签订,签字,签名,签署

⑧ sign a bill 签署法案

⑨ sign a certificate 签字证明

⑩ sign a contract 签约,签订合同

⑪ sign a pledge of repentance 责令具结悔过

⑬ sign a referendum contract 草签合同

⑮ sign bill 签署法案

⑯ sign of official 公务标志

⑰ sign or seal 签名或盖章

⑱ sign post 标志牌

⑲ sign the contract 签署合同

⑳ signatory 签订,签约人,签字方,签字者,签字国,签字人

㉒ signatory organization 签字组织

㉓ signatory party 签字一方

㉔ signatory representative 签约代表

㉖ signature 署名,签字,签名,签署,印鉴

㉘ signature ad referendum 尚待核准的签署,暂签

㉚ signature guaranteed 担保签字

㉛ signature of treaty 条约的签署

㉜ signature unknown 签名不详

㉝ signed instrument 签约文件

㉞ signer 签字人,印章,私章

㉟ significance of social influence 社会影响

㊱ significant 有意义的

㊲ signing 签署

㊳ signing and issue of bill of lading 提单的签发

㊶ signing authority 签字权

㊷ signing of contract 签约

㊸ signing power 签字权

㊹ signtory 签署人

㊺ Silence does not constitute acceptance 沉默并不构成承诺

㊼ Silence may constitute misrepre-

sentation 沉默不能构成虚伪陈述

Silence shall not be deemed consent 沉默不能当做同意看待

silent partner 隐名合伙人

dormant partner 隐名合伙人

sill 窗台

silver standard 银本位

similar 同类的

similar clauses 类似商品,类似条款

similar facts 同类事实

simple 简单

simple administrative measure 简单的行政措施

simple and easy case 简易案件

simple commodity economy 简单商品经济

simple constitution of a crime 简单犯罪构成

simple contract 简单合同,简单契约,无签名的合同,单纯契约

simple count of a crime 简单罪状

simple encroachment 单纯侵占

simple facts of a crime 简单罪状

simple interest 单利

simple joint crime 简单共同犯罪

simple larceny 单纯盗窃罪

simple legacy 单纯遗赠

simple legal charge 单纯法律负担

simple license 普通许可协议

simple license contract 普通许可合同

simple majority 简单多数

simple majority votes 简单多数票

simple obligation 单一之债

simple proceeding in case of minors 少年诉讼简易程序

simple social criminal law 单纯社会刑法

simple state 单一国,单一制国家

simple trust (英) 单一信托

simpliciter acceptance 简单接受

simplified consultation 简化磋商

simplify 精简

(to) simplify administration 简政

simplify the formalities 简化手续

simplum (拉) 单一物

simulated civil act 假装行为

simultaneous existence of 并存

sin 罪过

sin money 赎罪金

sin of omission 不作为犯罪

sine die (拉) 无限期

sine qua non (拉) 必具的资格

single account 单边账户

single and several crimes 单一罪与数罪

single aspect block 单朝向的建筑群

single bedroom 单人卧室

single budget 单一预算

single constitution of crime 单一犯罪构成

single crime 单一罪

single election 一次选举

single factor theory of crime 犯罪单一因素论

single head type of organization 首长制

single interest and compound interest 单利与复利

single interests 单方权益

single legislative system 单一立法体制

single liability 单一责任

single mode of transport 单一运输方式

single money 单一货币

single occupancy 独门独户

single payment 一次付清,单一付款

single price 单一价格

single renvoi 一次反致

single socialist market 统一的社会主义市场

single sovereign state 单一主权国家

single standard 统一标准

single status 单一地位

single statutory penalty 单一法定刑

single tariff 单式税则，单一税则

single-candidate election 等额选举

single-candidate system 单一候选人制

single-chamber legislature 一院制立法机构

single-entry accounting 单式记账法

single-entry visa 一次入境签证

single-handed 独立

single-head system 首长制，一厂制

single-level legislative system 一级立法体制

single-level system of review 一级复议制

single-line operation 单一经营

single-member district system 单数选区制

single-name constituency system 单名选区制

single-nationality state 单一民族国家

single-party system 一党制

single-product economy 单一经济

single-room occupancy 单人套房

single-storey building 平房

sinking fund 偿债基金

sinking fund bond 偿债基本债券

sinking fund mortgage 偿债基金抵押

Sino-British joint declaration 中英联合声明

Sino-Indonesian treaty on dual nationality 中国和印尼关于双重国籍条约

sister ships 姐妹船

sister's ship clause 姐妹船条款

sit at assession of the court 到庭听审

sit in cases of summary procedure 紧急裁定

sit in judgment 审判

sit on (upon) the jury 参加陪审团

site 场地

site analysis 场地分析

site clearance activities 场地清理

site development 场地开发

site of factory 厂址

site of storage 保管场所

site value tax 地价税

sitting in camera 秘密开庭，非公开审讯

sitting(s) 议会开会期，席位，合议期

situation 情势

situation ethics 实用主义道德观

situational prevention 情境预防

sit-down protest 静坐示威

sit-down strike 静坐罢工

sit-in demonstration 静坐示威

size 规格

skeleton 草图

skeptical 不信任的

sketch 草图

skill grade 技术等级

skill-intensive products 技术密集型产品

skip bail 保释中逃跑

skyrocketing prices 物价飞涨

slack 怠工

slack law enforcement 执法不严

slacking off at work 怠工

slander calumny 诽谤

slander crime 口头诽谤罪

slander of property 财产诽谤之诉

slaughter tax 屠宰税

slavery 奴隶制度

slavery system 奴隶制度

slavish copying 原样复制

sleep walking 梦游症

sleeping intermediary 隐名居间

sleeping partner 隐名合伙人

slide price 浮动价格

sliding duties 机动税

sliding duty 滑动关税

sliding royalty 递减提成

sliding tariff 滑动关税

sliding-scale duty 滑动税

sliding-scale price 浮动价格

slight 轻微的,不稳固的

slight damage 轻微损失

slight fault 轻微过失

slight loss 轻微损失

slip rule 错漏规则

slow down 怠工,消极怠工

slump 经济萧条

small agreement 小额协议

small and medium-sized business 中小企业

small business 小型企业,个体户

small business investment act 小企业投资法

small business of industry and commerce 个体工商户

small businessman 个体工商户

small claim court 和解法庭

small claims 小额赔款

small constituency system 小选区制

small handicrafts man 小手工业者

small holder of land 小土地私有者

small industrial or commercial business 个体工商户

small land holder 小土地私有者

small peasant economy 小农经济

small private economy 小私有经济

small profit and quick return 薄利多销

small proprietors 小私有者

small reduction 稍许减价

small town 市镇

small wares (英) 小商品

smart money 赔偿金

smash the bonds of tradition 冲破传统观念的束缚

smash the old state apparatus 摧毁旧的国家机器

smash the old state machinery 打碎旧的国家机器

Smith act 史密斯法(外侨登记法)

Smithsonian institution agreement 史密森学会协定

Smith-Connally act 史密斯-康纳利法(战时劳工纠纷法)

smooth over a fault 弥补过失

smooth the trade 稳定交易

smuggling and trafficking in contraband 走私犯私活动

smuggling ring head 走私集团首要分子

snap check 抽查检验

So use your own property as not to injure your neighbour's 使用自己财产应不损及他人的财产

soaring prices 物价飞涨

social affairs 社会事务

social assistance 社会救济

social audit 社会审计

social auditing agency 社会审计机构

social auditing organization 社会审计机构

social basis 社会基础

social bond 社会联系,社会结合

social compact 社会契约,社会契约

social conflicts 社会斗争

social contract theory 社会契约论

social contradiction(s) 社会矛盾

social control 社会控制

social disharmony 社会失调

social disorganization 社会失控

social division of labor 社会分工

social dumping 社会倾销

social duty 社会义务

social economic order 社会经济秩序

social economic program 社会经济活动计划

social economy organization 社会经济组织

social effect 社会效益

social effects of pollution 公害

social engineering 社会工程

social environment 社会环境

social estate system 等级制度

social ethics 社会伦理学

social factors of crime 犯罪社会因素

social groupings 社会集团

social history of development 社会发展史

social influential measure 社会影响措施

social institution 社会制度

social integration 社会一体化

social interests 社会利益

social justice 社会正义

social legislation 社会立法

social life 社会生活

social morality 社会道德

social morality 公德

social morals 社会公德

social needs 社会需要

social norm 社会规范

social order 社会秩序

social organization 社会集团，社会团体

social organization as legal person 社会团体法人，社团法人

social origin 社会根源

social phenomenon 社会现象

social philosophical school of law 社会哲学法学派

social policy 社会政策

social policy rule 社会政策规则

social policy theory of taxation 课税的社会理论

social position 社会地位

social prevention of criminality 社会预防犯罪

social problem 社会问题

social protection 社会保护

social regulation 社会规范

social relations 社会关系

social relief 社会保险

social research 社会研究，社会调查

social rights 社会权利

social science 社会科学

social security 社会保障

social security act（U.S.） 社会保险法（美）

social security system 社会保障制度

social services 社会工作

social solidarism jurisprudence 社会连带主义法学

social solidarist school of law 社会连带主义法学派

social stability 社会稳定

social status 社会地位

social structure 社会结构

social supervision 社会监督

social survey 社会调查

social system 社会制度，社会体系

social transformation 社会转型

social upheaval 社会动乱

social usage 社会习俗

social usage of law 法的社会作用

social utilitarian jurisprudence 社会功利主义法学

social welfare 社会福利，社会福利救济

socialism 社会主义

socialism with Chinese characteristics 有中国特色的社会主义

socialist 社会主义的

socialist cause of modernized construction 社会主义现代化建设工业

socialist collective ownership 社会主义集体所有制

socialist constitution 社会主义宪法

socialist construction 社会主义建设

socialist construction of modernization 社会主义现代化建设

socialist country 社会主义国家

socialist criminal law 社会主义刑法

socialist democracy 社会主义民主

socialist discipline of labo(u)r 社会主义劳动纪律

socialist economic system 社会主义经济制度

socialist economy 社会主义经济

socialist jurisprudence 社会主义法学

socialist jurist 社会主义法学家

socialist labor emulation 社会主义劳动竞赛

socialist labouring masses 社会主义劳动群众

socialist law 社会主义法律

socialist legal order 社会主义法律秩序

socialist legal system 社会主义法制,社会主义法制国家

socialist legal system with Chinese character 中国特色的社会主义法制

socialist legality 社会主义法制

socialist market economy 社会主义市场经济

socialist material civilization 社会主义物质文明

socialist mode of production 社会主义生产方式

socialist modernization 社会主义现代化建设

socialist nationalization 社会主义国有化

socialist ownership by the entire people 社会主义全民所有制

socialist ownership by the state 社会主义国家所有制

socialist party 社会党

socialist political power 社会主义政权

socialist property owned by the whole people 社会主义全民所有的财产

socialist public economy 社会主义公有制经济

socialist public ownership 社会主义公有制

socialist public ownership of the means of production 生产资料的社会主义公有制

socialist public property 社会主义公有财产,社会主义公共财产

Socialist public property is sacred and inviolable 社会主义公有财产神圣不可侵犯

socialist relation(s) of equality 社会主义平等关系

socialist revolution 社会主义革命

socialist road 社会主义道路

socialist rule of law 社会主义法制

socialist sector of economy 社会主义经济成分

socialist spiritual civilization 社会主义精神文明

socialist state 社会主义国家

socialist superiority 社会主义优越性

socialist system 社会主义制度

socialist transformation 社会主义改革

socialist working people 社会主义劳动者

socialization of agriculture 农业社会化

socialization of law 法律的社会化

socialized large-scale production 社会化大生产

socializing agriculture 农业社会化

socially organized sanction 社会有组织的制裁

sociological school of law 社会学法学派

society with rule of law 法治社会

sociocultural cohesion 社会文化一致性

sociocultural mainstream 社会文化主流

sociological jurisprudence 社会法学,社会学法学

sociological jurist 社会法学家

sociology 社会学

sociology of law 法社会学

socio-economic system 社会经济制度

socket 插座

sock-print 袜足迹

sodomy 鸡奸罪

softening process of conflict of laws 冲突规范软化处理

softening process of connecting points 连结点软化处理

soil desertification 土地的沙漠化

soil erosion 水土流失

soldier on reserve service 预备役士兵

sole agency 独家代理权

sole arbitrator 独任仲裁员

solemn 正式的,庄严的,严肃的

solemnity formal 要式

solicitor: office-practice lawyer 咨询律师(注:英国指出席下级法院的律师,美国则指法务官)

solicitress(英) 女诉状律师

solid evidence 证据确凿,实证

solid vote 全体一致的投票

solidarity by similitude 同求连带关系

solitary confinement 单独监禁

solitary perpetrator 单独正犯

solitary principal offender 单独正犯

solve a criminal case 破案

solvency 偿付能力,有请偿能力,偿债能力,支付能力

solvent 有偿债能力的

solvent debtor clause 有偿还能力债务人条款

somnambulism 梦游症

sophisticated equipment 先进设备

sophisticated industry 尖端工业

sophisticated technique 尖端技术

sorts of acts violating the administration of public security 违反治安管理行为的种类

sound 健全,合理

sound condition 完好状态

sound goods 完好货物

sound investment 稳妥投资

sound market value 完好货物市价

sound market 合理市价

sound quality 完好质量

sound value 合理市价

source 出处,渊源

source jurisdiction 来源地管辖权

source of administrative law 行政法渊源

source of auditing evidence 审计证据来源

source of criminal law 刑法渊源

source of evidence 证据来源

source of finance 经济来源

source of goods 货源

source of law 法律渊源

source of tax 税源

sources of civil law 民法渊源

sources of goods for import or export 进出口货源

sources of international law 国际法渊源

South-South cooperation 南南合作

sovereign 皇帝,君主

sovereign equality 主权平等

sovereign government 主权政府

sovereign right over territory 领

土主权

sovereign rights 主权

sovereign state 主权国家

sovereignty 君权,主权,统治权

sovereignty over air (/space) 空中主权

Soviet 苏维埃

sox-print 袜足迹

space crime 空间罪行

space law 空间法

space object 空间实体

space of time 期间

space power 航天国家

space resources 空间资源

space station 空间站

spare 赦免

spatial approach 空间论即外层空间的界限

speak in defense of 辩护

speaker 议长

speakers of the houses of parliament 国会两院议长

special accomplice 特殊共犯

special additional risk 特别附加险

special administration 特别管理

special administrative region/SAR (中) 特别行政区 (中)

special advantage 特别利益

special agent 特别代理人

special aggravated bodily injury 特别加重伤害罪

special amount-limited tax credit 税收专项限额抵免

special appeal 非常上诉

special assumption 不履约赔偿诉讼

special attempt 特殊未遂

special auditing commissioner 审计特派员

special bid 特别购进

special bill 特别法案

special business 特别业务

special cargo 特殊货物

special charge 特别费用

special circumstances 特别情况

special clause 特殊条款

special committee 专门委员会

special committees of the National People's Congress 全国人民代表大会各委员会

special commodity 特殊商品

special commodity rate 特定货物运费率

special compensation 特别补偿

special compensation clause 特殊保障条款,特殊补偿条款

special constable 临时警察

special constitution of crime 特殊犯罪构成

special constitutional guarantee 特别的宪法保证

special constitutive elements of crime 犯罪构成特殊要件

special contingency reserve 特别意外准备

special contract 特别合同,特别契约,个别契约

special court 特别法院

special custom 特别惯例,特别习惯

special damages 特别损害赔偿金,特别损失赔偿

special delivery 快递邮件

special demurrer 特定抗辩

special devise 特别不动产遗赠

special diplomatic courier 特别外交信差

special disposing capacity 特殊行为能力

special drawing rights (SDR) 特别提款权

special economic zone 经济物区,特区

special effect of administrative procedure law 行政诉讼法的空间效力

special effect of criminal law 刑法的空间效力,刑法空间效力

special envoy 特使

special error 特别过错

special formality 特殊手续

special goods 特殊货物

special group for handling a case

办案组

special guaranty 特别保证

special helr 特别继承人

special international law 特殊国际法

special items 特别项目

special jury 特别陪审团

special law 特别法

special legacy 特定物遗赠

special legal status 特殊的法律地位

Special legate 特别教庭代表

special letter of authority 特别授权书

special license 特别许可证

special lien 特别留置权

special majority 特别多数

special malignant mankiller 特种恶性杀人犯

special meaning 特殊意义

special measure 特殊措施,特别办法

special mission 特别使团

special mortgage 特定抵押

special natural condition 特殊自然条件

special negligence 特别过失

special object 特殊客体

special offender 特别犯

special offer 特别报价

special ordinance 特别法令

special partner 特别合伙人

special partnership 特别合伙

special people's court 专门人民法院

special people's procuratorate 专门人民检察院

special permission export 出口特许证

special plea 特殊抗辩

special policies 特别政策

special postal article 邮政专用品

special postal mark 邮政专用标志

special power(s) 特别的权力,特殊权力

① special preference 特殊优惠

② special preferential treatment 特别优惠待遇

④ special prevention 特殊预防

⑤ special price 特别价格

⑥ special privilege 特殊权益

⑦ special privilege monopoly 特权垄断

⑨ special procedure 特别程序

⑩ special property 特有物权,物有物权

⑫ special protection 特别保护,特殊保护

⑭ special protection of state property night by the civil law 民法对国家所有权的特殊保护

⑰ special proviso 特别但书

⑱ special purpose trust 特殊目的信托

⑳ special recidivist 特别累犯

㉑ special regional agreement 特殊区域协定

㉓ special regulation in foreign civil procedure 涉外民事诉讼程序特别规定

㉖ special relationship 特殊关系

㉗ special relationship of rights and obligations 特定权利义务关系

㉚ special rights 特殊权利

㉛ special risk 特别风险

㉜ special sale agency 特约经销处

㉝ special service 特殊常务

㉞ special session 国会特别会议

㉟ special session of the United Nations general assembly 联合国大会特别会议

㊳ special statute 特别法规

㊴ special subject 特殊主体

㊵ special survey 特别检查,特别检验

㊷ special tax credit of limited amount 税收专项限额抵免

㊹ special thing 特定物

㊺ special tort conduct 特殊侵权行为

㊻ special trade 特种买卖,专门贸

易

specific industries at home　国内特定产业

special trust　特约信托,特殊信托

specific legacy　特定动产遗赠

special verdict　特别裁决

specific licence　特种进口许可证

special vigilance　特别保护,特殊保护

specific modalities of domestic support　国内支持的具体模式

special voluntary surrender　特殊自首

specific modalities of market access　市场准入的具体模式

specialist　特种经纪人

specific object　特定物

speciality　特性

specific ordinance　单行条例

speciality contract　盖印合同

specific performance　特定履行,强制履行,具体履行,(英)特定履行令,实际履行

specialization in agricultural production　农业专业化

specialized foreign exchange bank　外汇专业银行

specific performance　强制履行

specific performance of contract　(英)强制组织履行

specialized international organization　专门性国际组织

specific policy　特殊政策

specialized salvage service　专业救助

specific provisions of criminal law　刑法分则

specially protected area　特别保护区

specific regulation(s)　单行法规,单行条例

specialty　依式契约

specific risk guaranty　特种风险保证

specialty contract　依式契约

special-type license　特种许可证

specific sample survey　典型抽样调查

species protection　物种保护

specific service　特定服务

specific administrative act　具体行政行为

specific tax　特定目的税

specific administrative act of the customs　海关具体行政行为

specific trust　特定资金信托

specification　说明书,规格

specific agreement　特殊协定

specific charge　特定负担责任

specificity of the counterclaim object　反诉对象的特定性

specific cheque　记名支票

specified　限定

specific consumption tax on cars　小轿车特别消费税

specified area　特定地区

specified by　由…规定

specific consumption tax on color TV sets　彩电特别费税

specified criterion　明细规范

specified in　由…规定

specific contract　特定合约

specified period of time　特定期限

specific delivery date　特定交货日期

specified service trades at home　国内特定的服务行业

specific devise　特定土地遗赠

specify　规定

specific duties　从量税

specimen　样品

specific factors of production　特殊生产要素

specimen computation　抽样计算

specimen of breath　呼吸检样

specific goods　特定的货物,特定物

specimen of draft　汇票样本

specific gravity　比重

specimen of signature　印鉴样

specific guarantee　特殊担保

本,签字范本

specimen sample book 样本

specimen signature 印鉴样本

speculate 投机倒把

speculate on the rise and fall of price 买空卖空

speculation 投机倒把,投机买卖

speculation and swindling 投机诈骗

speculative activities 投机倒把活动

speculative damage 预期损害

speculative motive 投机动机

speculative trade 投机买卖

speculative transaction 投机交易

speculator 外汇投机者,投机者

speeding up the work 加快工程进度

speedy clearance 即时结算

sphere 外销

sphere of application 适用范围,适合范围

sphere of influence 势力范围

spiral stair 螺旋楼梯

spirit of constitution 宪法精神

spirit of law 法的精神

spirit of legality 法制的精神

spirit of the times 时代精神

spirit one's money away 抽逃资金

spiritual accessory 精神从犯

spiritual civilization 精神文明

split 便衣警察

split order 分散出货

split-down stock consolidation 股票合并

split-up of state 国家的分立

spoken and written language 语言文字

spokesman 代言人

spoliation of evidence 窜改证据

sponsor 保证人

spontaneous agency 无因管理

sporadic dumping 偶发性倾销

spot 当场

① spot cash 即付

② spot cash transaction 股票现货交易

④ spot check 抽查检验

⑤ spot commodity 现货

⑥ spot delivery 现货交割,当场交货,当场交付,即期交割

⑧ spot exchange 现汇

⑨ spot exchange rate 即期汇率

⑩ spot goods 现货

⑪ spot market 解除市场

⑫ spot price 现售价格,现货价格

⑬ spot sale 现货销售

⑭ spot test 抽查检验

⑮ spot trading 现货交易

⑯ spot transaction 即期交易,现汇交易,现货交易

⑱ spots 现货

⑲ spouse 配偶

⑳ spread 价差,利息率

㉑ spread delivery 分期交货

㉒ spread or margin 加息率

㉓ spread the scope of the application 推广应用范围

㉕ springing use 未来使用权,有条件的使用权

㉗ spurious class action 假群体诉讼

㉙ spy 间谍

㉚ spy out 秘密监视

㉛ squander 滥用

㉜ square deal 公平交易

㉝ squatter 擅自占地人

㉞ squatter's title 擅自占地人的所有权

㉟ squatters community 贫民区

㊱ squatting 违章建筑

㊳ stab 戳伤

㊴ stability 稳定性

㊵ stabilization of currency 通货稳定

㊷ stabilize prices 平抑价格

㊸ stable currency 稳定的货币

㊹ stable deposit 稳定性存款

㊺ stable money 稳定的货币

㊻ stable-money-concept 稳定的货币单位概念

staff 参谋部

staff section 参谋处

stage of an intermittence of psychosis 精神疾病间歇期

stage of application of punishment 刑罚适用阶段

stage of court debate 辩论阶段

stage of criminal proceedings 刑事诉讼阶段

stagnation 停滞膨胀

stain the law 歪曲法律

stair 楼梯

stalrway 楼梯

stakeholder 保证金保存人

stall keeper 摊贩

stallage 摊位税

stall-holder 摊贩

stamp 印章,图章

stamp act 印花税条例

stamp clause 印戳条款

stamp date 邮戳日

stamp tax/duty 印花税

stamp tax rate 印花税率

stamped clauses 盖戳条款

stamped seal 封印

stamped signature 签字盖章

stand (for election) 参加竞选

stund by 遵守

stand convicted (of) 被确证有罪,被认定有罪

stand mute 不作答辩

stand of testification 证明标准

stand still 停滞

stand surety for sb 为某人做保证人

stand to one's promise 遵守诺言

stand up for 辩护

standard 标准,规范

standard clause 条文的范例

standard contact 标准合同

standard contract form 标准合同格式,标准契约格式

standard contract of towage 拖航合同格式

standard contract provisions 标准合同条款

standard documents outside administrative legislation 行政法规、规章以外的行政规范性文件

standard flat type 标准房型

standard for computation of compensation 赔偿计算标准

standard form contract 固定格式合同,标准合同

standard form of agreement on arbitration over collision 船舶碰撞仲裁标准格式

standard form of copyright contract 合同标准样式

standard forms of charter party 租船合同标准格式,标准租船合同格式

standard housing unit 标准住房单元

standard international trade classification (SITC) 国际贸易标准分类号

standard material 标准材料

standard of classification 分类标准

standard of conduct 行为准则

standard of interpretation 解释标准

standard of justice 正义标准

standard of measurement 计量标准器具

standard of no responsibility 免责的标准,免责标准

standard of performance 经营成绩标准

standard of price 价格标准

standard of production quota 劳动定额标准

standard of proof 证明标准

standard of right 权利本位

standard of severe injury certification 重伤鉴定标准

standard of taxation 课税标准

standard omission offense 纯正不作为犯

standard practice instructions 标准操作规程

standard price 标准价格

standard provision 标准条款

standard purchase price 标准购价

standard quality 标准品质

standard specifications 标准规格

standard terms 格式条款

standard weight 标准重量

standardization act 标准化法

standardization law 标准化法

standardization measures 标准化措施

standardization of tariff 统一运价表

standardized contract 标准化契约

standardized tax returns 纳税申请表

standards 规格

standards and rules for construction projects 建筑工程规范和规程

standards for grading skills 技术等级标准

standards of administrative compensation 行政补偿的标准

standards of administrative indemnity 行政赔偿标准

standards of feasibility 可行性标准

standby arrangement 备用安排

standby credit 担保信用证

standby equipment 闲置设备

standby L/C 备用信用证

standby letter of credit 备用信用证

standby plan 备用计划

standing 常设,地位

standing administrative organ 常设行政机关

standing aside juror 排除陪审员

standing body 常设机构

standing committee 常设委员会,常委会,常务委员会

standing committee member 常委

Standing Committee of the National People's Congress 全国人大常委会

standing committee of the people's congress at the corresponding level 本级人大常委会

standing criminal 状态犯罪人

standing institution 常设机构

standing offer 持续性要约

standing order 长期订单,长期有效订单

standing organization 常设机关

standstill 维持现状,停止

standstill agreement 就地协议

standstill cease-fire 就地停火

stand-by equipment 备用设备

stand-by letter of credit 备用信用证

staple 主要商品

staple commodity 大宗产品

staple goods 主要商品

staple industry 基本工业

staple market 主要市场

staple product 主要产品,重要产品

staple theory 大宗产品论

stare decisis（拉）依照先例,遵循先例

stare in judicio（拉）出庭

starting place of carriage 起运地

starting point of the limitation 时效期的起算点

star-chamber 星座法院

state 说明,陈述,国家,阐明

state act 国家行为

state adjudicatory 国家审判机关

state adjudicatory organization 国家审判机关

state administration 国家行政管理

state administration for commodity inspection 国家商检部门

state administration of commodity prices 物价局

state administration of supplies
国家物资局

state administrative agency 国家
管理机关

state administrative department of
marine affairs 国家海洋管理
部门

state administrative law 国家行
政法

state administrative organization
国家行政管理活动,国家行政
机关

state administrative organization
at the higher level 上级国家
行政机关

state administrative organization
at the next higher level 上一
级国家行政机关

state agency 国家机构,国家机
关

state agricultural commission 国
家农业委员会

state aircraft 国家航空器

state approval 国家批准

state auditing administration 国
家审计署

state authorities/authority 国家
权力机关

state authority in charge of national defense communications 国
家国防交通主管机构

state boundary 国家边境

state budget 国家预算

state budget and the final state accounts 国家预算和决算

state budget expenditure 国家预
算支出

state budget revenue 国家预算
收入

state bureau of oceanography 国
家海洋局

state capital construction commission 国家建议委员会

state capitalism 国家资本主义

state civil service（servant） 国家
公务员

state civil service examination 国

家公务员考试

state civil service law 国家公务
员法

state commerce 国营商业

state commercial vessel 国有商
船

state compensation 国家赔偿

state compensation action 国家
赔偿诉讼

state compensation law 国家赔
偿法

state compensation obligation 国
家赔偿责任

state compensation system 国家
赔偿制度

state conference 国务会议

state construction 国家建设

state contract 国际契约,国家契
约

state contract theory 国家契约
论

state control 国家控制

state controlled country 国家管
制经济的国家

State Council 国务院

state councillor 国务委员

state crime 国事罪

state criminal 状态犯罪人

state debt 国家债务

state economic commission 国家
经济委员会

state economic order 国家经济
秩序

state economic plan 国家经济计
划

state economy 国营经济

state enterprise 国营企业

state enterprises adopting share
holding system 国有股份制企
业

state forest farm 国营林场

state frontier 国家边境

state functionaries 国家工作人
员

state general 国会

state general bureau of metrology
国家计量总局

state general bureau of price control 国家物价管理局

state general bureau of standardization 国家标准总局

state general bureau of surveying cartography 国家测绘总局

state guarantee 国家保护

state guest 国宾

state health standards 国家卫生标准

state immunity 国家豁免

state in abeyance 所有权未定的房地产

state institution 国家制度

state interest 国家利益

state investment 国家投资

state judicial organization 国家司法机关

state military organization 国家军事机关

state monopoly 国家垄断

state monopoly on imports and exports 进出口国家垄断

state nationalities affairs commission 国家民族事务委员会

state notarial organ 国家公证机关

state of curfew 戒严状态

state of economy 经济状况

state of emergency 紧急状态

state of martial law 戒严状态

state of national emergency 国家紧急状态

state of necessity 危急状态

state of operation 经营状况

state of registry 登记国

state of the city of Vatican 梵蒂冈市府国

state of the international court of justice 国际法院规约

state of the nation 国情

state of war 战争状态

state one's views 陈述自己的观点

state orders for goods 国家订货

state organ 国家机关

state organ of legal supervision 国家监察机关

state organization of family planning administration 国家计划生育行政委员会

state organization of legal supervision 国家法律监督机关

state organization of public security 国家公安机关

state organizations of supervision 国家监察机关

state organs 国家机构,国家机关

state ownership 国家所有制,国家所有,国有制,国家所有权

state ownership by provision of law 由法律规定为国有的

state ownership of mineral resources 矿产资源的国家所有权

state personnel 国机关工作人员,国家机关工作人员

state plan 国家计划

state planning commission 国家计划委员会

state police 国家警察

state policy 国家政策,国策

state political power 国家政权

state power 国家政权,政权,国家权力

state pricing organization 国家物价机关

state pricing organs 国家物价机关

state property 国家所有权,国家财产,全民财产

state prosecuting organizations 国家检察机关

state prosecutorial apparatus 国家检察机关

state prosecutorial organization 国家检察机关

state provisions for foreign exchange control 国家外汇管理规定

state purchasing order 国家订货任务

state quality standards 国家质

量标准

state race 法定利率

state reimbursement 国家补偿

state responsibility 国家责任

state room 大厅

state sector of the economy 国营经济

state security 国家安全

state security organization 国家安全机关

state statistical bureau 国家统计局

state statistical standard 国家统计标准

state structure 国家结构

state succession 国家继承

state subsidies 财政补贴

state supervision of economic contracts 国家的经济合同管理

state supervisory organization 国家监察机关

state supremacy 国家最高权

state survey and drawing bureau 国家测绘局

state system 国体

state tariff committee 关税税则委员会

state tax 国税

state taxation authorities 国税局

state technical supervision bureau 国家技术监督局

state territory 国家领土

state the reason 说明理由

state trading enterprises 国营贸易企业

state treason 国事罪

state treasury bond 国库证券

state trial 国家审判

state under protectorate 被保护国

state victim 国家被害人

state will 国家意志

state with centralized power 中央集权的国家

state's administrative organization in the localities 地方国家行政机关

state's mandatory plan 国家指令性计划

state's will 国家意志

stateless 无国籍的

stateless person 无国籍人

statelessness 无国籍

statelike entity 类似国家的实体

statement 说明,供述

statement ability of witness 证人的陈述能力

statement and exculpation of the victim 被害人的供述和辩解

statement and exculpations of a suspect and defendant 犯罪嫌疑人、被告人供述和辩解

statement based on collusion 串供

statement made under examination 供词

statement of a case 案情陈述

statement of a victim 被害人陈述

statement of affairs 清算资产负债表

statement of changes in financial position 财务状况变动表

statement of changes in stockholder equity 股东权益变动表

statement of claim 索赔清单,请求书

statement of confession 认罪书

statement of defense 被告的抗辩声明,辩护状,答辩书,辩护词

statement of law 法律申明

statement of public prosecution 公诉词

statement of realization and liquidation 变产清算表

statement of reasons for judicial decision 司法裁判理由的陈述

statement of stockholder investment 股东权益计算书

statement of stockholder networth 股东权益净值计算书

statement of the accused 被告陈

述

statement of the victim 被害人陈述

state-operated economy 国营经济

state-operated enterprises 国营企业

state-operated mining enterprise 国营矿山企业

state-owned assets 国有资产

state-owned but locally administered 地方国营

state-owned economy 国营经济,国有经济

state-owned enterprise 国有企业,国营企业

state-owned enterprises under the charge of local authorities 地方国营企业

state-owned industrial enterprise 国有工业企业

state-owned land 国有土地

state-owned property 国有财产

state-owned property administration 国有资产管理

state-owned property administration law 国有资产管理法

state-owned property right 国有产权

state-private joint company 公私合营公司

static budget 固定预算

static inquisition and survey 静态勘验

static state traces 静态痕迹

statistical index 统计指标

statistical inference 统计推理

statistical inspector's certificate 统计检查员证书

statistical investigation 统计调查

statistical investigation form 统计调查表

statistical investigation item 统计调查项目

statistical method 统计方法

statistical organ 统计机构

statistical personnel 统计人员

statistical reasoning 统计推理

statistical report 统计报告

statistical scientific study 统计科学研究

statistical service 统计事项

statistical standard 统计标准

statistical supervision 统计监督

statistical system 统计制度

statues of market supervision law 市场管理法的地位

status 身份

status crime 身份犯

status in litigation 诉讼地位

status of a Chinese legal person 中国法人资格

status of a legal person 法人身份,法人地位

status of aliens 外国人民事法律地位,外侨地位

status of document 单据效力

status of economic law 经济法的地位

status of state civil service 国家公务员身份

status of women 妇女地位

status quo ante（拉）原状

status quo of economic law 经济法学的现状

statuta realia（拉）物的法则,物法

statute 法律,制定法,规约,法令,条例

statute book 法典

statute of a subject 主体资格

statute of citations 传讯法（英 1531）

statute of frauds amendment act 修正防止诈欺法

statute of frauds（英）防止欺诈条例

statute of Gloucester 格罗斯特法

statute of limitations 法定时效,时效,法令限制

statute of Merton 麦尔登条例

statute of the international court

of justice 国际法院规约

statute of Westminster 威斯特敏斯特条例(英)

statute of wills (英) 遗嘱法

statutes at large 联邦法规汇编

statute-barred debt 逾诉讼时效期限的债务

statutory 法定的,法定

statutory agency 法定代理

statutory agent 法定代理人

statutory assignment 法定转让

statutory audit 法定检查

statutory audit responsibilities 法定的审计责任

statutory authority 法定权限

statutory corporation 法定法人

statutory crime 法定犯罪

statutory domicile 法定住所

statutory duty 法定责任,法定职责

statutory extortion 制定法勒索罪

statutory fine 法定罚金

statutory force 法定效力

statutory form of conditions of sale 买卖条件的法定格式

statutory guarantee 法定担保

statutory holiday 法定假日

statutory instruments 制定法文件

statutory interpretation 法定解释

statutory limitation 法定时效

statutory limits on debts 法定债务限额

statutory majority 法定多数

statutory merger 法定兼并

statutory oath 法定宣誓

statutory offense 法定犯,法定罪行

statutory penalty 法定处罚

statutory period 法定期间

statutory power 法定权力

statutory prescription 法定时效

statutory provisions 法定条文

statutory punishment 法定刑罚

statutory rape 奸淫少女罪,法定强奸罪

statutory referendum 法定复决投票

statutory regulation 法律管制

statutory remedies 法定救济手段

statutory representative 法定代表人

statutory restrictions 法定限制

statutory review 法定视察

statutory right 法定权利

statutory rules 法定条例

statutory rules and orders 制定法规和法令

statutory sentence 法定刑

statutory share 特留份,物财产

statutory succession 法定继承

statutory tariff 法定税则,法定关税税率,法定税率

statutory tenancy 法定租赁

statutory time limit for hearing 法定审理期限

stay away from work without leave or good reason 旷工

stay of collection 延期收款

steady growth 稳步增长

steal 盗窃

steal intelligence 窃取情报

stealing 偷窃行为

stealing ring 盗窃集团

steep increase in prices 物价飞涨

stem from 出于

step 措施

Sterling area 英镑区

stern 严厉的

stevedore 装卸

stevedore damage clause 装卸损坏条款

stick to conventions 墨守成规

still tool mark 静态工具痕迹

stillbirth 死产

Stimson doctrine 史汀生主义

stimulation-response theory 刺激-反应说

stimulation-seeking theory 刺激-寻求论

stimulus of crime 犯罪刺激

stipulate 规定

stipulated 合同规定的

stipulated place 约定地点,约定价金

stipulatio(拉) 要式口头合同

stipulatio poenae(拉) 违约金

stipulation by samples 列举式规定

stipulation in favour of a third party 有利第三者的条款

stipulation(s) 若干规定,约定合同

stipulations of contract 合同规定,合同惯例

stock 股票

stock (/capital) issue 股票发行

stock (/capital) issue price 股票发行价格

stock (price) averages 股票价格平均数

stock and share broker 股票经济人

stock arbitrage 股票套利,股票投机

stock average 股票平均价格

stock bonus 股份红利

stock certificate 股份凭证

stock clearing corporation 股票交割公司

stock company 股份公司

stock discount 股本折价

stock dividend(s) 股份分红,股票红利,股息票,股票股利

stock economy 股份经济

stock exchange 证券交易所,股票交易所

stock exchange transaction 证券交易所

stock fraction 股票分割

stock holder 股东

stock in trade 待售商品

stock index futures 股票指数期货

stock index futures transaction 股票指数期货交易

stock index options 股指期权

权

stock investment 股份投资,股票投资

stock issue 股票发行

stock ledger 股东名册

stock loan 股票贷款

stock management 股份经营

stock margin trading 股票保证金信用交易

stock market 证券市场,股票市场

stock ownership 股份所有权,股份所有制

stock power 股票转让授权书

stock price 股票价格

stock price average 股票平均价格

stock price index 股票价格指数

stock split 股票分股

stock split-up 股票分割

stock subscription 股份认购

stock swap 股票交换

stock to bearer 无记名股票

stock transfer 股票过户

stock valuation 股票估价

stock with par value 有面值股票

stock without par value 无面值股

stockbroker 股票经济人

stockholder equity 股东拥有的资产净值

stockholder's contribution 股东缴资

stockholder's equity 股东权益

stockholder's right 股东权利

stockholding equity holding 股份持有

stockjobber 股票经济人

stool of repentance 悔罪席

stop business 停止营业

stop consignment 停止托运

stop criminal activities absolutely 彻底停止犯罪

stop delivery of goods 停止交货

stop doing business 停业

stop doing business for internal

rectification 停业整顿

stop infringement 停止侵害

stop order 停止委托,停止订货,阻止指令

stop payment 停止付款

stop payment order 停止付款通知书

stop production 停产

stop supplies 停止供应

stop the acts of infringement 停止侵权

stop the discharge of pollutant 停止排放污染物

stop the sale 停止出售

stoppage 扣留,抵消

stoppage at source 从源扣缴税款

stoppage in transit 停运权,(英)中途停运权

stoppage time 停工期间

stop-loss 停止损失

stop-out price 截止价

stop-payment notice 停付通知书

storage and transport management of dangerous articles 危险品储运管理

storage certificate 保管凭证

storage charges 存储费

storage contract 保管合同

storage expenses 保管费

storage fee 保管费

store room 储藏室

stored article 保管物

storefront 店面房屋,铺面房屋

storekeeper 仓储者

storeroom expense 货栈费用

storey 楼层

storied house 楼房

storing party 寄存人

stow away from heat 切勿受热

stowage survey 积载鉴定

straddle 对敲、双向期权

straight B/L 记名提单

straight baseline 直线基线

straight bill of lading 记名提单

straight bonds 国定利率债券

straight unit price contract 纯单价合同

straight-term mortgage loan 定期抵押贷款

strain 滥用

straits used for international navigation 用于国际航行的海峡

strangle 扼杀

strap to death 勒死

strategic blockade 战略封锁

strategy 策略

strategy of economy development 经济发展战略

stray animals 失散的饲养动物,失散的动物

streamline government organization 精简政府机构

street front 沿街门面

strengthen 健全,强化

strengthen labour protection 加强劳动保护

strengthen socialist democracy 健全社会主义民主

strengthen the national unity 加强民族团结

strengthen the socialist legal system 加强社会主义法制

strengthen the state apparatus 强化国家机器

strengthening of criminal motives 犯罪动机的强化

stress crime 应激性犯罪

stress of criminal mind 犯罪心理紧张

stress on practical results 注重实效

Stress should be laid on evidence, investigation and study and one should not be too ready to believe confessions 重证据,重调查研究而不轻信口供

stretch 滥用,徒刑

striated mark 插划痕迹

strict 严格

strict administrative act 羁束行政行为

strict construction 狭义解释

strict criminal liability 严格刑事责任

strict enforcement of law 严格执法

strict execution of orders and prohibitions 令行禁止

strict interpretation 严格解释

strict law 严格的法律

strict law enforcement 执法必严

strict liability 严格赔偿责任,严重责任,严格责任

strict neutrality 严格中立

strict observance of the law of the state 严格遵守国家法律

strict product liability 严格产品责任

stricti juris (拉) 依照严格的法律

strictly abide by contract 重合同

strictly adhere to the agreement 忠于协议

strictly enforce and abide by the law 执法守法

strictly implement the terms of the agreement 严格履行协定条款

strictly prohibit 严格禁止

strike 罢工

strike an agreement 缔结合同

strike to conventions 墨守成规

striking 显著

stringent 严厉的

strip development zone 带状商业发展区

stripe 鞭刑

stripping of medals, decoration or honorary titles (punishment specially for armymen) 剥夺勋章、奖章和荣誉称号

striving for independent nation 争取独立的民族

striving nation striving for independence 争取独立的民族

strong man 实权派

structural change of criminal behavior 犯罪行为结构变化

structural change of subject of crime 犯罪主体结构变化

structural element 承重构件

structural establishment 机构设置

structural form of state 国家结构形式

structural form of state political power 国家政权组织形式

structural reform 体制改革

structural reform of the economy 经济体制改革

structure 体制

structure of criminal law 刑法结构

structure of criminal mind 犯罪心理结构

structure of criminal proceedings 刑事诉讼结构

structure of economic administration 经济管理体制

structure of investment 投资结构

structure of legal action 法律行为的结构

structure of macro-control law 宏观调控法的体系结构

structure of market supervision law 市场管理法的结构

structure of ownership 所有制结构

structure of the state 国家机构

structure of the system of subjects in economic law 经济法主体的体系结构

struggle against capitalist bribery of goverment workers, tax evasion, theft of sate property, cheating on government contracts, and stealing economic information for industrial and commercial enterprises 反对行贿、反对偷税漏税、反对盗窃国家财产、反对偷工减料和反对盗窃经济情报(五反)

struggle against corruption, waste and bureaucracy 反贪污,反

浪费,反官僚主义(三反)

struggle against hegemonism 反霸斗争

Stuart Dynasty 斯图亚特王朝

stubs of a checkbook 票根

student consul 随行领事

student's identity card 学生证

students of returned overseas Chinese 归侨学生

studies of legal history 立法研究

studio-apartment 单间公寓房

study report for investment feasibility 可行性投资研究报告

style 样式

stylization 程式化

sub(拉) 在胁迫之下

sub colore juris(拉) 在权利的伪装下

sub conditione(拉) 在某种条件下

sub contractor 分包人

sub modo(拉) 在限制条件下

sub suo periculo(拉) 自己承担风险

subagency 分代理处,次代理人

subagent 分代理人

subcompany 子公司

subconditional offer 附条件要约

subcontract 分包合同,分契,转契

subcontracted work 分包工程

subculture of violent behaviour 暴力亚文化理论

subdistrict office 街道办事处

subdivision fees 土地变更使用费

subduct(美) 撤回

subinfeudation 分封采邑制

subject 臣民,体,国民

subject activity 主观能动性

subject and object 主体与客体

subject criminal psychology 主观犯罪心理学

subject in the relations of ownership 所有制关系主体

subject matter 标的物

subject matter jurisdiction 级别管辖

① **subject matter jurisdicton of economic controversives at various levels** 经济纠纷级别管辖

④ **subject matter of action** 诉讼标的物

⑥ **subject matter of constitutional law** 宪法调整对象

⑧ **subject of administration** 行政管理主体

⑩ **subject of administrative** 行政主体

⑫ **subject of administrative law** 行政法主体

⑭ **subject of administrative legal relationship** 行政法律关系主体

⑯ **subject of administrative power** 行政权主体

⑱ **subject of civil jural relations** 民事法律关系主体

⑳ **subject of civil relation** 民事法律关系主体

㉒ **subject of civil right** 权利主体

㉓ **subject of civil right or duty** 权利义务主体

㉕ **subject of constitution** 宪法主体

㉖ **subject of crime** 犯罪主体

㉗ **subject of criminal proceedings** 刑事诉讼主体

㉙ **subject of duty** 义务主体

㉚ **subject of economic legal (relation) nexus** 经济法律关系主体

㉝ **subject of education** 教育主体

㉞ **subject of financial law** 财政法主体

㊱ **subject of imposing fines** 执行罚款主体

㊳ **subject of international law** 国际法主体

㊵ **subject of international legal responsibility** 国际法律责任的主体

㊸ **subject of jural relation of administrative procedure** 行政诉讼法律关系主体

㊻ **subject of jural relation of auditing** 审计法律关系主体

subject of jural relation of labour 劳动法律关系主体

subject of labour 劳动对象

subject of law enforcement 执法主体

subject of law in the contract responsibility system 承包制法律主体

subject of legal regal relationship of taxation 税收法律关系主体

subject of legal relation 法律关系主体

subject of legal relationship in criminal proceedings 刑事诉讼法律关系主体

subject of legal relationship of administrative procedure 行政诉讼法律关系主体

subject of legal relationship of auditing 审计法律关系主体

subject of legal relationship of labour 劳动法律关系主体

subject of legal relationship of revenue 税收法律关系主体

subject of legal responsibility 法律责任主体

subject of liabilities for compensation 赔偿责任主体

subject of obligation 债的主体

subject of offense 违法主体

subject of punishment 刑罚主体

subject of state compensation 国家赔偿主体

subject of supervision 监督主体

subject of tax payment 纳税主体

subject of taxation 课税主体,税出主体,征税人/征税主体,征税主体

subject of the right 权利主体

subject of the right of action 诉权主体

subject of the right of ownership 所有权主体

subject of treaty 条约的主体

subject sb to discipline 管教

subject to approval 以确认为准

subject to changes at a later date by mutual agreement 以日后双方同意变更为准

subject to confirmation 以确认为准

subject to contract 以签订的合同为条件

subject to final confirmation 以最后确认为准

subject to goods available 以有货为条件的报价

subject to no appeal 不得上诉

subject to one's confirmation 确认有效

subject to prior approval 须经预先批准

subject to tax subject to taxation 负缴税义务

subject to the law 受法律管辖

subject to the provisions of (this law) 除(本法)另有规定外

subjective incapacity 主观不能

subjective initiative 主观能动性

subjective responsibility 主观责任

subjectivist theory of complicity 主观主义共犯理论

subject-matter of contract 契约标的

submission 辩护词

submission of a tender 投标

submit 呈递

submit a report (asking) for review 报请复核

submit evidence 提供证据

submit to 服从

subordinate 归所属,隶属,部属

subordinate body 下属机构

subordinate enterprise group 集团所属企业

subordinate legislation 附属立法

subordinate relationship 从属地位

subordinate to a ministry 部属的

subordinate unit 下级单位

subordinated debt 附属债务

subordination 从属之债

subordination relations among enterprise 企业的隶属关系

suborn subordination 唆使犯法

subpoena（拉）传票，传唤

subpoena duces tecum（拉）出庭出示证明的传票

subprinciple 分委托人

subpurchase 转买

subpurchaser 转买人

subqualify product 不合格产品

subrogation 代位求偿，代位行使，代位权，代位求偿，代位权，债务转移，代位

subrogation form 转利转让证书

subrogation of compensation 代位赔偿

subrogation right 代位求偿权

subrogation to right under a contract 以代位取得合同上的权利

subscribe 签名，认购，签署

subscribe an act 签署法案

subscriber 认购者

subscription 签署，认购，预约金，预约

subscription agreement 认购协议

subscription of shares 股份认购

subscription pay 约定报酬

subscription right 认购权

subsequent crime 后罪

subsequent endorser 后手

subsequent mortgage 次抵押，后续抵押

subsequent ratification 事后追认

subsequent supervision 事后监督

subshare dividend warrant 股息单

subsidiary 子公司，附带，附属机构

subsidiary body 附属机构，辅助机构

subsidiary coin/note/money 辅币

subsidiary corporation 子公司

subsidiary organ 附属机构

subsidies for commodity prices 物价补贴

subsidies for the purchase prices 价格补贴

subsidies granted for policy consideration 政策性补贴

subsidized price 补助价格

subsidy 补贴

subsidy in work points 补贴价格

subsisting contract 现存，现有契约，有效合同

substance 原物，实质

substandard goods 不合格商品

substandard housing 不合标准住房

substantial 有效的，实际的

substantial capacity rule（美）实际能力规则

substantial charge of circumstances 情势的重大变化

substantial connection 实质联系

substantial control 实际控制

substantial damages 实质赔偿

substantial defence 实体法上的抗辩

substantial existence 实际存在

substantial interest 实际利害关系

substantial law 实体法

substantial offense 实质犯

substantial performance 实物履行，实质性履行，实际履行

substantial transformation criterion 实质性改变标准

substantial true 实质真实

substantialization 实体化

substantially modify 实质性更改

substantive administrative law 行政实体法

substantive agreement 实质性协议

substantive change 实质性改变

substantive clause 实质条款

substantive constitution of crime 实质犯罪构成

substantive criminal law 实体刑法,实质刑法,刑事实体法

substantive damage 实质损害

substantive decision 实质性决定

substantive distinguishing features 实质性特点

substantive features 实质性特点

substantive hearing 实体审

substantive hindrance 实质阻碍

substantive legal norms of administration 行政实体法规范

substantive matter 实质问题

substantive natural law 实体自然法

substantive offense 实体罪

substantive part 实估部分,实质部分

substantive provision(s) 实质性规定,实质条款

substantive punishment 实体刑罚

substantive requirements of form 形成要求

substantive right 实体权利

substantive rules 实体法性质的法规

substantive source 实质渊源

substantive trend 实质趋向

substantive ultra vires 实体越权

substitute 替代物,替代

substitute arbitrator 代理仲裁员

substitute articles 替代商品

substitute carrier 替代承运人

substitute fines for criminal punishment 以罚代刑

substitute material 替代材料

substitute money 代用货币

substitute obligation 替代义务

substitute one's words for legal provision 以言代法

substitute organization 替代组织

substitute product 代替品

substitute security 替代担保

substitute service 替代性服务

substitute things 代替物

substituted expenses 代替费用

substituted goods 替代商品

substituted service 代理送达,间接送达,替代送达

substituted service of writ 代理送达令状

substitutio pupillaris(拉) 未成年人的补充继承人

substitutio vulganis(拉) 通常补充继承

substitution 合同替代

substitution performance 代执行

substitutional legacy 代位继受遗赠

substructure 地下建筑

subsurface right 地下权

subterranean work 地下工程

subtraction 不履行义务

subtrust 次信托

suburban community 城市外围的居住点

subway 地下人行过道

succeed oneself 连任

succeed sb as president 继位总统

succeed to the throne 继位

success in salvage 救助效果

successful party 胜诉方当事人

succession duty 遗产税

succession in international law 国际法上的继承

succession in respect of immovable state property 国家不动产的继承

succession in respect of matters other than treaty 条约外事项的继承

succession in respect of movable state property 国家动产的继承

succession in respect of state debts 国家债务的继承

succession in respect of state property 国家财产的继承,国家

的继承

succession in respect of treaty 条约的继承

succession of international organization 国际组织的继承

succession of law 法的继承，法律的继承

succession of status 身份继承

succession tax 遗产税

succession to the crown 王位继承

successive 连续

successive ballots 连续投票

successive buyers and sellers 连续买卖双方

successive election 连续选举

successive joint crime 继承共犯

successive losses 连续损失

successor in total 完全继承人

sudden injury 突发性伤害

sue and labor expenses 施救费用

sue and labour charges 损害防止费用

sue and labour clause 损害防止条款，诉讼与营救条款

Suez canal 苏伊士运河

suffer a loss 受损失

suffer damage 受到损害

suffer for 因…而受到惩罚

suffer heavy losses 遭受巨大损失，遭受重大损失

suffer losses 遭受损失

sufferer 受害者

sufficiency of consideration 有效代价

sufficiency of evidence rule 充分证据原则

sufficient 充分

sufficient condition 充分条件

sufficient consideration 有效代价

sufficient evidence 充分证据

sufficient grounds 有充分理由

sufficient reason 充足理由

suffrage 参政权

suggest motion 提议

suggested price 建议价格

suggesting theory of crime 犯罪暗示论

suggestion 提议

suggestion from prosecutorial organizations 检察建议

suicide clauses 自杀条款

suicide prevention centre 防止自杀中心

suit 诉讼，切合

suit at law 民事案件

suit for contract 关于合同的诉讼

suit in marriage 婚姻诉讼

suit of civil nature 民事性质的诉讼

suitor 请求人

sultan 元首

sum 总额

sum of claim 索赔额

sum of indemnity 补偿金

sum of money gained from a sale 变卖所得的款项

sum total 总额

sum up 概括

summarize 概括

summary 概括，即决

summary action 简易诉讼

summary administrative act 行政即决行为

summary arrest 即时逮捕

summary conviction 即决裁定，简易判罪

summary court （日）简易裁判所，(英)即决法院

summary crimes 简易审决罪

summary dismissal 即决驳回

summary execution 立决

summary hearing 简易程序听审

summary instigation 概然性教唆

summary judgment 即决裁判，简易审判权

summary justice 即决裁判，简易程序裁判

summary of executive meeting

行政会议纪要

summary of leading case and decisions 判例汇编索引

summary offense (英) 即决犯罪

summary one-crime 概括一罪

summary procedure 即决裁判程序,简易程序,简易诉讼

summary procedure for administrative penalties 行政处罚的简易程序

summary procedure for administrative punishment 行政处罚的简易程序

summary proceeding 简易程序

summary proceedings for administrative punishment concerning public security 治安管理处罚简易程序

summary punishment 惩戒性惩罚

summary questioning 即决审讯

summary record 摘要记录

summary session 简易法庭

summary trial 简易程序裁判,即决审讯,即决审判

summation 辩论总结,判决前法庭辩论总结

summon a defendant 传唤被告出庭

summon to court 传唤

summoned in person 受送达人,被传当事人

sumption 大前提

sundry 各种

sundry creditors 各种债权人

sunset clause 届满条款

supecificatio specificatio (拉) 加工

super highrise building 超高层建筑

super standard 超级标准

super state 超国家

super tax 额外税收

supera-national goverment 超国家政府

supera-national law 超国家法律

supercargo 货物管理人,货运监

① 督

② superconstitutional effect 超宪法的效力

④ superconstitutional power 超宪法的权力

⑥ superficial phenomenon 表面现象

⑧ superficiary 租地造房者

⑨ superheating 景气过度

⑩ superimposed cause on bill of lading 提单附加条款

⑫ superimposed clause 附加条款

⑬ superintend 监管,监督

⑭ superintendent of banks (美) 银行督察

⑯ superintendent office 监督部门

⑰ superintending and surveying services 公证鉴定

⑲ superior court 高级法院

⑳ superior force 不可抗力

㉑ superior people's court 高级人民法院

㉓ superior people's prosecutor's office 高级人民检察院

㉕ superior title 优越所有权

㉖ supernational government 超国家政府

㉘ supernatural power 法力

㉙ supernaturalism 超自然性

㉚ superpower 超级大国

㉛ supersede 替代

㉜ superseded suretyship riders 替代担保附加条款

㉞ superstious 迷信

㉟ superstious behavior 迷信行为

㊱ superstition 迷信

㊲ superstitious belief 迷信

㊳ superstitious offense 迷信犯

㊴ superstitious sects and secret societies 会道门

㊶ supervening impossibility of performance 给付不能,后履行不可能

㊹ supervening negligence 后发过失

㊻ supervise 监督,监察

㊼ supervise in accordance with law

法律监督

supervise the enforcement of the constitution 监督宪法的实施

supervise through auditing 审计监督

supervisery mechanism 监督机制

supervision 仲裁监督,监督,监察官,监察

supervision after the event 事后监督

supervision afterwards 事后监督

supervision and administration 监督管理

supervision and control 监督管理

supervision and control over imports and exports 进出口货物监管

supervision and control over transshipment cargo 转运货物监管

supervision and inspection on safety 安全监督检验

supervision and management of mineral resource 矿产资源监管

supervision and management of the prevention and control of water pollution 水污染防治的监管

supervision before the event 事前监督

supervision by administration 行政监督

supervision by administrative bodies 行政机关的监督

supervision by public opinions 舆论监督

supervision by statistical means 统计监督

supervision by the executive branch 行政监督

supervision commission contract 委托监理合同

supervision in advance 事先监督

督

supervision ministry 监察部

supervision of adjudication 审判监督

supervision of advertising 广告管理

supervision of banks over credits 银行信贷管理

supervision of constitution 宪法监督,施工监督

supervision of election 选举监督

supervision of fire prevention and control 消防监督

supervision of investigation 侦查监督

supervision of plan implementation 计划执行的监督

supervision of the mass 群众监督

supervision of the party 党的监督

supervision on product quality 产品质量的管理

supervision organization of product quality 产品质量监督机构

supervision over administration 行政监察

supervision over administrative legislation 行政立法的监督

supervision over enforcement of law and discipline 法纪监督

supervision over execution 执行监督

supervision over parole 假释监督

supervision over pharmaceutical 药品监督

supervision over prisoners 犯人监管

supervision over probation 缓刑监督

supervision prescribed by law 法定监督

supervision subject over public administration 行政法制监督主体

supervision system 监督制度	supplementary specification 补充规定
supervisior of election 选举监督人	supplement 加以补充,补充
supervisor(s) 警督,管理人员,监察工作人员,监事会监事	supplemental agreement 补充协议
supervisory 监督的,监管	supplemental bill 补充诉状
supervisory activity 监督活动	supplemental claim 补充指控
supervisory agency over administration 行政监察机构	supplemental complaint 补充诉状,补充指控
supervisory and management department 监督管理部门	supplemental deed 补充契据
supervisory authority 监察权	supplementary 辅助
supervisory board 监察委员会	supplementary accusation 补充起诉
supervisory body 监督机构,监察机关	supplementary act 补充文件
supervisory committee 监察委员会	supplementary administrative regulation 补充的行政法规
supervisory decision 监察决定	supplementary answer 补充答辩
supervisory department 监察机关	supplementary civil action in administrative proceedings 行政诉讼附带民事诉讼
supervisory jurisdiction 监察权,监督管辖权	supplementary civil compensation 附带民事赔偿
supervisory measure 监督措施,监督方法	supplementary claim 补充诉求
supervisory notice 监察通知书	supplementary clause 补充条款
supervisory organ 监察机关,监察机构	supplementary contract 补充契约
supervisory organization 监督机构	supplementary declaration 补充说明
supervisory organization of a higher level 上级监察机关	supplementary document 补充文件
supervisory organization of state power 国家权力监督机关	supplementary election 补选,补缺选举
supervisory organization over administration 行政监察机关	supplementary expense 追加支出
supervisory personnel 监察工作人员	supplementary financing facility 补充金融资助
supervisory power 监察权	supplementary guarantee 补充担保
supervisory power over pharmaceutical 药品监督职权	supplementary income tax 追加所得税
supervisory procedure over adjudication of administrative cases 行政审判监督机关	supplementary investigation 补充侦查
supervisory proposal 监察建议	supplementary judgment 补充判决
supervisory proposal letter 监察建议书	supplementary order 追加订货
supervisory system 监察制度	supplementary pleading 补充答辩

supplementary proceedings 补充程序,补充诉讼程序

supplementary prosecution 补充起诉

supplementary provisions 附则,补充规定

supplementary regulation(s) 补充办法,补充规定

supplementary sentence 补充判决

supplementary specification 补充说明

supplementary standard 增补标准

supplementary statement 补充陈述

supplementary terms 补充条件,补充条款

supplemented by other sectors and other modes 其他经济成分和分配方式为补充

supplier's credit 卖方退货

supplicatio(拉) 被告对原告的第二次答辩

supplication 被告对原告的第二次答辩

supplier 供货人,供应商

supplier's credit 卖方信贷

supplies 物料

supply a demand 满足需要

supply and marketing contract 供销合同

supply and marketing co-operative 供销社

supply contract 供货合同

supply in full sets 成套供应

supply price 供应价格

supplying and requisitioning parties 供需双方

supplying party 供货方

support 承重,抚养,赡养

support and assist 赡养扶助

support area 维持价格范围

support price 支持价格,保障价格,维持性价格

supported elderly 被赡养人

supporting material 附属资料

suppress 扣留,钳制

suppress drugs 禁毒

suppress law with power 以权压法

suppress the truth 隐瞒事实,隐瞒真相

suppression of drugs 禁毒

suppression of violence 残酷镇压

supremacy 无上权力

supremacy of international law 国际法高于国内法

supreme 最高

supreme authority 最高权威

supreme court(日) 最高裁判所

supreme court of judicature 英国最高法院,最高法院

supreme court of the U.S.A. 美国联邦最高法院

supreme court of the United States (US S.C.) 美国最高法院

supreme federal court 联邦最高法院,联邦最高法院(美)

supreme interests 最高利益

supreme law 最高法

supreme legal authority 最高法律效力,最高法律权威

supreme people's court 最高人民法院

supreme people's procuratorate 最高人民检察院

supreme power 无上权力,最高权力

supreme state conference 最高国务会议

surcharge 附加税

surety 担保人,保证人,可靠性

surety bond 担保保证金,担保书

surety company 担保公司

surety of tax payment tax guarantor 纳税担保人

surety system for punishments in respect to management of public security 治安管理处罚担保人制度

suretyship 保证人的地位,保证

人的责任,保证

suretyship contract 保证合同

suretyship obligation 保证债务

surface 表面

surface crack 表面裂缝

surface mail 平信

surface right 地上权

surmount 超越

surmount an obstacle 超越障碍

surpass 超越

surplus 顺差

surplus assets 过剩资产

surplus capital 过剩产品,过剩资本

surplus product 过剩产品

surplus value 剩余价值

surrebut (by a plaintiff) 第三次驳复被告

surrejoin 第二次驳复被告

surrejoinder 第二次驳复被告

surrender 投降

surrender of lease 放弃租赁,放弃租约

surrender one's privilege 放弃特权

surrender to one's bail 保释后如期出庭

surrendering criminal 自首犯

surrey clause 公证条款

surrogate 替代国,地方法官

surtax 累进附加所得税,附加税

surtax/supertax additional tax 附加税

Suruga Bank (Nunazu) 骏河银行(沼津)

surveillance 监督

surveillance by the masses 群众监督

surveillant 看管人

survey and inspection organization 检验机构

survey before shipment 装船前检验

survey clause 检验条款

survey fees 勘察费

survey of ships 船舶检验

survey of the law of the united state 美国法律概况

survey of wildlife resource 野生动物资源调查

survey report on quality 品质鉴定证书

survey report on weight 重量鉴定证明书

survey services 鉴定业务

survey (/investigation) of aviation accident 航空事故调查

surveying and mapping 测绘

surveyor 鉴定人

surveyor's report 公证人报告,鉴定书,鉴定证明

survivals of feudalism 封建残余

surviving building 残存的建筑

suspected murder 杀人嫌疑犯

suspects in a crime 涉嫌人犯

suspend 无力支付

suspend business 停止营业,停业

suspend one's performance 中止履行

suspend order 停止订货

suspend payment 暂停付款,无力支付

suspend performance of contract 中止履行合同

suspend production or business operation and rectification 停产停业整顿

suspend sentence 缓期处刑

suspend the bankruptcy proceedings 中止破产程序

suspend the carriage 中止运输

suspend to pay 中止支付

suspended announcement of punishment 刑罚宣告犹豫制

suspended ceiling 吊顶

suspended problem 没有理决的问题

suspension 无力偿债,停止支付

suspension of action limitation 诉讼时效中止

suspension of business license 暂扣执照

suspension of crime 犯罪中断

suspension of execution 缓执行

suspension of hire　租赁中止条款

suspension of license　暂扣许可证

suspension of performance　履行中断

suspension of pronouncement of condemnation　缓宣告

suspension of punishment　留刑警告制

suspension of treaty　条约的中止,条约的暂停施行

suspensive　未确定的

suspensive condition　停止条件

sustain　维持,确认

sustain a great loss　蒙受重大损失

sustainable development　可持续的发展

sustained　持续

sustained development　持续发展

sustained losses　连续亏损

suzerain state　宗主国

suzerainty　宗主权

swallow one's words　取消诺言

swamp the market　扰乱市场

swap　互换交易

swap credits　互惠信贷

swap transaction　掉期交易

swapping shortage and surpluses　调剂气缺

swear　发誓

swear a crime against sb　发誓控诉某人犯罪

sweat damage　受潮损失

sweating and/on heating　受潮受热

sweep away the old influences　摧毁旧势力

sweep away the old legal system　摧毁旧法制

swindle through credit cards or letters of credit　利用信用卡或信用证进行诈骗

swindler　拐骗犯

swindling act　诈骗行为

swindling gang　诈骗团伙

swing credits　互许贸易差额

swinging limit　摆动额

switch　转ese

switch trade　转口贸易

swith selling　(英)诱饵售法

sword oath　剑誓

syllabus　判词前的说明,判决理由概要

symbol　象征物,标志性建筑

symbol of state　国家象征

symbolic delivery　象征性交付

symbolic delivery terms　象征性交货条件

symptomatic psychosis　症状性精神病

sympton test　征表说

syndrome of similar psychopathic personality　类变态人格综合症

synopsis　说明书

synthesis of the price indices　综合物价指数

synthetic price index　综合物价指数

synthetic study　综合研究

system　体制,系统制度,制度

system development　系统开发

system for officers on reserve service　预备役军官制度

system for safe-keeping of a criminal's properties　罪犯财产保管制度

system for the recourse of administrative compensation　行政赔偿的追偿制度

system for the use of weapons by the people's police　人民警察使用警械制度,人民警察使用武器制度

system guaranteeing the human rights for the disabled　残疾人人权保障制度

system integrated distribution floor　综合分布的楼面系统

system management　系统管理

system of administrative　行政制度

system of administrative jurisprudence 行政法学体系

system of administrative law 行政法体系

system of administrative law system 行政法制监督制度

system of administrative review 行政复议制度

system of advocacy 辩护制度

system of alternative imposition of penalties 易科罚金制

system of amount 金额制度

system of annual survey on business registration 企业登记年检制度

system of being elected with absolute majority 绝对多数当选制

system of bond for punishments in respect to management of public security 治安管理处罚保证金制度

system of capitalist ownership 资本主义所有制

system of centralization 集权制

system of civil entries 民事案由制度

system of civil justice 民事审判体制

system of collective leadership with each person responsible for a particular field of work 集体领导下的分工负责制

system of collective ownership by labourers 劳动群众集体所有制

system of collective security 集体安全体系

system of combination of collective leadership and division of labour with personal responsibility 集体领导和个人负责相结合制度

system of composition with creditors 和解制度

system of concurrently imposing fines 并科罚金制

system of congress of workers and staff under the leadership of the Party committee 党委领导下的职工代表大会制

system of constitutional safeguard 宪法保障制度

system of consultation and dialogue 协商对话制度

system of contracted linked to output 家庭联产承包责任制

system of contracts 合同制度，契约制度

system of criminal justice 刑事审判体制

system of criminal law 刑法体系

system of decentralization 分权制

system of delegacy 代表团制

system of democratic centralism 民主集中制

system of discretionary action of sentencing 量刑制度

system of divinity evidence 神示证据制度

system of dual criminal sanctions 双重刑事制裁体系

system of economic administration 经济管理体制

system of economic law 经济法的体系

system of economic laws and decrees 经济法规体系

system of education 教育制度

system of evidence in ancient times 古代证据制度

system of execution 行刑制度

system of exploitation of man by man 人剥削人的制度

system of export licensing 出口许可制度

system of feudal tenure 封建的土地私有制

system of financial responsibility 经济责任制

system of fingerprint ridges 指纹纹线系统

system of fingerprints 指纹系统

system of food hygiene supervision

食品卫生监督制度

system of forced reform through labor 强迫劳动改造制度

system of government 政体

system of inspection for labour safety and hygiene 劳动安全卫生检查制度

system of international civil juris-diction 国际民事管辖权制度

system of international law 国际法体系

system of interpretation by general judicial institutions 普通司法机构解释制

system of interpretation by legislative institutions 立法机构解释制

system of investigating into mis-judged case 错案追究制度

system of Japanese emperor 天皇制

system of job responsibility 责任制,岗位责任制

system of judges 法官制度

system of land investigation 土地调查制度

system of legal evidence 法定证据制度

system of legal rules 法律规则体系

system of macroeconomic manage-ment 宏观经济管理体制

system of majority representation 多数代表制

system of manager assuming chief responsibility 经理负责制

system of manager assuming full responsibility under the leader-ship of party committee 党委领导下的经理负责制

system of managing the economic plans 计划管理

system of market supervision law 市场管理法的体系

system of multiple exchange rates 复汇率制度

system of multi-party co-operation 多党合作制

system of multi-party co-operation and political consultation system 多党合作与政治协商制度

system of multi-party co-operation and political consultation under the leadership of the Chinese Communist Party 中国共产党领导的多党合作和政治协商制度

system of notification 告知制度

system of overall responsibility by factory manager 厂长负责制

system of ownership 所有制

system of ownership of the means of production 生产资料所有制

system of personal responsibility for profit 自负盈亏制度

system of people's assessors 人民陪审员制

system of people's congress 人民代表大会制

system of people's mediation 人民调解制度

system of peoples's representative 人民代表制

system of perform 执行制度

system of personal responsibility 一厂制,岗位责任制

system of piecerate wage for above-quota output 超定额件工资制

system of planned management 计划管理体制

system of planning 计划体制

system of possession 占有制,预防制

system of production responsibility 生产责任制

system of promotion through ex-amination 考试晋升制

system of proof 证据体系

system of public bidding 招标承包制

system of public prosecution 检察制度

system of punishment 刑罚的体系,刑罚体系,刑罚制度

system of punishment after the event 追惩制度,事后审查

system of punishment against old offense 追惩制度

system of recourse 求偿制度

system of regional national autonomy 民族区域自治制度

system of report 报告制

system of responsibility for work 工作责任制

system of responsibility in agricultural production 农业生产责任制

system of retirement 退休制度

system of reviewing the performances of staff and workers 人事考核制度

system of rewards and penalties 奖惩制度

system of safety inspection inside prison 狱内安全检查制度

system of science and technology 科技体制

system of security measures 保安处分体系

system of separation of powers 分权制

system of separation of three powers 三权分立制度

system of ship-value 船价制度

system of single imprisonment 单人囚禁制

system of sole-judge proceedings 独任制

system of special permission 特许制

system of special responsibility for each person 个人负责制

system of subjects in economic law 经济法主体的体系

system of supervision over administration 行政监察体制

system of supervision over withdrawal of cases 撤案监督制度

system of supervision through auditing 审计监督制度

system of suspended pronouncement of sentence 缓期宣告制

system of suspended prosecution 缓期起诉制

system of suspension in combat situation 战时缓刑制度

system of tax division between central and local governments 分税制

system of the law of reform-through-labour 劳动改造法体系

system of the manager assuming full responsibility 经理负责制

system of three-level ownership of the people's commune (中) 人民公社三级所有制

system of two chambers with unequal powers 非均权二院

system of universal election 普遍选举制

system of university admission charges 大学招生收费制度

system of values 社会价值准则体系

system on passing of property of goods 货物所有权转移制度

system on passing of risks of goods 货物风险转移制度

system with fixed terms of office 任期制

systematic forecasting 系统销售

systematic interpretation 系统解释

systematic rule 系统规则

systematical interpretation 系统解释

systematization of administrative regulations 行政管理法规系统化

systems of contracted responsibilities on a household basis with remuneration linked to output (中) 家庭联产承包责任制

T

tabernacle 临时住所

table 搁置

table a motion 搁置动议

table of appraisal for outgoing prisoners 犯人出监鉴定表

table of cases 案件一览表

table salt monopoly 食盐专卖

tacit 默示的

tacit acceptance 默示承诺,默示接受

tacit admission 默认

tacit agreement 默示协议

tacit approval 默示

tacit approve, tacit acquiescence 默认

tacit confirmation 默示确认

tacit consent 默示同意,默许

tacit declaration 默示

tacit intention 默示意思

tacit mutual consent 默示相互同意

tacit ratification 默示批准

tacit recognition 默认

tacit recognition of government 对政府的默示承认

tacit renewal 默示重订

tacitly to agree to or to recognize 默认的承认

tag price 标明价目

Tai league 台盟

tail special 特别限定继承

Taiwan association 台联

Taiwan authorities 台湾当局

Taiwan residents 台湾居民

take 采取

take a bribe and prevent the law 受贿枉法

take a decisive step 采取决定性措施

take an oath 发誓

take delivery of goods 提货,收货

take delivery of the object 提取货物

take disciplinary measures against sb 给予纪律处分

take effect 发生法律效力

take for granted 认为当然

take in 收容

take into custody 逮捕,收监

take into custody for trial 羁押候审

take land as collateral for an obligation 以土地担保债务

take law as the criterion 以法律为准绳

take measures in advance to prevent losses 事先防止损失

take office 就职

take over 收购,收缴

take over an enterprise 收购企业

take over goods 收货

take over the goods 接收货物

take precaution against calamity 防患未然

take priority in compensation 优先受偿

take reasonable measure 采取合理措施

take responsibility for their respective work while dividing functions 分工负责

take revenge 打击报复

take sb into custody 拘留

take sb's name of the books 开除公职

take something out of pledge 赎回抵押品

take the bribe but not prevent the law 受贿不枉法

take the consequences 承担后果

take the debts out in goods 用货物抵偿债务

take the dimensions of field 丈量土地

take the law into one's hands 违法处罚

take the legal consequence 承担法律后果

take the rap 承担刑事责任

take the whole situation into account 顾全大局

take up a bill 赎票

retire 退休

take-it-or-leave-it contract 附延缓条件(民事)法律行为,附意合同

take-or-pay contract 提货或付款合同

take-over purchase 收购

taking into consideration the interests of the state, the collective and the ind ividual 兼顾国家、集体、个人三者利益

taking of evidence 取证

taking of oaths 进行宣誓

taking-in charge 承运

takings 收益

tales 补缺陪审员

talk 谈判

tallest 最高的

tally with 符合

tally with the facts 合乎事实

tamper 贿赂

tangible chattels 有形动产

tangible damage 有形损害

tangible form 有形形式

tangible goods 有形商品

tangible goods trade 有形商品贸易

tangible personal property 有形动产

tangle 涉及

tanker owner voluntary agreement concerning liability for oil pollution (TOVALOP) 油轮船东自愿承担油污责任协定

Taoism 道教

tardy 误期

tardy debtor 违约债务人

target of crime 犯罪对象

target of dictatorship 专政对象

target of taxation 税收指标

target price 指标价格,目标价格,计划价格

target, subject matter 标的

targeted technology 技术标的

targets of help and education as of delinquent children (in the PRC) 帮教对象

tariff 税则,关税

tariff alliance 关税同盟

tariff barrier 关税壁垒

tariff board 关税委员会

tariff committee 关税委员会

tariff concession 关税减让原则,关税减免

tariff concession table 关税减让表

tariff diminution 关税减免

tariff enforcement zone 关税执行区

tariff for foreign trade 国际贸易税则

tariff no. 税则号列

tariff nomenclature 关税税目,税则类别

tariff protection 关税保护

tariff quota(s) 关税配额

tariff regulation 关税税则

tariff retaliation 关税报复

tariff schedule 关税率,税则

tariff subheading 分税目

tariff union 关税同盟

tariff wall 关税壁垒

task of civil procedure law 民事诉讼法任务

task of the criminal procedural law 刑事诉讼法任务

tasks of criminal law 刑法的任务

tasks of inspection and assessment 检验评审任务

tattooing 墨刑

tax 税务,税收,税

tax abatement 减税

tax affairs 税务

tax agent 纳税代理人

tax amount 税额

tax amount payable 应纳税额

tax assessment 征税估值,纳税鉴定

tax authorities 税务机关,税收机关/税务机关

tax avoidance 避税,国际避税

tax avoidance investment(s) 避税投资

tax base 计税依据,课税依据

tax bearer 赋税分担者,负税人,纳税人

tax bill 征税单

tax bond 抵税公债

tax breaks 减税

tax bureau 税务局

tax capacity 纳税能力

tax category 税种

tax clause 税收条款

tax collected amount 征税额

tax collection 征税

tax collector 稽征员,税务官,税务员

tax court 税务法院

tax credit 抵免税费,抵免所得税,税收抵免,课税扣除

tax credit system 抵免所得税制度

tax crime(s) 税务犯罪

tax day 纳税日,征税日期

tax deception 骗税,课税减免

tax deductions 减税

tax disc 纳税证

tax dodge 逃税,偷税

tax equalization 纳税均等

tax evasion 偷税

tax evasion and refusal to pay taxes by violent means 偷税、抗税犯罪

tax exclusive price 不含税价格

tax exemption volume 免征额

tax exemptions 免税

tax file 税务档案,税务罚款

tax for maintaining and building city 城市维修建设税

tax for regulating differential income 级差收入调节税

tax for specific acts 特定行为税

tax gatherer 税务员

tax haven 避税地

tax holidays 免税期

tax in kind 实物税

tax inspection 查税

tax inspector 税务稽查员

tax invoice 纳税单据

tax item 税目

tax jurisdiction 税收管辖权

tax law concerning foreign affairs 涉外税法

tax law concerning foreign interests 涉外税收

tax law in a broad sense 狭义税法

tax law involving foreign elements 涉外税收

tax levy 纳税付款通知书,征税

tax lien 征税留置权

tax limit 课税限额

tax of adjustment for the orientation of fixed investment 固定资产投资方向调节税

tax of earnings 收益税/收益额课税

tax of gains 收益税/收益额课税

tax of proceeds 收益税/收益额课税

tax of profit 收益税/收益额课税

tax of yield 收益税/收益额课税

tax on agricultural and forestry specialties 农林特产税

tax on contract 契税

tax on dividends 股息税

tax on earned income 劳动所得税额

tax on industry and commerce returns 工商业所得税

tax on land price 地价税

tax on land revenue 土地收入税

tax on occupation of cultivated land 耕地占用税

tax on premises 房产税

tax on price of land 地价税

tax on revaluation 重估价税

tax on sales 产品销售税金

tax on the above-norm bonus 超额奖金税

tax on the sale of property 买卖产业税

tax or duty free 免税

tax paper 纳税通知书

tax payable 应纳税额

tax payment 税款,征税额

tax payment certificate 缴款凭证

tax payment deadline 纳税期限

tax payment place 纳税地点

tax payment receipt 纳税凭证

tax police 税务警察

tax rate 税率

tax receipt 税票

tax registration 税务登记,纳税登记工作

tax registration form 税务登记表

tax regulations 税则

tax relief 税款减免

tax report on wine tax 酒税报告书

tax reserve 纳税准备金

tax returns 报税单,报税表,纳税申报,纳税清册

tax revenue 税收

tax revenue administration 税收管理

tax revenue jurisdiction 税收管辖权

tax sale 私房公卖

tax shared by central and local governments 中央地方共享税

tax shield creator 设法逃税者

tax source 税源

tax sparing 税收饶让,税收饶让证

tax stamp 税章

tax surcharge on dumping 倾销关税

tax system 税制

tax technique 征税方法,课征方法

tax undertaker 纳税担保人

tax withholding certificate 扣缴税款凭证

tax year 纳税年度,征税年度

taxable 可征税的,应纳税

taxable amount of income 应纳税所得额

taxable commodities 征税品

taxable consumption goods 应税消费品

taxable earnings 应税收入

taxable income 应税所得,可征税收入,应纳税所得额

taxable item(s) 应税项目,税目

taxable products 应税产品

taxable resources 应税资源

taxable service 应税劳务

taxable unit 课税单位

taxable year 课税年度

taxation 征税,课税,纳税

taxation at the source 根据收入来源课税

taxation base 计税依据

taxation bureau 税务局

taxation clause 上税收条款

taxation form 报关单

taxation inspection 税务检查

taxation litigation 税务诉讼

taxation of foreign affairs 涉外征税

taxation payment 税款

taxation proceeding 税务诉讼

taxation review 税收复查

taxation standard 计税标准

taxation system 税制

taxed article 课税品

taxer 纳税人

taxes 赋税

taxes included in the calculated prices 价内税

taxes on enterprises 企业税

taxes withheld 扣缴税捐

taxing authorities 税收机关/税务机关

taxing officer 税务官

taxing power 课税权

taxpayer 纳税义务人,纳税人,小规模纳税人

taxpayer personally filling returns 自报纳税人

teacher's law 教师法

teachers' congress 教代会

teachers' representative assembly 教代会

teaching assistant 助教

teachings of international publicists 国际法学家的学说

team of supervision for reform-through-labour 劳动改造管教队

technical adviser 技术顾问

technical aid 技术援助

technical allowance or assistance 技术援助

technical amendments 技术补充性条款

technical and economic responsibility 技术经济责任制

technical assistance 技术援助

technical assistance fund 技术援助基金

technical assistance program 技术援助方案

technical certificate 技术证书

technical characteristics 技术性能

technical collaboration 技术协会

technical collaboration agreement 技术合作协议

technical commission 技术委员会

technical committee on rules of origin 原产地规则技术委员会

technical contract 技术承包

technical control 技术控制

technical cooperation 技术合作

technical data 技术数据

technical diffusion 技术扩散

technical directives 技术性指令

technical division of labour 技术分工

technical education 技术教育

① technical essential 技术要点
② technical exchange 技术交流
③ technical expert 技术
④ technical expertise 技术知识
⑤ technical features 技术物证
⑥ technical field 技术领域
⑦ technical file 技术文件
⑧ technical grade standard 技术等级标准
⑩ technical guidance 技术指导
⑪ technical improvement 技术创新
⑬ technical indicator 技术指标
⑭ technical information 技术信息
⑮ technical innovation 技术革新,技术改造
⑰ technical interest 技术权益
⑱ technical interpretation 技术解释
⑲ technical investigation and analytical evaluation 技术调查、分析评价报告
㉓ technical know-how 技术诀窍 F
㉔ technical legal rule 技术性法规
㉕ technical management 技术管理
㉖ technical manual 技术规范,技术手册
㉘ technical meaning 专门意义
㉙ technical measures for electric safety 电气安全技术措施
㉛ technical meeting 技术会议
㉜ technical norm 技术标准
㉝ technical organization 技术组织
㉞ technical performance 技术性能
㉟ technical plant 技术设备
㊱ technical problem 技术问题
㊲ technical progress theory 技术进步论
㊳ technical qualitative evaluation 技术质量鉴定
㊶ technical reconstruction 技术改造
㊸ technical regulations 技术规章,技术规程
㊺ technical requirements 技术要求
㊼ technical rule of interpretation

解释的技术规则

technical rule of interpretation of constitution　解释宪法的技术规则

technical rule of interpretation of law　解释法律的技术规则

technical secret　技术秘密,技术诀窍

technical service credit　技术服务融资

technical service period　技术服务期

technical services　技术服务

technical services income　技术服务收入

technical sophistication　技术复杂

technical specification　技术规范,技术说明

technical standards　复杂苛刻的技术标准

technical term　专门术语,技术词语

technical trade　技术贸易

technical trade barrier　技术性贸易壁垒

technical training　技术培训

technical training contract　技术培训合同

technical transformation　技术改造

technical victim　技术性被害人

technical visa　技术签证

technician　技术人员

techniques of law　法律技术

technological advance　技术进步

technological background information　技术背景材料

technological commodity　技术商品

technological competition　技术竞争

technological control　技术监督

technological cooperation　技术协会

technological development　技术发展,技术革新

technological equipment　技术设备

technological evaluation of tenders　技术评级

technological export administration　技术出口管理

technological follow-up improvements　技术后续改进

technological forecast　技术预测

technological innovation　技术改进,技术创新

technological leapfrogging　技术跳跃

technological life　技术有效期

technological market　技术市场

technological materials　技术资料

technological monopoly　技术垄断

technological process　技术规程,工艺流程

technological renovation　技术改造

technological research achievements　科技成果

technological specifications　技术规范

technological standards　技术标准

technological superiority　技术优势

technological superpower　技术大国

technological supervision　技术监督

technological transformation planning　技术改选规划

technologies contributed as investment　技术投资

technologist　技术人员,技术

technology　技术

technology and equipment　技术和设备

technology assessment　技术评估

technology consultant contract　技术咨询合同

technology contract　技术合同

technology development 技术开发

technology development contract 技术开发合同

technology export administration 技术出口管理

technology export contract 技术出口合同

technology failure 技术故障

technology files 技术文档

technology guarantee clause 技术担保条款

technology import administration 技术进口管理

technology import and export contract 技术进出口合同

technology introduction 技术引进

technology market 技术市场

technology policy 技术政策

technology research and development 技术研究与开发

technology service contract 技术服务合同

technology trade 技术贸易

technology transfer 技术转让

technology transfer clause 技术转让条款

technology transfer contract 技术转让合同

technology transferee 技术受让人

technology-intensive products 技术密集型产品

techno-economic policy 技术经济政策

telegraphic money order (/draft) 电汇汇票

telegraphic transfer (/money) 电汇

telegraphic transfer bought 电汇买进

telegraphic transfer rate (T/T rate) 电汇汇率

telegraphic transfer sold 电汇售出

telegraphic transfer (简写 T/T) 电汇

teleological interpretation 目的解释

teleological viewpoint 目的论观点

telephone ordering 电话订购

telephone purchasing 电话采购

telephone selling 电话售货

telephone telegram 电话保送电报

teletype 电传打字打电

teller 唱票人

temper justice with mercy 宽严并举

temporal limit liability 赔偿期限

temporal lords 贵族院普通议员(英)

temporary 暂时,暂行

temporary admission 临时许可进口

temporary alimony 临时托养费

temporary arbitration 临时执照

temporary building 临时性建筑

temporary business tax 临时营业税

temporary custody 暂时保管

temporary detention 临时拘留

temporary diplomatic mission 临时使用

temporary driving license 临时驾驶证

temporary free importation 暂时免税进口

temporary global bond 综合债券

temporary impossibility of performance 暂时不能履行

temporary interests 暂时利益

temporary loans 暂时借款,暂时贷款

temporary payment 暂时付款,临时付额

temporary repair 临时修理

temporary residence permit 临时户口

temporary resident population

上 temporary   554   terminal

暂住人口

temporary right of defence 暂时抗辩权

temporary service outside prison 暂予监外执行

ten chaotic years 十年动乱

ten commandments 十诫

ten principles of Asian-African conference 亚非会议十项原则

tenancy 租期,任职,租约

tenancy agreement 租借合约

tenancy at will 无定期租赁

tenancy for years 长期租赁

tenancy from month to month 按月租借

tenancy from year to year 按年租借,不定期租赁

tenancy in common 分别共有的财产权,共同租赁

tenant 租借人,承租人,佃户

tenant in common 共同租赁人

tenant's improvement 承租人的改建和改良

tend to 趋向

tendency 趋向

tendency towards compromise 妥协性

tender 招标,偿付,投标

tender bid 投标

tender bidding 投标买卖

tender bill,(英) treasury bill 国库证券

tender bond 投标保证金,投标担保

tender day 投标日

tender documents 投标文件

tender guarantee 投标担保,投标保证人

tender guarantor 投标保证人

tender of performance 提供汇付,准备履行合同

tender offer 提出要约,投标要约

tender price 开标价格,投标价格

tender procedures 投标手续

① **tenderer** 投标人

② **tendering party** 投标人

③ **tentative plan** 试行计划

④ **tentative purchase** 试购

⑤ **tenure** 保有条件,任期

⑥ **tenure of office** 任期

⑦ **ten-year program for national economy and social development** 国民经济和社会发展十年规划

⑧

⑨

⑩

⑪ **term** 用语,条件

⑫ **term day** 付款日期

⑬ **term implied by law** 法律默认条款

⑭

⑮ **term insurance** 定期寿险

⑯ **term loan agreements** 国际定期贷款协议

⑰

⑱ **term mortgage** 定期抵押贷款

⑲ **term of a labour contract** 劳动合同期限

⑳

㉑ **term of agreement** 合同有效期条款

㉒

㉓ **term of contract** 合同条款

㉔ **term of credit** 赊销期

㉕ **term of delivery** 交付条件

㉖ **term of detention** 拘留期限

㉗ **term of disappearance** 失踪期间

㉘ **term of imprisonment** 刑期

㉙ **term of imprisonment in the original sentence** 原判刑期

㉚

㉛ **term of lease** 租赁期限

㉜ **term of office** 任期

㉝ **term of payment** 清偿期

㉞ **term of penalty** 刑期

㉟ **term of price** 价格条件,价格术语

㊱

㊲ **term of punishment** 刑期

㊳ **term of redemption** 还债期限,偿还期限

㊴

㊵ **term of sentence actually served** 实际执行刑期

㊶

㊷ **term of time** 期限

㊸ **term of validity** 有效期间,有效期,有效期限

㊹

㊺ **term of validity of claim** 索赔时效

㊻

㊼ **terminal contract** 定期合同

terminate a contract 终止合同

terminate business 停业

terminate by agreement 协议解除

terminate contract before the date of expiration 提前终止合同

terminate effectiveness 终止生效

terminate the bankruptcy proceedings 终结破产程序

terminate the procedure for public summons exhortation 终结公示催告程序

termination compensation 终止赔偿金

termination forthwith clause 立即终止生效条款

termination of a business 歇业

termination of a contract 合同终止

termination of adventure clause 航程终止条款,运输终止条款

termination of agency business 代理关系终止

termination of business 停业

termination of contract 终止合同,合同期满,合同的解除

termination of contract of carriage clause 运输契约终止条款

termination of land use right 土地使用权终止

termination of membership 会员籍的终止

termination of partnership 合伙终止

termination of the pleadings 辩论终结

termination of the rights and obligation(s) of contracts 合同权利义务的终止

termination time period 附终止期限

terminology 用语,术语

terminology of price 价格术语

terminus ad quem（拉） 终止日期,到达目的地

terms for entry 加入条件

① terms of contract 合同条款

② terms of credit 信用证条件,贷款条件

③ terms of payment 付款条件

④ terms of reference 职权范围,委托的规定说明,职权范围

⑤ terms of sale 买卖条件,销货条件

⑥ terms of shipment 装运条件

⑦ terms of trade 进出口交换比率

⑧ terra firma（拉） 稳固的地位

⑨ terra nullius（拉） 无主地

⑩ terra putura（拉） 森林地

⑪ terrain 地势,地区

⑫ terrestrial wildlife animal 陆生野生动物

⑬ territorial acquisition 领土的取得

⑭ territorial asylum 领土庇护

⑮ territorial boundary 边境

⑯ territorial claim 领土要求

⑰ territorial effect of criminal law 刑法地域效力

⑱ territorial expansion 领土扩张

⑲ territorial integrity 领土完整

⑳ territorial jurisdiction 属地管辖权

㉑ territorial law 属地法

㉒ territorial scope of application of criminal law 刑法对地域的适用范围

㉓ territorial sea 领海

㉔ territorial status quo 领土现状

㉕ territorial strait 领峡

㉖ territorial subsoil 领土,地下领土

㉗ territorial title 领土所有权

㉘ territorial waters 领水

㉙ territories of China 中国领土问题

㉚ territory 地方,领土

㉛ territory of a judge 法官管辖区域

㉜ tertiary rules 第三级规则

㉝ tesimony 作证

㉞ test 考试

㉟ test case 判例案件

test marketing 试销

test of compatibility 适合性标准

test unit 试点单位

testament 遗嘱

testamentary will 遗嘱

testifying attitude of witness 证人的作证态度,证人作证行为

testimonial evidence 证明性证据,供述证据

testimonial session 听证会

testimonium clause (拉) 合同未了条款,合同末了条文

testimony 证言,证据

testimony rules 证言规则

testing and appointment system 考任制

testing conditions 检测条件

testing of equipment 设备调试

testing of machinery and installation clause 机器设备试车

text of court's decision 法院判决主义

text of judgment 判决正文,判决主文,判词

text of sentence 判决正文

that 该

That which is expressed makes that which is implied to cease 明示排除默示

the abetted 被教唆的人

the above-mentioned 上述

the accused 刑事被告,被控方,被控犯罪人

the accused (of a criminal case) 被告,被告人

the accused administrative department 被告行政机关

the act of agency 代理行为

the administrative agency for industry and commerce 工商行政管理机构

the African intellectual property organization (OAPI) 非洲知识产权组织

the aggregate amount of compensation 赔偿金额

① the aggrieved 受害者

② the aggrieved party 受害方

③ The agreement creates the law 协议产生法律

④

⑤ The agreement of private person cannot derogate from public right 私人间的协议不得有损于公共的权利

⑥

⑦

⑧

⑨ the allocation of funds 拨款

⑩ the american convention on human rights 美洲人权公约

⑪

⑫ the are laws and regulations to go by 有法可依,有章可循

⑬

⑭ the area of applicability of the civil law 民法调整范围

⑮

⑯ the area within which the civil law regulates 民法调整范围

⑰

⑱ the articles of association of the legal person 法人组织章程

⑲

⑳ the authorities 当局

㉑ the authorities concerned 有关当局

㉒

㉓ the authority in change of foreign exchange control 外汇主管机关

㉔

㉕

㉖ the bar 律师界

㉗ the basic law of hong kong special Administrative Region of the People's Republ ic of China 中华人民共和国香港特别行政区基本法

㉘

㉙

㉚

㉛

㉜ the best price 最高价

㉝ the big pot 大锅饭

㉞ the boundary dispute between China and India 中印边界问题

㉟

㊱

㊲ the boundary dispute between China and Russia 中俄边界问题

㊳

㊴

㊵ the British commonwealth of nations 英联邦

㊶

㊷ the carriage of postal matters 邮件运输

㊸

㊹ the carriage performed by the actual carrier 实际承运人承担的运输

㊺

㊻

㊼ the case 本案

The case goes against him 此案判他败诉

The case goes for him 此案判他胜诉

the central people's government commission 中央人民政府委员会

the certificate of origin 原产地证

the certificate of the right 使用权证书

the chairman of the creditor's meeting 债权人会议主席

the character of law 法的特征

the Chinese People's Political Consultative Conference 中国人民政治协商会议

the class feature of human rights 人权的阶级性

the commissioned party 受托方

the commodity inspection authority at the production site 产地商检机构

the common people 平民,民众

the communist party 共产党

the communist party of China 中国共产党

the competent departments concerned of the State Council (中) 国务院有关主管部门

the compositions of legal culture 法律文化的结构

the condition to be effective 有效条件

the conduct of constructive consent 推定承诺行为

the consciousness of category of jurisprudence 法学的范畴意识

the conservation party 保守党

the conservatives 保守派

the consolidation and growth of the state economy 国营经济的巩固和发展

the continental conference 大陆会议

the continental law system 大陆法系

the contract administration authority 合同管理机关

the contract letting party 发包人

the contracting parties 缔约方全体

the contracting party 承揽方

the convention establishing the world intellectual property organization (1967)年成立世界知识产权组织公约

the cost of construction 工程造价

the country's balance of international payments 国家外汇收支平衡

the court holds that...法庭认定

the creditable amount of tax 抵税额

the declaration on territorial asylum 领土庇护宣言

the defendant work unit 被告单位

the defendant 被告

the defense 被告方

the department of administration for industry and commerce 工商行政管理部门

the development zone for high and new technological industry 高新技术开发区

the diet 国会

the disabled 残废者,残疾人

the disciplined (person) 被惩戒人

the doctrine of liberal interpretation 从宽解释原则

the doctrine of limited sovereignty 有限主权论

the doctrine of observing new laws 从新原则

the doctrine of observing new laws and old ones when with lighter punishment 从新兼从轻原则

the doctrine of observing old laws 从旧原则

the doctrine of observing old laws and new ones when with lighter punishment 从旧兼从轻原则

the doctrine of strict construction 从严解释原则

the doctrine of territoriality of criminal law 刑法属地性原则

the doctrine of the equality of litigants 当事人地位平等原则

the doctrine of ultra vires 越权原则

the duma 国会

the economic integration of western europe 西欧经济一体化

the economic open area 经济开放地区

The effect of the law consists in the execution 法律的效力在于执行

the elect 当选人

the elected 被选人

the electoral system for deputies to the people's congress 人大代表选举制

the elements of rule of law 法治的要素

the ending of partnership 合伙终止

the Enlightenment 启蒙运动

the entering into partnership 入伙

the entrusting party 委托方

the equal protection clauses (美) 平等保护条款

the estimates (英) 财政预算

the European Investment Bank 欧洲投资银行

the exclusions of cargo insurance 货物保险除外责任

the expiration of the term 期限届满

the export credit guarantee department 出口信贷担保署

the express agreement of parties overcomes the law 双方当事人暗示的协议胜过法律

The expression of one thing is the exclusion of another 明示排除其它

the extension of suffrage 选举权的扩大

the extent to which the reform is acceptable to the people 人民对改革的承受能力

The fact has been fully proved 事实清楚

The fact was established after investigation 审查属实

The facts are corroborated and the evidence is irrefutable 事实清楚,证据确凿

the female accused 女性被告人

the Five-Starred Red Flag 五星红旗

the forestry department under the State Council (中) 国务院林业主管部门

the form of an official document 公文格式

the form of law 法律形式

the form of treaty 条约的格式

the forum rei doctrine (拉) 被告住所原则

the four cardinal principles 四项基本原则

the fourth market 第四市场

the freedom of person is inviolable 人身自由不受侵犯

the french revolution 法国大革命

the function of the thing 物的效用

the functions of legal culture 法律文化的功能

the fundamental law 大法,基本法

the general guaranty 一般保证

the general pattern 一般规律

the goal of monetary policy 货币政策目标

the goods to be valued 所估货物

the governed 被统治者

the government administration

councll 政务院

the government and the public 朝野

the government authorities 政府当局

the group of 77 七十七国集团

the guaranty law of the People's republic of China 中华人民共和国担保法

the handicapped 残疾人

the haulier 货物承运人

the high court 高等法庭

the highest bld 最高投标价

the highest price 最高价

the Hong Kong British authorities 港英当局

the house 下院,下议院

the house of commons 下院,下议院

the ideological sphere 意识形态领域

the industrial revolution 工业革命

the infringed 被侵权人

the injured party 受害方

The intention expressed is genuine 意思表示真实

the intention of the parties 当事人的意向

the interaction of jurisprudence and criminology 法理学与犯罪学的相互关系

the international center for settlement of investment disputes (注:简写为 ICSID) 国际投资争端解决中心

the international development association (IDA) 国际开发协会

the international financial corporation (IFC) 国际金融公司

The international regulations for preventing collision at sea 国际海上避撞规则

the joint liability guaranty 连带责任保证

the judiciary style of Ma Xiwu 马锡五审判方式

the justice of the supreme court 最高法院大法官

the Koran 可兰经

the latest allowable date 最迟允许日期

the latest date of shipment 最迟装货日期

the latest shipment date 最迟装货日期

the law 王法

the law never suffers anything contrary to truth 法律绝不容忍违反真理的事情

The law of nature are unchangeable 自然法则是不可改变的

the law of succession 继承法

the law of the land 王法

the law of the People's Republic of China on the protection of consumers rights and interests 中华人民共和国消费者权益保护法

the law of the place where the infringing act ls committed 侵权行为地质法

the law of the United States of America 美利坚合众国法

the lawful rights and interests 合法权益

the laws of Hong Kong 香港法例

the lawsuit 本案

the least time 最短期间

the legal obligation theory 法律义务论

the legalist school 法家

the local authorities 地方当局

the local people's governmcnts above the country level 县级以上政府部门

the local tax authorities 当地税务机关

the localization and adaptation of laws 法律的本土化和改写

the lowest selling price 最低出售价格

the main business place 主营业地

the maritime law of the People's Republic of China 中华人民共和国海商法

the masses of the people 民众

the maximum price 最高价

the measures of precaution 防范措施

the mechanism of rule of law 法治的机制

the ministry of punishment in the feudal China 刑部(中)

The minority is subordinate to the majority 少数服从多数

the missing person's registration 失踪人登记

the missing registration 失踪人登记

the models of legal culture 法律文化的模式

the name of firm 企业名称

the national economy and the livelihood of the people 国计民生

the nature of law 法的本质

the net of justice 法网

the new culture movement 新文化运动

the new political consultative conference 新政治协商会议

the New Testament 新约,新约全书

the number of deputies to local people's congress at different levels 地方各级人大代表名额

the number of duties to the people's congress 人大代表的数额

The object is an indispensable clause in any contract 标的是任何合同不可缺少的条款

the old testament 旧约全书

the old, weak, sick, and disabled criminals 老、弱、病、残罪犯

the Opium War 鸦片战争

the opposition 反对党

the ordering party 定作方

the other party 对方

the panty awarding the contract 发包方

the Paris Commune 巴黎公社

the Paris Commune committee system 巴黎公社委员会制

the partial payment clause 部分的

the particularity of contradiction 矛盾的特殊性

the party against whom an application is filed 被申请人

the party committee member 党委成员

the party committee of an enterprise 企业党委

the party concerned 有关方面

the party in power 执政党

the party's policy 党的方针,党的政策

the patent claim 权利要求

the penal code of Germany 德国刑法典

the people 人民

the people of all nationalities in China 中国各族人民

the people's congress of municipality directly under the central government 直辖市人民代表大会

the people's court where an insured event has occurred 保险事故发生地人民法院

the people's insurance company of China 中国人民保险公司

the people's liberation army 人民解放军

the people's postal service of China 中国人民邮政

the People's Republic of China 中华人民共和国

the period of carriage 运送期间

the period of carrier's responsibility 承运人的责任期间

the person 人身

the person directly responsible 直接责任人员

the personal freedom of another 他人人身自由

the place of injury 损害发生地

the place of the situation of the object 物之所在地

the place where a case has occurred 案件发生地

the place where the infringing act is committed 侵权行为地

the policy of opening to the outside world 开放政策

the Pope 罗马教皇

the populace 平民,民众

the power of agency expires 代理权终止

The practice of fixing and refixing the laws is a most dangerous one 惯于制定和修改法规是最有害的作法

the priciple that the polluter should pay 谁污染谁付款原则

the primary stage of socialism 社会主义初级阶段

the principle of economization of punishment 刑罚经济原则

the principle of freedom of contract 契约自由原则

the principle of good faith and fair dealing 诚实信用和公平交易原则

the principle of honesty and credibility 诚信原则

the priciple of humanitarism of punishment 刑罚人道主义原则

the principle of individualization of punishment 刑罚个别化原则

the principle of international cooperation for development 国际合作以谋发展的原则

the principle of law common to the parties 双方当事人公认的法律原则

the principle of lighter punishment 从轻原则

the principle of making compensation for equal value 等价有偿原则

the principle of men and women getting equal pay for equal work 男女同工同酬原则

the principle of no prosecution where it is impossible to investigate into the criminal responsibility 不能追究刑事责任不追诉的原则

the Principle of People's Livelihood 民生主义

the principle of protecting the legitimate rights of children 保护儿童合法权益原则

the principle of protecting the legitimate rights of the elderly 保护老人合法权益原则

the principle of protecting the legitimate rights of women 保护妇女合法原则

the principle of safeguarding the fundamental human rights 保障基本人权原则

the principle of safeguarding the fundamental rights of citizens 保障公民基本权利原则

the principle of utility of punishment 刑罚效益原则

the principle of voluntariness 自愿原则

the principle that no crime is borne from consented act 得承诺不为罪原则

the principle that the polluter shall be responsible for its elimination 谁污染谁防治原则

the principles of insurance 保险原则

the principles of the civil law 民法准则

the privilege of clergy 神职人员的特权

the procedure for collecting and

housing persons for reeducation-through-labour 劳教收容程序

the proletariat 无产阶级

the properties sealed up 查封的财产

the prosecuting party 控方

the public 公众

the public sector of the economy 公营经济

the purview of authority 职能范围

the quality of the construction 工程质量

the quality of the thing 物的质量

the ranking of the mortgage of ship 船舶抵押权顺序

the real conveyance of the thing 物的现实交付

the recall system for deputies to the people's congress 人大代表罢免制

the reform of the political structure 政治体制改革

the regulating function of the civil law 民法调整作用

the replacement of one historical mode of law by another 法的历史类型的更替

the replacement of one mode of production by another 生产方式的更替

the representative of a unit 单位代表人

the representative system 代议制

the requisite majority 必要多数

The rest may be deduced by analogy 依此类推

the right of beneficial use of a property 用益权

the right of inheritance 继续权

the right to criticize 批评权

the right to defence 辩护权

the right to development 发展权

the right to hold strike 罢工权

the right to make complain 申诉权

the right to make suggestions 建议权

the right to personal liberty 人身自由权

the right to stand for election 被选举权

the right to strike 罢工权

the right to the use of the site 土地使用权

the Roman catholic church 天主教会

the ruled 被统治者

the ruling party 执政党

the same as above 同上

the same court 该法院

the same kind of goods 同种商品

the same manner 同样方式

the same procuratorate 该检察院

the same prosecutors' officer 该检察院

the scope for guaranteed maintenance 质量保修范围

the scope guaranteed by the guaranty 保证的范围

the scope of cover and exclusions on hull insurance 船舶保险的责任范围与除外责任

the scope of insured perils 承保风险范围

the scope of marine underwriter 海上保险的责任

the scope of the power of agency 代理权范围

the set of multilaterally agreed equitable rules for the control of restrictive business practics 关于控制限制性商业法的多边协定的公平原则和规则

the shortest 最短期间

the south (/Antarctic) pole environment protection 南极环境保护

the special economic zone 经济

特区

the staff 参谋人员

the standing committee of the political bureau 政治局常委会

the state administration for commodity inspection（中） 国家商检局

the state administrative departments 国家机关

the state bureau of cultural relics（中） 国家文物局

the state capital construction commission（中） 国家基建委员会

the state functionaries 国家职能部门

the state organs at the ministerial level 中央一级国家机关

the status of aliens 外国人民事法律地位

The stipulations of parties constitute the law to the contract 当事人协议构成共有法律效力的合同

the storing party 有货方

the structure of constitution 宪法结构

The subject cannot be analogized 主体不能类推

the supplier of electricity 供电方

the sword of justice 司法权

the system of categories of jurisprudence 法学的范畴体系

the system of five powers 五权制度

the tax overpaid 多缴的税款

The term has expired 期满

the theory of imitation 模仿法则说

the third market 第三市场

the third party 第三人

the Third Reich 第三帝国

the third-party beneficiary doctrine 第三人受益学论

the thirty-nine articles 三十九条信纲

the three big mountains（imperialism, feudalism and bureaucratic-capitalism） 三座大山

the three principles of the people 三民主义

the time limit for action 诉讼时效

the time of validity of claim 索赔时效

the time period of guaranty 保证的期限

the town head 镇长

the trade union at a private enterprise 私营企业工会

the transferee of technology 技术受让方

the tremendous force of public opinion 舆论的威力

the Trial smelter arbitration 特雷尔冶炼厂仲裁案

the trustee 被委托方

the twenty-four histories 二十四史

the two-counsel rule 必须同时有两个诉讼代理人原则

the undersigned 签字人

the underworld 下层社会

The Uniform Law on International Sale of Goods 《国际货物买卖统一法公约》

the Uniform Law on the Formation of Contract for International Sale of Goods 《国际货物买卖合同成立统一法公约》

the United Nations environment program（UNEP） 联合国环境规划署

the universality of contradiction 矛盾的普遍性

the upset price 最低出售价格

the urban unemployed 城镇失业人员

the value of law 法律价值

the war of resistance against japan 抗日战争（中）

the whole staff 全体工作人员

the whole text of a law 法律全

文

the wife's first son 嫡长子

the will of the people 民意

the women's federation 妇联

the working class 工人阶级

the zone for economy and technology development 开发区

theft 盗窃罪,盗窃案件

theft act 盗窃犯罪

theft of wild creature 偷猎野生动物

then and there 当场

theocracy 神权统治

Theodosius 狄奥多西

Theodosius code 狄奥多西法典

theoretical base of administrative compensation 行政补偿制度的理论基础

theoretical criminal law 理论刑法学

theoretical jurisprudence 理论法学

theoretical jurisprudence school 理论法理学派

theoretical level of economic law 经济法理论水平

theory asserting act as the criterion of plural crimes 数罪行为说

theory asserting constitution of a crime as the criterion of plural crimes 数罪构成要件说

theory asserting objective facts as the criterion of plural crimes 数罪客观说

theory of asserting act as the criterion of accomplished offense 既遂行为说

theory of asserting purpose as the criterion of accomplished offense 既遂目的说

theory of born criminal 天生犯罪人论

theory of born criminal types 天生犯罪人类型说

theory of building socialism with Chinese characteristics 建设

有中国特色社会主义的理论

theory of conflicts of crime culture 犯罪文化冲突论

theory of contract 契约法

theory of correction and reform 教养改造说

theory of crime due to intelligence disturbance 智能障碍犯罪说

theory of criminal commonness 犯罪共同说

theory of criminal instinct 犯罪本能说

theory of criminal law 刑法理论

theory of criminal normalcy 犯罪正常论

theory of criminal punishment as a means of education 教育刑论

theory of criminal symptom 犯罪表征说

theory of criminal typification based on behavior mechanism 根据行为机制的犯罪类型论

theory of criminal typification based on formation process of personality 根据人格形成过程的犯罪类型

theory of criminal typification based on motives 根据动机的犯罪类型论

theory of criminal typification based on physiological diagnosis 根据生理诊断的犯罪类型论

theory of criminal typification based on psychoanalysis 根据精神诊断的犯罪类型论

theory of criminal typification based on standpoints of social pathology 根据社会病理学观点的犯罪类型

theory of diversification of economy 经济多样化论

theory of divine right 神权说

theory of economic determination 经济决定论

theory of economics on causation of crimes 经济犯罪原因论

theory of educative punishment

教育刑理论

theory of equal retaliation　同害报复论

theory of expandable principal　扩张正犯论

theory of explanatory criminal law　注释刑法

theory of geographical cause of crime　犯罪地理原因论

theory of indulgent conduct　放任行为说

theory of inherent crime　原罪说

theory of intention　故意论

theory of international law　国际法学说

theory of just trade　公正贸易论

theory of knowledge　认识论

theory of law　法学理论

theory of law as social engineering　法律社会工程说

theory of most real connection　最实际关联说

theory of negligence　疏忽说

theory of of asserting consequence as the criterion of accomplished offense　既遂结果论

theory of original evil of human nature　性恶说

theory of original sin　原罪说

theory of political causes of crime　政治学的犯罪原因论

theory of protecting agriculture　农业保护论

theory of protecting block's interest　集团利益保护论

theory of protecting industry　衰退产业保护论,工业保护论

theory of protecting infant industry　幼稚产业保护论

theory of punishment　刑罚论

theory of punitive function　刑罚功能说

theory of rational decision　理性决定说

theory of reasonable crime　犯罪有理论

theory of relative rise of crime　犯罪相对增长论

theory of remuneration　报酬论

theory of retribution　惩罚说,报应主义说

theory of social contract　社会契约论

theory of social interests　社会利益说

theory of solicitation of a crime　教唆犯罪论

theory of spiritual poor　精神贫困论

theory of swapping shortages and surpluses　调剂余缺论

theory of synchronous crime　犯罪同步论

theory of synchronous growth of crime and economy　犯罪与经济同步增长理论

theory of the presumption of innocence　无罪推定说

theory of ultimate popular sovereignty　人民主权论

theory of urbanism　都市化犯罪学说

theory of workable competition　有效竞争论

theory on the relationship of punishment, reason and feelings　刑理情关系说

There are laws but little observation of them　有法不依

There are no statutes to apply　无法可依

therefrom　从中

the "big" responsibility system　大包干

thief　窃贼

thievery　偷窃行为

thin layer　薄层

things corporeal　有体物

things fixed on land　土地定着物

things immovable　不动产

Things manifest do not require proof　明显的事情无需我证据

thing-thing definition　物-物主义

thinking 思想

third class 三等

third conviction 第三次定罪

third debtor 第三债务人

third market of stocks 股票第三市场,股票三级市场

third panty intervention 第三方干预

third party 第三方

third party acting in good faith 善意第三人

third party beneficiary contract 第三人利益合同

third party clause 第三者条款

third party complaint 被告向第三方提出赔偿的申请书

third party in administrative proceedings 行政诉讼第三人

third party in an administrative case 行政诉法第三人

third party in litigation 诉讼第三人

third party interests 第三方利益,第三者利益

third party liability 第三方责任,第三者责任

third party notice 第三者通知

third party settlement 第三方解决

third party shipper 第三者托运人

third reading 第三读

third world countries 第三世界国家

third-country dumping 第三国倾销

third-party claim 索赔涉及第三方的诉讼

this case 本案

this court 本院

this crime 本罪

this lawsuit 本案

this region of administration 本行政区域

thought 思想

thoughtlessness 盲目

thousand 千

① threat and coercion 恐吓胁迫

② threaten 威吓

③ three days of grace（英） 延期三

④ 天支付

⑤ three factors of production argu-

⑥ ment 生产三要素论

⑦ three guarantees（for repair, re-

⑧ placement and compensation of

⑨ faulty products） 三包（包修、

⑩ 包换、包赔）

⑪ three kinds of investment enter-

⑫ prises 三资企业

⑬ Three People's Principles（nation-

⑭ alism, democracy and the peo-

⑮ ple's livelihood） 三民主义

⑯ three readings 三读制

⑰ three zi's and one contract 三自

⑱ 一包

⑲ three-chamber system 三院制

⑳ three-level collective ownership

㉑ 三级集体所有制

㉒ three-level government 三级所

㉓ 有

㉔ three-mile rule 三海里规则

㉕ three-stage 三级

㉖ three-tier 三级

㉗ three-tier system 三层次制度

㉘ threshold price 入门价格

㉙ throne 王位

㉚ through agent 通过代理人

㉛ through air transport 航空联运

㉜ through bill of lading 联运提单

㉝ through cargo 直达货场

㉞ through cargo manifest 过境货

㉟ 物明细单

㊱ through carriage 联运,全程运

㊲ 输

㊳ through consultation 通过协商

㊴ through fault 由于过错

㊵ through freight traffic 货物联运

㊶ through rate 全程运价

㊷ through the fault of the victim

㊸ 由于受害人过错

㊹ through traffic 联合运输

㊺ through transport 联运

㊻ through various channels and in

㊼ various ways 通过各种途径

和形式

thumb impression 拇指印

thumb print 拇指印,拇指纹

ticket-fare 运费

tie 约束

tie down 约束

tie up 停滞

tied loan 限制性贷款,约束性贷款

tied purchase clause 搭售条款

tied sale 搭售

tied-in 搭卖品

tied-in clause 搭售条款

tied-in sale 搭售

tied-in sale clause 搭卖条款

tier building 多层建筑

tie-in clause 一揽子交易条款

tie-in contract 搭售合同

tight monetary policy 紧缩信用政策

tight money 限定贷款,紧缩银根

tight money market 银根紧缩的金融市场

tight money policy 紧缩信用政策,银根紧缩政策

tile 瓷砖

timber forest 用材林

timber reserves 森林资源

time 期间,时间,时期,时代

time and crime 时日与犯罪

time and space factors and crime 时空因素与犯罪

time bar 时限,时效期间

time bar in maritime action 海事诉讼时效

time bargain 定期交易

time bill 期票

time charter 定期租船合同,期租

time charter on trip basis 航次期租合同

time charter party 定期租船合同

time delivery 定期交货

time deposit 定期存款

time determined by contract 合

同规定期限

time draft 远期汇票

time effect 时效

time effect of criminal law 刑法的时间效力

time effect of of administrative procedure law 行政诉讼的时间效力

time for loading and discharge 装卸期限

time for payment 付款期限

time limit 时限,时效

time limit expires 时限届满

time limit for a project 工程工期

time limit for acceptance 承诺期限

time limit for accepting administrative cases 行政诉法的受理期限

time limit for adjudication 审判期限

time limit for commencement 起诉期限

time limit for examination and approval 审批期限

time limit for filing claims 索赔时限,索赔期限

time limit for first instance 第一审期限

time limit for handling a case 办案期限

time limit for handling a criminal case 刑事案件办案期限

time limit for performance 履行期限

time limit for reeducation-through-labour 劳动教养期限

time limit for tax payment 纳税期限

time limit of appeal 上诉期限

time limit of claim 索赔期限

time limit of defense 防卫时限

time limit of general average 共同海损时限

time limit of investigation and custody 侦查羁押期限

time limit required for an answer 承诺期限

time limits for submission of claims 提出索赔的时限

time loam 定期放款

time of a crime 犯罪时间

time of arrival 到达时间

time of birth 出生时间

time of death 死亡时间

time of delivery 交付期限

time of effect 有效期间

time of efficiency 有效期限

time of legal memory 法定追溯期

time of payment 付款期

time of performance 履行期限

time of shipment 装船期

time of supervision 监督时间

time of validity of a claim 索赔有效期间

time payment debts 定期偿还的债务

time period for investigation 侦查期限

time periods designated by a people's count 指定期间

time periods prescribed by law 法定期间

time purchase 分期付款购买

time range 时间范围

time risk 时间风险

timely completion 按时竣工

timetable of trains 列车时刻表

time-period concept 期间概念

time-schedule float 预定浮动

time-worn building 旧住房

tire mark 运输工具痕迹,车轮压痕

title 所有权证,所有权

title deed for land 地契

title deed(s) 所有权契据,田契,地契,契约

title defect 所有权瑕疵

title of a case 案件名称

title of administrative case 行政案由

title of honor 荣誉称号

title of possession 所有权

title of punishment 刑名

title retention 所有权保留

title to property 物权所有权

title to the goods 货物所有权

titles of securities 有价证券所有权

titular possession 有权占有

to apply for tax exemption 申请免税

to apply stern sanctions against sb 严厉的制裁

to arrival term 到货条件

"to arrive" contract 目的地交货合同

to be protected from cold 切勿受冷

to be protected from heat 切勿受热

to bear a joint to liability for repayment of a debt 负连带清偿债务责任

to bear civil responsibility 承担民事责任

to bear financial responsibility 承担经济责任

to beaver 交与持票人

to call for tenders 招标

to cancel 退保

to cancel one's registration 注销登记

to carry out autonomous operation and assume sole responsibility for profits or losses 自主经营,自负盈亏

to cavil at the price 驳价

to claim for tax refund 申请退税

to close down 倒闭

to conserve 保全

to cross the border 进出国境

to declare goods for duty 报税

to declare sth at customs 报关

to defraud the revenue 漏税

to discharge poisonous and harmful waster water 排放有害有

毒废水

to do business on one's own account 自营商业

to engage in 经营

to enter and exit or leave the country 进出国境

to evade paying income tax 避付所得税

to evade payment of a tax 漏税

to evade taxation 漏税

to examine 审查

to exceed the competence 在权限以外

to excise 收税

to expand or enlarge the decision-making powers of enterprises 扩大企业自主权

to exploit natural resources 开发自然资源

to falsity accounts 伪造账目

to file one's tax return and pay the tax 报缴税款

to fix a price for sth 作价

to give greater autonomy to enterprises 扩大企业自主权

to honour one's liability 承担赔偿责任

to impose a duty on sb 对某人课税

to impose import tax 征收进口税

to investigate 审查

to issue a drawback 发还退税

to levy a tax 抽税

to levy a tax on sb 对某人课税

to levy charges 收税

to levy heavy tax 课以重税

to levy tax(es) 征收赋税,课税

to make a statement of dutiable goods 报税

to manage 经营

to operate 经营

to order 凭指示,不记名人

to order of 凭某人指示

to order of bank 银行抬头

to pay an overdue tax 补交税款

to pay in advance in quarterly instalment 分季预缴

to pay income tax instead of delivery of profits to the state 利改税

to pay income tax instead of delivery of profits to the state-owned enterprises 国有企业利改税

to pay tax(es) 交纳税款,缴纳税款,缴税,付税,完税

to pay taxes in arrears 补交税款

to price 定价

to punish sb with severity 严厉的惩罚

to pursue the tax payment 追缴税款

to quote 报价

to receive business license 领取营业执照

to receive business license of legal person 领取商业法人营业执照

to recover debts 追偿损失

to refuse to pay tax 抗税

to register to start operation 开业登记

to run 经营

to run at a loss due to poor operation 经营性亏损

to seek private gains through power 以权谋私

to standardize 标准化

to start business registration 企业开业登记

to submit tender 投标

to suspend payment 无力偿债

to the order of the bank 银行指示

to the order of the consignee 收货人指示

to the order of the shipper 有托运人指示

to transit goods 转口货物

to transport 转运

to transship cargo 转运货物

to undertake independent accounting and assume sole responsibility 独立核算, 自负盈亏

to wangle accounts 伪造账目

tobacco monopoly administration 烟草专卖管理

tobacco monopoly commodities 烟草专卖品

tobacco tax 烟草税

toilet bowl 抽水马桶

token money 名义货币

Tokyo trial 东京审判

toll 税收

toll of road 公路税

toll turn 牲畜市场税

tollage 税

tombstone announcement 墓碑式公告

tonnage rent 矿产采掘税

tonnage tax(es) 吨位税

too heavy sentencing 处刑过重

too light sentencing 处刑过轻

tool finishing 机械加工

tool for criminal purpose 作案工具

tool marks 工具痕迹检验样本

top bond 国库债券

top price 高价

topic for discussion 议题

Torquay 英国托基

tort 侵权, 民事侵害, 侵权行为, 侵害方

tort action against government 行政侵权诉讼

tort by anti-dated B/L 倒签提单

tort law 侵权法

tort liability for compensation 侵权行为的赔偿责任

tort liability 侵权赔偿责任, 过错责任

tort liability of a guardian 监护人的债权责任

tort liability of environmental pollution 环境污染的权责任

tort of negligence 疏忽的侵权行为

tortious 侵权行为的

tortious act 侵权行为

① tortious liability 侵权行为性的责任, 侵权行为责任, 侵权责任

④ torture 酷刑, 刑讯

⑤ torture chamber 刑讯室

⑥ total 总额

⑦ total abolition 全部废除

⑧ total absorption 全部吞并

⑨ total amount 总额

⑩ total and uncritical acceptance 全盘接受

⑫ total annexation 全部合并

⑬ total discharge 全部履行

⑭ total export 出口总额

⑮ total in corporation 全部合并

⑯ total investment 总投资

⑰ total loss 全部损失, 全损, 全部损失, 总损失

⑲ total merger 全部合并

⑳ total mobilization 总动员

㉑ total nonperformance of obligation 债的全部不履行

㉓ total payment for honour 全部参加付款

㉕ total price 总价

㉖ total productive capacity 总生产能力

㉘ total quantity 总数量

㉙ total repudiation 全盘否定

㉚ total sum 总额

㉛ total term (of sentences) 总和刑期

㉝ total value involved in a case 案值

㉟ totalitarian state 极权主义国家

㊱ totalitarianism 极权主义

㊲ touch common interest 涉及共同利益

㊴ touch upon 涉及

㊵ tough policy 强硬政策

㊶ tour operator 旅游公司

㊷ tourism 旅游业

㊸ tourist agency 旅行社

㊹ tourist industry 旅游业

㊺ tow and assist 施救

㊻ towage contract 海上拖航合同

㊼ towing contract 拖带契约

town 城镇,镇,集镇,乡镇	**trade investment** 商业投资
town dweller 城镇居民	**trade mark** 商标
town house 城市住宅,城镇住房	**trade mark license contract** 商标许可合同
town people's congress 镇人民代表大会	**trade monopoly** 贸易垄断
town people's government 镇人民政府	**trade names** 商号,厂商名称
town site 城市建设用地	**trade of payment by installments** 分期付款买卖
town tax 城镇税	**trade on spot** 境外贸易
town toll 入市税	**trade pact** 贸易协定
township 乡,乡镇	**trade policy review body** 贸易政策审查机构
township enterprises 乡镇企业	**trade preference** 贸易互惠
township government 乡政府	**trade promotion centre** 贸易促进中心
township people's congress 乡人民代表大会	**trade protection** 贸易保护
township regime 乡政权	**trade protocol** 贸易议定书
toxic pollutant 有毒污染物	**trade regulations** 贸易条例
toxic psychosis 中毒性精神障碍	**trade relation** 贸易关系
trace 追查	**trade safeguarding act trade protecting law** 贸易保护法
trace back to 追溯	
trace expertise 痕迹学鉴定	**trade safe-guarding act** 通商保护法
track down and apprehend criminals 查缉人犯	
track down and arrest 搜捕	**trade secret** 商业秘密
trade 商业	**trade standards** 行业标准
trade act 贸易法(美)	**trade tax** 交易税
trade agreement 贸易协定	**trade terms** 贸易术语或贸易条件
trade agreements act (of the U.S.A.) 美国贸易协定法	
	trade union act (英) 工会法
trade and payments agreement 贸易支付协定	**trade union activities** 工会活动
	trade union federation 工会合会
trade barrier 贸易壁垒	**trade union official** 工会干部
trade by agreement 协定贸易	**trade war** 贸易战
trade by airway 空运贸易	**traded option** 可买卖期权
trade by mail order 邮购贸易	**trademark** 商标
trade by roadway 陆路贸易	**trademark falsely represented as registered** 冒名注册商标
trade by seaway 海路贸易	
trade custom 贸易惯例	**trader** 交易商
trade deficit 贸易逆差	**trader's price** 居间价格
trade description 商品说明	**trader's transaction** 同业交易
trade discount(s) 商业折扣,交易折扣,同业折扣	**trading** 交易
	trading account 贸易账户
trade discrimination 贸易歧视	**trading clause** 航区条款
trade disputes act 商业纠纷法	**trading licence** 营业执照
trade embargo 贸易禁运	**trading market** 流通市场
trade in technology 技术贸易	**trading on equity** 举债经营
	trading partners 商业合伙人

trading risk 经营风险

trading tax 交易税

tradition 传统

tradition of law 法律传统

tradition of law system 法制传统

traditional architecture 传统建筑

traditional ideas 传统观念

traditional ideas of law 传统法律观念

traditional law system 传统法制

traffic 交通,运输

traffic accident 交通事故

traffic control 交通管制

traffic control rules 交通管理法规

traffic in transit 中转运输

traffic in women 贩卖妇女

traffic on inland waters 内河交通

traffic police 交通警

traffic regulations 交通规则

traffic rules 交通规则

traffic safety code 交通安全法规

traffic sign 交通标志

traffic signal 交通信号

traffic violation 交通违章

train safety rules 列车安全规则

train schedule 列车时刻表

training 教育

traitor's property 逆产

tramp 不定期船舶

trample on democracy 摧残民主

transacted price 成交价格

transaction 买空卖空,交易

transaction at buyer's option 由买方选择的交易

transaction cost 交易费用

transaction exposure 交易风险

transaction in security 证券交易

transaction of postal material 邮件的运输

transaction practices 交易习惯

transaction tax 交易税

transaction through agent 代理交易

transaction value 交易价格,成交价格

transaction value of identical goods 相同货物成交价格,同类商品的成交价格

transaction value of similar goods 类似商品成交价格

transaction with credit 信用交易

transactions tax 营业税

transboundary crime 跨境犯罪

transcend 超越

transcript 笔录供词

transcript of an oral confession 口供笔录

transcript on appeal 上诉副本

transfer 出让,转移,转让,让步,让受,划拨

transfer agent 过户代理,转让代理人

transfer clause 转让条款

transfer contract 转让契据

transfer deeds of property right 产权转让契约

transfer discount 转贴现

transfer in transit 运送中的转移

transfer mortgage 转抵押

transfer of a case (to another court at the same level) 案件的移送

transfer of bill of lading 提单的转让

transfer of criminals 罪犯移送

transfer of mortgage 抵押品的转让

transfer of obligations 转移义务

transfer of ownership 所有权转让,所有权过户

transfer of portfolio 未满期责任移转

transfer of possession 占有权转移

transfer of power 权力转让

transfer of property 财产转让

transfer of real right　物权的移转

transfer of resources　资源转移

transfer of rights　权利的转移

transfer of shares　股份转让,股票过户

transfer of the land　土地转让

transfer of the right of action　诉权转移

transfer on a lien　出典

transfer ownership　转移所有权

transfer payment　转让性付款

transfer power to a lower level　权利下放

transfer price　转让价格,调拨价格

transfer pricing　转移定价,调拨定价

transfer property title　转让财产契据

transfer risk　转移险

transfer the ownership　转让所有权

transfer the possession　转移占有

transfer the right　转让权利

transfer through bank　银行划拨

transfer with compensation　有偿转让

transferable　可转让的

transferable L/C　可转让信用证

transferable right　转让权

transferable without restrict　无限制转让

transferee　受让人,受让方

transference　让步,转让,权利转移

transference of debt　债务转移,债务承担

transference of obligation　债的转移

transference of obligatory right and debt　债权债务全部转移

transferor　出让人,让步人,转让人

transferor of technology　技术转让方

transferred malice　恶意转移

transform　转换,改造,改变,改造

transform criminals through reform-through-labour　劳动改造罪犯

transform into an enterprise　企业化

transformation　改造,转换

transformation of capitalist industry and commerce　改造资本主义工商业

transgress　违反

transgress a ban　违禁

transgress one's competence　超越职权范围,超职权范围

transgression　违背道德规范

transgression of the law and neglect of duty　违法失职

transgressor　违犯者

transhipment cargo　转运货物

Transhipment is permitted　准许转运

transient disturbance of consciousness　短暂性意识障碍

transit　过境

transit cargo　过境货物

transit clause　运输条款,转运条款

transit company　中转公司

transit country　过境国

transit declaration　过境报关单,过境报关单

transit depot　转运仓库

transit document　过境单据

transit duties　过境税,中转税,转口税,过境税

transit flight　过境飞行

transit goods　过境货物

transit interest　中转利息

transit letter of credit　转口信用证

transit passage on strait　海峡的过境通行

transit period　转运期

transit permit　过境通行证

transit quarantine　过境检疫

transit shipment 过境转运

transit trade 过境贸易

transit visa 过境签证

transition cabinet 过渡内阁

transition period 过渡时期

transitional government 过渡政府

transitional measure 过渡措施

transitional safeguard 过渡性保障

transitive regime 过渡政权

transmission of shares 股份移转

transnational 超越国家的

transnational agreement 跨国协定

transnational associated enterprise 跨国联属企业

transnational bank 跨国银行

transnational company 跨国公司

transnational contract(s) 跨国契约

transnational currency 跨国货币

transnational enterprise 跨国企业

transnational income from investment 跨国投资款

transnational lease 跨国租赁

transnational operation 跨国经营

transnational related enterprise 跨国关联企业

transparency 透明度原则

transport 装运

transport by air 空运

transport by water 水路运输

transport charge 运输费

transport document 运输单据

transport law 运输法

transport license 运输许可证

transport licensing 运输许可证的颁发,运输许可

transport loss 运输损失

transport management fee 运输管理费

transport of dangerous goods 危险货物运输

transport operation 运输业务

transport rental company 运输租赁公司

transport service 运输业

transport service licence 运输服务许可证

transport tracks 运输工具痕迹

transportation 运输,运输业

transportation capacity 运输能力

transportation document 运输单据

transportation efficiency 运输效益

transportation expense 运费

transportation facility 交通工具

transportation of tobacco product 烟草制品的运输

transportation permit 转运许可证

transship 转运

transshipment B/L 或 through B/L 转船提单或联运提单

transshipment bill of lading 转运提单

transshipment cargo rule 中转货物规则

transshipment entry 转运报单

trauma 创伤

traumatic shock 外伤性休克

travel agency 旅行社,旅游代理处

travel certificate 旅行证

travel service 旅行社

traverse 抗辩

traverse upon a traverse 对反驳的再反驳

traverser 抗辩者

treachery 叛逆

treason 叛逆罪,叛逆

treason and heresy 大逆不道

treasure bill market 国库券市场

treasure trove 埋藏物

treasury attache 财务专员

treasury bill futures contract 国

库期货契约

treasury bonds　国库券,长期债券,国库证券

treasury bonds investment series　投资债券

treasury certificate（美）　国库证券

treasury notes　中期债券

treasury regulation　财政法规

treat　谈判

treaties　一揽子合同

treatment of aliens　外国人待遇

treatment of prisoners of war　战俘待遇

treatment of sick and wounded soldiers　伤病员待遇

treatment on maritime dispute by the port and shipping administration　港航行政机关对海事纠纷的处理

treatment standard　待遇标准

treaty　条约

treaty in simplified form　简式条约

treaty of amity and commerce　友好通商条约

treaty of cession　割让条约

treaty of commerce and navigation　通商航海条约

treaty of confederation　邦联条约

treaty of extradition　引渡条约

treaty of mutual defence　共同防御条约

treaty of Nanking　南京条约（1843 年）

treaty of peace　和平条约

treaty of Versailles　凡尔赛和约

treaty on Antarctica　南极条约

treaty on principles governing the activities of states in the exploration and use of outer space, including the moon and other celestial bodies　关于各国探索和利用包括月球和其他天体在同内的外层空间活动的原则条约(外层空间条约)

treaty on the non-proliferation of Nuclear weapons　核不扩散条约

treaty participant　条约参加国

treaty port　通商口岸

treaty power　约权

treaty procured through fraud　诈欺性条约

treaty tariff　约定关税

treaty wording　合同文本

treble damages　赔偿金

tree farm　林场

tree preservation order　保护树木令

trend　趋势

trend analysis　趋势分析

trend of events　情势

trespass　侵犯

trespass to chattels　侵犯动产

trespass to goods　侵物行为

trespass to person　对人身的侵犯行为

trespass to residence　侵入住宅罪

trespasser of land and property　侵犯私产者

triad　三元体系

trial　听审

trial by battle　决斗裁判

trial by certificate　根据证书的审判

trial by grand assize　大巡回法庭审判

trial by inspection or examination　纠问式审判

trial docket　法院待审案件清单

trial in camera　秘密审讯

trial judge　初审法官

trial jurisdiction　审判管辖,审判管辖权

trial lawyer　诉讼律师

trial mode of second instance　二审审理形式

trial of first instance　初审

trial of second instance　二审

trial on the merits　实体审

trial order　试订单

trial product 试制品

trial sale 试销

trial trade 试验买卖

tribal law 部落法

tribunal 法官席,裁判庭

tribunal de grande instance（法、英）大审法庭

tribunal of conflict 冲突法庭

tribunal of inquiry 调查法庭

tribunal of second hearing 第二审法庭

tribunal of summary jurisdiction 即决裁判庭

trifling loss 轻微损失

trigger price 机动价格,引发价格

trigger price mechanism-TPM 启动价格制

trinity term 三位一体节开庭期（英）

tripartite agreement 三方协定,三方协议

tripartite indenture 三方合同

triple agreement 三方协议

trivial loss 轻微损失

truce negotiations 停战谈判

trucking 货运

true 忠实,真实

true bill 核定诉状

true intention 真实意思

true meaning 真实意义

true price 真正价格

true verdict 公正的裁决

Truman proclamations 杜鲁门公告

trump up 捏造

trump up a charge against sb 捏造罪名

truss up a criminal 捆绑罪犯

trust 信托

trust accounting 信托会计

trust administration（/management）信托管理

trust agreement 信托协定

trust and investment business 信托投资业务

trust and saving's bank 信托储蓄银行

trust assets 信托资产

trust bank 信托银行

trust business 信托业,信托业务

trust certificate 信托证书

trust company 信托公司

trust corporation 信托公司

trust deed(s) 信托契约,信托书,信托契据,信托契

trust deposit 信托保证金,信托金,信托存款

trust for sale 信托售卖

trust for sale of land 土地售卖信托

trust fund ledger 信托基金分类账

trust fund(s) 信托基金

trust indenture 信托契据,信托契

trust inspection 信托检查

trust institution 信托机构

trust instrument 信托文件

trust investment 信托投资

trust law 信托法

trust liabilities 信托负债

trust money 托管金,信托款项

trust obligation 信托合约,信托职责,信托责任

trust or commission clause 信托或代理条款

trust process 信托手续

trust property 信托财产

trust receipt（注：简称 T/R）信托收据

trust revolving fund 信托周转金

trust service 信托服务

trust share certificate 信托股份证

trust stock company 股份信托公司

trust territories 托管领土

trust under agreement 根据协议设立的信托

trustee 受托管理人,保管人

trustee act 信托法例,(美)受托人管理法

trustee bank　信托银行

trustee company　受托公司

trustee for sale　售卖信托人

trustee in bankruptcy　破产管理人

trustee investments　受托人投资

trustee securities　受托人报告

trustee's account　受托人账户

trustee's cash account　托管人现金账户

trusteeship council　托管理事会

trusteeship function　托管人职责

trusteeship management　受托管理制度

trusting to luck　侥幸心理

trustless　不可信任的

trustor　信托人

trustworthy　忠实

trying the case　要因

tub-man（英）财政律师

turbulence　动乱

turmoil　动乱

turn　转手,改变

turn loss into gain　扭亏为盈

turn-key　统包

two civilizations　两个文明

two conceptual system of ownership in the civil law　民法上的所有权制度

two different kinds of contradictions　两类不同性质的矛盾

two family duplex　独立双户住宅

two laws opposition　两法相反

two parties　双方当事人

two texts being equally authentic　两种文字具有同等效力

two thirds majority　三分之二多数

two thirds majority rule　三分之二多数制

tying clause　搭售条款

tying contract　搭售合同,附条件合同

type　样式

type of business　企业类型

type of business organization　企业组织类型

type of contract　契约种类

type of evidence for criminal procedure　刑事诉讼证据的种类

type of operation　经营方式

type of punishments　刑罚类型

type of victims　被害人类型

type of volitional unstableness　意志不稳定型

types of constitution　宪法类型

types of evidence　证据的种类

types of law　法的类型

typical　代表性的

typical case　典型案件

typical model　典型模式

typical-case investigation　典型调查

tyrannical　暴虐

tyrannical government　虐政

tyrannism　虐待狂

tyrannize　虐待

tyranny　暴行,暴政,苛政

tyranny in conviction and sentencing　罪刑擅断主义

tyranny of the majority　多数暴政

tyrant　暴君

U

uberrima fides（拉） 最大善意，出于至诚

ubi jus, ibi officium（拉） 有权利即有义务

ubi jus, ibi remedium（拉） 有权利就有补救办法

ubi remedium ibi jus 有补偿便是有权利

ubicunque est injuria, ibi damnum sequitur（拉） 有侵权必有损害

ubiquity 普遍存在

ugly 丑恶

ulterior destination 最后目的地

ultimate 根本

ultimate consignee 最终收货人

ultimate consumer 最终消费者

ultimate destination 最终目的地

ultimate facts 最终受理的事实

ultimate liability 最终责任，主要责任

ultimate purchaser 最终购买者

ultimate risk for audit 审计的最大风险

ultimate rule of recognition 最终承认规则

ultimatum 最后通牒

ultimum supplicium（拉） 极刑

ultra damages 额外损害赔偿

ultra licitum（拉） 超过合法范围的

ultra vires 越权

ultra vires act 越权行为

ultra vires agency 越权代理

ultra vires doctrine 越权原则

umbrella articles 总括条款

umbrella project 大型项目

umpirage 裁决书

umpire 裁决，裁判，裁判官

umpire（the third arbitrator） 裁决人

unacceptable 不可接受的，不能接受的，无法接受的

unaccountable 无责任的

unadvent 无意识

unalienable 不可转让的

unallocated quotas 全球配额

unanimity 全体一致

unanimity rule of five great powers 五大国一致原则

unanimous 一致的

unanimous ballot 一致投票

unanimous vote 一致表决

unanswerable 无责任的

unapproved 未批准的

unascertained goods 未确定货物，不确定物，未经确定之货物，未确定的货物，非特定物

unauthorized 未授权，未经许可

unauthorized agency 无权代理

unauthorized broadcasting from the high seas 公海上的非法广播

unauthorized carving of an official seal 私刻公章

unauthorized construction 违章建筑

unauthorized representation 未经授权的代理

unavoidable 不可避免的，不能避免

unavoidable accident 不可避免的意外

unavoidable cause 不可避免的原因

unavoidable delay 不可避免的延迟

unavoidable risk 不可避免的风险，不可避免的延迟

unaware 无意的

unbinding engagement 无约束力

unbridled competition 盲目竞争

uncertain 不明确的，不确定的

uncertain interest 不确定的权益

uncertain limitation of time 不确定期限

uncertain nationality 国籍不明

uncertainty 不明确,不确定性

uncertainty condition 不确定条件

uncivilized 野蛮

unclaimed 无人认领的,无人领取的,未要求索赔的

unclaimed cargo 无人领取的货物

unclaimed property 无主物

unclean (/foul) bill of lading 不清洁提单

unclean B/L 或 Foul B/L 不清洁提单

unclear 不能补偿的,不明确的

uncleared 未签署的

uncommitted 不负义务的,未受委托的

uncommitted contract 不受约束的合同

uncompleted 未完成的

uncompleted contract 未完成契约,未完成合同

uncomplicated 简单的

unconditional 无条件的

unconditional acceptance 无条件承诺

unconditional delivery 无条件交付

unconditional equality 无条件平等

unconditional guaranty 不附条件保证

unconditional interpretation 无条件解释

unconditional obligation 无条件义务

unconditional promise 无条件允诺

unconditional surrender 无条件投降

unconfirmed L/C 不保兑信用证

unconscionable 不合理的

unconscionable award 不合理的裁决

unconscionable bargain 违背良心的契约,违背良心的合同,不公平合同,不合理的合同

unconscionable contract 极不公平的合同

unconscionable judicial decision 不当判决

unconscious 无意识

unconscious negligent 无认识的过失

unconsciousability 不合理

unconstitutional 违宪的

unconstitutional act 违宪行为,违宪的法令

unconstitutional law 违宪的法律

unconstitutional ordinance 违宪的法令

unconstitutional party 违宪政党

unconstitutional presumption 违宪性推定

unconstitutional ratification 违宪批准

unconstitutional statute 违宪制定法

unconstitutional treaty 违宪条约

uncontrollable impulse 难压制的刺激

uncontrolled price 非控制价格

uncover 无担保,无抵押品

uncovered 无担保的,无抵押品的

UNCTAD 联合国贸易与发展会议

uncultivated land 未开垦土地,荒地

undecided 未定

undeclared war 不宣而战

undefined 未定的,不明确的

undeliverable 无法交付的,无法投递的

under a legal incapacity 缺乏法律上的行为能力

under collective ownership 集体所有

under conditions　下列情形

under duress　在胁迫之下

under emergency conditions　在紧急需要的情况下

under fair and just terms　在公平合理的条件下

under his hand and seal　由他原名盖印

under insurance　不足额保险

under my hand and seal　由本人签名盖章

under normal circumstances　依通常情形

under offer　在出售中

under one's hand and seal　签名盖章,亲笔签名

under par　折价发行

under pricing　定价偏低

under proper conditions　在适当条件下

under repair　在修理中

under seal　加封

under shipment　在装运中

under some incapacity　缺乏行为能力

under surveillance　监视居住决定书

under taxation　征税过低

under test　在试验中

under the condition　在某种条件下

under the existing condition　在目前条件下

under the guise of legitimate acts　合法形式下

under the name of/in the name of　用…名义

under the premise　在某种条件下

under the pretext of his official power　假借职权

under the prevailing condition　在目前条件下

under the principle of...　在…原则下

under the terms of the contract　依合同要求

under unified management　共同管理

under unified use　共同使用

under way　在途中

underground mining method　地下开采法

underground organization　秘密组织

underground parking　地下停车场

underground water resources　地下水资源

underleesee　重承担人

underlying and fundamental fact　基本事实

underlying contract　基础合同

underlying lien　第一置管权

underlying mortgage　第一抵押,第一担保,优先抵押

underlying right　原属权利

underprivileged　没有基本社会权利的

underpunishment　重罪轻判

understanding on rules and procedures governing the settlement of disputes　关于争端处理规则和程序谅解

undertake　承担,保证,承办

undertake the responsibility　承担责任

undertake to do　承诺

undertaking　事业单位,义务承担

undertaking for profit　营利企业

underweight　重量不足

underwrite　承销,承购行为

underwriter　证券承购人,承购商,证券经纪人,证券经销人,承销人

underwriting agreement　承购协议,证券包销协议

underwriting group　证券包销集团,承销集团

underwriting syndicate　证券经销辛迪加,承销辛迪加,包销集团

undetermined intention　不确定

故意

undeveloped area 未开发地区

undeveloped estate 未开发的土地

undisclosed agency 不披露的代理方法

undisclosed factor 隐名代办人

undisclosed factoring 隐名代办

undisclosed information 未披露信息

undisclosed principal 不公开的本人,未公开的委托人,不公开身份的本人,(英美)未被披露的本人,隐名委托人

undiscovered loss 未发觉的损失,未发觉损失

undiscovered loss clause 未发现损失条款

undistributed profit 未分配利润

undivided 不可分割

undivided co-ownership (美) 共同共有

undivided matter 不可分物

undivided responsibility 单独承担的责任

undivided shares 未分割的份额

undue 未到期的,不当的

undue delay 不应有的延误

undue enrichment 不当得利

undue harm 不必要的损失,不应有损害

undue influence 不正当影响

undue judgment 不当的判决,不当判决

undue punishment 不当的处罚,罚不当罪

unearned increment tax 土地增值税

unearned premium reserve 未到期责任准备金

unearthed relics 出土文物

unemployed workers' department act (英) 失业工人家属暂定法

unemployment benefit 失业救济

unemployment compensation system 失业救济制度

unemployment insurance 待业保险

unemployment register 待业登记

unemployment relief 待业救济金

unemployment workman act (英) 失业劳动者法

unencumbered property 无债权财产

unequal 不公平的

unequal election 不公平选举

unequal exchange 不等价交换

unequal treaty 不平等条约

unerring 无过失的

unexecuted 未根据条款履行的,未实行的

unexpected 意外的

unexpected accident 意外事故

unexpected crime 突发性犯罪

unexpected hindrance 意外障碍

unexpected obstacle 意外障碍

unfair 不当的,不公平的

unfair advantage 不当得利

unfair competition 不公平竞争,不合理竞争,非公平竞争,不正当竞争

unfair consumer goods practices 不公平消费品贸易惯例

unfair contract terms act 不公平合同条款法 1977 (英)

unfair hearing 不公平审理

unfair means of competition 不正当竞争

unfair practices in competition 不正当竞争

unfair price 不合理价格

unfair trade practice(s) 不公正的商业做法,不正当商业行为

unfair trial 不公平审理

unfair verdict 不公正裁决,不当的裁决

unfettering of discretionary power 无拘束的自由裁量权

unfilled orders 未发货订单

unfinished 粗糙的

unfixed lease 不定期租贷

unforeseeable 不能预见的,不可预见的

unforeseen 意外的,不能预见的

unforeseen event 不能预见的事件

unforeseen expense 不能预见费用

unforeseen loss 不能预见的损失

unfounded 没有根据的

unfounded accusation of informers 检察失实

unhealthy dwelling place 不良居住环境

unicameral system 一院制

unidentified goods 未特定化的货物

unidirectional 单行的

unification 一体化

unification of law 法律的统一

unification of rules 统一规则

unified budget 统一预算

unified foreign trade system 统一的对外贸易制度

unified joint economic legal relation 统一连带经济法律关系

unified judicial supervision 统一的司法监督

unified leadership 统一领导

unified management 统一管理

unified purchase and sale 统购包销

unified state control 国家统一管理

uniform 一致

uniform accounting system 统一会计制度

uniform bill of landing act 统一载货法

uniform commercial code (VCC) 美国统一商法典

uniform conditional sales act (美) 统一附条件买卖法

uniform conditions 同样条件,相同条件

uniform crime report 统一犯罪报告

① uniform custom 统一惯例

② uniform customs and practice for documentary credit 跟单信用证统一惯例

⑤ uniform expert evidence act 鉴定证据统一法

⑦ uniform general charter 统一杂货租船合同,标准杂货租船合同

⑩ uniform interpretation 统一解释

⑫ uniform law 统一法规

⑬ uniform level of liability 统一责任标准

⑮ uniform liability system 统一责任制

⑰ uniform monetary limitation of liability rule 统一赔偿责任限额规则

⑳ uniform negotiable instruments act (美) 统一流通证券法,统一票据法

㉓ uniform partnership act (美) 统一合伙法

㉕ uniform price 统一价格

㉖ uniform price set by the state 国家统一定价

㉘ uniform product liability law 统一产品责任法

㉚ uniform rules for collections 托收统一规则

㉜ uniform safety standards 统一安全标准

㉞ uniform sales act 统一买卖法

㉟ uniform sales law 统一销售法

㊱ uniform system of liability 统一责任制

㊳ uniform time charter 统一定期租船合同

㊵ uniform trust receipts act (美) 统一信托收据法

㊷ uniformity 一致性

㊸ uniformity and dignity 统一和尊严

㊺ uniformity of law 法律的统一性

㊼ unilateral 片面的,单方面的

unilateral abrogation 单方面废除

unilateral act 单方行为

unilateral action 单方行为,单边行为

unilateral administrative act 单方行政行为

unilateral agreement 单边协定,单方面承担义务的协议

unilateral character of administrative act 行政行为的单方性

unilateral conflict rules 单边冲突规范

unilateral contract 单方合同,单方契约,单边契约

unilateral declaration 单方宣言

unilateral denunciation 单方废除

unilateral denunciation of treaty 单方面废约

unilateral discharge 单方向的解除

unilateral importation 单边进口

unilateral international legal act 单方国际法律行为

unilateral interpretation 片面解释

unilateral mistake 单方错误

unilateral notice 单方通知

unilateral obligation 单方面的义务

unilateral preliminary agreement 片面预约,单方草约

unilateral price 单一价格

unilateral repudiation of debt 单方面不履行债务

unilateral requirements 单方要件

unilateral restitution 单方返还

unilateral stipulation 片面规定

unilateral termination 单方终止

unilateral transfers 单方转让

unimpeachable 无过失的,无缺陷的

unin cooporated private enterprise 非公司私营企业

unincooporated 未组成法人的

uninhabitable 不能居住的

unintentional 无意的

union 联邦

union dues 工会会费

union member 工会会员

union mortgage clause 标准抵押条款

union organization 工会组织

union representative 工会代表

unit 单位,基层单位

unit design 单元设计

unit furniture 成套家具

unit in charge of construction 施工单位

unit in operation 经营单位

unit limitation of liability 单位责任限制

unit of measurement 计量单位

unit of plan 计划单位

unit of possession 恢复占有金

unit of restitution 恢复物权令

unit owned by the whole people 全民所有制单位

unit price 单价,单位价格

unit price contract 单价合同,单价契约

unit rent 单元租金

unit system 成套灶具

unit under auditing 被审计单位

unit under collective ownership 集体所有制单位

unit under ownership by the whole people 全民所有制单位

unit undertaking projects 建设单位

unit value index 单价指数

unitary 不可分割

unitary constitution 单一宪法

unitary criminal law 单一刑法

unitary exchange rate 单一汇率

unitary government 单一制政府

unitary head of state 个体元首,单一元首

unitary legal system 单一法律体系

unitary multinational state 统一的多民族国家

unitary state 单一国,单一制国家

unitary system 单一制

unite rule 单元选举制

united front 统一战线

United Nations administrative tribunal 联合国行政法庭

United Nations commission on human rights 联合国人权委员会

United Nations conference on trade and development (UNCTAD) 贸易与发展会议,联合国贸易和发展会议

United Nations convention on international multimodel transport of good (1980) 联合国（国际货物）多式联运公约（1980）

United Nations convention on the carriage of goods by sea, 1978 联合国海上货物运输公约（1978）

United Nations convention on the law of the sea (1982) (1982年)联合国海洋法公约

United Nations convention on the special mission 联合国特别使团公约

United Nations declaration 联合国家宣言

United Nations declaration of the human environment 联合国人类环境会议宣言

United Nations draft for international code of conduct on the transfer of technology 联合国国际技术转让行动守则（草案）

United Nations educational, scientific and cultural oriantation 联合国教育、科学及文化组织

United Nations environment fund 联合国环境基金

United Nations environment programme 联合国环境规划署

United Nations flag 联合国旗帜

United Nations forces 联合国部队

United Nations peace keeping forces 联合国维持和平部队

United Nations peace-keeping operation 联合国维持和平行动

United Nations standards international trade classification 国际贸易标准分类

United Nations' day 联合国日

United Nations conference on the law of the sea 联合国海洋法会议

United State code supplement 美国法典补编

United States arbitration act (USAA) 美国仲裁法

United States attorney 联邦律师

United States circuit court (USCC) 美国巡回法庭

United States circuit court of appeals (USSCA) 美国巡回上诉法院

United States citizens rights association (USCRA) 美国公民权利协会

United States code (U.S.C) 美国法典（1926）

United States code annotated (U.S.C.A) 美国法典注释

United States congress (U.S.C) 美国国会

United States court of appeals 美国联邦上诉法院

United States court of claims 美国联邦索赔法院

United States court of customs and patent appeals 美国关税及专利权上诉法院

United States customs court (USCC) 美国关税法院

United States district courts 美国联邦地区法院

United States tax court 美国联邦税务法院

United States treasury regulations 美国财政条例

unitized cargo 单位货物
unitized shipment 单位代运输
unity of the nationalities 民族团结
unity property system 统一财产制
unity state 统一国家
universal 普遍
universal adult franchise 成年人普选权
universal agent 全权代理人
universal copyright convention 世界版权公约
universal declaration of human rights 世界人权宣言
universal election 大选
universal jurisdiction 普遍管辖权,普遍性管辖
universal law 普遍规律,世界法
universal legal order 普遍的法律秩序
universal malice 不确定的信息
universal postal union 万国邮政联盟
universal property 概括财产
universal respect for and observance of human rights 普遍尊重和遵守人权
universal succession 全面继承
universal suffrage 普遍选举,普选制
universal truth 普遍真理
universality 普遍性
universality of human rights 人权的普遍性
universally accepted principle 普遍承认的原则
university court (英) 大学法庭,大学法院
unjust 不公平的,不当
unjust acquittal 不当的释放,不公正的判决
unjust arrest 不当的逮捕
unjust case 冤假错案
unjust enrichment 不正当获利,不当得利
unjust judge 不公正的法官

① unjust sentence 不当的判决,不当判决,不公正地宣判无罪释放
④ unjustifiable self-defense 防卫过当
⑥ unjustified 不当
⑦ unjustified benefit 不当得利
⑧ unjustified financial levies 乱摊派
⑩ unjustified fines 乱罚款
⑪ unknown clause "不知"条款
⑫ unlandful possession of cultivated land 乱占耕地
⑭ unlawful 不合法的,违章的,非法的,不法的
⑯ unlawful act 违法行为,不法行为
⑱ unlawful act in taxation 税收违法行为
⑳ unlawful activities 非法活动,不法活动
㉒ unlawful assembly 非法集会
㉓ unlawful attack 不法侵害
㉔ unlawful deprivation or restriction 非法剥夺或限制
㉖ unlawful detention 非法拘留,不法拘留
㉘ unlawful human experimentation 非法人体试验罪
㉚ unlawful infringement 不法侵害
㉛ unlawful interest(s) 非法权益
㉜ unlawful interference 非法干预,不法干预
㉞ unlawful intrusion 非法侵入
㉟ unlawful practice in taxation 税收违法行为
㊲ unlawful punishment 非法处罚
㊳ unlawful regime 非法政权
㊴ unlawful restraint of another person's liberty 非法限制他人人身自由
㊷ unlawful search of the person of a citizen 非法搜查公民的身体
㊹ Unlawful search of the person of citizens is prohibited 禁止非法搜查公民的身体
㊼ unlawful seizure 非法劫持

unlawful trading　非法交易

unlawful trust　不合法的信托

unlawful use of weapons　非法使用武器

unlawful wounding　不法伤害

unlawfully intrude into the residence of another person　非法侵入他人住宅

unless the law stipulated otherwise　除法律另有规定者外

unlimited amount guarantee　非限额保证

unlimited damages　未限定的违约损害赔偿金

unlimited duration　无限期

unlimited duration guarantee　非定期保证

unlimited flexibility　无限制浮动

unlimited full powers　无限全权

unlimited guarantee　无限担保,无限额担保函,无限额担保函

unlimited mortgage　无限抵押

unlimited partnership　无限合伙,普通合伙

unlimited transhipment　无限制性转运

unlimited warranty　无限责任担保

unliquidated　未清偿的,未偿还的,未清算的

unliquidated debt(s)　未清偿债务

unliquidated obligation　未经付款的债务

unliquidated obligations　未偿债务

unload　倾销

unloading breaking bulk　卸货

unloading charge　卸货费

unloading point　卸货地点

unloading port　卸货港

unloading unit　卸货单位

unmake law　取消法律

unnatural　违背人道的

unnatural crimes　违背自然罪

unnatural offender　兽奸犯,鸡奸犯

① unnaturalized　没有公民权的

② unnecessary delays　不必要的迟延

③ unnecessary restrictions　不必要的限制

⑥ unoccupied house　无人住的房子

⑧ unofficial interpretation　非正式解释

⑩ unowned　无主的

⑪ unpaid　未付的,未偿付的

⑫ unpaid balance　未付差额

⑬ unpaid expense　未付费用

⑭ unpaid seller　未收到货款的卖方

⑯ unplanned investment project　计划外投资项目

⑱ unpredictable behavior　不可预测行为

⑳ unpredictable event　不可预测事件

㉒ unpredictable factor　不可预测的因素

㉔ unprofessional operation　违章操作

㉖ unprofitable　无益

㉗ unpunished　没有受到惩罚的

㉘ unqualified　不合格的

㉚ unqualified acceptance　无条件接受

㉜ unqualified measuring instrument　不合格的计量器具

㉝ unqualified party　不合格当事人

㉞ unratified　未批准的

㉟ unrealized offense　不能犯

㊱ unreasonable　不合理的

㊲ unreasonable action　不合理行为

㊳ unreasonable charge　不合理的搜查

㊵ unreasonable danger　不合理的风险

㊷ unreasonable delay　无理拖延

㊸ unreasonable demands　无理要求

㊺ unreasonable price　不合理价格

㊻ unrecorded　未登记的

㊼ unregistered　未登记的

unregistered land 未登记的土地

unregistered shares 无记名股票

unrepealed contract 有效合同

unreserved acceptance 无保留接受

unrestricted random sampling 无限制任意抽样法

unsafe building 不安全建筑,危房

unsafe condition 不安全条件

unsaleable product 没有销路的产品

unsatisfactory product 不合格产品

unscheduled call 意外停泊

unsecured 无担保的,没有担保的

unsecured credit 无担保债权

unsecured creditor 无保证债权人,无担保债权人

unsecured liability 无担保负债

unsecured loan 无担保负债

unsentenced prisoner 待决犯

unsettled 未偿付的,未偿付的

unsigned 未签名的,未签署的

unsolicited offer 主动报价

unsound 有瑕疵的

unstamped 未盖戳的

unsuccessful party 败诉方

unsuitable packing 包装不当

unsystematic risk 可避免的风险

untenable 不能成立的

until further notice 在另行通知以前

untimely emergency measure 避险不适时

untimely prevention of imminent peril 避险不适时

untimely recognition 不适时的承认

unused land tax 土地闲置税

unusual 非常的

unusual time 非常时期

unvalued insurance 不定值保险

unvalued policy 不定值保单

unwanted house 不合适的房子

unwarranted 莫须有的,未经保证的

unwarranted charge 莫须有的罪名

unwarranted claim 无担保债权

unwarranted intervention 不当干预

unwritten constitution 不成文宪法

unwritten convention 不成文惯例

unwritten law 不成文法

unwritten rule 不成文规则

update 现代化

upheaval 动乱

uphold 维护

uphold a verdict 确认陪审团的裁决

uphold national unity and territorial integrity 维护国家的统一和领土的完整

uphold the principle that all men are equal before the law 维护法律面前人人平等的原则

upholsterer 室内装修工,室内装潢商

upholstery 室内装潢业

upon nomination by sb 根据…的提名

upon the spot 用现货

upper house 上议院

upright and honest law enforcement 廉正执法

upset price 最低价格,最低拍卖限价,底价,开盘价格,拍卖底价

upstream 上游

urban and rural individual industrial and commercial household income tax 城乡个体工商户所行税

urban area 城区

urban conservation 城市保护

urban construction 城建

urban construction and environmental protection 城市建设和环境保护

urban construction license 城市建设许可证

urban crime rate 市区犯罪率

urban design 城市设计

urban drift 城市人口流向

urban dweller 城市居民

urban fringe 城市边缘居住区

urban growth 城市扩展

urban infrastructure 城市基础设施,城市设施

urban inhabitant 城市居民

urban land utilization 城市土地利用

urban maintenance & construction tax 城市维护建设税

urban network 城市网络

urban planning 城市规划

urban planning law 城市规划法

urban pollutant 城市污染物

urban problem 城市问题

urban redevelopment 城市重建,城市改建

urban residential land 城市住宅用地

urban residential trial quarter 城市住宅试验小区

urban residents' committee 居民调解委员会

urban road network 城市道路网络

urban unemployment rate 城镇失业率

urbanism 城市居民生活方式

urbanite 城市居民

urbanization 城市化

urge 促使

urgency 迫切性

urgency order 紧急拘禁令

urgent emergent 紧急

urgent motion 紧急动议

urgent order 紧急命令

urgently needed articles 急需物品

Uruguay Round 乌拉圭回合

U. S. court of appeal （USCA） 美国上诉法院

U.S. court of claims 美国求偿法院

U. S. court of international Trade 美国联邦国际贸易法院

U. S. department of commerce 美国商务部

U. S. federal civil justice reform law of 1979 美国联邦民事司法改革法(1979)

U. S. federal communication act 美国联邦交通法

U. S. federal constitution 美国宪法

U. S. federal judicial centre 美国联邦司法中心

U. S. federal magistrate 美国联邦行政司法官

U. S. federal register act 美国联邦登记法

U. S. federal rules of appeal procedure 美国联邦上诉程序规则

U. S. federal rules of civil procedure 美国联邦民事诉讼规则

U. S. federal rules of criminal procedure 美国联邦刑事诉讼规则

U. S. federal trade commission （FTC） 美国联邦通商委员会

U.S. reports 美国判例汇编

U.S. senate （USS） 美国参议院

U.S. statutes at large 美国法律汇编

U.S. taiwan relations act 美国对台湾关系法

usable floor area 使用面积

usage 用途

usage of the particular trade 特定商业习惯

usage of trade 贸易惯例

use 用途

use and occupation 使用和占用

use classes 使用类别

use land to guarantee an obligation 以土地担保债务

use of quality controls 使用质量控制方法的限制

use of undue authority 滥用权

利

use permit 使用证

use power 行使权力

use public office for private gain 假公济私

use the right of beneficial use of a thing 用益权

use the threat of violence 以暴力相威胁

use torture to coerce a statement 刑讯逼供

use upon a use 用益权上的用益权

use without compensation 无偿使用

used house 旧房

useful life 使用寿命,使用年限

usefulness 效用

useless 无益的

user 受益权人,用益权人

user contracting party 使用者缔约方

usual conditions 通常条件

usual covenants 习惯规约

usual meaning 通常意义

usual packing 惯常包装

① **usual residence** 惯常居所

② **usucaptio**(拉) 凭时效取得财产权

④ **usurer** 高利贷者

⑤ **usurp** 篡权

⑥ **usurp decision-making by a few men** 由少数人擅自决定

⑧ **usurp the throne** 篡位

⑨ **usurpation** 篡权

⑩ **usurper** 篡权者

⑪ **usury** 高利贷业,高利贷,暴利罪

⑬ **ut most limit** 最大限额

⑭ **uti frui**(拉) 对物的用益权

⑮ **utilitarian crimes** 功利性犯罪

⑯ **utilization of a loan** 贷款使用,使用贷款

⑱ **utilization of land** 土地的利用

⑲ **utilization of losses to avoid tax** 利用亏损逃税

㉑ **utilize resources rationally** 合理利用资源

㉓ **utmost good faith** 最大诚信

㉔ **utmost limit** 最高限额

㉕ **utopian socialism** 空想社会主义

㉖ **utter bar** 外席法庭(英)

V

vacancy 缺额,空房
vacancy of succession 无人继承
vacant 无继承人的
vacant land tax 土地闲置税
vacant succession 无人继承
vacate 使无效,取消,让出房屋（或场地）
vacation 法院休庭期
vacation of the premises 搬出房屋
vades 抵押
vadium （拉）以财产抵押作担保,典权
vadium mortuum（拉）典权
vadium vivium（拉）质权
vagabond offender 流窜犯
vagabond to commit crimes 流窜作案
valid 有效的,有效
valid act 有效行为
valid contract 有效合同
valid entry and exit certificate 有效出境入境证件
valid entry certificate 有效入境证件
valid guaranty 有效担保
valid law 有效的法律
valid period 有效期限
validate 使生效,使有法律效力
validated license 有效许可证
validity 有效性
validity in terms of person 人的效力
validity in terms of time 时间效力
validity of audit evidence 审计证据的有效性
validity of basic law 基本法效力
validity of civil law 民法效力
validity of civil procedure law 民事诉讼法效力
validity of contract 合同效力

validity of court mediation 法院调解效力
validity of criminal law 刑法效力
validity of criminal procedure law 刑事诉讼法的效力
validity of law 法律效力
validity of tender 投标有效期
validity of treaty 条约效力
valuable (/negotiable) securities 有价证券
valuable (/negotiable) securities trust 有价证券信托
valuable cargo 高价货物
valuable consideration 有价格的报酬,有价约因,有值对价
valuable goods 高价货物
valuable documents (/papers) 有价证券
valuable historical relics 珍贵文物
valuation 计价
valuation at cost 按成本计价
valuation of goods 货物估价
valuation of work in process 在建工程估价
valuator 价格核定人
value added tax 增值税
value added tax unpaid 完税后交货,增值税未付
value in collections 托收价值
value in pledge 抵押品价值
value of constitution 宪法价值
value of foreign trade 对外贸易额
value of international trade 国际贸易价格
value of sales of goods 货物销售价值
value of tax （计）课税价格
value securities 有价证券
valued insurance 定值保险
value-added criterion 增值标准

（指确认原产地）

van 搬运车

vanquished country 战败国

variable budget 变动预算

variable import levy 差价关税，非固定进口税

variable levy 差价税，差额税，差额税率

variation 差额

variation from the order 与订单不符

variation in packing 包装不符

variation in prices 价格不符

variation margin 价格变动保证金

variation of contract 合同的变更

variation order 变更设计文件

various economic sectors coexist 多种经济成分并存

vas（拉）抵押

vassal state 附庸国

vault 储藏室，地下室

vector of infection 传染媒介

vegetution of grassland 草原植被

vehicle and vessel license and plate tax 车船使用牌照税

vehicle and vessel usage tax 车船使用税

vehicle purchase surcharge 车辆购置附加费

venal practices 贿赂行为

vender 叫卖商

vent 出烟道

venture 代销货

venture capital 投入资本，投资资本

venture of competition 竞争风险

ventures with overseas Chinese investment 侨资企业

verbal complaint 口头起诉

verbal confession 口供

verbal contract 口头契约

verbal evidence 言词证据

verbal promise 口头承诺

verbal stipulations 口头约定

verbal summons 口头传唤

verbal understanding 口头协议

verbatim record 逐字记录

verdict of guilty （陪审团）的有罪裁决

verdict of not guilty （陪审团）的无罪裁决

verification 鉴定

verification of a contract 合同鉴证

verification of degree of disability 劳动能力丧失程度鉴定

verification of documents 档案鉴定

verification of the person 人身检查

verification of traces 痕迹检验

Versailles peace treaty 凡尔赛和约

version 修改

versus（拉）与…相对

vertical accomplice 纵向共犯

vertical cartel 纵向卡特尔

vertical integration 纵向合并，垂直一体化，纵向联合

very complicated 错综交杂

very weak in the understanding of law 法制观念薄弱

vessel flag nation 船旗国

vessels flying flags of convenience 方便旗船

vest 授权

vest to 赋予

vested capital 投入资本

vested in interest 将来可得的权利，将来可行的利益

vested in possession 现有的占有权

vested interest 归序权益，既得权益

vested interest acquired right 既得利益

vested interests 利益集团

vestibule 门厅

vestiges of the ideology of the feudal age 封建时代思想残余

vesting assent　授权认可

vesting deed　授权契据,授予契据

vesting instrument　授权证书

vesting of right　授予权利

vesting order　财产转移令

veto　否决,禁止

veto bill　否决议案

veto power　否决权

vexatious action　滥用诉讼,滥用的诉讼

vicarious liability　替代责任,转承责任

vicarious performance　替代履行,转承履行,替代偿付

vicarious punishment　替受惩罚

vicarious responsibility　转承责任,转嫁责任

vice　瑕疵,恶习

vice-chairman　副主任委员,副主席

vice-chairperson　副主席

vice-chairwoman　副主席

vice-chancellor　副大法官(英)

vice-consul　副领事

vice-mayor　副市长

vice-minister　副部长

vice-of constitution　宪法的瑕疵

vice-premier　副总理

vice-premier of the State Council　国务院副总理

vice-president　副院长,副主席

vice-president of the People's Republic of China　中华人民共和国副主席

viceroy　总督

vicinity　周围地区

vicious circle　恶性循环

vicious crime　恶性犯罪

vicious power　恶势力

vicious transformation of criminal motives　犯罪动机的恶性转化

victim　受害人

victim compensation　被害人的赔偿

victimize　契纸

vie with one another to raise prices　竞相提价

Vienna convention on consular relations　维也纳领事关系公约

Vienna convention on succession of states in respect of state property archives and debts　关于国家在国家财产、档案和债务方面继承的维也纳公约

Vienna convention on succession of states in respect of treaties　关于国家在条约方面继承的维也纳公约

Vienna convention on the law of treaties　维也纳条约法公约

vile　丑恶

vile social evils　丑恶现象

villa　别墅

village　村庄

village agricultural production cooperative　村农业生产合作社

village enterprises　村办企业

village fairs　集市贸易

villagers' committee　村民委员会

villages and small towns　村镇

villages committees　村民委员会

villain　农奴

villainy　恶行

violate　违反,违背,触犯,违犯

violate (a law) knowingly and willfully　明知故犯

violate a ban　违禁,犯禁

violate a principle　违背原则

violate a prohibition　冒犯禁令,违禁

violate a regulation　违章

violate contract　违约,违反合同

violate discipline　违反纪律

violate law　侵犯法律

violate lawful rights　侵犯合法权利

violate rules and regulations　违反规章制度,违章

violate the criminal law　触犯刑律

violate the law　犯法,触犯法律

violate the provisions 违反规定

violating party 违犯一方

violation of constitution 违宪

violation of contract 违约行为

violation of human rights 侵犯人权

violation of law of administrative procedure 行政程序违法

violation of legal procedure 违反法定程序

Violation of the freedom of marriage is prohibited 禁止破坏婚姻自由

violation of regulations 违章

violations against decrees on public order 违反治安管理禁令

violations against duties of the armymen 违反军人职责行为

violations against public order control 违反治安管理行为

violations against traffic control 违反交通管理行为

violations of law to authorities 检举权

violator 违犯者

violent accident 意外事故

violent behaviour 暴力行为

violent criminal 暴力犯罪分子,强暴性罪犯

violent death 暴力死亡

violent offense 暴力犯罪,暴力犯

virtual acceptance 事实上的接受,事实上的承诺

virtute officii (拉) 依据职权

virus control measures 病毒控制办法

visa 签证,加签

visa application 签证申请书

visa office 签证机关

visible parties to crime 有形共犯

visible trade 有形贸易

visible trend 明显趋势

vision-light door 带观察窗的门

visit by a deputy 委员视察

visitiation 临检

visual inspection 外观检验

vital change of circumstances 情况重大变迁

vital interests 重大利益,切身利益

vocational education 职业教育

vocational education law 职业教育法

void 无效,失效,使无效

void ab initio (拉) 自始无效

void act 无效民事行为,无效行为,无效法律行为

void after the fact 事后无效

void and of no effect 无效力

void before the fact 事前无效,自始无效,当始无效

void contract 无效合同

void in part 一部无效,部分无效

void in whole 全部无效

void law 无效的法律

void trust 无效信托

voidable 可撤销的

voidable contract 可撤销合同,可归无效的合同,可作废合同

voidable title 可归无效的物权

voidance of contract 合同的废除

voidance of election 当选无效

volatile deposit 易变性存款

volenti non fit injuria (拉) 对同意者不构成侵害

volume discount 数量折扣

volume of total investment 投资总规模

voluntary 自愿,无偿的,任意

voluntary abandonment 自愿中止

voluntary agency 任意代理

voluntary assignment 自愿让与

voluntary association 自由意志的团体

voluntary auction 任意性拍卖

voluntary bankruptcy 自行申请破产,自愿破产

voluntary conveyance 任意让步,无偿让与,自愿让与,无偿

转让

voluntary domicile 意定住所,任意住所

voluntary export quotas 自动出口配额制

voluntary jurisdiction 自愿管辖

voluntary liquidation 自愿清算

voluntary obligation 任意之债

voluntary payment 自动付款

"voluntary" restriction of export "自动"限制出口

voluntary sanction 任意性制裁

voluntary termination of crime 自动停止犯罪

voluntary trust 自愿信托

voluntary waste 积极毁损

volunteer 无偿者

volunteer corps 志愿军

vote 投票,投票选举

vote by ballot 投票表决

vote by roll call 唱名表决

vote by show of hands 举手表决

vote down 否决

① vote in the affirmative 赞成票

② vote secretly 秘密投票

③ voter 投票日,选举人,选民

④ voter's card 选民证

⑤ voter's roll 选民名单

⑥ vote-count system 当选计票制度

⑦

⑧ voting formula 表决方式

⑨ voting power 表决权

⑩ voting procedure 表决程序

⑪ voting register 选民名单

⑫ voting rule 表决规则

⑬ voting trust 授权信托

⑭ votum (拉) 承诺

⑮ vouch 保证

⑯ voucher 担保人

⑰ voyage charter 航次租船合同

⑱ voyage charter party 航次租船合同

⑲

⑳ voyeurism 观淫癖

㉑ vulgar law 平民法

㉒ vulnerable 弱点

㉓ vulnerable to fraud 易受骗

W

wage (/hired) labour　雇用劳动

wage for piecework　计件工资

wages council　工资委员会

waiting list　候补名单

waive　弃权

waive a right　放弃权利

waiver of obligation　债务免除

waiver of sanction　免除处分

walking delegate　工会代表

walk-out　罢工

wall garden　垂直花园

wall painting　壁画

wall-hung fixtures　壁挂式器具

want of form　不合程式

want of warrant of authority　缺乏授权

wanton and reckless negligence　有意的粗心过失

wanton exercise of power　滥用权利

war　战争

war cabinet　战时内阁

war crimes　战争犯罪,战争罪行

war criminal　战争罪犯,战犯

war disputes act　战时劳工纠纷法(1943)

war indemnity　战争赔偿

war of independence　独立战争

war of self-defence　自卫战争

war preparedness　战备

war proclamation　战争宣言

war profit tax　战时利得税

war risk　战争险

ward　监督

warden　监狱长

warder　监狱看守

wardress　女看守

ware house receipt clause　仓单条款

warehouse to warehouse clause　仓到仓条款

warehouse voucher　仓单

warehouse warrant　货仓保证书

warehousing fee　仓储费

warehousing goods　仓储物

warfare of poison gas　毒气战

warning　警告

warning device　报警装置

warning sign　警告标志

warrant　授权令,付款凭单,许可证,权利,授权

warrant for apprehension　逮捕令

warrant of appearance　出庭令

warrant of arrest　拘捕状,逮捕证

warrant of attorney　授权委托书

warrant of commitment　关押令,拘押证

warrant of commitment to prison　收监令

warrant of seizure　没收令

warrant of summons　传审令,传讯令

warranted free　特约不赔

warrantee　被担保人

warrantee guaranteed person　被保证人

warranter　保证人

warranties and guarantee　不担保条款与担保条款

warranties under the contract　合同保证条款

warranty　保证,担保,承诺

warranty against defects of thing　物的瑕疵担保

warranty clause, guarantee clause　保证条款

warranty for goods purchased　产品级证书

warranty of goods safety　货物的安全保证

warranty of legality　保证合法

warranty of quality　质量保证,品质保证书

warranty of title 对所有权之担保,权利担保

warranty period 保证期限,抵押期,保证期间

Warsaw rules 华沙规则

Warsaw-Oxford rules 1932 牛津-华沙规则·1932

warship passage of territorial sea 军舰通过领海

wartime administrative law 战时行政法

wartime cabinet 战时内阁

wartime constitution 战时宪法

wartime medical workers 战时医务人员

wartime recruitment 战时征集

wartime requisition 战时征用

wash sale 虚卖

waste 荒地

waste disposal 废料处理

waste gas emission standard 废气排放标准

waste gas pollution control 废气污染控制

waste product 工业废物

waste treatment 废料处理

waste water 废水

waste water treatment 废水处理

waster water utilization 废水利用

wasteland 荒地

wasting manpower and material resources 浪费人力物力

watch house 看守所

water act 水法

water and electricity supply 水电供应

water and soil conservation 水土保持

water charge 水费

water conservancy administration department 水利管理部门

water course 水路

water down 打折扣

water environment quality standard 水环境质量标准

water law 水法

water pollution 水污染

water pollution accident 水污染事故

water pollution loss 水污染损失

water power resources 水力资源

water quality 水质

water quality protection 水质保护

water rate 水费

water resources 水利资源

water route 水路

water source protection agency 水源保护机关

water traffic control 水路交通管理行为

water transport 水路运输

water transport enterprise 水路运输企业

water transport management 水路运输管理

water transport service enterprise 水路运输服务企业

water transport through the country 全国水路运输业

waterborne police 水上警察

waterborne police station 水上派出所

waters 水流

waterway 水路

waterway pollution 水道污染

way bill 运货单,铁路运单,运单

ways and means of taxation 赋税方法

ways of compensation 赔偿方式

ways of indemnity 赔偿方式

ways of international technology transfer 国际技术转让方式

WB 世界银行

weak evidence 不充分证据

weakness 弱点

weaponry 枪支

weapons of offense 作案凶器

wear and tear 自然磨损

weather working days 晴天工作日

weather working days of 24 consecutive hours 连续 24 小时及星期天工作日

Web-Pomerene export trade act 韦布—波默标出口贸易法

weigh 权衡

weigh gains and losses 权衡得失

weigh the advantages and disadvantages 权衡利弊

weighing 权衡

weighing and measures law 计量法

weight 重量,权衡

weight ascerntained by shipper 发货人确定重量

weight certificate 重量证明书

weight declaration 重量声明

weight limit 重量限制

weight of evidence 证据力

weight of proof 证据力,证明力

weight survey of import and export commodities 进出口商品的重量鉴定

weight the advantages and disadvantages 权衡利弊

weight the liabilities 加重责任

weight up the consequences 权衡后果

weighted voting system 加权表决制

weighthouse 计量所

weighty responsibility 重大责任

welfare 福利

welfare interest 福利

welfare state 福利国家

well-appointed residence 设备完善的住宅

well-defined goals 明确目标

Welsh mortgage 威尔士式抵押

wet module 浴室、厕所和厨房部分

whaling regulation 捕鲸管理

wheel trace 车轮压痕

when the circumstances are particularly serious 情节特别严重

when the circumstances are particularly wicked 情节特别恶劣

when the circumstances are rather serious 情节较重的

when the circumstances are so serious as to constitute a crime 情节严重、构成犯罪的

whereabouts 下落

Whereabouts are unknown 下落不明

whereas 鉴于条款

whether in berth or not (WIBON) "不论靠泊与否"条款

while counting ballot-slips 唱票

white book 白皮书

white collar defense bar 白领阶层的辩护律师

white paper 白皮书

white paper on human rights in China 中国的人权状况白皮书

White plan 怀特计划(1943 年)

white-collar crimes 白领犯罪,绅士犯罪

WHO 卫生组织

whole life insurance 终生寿险

wholesale license 批发执照

wholesale loan 批发放款

wholesale trade of tobacco product 烟草制品批发业务

wholly foreign-owned enterprise 外商独资企业

wholly produced criterion 整件生产标准

whore 妓女

whorl 斗型纹

widespread 普遍

widows's election 寡妇取得丈夫遗产的选择权(美)

wife's equitable separate estate 妻子的衡平法上的独立财产

wife's power ot dispose of equitable separate estate 妻子在衡平法上的独立财产的处分权

wild animal conservation law 野生动物保护法

wild animal migration 动生动物迁徙

wild animals 野生动物
wild land 荒地
wild life protection law 野生动植物保
wild plants 野生植物
wilful act 故意的行为
wilful neglect 有意的疏乎
wildlife 野生动物
wildlife conservation 野生动物保护
wildlife conservation law 野生动物保护法
wildlife resource 野生动物资源
wildlife under first class protection 一级保护野生动物
wildlife under second class protection 二级保护野生动物
wildlife under special local protection 地方重点保护野生动物
wildlife under special state protection 国家重点保护的野生动物
wilful negligence 有意的疏乎,有意的粗心过失
will 遗嘱
will act (英) 遗嘱法
will of the public 公意
willful act to damage public utilities 故意损毁公用设施行为
willful damage to properties 故意损害财产
willful inflation of prices 随意涨价
willful negligence 故意过失
Wilson doctrine 威尔逊主义
wind up a case 结案
wind up business 停业
windfall loss 意外损失
winding-up 清理
window frame 窗框
window tax (英) 窗户税
wine tax 酒税
wine tax bill 酒税票
winter circuit 冬季开庭的巡回法院
with a need to know 有需要知情

① with a two-year reprieve 缓期二年执行
③ with all faults 损伤概不负责
④ with average 水渍险
⑤ with circumstances remaining as they are 情势不变
⑦ with documentation 有单据
⑧ with due care 以应有的谨慎
⑨ with equal authenticity 具有同等效力
⑪ with equal status 平等地位
⑫ with holding at source 从源扣缴税款
⑭ with intent 有意
⑮ with one's authority 经…授权
⑯ with recourse 有追索权
⑰ with reference 根据
⑱ with the purposes of business 以生产经营为目的
⑳ with the rent 在租金以内
㉑ with valuable thing as a stake 以有价金额作赌金
㉓ withdraw 撤回,撤销
㉔ withdraw a bid 撤销投标
㉕ withdraw a bill 撤销议案
㉖ withdraw a case 撤销案件
㉗ withdraw a charge 撤回指控,撤回告诉
㉙ withdraw a claim 撤回诉讼,放弃权利
㉛ withdraw a confession 翻供
㉜ withdraw a request 取消请求
㉝ withdraw an accusation 撤回告诉
㉟ withdraw an action 撤诉
㊱ withdraw an appeal 撤回上诉
㊲ withdraw an application 撤回申请
㊳ withdraw an indictment 撤回起诉
㊶ withdraw an offer 撤回要约,取消报价
㊸ withdraw from partnership 退伙
㊹ withdraw one's bid 收回投标
㊺ withdraw private prosecution 撤回自诉
㊻ withdraw prosecution 撤回起诉

withdraw record （of a plaintiff） 撤回案件记录

withdrawal 退约,撤回

withdrawal by notice 通知退约,通知退出

withdrawal from partnership 退伙

withdrawal of a protest 撤回抗诉

withdrawal of appearance 回避出庭

wither away 消亡

withering away of law 法的消亡

withhold 预扣,扣留

withhold payment 拒绝支付

withhold the truth 隐瞒事实

withholding 预扣

withholding agent 扣缴义务人

withholding income tax return 扣缴所得税报告表

withholding of evidence 证据的拘留

withholding of the truth 隐瞒真相

withholding offer 暂停发盘

withholding tax 预提税,预扣税,扣除税

withholding the truth in reports 隐瞒真实情况

within a specified time limit 在规定期限内

within an appropriate time 在适当期限内

within limits 在范围内,在限定范围内

within one's competence 权力范围内

within the allotted time 在规定时间内

within the borders 境内

within the boundaries 境内

within the bounds of possibility 在可能范围内

within the delegation extent 授权范围内

within the designated scope 在指定的范围内

within the framework of agreement 在协议范围内

within the jurisdiction of China 在中国辖区内

within the law 在法律的范围内

within the limits expressly stated by law 在法律规定的限度内

within the limits laid down by law 在法律规定的范围内

within the maximum obligatory right amount 最高债权额限度内

within the power of 权限之内

within the prescribed limit 在规定限额内

within the range as approved and registered 在核准范围内

within the required time 在规定时间内

within the scope of its competence and functions 在职权范围内

within the scope of the power of agency 代理权限范围之内

within the specified time 在限期内

within the sphere permitted by law 法律允许的范围内

within the term of validity of the document 在证件有效期内

within the territory of China 在中国境内

within the time limit 在期间内,在规定期限内

within the time limit of not delaying shipment 在不延误装运的期限内

without （or, not） capacity of civil conduct 无民事行为能力

without approval 未经批准

without authorization 擅自

without benefit 无益

without consideration 无对价

without value 无对价

without day 无期限的

without engagement 未承诺,不承担义务,无承诺

without fault 无过失

without justified reasons 无正当理由

without notice 未经通知

without obligation 无义务

without party affiliation 无党派

without permission 未经许可

without personal freedom 没有个人自由的

without personal responsibility 无人负责现象

without prejudice to 不受损害

without prejudice to the right 不使权利受伤害

without right 无权

without sb's consent 未经某人同意

without the consent 未经同意

without the power of disposal 无处分权

witness 证人

witness box 证人席

witness for the defense 被告证人

witness in criminal proceedings 刑事诉讼中的证人

witness of making expert evaluation before filing a case 鉴定证人

witness stand 证人席

witness tampering 阻拦或恫吓证人罪

witness' testimony 证人证言

witnessing 作证

woman 成年女子,妇女

woman attorney 女律师

woman deputy 妇女代表

woman judge 女法官,女审判员

woman lawyer 女律师

woman police officer 女警官

woman power 女权

woman prosecutor 女检察官

woman suitor 女起诉人

women rights 妇女权利

women's rights 妇女权利

wooded mountain 山林

words treason 言辞叛逆罪

work 加工承揽合同

① work area 工作区

② work cabinet 事务内阁

③ work capacity 工作能力

④ work contract 承揽合同

⑤ work discipline 劳动纪律

⑥ work force 劳动力

⑦ work of environmental protection 环境保护工作

⑧ work of reconsideration 复议工作

⑪ work out the final state accounts 编制国家决策

⑬ work progress 工程进度

⑭ work quality 工作质量

⑮ work rules 工作规则

⑯ work seniority 工作年限

⑰ work sheet 加工单

⑱ work specification 工作规范

⑲ work task 工作任务

⑳ work together 合作

㉑ work's inspection certificate 工厂检验证明书

㉔ workable competition 有效竞争

㉕ workday 劳动日

㉖ worked materials 加工材料

㉗ worker 劳动者

㉘ worker director 工人董事

㉙ worker's congress 职工代表大会

㉚ worker's representative 工人代表

㉜ worker's supervision 工人监督

㉝ workers compensation and employer liability insurance 劳工保险和雇主责任保险

㊱ workers under labour contract system 劳动合同制工人

㊳ workers' autonomy 工人自治

㊴ workers' conference 工人会议

㊵ workers' management 工人自治

㊷ working area 工作区

㊸ working body 办事机构

㊹ working class 工人阶级

㊺ working commission 工作委员会

㊼ working committee 工作委员会

working conditions　劳动条件
working control　有效控制
working day　劳动日
working fund　周转定金
working hours, labour time　劳动时间
working order　加工单
working partner　经营合伙人
working period　劳动期间
working quality of case handling　办案质量
working rules　岗位责任制
working space　工作区
working style of the party　党风
world bank credit　世界银行贷款
world commerce　世界贸易
world culture　世界文化
world economy　世界经济
world environment day　世界环境日
world environment situation (／conditions)　世界环境状况
world government　世界政府
world health organization　世界卫生组织
world law　世界法
world legal order　世界法律程序,世界法律秩序
world market　世界市场
world market price　世界市场价格
world meteorological organization　世界气象组织
world rule of law　世界法治
world trade　世界贸易
world trade organization, WTO　世贸组织
world war　世界大战
worldwide express mail service　全球邮政特快专递
worldwide international organization　世界性国际组织
worship　崇拜
wound　创伤,损害,戳伤
wound and disability pension　伤残抚恤金

wound ballistics　创伤弹道学
wounding and maiming　伤害致残
wreck　破坏
wreck commissioner　法庭调查船舶失事人员
wrecker　拆房者
wring　强权
writ　令状
writ department　令状交待处
writ of arrest　逮捕令
writ of capias (拉)　拘捕令状
writ of covenant　因违约而请求赔偿损失的令状
writ of custody　拘禁令
writ of error　纠正错误令状
Writ of Error　调案令(英)
writ of exigent　催告令
writ of inhibition　禁审令
writ of possession　土地归还所有人判令
writ of quo warranto (拉)　证明令状
writ of reinstitution　发还令
writ of sequestration　查封令状
writ of specific performance　强制履行金
write off　冲销
write out　书面写出,全部写出合同或契约条款等
writing　笔迹
writings on the civil law　民法著作
written　成文的
written administrative appeal　行政上诉状,行政申诉状
written administrative judgment of first instance　第一审行政判决书
written administrative judgment of second instance　第二审行政判决书
written administrative ruling of first instance　第一审行政裁定书
written administrative ruling of second instance　第二审行政

裁定书

written agreement 书面协议,书契,书面协定

written agreement on arbitration 书面仲裁协议

written application for reconsideration 复议申请书,申请复议书

written arbitral mediation 仲裁调解书

written award 裁决书

written bidding 书面投标

written civil judgment of second instance 第二审民事判决书

written civil ruling 民事裁定书

written civil ruling of second instance 第二审民事裁定书

written commission 书面委托

written complaint 书状起诉

written confession 笔供,供状

written confirmation 书面凭证,书面确认,成文宪法

written constitution system 成文宪法制

written contract 书面合约,书面契约

written criminal appeal 刑事申诉状

written criminal ruling of first instance 第一审刑事裁定书

written criminal ruling of second instance 第二审刑事裁定书

written decision of administrative penalty 行政处罚决定书

written decision of administrative reconsideration of the customs 海关行政复议 决定书

written decision of civil sanctions 民事制裁决定书

written decision of disapproving an arrest 不批准逮捕决定书

written decision of exemption from prosecution 免予起诉决定书

written decision of living at home 监视居住决定书

written decision of no case-filing 不立案决定书

written decision of reconsideration 复议决定书

written decision of review 复核决定书

written decision of withdrawing a nol-pros order 撤回不起诉决定书

written decision of withdrawing an indictment 撤回起诉决定书

written decision on bail pending trial with restricted liberty of moving 取保候审决定书

written decision to exempt from prosecution 免予起诉决定书

written decision to quash a protest filed by the prosecutor 撤销抗诉决定书

written decision to quash an arrest 撤销逮捕决定书

written decision to revoke an apprehension 撤销逮捕决定书

written defense in arbitration 仲裁答辩书

written form of appraisal prepared for a leaving prisoner 罪犯出监鉴定表

written inquiry 书面询价

written inspection report 检验报告书

written interrogatories 书面质询

written judgment 判决书

written justification 辩护书

written law 成文法

written negotiation 书面谈判

written notice 书面通知

written notification 书面通知

written opinion on exemption from prosecution 免予起诉意见书

written plea 答辩书

written plea against a criminal appeal 刑事被上诉答辩状

written proposal of supervision over administration 行政监察建议书

written quotation 书面报价

written report submitted for ap-

proval of extending custodial terms 澄清延长羁押期限报告书

written resignation 辞职书

written sentence 判决书

written sentence of first instance 第一审刑事判决书

written sentence of second instance 第二审刑事判决书

written sentence of "not guilty" of first instance 第一审刑事无罪判决书

written sentence of "guilty" of first instance 第一审刑事有罪判决书

written statement 供述书

written wider clause 手写追加条款

writ-server 令状传达人

wrong adjudication 错误裁判

wrong civil 民事不法行为

① wrong judgment 错误裁判

② wrongdoer 过错方

③ wrongful act 不法行为,过错行为,侵害行为

⑤ wrongful act in taxation 税收违法行为

⑦ wrongful communication of information 错误传播资料罪

⑨ wrongful conduct 过错行为

⑩ wrongful conduct against one's duties 违反职责行为

⑫ wrongful dealing 不公平的交易,不公平交易

⑭ wrongful detention 拘留不当

⑮ wrongful hot pursuit 紧追不当

⑯ wrongful possession 非法占有人

⑰ wrongfully declared cargo 误报货物

⑲ wrongly accuse 错告

⑳ wrong-doing 恶行

Y

Yalta conference 雅尔塔会议

Yalta formula 雅尔塔方式

Yankee bond 扬基债券

yard transportation expenses 厂内运输费

year of assessment 课税年度,评税年度

year of discretion 责任年龄

yearbook 年鉴

years of discretion 责任年龄

yellow dog contract 黄狗规约

yellow fever 黄热病

yield 让步,收益

yield net 纯收益

yield possession 让渡占有权

yield rate of bonds 债券收益率

yield the maximum benefit 充分发挥效益

yoke cover 隐蔽

yoke of a judgment 判决的约束力

York-Antwerp rules 约克·安特卫普规则

youngsters 青少年

your honor 法官阁下

your lordship 法官阁下

youth correction act 青少年教养法(美)

youth rights 青年权利

Z

zero tax rate 零税率
zero-coupon bond 零息票债券
zip code 邮政编码
zone 地区
zone code 邮政代码

zone of fishery 渔区
zone price 区域价格
zoo sea miles maritime right 二百海里海洋权

暴君政治 181㊵
暴力犯 157⑭,593㉛
暴力犯罪 157⑭,593㉛
暴力犯罪分子 593㉘
暴力干涉婚姻自由行为 305②
暴力机关 403⑲,404③
暴力殴打 160⑦
暴力取证罪 154④
暴力死亡 170㊶,593㉚
暴力行使私权罪 211⑬
暴力行为 12㉓,593㉗
暴力亚文化理论 533㉜
暴力越狱罪 154⑯
暴力罪案 81㊱
暴利罪 589⑪,396⑦
暴民法 371㉚
暴民政治 371㊲
暴虐 577㉘
暴行 12㉓,373㊱,577㉜
暴政 181㊷,577㉜
爆炸损害建筑物、货物罪 149㊸
爆炸案 81②
爆炸物 229㊻
爆炸物品安全生产许可证 345⑲

bei

北大西洋公约组织 388⑤
北美自由贸易区 388②
备案 212⑮,⑰,248⑩,⑪,⑬,326⑥,508⑧
备案事项 364⑰
备查 248②
备用安排 524㉜
备用计划 524㊳
备用设备 524⑰
备用税率 175⑬
备用信用证 524⑱,㉟,㊱
备有家具的出租住房 260⑳
背对背贷款 55㉙
背对背信用证 55⑲,㉗
背教罪 41㉕
背景资料 55㉑
背离 179④,183㉜
背弃 2⑲
背书 210⑩
背书担保 272㉛
背书人 210⑱,296⑭
背书支票 55⑩
背信罪 70㉑
悖德狂 374⑯
悖德狂犯罪人 374⑲
悖德型人格障碍 176㉟
被保护的建筑 438⑬
被保护国 527㊴
被保留的建筑 118㉟
被保险人 48㉗,303①,㊼
被保证的 272㉗
被保证的租赁 48㉘
被保证人 595㉙
被背书人 210⑧,296⑫
被变换的租赁 132⑪
被剥夺政治权利的人 423㉖
被剥削阶级 229㊲
被捕 60㉟,62㊸
被查封的财产 502⑫
被承兑人 6㉟
被惩戒人 557㉟
被处绞刑 61㉝,375㊸
被处死刑 62⑱,266㊻
被处无期徒刑 62㉑
被处有期徒刑 62⑲
被传当事人 538㉛
被传到庭 60⑧
被传唤作证 60⑦
被代理人 442㊷
被担保的 272㉗,504⑥
被担保人 595㉘
被动的警察(指自由贸易论中的国家)414⑩
被动犯罪 413㊼
被动攻击型人格障碍 423⑨
被动型人格障碍 414⑧
被动性犯罪 413㊼
被动性犯罪人 414②
被动性同性恋 414④
被废黜君主 179㊸,㊺
被封锁国家 67㉘
被复议机关 22⑧
被告 174⑬,⑭,㉚,556㉟,557㉕
被告被监禁地法院 138㉔
被告被劳动教养地法院 418⑤

ben

biao

查十丁尼安皇帝 208㉓
查士丁尼法典 99⑭
查税 549⑤
查账 50㉞,50㊺
查账验证业务 8㊻
查证属实 60⑯
差别 184㉒,189②,190㊸
差别待遇 184⑥,184㉟,188㊷
差别待遇税则 188⑥
差别定额税率 184㊻,188㉞
差别对待 188㊳
差别工资 184③
差别关税 184㊴,184㊵,188㉚
差别关税率 184①
差别税 188㊶
差别税率 184④,188㊲
差别税则 184④,188㊲
差别税制 188⑧
差别投票制 184⑨
差别选举制 184⑨,㊷
养额 55㊵,361㊺,591⑨
差额税 591⑦
差额税率 591⑦
差额选举 123⑧,184⑧
差价 184㉖,441②
差价调房 224㉘
差价关税 591⑤
差价税 591⑦

chai

拆房者 601⑦
拆毁 178⑥,178⑦
拆毁许可证 502㉒
拆平房屋 330⑨
拆迁费用 178⑧

chan

掺假 28⑩,28⑪
掺杂 28⑪
掺杂使假 371⑩
缠讼 376㊵
产出税 406⑪
产地商检机构 557㉑
产地证明书 A 格式 86㉔

产地证明书 DA59 格式 86㉖,172㉓
产妇分娩津贴 364①
产假 364②
产假工资 364③
产品保证书 451㊶
产品标准 451㉚
产品标准侵权损害赔偿纠纷 190㉖
产品到手 452⑥
产品返销 451⑮
产品级证书 595㊶
产品类别 83㉕
产品赔偿责任 451㉓
产品缺陷 451⑯
产品设计 451⑲
产品识别 451⑳
产品试验 451㊴
产品税 451㊴
产品销售税金 550②
产品信誉 140⑬
产品形状 510㉒
产品性能 454㊵
产品责任 360㊺,451㉓
产品责任保险 451㉕
产品责任法 451㉗
产品质量 451㉛
产品质量标准 451㉛
产品质量的管理 539㉒
产品质量监督机构 539㉔
产品质量检验 452㉟
产品质量检验机构 451㉞
产品质量纠纷 451㉚
产品质量认证管理 18⑫
产品质量责任法 451㉗
产权 454㉟
产权变更 88㉒
产权不清 98⑰
产权抵押贷款 198㉞
产权审查书 401⑫
产权审查意见书 86㉕
产权市场 362⑩
产权说明 5㊷
产权诉讼 14⑩
产权要求 454②
产权与使用权分离 507㊷

chang

常规抵押贷款 102⑭
常设 420⑫,524㊴
常设公断法院 420⑦
常设机构 420①,⑮,㉚,421⑥,524
　⑨,524⑭
常设机关 420①,524⑩
常设委员会 420③,524㊺
常设行政机关 420㊸,524㊵
常设仲裁法院 420⑦
常识 431㊴
常事犯 403㉓
常委 366㊷,524㊹
常委会 524㊺
常委会会议 509③
常务会议 226⑤
常务委员会 225㊴,524㊺
常习犯 274⑱,421③
常习累犯 274⑲
常住地 393㉘
常住房屋 420⑰
常住居民 299③
常住人口 420㉜
常驻 411㊵
常驻公安派出所 429①
常驻使团 420㉚
厂长负责制 545⑪
厂长聘任制 43㉚
厂长任期目标责任制 392㉒
厂长任期终结审计制 50⑭
厂方证明书 86⑬
厂房和设备的处理 189㉓
厂价 348㉘,383①,441③
厂内运输费 604⑧
厂商代理人 361⑥
厂商广告 302㊲
厂商名称 571⑥
厂址 352⑥,514⑰
场到场 167⑲
场到门 167⑳
场到站 167⑱
场地 514⑫
场地分析 514⑬
场地开发 514⑯
场地清理 514⑭
场所 351②,352⑭,425㊹,437㊱
场外交易 165㉔

场外经纪人 326㊸
倡导 300㉑
唱名表决 594㉑
唱票 76⑨,597⑫
唱票人 553⑫

chao

钞票汇率 388㊷
超标准 406㊸
超标准排污费 239㉖
超长货物 343㉕
超出法律范围 406⑲
超出法律范围的 406⑮
超出法律权限的 233㊻
超出面值 3㊸
超大货物 73㊵
超大货物运费 73㊶
超定额件工资制 545㉛
超额保险 406⑨
超额偿付 406㊷
超额偿还 223㉒
超额贷款 406㊶
超额公司利得税 233㉕
超额奖金税 550③
超额累进税率 453⑥
超额利得税 233㉕
超额利润税 223㉟
超额赔款 223㉙
超额赔款合同 223㉚
超额损害赔偿 223㊷
超额征税 407㊸
超额支付 223㉓,⑳
超额准备金 223㊳
超发、滥发林木采伐许可罪 145㊺
超法规紧急避险 382㊹
超付 223㉜,406㊸
超付价值 390㉓
超高层建筑 538⑨
超国家 538㊷
超国家法律 538㊻
超国家政府 538㉖,㊹
超过必要限度 222㊸
超过合法范围的 578㉞
超过或不足条款 374㊵
超过权限 64㉚,222㉟

chong

chou

chuan

独占使用 225⑫
独占许可 224㊱
独占许可合同 224㊳
独占优势 4㊲
独资公司 134㉜
赌博契约 261㉒
赌博罪 261㉑
杜鲁门公告 576㉞

duan

短尺少秤 237㉝
短期国库券 66⑩
短期价格 512⑯
短期价格协议 512㉘
短期价值 512⑰
短期借款 69⑯
短期经济活动 201㉛
短期经济政策 512㉑
短期效应 512㉓
(消费者)短期信贷 122⑲
短期信贷综合担保 111③
短期行为 512⑱
短期性倾销 512⑲
短期债券 165⑪,⑳
短期资金清偿能力 512㉔
短缺 500⑩,511㉟,512⑩
短刑犯 163③
短暂性意识障碍 573㉔
段 410㊻
断定 47㉔,252⑱
断交 509㊵
断头台 272㊲

dui

对…负责 62⑨
对…起鼓励作用 60㉖
对…提出抗议 212⑲
对比分析 107②
对财产的查封、扣押、冻结 502⑰,505⑬
对财产的管辖权 324⑤
对裁决提出异议 87⑬
对策 136㉘,㊳
对冲基金 276㊻

对等 215㊴
对等抵消 217㉝
对等关系的法律 333㊷
对等价格 411③
对等原则 445㊸
对第三人的责任 345①
对法官的奖励 54⑱
对反驳的再反驳 574㊲
对方 136㉜,411②,560③
对方当事人 28⑲,401⑱,405⑦
对妨害民事诉讼的强制措施 99⑭,99⑰
对妨害行政诉讼的强制措施 99⑩
对非法或不道德的对价不能诉诸履行 405㉔
对管辖权的管辖权 324⑭
对管辖权的抗辩 427⑲
对价(注:指英美法中)118㊵
对价必须合法 118③
对价必须有价值 118⑤,⑦,118⑩
对价不充分 302㉞
对价可以是来付的和已付的 118㊷,㊻
对经营活动管理权 434㊻
对抗策略 136㊵
对抗措施 136①
对抗关税 136③
对抗性矛盾 40㉙
对抗制 28㉗
对空中劫持的管辖权 324㊻
对立 60㉘,401⑮
对立统一规律 334㊴
对流条件 113㉛
对某人课税 569㉘,㉟
对内负责 306⑥
对内行政法规 306①
对内政策 195⑩
对内主权 306㊷
对内最高权 307①
对偶婚 137⑥
对偶家庭 137⑤
对敲、双向期权 531㊸
对权利的侵犯 209⑬
对人的管辖权 324㉑
对人管辖 324⑪
对人捐税 422㉚

fang

gei

给…合法地位 342⑭
给…下定义 175㊳
给付 265④,414㊸,419㊷
给付不能 538㊶
给付迟延 175㊳
给付定金 337㊵

gen

根本 58⑰,㊷,79㉑,218⑫,259㊵,578⑲
根本不算损失 38⑤
根本大法 59㉔,120⑰,260⑰
根本的行为准则 59㊵
根本法 59㉔,120⑰,260⑰
根本利益 260⑯
根本任务 59㉟
根本违反合同 259㊷
根本违约 260②
根本问题 218㉗
根本原因 59⑰,79㉑,83㊲
根本制度 59㉘
根据人格形成过程的犯罪类型论 564㉒
根据 8㊲,289㊹,290㊵,398㊲,598⑰
根据…的提名 587㉘
根据本身利益 448㉑
根据动机的犯罪类型论 564㉗
根据法规 75㊶
根据法律的 221㊹
根据合同 289③
根据合同提起的诉讼 13㉑
根据精神诊断的犯罪类型论 564㉝
根据具体情况 289⑩
根据社会病理学观点的犯罪类型 564㊱
根据生理诊断的犯罪类型论 564㉚
根据时效的抗辩 427㊵
根据事实判断 321④
根据收入来源课税 550㉒

根据推理 75⑲
根据委托契约的诉讼 13㉖
根据习惯 59㊼,222⑤
根据协议设立的信托 576㊸
根据行为机制的犯罪类型论 564㉕
根据血统 75㉜
根据招供作出的判决 321㉛
根据这种权限 279㉕
根据证书的审判 575㉚
根据租船合签发的提单 65⑫
跟单承兑 194㊻
跟单承兑汇票 194①
跟单承兑信用证 194③
跟单汇票 194⑤,⑧,⑬
跟单汇票把收委托书 29⑱
跟单票据 66③,194㉚
跟单托收 194⑥,⑩
跟单信用证 194⑮,⑯
跟单信用证统一惯例 582②

geng

更迭 87⑰
更改 36㊳,87㊼,300㉘
更改原判 88㉝
更生保护 30㉝
更生保护处分 30㉞
更生保护组织 2㉒
更市 383㊴
更新改造 357㉕
更新合同的优先权 436㉑
更正的权力 109⑧
庚子赔款(中国 1900 年)69㉟
耕地 164②
耕地占用税 549㊹
耿多巴德法典 99㉕

gong

工长 261㉟
工厂订单 511㉘
工厂法 235⑥
工厂法 235⑲
工厂管理委员会 235㉒
工厂和车间法 235⑦

gua

寡妇取得丈夫遗产的选择权（美）597㊱

寡头垄断售价与购价 398㉓

寡头政治 398㉑

挂名全伙人 387㊷,405㊺

guai

拐卖妇女、儿童罪 141㉒

拐卖人口 3㉑

拐卖人口案件 81㊵

拐卖人口罪 141㉒

拐骗犯 3㉓,543㊺

拐骗未成年人罪 81㊳

guan

关键部门 326⑪

关键风险 326⑩

关键工业 326⑤

关键技术 326⑫

关键契约 326㊺

关境（关税地位）166㊱

关联产品 320⑪,348⑲

关联公司 48㉚

关联银行 134㉙

关贸总协定 261⑧

关税 166⑫,548⑨

关税保护 548㉖

关税报复 548㉕

关税壁垒 548⑪,㉝

关税费用 166㊶

关税分类 166㉒

关税国境 166㉕

关税合作理事会税则目录 166㊷

关税豁免 166㉔,285㉟

关税减免 548⑭,⑱

关税减让表 548⑯

关税减让原则 548⑭

关税领土 167⑱

关税率 167⑯,548㉚

关税配额 548㉗

关税普遍优惠制 263⑪

关税收入 167⑨

关税税目 548㉔

关税税则 167⑯,548㉘

关税税则委员会 527㉖

关税特惠制 436㉔

关税条约 167⑲

关税同盟 167㉑,548⑩,㉜

关税委员会 548⑫,⑬

关税与贸易总协定 261㉝

关税执行区 548⑲

关税专约 166㊻

关税转嫁 510㊴

关系计民生 316㉟

关系聚集地 271⑱

关系密切亲戚 98③

关系企业 29㉘

关系人 29㉟,413㉛,448⑩

关系银行 134㉙

关押 166③,288㊸

关押令 595㉑

关于 112㉜

关于 398㊼

关于保护占有动产的诉讼 304㉚

关于抵押财产索赔权的诉讼 282①

关于防止因倾倒废料及其他物质造成海洋污染的公约 131㊷

关于港口国际制度公约 131⑯

关于各国内政不容干涉及独立与主权之保护宣言 173⑦

关于各国探索和利用包括月球和其他天体在同内的外层空间活动的原则条约（外层空间条约）575㊵

关于国籍法冲突的若干问题的公约 131㉙

关于国际承认对航空器的权利的公约 131⑫

关于国际经营活动中的反托拉斯指南 40㉖

关于国家在国家财产、档案和债务方面继承的维也纳公约 592⑤

关于国家在条约方面继承的维也纳公约 592⑩

关于国家责任的条文草案 197①

关于合同的诉讼 537⑫

guo

hua

huai

huan

hun

huo

基建任务书 121⑫
基金 259⑧
基金贷款 260㊹
基金管理人 259㊲
基金扣押令 88㉚
基金联合投资 259㊸
基罗亚 264㊹
基于胁迫行为诉 13㉝
基于义务的赠与 196⑫
箕型纹 353⑧
稽查 315②
稽查部门 50㊵
稽查员 228⑲
稽查证 315⑬
稽核 50㉞,89⑦,111⑱,222⑭
稽核长 90⑯
稽核账目 50㉟
稽核制度 51⑨
稽征员 549㉑
激励机制 291⑰
激情犯 208㊵
激情犯罪 141㊳
激情故意 208㉑
激情危象 29㉘
激情与犯罪 413㊷
羁束行政行为 531㊺
羁押场所 425⑫
羁押犯 447⑨
羁押候审 547⑫
羁押令 371⑧
及时 289㉝,290⑪,㉓
及时到达 198㉑
及时发生 198㊺
及时付清 415③
及时审批 266⑨
及时性 454⑥
及早控诉 201⑩
级别管辖 269㊺,533㊻
级差收入调节税 549㊺
给予 265④
给予 8㉜,270⑪
给予惩罚 298㉞
给予贷款 270⑬,⑭
给予公正裁判 265⑥
给予纪律处分 547⑥
给予适当补偿 265㉕,357㊲

给予一个期限 266①
给予优先权 8㉟
给予折扣 187㉝
给予正式承认 265㊲
给予政治庇护 270㉕
给予殖民地国家和人民独立宣言 172①
即成犯 187㉔
即付 285⑰,522①
即付交易 58㉟
即付票据 65㊵,388㊻
即付现金 453㊺
即将到期的负债 364㉔
即决 537㉗
即决驳回 537㊲
即决裁定 537㉜
即决裁判 537㊸,㊺
即决裁判程序 138③,538⑥,576⑫
即决法院 424㉝
(英)即决法院 537㉞
即决犯罪 538④
即决审判 538④
即决审讯 538㉑,㉔
即期 285⑯,512③
即期本票 177㉚
即期付款 285㊴,512⑤
即期汇率 177⑨,522⑨
即期交割 522⑯
即期交货 177⑦,㉜,285⑭,453㊹
即期交易 522⑯
即期票汇汇率 398⑱
即期票据 65⑰
即期外汇业务 223㉘
即期信用证 512④
即期装运 201⑮,285㊺,453㊷
即期资金 285㉚
即时答辩 285㊹
即时代执行 454②
即时逮捕 537㉛
即时的 285㉔
即时订货单 285㉟
即时犯 187㉔,301㊻
即时付款 285㊴,415③
即时加工 453㊷
即时结算 522㉑
即时解雇 301㊺

jiang

jie

可勘探性 229㊶
可靠的担保 272②
可靠性 179㉑,541㊲
可可生产者联盟 99②
可扣除的税额 173⑫
可兰经 559④
可流通性 383⑥
可买卖期权 571㉞
可免除的 225㉕
可免税的收入 47㉘
可能犯罪者 434⑧
可能性 432㊲
可能用竭的国内资源 195㉟
可能预见 54②
可赔偿 107㊳
可批准的 51㊲
可强制执行的合同 210㉒
可燃物 298⑳
可燃性纤维法 246㉞
可让与的 35②,47㉑
可让与性 35㉛
可识别性 283㉕
可实施性 229㊱
可收回的 100㊱
可售债券 362⑲
可授权的 51⑫
可税资产 27⑫
可说明性 8⑱
可替代 260⑬
可贴现 188①
可退货经销 498㊳
可销售的质量 367㊱
可销售品质 367㊴
可信赖的 314㉗
可行 238⑧
可行的 238㊻,435㊲
可行方案 238⑩
可行合同 206④
可行性 206④
可行性标准 524㉚
可行性分析 238㊼
可行性论证 238④
可行性条件 238①
可行性投资研究报告 533⑫
可行性研究 53⑨,238③,④
可行性研究报告 238⑥

可选择的合同条款 401⑧
可延长的 231⑪
可要求清偿的债务 170㊹
可依法占有而实际占有的动产抵
押 374⑫
可以起诉 294⑤
可以起诉的罪行 294⑨
可以受理的抗辩 27⑬
可引渡之罪 233㉝
可用法律强制执行的 210㉑
可由法院裁判的争执 325⑰
可予起罪的轻罪 294⑥
可与黄金兑换的货币 132⑯,275⑪
可预测性 436㉘
可预见的 251㊷
可预见损失 251㊸,㊹
可征税的 550⑥
可征税收入 550⑬
可支配价格 189⑰
可执行性 210⑰
可直接适用的法律 186⑨
可转换的优先股 132⑱
可转让存单 383⑧
可转让的 383⑦,573㉚
可转让的合同 47㉒
可转让定期存单 383⑧
可转让信用证 573㉛
可作废合同 593㉔
克莱顿法 97㉛
克莱顿反托拉斯法 97㉜
克莱灵顿法(12C 英国)120⑯
克洛维斯 98⑱
客观犯罪心理学 392⑪
客观规律 392⑰
客观解释 392⑮
客观情况 392⑥
客观实际 392⑲
客观事实 392⑬
客观条件 392⑩
客观性 392⑫
客观因素 392⑭
客观原因 392⑤
客观原则 392㊱
客观责任 392⑳
客观中立 392⑱
客观主义 392㉖

le

lei

lian

luan

lüe

lun

mei

men

meng

mi

nu

nü

nüe

pan

qi

契约 ⑯,409⑧,㊲,425㉚,568㊷
契约必须遵守约定必须信守原则
　(拉)409㊸
契约编号 126㉑
契约标的 534㉘
契约不能产生于不法行为 221㊼
契约采购 126⑫
契约成立要素 218⑩
契约当事人 412㊲
契约的 409⑨
契约的相互关系 446⑯
契约登记簿 345⑱
契约缔结地法院 253①
契约订立地法 344⑨
契约订约人 130②
契约对第三方无损害 409⑤
契约法 124㊺,333㊴
契约法 564④
契约方案 111①
契约废止 178㊷
契约格式 252㊶
契约规定 128③
契约过失 164⑦
契约见证人 49㊷
契约里大家同意的条款 138㊶
契约理论 126㉞
契约留置权 125②
契约履行 80②
契约落空 258㉛
契约买卖 124⑥
契约目的 304㊹
契约上的 221㉟
契约上的相互关系 377㉑
契约上的义务 127㉔
契约生效 225⑰
契约式合营农业 127⑬
契约式合营企业 127⑬
契约式联营 128⑪
契约收入 127⑧
契约收益 127㊻
契约受约人 139⑦
契约书 88㊴
契约诉讼 13㊳
契约所规定的义务 67㊵
契约条件 114⑲
契约条款 97⑨

契约外效果 234⑤
契约无效 390⑨
契约细节 182⑱
契约协议 127㊷
契约型基金 128⑥
契约性不法行为 127①
契约性求偿 127㊸
契约性条款 127㊹
契约性投资 127⑨
契约性行为 127㊶
契约性责任 127㊹
契约性债务 127㊻
契约性直接投资 127④
契约许可证 127⑰
契约义务 127㉗
契约有效期间 199㉘
契约债权人 68③
契约债务 170㉟,392⑰
契约之履行 419⑫
契约之相互关系 448③
契约制度 544⑩
契约种类 577⑫
契约转让 47㉟
契约自由 256⑮,345㊱
契约自由原则 443⑲,561㉘
契纸 171③,⑤,⑯,254⑭,592㊼

qia

恰当的规定 43㉘
恰当性标准 16㉞

qian

千 566㊼
迁户口 88㉗,369⑩,375⑨
迁居 88㉗,369⑩,375⑨
迁入地公安局 461⑬
迁徙 88㉘,369⑩
迁徙自由 256⑫,㉞
迁移出境 208⑩,⑪
迁移费 108⑫
牵连 286㉘,316㉞
牵连犯 286㉚
牵头经理人 336⑨
牵头银行 336⑨

qing

que

缺度裁决 54⑮
缺额 512⑩,⑭,590⑤
缺乏 62㉓,329⑱
缺乏偿还能力 329㉗
缺乏对价 4㉖,236㉗,329㉙
缺乏法定形式 329㉑
缺乏法定形式的 298㊸
缺乏法律上的行为能力 579㊹
缺乏经验 329⑲
缺乏理性 174㊵
缺乏能力 329㉚
缺乏授权 595⑲
缺乏行为能力 580㉔
缺乏约因 4㉖
缺乏证据 4㉙
缺斤少两 512①
缺量 512⑨,⑩
缺少 61㊷,329⑱,512⑭
缺席判决 174㉒
缺陷产权 55㊸
缺陷规则 370③
缺陷责任 174⑤
确定不移的结论 38㊹
确定承诺 175⑬
确定的 29㊸,183⑲,246④,432⑦
确定的故意 195⑭
确定的权利 218㊸
确定的时效 432㊴
确定的销售合同 244㊸
确定的要约 244㊶
确定合同等 378⑥
确定价格 244㊺,440㊹
确定期限 184⑭
确定契约 244㊸
确定损害赔偿金 365㊶
确定问题之所在 283⑮
确定物 46⑥
确定性的推断 113㊸
确定性规范 219①
确定在合同项下 283⑰
确定债务 119⑤,170㊸,392④
确立的原则 218㊺
确盘 115㊳,244㊶

确切 175㊴,222㉚
确切的定义 2⑬
确切的解释 1㉔
确切通知 175㊵
确切证据 113㊸
确权之诉 313⑫
确认 29㊺,㊻,115㊶,283㉓,543⑮
确认保证 30⑪
确认承运人条款 283㉔
确认的债务 457㉜
确认订单 244㊸
确认陪审团的裁决 587⑰
确认书 1㊳,115㊶,343⑦
确认所有权 116⑤
确认通知书 116⑧
确认协议 115㊲
确认行为 30①
确认样品 116⑪
确认要求 6⑲
确认有效 534⑭
确认者 51㊷
确实性 51㊸,139⑤
确信 62㊱,63㊵,244②,401⑩
确凿的证据 4㊵,113㊸
确凿事实 4⑭
确证 53⑭,97㉔,113②,178㉔,296⑮

qun

群岛国 45⑬
群岛基线 45⑫
群岛水域 45⑭
群管制 363㊵
群集犯罪 404⑯
群体犯罪心理学 459⑰
群众集会 363④
群众监督 461㊹,539⑱,542㊲
群众体育 363⑪
群众团体 363㊱,㊺
群众性体育活动 363⑫
群众性自治组织 363②
群众自治组织 505㉒

社会主义宪法 517③
社会主义刑法 517⑩
社会主义优越性 517㉝
社会主义政权 517③
社会主义制度 517㉟
社会转型 516㉜
社团 48㉟
社团法人 106㊶,134㉔,㉕,31㊱,
　323㊸,516㊵
涉及 112㉘,212⑬,275㊷,305㉞,
　316㉞,423㉟,548㊳,570㊴
涉及干扰司法公证罪 395⑭
涉及共同利益 570㊲
涉枪犯罪 273④
涉外保险关系准据法 454㉘
涉外产品责任准据法 454㉚
涉外工程承包 250㉓
涉外合同 124㊴
涉外经济法 249㉗
涉外经济贸易合同 202⑤
涉外民事法律关系 94⑩
涉外民事关系 94㉗
涉外民事关系的法律适用 42⑭,
　⑰
涉外民事诉讼程序特别规定 520
　㉓
涉外税法 549⑩
涉外税收 250㊷,⑫,549⑯
涉外投资法 250㊷
涉外刑事诉讼 159㊳
涉外刑事诉讼程序 162①
涉外行政诉讼 18㉝
涉外因素 249㉛
涉外征税 550㉚
涉外仲裁 44㉙
涉嫌人犯 542⑱
赦免 5⑨,38⑧,225㉘,269㉓,293
　㉖,410㉔,519⑯
赦免法 11④
赦免权 189⑪
赦免特权 437㉚
摄政 10㉑
摄政时期 457⑱
摄政王 442㊶

shen

申报表 172㊶
申报纳税身份 240㉞
申报所得税截止期 170⑤,241⑭
申报义务 200㉑
申请 42⑩,42㉕,46㊹,424①,436
　㊺
申请保险人 303⑨
申请缔约方 42⑥
申请复议 42㉜,㊷
申请复议书 602⑥
申请公证 42③
申请货款 349㊵
申请货款人 349㊳
申请加入国籍 42㊹
申请检验 42㉞
申请借款人 349㊳
申请免税 568⑩
申请免税额 42⑲
申请顺延期限 42㉙
申请退还税款 42㉞
申请退税 568㉜
申请宣告合同无效 42㉑
申请延期 42⑭
申请仲裁 240㉚
申述自己的观点 230㊵
申诉权 562①
申诉权利 6㊼
身份 528⑫
身份犯 528⑬
身份关系 423㊸
身份继承 537⑧
身份证 283㉚
身体伤害 425⑤
身体刑 462⑬
绅士(君子)协定 264㊸
绅士犯罪 597㉑
深入调查 502㉓
神经错乱罪犯 354㉗
神经症犯罪 396③
神权说 564㊷
神权统治 564⑬
神审 401㊵
神圣 279⑩,316㉖,㊶,㊸,497⑨

shou

shu

shui

shun

shuo

si

tou

wan

wen

xing

xue

xun

夜入私宅罪 395㉘

yi

yin

ying

yue

zan

zhi

zhuan

参考书目

英汉—汉英法律词汇　法律出版社,1999 年

英汉银行词典　浙江大学出版社,1989 年

汉英法律词典　法律出版社,1998 年

英汉双解法律词典　世界图书出版公司,1998 年

常用汉英法律词典　法律出版社,1998 年